50% OFF

Online NCMHCE Prep Course!

by Mometrix

Dear Customer,

We consider it an honor and a privilege that you chose our NCMHCE Study Guide. As a way of showing our appreciation and to help us better serve you, we are offering **50% off our online NCMHCE Prep Course**. Many NCMHCE courses are needlessly expensive and don't deliver enough value. With our course, you get access to the best NCMHCE prep material, and **you only pay half price**.

We have structured our online course to perfectly complement your printed study guide. The NCMHCE Prep Course contains **in-depth lessons** that cover all the most important topics, **30+ video reviews** that explain difficult concepts, over **600 practice questions** to ensure you feel prepared, and more than **500 digital flashcards**, so you can study while you're on the go.

Online NCMHCE Prep Course

Topics Included:

- Professional Practice and Ethics
- Intake, Assessment, and Diagnosis
- Areas of Clinical Focus
- Treatment Planning
- Counseling Skills and Interventions
- Core Counseling Attributes

Course Features:

- NCMHCE Study Guide
  - Get content that complements our best-selling study guide.
- Full-Length Practice Tests
  - With over 600 practice questions, you can test yourself again and again.
- Mobile Friendly
  - If you need to study on the go, the course is easily accessible from your mobile device.
- NCMHCE Flashcards
  - Our course includes a flashcard mode with over 500 content cards to help you study.

To receive this discount, visit us at mometrix.com/university/ncmhce or simply scan this QR code with your smartphone. At the checkout page, enter the discount code: **ncmhce50off**

If you have any questions or concerns, please contact us at support@mometrix.com.

FREE Study Skills Videos/DVD Offer

Dear Customer,

Thank you for your purchase from Mometrix! We consider it an honor and a privilege that you have purchased our product and we want to ensure your satisfaction.

As part of our ongoing effort to meet the needs of test takers, we have developed a set of Study Skills Videos that we would like to give you for FREE. These videos cover our *best practices* for getting ready for your exam, from how to use our study materials to how to best prepare for the day of the test.

All that we ask is that you email us with feedback that would describe your experience so far with our product. Good, bad, or indifferent, we want to know what you think!

To get your FREE Study Skills Videos, you can use the **QR code** below, or send us an **email** at studyvideos@mometrix.com with *FREE VIDEOS* in the subject line and the following information in the body of the email:

- The name of the product you purchased.
- Your product rating on a scale of 1-5, with 5 being the highest rating.
- Your feedback. It can be long, short, or anything in between. We just want to know your impressions and experience so far with our product. (Good feedback might include how our study material met your needs and ways we might be able to make it even better. You could highlight features that you found helpful or features that you think we should add.)

If you have any questions or concerns, please don't hesitate to contact me directly.

Thanks again!

Sincerely,

Jay Willis
Vice President
jay.willis@mometrix.com
1-800-673-8175

NCMHCE

Secrets Study Guide

Covers the 2022 Outline and Question Format

Exam Review and NCMHCE Practice Test for the National Clinical Mental Health Counseling Examination

2 Full-Length Practice Tests

Written and edited by Mometrix Test Prep

Printed in the United States of America

This paper meets the requirements of ANSI/NISO Z39.48-1992 (Permanence of Paper).

Paperback
ISBN 13: 978-1-5167-3171-8
ISBN 10: 1-5167-3171-9

Ebook
ISBN 13: 978-1-5167-1684-5
ISBN 10: 1-5167-1684-1

Hardback
ISBN 13: 978-1-5167-1877-1
ISBN 10: 1-5167-1877-1

Dear Future Exam Success Story

First of all, **THANK YOU** for purchasing Mometrix study materials!

Second, congratulations! You are one of the few determined test-takers who are committed to doing whatever it takes to excel on your exam. **You have come to the right place.** We developed these study materials with one goal in mind: to deliver you the information you need in a format that's concise and easy to use.

In addition to optimizing your guide for the content of the test, we've outlined our recommended steps for breaking down the preparation process into small, attainable goals so you can make sure you stay on track.

We've also analyzed the entire test-taking process, identifying the most common pitfalls and showing how you can overcome them and be ready for any curveball the test throws you.

Standardized testing is one of the biggest obstacles on your road to success, which only increases the importance of doing well in the high-pressure, high-stakes environment of test day. Your results on this test could have a significant impact on your future, and this guide provides the information and practical advice to help you achieve your full potential on test day.

Your success is our success

We would love to hear from you! If you would like to share the story of your exam success or if you have any questions or comments in regard to our products, please contact us at **800-673-8175** or **support@mometrix.com**.

Thanks again for your business and we wish you continued success!

Sincerely,
The Mometrix Test Preparation Team

Need more help? Check out our flashcards at:
http://mometrixflashcards.com/NCMHCE

TABLE OF CONTENTS

Introduction

Thank you for purchasing this resource! You have made the choice to prepare yourself for a test that could have a huge impact on your future, and this guide is designed to help you be fully ready for test day. Obviously, it's important to have a solid understanding of the test material, but you also need to be prepared for the unique environment and stressors of the test, so that you can perform to the best of your abilities.

For this purpose, the first section that appears in this guide is the **Secret Keys**. We've devoted countless hours to meticulously researching what works and what doesn't, and we've boiled down our findings to the five most impactful steps you can take to improve your performance on the test. We start at the beginning with study planning and move through the preparation process, all the way to the testing strategies that will help you get the most out of what you know when you're finally sitting in front of the test.

We recommend that you start preparing for your test as far in advance as possible. However, if you've bought this guide as a last-minute study resource and only have a few days before your test, we recommend that you skip over the first two Secret Keys since they address a long-term study plan.

If you struggle with **test anxiety**, we strongly encourage you to check out our recommendations for how you can overcome it. Test anxiety is a formidable foe, but it can be beaten, and we want to make sure you have the tools you need to defeat it.

Secret Key #1 – Plan Big, Study Small

There's a lot riding on your performance. If you want to ace this test, you're going to need to keep your skills sharp and the material fresh in your mind. You need a plan that lets you review everything you need to know while still fitting in your schedule. We'll break this strategy down into three categories.

Information Organization

Start with the information you already have: the official test outline. From this, you can make a complete list of all the concepts you need to cover before the test. Organize these concepts into groups that can be studied together, and create a list of any related vocabulary you need to learn so you can brush up on any difficult terms. You'll want to keep this vocabulary list handy once you actually start studying since you may need to add to it along the way.

Time Management

Once you have your set of study concepts, decide how to spread them out over the time you have left before the test. Break your study plan into small, clear goals so you have a manageable task for each day and know exactly what you're doing. Then just focus on one small step at a time. When you manage your time this way, you don't need to spend hours at a time studying. Studying a small block of content for a short period each day helps you retain information better and avoid stressing over how much you have left to do. You can relax knowing that you have a plan to cover everything in time. In order for this strategy to be effective though, you have to start studying early and stick to your schedule. Avoid the exhaustion and futility that comes from last-minute cramming!

Study Environment

The environment you study in has a big impact on your learning. Studying in a coffee shop, while probably more enjoyable, is not likely to be as fruitful as studying in a quiet room. It's important to keep distractions to a minimum. You're only planning to study for a short block of time, so make the most of it. Don't pause to check your phone or get up to find a snack. It's also important to **avoid multitasking**. Research has consistently shown that multitasking will make your studying dramatically less effective. Your study area should also be comfortable and well-lit so you don't have the distraction of straining your eyes or sitting on an uncomfortable chair.

The time of day you study is also important. You want to be rested and alert. Don't wait until just before bedtime. Study when you'll be most likely to comprehend and remember. Even better, if you know what time of day your test will be, set that time aside for study. That way your brain will be used to working on that subject at that specific time and you'll have a better chance of recalling information.

Finally, it can be helpful to team up with others who are studying for the same test. Your actual studying should be done in as isolated an environment as possible, but the work of organizing the information and setting up the study plan can be divided up. In between study sessions, you can discuss with your teammates the concepts that you're all studying and quiz each other on the details. Just be sure that your teammates are as serious about the test as you are. If you find that your study time is being replaced with social time, you might need to find a new team.

Secret Key #2 – Make Your Studying Count

You're devoting a lot of time and effort to preparing for this test, so you want to be absolutely certain it will pay off. This means doing more than just reading the content and hoping you can remember it on test day. It's important to make every minute of study count. There are two main areas you can focus on to make your studying count.

Retention

It doesn't matter how much time you study if you can't remember the material. You need to make sure you are retaining the concepts. To check your retention of the information you're learning, try recalling it at later times with minimal prompting. Try carrying around flashcards and glance at one or two from time to time or ask a friend who's also studying for the test to quiz you.

To enhance your retention, look for ways to put the information into practice so that you can apply it rather than simply recalling it. If you're using the information in practical ways, it will be much easier to remember. Similarly, it helps to solidify a concept in your mind if you're not only reading it to yourself but also explaining it to someone else. Ask a friend to let you teach them about a concept you're a little shaky on (or speak aloud to an imaginary audience if necessary). As you try to summarize, define, give examples, and answer your friend's questions, you'll understand the concepts better and they will stay with you longer. Finally, step back for a big picture view and ask yourself how each piece of information fits with the whole subject. When you link the different concepts together and see them working together as a whole, it's easier to remember the individual components.

Finally, practice showing your work on any multi-step problems, even if you're just studying. Writing out each step you take to solve a problem will help solidify the process in your mind, and you'll be more likely to remember it during the test.

Modality

Modality simply refers to the means or method by which you study. Choosing a study modality that fits your own individual learning style is crucial. No two people learn best in exactly the same way, so it's important to know your strengths and use them to your advantage.

For example, if you learn best by visualization, focus on visualizing a concept in your mind and draw an image or a diagram. Try color-coding your notes, illustrating them, or creating symbols that will trigger your mind to recall a learned concept. If you learn best by hearing or discussing information, find a study partner who learns the same way or read aloud to yourself. Think about how to put the information in your own words. Imagine that you are giving a lecture on the topic and record yourself so you can listen to it later.

For any learning style, flashcards can be helpful. Organize the information so you can take advantage of spare moments to review. Underline key words or phrases. Use different colors for different categories. Mnemonic devices (such as creating a short list in which every item starts with the same letter) can also help with retention. Find what works best for you and use it to store the information in your mind most effectively and easily.

Secret Key #3 – Practice the Right Way

Your success on test day depends not only on how many hours you put into preparing, but also on whether you prepared the right way. It's good to check along the way to see if your studying is paying off. One of the most effective ways to do this is by taking practice tests to evaluate your progress. Practice tests are useful because they show exactly where you need to improve. Every time you take a practice test, pay special attention to these three groups of questions:

- The questions you got wrong
- The questions you had to guess on, even if you guessed right
- The questions you found difficult or slow to work through

This will show you exactly what your weak areas are, and where you need to devote more study time. Ask yourself why each of these questions gave you trouble. Was it because you didn't understand the material? Was it because you didn't remember the vocabulary? Do you need more repetitions on this type of question to build speed and confidence? Dig into those questions and figure out how you can strengthen your weak areas as you go back to review the material.

Additionally, many practice tests have a section explaining the answer choices. It can be tempting to read the explanation and think that you now have a good understanding of the concept. However, an explanation likely only covers part of the question's broader context. Even if the explanation makes perfect sense, **go back and investigate** every concept related to the question until you're positive you have a thorough understanding.

As you go along, keep in mind that the practice test is just that: practice. Memorizing these questions and answers will not be very helpful on the actual test because it is unlikely to have any of the same exact questions. If you only know the right answers to the sample questions, you won't be prepared for the real thing. **Study the concepts** until you understand them fully, and then you'll be able to answer any question that shows up on the test.

It's important to wait on the practice tests until you're ready. If you take a test on your first day of study, you may be overwhelmed by the amount of material covered and how much you need to learn. Work up to it gradually.

On test day, you'll need to be prepared for answering questions, managing your time, and using the test-taking strategies you've learned. It's a lot to balance, like a mental marathon that will have a big impact on your future. Like training for a marathon, you'll need to start slowly and work your way up. When test day arrives, you'll be ready.

Start with the strategies you've read in the first two Secret Keys—plan your course and study in the way that works best for you. If you have time, consider using multiple study resources to get different approaches to the same concepts. It can be helpful to see difficult concepts from more than one angle. Then find a good source for practice tests. Many times, the test website will suggest potential study resources or provide sample tests.

Practice Test Strategy

If you're able to find at least three practice tests, we recommend this strategy:

Untimed and Open-Book Practice

Take the first test with no time constraints and with your notes and study guide handy. Take your time and focus on applying the strategies you've learned.

Timed and Open-Book Practice

Take the second practice test open-book as well, but set a timer and practice pacing yourself to finish in time.

Timed and Closed-Book Practice

Take any other practice tests as if it were test day. Set a timer and put away your study materials. Sit at a table or desk in a quiet room, imagine yourself at the testing center, and answer questions as quickly and accurately as possible.

Keep repeating timed and closed-book tests on a regular basis until you run out of practice tests or it's time for the actual test. Your mind will be ready for the schedule and stress of test day, and you'll be able to focus on recalling the material you've learned.

Secret Key #4 – Pace Yourself

Once you're fully prepared for the material on the test, your biggest challenge on test day will be managing your time. Just knowing that the clock is ticking can make you panic even if you have plenty of time left. Work on pacing yourself so you can build confidence against the time constraints of the exam. Pacing is a difficult skill to master, especially in a high-pressure environment, so **practice is vital**.

Set time expectations for your pace based on how much time is available. For example, if a section has 60 questions and the time limit is 30 minutes, you know you have to average 30 seconds or less per question in order to answer them all. Although 30 seconds is the hard limit, set 25 seconds per question as your goal, so you reserve extra time to spend on harder questions. When you budget extra time for the harder questions, you no longer have any reason to stress when those questions take longer to answer.

Don't let this time expectation distract you from working through the test at a calm, steady pace, but keep it in mind so you don't spend too much time on any one question. Recognize that taking extra time on one question you don't understand may keep you from answering two that you do understand later in the test. If your time limit for a question is up and you're still not sure of the answer, mark it and move on, and come back to it later if the time and the test format allow. If the testing format doesn't allow you to return to earlier questions, just make an educated guess; then put it out of your mind and move on.

On the easier questions, be careful not to rush. It may seem wise to hurry through them so you have more time for the challenging ones, but it's not worth missing one if you know the concept and just didn't take the time to read the question fully. Work efficiently but make sure you understand the question and have looked at all of the answer choices, since more than one may seem right at first.

Even if you're paying attention to the time, you may find yourself a little behind at some point. You should speed up to get back on track, but do so wisely. Don't panic; just take a few seconds less on each question until you're caught up. Don't guess without thinking, but do look through the answer choices and eliminate any you know are wrong. If you can get down to two choices, it is often worthwhile to guess from those. Once you've chosen an answer, move on and don't dwell on any that you skipped or had to hurry through. If a question was taking too long, chances are it was one of the harder ones, so you weren't as likely to get it right anyway.

On the other hand, if you find yourself getting ahead of schedule, it may be beneficial to slow down a little. The more quickly you work, the more likely you are to make a careless mistake that will affect your score. You've budgeted time for each question, so don't be afraid to spend that time. Practice an efficient but careful pace to get the most out of the time you have.

Secret Key #5 – Have a Plan for Guessing

When you're taking the test, you may find yourself stuck on a question. Some of the answer choices seem better than others, but you don't see the one answer choice that is obviously correct. What do you do?

The scenario described above is very common, yet most test takers have not effectively prepared for it. Developing and practicing a plan for guessing may be one of the single most effective uses of your time as you get ready for the exam.

In developing your plan for guessing, there are three questions to address:

- When should you start the guessing process?
- How should you narrow down the choices?
- Which answer should you choose?

When to Start the Guessing Process

Unless your plan for guessing is to select C every time (which, despite its merits, is not what we recommend), you need to leave yourself enough time to apply your answer elimination strategies. Since you have a limited amount of time for each question, that means that if you're going to give yourself the best shot at guessing correctly, you have to decide quickly whether or not you will guess.

Of course, the best-case scenario is that you don't have to guess at all, so first, see if you can answer the question based on your knowledge of the subject and basic reasoning skills. Focus on the key words in the question and try to jog your memory of related topics. Give yourself a chance to bring the knowledge to mind, but once you realize that you don't have (or you can't access) the knowledge you need to answer the question, it's time to start the guessing process.

It's almost always better to start the guessing process too early than too late. It only takes a few seconds to remember something and answer the question from knowledge. Carefully eliminating wrong answer choices takes longer. Plus, going through the process of eliminating answer choices can actually help jog your memory.

Summary: Start the guessing process as soon as you decide that you can't answer the question based on your knowledge.

How to Narrow Down the Choices

The next chapter in this book (**Test-Taking Strategies**) includes a wide range of strategies for how to approach questions and how to look for answer choices to eliminate. You will definitely want to read those carefully, practice them, and figure out which ones work best for you. Here though, we're going to address a mindset rather than a particular strategy.

Your odds of guessing an answer correctly depend on how many options you are choosing from.

Number of options left	5	4	3	2	1
Odds of guessing correctly	20%	25%	33%	50%	100%

You can see from this chart just how valuable it is to be able to eliminate incorrect answers and make an educated guess, but there are two things that many test takers do that cause them to miss out on the benefits of guessing:

- Accidentally eliminating the correct answer
- Selecting an answer based on an impression

We'll look at the first one here, and the second one in the next section.

To avoid accidentally eliminating the correct answer, we recommend a thought exercise called **the $5 challenge**. In this challenge, you only eliminate an answer choice from contention if you are willing to bet $5 on it being wrong. Why $5? Five dollars is a small but not insignificant amount of money. It's an amount you could afford to lose but wouldn't want to throw away. And while losing $5 once might not hurt too much, doing it twenty times will set you back $100. In the same way, each small decision you make—eliminating a choice here, guessing on a question there—won't by itself impact your score very much, but when you put them all together, they can make a big difference. By holding each answer choice elimination decision to a higher standard, you can reduce the risk of accidentally eliminating the correct answer.

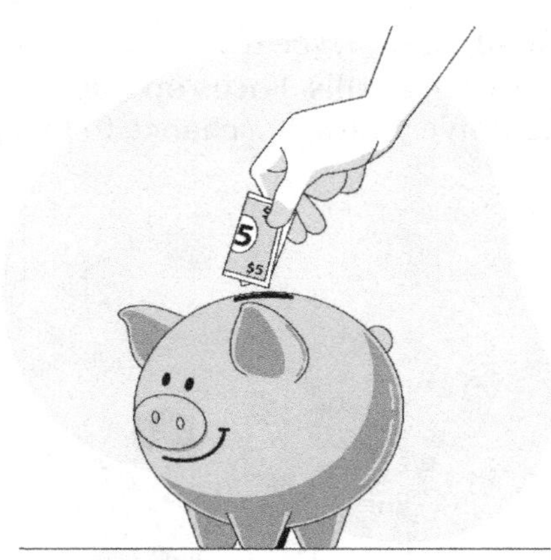

The $5 challenge can also be applied in a positive sense: If you are willing to bet $5 that an answer choice *is* correct, go ahead and mark it as correct.

Summary: Only eliminate an answer choice if you are willing to bet $5 that it is wrong.

Which Answer to Choose

You're taking the test. You've run into a hard question and decided you'll have to guess. You've eliminated all the answer choices you're willing to bet $5 on. Now you have to pick an answer. Why do we even need to talk about this? Why can't you just pick whichever one you feel like when the time comes?

The answer to these questions is that if you don't come into the test with a plan, you'll rely on your impression to select an answer choice, and if you do that, you risk falling into a trap. The test writers know that everyone who takes their test will be guessing on some of the questions, so they intentionally write wrong answer choices to seem plausible. You still have to pick an answer though, and if the wrong answer choices are designed to look right, how can you ever be sure that you're not falling for their trap? The best solution we've found to this dilemma is to take the decision out of your hands entirely. Here is the process we recommend:

Once you've eliminated any choices that you are confident (willing to bet $5) are wrong, select the first remaining choice as your answer.

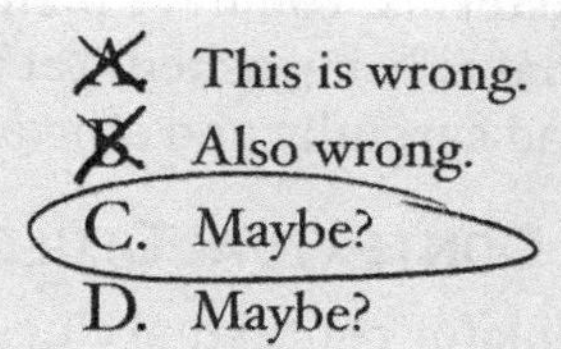

Whether you choose to select the first remaining choice, the second, or the last, the important thing is that you use some preselected standard. Using this approach guarantees that you will not be enticed into selecting an answer choice that looks right, because you are not basing your decision on how the answer choices look.

This is not meant to make you question your knowledge. Instead, it is to help you recognize the difference between your knowledge and your impressions. There's a huge difference between thinking an answer is right because of what you know, and thinking an answer is right because it looks or sounds like it should be right.

Summary: To ensure that your selection is appropriately random, make a predetermined selection from among all answer choices you have not eliminated.

Test-Taking Strategies

This section contains a list of test-taking strategies that you may find helpful as you work through the test. By taking what you know and applying logical thought, you can maximize your chances of answering any question correctly!

It is very important to realize that every question is different and every person is different: no single strategy will work on every question, and no single strategy will work for every person. That's why we've included all of them here, so you can try them out and determine which ones work best for different types of questions and which ones work best for you.

Question Strategies

☑ Read Carefully

Read the question and the answer choices carefully. Don't miss the question because you misread the terms. You have plenty of time to read each question thoroughly and make sure you understand what is being asked. Yet a happy medium must be attained, so don't waste too much time. You must read carefully and efficiently.

☑ Contextual Clues

Look for contextual clues. If the question includes a word you are not familiar with, look at the immediate context for some indication of what the word might mean. Contextual clues can often give you all the information you need to decipher the meaning of an unfamiliar word. Even if you can't determine the meaning, you may be able to narrow down the possibilities enough to make a solid guess at the answer to the question.

☑ Prefixes

If you're having trouble with a word in the question or answer choices, try dissecting it. Take advantage of every clue that the word might include. Prefixes can be a huge help. Usually, they allow you to determine a basic meaning. *Pre-* means before, *post-* means after, *pro-* is positive, *de-* is negative. From prefixes, you can get an idea of the general meaning of the word and try to put it into context.

☑ Hedge Words

Watch out for critical hedge words, such as *likely, may, can, sometimes, often, almost, mostly, usually, generally, rarely,* and *sometimes.* Question writers insert these hedge phrases to cover every possibility. Often an answer choice will be wrong simply because it leaves no room for exception. Be on guard for answer choices that have definitive words such as *exactly* and *always.*

☑ Switchback Words

Stay alert for *switchbacks.* These are the words and phrases frequently used to alert you to shifts in thought. The most common switchback words are *but, although,* and *however.* Others include *nevertheless, on the other hand, even though, while, in spite of, despite,* and *regardless of.* Switchback words are important to catch because they can change the direction of the question or an answer choice.

✓ Face Value

When in doubt, use common sense. Accept the situation in the problem at face value. Don't read too much into it. These problems will not require you to make wild assumptions. If you have to go beyond creativity and warp time or space in order to have an answer choice fit the question, then you should move on and consider the other answer choices. These are normal problems rooted in reality. The applicable relationship or explanation may not be readily apparent, but it is there for you to figure out. Use your common sense to interpret anything that isn't clear.

Answer Choice Strategies

✓ Answer Selection

The most thorough way to pick an answer choice is to identify and eliminate wrong answers until only one is left, then confirm it is the correct answer. Sometimes an answer choice may immediately seem right, but be careful. The test writers will usually put more than one reasonable answer choice on each question, so take a second to read all of them and make sure that the other choices are not equally obvious. As long as you have time left, it is better to read every answer choice than to pick the first one that looks right without checking the others.

✓ Answer Choice Families

An answer choice family consists of two (in rare cases, three) answer choices that are very similar in construction and cannot all be true at the same time. If you see two answer choices that are direct opposites or parallels, one of them is usually the correct answer. For instance, if one answer choice says that quantity *x* increases and another either says that quantity *x* decreases (opposite) or says that quantity *y* increases (parallel), then those answer choices would fall into the same family. An answer choice that doesn't match the construction of the answer choice family is more likely to be incorrect. Most questions will not have answer choice families, but when they do appear, you should be prepared to recognize them.

✓ Eliminate Answers

Eliminate answer choices as soon as you realize they are wrong, but make sure you consider all possibilities. If you are eliminating answer choices and realize that the last one you are left with is also wrong, don't panic. Start over and consider each choice again. There may be something you missed the first time that you will realize on the second pass.

✓ Avoid Fact Traps

Don't be distracted by an answer choice that is factually true but doesn't answer the question. You are looking for the choice that answers the question. Stay focused on what the question is asking for so you don't accidentally pick an answer that is true but incorrect. Always go back to the question and make sure the answer choice you've selected actually answers the question and is not merely a true statement.

✓ Extreme Statements

In general, you should avoid answers that put forth extreme actions as standard practice or proclaim controversial ideas as established fact. An answer choice that states the "process should be used in certain situations, if…" is much more likely to be correct than one that states the "process should be discontinued completely." The first is a calm rational statement and doesn't even make a definitive, uncompromising stance, using a hedge word *if* to provide wiggle room, whereas the second choice is far more extreme.

⊘ Benchmark

As you read through the answer choices and you come across one that seems to answer the question well, mentally select that answer choice. This is not your final answer, but it's the one that will help you evaluate the other answer choices. The one that you selected is your benchmark or standard for judging each of the other answer choices. Every other answer choice must be compared to your benchmark. That choice is correct until proven otherwise by another answer choice beating it. If you find a better answer, then that one becomes your new benchmark. Once you've decided that no other choice answers the question as well as your benchmark, you have your final answer.

⊘ Predict the Answer

Before you even start looking at the answer choices, it is often best to try to predict the answer. When you come up with the answer on your own, it is easier to avoid distractions and traps because you will know exactly what to look for. The right answer choice is unlikely to be word-for-word what you came up with, but it should be a close match. Even if you are confident that you have the right answer, you should still take the time to read each option before moving on.

General Strategies

⊘ Tough Questions

If you are stumped on a problem or it appears too hard or too difficult, don't waste time. Move on! Remember though, if you can quickly check for obviously incorrect answer choices, your chances of guessing correctly are greatly improved. Before you completely give up, at least try to knock out a couple of possible answers. Eliminate what you can and then guess at the remaining answer choices before moving on.

⊘ Check Your Work

Since you will probably not know every term listed and the answer to every question, it is important that you get credit for the ones that you do know. Don't miss any questions through careless mistakes. If at all possible, try to take a second to look back over your answer selection and make sure you've selected the correct answer choice and haven't made a costly careless mistake (such as marking an answer choice that you didn't mean to mark). This quick double check should more than pay for itself in caught mistakes for the time it costs.

⊘ Pace Yourself

It's easy to be overwhelmed when you're looking at a page full of questions; your mind is confused and full of random thoughts, and the clock is ticking down faster than you would like. Calm down and maintain the pace that you have set for yourself. Especially as you get down to the last few minutes of the test, don't let the small numbers on the clock make you panic. As long as you are on track by monitoring your pace, you are guaranteed to have time for each question.

⊘ Don't Rush

It is very easy to make errors when you are in a hurry. Maintaining a fast pace in answering questions is pointless if it makes you miss questions that you would have gotten right otherwise. Test writers like to include distracting information and wrong answers that seem right. Taking a little extra time to avoid careless mistakes can make all the difference in your test score. Find a pace that allows you to be confident in the answers that you select.

✅ Keep Moving

Panicking will not help you pass the test, so do your best to stay calm and keep moving. Taking deep breaths and going through the answer elimination steps you practiced can help to break through a stress barrier and keep your pace.

Final Notes

The combination of a solid foundation of content knowledge and the confidence that comes from practicing your plan for applying that knowledge is the key to maximizing your performance on test day. As your foundation of content knowledge is built up and strengthened, you'll find that the strategies included in this chapter become more and more effective in helping you quickly sift through the distractions and traps of the test to isolate the correct answer.

Now that you're preparing to move forward into the test content chapters of this book, be sure to keep your goal in mind. As you read, think about how you will be able to apply this information on the test. If you've already seen sample questions for the test and you have an idea of the question format and style, try to come up with questions of your own that you can answer based on what you're reading. This will give you valuable practice applying your knowledge in the same ways you can expect to on test day.

Good luck and good studying!

Professional Practice and Ethics

Ethics

History and Development of Ethical Standards

In 1961, the American Personnel and Guidance Association (APGA) adopted **ethical standards** of the mental health counseling profession. In 1964, the Association for Counselor Education and Supervision (ACES) provided training standards for secondary school counselors. In 1973, the Standards for Preparation of Counselors and other Personnel Services Specialists were embraced by the ACES association. In 1977, standards were agreed on that met master's and doctoral degree requirements.

The American Mental Health Counselors Association (AMHCA) also wrote standards for mental health counseling programs. In 1995, these ethical standards went through a thorough process of revision. These new standards have been adopted by other groups that provide certification. AMHCA Standards are applied and enforced by the AMHCA Ethics Committee. The most stringent of these enforcements are found in the regulations that allocate expulsion from the association.

Review Video: Code of Ethics
Visit mometrix.com/academy and enter code: 629669

Incorporation of Ethics into Curricula

It was not until after 1990 that **ethics courses** were incorporated into the counselors' graduate degree programs. The American Psychological Association played an important part in the 1970's to change the curricula offered in doctoral programs by requiring colleges to teach ethics. This requirement was necessary before the college could be granted accreditation privileges. Those in the field prior to 1990 had to depend upon their supervisors' ability to both model and train in ethical procedures and conduct. This was an inefficient method for a number of reasons. The supervisor may not have been aware of the ethical code that applied to a given situation, or the supervisor may not have had a good understanding of sound ethical principles. Instruction in ethical principles should not be the sole responsibility of the clinical supervisor.

History and Development of the Code of Ethics

The original **Code of Ethics** for counselors was introduced in 1990 and gave specific solutions to specific problems; however, it had ambiguous interpretations in areas not specifically spelled out. The ambiguity is seen in the way that the code does not specify the meaning of exact terms. The National Board for Certified Counselors sought in 1997 to provide a less ambiguous wording for the Code of Ethics, so it is no longer seen as abstract rules that do not apply to real situations and real people. Problem-solving models and appreciation for the philosophical basis of each code has been applied to the more comprehensive ethical courses available in colleges today. The American Counseling Association's most recent Code of Ethics was released in 2014 to include the elements of distance counseling, technology, and social media. This code is very similar to the National Board for Certified Counselors Code of Ethics (2016), which contains 95 directives for ethical standards to be upheld by all certified counselors.

ACA's 2014 Code of Ethics

Elements addressed within the American Counseling Association (ACA) Code of Ethics (2014) include the following:

- **Counseling relationship**: Informed consent, prohibited sexual and/or romantic relationships, professional boundaries, roles with individuals and groups, payment issues, business practices, and termination and referrals.
- **Confidentiality and privacy**: Right to privacy and exceptions, such as the serious and foreseeable harm requirements, information sharing, record keeping, and client access.
- **Professional responsibility**: Issues of competency, advertising, soliciting clients, professional qualifications, and responsibilities to public.
- **Relationships with other professionals**: Respect and equity in professional relationships with colleagues, employers, and employees, and provisions of consultation.
- **Evaluation, assessment, and interpretation**: Assessment, diagnosis, instrument selection, and conditions and issues related to assessment.
- **Supervision, training, and teaching**: Responsibilities of the supervisor and educator roles.
- **Research and publication**: Guidelines for carrying out research, informing clients, and protecting clients.
- **Distance counseling, technology, and social media**: Laws/regulations for both the counselor's place of work and client's place of residence may apply. Clients should be aware that privacy and security of electronic transmission may be breached. The counselor must verify the client's identity at every session.
- **Resolving ethical issues**: Reporting violations and cooperating with ethics committees.

Informed Consent

Provisions of the ACA Code of Ethics (2014) regarding **informed consent** in the counseling relationship include the following:

- Clients should be informed of the nature of all services both in writing and verbally and should be apprised of fees. Clients should be included in discussions even if they are themselves unable to give informed consent.
- Language used to obtain informed consent must be clear, understandable, and culturally appropriate.
- Informed consent must be obtained for all assessments, and recipients of assessment results must be identified.
- If supervising another counselor, the supervisee must be made aware of clients' rights, and the client must give consent for supervision.
- Clients must have informed consent for any research they are involved in and have the right to refuse participation.
- Clients must be informed about risks of breach of security when utilizing distance counseling and should be apprised of the location of the counselor's practice, risks and benefits of participation, anticipated response times (such as for text messaging), times when counselor is available, and issues related to payment or nonpayment of third-party payors.

Ethical Dilemmas

Ethical Issues that Counselors May Face

The counselor is obligated to uphold ethical standards. The nature of the work presents the counselor with ongoing **challenges that test the counselor's ethical positions** about a problem.

Counselors not only have to consider the ethical position they should take when a problem presents, but must also consider how the solution will be of benefit to the client. The client cannot be damaged from the solution. Therefore, the consequences of the solution should be weighed carefully. There does exist a tendency for counselors to do nothing when an ethical issue is involved. This tendency may be due to the fact that the counselor feels unsure of how to proceed in the situation, or it may be that the counselor is reluctant to proceed in general. Self-awareness when this hesitation occurs is vital in ensuring proper handling of ethical dilemmas.

Problem-Solving for Ethical Dilemmas

There are nine steps used in the problem-solving model for ethical dilemmas designed by Koocher and Keith-Spiegel in 1998:

- **Step 1**: Determine the ethical problem.
- **Step 2**: Review the ethical guidelines available that pertain to the problem at hand, including possible solutions that have previously worked with other clients.
- **Step 3**: Peruse the impact that other sources may have on the decisions that should be made to resolve the problem.
- **Step 4**: Consult with trusted professionals about the problem and possible solutions.
- **Step 5**: Assess the human rights and civil liberties of the client, which may be impacted by the solution to the problem, and consider possible consequences of the solution for the problem at hand.
- **Step 6**: Create a number of avenues that may be explored in the solution to the problem.
- **Step 7**: Evaluate the possible consequences that can be the result of each solution applied to the problem at hand.
- **Step 8**: Make a decision about one solution to be implemented.
- **Step 9**: Follow through with the decision that was made.

Koocher and Keith-Spiegel's approach can be applied to many ethical dilemmas that a counselor faces in his or her daily professional life. This model is currently in use in the instruction of ethical principles in degree programs throughout the country.

Multiple Relationships

In 1974, Arnold Lazarus was a renowned psychotherapist who supported **multiple relationships** in his ethical decision-making model (multi-modal therapy). Lazarus thought that the client could benefit from the development of both a therapeutic and social relationship with the counselor. In 1993, M.C. Gottlieb responded with his own five-step model:

- **Step 1**: Consider the element of power, where the client feels inferior to the counselor and may find a long-standing relationship harmful.
- **Step 2**: Consider the duration of the relationship by predicting how the relationship and the balance of power may change over time.
- **Step 3**: Consider the clarity of termination, which involves compatibility between the client and the counselor, and consequences that can occur when the client and counselor roles are conflicting and harmful.
- **Step 4**: Gain the perspective and advice of a professional associate.
- **Step 5**: Present the relationship change to the client, and give him or her time to make a decision about this change in the relationship.

Small-Town Phenomenon

Some multiple relationships are unavoidable. For instance, the **small-town phenomenon** describes a situation in which the therapist may have to come into contact with clients within the social structures of a community. A small-town therapist may belong to the same religious organization as a client. The small-town therapist may find that their clients live in the same neighborhood or have children in the same school as their own. The small-town therapist may belong to the same charitable organizations or attend the same functions.

Deontology vs. Utilitarianism

Two of the most common schools of thought when approaching ethical decision-making and ethical dilemmas are the deontological view and the utilitarian view.

- Immanuel Kant is most commonly associated with the **deontological view** of ethics. One foundational philosophy developed by Kant was his categorical imperative. Deontological perspectives deal in universal truths, where everyone receives equal treatment. Therefore, when a counselor believes that privacy should be part of their service, then that privacy is applied to all clients in every situation. There is no room for exceptions to the rule. Likewise, there is no need to consider consequences in this philosophy, as all people are treated equally. The Golden Rule is at the heart of deontology ("Do unto others as you would have them do unto you").
- **Utilitarianism** was presented by John Stuart Mill. He believed that the consequences had to be looked at in relation to the resulting outcomes. The overall goal is to create as many constructive and positive consequences as possible for the majority of people.

Confidentiality in the Counselor-Client Relationship

Application of HIPAA Concepts in the Counseling Profession

Counselors who electronically submit any type of protected health information for third-party payments for services must be **HIPAA** compliant with the privacy rule, which then applies to all protected health information (PHI), even that not transmitted. Once compliance with the privacy rule is triggered, compliance with the security rule is also required:

- **Privacy rule**: Protected information includes any information included in the medical record (electronic or paper), conversations between the doctor and other healthcare providers, billing information, and any other form of health information. Procedures must be in place to limit access and disclosures.
- **Security rule**: Any electronic health information must be secure and protected against threats, hazards, or non-permitted disclosures, in compliance with established standards.

Individual states may have even more restrictive regulations and may have consent requirements, so the counselor must be aware of all pertinent laws and regulations. Therapy notes that are separate from the rest of the medical record have increased protection from disclosure. PHI may be disclosed without consent to report abuse, to prevent serious harm to person or public, and in response to legal subpoenas or court orders.

> **Review Video: What is HIPAA?**
> Visit mometrix.com/academy and enter code: 412009

Breaking Confidentiality

John Stuart Mill proposed that the utilitarian should **break confidentiality** when it benefited the majority of the people. In 1976, a lawsuit was brought to the California Supreme Court to contest the deontological perspective against the utilitarian perspective. In the case of *Tarasoff versus the Board of Regents of the University of California*, the courts supported the utilitarian perspective on breaking confidentiality for the good of the majority. The court allowed that keeping confidentiality in this case could have caused injury to others. However, some counselors do tend to believe that confidentiality should be an absolute right of the client.

Review Video: Ethics and Confidentiality in Counseling
Visit mometrix.com/academy and enter code: 250384

Virtue Ethics

The **virtue ethics** philosophy holds that people with high ethical standards have the ability to make good ethical judgments. This philosophy is also known as value ethics or principle ethics. Lazarus' decision-making model is based on the virtue ethics philosophy. The counselor can find that having a strong philosophy of virtue ethics can assist them in their work. Virtue ethics helps the counselor to be motivated to make the best decision for their client and helps the counselor to understand their responsibility to act in a positive manner and to implement an ethical solution to a problem. Virtue ethics help the counselor in their appraisal of possible consequences that can arise in a given solution. The counselor with a strong philosophy in virtue ethics has a strong moral character. Virtue ethics is based on **beneficence** and **nonmaleficence**, which are the basis of the **Hippocratic Oath** that states, "First, do no harm." This means that the counselor works to help the client and does not want any damage to come to the client. The decisions that are made in counseling must not disregard the principles maintained in virtue ethics.

Role of Care and Compassion in Virtue Ethics and Counseling

Care and compassion take the principles behind beneficence one step further. In 1982, Gilligan described caring as a bonding process that created a sense that the counselor had the ability to understand and to identify with how the client was feeling. Gilligan also proposed that the counselor was able to react quickly and favorably in meeting the needs of the client. Gilligan went on to state that the counselor exhibited a compassionate and concerned commitment to their client. The counselor performs these acts of caring in a professional manner. The counselor should not try to practice counseling methods that fall outside their scope of expertise and training. The counselor may violate an ethical principle by not realizing their own incompetence in an area. Some violations occur out of arrogance, over-involvement, or control issues with the client.

Inherent Dangers Associated with Virtue Ethics and Ways to Enhance an Ethical Perspective

Virtue ethics are essential in the role that the counselor performs. However, a note of caution: No one source can be trusted to **maintain a virtue ethics perspective**. Therefore, supervisors, ethical codes, decision-making models, utilitarian perspectives, and deontological perspectives should all be understood and reviewed when making ethical decisions.

- The counselor should seek to internalize sound virtue ethics principles.
- The counselor should recognize virtue ethics and seek to live by those ethics in all areas of life.
- The counselor should seek to gain additional education and training to ensure that they gain competency in a variety of areas.
- The counselor should seek out an ethical support group.
- The counselor should seek to establish sound ethical philosophies that reflect virtue ethics principles.

COMPETENCE

Competence is the ability to do something to a compulsory set of standards. However, this denotes the most basic level of competency. In the counselor's role, **competence** must be reached at its uppermost levels. This regard for excellence in performance levels follows the perspective held in virtue ethics. Therefore, the counselor takes on a life-long commitment to achieving competency levels in their profession. In 1996, Pope and Brown proposed that there were two types of competence to be achieved.

- The first type involves **intellectual competence**, which consists of education and training.
- The second type involves **emotional competence**. The counselor is self-aware of prejudices held, emotional stability, and competence levels. The counselor seeks professional supervision and referrals when it is necessary.

SELF-KNOWLEDGE

Self-knowledge is an area in which a counselor should make a daily assessment. Some psychoanalytically-trained therapists must undergo counseling therapy as part of their training. This is not always the case, however. **Self-knowledge** is essential in developing competency in an area. Competency is a considerable part of value ethics. Self-knowledge is also supported by supervisory personnel in the field. Peers or colleagues can be sought out to gain advice on ethical dilemmas. Some counselors violate virtue ethics by becoming too absorbed in the client's problem. Caring and compassion is taken to unhealthy emotional levels. One condition that can arise from this violation is post-traumatic stress disorder. The counselor has the tendency to develop hypervigilance in response to stressful situations that arise daily. The counselor may experience burnout or withdraw from their family. The counselor may also experience physical or emotional symptoms.

RESPECT

The counselor must treat all clients with **respect**. Respect involves accuracy in reporting details, loyal devotion, honesty, confidence, reliability, keeping promises, and valuing the client's personal independence. The counselor relays to the client an accurate representation of the counselor's role, the client's rights, confidentiality rights, and any negative consequences that can result in a prescribed treatment plan. A handout and simple explanation do not ensure client understanding. The client and legal guardians must give informed consent before treatment can be applied. Clients with a legal guardian must have the guardian's consent to the therapy. Informed consent involves confidentiality in the counselor-client relationship. Confidentiality is maintained in individual counseling sessions unless the client is a danger to himself or others. This harm must be identified by method and time. Confidentiality is not assured in a group setting or in cases of child abuse.

JUSTICE AND ACCOUNTABILITY

The counselor is aware of their role in providing clients with a fair and just program of treatment. Fairness involves the same equal treatment of all clients, as each receives a fair amount of the counselor's time and attention. The virtue of **justice** may be violated when the counselor is in denial or when the counselor tries to rationalize their actions.

Accountability is part of the virtue ethics philosophy. This means that the counselor takes responsibility for their actions and that of others in their field. Unethical behavior in others can be handled professionally and emphatically. Confrontations need to be approached with respect and a sense of fair play. The goal of the confrontation is to achieve a positive result. The counselor should role-play or rehearse confrontations to ensure that possible responses and consequences can be responded to on a professional level.

Ethics-Based Approaches when Services a Client Requires are Limited

Many HMO's and other third-party influences may cause the counselor to question whether virtue ethics principles are being followed in the client's care. The counselor may believe that the client is in need of more sessions that are not covered under the client's insurance policy. The counselor can follow a series of actions to maintain the virtue ethics principles of beneficence and nonmaleficence. The counselor may appeal to the insurance company for additional sessions. The counselor may also continue to see the client at a reduced price, giving additional sessions at an affordable rate, or issue a referral to the client to seek free services from a government agency or reputable charity. These actions reflect a sense of caring for the client that follows ethical guidelines.

Regulatory Standards

History of Professional Counseling Certification

The **Commission on Rehabilitation Counselor Certification (CRCC)** was established in 1973. In 1976, the CRCC initiated its first national assessment. Currently, the CRCC boasts over 30,000 certifications and over 15,000 valid certification holders.

The **National Academy of Certified Clinical Mental Health Counselors** was founded by AMHCA in 1979. The first 50 candidates had to provide a clinical work sample and pass the national assessment exam. Throughout the years, the exacting standards for this voluntary credential have kept the numbers of credentialed counselors low.

In 1982, the **National Board of Certified Counselors (NBCC)** was established under the APGA. This organization offered a generic counseling certificate to mental health counselors. In 1983, the NBCC gave the assessment to certify over 2,200 mental health counselors.

In 1985, the **National Counsel for the Credentialing of Career Counselors (NCCC)** offered a professional certification. However, this certification is no longer available. The NCCC does maintain the NCCC credential previously achieved by its candidates who passed the assessment given.

In the latter part of the 1990s, the National Academy of Certified Clinical Mental Health Counselors joined the National Board for Certified Counselors. The joint entity offers the National Certified School Counselor (NCSC) and the Master Addictions Counselor (MAC) certificates. There is now one generic certification available to mental health counselors, which remains suitable for a broad range of positions. There are now five specialty certifications available on a national or international level, in addition to minor types of certification in place.

Credentialing Process

The credentialing process depends on the counselor's work setting and specialty. Generally, credentialing begins with the student obtaining a master's degree of 48-60 semester hours in psychology or education. Some states still accept a bachelor's degree with additional post-graduate courses in counseling, or for substance abuse and behavior counselors in certain settings, a high school diploma and certification. There are generally eight **core areas of study**:

- Professional counseling orientation and ethical practice
- Social and cultural diversity
- Human growth and development
- Career development
- Counseling and helping relationships
- Group counseling and group work
- Assessment and testing
- Research and program evaluation

Student counselors complete a supervised clinical experience, usually 3,000 hours or 2 years, and obtain two letters of professional endorsement. Licensure differs state by state. The candidate must pass a state exam. Most licenses require annual continuing education credits for maintenance. The counselor agrees to follow certain standards and ethical codes. Some jobs require additional credentials, for example, a school counselor must have both a teaching certificate and a counseling certificate, in addition to teaching experience.

Accreditation

Accreditation is quality control for the programs that train mental health counselors. Most universities observe **accreditation standards** in each academic department. Not all private schools, colleges, and universities that offer counseling courses are accredited. A student will probably not be able to obtain an internship to complete their practicum or obtain a license if they did not attend an accredited school. Internship positions are usually found in organizations such as hospitals, community mental health centers, clinics, and schools, many of which require accreditation. The stakeholders involved in accreditation include the following:

- Pre-service programs
- Professional preparation programs
- Local agencies
- State agencies
- Federal agencies

Accreditation is founded on a set of standards that can be tied to either the professional standards or to a general set of standards. The program and the standards must be defined in such a way that the accreditation is acceptable to future employers.

CACREP Accreditation

The ACES (Assessment, Counseling, and Educational Services) developed a manual for training counselors in the field of mental health in 1978. This manual was used in five regional workshops in 1979 for a pilot program. Then, the American Personnel and Guidance Association (APGA) and ACES began developing an accreditation program for mental health counselors. In 1981, the **Council for the Accreditation of Counseling and Related Educational Programs (CACREP)** was founded as an independent organization that could provide accreditation to the mental health counselor. As of 2018, over 400 universities boast of CACREP accredited educational programs in their schools. These universities have increased the number of master's and doctoral level programs that they now offer. Many other universities are in pursuit of the CACREP accreditation for their programs. Many states mandate the necessity of the CACREP accreditation as a requirement for obtaining a license.

Changes in the Counseling Education and Program Accreditation

The increase in both long- and short-term psychotherapies wrought a number of **changes in the education system**. Those responsible for the educational needs of counselors changed curricula and techniques to improve the quality of education. Education counselors added the courses to the counselor's curricula to address the changing demographics and needs of the country, with courses focused on multicultural counseling, brief therapy, and ethical issues. Counselors began learning about conflict resolution, community consultations, case management, and client advocacy, in addition to sound business practices. Counselor education programs have been encouraged to seek accreditation privileges from the Council for Accreditation of Counseling and Related Educational Programs (CACREP). The accredited program's objectives and curriculum must follow approved standards with clinical instruction. Faculty and staff must meet prescribed CACREP standards regarding organizations and administrative structures. In addition, the college must be willing to undergo program evaluations set by CACREP standards.

CACREP Standards for Professional Counseling Education Programs

In 2016, the **Standards of the Council for the Accreditation of Counseling and Related Educational Programs (CACREP)** were organized into six sections. These six sections include:

- The learning environment
- Professional counseling identity
- Professional practice
- Evaluation in the program
- Entry-level specialty areas (including addictions, career, clinical mental health, clinical rehabilitation, college counseling and student affairs, marriage/couple/family, and school counseling)
- Doctoral standards for counselor education and supervision

According to the CACREP, these standards were written "with the intention to simplify and clarify the accreditation requirements and to promote a unified counseling profession." The CACREP standards provide sequencing and clinical experience that can make a solid foundation for the professional counselor's education. The standards help the counselor to develop a professional identity. The student learns about social and cultural diversity, human development and growth, career development, helping relationships, group work, assessment, research, and program evaluation. The student receives clinical instruction and experience at a supervised practicum and internship opportunities, in addition to the theory. The number of clinical hours, the type of supervision, and supervisory credentials are included in the **CACREP standards**. Curriculum development can also be improved with contributions made by counseling practitioners.

Standards of Professional Practice

The professional practice standards for counselors require significant command of mental health care theory and its application. Graduate students must be prepared to accept entry level positions to become proficient and competent in all skills. A standard set of criteria is used to assess whether or not the graduate student has reached the level of professional proficiency. The criteria include the following:

- Meeting accreditation requirements
- Following ethical practice standards* for the public good
- Achieving competencies required in entry level positions
- Satisfactory completion of all academic classes
- Satisfactory completion of a supervised clinical experience (usually 3,000 hours)
- Meeting all certification provisions (e.g., two professional endorsement letters)

*Ethical standards apply to testing of humans and animals and refraining from sexual or other harmful relationships with clients. Ethical standards stipulate scrutiny and disciplinary actions for violators.

Licensing

State Licensing Boards

State licensing boards supervise mental health professionals in their work. **State licensing boards** set internship hours, supervisor qualifications, and the amount of direct client contact required, as well as monitor ethics. When a board finds that a counselor acted unethically, then the state can suspend or revoke the counselor's license and apply penalties. Counselors who wish to renew their licenses may be required to complete continuing education credits and pay additional fees to the state board. If a counselor is discovered practicing without a legal license, then he or she can be charged and prosecuted. Each state posts its minimum education and work experience standards for statutory certification, and every counselor in the state must meet them. The counselor can use the civil law system to fight the state board's charges and to sue for monetary restitution.

Licensure and Professional Certification Requirements

Counselors receive state authorization to work as mental health practitioners either through **licensure** or **professional certification**. Licensure is the law in most of the country. Some states do not issue licenses; instead, they recognize professional certification as the practice credential, meaning the candidate obtained the National Certified Counselor designation through the National Board for Certified Counselors, Inc. National certification is voluntary. It is distinct from a state license and requires a separate exam and 100 hours of continuing education every 5 years. The Commission on Rehabilitation Counselor Certification is required for rehab counselors, and includes an exam every 5 years or 100 hours of education, an internship, and work experience in rehabilitation if the counselor graduated with another specialization.

Licensure Laws

In 1976, the Virginia Counselors Association passed **licensure laws**. This was the result of a lawsuit by an unlicensed counselor. In 1979, Arkansas and Alabama passed licensure laws also. By the end of 1985, more than 13 states had passed similar licensure laws. Currently, all states, the District of Colombia, and Puerto Rico now have counseling licensure laws. Licensure laws give the public a sense of protection that their therapists are qualified professionals who have met the requirements of the state to hold those positions. All states mandate a written assessment and some also have oral assessments in place. The professional who gains a license is a Licensed Professional Counselor, Licensed Clinical Mental Health Counselor, or Certified Professional Counselor. Ethical violators are penalized by the legal system. Exemptions are given to those in private and public practice who counsel in related professional groups.

Future of Counselor Credentialing

The efforts of the AMHCA have had a profound affect upon the licensure laws for counselors in the mental health field. Counselor education programs have applied more exacting standards to their courses. Managed care options in the insurance industry have also changed the counselor's standing within the profession. This change has benefited the equality that mental health counselors desire to be accepted by other professionals. Legislation has also been passed to grant professional counselors equal standing. The credentials and licensure laws will continue to change as government bodies are influenced by the efforts of AMHCA. The future promises to be one in which more opportunities are presented to the counselors who have achieved the appropriate credentials required in their state of operation. New counseling professions will emerge as the need for more specialized counselors arises.

Legal and Political Issues

Legislative Process

Proposing and Promoting a Bill

The **legislative process** begins with a proposed bill. This proposed bill must be assessed to determine what strategies are applicable to get the bill to pass and become law. The bill must be presented to the legislature. This calls for some consideration about the most receptive body. Some bills do well in the House of Representatives, and other bills are more suited to the Senate. Still others perform well in both the House and the Senate. The political representative who is chosen must be the best advocate for the particular cause. Special interest groups may help promote the bill through legislative contacts, after it has been presented to the legislative body. Lobbyists work to establish relationships with key committee members. The bill must go through the committee before it can be voted on.

Passing a Bill to Become Law

Most bills that are introduced to a legislative body never make it out of committee. The bill that does make it out of committee must still be given support by the majority of the legislative body to be **approved**. The approved bill can then be sent to the **executive branch** of the government. The executive branch on the state level is the governor. The executive branch on the national level is the president. The executive branch representative has the responsibility of signing the bill into law and may veto or reject a bill. The executive branch is subject to lobbying efforts. The **legislative process** is expensive and time-consuming. The American Mental Health Counselors Association (AMHCA) sees it as their responsibility to take on this complex process to ensure that counselors are recognized and credentialed by each state.

Influences of the Political System on Counseling

The United States has a **political system** that allows its citizens to voice their issues and concerns publicly. A wide spectrum of communication systems is available to help in this endeavor. The individual may present their issues/concerns to others through speeches, telephone calls, emails, or the internet (blogs, social media, etc.). The AMHCA recognizes the need to bring issues important to mental health counselors to light and works jointly with the American Counseling Association (ACA) to send lobbyists to Washington D.C. to represent mental health counselors. As early as 1982, the AMHCA has managed to enlist the services of a renowned lobbyist to represent its interests in the political arena. Today, the AMHCA continues on this endeavor, and provides resources to mental health counselors on how to stay informed on proposed legislation, contact their local legislator, and appropriately lobby either as an individual or part of a group.

Avenues the AMHCA Established in their Political Network

Mental health counselors were taught how to represent themselves as **political advocates and lobbyists** in the grassroots campaigns set up by the AMHCA. The AMHCA and the ACA have worked diligently to establish a network that is competent in issuing timely emails, written correspondence, phone calls, and face-to-face communications to promote its political agenda. The successes of the lobbying efforts have been critical in the licensure legislation set up in the majority of states, and it is expected that the AMHCA and the ACA will turn their efforts to equality issues for the mental health counselor. The problem of recognition exists on the corporate level. Private corporate third-party payers and some insurance companies have yet to recognize the high standards and expertise that exist in the mental health counselors' professional credentials.

Establishing Relationships of Influence with Political Officials

Mental health professionals may consider a relationship that is built on campaign contributions as ethically suspect. However, the time-honored tradition of donating money to a candidate's election campaign is effective in gaining the attention of **elected government officials**. The government official takes a donation to mean that an individual or group is a member of their campaign and that they support their position as a representative for the state. This puts the contributor in a privileged and influential position. A campaign donation may be enough for one to gain faster access into the government official's office. Any relationship that is built should be given the necessary attention to maintain it. Be persistent with communication efforts, even when no lobbying agenda is in place.

Relationships that Unpaid Lobbyists Must Develop

The **unpaid lobbyist** works to influence political entities and representatives who have the power to pass a bill. The counselor assigned as a lobbyist creates a rapport with elected government officials face-to-face and develops it through telephone calls, letters, and email correspondence. The intended result of this diligent communication effort is to remind the official about issues that are important to the counselor. The face-to-face visit can be accomplished during visits to the official's office in the home state. This setting gives the official a chance to connect with their constituents and to engage in conversation on key issues.

Importance of Votes and Financial Backing in Lobbying Efforts

Politicians are elected based on how many votes they receive from their constituents. This means that the politician finds great worth in the **power of the voter**. Constituents who are part of an organized group can mean a great many votes on election day. The politician will pay attention to the lobbyist who represents large numbers of constituents. The Political Action Committees (PAC) had a strong influence on the political system in the past. However, today this influence has diminished. PACs and many lobbying committees are careful to keep a low profile because of the negative attitudes that voters have about paid lobbyists and large corporations. Counselor lobbyists do not have much in the way of financial resources but do have the grassroots support of other counselor voters that are responsible for electing government officials into office.

Presenting Issues to Policy Makers

Communication Style

The importance of **communicating to policy makers in succinct terms** cannot be overstated. The unpaid lobbyist must make his or her point quickly and succinctly to be heard. Otherwise, the unpaid lobbyist risks "the brush off," or is not understood by the official. The best way to present an issue is through brief telephone calls, emails, or formally written letters. Hand-written notes should be written on paper that bears personal letterhead. Emails are not as effective but benefit from an appropriate subject and respectful tone. Communication should clearly state how the bill will make a positive impact on the voting constituents. Data points, signature lists of supporters, and other attachments are helpful to include in these communication efforts. Keep the client's needs at the forefront of one's mind. Represent these needs accurately to the elected government official. The official needs to understand how the bill will improve counseling services for the client.

Timing

Timing is another issue that should be addressed in the life of an unpaid lobbyist. Activate the communication network system among fellow counselor supporters whenever there is a vote in front of a legislative committee. The support of other counselors within the organized network should impact this vote in a positive way. The bill cannot go to the floor for a vote by the larger body of legislators until it is passed by the committee. The chain needs to be activated again when the bill comes up for a vote on the floor. This is a critical time, as the vote must pass to go on to the next step in the legislative process. The final stop is at the executive branch. This is also a critical time for the communication network to make their opinions known to their elected governmental leader.

Research

Research Process

The key steps in the research process are as follows:

1. **Problem or issue identification**: Includes a literature review to further define the problem and to ensure that the problem has not already been studied
2. **Hypothesis formulation**: Creating a clear statement of the problem or concern, worded in a way that it can be operationalized and measured
3. **Operationalization**: Creating measurable variables that fully address the hypothesis
4. **Study design selection**: Choosing a study design that will allow for the proper analysis of the data to be collected

Data

Objective vs. Subjective Data

Both **subjective (qualitative)** and **objective (quantitative)** data are used for research and analysis, but the focus is quite different:

Subjective Data	Objective Data
Subjective data depend on the opinions of the observer or the subject. Data are described verbally or graphically, depending upon observers to provide information. Interviews may be used as a tool to gather information, and the researcher's interpretation of data is important. Gathering this type of data can be time-intensive, and it usually cannot be generalized to a larger population. This type of information gathering is often useful at the beginning of the design process for data collection.	Objective data are observable and can be tested and verified. Data are described in terms of numbers within a statistical format. This type of information gathering is done after the design of data collection is outlined, usually in later stages. Tools may include surveys, questionnaires, or other methods of obtaining numerical data.

Data Collection

Key points in data collection include the following:

- Data should ideally be collected close to the time of intervention (delays may result in variation from forgetfulness, rather than from the intervention process).
- Frequent data collection is ideal, but subject boredom or fatigue must be avoided as well. Thus, make the data collection process as easy as possible (electronic devices can sometimes help).
- Keep the data collection process short to increase subject responsiveness.
- Standardize recording procedures (collect data at the same time, place, and method to enhance ultimate data validity and reliability).
- Choose a collection method that fits the study well (observation, questionnaires, logs, diaries, surveys, rating scales, etc.) to optimize the data collection process and enhance the value of the data obtained.

Study Designs

Selecting a Study Design

Key considerations that guide the selection of a study design include the following:

- **Standardization**: Whether or not data can be collected in an identical way from each participant (eliminating collection variation)
- **Level of certainty**: The study size needed to achieve statistical significance (determined via power calculations)
- **Resources**: The availability of funding and other resources needed
- The **time frame** required
- The capacity of subjects to provide **informed consent** and receiving **ethics approval** via Human Subjects Review Committees and Institutional Review Boards

Common Study Designs

The three common study designs used in the research process include the following:

- An **exploratory research design** is common when little is known about a particular problem or issue. Its key feature is flexibility. The results comprise detailed descriptions of all observations made, arranged in some kind of order. Conclusions drawn include educated guesses or hypotheses.
- When the variables chosen have already been studied (e.g., in an exploratory study), further research requires a **descriptive survey design**. In this design, the variables are controlled partly by the situation and partly by the investigator, who chooses the sample. Proof of causality cannot be established, but the evidence may support causality.
- **Experimental studies** are highly controlled. Intervening and extraneous variables are eliminated, and independent variables are manipulated to measure effects in dependent variables (e.g., variables of interest)—either in the field or in a laboratory setting.

Ethical Concerns with Study Design Selection

Ethical concerns involved with selecting a study design include the following:

- Research must not lead to harming clients.
- Denying an intervention may amount to harm.
- Informed consent is essential.
- Confidentiality is required.

Single System Study Designs

Evaluation of the efficacy and functionality of a practice is an important aspect of quality control and practice improvement. The most common approach to such an evaluation is the **single system study approach**. Selecting one client per system ($n = 1$), observations are made prior to, during, and following an intervention.

The **research steps** are:

1. Selection of a problem for change (the target)
2. Operationalizing the target into measurable terms
3. Following the target during the baseline phase, prior to the application of any intervention
4. Observing the target and collecting data during the intervention phase, during which the intervention is carried out (There may be more than one phase of data collection.)

Data that are repeatedly collected constitute a single system study "time series design." Single system designs provide a flexible and efficient way to evaluate virtually any type of practice.

Basic Single System Design and Additional Types of Case Study or Predesigns

The most basic single system design is the **A-B design**. The baseline phase (A) has no intervention, followed by the intervention phase (B) with data collection. Typically, data are collected continuously through the intervention phase. Advantages of this design include the following:

- Versatility
- Adaptability to many settings, program styles, and problems
- Clear comparative information between phases

A significant limitation, however, is that causation cannot be demonstrated.

Three additional types of **case study or predesigns** are:

- **Design A**, an observational design with no intervention
- **Design B,** an intervention-only design without any baseline
- **Design B-C**, a "changes case study" design (where no baseline is recorded, a first intervention [B] is performed and then changed [C] and data are recorded)

Common Single System Experimental Designs

Common single system experimental designs are described below:

- The **A-B-A design** begins with data collection in the pre-intervention phase (A) and then continuously during the intervention phases (B). The intervention is then removed (returning to "A") and data are again collected. In this way an experimental process is produced (testing without, with, and then again without intervention). Inferences regarding causality can be made, and two points of comparison are achieved. However, the ethics of removing a successful intervention leaves this study poorly recommended.
- The **A-B-A-B study** overcomes this failure by reintroducing the intervention ("B") at the close of the study. Greater causality inferences are obtained. However, even temporary removal of a successful intervention is problematic (especially if the client drops out at that time), and this design is fairly time-consuming.
- The **B-A-B design** (the "intervention repeat design") drops the baseline phase and starts and ends with the intervention (important in crisis situations and where treatment delays are problematic), saving time and reducing ethical concerns.

Sampling

Terms Used in Sampling

In sampling, the following concepts are considered:

- A **population** is the total set of subjects sought for measurement by a researcher.
- A **sample** is a subset of subjects drawn from a population (as total population testing is usually not possible).
- A **subject** is a single unit of a population.
- **Generalizability** refers to the degree to which specific findings obtained can be applied to the total population.

Sampling Techniques

The following are types of sampling techniques:

Simple random sampling	Any method of sampling wherein each subject selected from a population has an equal chance of being selected (e.g., drawing names from a hat).
Stratified random sampling	Dividing a population into desired groups (age, income, etc.) and then using a simple random sample from each stratified group.
Cluster sampling	A technique used when natural groups are readily evident in a population (e.g., residents within each county in a state). The natural groups are then subjected to random sampling to obtain random members from each county. The best results occur when elements within clusters are internally heterogeneous and externally (between clusters) homogeneous, as the formation of natural clusters may introduce error and bias.
Systematic sampling	A systematic method of random sampling (e.g., randomly choosing a number *n* between 1 and 10—perhaps drawing the number from a hat) and then selecting every *n*th name of a randomly generated or already existing list (such as the phone book) to obtain a study sample.

Measurements

Categories of Measurement

The four different categories of measurement are as follows:

Nominal	Used when two or more named variables exist (male/female, pass/fail, etc.)
Ordinal	Used when a hierarchy is present but when the distance between each value is not necessarily equal (e.g., first, second, third place)
Interval	Hierarchal values that are at equal distance from each other
Ratio	One value divided by another, providing a relative association of one quantity in terms of the other (e.g., 50 is one half of 100)

Statistics and Measures of Central Tendency

A statistic is a numerical representation of an identified characteristic of a subject.

- **Descriptive statistics** are mathematically derived values that represent characteristics identified in a group or population.
- **Inferential statistics** are mathematical calculations that produce generalizations about a group or population from the numerical values of known characteristics.

Measures of central tendency identify the relative degree to which certain characteristics in a population are grouped together. Such measures include:

- The **mean**, or the arithmetic average
- The **median**, or the numerical value above which 50% of the population is found and below which the other 50% is located
- The **mode**, or the most frequently appearing value (score) in a series of numerical values

Review Video: Mean, Median, and Mode
Visit mometrix.com/academy and enter code: 286207

Measures of Variability and Correlation

Measures of variability (or variation) include the following:

- The **range**, or the arithmetic difference between the largest and the smallest value (idiosyncratic "outliers" often excluded)
- The **interquartile range**, or the difference between the upper and lower quartiles (e.g., between the 75th and 25th percentiles)
- The **standard deviation,** or the average distance that numerical values are dispersed around the arithmetic mean

Correlation refers to the strength of relatedness when a relationship exists between two or more numerical values, which, when assigned a numerical value, is the **correlation coefficient** (*r*). A perfect (1:1) correlation has an *r* value of 1.0, with decimal values indicating a lesser correlation as the correlation coefficient moves away from 1.0. The correlation may be either positive (with the values increasing or decreasing together) or negative (if the values are inverse and move opposite to each other).

Review Video: Standard Deviation
Visit mometrix.com/academy and enter code: 419469

Statistical Significance

Statistical tests presume the null hypothesis to be true and use the values derived from a test to calculate the likelihood of getting the same or better results under the conditions of the null hypothesis (referred to as the "observed probability" or "empirical probability," as opposed to the "theoretical probability"). This likelihood is referred to as **statistical significance**. Where this likelihood is very small, the null hypothesis is rejected. Traditionally, experimenters have defined a "small chance" at the 0.05 level (sometimes called the 5% level) or the 0.01 level (1% level). The Greek letter alpha (α) is used to indicate the significance level chosen. Where the observed or empirical probability is less than or equal to the selected alpha, the findings are said to be "statistically significant," and the research hypothesis would be accepted.

Tests

Three examples of tests of statistical significance are:

- The **chi square test** (a nonparametric test of significance), which assesses whether or not two samples are sufficiently different to conclude that the difference can be generalized to the larger population from which the samples were drawn. It provides the degree of confidence by which the research hypothesis can be accepted or rejected, measured on a scale from 0 (impossibility) to 1 (certainty).
- A ***t*-test** is used to compare the arithmetic means of a given characteristic in two samples and to determine whether they are sufficiently different from each other to be statistically significant.
- **Analysis of variance**, or **ANOVA** (also called the "***F* test**"), which is similar to the *t*-test. However, rather than simply comparing the means of two populations, it is used to determine whether or not statistically significant differences exist in multiple groups or samples.

Statistical Error

Types of statistical error include the following:

- **Type I error**: Rejecting the null hypothesis when it is true
- **Type II error**: Accepting the null hypothesis when it is false and the research hypothesis is true (concluding that a difference doesn't exist when it does)

Data Analysis

Data analysis involves the examination of testing results within their context, assessing for correlations, causality, reliability, and validity. In testing a hypothesis (the assertion that two variables are related), researchers look for correlations between variables (a change in one variable associated with a change in another, expressed in numerical values). The closer the correlation is to +1.0 or −1.0 (a perfect positive or negative correlation), the more meaningful the correlation. This, however, is not causality (change in one variable responsible for change in the other). Since all possible relationships between two variables cannot be tested (the variety approaches infinity), the "null hypothesis" is used (asserting that no relationship exists) with probability statistics that indicate the likelihood that the hypothesis is "null" (and must be rejected) or can be accepted. Indices of "reliability" and "validity" are also needed.

Reliability and Validity

Reliability refers to consistency of results. This is measured via test–retest evaluations, split-half testing (random assignment into two subgroups given the same intervention and then comparison of findings), or in interrater situations, where separate subjects' rating scores are compared to see if the correlations persist.

Validity indicates the degree to which a study's results capture the actual characteristics of the features being measured. Reliable results may be consistent but invalid. However, valid results will always be reliable. **Methods for testing validity** include the following:

Concurrent validity	Comparing the results of studies that used different measurement instruments but targeted the same features
Construct validity	The degree of agreement between a theoretical concept and the measurements obtained (as seen via the subcategories of (a) convergent validity, the degree of actual agreement on measures that should be theoretically related, and (b) discriminant validity, the lack of a relationship among measures which are theoretically not related)
Content validity	Comprising logical validity (i.e., whether reasoning indicates it is valid) and face validity (i.e., whether those involved concur that it appears valid)
Predictive validity	Concerning whether the measurement can be used to accurately extrapolate (predict) future outcomes

Review Video: Testing Validity
Visit mometrix.com/academy and enter code: 315457

Research in Counseling

Relevance of Research to Counseling Therapy

All counselors today receive training in how to apply theories and methods that have been discovered through **research.** The foundations to applying research to counseling are as follows:

- The counselor learns how to **evaluate** the clinical interventions that have been applied in therapy.
- The counselor **remains objective** in their examination of the data.
- The counselor maintains **ethical procedures** and is **accountable** for their actions. This means that the counselor is careful to document their work.
- The counselor is **competent** in their use of terminology and can make a sound interpretation of the research obtained.
- The counselor and the researcher work for the **client's benefit**. The client must not be harmed. The counselor and the researcher recognize that the client has a choice to determine his or her own actions. The counselor and the researcher are fair and loyal to the client. Both desire to help the client develop steps that will assist in the solution of the problem.

Steps Researchers Take to Help Clients

The researcher takes different steps than the counselor in helping the client:

1. The first research step is to **identify the problem** with a series of questions. These questions are used to formulate a research design.
2. The **research design** will utilize the goals that are essential to the researcher's investigation process.
3. The **treatment or interventions** that will be applied are considered in the choice of measuring instruments to be used. The interventions are implemented so that the researcher can collect data on the various interventions and results of each.
4. The **data is then evaluated** to determine the desired outcome. The data is interpreted in accordance with prescribed criteria.
5. The **conclusions** that are reached are used to help increase the knowledge that the research was used to develop. Counselors may use knowledge gleaned from previous research to help a client with his or her problem.

Positivistic Research

Positivism is a scientific method that can be applied in social science research. The researcher uses the method to make predictions about what may happen in the future. The researcher takes care in designing experiments that can be disproved or supported by observations of the conditions that occur. The research is accomplished by comparing groups. The numerical data obtained is taken from random samples of a population. The numerical data is compared to the group findings. **Positivistic research** investigates causality by comparing the group members in one group with another group. The variables that are different in each group are known as variable X or variable Y. Typically, variable X refers to an independent variable. Variable Y is known as the dependent variable that can change with the application or the withdrawal of variable X.

Post-Positivism Paradigm Applied to Social Science Research

The belief of those researchers who support **post-positivism** is that truth cannot ever be fully revealed. The post-positivist will collect data and perform methodical examinations of the data. These examinations help the researcher to develop a probability about the results. Probability is defined as a prediction, which is founded on hypothesized truths that are generally believed. The post-positivism researcher does not deal in absolutes. Instead, the researcher will apply statistical tests that will support their hypothesized and inconclusive information. They refrain from making an assertion about the absolute truth of an answer to the problem. The researcher will state a number of close approximations to the truth based on quantitative research. The term "quantitative" refers to the quantity or the amount, which is described in numerical terms of measurement. Qualitative research is different, in that it uses narrative forms of data.

Lab Research Versus Field Research

Lab research has a high internal validity value because it is more easily controlled in terms of the cause-and-effect relationships of the variables applied under specific conditions. It also eliminates other explanations that can be attributed to a change in the results. However, lab research has a low external validity, in that generalization to other people, places, or time frames may not be so easy to accomplish. Generalization means that the action can be repeated in other situations.

Field research is more easily accomplished because it is done in a natural setting or environment; the researcher travels to the field of study. Field research demonstrates low internal validity because of the lack of control over external variables. Field research has high external validity because it can be generalized to other situations and settings.

Barriers to Research Efforts

Cost has become an issue in the mental health care system, directly affecting the **research efforts** in this field. This issue has increased the need for counselors to be accountable in their work. Accountability is found in the documentation and data collection methods used by counselors. The National Institute of Mental Health (NIMH) issues funding grants to various research institutions. The research is performed on clients in the daily practice of mental health counselors. The research is concerned with gaining insight into the practicality of the counseling interventions applied in the daily life of the client. Therefore, it is necessary for research courses to be offered in college programs. Research courses may be used to instruct the student in standardized tests and evaluation, experimental research design, descriptive and inferential statistics, and the critique of research designs.

Careers in Counseling

Evolution of Perceptions of Counseling

Counselors have had an influx of clients in recent years. Part of the reason for this influx in clients can be found in the **changes in attitudes and perceptions** of other professionals towards counseling:

- **Human resources departments** recognize that counselors can assist employees by providing short-term counseling to address work performance issues.
- **Psychiatrists** recognize that counselors provide a necessary component in treatment, along with input regarding medications and capacity for compliance to medication regimens.
- **Managed care plans** pushed for counseling treatments.
- Organizations, such as **Mothers Against Drunk Driving (MADD)**, have worked toward increasing alcohol and drug programs provided by counselors.
- The **internet** has provided counselors with different counseling formats, particularly through telehealth.
- **State licensure boards** give clients reassurance about the treatment they will receive under the care of a licensed professional counselor.

Professional Counselors

Professional counselors provide similar services to those of the psychologist or social worker. However, the professional counselor does provide a distinctive professional service in its own right. The nature of a professional counselor is defined by the following **criteria**:

- A clear list of **objectives** for the professional counselor position and instruction on how to meet those defined objectives
- **Training techniques** to be applied to meet an individual's needs (These techniques are part of a subset of intellectual procedures. These intellectual procedures or techniques are founded within the principles of science, theology, and law, and these procedures cannot easily be applied by untrained personnel.)
- **Membership** in a professional organization
- **Ethical operation** that is service-oriented for the betterment of others

Review Video: Becoming a Professional Counselor
Visit mometrix.com/academy and enter code: 334798

Mental Health Counselors

The mental health counselor only received limited recognition in the early 1980's. This limited recognition originated from the efforts of the Office of Civilian Health and Medical Program for the Uniformed Services (now known as TRICARE), who refused to recognize the **mental health counselor** as the fifth core service provider. Opponents found the lack of a universal licensure or certification system for mental health counselors to be problematic. However, managed care programs have helped this process. The managed care systems' demand for licensed mental health counselors caused the states to appropriately respond by passing licensure legislation.

The professional counselor and mental health counselor titles gained popularity from 1980-1990. The mental health counselor's role was defined in the AMHCA's 1981 manual. In 1984, the mental health counselor's job description was listed in the Dictionary of Occupational Titles and the Occupational Outlook Handbook. This allowed the role of counselor to then be added to the core provider list for mental health services. Previously, the list included only psychiatrists, psychologists, psychiatric nurses, and clinical social workers. Today, the list has been expanded to include licensed professional counselors, family counselors, pastoral counselors, and marriage counselors. Recognition can now be given to the counselor in forms of reimbursement payments for services rendered.

Review Video: Careers in Counseling
Visit mometrix.com/academy and enter code: 363115

Counselor Educators

Counselor educators can become bridge builders who create an understanding between mental health practitioners and those that do research. Educators seek to help their students see the rationale behind research. Likewise, the educator strives to help the researching student to see the relevance of understanding sound counseling practices. One way that this is accomplished is to provide the student with an assignment that delves into the procedures used in cognitive therapy. The student counselor learns to appreciate research and its applications. The research student will find that an assignment in qualitative research provides ample opportunity to use counseling techniques. The current accountability movement makes it imperative for the counselor and the research student to share outcome data obtained in these areas. The practicing counselor will find that research is relevant to client counseling and the techniques used.

Psychiatrists

Psychiatrists are medical doctors with four years of residency in psychiatry. **Psychiatrists** assess and prescribe treatment for more complex mental disorders, and provide expert consultation for other mental health service providers. Psychiatrists are qualified to conduct psychotherapy and psychoanalysis, to order laboratory tests, to hospitalize clients, and prescribe all legal drugs. Psychotherapy provides the client and family with a series of discussions involving treatment methods proven to be effective in resolving behavioral problems. Psychoanalysis includes psychotherapy and medications for an extended period of time. Prescription drugs help correct chemical imbalances at the root of emotional problems. In cases where medication is ineffective, the psychiatrist provides an alternative treatment, such as electroconvulsive therapy.

Psychiatric Nurses

Psychiatric nurses are the only mental health professionals besides psychiatrists who have experience in the medical field, along with mental health instruction and training. The **psychiatric nurse** works closely with individuals suffering from severe emotional problems. The psychiatrist holds the psychiatric nurse responsible for providing quality medical care and for the administration of prescribed medications. The psychiatrist may delegate some therapeutic counseling and intervention program responsibilities to the psychiatric nurse. A psychiatric nurse can provide a client with outpatient care that is easily accessible. Insurance accepts claims for these services because of the licensure and training requirements associated with this position. Usually, psychiatric nurses do not open independent private practices within a community.

Clinical Psychologists

Clinical psychologists work in the following settings to assist a wide range of individuals/groups: physical rehabilitation departments, family or marriage counseling centers, independent practices, group practices, and hospitals. **Clinical psychologists** may be needed after a surgical procedure or other life-altering event, such as divorce, separation, death of a loved one, stroke, brain injury, paralysis, spinal cord injury, or debilitating illnesses. Psychologists conduct psychotherapy, but cannot order lab tests, and most cannot prescribe drugs. Only the states of New Mexico, Illinois,

Idaho, Iowa, and Louisiana have laws that give clinical psychologists permission to prescribe medications.

Social Workers

Demand for social workers increased when their roles expanded to providing care in the community. They are classified as Clinical or Licensed Clinical Social Workers. Educational requirements are stringent. Most **social workers** obtain a master's degree in social work, with a specialization in psychiatry, as the minimum requirement for employment. Most social workers provide assistance to children and families in schools, homes, or within the community. Some social workers assist with support groups geared to teenage mothers, the elderly, at-risk students, and unemployed or untrained workers. Social workers can hold the titles of child welfare social worker, family service social worker, child protective social worker, occupational social worker, or gerontology social worker.

Counseling Settings

Elementary and Secondary School Setting

In the past, certified school counselors filled guidance positions in both the **elementary and secondary school systems**. Over the past two decades, special programs have been initiated to counter non-educational problems that students experience, such as drug and alcohol addictions and teenage pregnancy, which both lead to student drop out. Individual counseling is usually conducted on a weekly basis to help students cope with problems they are having at home, school, or in their communities. Some students benefit from group therapy counseling sessions that present skills in socialization, behavior management, and problem solving in the context of their family situations.

Mental health counselors may consult with educators, principals, administrators, guidance counselors, and other school staff to help a child deal with life roles. Some students require specialized interventions to alleviate a crisis situation. Crisis services may help a student who has a behavior problem at school, who is on the verge of committing suicide, or who is inflicting self-injury. Crisis situations cause the student's educational performance to deteriorate. Therefore, the school counselor has a responsibility to evaluate students' academic successes and failures. The mental health counselor seeks to identify the career interests and aptitudes of at-risk students. The counselor assists in college selection and in the general social development of the student. In some states, Licensed Professional Counselors (LPC's) are engaged for teen pregnancy preventions, employment, GED testing, individual and group counseling, support groups, and classroom education.

College Setting

Counselors may seek employment with **college students** in individual or group counseling, on a consultation basis, or as a liaison between the faculty and students. Students self-refer to the counselor. However, if a student is in significant need of ongoing care, the counselor may refer the student to an outside agency for mental health care services. Cost-cutting has reduced college staffing, yet the need still exists to provide qualified counselors to cope with emergency situations and make the needed referrals. Career center counselors may prepare resumes, interest and aptitude assessments, job placement services, and career counseling services. Some counselors specialize in proactive drug and alcohol prevention programs.

Hospice Setting

Hospice centers opened in the 1970's. The professional counselor seeking a **hospice care position** can expect to deal with families experiencing a crisis situation of catastrophic illness and the impending death of a loved one. The professional counselor helps the family through the end-of-life experience and grieving. Ideally, the family comes to terms with the situation prior to the death, and the client gains insights and coping skills regarding death and dying. The counselor helps the client deal with living wills, financial concerns, family of origin issues, and other associated problems that may need to be handled. The goal of the counselor is to help the client and his or her family to experience caring in the dying process and to maintain their dignity.

Medical Rehabilitation Setting

Counselors may seek employment in a **rehabilitation program**. Rehabilitation counselors work to help a person gain skills to compensate for a disability. The effects of the disability may impair the person's personal, occupational, or social life and psychological well-being. The counselor must examine the strengths and weaknesses of the client to determine the course of treatment to be followed. The counselor works to collect personal information and data regarding training programs that will fit the individual's needs. Long range planning goals are established. The title of these counselors is **Certified Rehabilitation Counselor (CRC)**. Most CRC's have a graduate degree in rehabilitation counseling. Rehabilitation work is a growth area for counselors because of the increasing age of the population.

Community Mental Health Setting

Community mental health counselors can expect to have a variety of age groups in their treatment programs. One specialized area where the young and the old alike need treatment is domestic abuse. **Community mental health counselors** also work to provide assessment and treatment for clients with drug and alcohol addictions. Some community mental health counselors help families during child adoption interviews and the assessment process. Some counselors work in geriatric treatment centers with the elderly, while others may work in AIDS treatment and support service centers. Some families require conflict resolution and psychoeducational services. Still other counselors find work as employment counselors, helping others to find work by assessing clients' interests and aptitudes. Community mental health counselors must understand the community within which they function.

Elder Care Settings

The skills that a professional counselor needs in positions which serve the **elderly** are numerous. The counselor must receive training in the following:

- Cognitive and emotional assessments specifically geared to the elderly population
- Grief and bereavement counseling procedures
- How to establish a good rapport with an elderly individual
- Looking at the client holistically and noting any medical problems or medications that impact a client's daily functioning
- Laws that apply to treatment

The counselor listens to the concerns of family members involved in the client's care. The counselor is aware of the services and facilities that would benefit the client, and acts as a referral resource regarding lawyers, medical doctors, financial advisors, insurance specialists, and community support services.

Business and Industry Settings

Employers hire professional counselors to help improve job performance through **employee assistance programs**. Ongoing counseling in the business/industry setting helps to do the following:

- Alleviate job discontent
- Enhance coping skills for dealing with family problems
- Provide drug and alcohol addiction treatment
- Resolve work problems
- Ameliorate retirement issues

Some counselors provide contract training and educational workshops and seminars addressing job satisfaction, work productivity, and family and personal problems. The counselor may work as a consultant to directly support supervisors, managers, and employees, and refers them to outside resources when necessary. Some counselors work on-call to provide crises interventions on job sites, including catastrophic workplace accidents, deaths on the job, violence at work, sexual harassment, and layoffs or terminations of employees. Brief counseling is a cost-effective way to help employees cope with the transition process.

Criminal Justice System Setting

The number of professional counselors in the state-run criminal justice system has recently increased to alleviate some of the overpopulation found in prisons. The **criminal justice counselor** serves the following individuals:

- Prison inmates
- Detainees
- The accused on trial
- Recovering drug addicts and alcoholics

The job titles for this counselor include probation officer, juvenile offender officer, and prison counselor. The entry requirement is a bachelor's degree including criminology, counseling, psychology, social work, family relations, or theology, and a one-year internship. The counseling segregation trend replaces models that previously incarcerated all prisoners together, regardless of the nature of their crimes. Addiction centers are specifically designed to treat criminals with drug addictions who commit crimes to support their habits. Career criminals and sexual predators are now separated from young offenders. Criminal justice counselors have high-stress but rewarding jobs.

Personal Coaching

Professional counselors may find employment as a **personal coach**. Coaching certification, insurance, and job restrictions vary from state to state. Generally, a coach provides a client with the following services:

- Provides advice and coping strategies for specific issues
- Helps the client to focus on life goals
- Helps the client to realize potential
- Helps the client recognize their own value and self-worth

The coach can perform his or her duties in face-to-face interviews, online, or on the telephone, so the coach has more freedom than a licensed professional counselor. The coach may expect to find an increase in employment opportunities in the future.

Private Practices

Private Practitioner

Consultation Services

The private practitioner engages in two kinds of **consultation services**: unpaid and paid.

- **Unpaid consultation** involves communication between two professionals about the private practitioner's client. The counselor does not pay for or accept money for this exchange of information. The counselor that requested consultation must obtain a signed release of information consent form to protect the client's right to privacy. The consultation relationship with other professionals can lead to additional referrals for services.
- The private practitioner offers **paid consultations** to schools, agencies, industries, hospitals, vocational programs, nursing homes, or community organizations. These services can benefit those who cannot afford full-time counseling services. Payment may be received based on renewable contractual agreements made for a specific period of time.

Counseling Services

Counseling is the main source of income for the private practitioner. The counselor must evaluate potential needs to be addressed in the community being served. Good contacts to make within the community include pastors, social workers, school counselors, medical personnel, helping agencies, and employers. Other private practitioners in nearby geographic areas, (that are not competitors), may provide additional insights into the business. Some counselors are generalists. Others specialize in individual or group counseling sessions, marriage or family counseling, children/teenagers, elders, rehabilitation counseling, and drug and alcohol abuse counseling. It is also an option to choose a variety of different deliveries to ensure a more lucrative practice.

Community Involvement

Visibility within the community is good for the business. If a private practitioner provides some free services to **community groups**, it creates bonds and respectful relationships with the community members that could lead to paying referrals. Some organizations that may be in need of free services include Parent Teacher Associations, diabetes and other illness support groups, and local church groups. Groups may require the services of a counselor to conduct seminars on bereavement, violence, or other social problems experienced in the community. All counselors should provide some community service as a demonstration of their ethics, but it can be especially difficult to fit volunteerism into a private practitioner's role.

Supervisory Roles

The private practitioner performs **supervisory roles** to obtain additional credentials, or education credits required for licensing. When providing clinical advice and supervision to other professionals in the field, the private practitioner must keep their own skills up to date. The complexity of some client's cases requires the counselor to seek advice from peer supervision groups. These groups meet periodically to converse about cases and to review procedures. Insurance carriers and HMOs often require private practitioners to have some supervision by a licensed psychologist or psychiatrist. The licensed professional counselor, clinical social worker, or marriage and family therapist receives payments based on the decisions of the overseeing psychologist or psychiatrist and the insurer. Not every private practitioner finds supervision acceptable, and many turn down work that necessitates this relationship with a supervisor.

Work Settings

The three work settings of the private practitioner include the following:

- **Incorporated office groups** share the same workspace, and the members are not personally liable for legal judgments against the corporation.
- **Expense-sharing groups** share resources and costs but not office space. Counselors can benefit from local, state, and national counseling group relationships. Group practice gives the counselor an outlet from the isolation and burnout associated with private practice.
- **Sole proprietorship** indicates a single person is in charge of the business and is liable to pay business damages out of personal funds, if sued successfully. This business owner is not entirely alone, as he or she must continue to network with other mental health professionals.

The private practitioner should select a work setting based on which type of work fits their life and occupational goals. Choices will be influenced by the opportunities available in the geographic region and limited by the practitioner's type of training and licensing.

Recommendations for Day-to-Day Business

Recommendations for the private practitioner in running day-to-day business include the following:

- Have a **set schedule** that includes face-to-face therapy time with clients, research and preparation time, answering client phone calls and emails, coping with ethical issues, and handling everyday paperwork and operations.
- **Plan** ahead and **budget** for cancellations and payment problems that cause financial losses.
- Do not **overextend** resources, either in time or in financial considerations.
- Make **referrals** based on confidence in one's level of training and understanding of the client's needs.
- Evaluate what **types of mental health services** are delivered in the community. There are four types of services, which include counseling, consultation, supervision, and community involvement.
- Provide a **flexible model** to make services more attractive to the community.

Billable Hours

The **private practitioner** must be dedicated to the business at hand, whether it is run as a part-time or full-time operation, because the start-up time and effort is significant in both cases. Use the following standard calculation to determine the number of hours needed to bill for: Multiply the hours spent directly with the client by two to account for the additional office hours not in the company of the client spent doing paperwork and preparing for treatment. For example, if a practitioner has 15 clients, each of whom is booked weekly for an hour-long session, then they will spend 30 hours a week working. Make a realistic commitment for work-life balance.

Considerations Important in the Decision to Open a Private Practice

When deciding whether to open a private practice, the counselor must consider the following:

- Consider **problems associated with charging fees** for services in the mental health industry in perspective. A counselor in private practice must first find out which services are offered free in their community and not duplicate them.
- They must survey the surrounding geographic areas to find out which **mental health service models** colleagues use. Assess how to deliver mental health services to the consumer based on this comparative survey. Private practice has a multitude of service options for the counselor to explore. They should make practical decisions about the delivery model that will be used, because the model selected has financial implications for the business.
- Thoroughly understand the **advantages and disadvantages** of setting up and running a private practice and understand how insurance companies work in regard to reimbursement for services delivered.
- Balance **financial concerns** with sound ethical background.

Practical Considerations for Beginning a Private Practice

The first practical consideration for beginning a private practice is the type of office space required. The next consideration should be the length of time the practitioner plans to remain in private practice. They may rent space on a part-time basis from other mental health providers in the area, which would provide them with an already established location and recognized business address that may be more prestigious than what could be afforded alone. Sharing office equipment will minimize start-up costs. However, if financial resources permit, a practitioner may choose to purchase office space or a separate building. They may also choose to open a home office if space and money for office furniture, a computer, phone and internet service, answering machine, fax, office supplies, liability insurance, and restroom facilities for clients and their families are all available.

Practical issues associated with opening a private practice decrease the time spent on personal activities and with paying clients:

- A home business opens the family to intrusions by insistent clients, undesirables, or criminals.
- Time may be spent making structural changes to satisfy the insurance company and accountant. Set up a record keeping system to last at least seven years from the last time the client was seen.
- Avoid feeling shut off from the mental health network by establishing connections and maintaining contacts.
- Keep equipment functional and learn new software that meets the growing needs of the office. It is legally required that you record a referral number for clients who cannot contact you by phone in an emergency (usually the nearest hospital that offers 24-hour mental health services or the locum tenens).
- Instruct answering services in all procedures to be followed during emergency situations, and how to contact locum tenens when sick, on vacation, or attending training.

Incorporated Office Group

Incorporated office groups are mental health specialists who have signed on as legal partners with shares in a business. The specialists can include psychologists, psychiatrists, social workers, and professional counselors. Their salaries can be weekly, bi-weekly, or monthly payments, based on time spent on the job, the status of the specialist in the business, and the initial investment of the professional as a partner. The legal arrangements include an exit plan for leaving the practice, relocation of the practice, and expected changes in the practice. Consult an attorney to help thoroughly scrutinize and understand all aspects of the legal contract before making the commitment to become a partner. This understanding may prevent the business from making costly and illegal decisions.

Benefits and Risks Associated with Practicing in a Group Setting

Benefits associated conducting private practice in a group setting include having:

- Vacation and sick coverage by a trusted colleague (locum tenens)
- Quick access to consultation and referrals by other members
- Specialized services offered by other members
- Protection if a client becomes violent or makes threats
- Centralized bookings, accounting, and filing, if a clerk is affordable
- Higher group practice rates negotiated with insurance companies under a single tax number
- Better equipment than afforded alone

There are also **risks** involved in working with a group:

- If a group member is sued or has legal issues, the consequences impact the whole group.
- Staff supervision, consultations, and office meetings detract from therapy time with the clients.

Ask an attorney and accountant to address these possible risks in the initial business legal documents. Write a clear policies and procedures manual for staff.

Expense Sharing Groups

Expense sharing groups consist of mental health specialists who have not signed on as legal partners in a corporation. Their contractual agreements should define their financial and business relationships and costs incurred by each person in the group. A clear understanding prevents future misunderstandings and legal entanglements. The specialists can include psychologists, psychiatrists, social workers, and professional counselors. Their salaries are paid in the same way that a sole proprietor is paid. The group fees pay for office expenses and any consulting fees charged by other professionals. However, the private practitioner does not share his or her counseling payments received from clients or other agencies for services rendered. The legal options for the private practitioner include remaining in the group, incorporating the group, or leaving to start his or her own private practice.

GOAL SETTING

Goal setting involves a yearly evaluation. The private practitioner should set goals in the following areas:

- Gear **professional growth goals** to those that can be accomplished within one year's time. Determine how many cases or clients will be served annually and break that figure into monthly and weekly averages. Evaluate the types of clients the business will be willing to handle. The types include individuals, couples, families, and groups. Evaluate which skills must be improved or gained in order to obtain these clients. Monitor supervision to determine if enough time has been devoted to this task.
- The private practitioner should set goals for **financial growth** by the number of clients that they have the ability to serve. The number is limited by opportunities, time constraints, and voluntary performance.
- **Skill development** requires the practitioner to make a financial and time investment in university courses or seminar training. Professional organizations within the mental health community may make demands for professional counselors to obtain increased training in specialized areas.
- Plan time for **family and personal life activities**, because clients model their behavior of "wellness" after that of their counselor. The professional counselor must stay balanced in both professional and personal life.

ESTABLISHING A REFERRAL BASE

The practical needs of setting up an office cannot overshadow the need to establish a **referral base**. A private practice will grow out of referrals from the community. Referrals can come from educational facilities, private and public organizations, churches, corporations, manufacturing firms, other mental health providers, hospitals, medical physicians, and rehabilitation programs. Professional counselors increase public awareness of their services by writing for publications. Enhance public image by volunteering individual or group counseling, consultation services, support groups, workshops, or seminars. School personnel, medical professionals, and other community professionals seeking free services for an individual are good contacts to widen a referral base. A strong referral system is an investment in future revenue opportunities.

MENTAL HEALTH INSURANCE OPTIONS AND PAYMENT SYSTEMS

Mental health insurance coverage and payment options are complex. There are three kinds of insurance plans in which the client may be involved:

- **Indemnity plans** reimburse the client directly after the client has paid for a service. The client usually pays a deductible as a qualification before any additional reimbursements are paid by the insurance company.
- A **preferred provider organization (PPO)** offers the client the ability to visit any caregiver within their network provider list at a low fee, but if the client goes to a caregiver not on the list, the client must pay more. The PPO establishes set fees that the counselor can charge the client.
- A **health maintenance organization (HMO)** contracts with the provider for bulk discount care. A referral must be obtained from the client's general practitioner or other gatekeeper before commencing service. Outpatient mental health care is extremely limited at an HMO.

PPOs AND HMOs

The **PPO** establishes what fees the counselor can charge the client. The client usually pays co-payments and deductibles to the provider, and the PPO pays the remainder owed to the provider.

The **HMO** is like a PPO, except that the primary care physician pre-certifies the need for mental health services in an HMO. Some health maintenance organizations demand that the counselor submit a prescribed treatment plan as part of the pre-certification process. The provider sends the plan to the insurance company for pre-certification. The care and insurance coverage restricts the client to only going to an in-network provider for services. The HMO has a set fee for services. There usually is not a deductible with an HMO, but there is co-pay required. Normally, the premiums for an HMO are lower than other insurance plans.

Liability Insurance, Malpractice Insurance, and Attorney Services

Liability insurance is a policy that provides protection against negligent acts and omissions, such as failure to remove ice from a walkway that results in a client's accidental injury. **Malpractice insurance** provides protection against injurious conduct by the counselor when acting in his or her professional capacity, like misdiagnosis or incorrect treatment. Office equipment and the office space itself need separate policies. Most groups require a new partner to obtain these types of insurance before work begins.

Attorney services are enlisted to protect the practitioner's business and financial investments. Hire an attorney who is knowledgeable about mental health legalities. Ask the attorney to explain HIPAA duties (a law that protects the privacy of the client). The attorney may hire counselors to consult in custody or abuse cases, which can bring in revenue for the business as well.

Role of an Accountant in Private Practice

An accountant helps the professional counselor to set up and maintain accounting and billing systems for the business, to fill out Internal Revenue Service (IRS) paperwork and file income taxes. An accountant offers good advice regarding sound financial investments, selecting a retirement plan, business goals and growth plans for the business. An accountant can help the counselor determine projected income for the following year. Projected income is vital to know how much time should be allocated to counseling services, consultation services, and other professional time use. The IRS will not consider the practice to be a viable business if it does not make income within three years of operation.

Managed Care

Integrated Care Model of Managed Care

Integrated care is defined by AHRQ as "the care a patient experiences as a result of a team of primary care and behavioral health clinicians, working together with patients and families, using a systematic and cost-effective approach." The **integrated care model** for treatment is increasing in mental health service delivery and is directed towards providing services to those in underserved populations. Within the integrated care module of a managed care program, the counselor is responsible for:

- Giving an appropriate assessment and diagnosis of the client's mental state
- Supplying psychoeducational services
- Offering brief-structured counseling sessions

Integrated care models require the counselor to be able to do the following:

- **Accurately diagnose** the mental health of the client
- Be apprised of brief-structured **counseling methods** that utilize **pharmacological interventions** and individual and group approaches
- Follow specific guidelines in **reporting procedures**
- **Write a grant application** to compete for contractual agreements
- **Network and collaborate** with other service professionals

Impact of Managed Care on Service Delivery System

Mental health services are impacted by the need for cost-effective service deliveries. Managed care programs implement treatment plans that are supervised under case managers and review boards. Under the managed care programs, it is not uncommon for treatment plans to be restricted to a limited number of visits. Many counselors have switched to fee-for-service contractual agreements. These agreements are made with medical facilities, agencies, and private businesses to reduce the cost of having a salaried counselor on staff. Counselors had to change their business plans to compete for government contracts and insurance reimbursements. This change provides the counselors with a more secure source of income for services rendered.

Ethical Issues That May Be Influenced Under Managed Care Programs

Managed care programs have strict guidelines for treatment plans. These guidelines are used to restrict and limit the number of visits that a counselor can prescribe for treatment. Due to these restrictions, the counselor may face ethical dilemmas in being able to fully provide for the needs of the client. Dilemmas may include the following:

- These guidelines do not take into account any difficulties that may need to be addressed in establishing relationships between different cultures or races.
- These guidelines may not allow for differentiation specific to the competing needs of the client.
- The managed care program's reporting structure may compromise the confidentiality of the client.

The counselor may need to review their own personal identity principles to alleviate the stress that results from these types of compromises. To alleviate some of these stresses, the counselor should receive instruction in therapeutic relationships, contextual care in the community or private practice, writing case notes, informed consent issues, treatment plan development, selection of counseling interventions, and applying ethical decisions.

Components of Managed Care within Counseling Education Programs

Mental health counseling education programs should include these topics in relation to **managed care treatment**:

- Diagnosis and treatment of clients
- Treatment plans
- Methods of brief and goal directed counseling sessions
- Standards of practice for groups and families
- Pharmacological interventions that can be offered to the client
- Networking and consultation skills
- Record keeping procedures
- Understanding evidence-based research
- Practicum placement in a managed care setting during their internship experience

Incorporation of Managed Care into Curriculum

Counselor educators have not been strong supporters of incorporating the managed care component into the **curriculum**. There have been some attempts to include the managed care component, but overall, the changes to the curriculum have not been enough. A stronger component that addresses the following concerns in managed care restrictions is imperative:

- Minimum competencies
- Ethical standards
- Informed consent
- Confidentiality issues
- Reporting procedures
- Citing appropriate diagnosis
- How to terminate management when problems cannot be resolved

If managed care is incorporated into the curriculum, then the counselor will be better prepared to work in that setting.

Technology in Counseling

Advancements in Technology

Technical advancements over the last century have resulted in changes to almost every professional field of study. Mental health professionals can expect to see these technological advancements applied in a number of ways. Clients have new ways to access services. Counselors and clients will continue to find new formats for interaction. Management procedures may also change to support the technological structures. Training may be altered or delivered via different formats or systems. The latest research may increase in consumption due to the methods of accessing research data. The counselor will need to be competent in technological literacy and the applications of technology in the field.

Technological Advances in Counseling

Technological advances allow clients to have more control over their therapy and allow the counselor/client to better track progress. **Technological advances** include the following:

- **Greenspace**: This website matches clients and counselors and allows clients to plot their own progress by answering questions, such as about their level of depression, through email or messaging. The result graphs can be accessed by both client and counselor.
- **Apple Watch and other devices**: Can be used to track behavioral changes and to send information to the counselor. For example, Muse is a headband that is used to facilitate meditation through sensing brain activity.
- **Mobile device apps**: Multiple apps, such as MoodTracker, Mood Path, Calm, Calming Circles, and Mind Body Awareness Project, can be used to help clients relax, sleep, or carry out exercises. Alarm apps can remind the clients to take medications or keep appointments. Many apps, such as LoseIt, are available to assist with weight loss.

Technological Literacy

Technological literacy can be described as the ability to comprehend the use of technology and to select the appropriate applications used in a variety of systems.

- The counselor who is technologically literate will be able to make an **informed decision** about the use of technology in a given area.
- The technologically literate counselor will have the **basic skill level** that is needed in a variety of technological environments.
- The technologically literate counselor will be able to **access technology** at work, at home, and in the community environment.
- The technologically literate counselor will understand that there are certain **security risks** associated with the use of technology and will be able to make sound judgments about ethical dilemmas that can arise through the use of technology.
- The technologically literate counselor will be able to **critically examine new advancements** for their potential counseling uses.

Integration of Technology into Consultation, Collaboration, and Shared Decision-Making

The counselor must be able to collaborate and work with a wide group of people through **technologically-based systems**. The counselor can access others through electronic devices such as the internet or intranet. Email is used on a day-to-day basis by many individuals. Electronic communications can be accomplished on anywhere from internal to global scales.

- In the **discussion group format**, units are formed to talk about topics regarding specific activities, goals, or projects.
- In the **data collection and organizational activities format**, databases are used to organize, share, and retrieve information. Information can be given in the form of references, curriculum projects, research papers, and an exchange of contact information.
- In the **document or file sharing format**, the capability exists to allow each person in the group to work on a project at the same time, in synchronous collaboration.

Integrating Social Media into the Business of Counseling

It's essential that personal and professional **social media** accounts be kept strictly separate and that clients never be "friended" or accepted as friends on personal sites. The counselor should use privacy settings to shield personal information. The counselor should always avoid making any comments about work or clients on personal sites. For professional sites, such as LinkedIn, counselor should make a clear plan for use, ensuring that confidentiality is maintained. For example, the counselor may use social media to post information about office hours, to provide information (such as articles about treatment and mental health), and to schedule appointments. If clients can interact with the counselor on social media sites, such as by making Facebook posts, this can establish a legal responsibility to respond. Additionally, if non-clients post questions asking for advice to which the counselor responds, this can establish a counselor-client relationship that the counselor did not intend.

Synchronous and Asynchronous Communication

In **synchronous communication**, real time is incorporated to allow users to accomplish text chats with each other or video conferences between the counselor and the client. When documents are involved, annotations systems (such as in Microsoft Word) can be employed to allow the users to comment and edit the project. Online communication brings people together in an electronic format. A network of colleagues is formed to alleviate some of the isolation many counselors experience. Inclusion is promoted.

Asynchronous communication is a sharing of ideas at different times. This can be a benefit to the counselor who needs an opportunity to reflect on new ideas. Social media platforms, such as Twitter, Facebook, Snapchat, or LinkedIn, allow for the asynchronous communication of ideas, along with online blogs. An additional benefit is found in the sharing of solutions within the collaborative community. Online collaboration can save time and money. It is easily accessible and increases productivity, as the counselor doesn't have to leave their own office.

Collaboration Tools for Online Communication

With the technology boom, many free **video chat options** are available for clients to meet with their counselors through a digital avenue. The most important consideration in these various options is that **HIPAA privacy laws** are maintained. While there are different specifics to each video chat product, most will incorporate audio, video, and text communication. The user can exchange information in various ways. Graphics are exchanged on an electronic whiteboard. Files can be transferred. The benefits to video conferences include flexibility, comfort, price (perhaps simply saving on transportation costs), and an increased likelihood of consistently making scheduled meetings.

Online Surveys

Online surveys can be used for a number of different purposes:

- **To assess needs in a community**: The survey may be targeted to a specific population or to the community as a whole to help, for example, to determine the need for certain types of programs.
- **To gain specific feedback**: A counselor may ask brief post-counseling questions to ascertain the client's perceived reaction to the session and to plan further sessions.
- **To assess satisfaction**: A survey may be sent to all clients to ask about satisfaction with services provided as part of a quality improvement initiative.

Careful consideration must be given to development of the survey, the target population, and issues of privacy and confidentiality. The goal of the survey and how the results will be utilized should be clearly established and the survey written clearly, avoiding medical jargon, leading questions ("How helpful is our messaging service?"), double questions, and open-ended questions, which are difficult to quantify. When possible, the counselor should establish **benchmarks** in order to better interpret results.

Web Counseling

Web counseling is a popular format for counselors working in the current technological age and working specifically with clients of the generations raised on technical literacy. The American Counseling Association recommends that counselors who are providing assistance through **web counseling** always assess the client prior to offering this service to ensure it is the appropriate method of care. Counselors must also warn clients of the limitations, risks, and benefits of web counseling prior to initiating the service. There is a mixture of perceptions about how web counseling is performed, but there is no formal definition for this structure. Some think that this is not a viable way to accomplish counseling, because there is limited body language visible on a web cam. Some fear that online personalities differ from personalities encountered in real life. Others fear that generalization of coping strategies may not allow them to materialize in the life of the client. Some see web counseling as being beneficial as a supplemental tool to face-to-face counseling sessions, and are embracing this new structure.

Advantages to Web Counseling

There are many advantages to web counseling, including the following:

- Web counseling has increased both the **efficiency and accessibility** for persons seeking counseling services. For instance, individuals with physical disabilities or those located in remote locations may find that this medium is more accessible. Limitations of the worldwide COVID-19 pandemic required many counseling services to move to a web-based format. This was a necessary transition as mental health was greatly impacted by the isolation and loss experienced during the pandemic, in addition to the focus placed on struggling marriages/relationships that were forced to face issues head on during shutdowns.
- Some individuals may find that this medium is **less intrusive** upon their privacy, especially if it is by text alone. These clients may be more comfortable in disclosing private thoughts and feelings in the virtual environment.

- Counselors can provide **electronic file transfers** or links that connect clients to available research, or other information, in a direct manner.
- Counselors can seek help from colleagues in **collaborative efforts**.
- Assessment, instruction, and informational **resources** are available via the internet.
- Virtual environments give counselors and clients a **forum** to answer questions, gain social support, and conduct virtual counseling sessions.
- Marriage and family counseling can be conducted with clients from **different parts of the globe**.
- **Supervision** can be conducted through anecdotal evidence shown in emails. Increased communication between student counselor and supervisor counselor can be accomplished.

Disadvantages of Web Counseling

Disadvantages of web counseling also exist, and must be considered when deciding on the best medium for counseling services:

- **Certification and licensure issues** pose a complication to the concept of web counseling, as the counselor may be licensed in one state, while treating a client in another.
- Virtual environments **may not be conducive to building trust, concern, and authentic working relationships** between client and counselor.
- The **client's identity cannot be established** with verification procedures in the virtual environment. Clients could potentially disguise their gender, race, or other pertinent details about their life.
- The client's identity is at risk for **breaches of privacy**. Encryption and security measures can fail, increasing the risk that confidentiality is breached. Counselors must provide all possible and reasonable security measures in an effort to protect their clients.
- **Ethical standards** as they apply to web counseling have yet to be fully established.
- The counselor and the client **may not be proficient in their computer skills**. Keyboarding, electronic file transfers, and other computer skills are required.
- The **fluidity of the internet** and the changes that can occur in technology may have future implications on mental health service delivery that have yet to be realized. Therefore, training and educational programs may not be effective in preparing the mental health counselor to conduct web counseling.
- **Geographical, community, or cultural factors** may be ignored. Natural disasters in one part of the country may not be so readily understood in other parts of the country. The counselor should research the client's locale to anticipate geographical factors that may be of significance to the client.
- Web counseling inherently caters to individuals with the means to have access to a computer, internet, or other form of technology, therefore **disadvantaging those in lower socioeconomic categories**.
- The internet has also introduced new **negative habits** that the counselor must be aware of and prepared to assist with, such as compulsive shopping, gambling, pornography, online marital affairs, online bullying, online stalking, and hatred-based websites.

Virtual Meetings

Virtual meetings allow counselors and clients to conduct audiovisual meetings using the internet and video conferencing. Options include:

- **WebEx**: Allows voice and video conferencing and the ability to not only see each other but to share a screen so that both can, for example, discuss a graph showing a client's progress. Multiple individuals in different areas can participate in group discussions.
- **BetterHelp**: This online counseling service with over 15,000 counselors allows clients to pay a flat fee to unlimited sessions with a counselor at the times of their choosing. BetterHelp allows 24-hour a day texting that is not in real time but also offers real-time texting, and video sessions. Unlimited access costs $60-90 per week but is usually not covered by insurance.
- **Talkspace**: This site is similar to BetterHelp, and costs are similar. It offers matching with a personal counselor, unlimited text messaging, and video conferencing on request.

Ethical Considerations when Integrating Technology into Counseling

The ethical considerations critical to the integration of technology into counseling remain similar to those for other aspects of counseling:

- **Beneficence/Nonmaleficence**: The use of technology should not result in harm to the client. The counselor should assess the client to determine appropriateness of technology and should assess the remote location for videoconferencing to determine if privacy can be assured.
- **Fidelity/Responsibility**: Technology should promote trust and responsibility rather than impairment. The counselor should do a risk assessment regarding technology to ensure it is secure and the client's information is protected.
- **Integrity/Justice**: The counselor should keep commitments, be honest with clients, and be fair. The counselor must ensure that information exchanged through technology cannot be misused.
- **Privacy/Confidentiality**: Technology must have secure settings if information is exchanged. Counselors should obtain written permission to use technology, such as video conferencing, and should use only secure networks and password protected access. If information exchange (text messages, video/audio messages) is to be retained as part of client records, the clients should be made aware of this.

Professional Practice and Ethics Chapter Quiz

1. The reflection of the subject matter in the content of the test is known as:

a. Content validity
b. Face validity
c. Predictive validity
d. Construct validity

2. The immediate comparison of test results with the results from other sources that measure the same factors in the same short time span is known as:

a. Construct validity
b. Face validity
c. Concurrent validity
d. Content validity

3. How many steps are included in Koocher and Keith-Spiegel's problem-solving model for ethical dilemmas (1998)?

a. 9
b. 7
c. 5
d. 3

4. Which of the following is at the heart of the deontological view of ethics?

a. Jung's "Shadow" archetype
b. Gottlieb's multi-modal therapy
c. Mill's *A System of Logic*
d. "The Golden Rule"

5. Which court case supported the utilitarian perspective on breaking confidentiality for the good of the majority?

a. *United States v. Hearst*
b. *Tarasoff v. Regents of University of California*
c. *Jaffee v. Redmond*
d. *Roper v. Simmons*

6. Which of the following is the most basic single system experimental designs?

a. A-B-A-B design
b. A-B design
c. B-C design
d. B-A-B design

7. Which of the following is NOT a key step in the research process?

a. Problem or issue identification
b. Hypothesis formulation
c. Generalization
d. Study design selection

8. Which of the following is NOT one of the three common study designs used in the research process?

a. Exploratory research
b. Confirmation analysis
c. Descriptive survey
d. Experimental study

9. The total set of subjects sought for measurement by a researcher refers to which of the following?

a. Sample
b. Habitat
c. Population
d. System

10. Which of the following *r* values refer to a perfect correlation?

a. 1.0
b. 10.0
c. 100.0
d. 1,000.0

Intake, Assessment, and Diagnosis

Human Growth and Development

Maslow's Hierarchy of Needs

American psychologist Abraham Maslow defined human motivation in terms of needs and wants. His hierarchy of needs is classically portrayed as a pyramid sitting on its base divided into horizontal layers. He theorized that, as humans fulfill the needs of one layer, their motivation turns to the layer above.

Level	Need	Description
Physiological	Basic needs to sustain life—oxygen, food, fluids, sleep	These basic needs take precedence over all other needs and must be dealt with first before the individuals can focus on other needs.
Safety and security	Freedom from physiological and psychological threats	Once basic needs are met, individuals become concerned about safety, including freedom from fear, unemployment, war, and disasters. Children respond more intensely to threats than adults.
Love/Belonging	Support, caring, intimacy	Individuals tend to avoid isolation and loneliness and have a need for family, intimacy, or membership in a group where they feel they belong.
Self-esteem	Sense of worth, respect, independence	To have confidence, individuals need to develop self-esteem and receive the respect of others.
Self-actualization	Meeting one's own sense of potential and finding fulfillment	Individuals choose a path in life that leads to fulfillment and contentment.

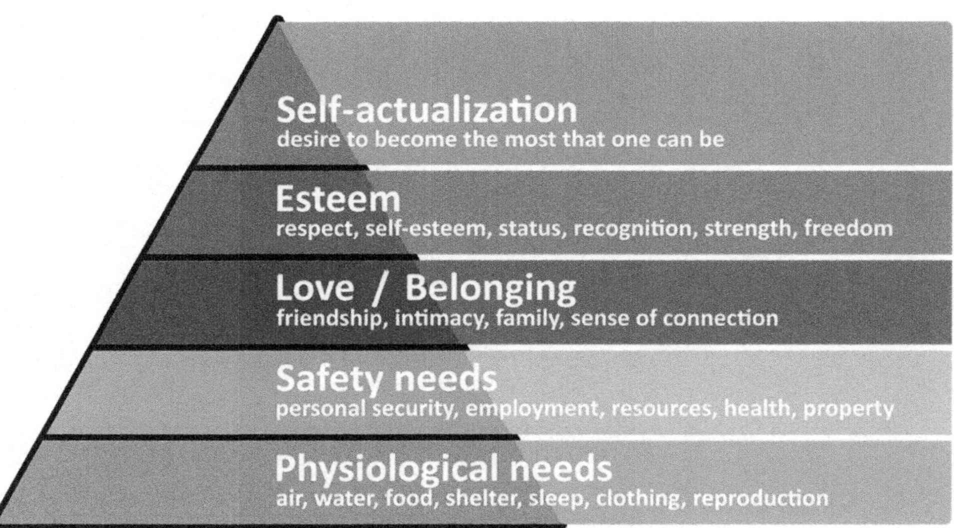

Review Video: Maslow's Hierarchy of Needs
Visit mometrix.com/academy and enter code: 461825

Freud's Psychoanalytic Theory

Motivational Forces of the Unconscious Mind That Shape Behavior

Freud's psychoanalytic theory postulates that behavior is influenced not only by environmental stimuli (i.e., physical influences) and external social constrains and constructs (i.e., taboos, rules, social expectations), but also by four specific unconscious elements as well. These elements exist only in the unconscious mind, and individuals remain substantively unaware of all the forces, motivations, and drives that shape their thoughts and behavioral decisions. The **four elements** are:

- Covert desires
- Defenses needed to protect, facilitate, and moderate behaviors
- Dreams
- Unconscious wishes

Levels of the Mind

The three levels of the mind that Freud proposed include the following:

- The **conscious mind** is comprised of various ideas and thoughts of which we are fully aware.
- The **preconscious mind** is comprised of ideas and thoughts that are outside of immediate awareness, but can be readily accessed and brought into awareness.
- The **unconscious mind** is comprised of thoughts and ideas that are outside of our awareness and that cannot be accessed or brought into full awareness by personal effort alone.

Primary Focus of Psychoanalysis

The primary focus of psychoanalysis is on the unconscious mind and the desires, defenses, dreams and wishes contained within it. Freud proposed that the key features of the unconscious mind arise from experiences in the past and from problems in the development of the personality. Consequently, a focus on the unconscious mind requires the psychoanalytic process to also focus on the **past**—specifically on those repressed infant and childhood memories and experiences that served to create the desires, defenses, dreams, and wishes that invariably manifest through the thoughts and behaviors of every individual.

Freud's Structural Theory of Personality Development

Freud proposed a three-level structure of personality, composed of the id, the ego, and the super-ego:

Id	The level of personality that comprises basic instinctual drives and is the only part of personality present at birth. The id seeks immediate gratification of primitive needs (hunger, thirst, libido) and adheres to the "pleasure principle" (i.e., seek pleasure, avoid pain).
Ego	Develops secondarily and allows for rational thought, executive functions, and the ability to delay gratification. The ego is governed by the "reality principle" and mediates the desires of the id with the requirements of the external world.
Super-ego	Develops last and incorporates the higher concepts of morality, ethics, and justice into the personality, allowing concepts of right, wrong, and greater good to override base instincts and purely rational goals.

Super-Ego, Conscience, and Ego Ideal

The **super-ego** is comprised of the conscience and the ego ideal, which are constructed from the restraints and encouragements provided by caregivers (parents, teachers, other role models). The **conscience** focuses on cognitive and behavioral restrictions (i.e., the "should nots") while the **ego ideal** focuses on perfection, including spiritual attainment and higher-order goals (the "shoulds" of thought and behavior).

The super-ego works in opposition to the id, produces feelings of guilt for inappropriate drives, fantasies, and actions, and encourages refinement, aspirations, and higher-order goals. Freud theorized that the super-ego emerges around age five, and is not the dominant feature of the personality in a healthy person (which would result in overly-rigid, rule-bound behavior).

The strongest part of the personality is the ego, which seeks to satisfy the needs of the id without disrupting the super-ego.

Psychosexual Stages of Development

Freud proposed that children develop through five stages that he referred to as the psychosexual stages of development. They are as follows:

Stage	Description
Oral (Birth to 1.5 years)	Gratification through mouth/upper digestive tract.
Anal (1.5 to 3 years)	The child gains control over anal sphincter and bowel movements.
Phallic (3 to 6 years)	Gratification through genitalia. Major task is resolution of Oedipal complex and leads to development of superego, which begins about age 4. During this time child's phallic striving is directed toward the opposite-sex parent and in competition with same-sex parent. Out of fear and love, child renounces desire for the opposite sex parent and represses sexual desires. Child then identifies with same-sex parent and internalizes their values, etc. This leads to development of superego and ability to experience guilt.
Latency (6 to 10 years)	Sublimation of the oedipal stage, expression of sexual-aggressive drives in socially acceptable forms
Genital (10 years to adulthood)	Acceptance of one's genitalia and concern for others' wellbeing.

Adult Personality Types

Freud's adult personality types are based on his psychosexual stages and include the following:

Personality Type	Characteristics
Oral	Infantile, demanding, dependent behavior; preoccupation with oral gratification.
Anal	Stinginess, excessive focus on accumulating and collecting. Rigidity in routines and forms, suspiciousness, legalistic thinking.
Phallic	Selfish sexual exploitation of others, without regard to their needs or concerns.

Processes and Stages Relevant to Development of the Personality

Freud identified two primary elements that contribute to the development of the personality:

1. Natural growth and maturational processes (biological, hormonal, and time-dependent processes)
2. Learning and experiential processes (coping with and avoiding pain, managing frustration, reducing anxiety, and resolving conflicts).

According to Freud, psychopathology will result if all 5 stages of psychosexual development are not fully mastered, or if fixation at a particular stage develops (resulting if needs at a particular stage are either over- or under-gratified). If significant developmental frustration is experienced in a later stage, the developmental process may fall back to an earlier stage by means of the defense mechanism known as regression.

Cathexis and Anti-Cathexis

According to Freud's theory, the individual's mental state emerges from the process of reciprocal exchange between two forces: cathexis and anti-cathexis:

- Freud used the term **cathexis** to refer to the psychic energy attached to an object of importance (i.e., person, body part, psychic element). He also used this term to refer to what he called urges, or psychic impulses (e.g., desires, wishes, pain), that drive human behavior.
- In contrast to the driving urges of cathexis, there is a checking force he referred to as **anti-cathexis**. It serves to restrict the urges of the id and also to keep repressed information in the unconscious mind.

Erik Erikson's Psychosocial Stages of Development

Erik Erikson was one of the first theorists to address human development over the entire life span. The eight developmental stages in his theory of psychosocial development are:

Stage	Description
Trust vs. Mistrust (Birth to 1.5 years)	• Same ages as Freud's oral stage. • Infants develop a sense of trust in self and in others. • Psychological dangers include a strong sense of mistrust that later develops and is revealed as withdrawal when the individual is at odds with self and others.
Autonomy vs. Shame (1.5 to 3 years)	• Same ages as Freud's anal stage. • In this phase, rapid growth in muscular maturation, verbalization, and the ability to coordinate highly conflicting action patterns is characterized by tendencies of holding on and letting go. • The child begins experiencing an autonomous will, which contributes to the process of identity building and development of the courage to be an independent individual. • Psychological dangers include immature obsessiveness and procrastination, ritualistic repetitions to gain power, self-insistent stubbornness, compulsive meek compliance or self-restraint, and the fear of a loss of self-control.

Stage	Description
Initiative vs. Guilt (3 to 6 years)	• Same ages as Freud's phallic stage. • Incursion into space by mobility, into the unknown by curiosity, and into others by physical attack and aggressive voice. • This stage frees the child's initiative and sense of purpose for adult tasks. • Psychological dangers include hysterical denial or self-restriction, which impede an individual from actualizing inner capacities.
Industry vs. Inferiority (6 to 11 years)	• Same as Freud's latency stage. • The need of the child is to make things well, to be a worker, and a potential provider. • Developmental task is mastery over physical objects, self, social transaction, ideas, and concepts. • School and peer groups are necessary for gaining and testing mastery. • Psychological dangers include a sense of inferiority, incompetence, self-restraint, and conformity.
Identity vs. Role Confusion (Adolescence)	• Same age range as Freud's genital stage. • Crucial task is to create an identity, reintegration of various components of self into a whole person—a process of ego synthesis. • Peer group is greatly important in providing support, values, a primary reference group, and an arena in which to experiment with various roles. • Psychological dangers include extreme identity confusion, feelings of estrangement, excessive conformity or rebelliousness, and idealism (a denial of reality, neurotic conflict, or delinquency).
Intimacy vs. Isolation (Early adulthood)	• Task is to enter relationships with others in an involved, reciprocal manner. • Failure to achieve intimacy can lead to highly stereotyped interpersonal relationships and distancing. Can also lead to a willingness to renounce, isolate, and destroy others whose presence seems dangerous.
Generativity vs. Stagnation (Adulthood)	• Key task is to develop concern for establishing and guiding the next generation, and the capacity for caring, nurturing, and concern for others. • Psychological danger is stagnation. Stagnation includes caring primarily for oneself, an artificial intimacy with others, and self-indulgence.
Ego integrity vs. Despair (Late adulthood)	• Task is the acceptance of one's life, achievements, and significant relationships as satisfactory and acceptable. • Psychological danger is despair. Despair is expressed in having the sense that time is too short to start another life or to test alternative roads to integrity. • Despair is accompanied by self-criticism, regret, and fear of impending death.

The stages are hierarchical and build upon each other. The resolution of the fundamental "crisis" of each prior stage must occur before one can move on to the next stage of growth. Although individual attributes are primary in resolving the crisis associated with each stage, the social environment can play an important role as well.

Erikson's Ego Strength

The ego essentially mediates irrational impulses related to the id (drives, instincts, needs). The concept of ego strengths derives from Erikson's (1964, 1985) 8 psychosocial stages and includes hope, will, purpose, competence, fidelity, love, care, and wisdom. Ego strength results from the overcoming of crises in each stage of development and allows the individual to maintain good mental health despite challenges and cope with conflict. Ego strength is assessed through questioning and observation. Characteristics of **ego strength** include the ability to:

- Express a range of feelings and emotions without being overwhelmed by them
- Deal effectively with loss
- Gain strength from loss
- Continue to engage in positive and life-affirming activities
- Exhibit empathy and consideration of others
- Resist temptation and exercise self-control
- Admit responsibility for own actions and avoid blaming others
- Show acceptance of the self
- Set limits in order to avoid negative influences and outcomes

Jean Piaget's Theory of Cognitive and Moral Development

Key Concepts

Jean Piaget believed that development was progressive and followed a set pattern. He believed the child's environment, their interactions with others in that environment, and how the environment responds help to shape the child's cognitive development. **Key concepts of Piaget's theory of cognitive and moral development** are defined below:

- **Action** is overt behavior.
- **Operation** is a particular type of action that may be internalized thought.
- **Activity in Development** refers to the fact that the child is not a passive subject, but an active contributor to the construction of her or his personality and universe. The child acts on her or his environment, modifies it, and is an active participant in the construction of reality.
- **Adaptation** includes accommodation and assimilation. Accommodation entails adapting to the characteristics of the object. Assimilation is the incorporation of external reality into the existing mental organization.

Stages of Cognitive and Moral Development

The stages of Piaget's theory of cognitive and moral development are as follows:

Stage	Description
Sensorimotor (Birth to 2 years)	• Infant cannot evoke representations of persons or objects when they are absent—symbolic function. • Infant interacts with her or his surroundings and can focus on objects other than self. Infant learns to predict events (door opening signals that someone will appear). Infants also learn that objects continue to exist when out of sight and learn a beginning sense of causality.
Pre-operational (2 to 7 years)	• Developing of symbolic thought draws from sensory-motor thinking. • Conceptual ability not yet developed.
Concrete operational (7 to 11 years)	• Child gains capacity to order and relate experience to an organized whole. • Children can now explore several possible solutions to a problem without adopting one, as they are able to return to their original outlook.
Formal operational (11 years to adolescence)	• Child/youth can visualize events and concepts beyond the present and is able to form theories.

Lawrence Kohlberg's Theory of Moral Development

Lawrence Kohlberg's theory of moral development is characterized as the following:

- Kohlberg formulated his theory to extend and modify the work of Piaget, as he believed that moral development was a longer and more complex process. He postulated that infants possess no morals or ethics at birth and that moral development occurs largely independently of age. Kohlberg asserted that children's experiences shape their understanding of moral concepts (i.e., justice, rights, equality, human welfare).
- Kohlberg suggested a process involving three levels, each with two stages. Each stage reveals a dramatic change in the moral perspective of the individual.
- In this theory, moral development is linear, no stage can be skipped, and development takes place throughout the life span.
- Progress between stages is contingent upon the availability of a role model who offers a model of the principles of the next higher level.

Levels and Stages of Moral Development

The levels and stages of Kohlberg's theory of moral development are as follows:

Stage	Level	Description
1	Pre-conventional	The individual perspective frames moral judgments, which are concrete. The framework of Stage 1 stresses rule following, because breaking rules may lead to punishment. Reasoning in this stage is egocentric and not concerned with others.
2	Pre-conventional	Emphasizes moral reciprocity and has its focus on the pragmatic, instrumental value of an action. Individuals at this stage observe moral standards because it is in their interest, but they are able to justify retaliation as a form of justice. Behavior in this stage is focused on following rules only when it is in the person's immediate interest. Stage 2 has a mutual contractual nature, which makes rule-following instrumental and based on externalities. There is, however, an understanding of conventional morality.
3	Conventional	Individuals define morality in reference to what is expected by those with whom they have close relationships. Emphasis of this stage is on stereotypic roles (good mother, father, sister). Virtue is achieved through maintaining trusting and loyal relationships.
4	Conventional	In this stage, the individual shifts from basically narrow local norms and role expectations to a larger social system perspective. Social responsibilities and observance of laws are key aspects of social responsibility. Individuals in this stage reflect higher levels of abstraction in understanding laws' significance. Individuals at Stage 4 have a sophisticated understanding of the law and only violate laws when they conflict with social duties. Observance of the law is seen as necessary to maintain the protections that the legal system provides to all.
5	Post-conventional	The individual becomes aware that while rules and laws exist for the good of the greatest number, there are times when they will work against the interest of particular individuals. Issues may not always be clear-cut and the individual may have to decide to disregard some rules or laws in order to uphold a higher good (such as the protection of life).
6	Post-conventional	Individuals have developed their own set of moral guidelines, which may or may not fit with the law. Principles such as human rights, justice, and equality apply to everyone and the individual must be prepared to act to defend these principles, even if it means going against the rest of society and paying the consequences (i.e., disapproval or imprisonment). Kohlberg believed very few, if any, people reached this stage.

Parenting Styles

Although children are born with their own temperament, the parenting style they grow up with can influence how this temperament manifests over time.

Authoritarian (autocratic) parents desire obedience without question. They tend toward harsh punishments, using their power to make their children obey. They are emotionally withdrawn from their children and enforce strict rules without discussing why the rules exist. These children tend to have low self-esteem, be more dependent, and are introverted with poor social skills.

Authoritative (democratic) parents provide boundaries and expect obedience, but use love when they discipline. They involve their children in deciding rules and consequences, discussing reasons for their decisions, but they will still enforce the rules consistently. They encourage independence and take each child's unique position seriously. These children tend to have higher self-esteem, good social skills, and confidence in themselves.

Indulgent (permissive) parents stay involved with their children, but have few rules in place to give the children boundaries. These children have a difficult time setting their own limits and are not responsible. They disrespect others and have trouble with authority figures.

Indifferent (uninvolved) parents spend as little time as possible with their children. They are self-involved, with no time or patience for taking care of their children's needs. Guidance and discipline are lacking and inconsistent. These children tend toward delinquency, with a lack of respect for others.

Attachment and Bonding

Attachment is the emotional bond that develops between an infant and parent/caregiver when the infant responds to the nonverbal communication of the parent/caregiver and develops a sense of trust and security as the infant's needs are met. Nonverbal communication includes eye contact, calm and attentive facial expressions, tender tone of voice, touch, and body language.

Bonding is especially important during the child's first 3 years, and the failure to develop an attachment bond may impact the child's development and the family dynamics. Infants that have bonded generally exhibit stranger anxiety at about 6 months and separation anxiety by one year. While the parent/caregiver can nurture the emotional connection with the child at later ages, those infants who failed to attach in the first year may have increased difficulty doing so later. Children who have bonded with parents/caregivers tend to develop according to expectations, meeting expected milestones, while those who are deprived may exhibit growth and development delays as well as poor feeding.

Review Video: Factors in Development
Visit mometrix.com/academy and enter code: 112169

Learning Theory and Behavior Modification

Pavlov's Work

Pavlov learned to link experimentally manipulated stimuli (or conditioned stimuli) to existing natural, unconditioned stimuli that elicited a fixed, **unconditioned response**. Pavlov accomplished this by introducing the **conditioned response** just prior to the natural, unconditioned stimulus. Just before giving a dog food (an autonomic stimulus for salivation), Pavlov sounded a bell. The bell then became the stimulus for salivation, even in the absence of food being given. Many conditioned responses can be created through continuing reinforcement.

Skinner's Work

B. F. Skinner developed the **empty organism concept**, which proposes that an infant has the capacity for action built into his or her physical makeup. The infant also has reflexes and motivations that will set this capacity in random motion. Skinner asserted that the **law of effect** governs development. Behavior of children is shaped largely by adults. Behaviors that result in satisfying consequences are likely to be repeated under similar circumstances. Halting or discontinuing behavior is accomplished by denying satisfying rewards or through punishment. Skinner also theorized about **schedules of reinforcement**. He posited that rather than reinforcing every instance of a correct response, one can reinforce a fixed percentage of correct responses, or space reinforcements according to some interval of time. Intermittent reinforcement will reinforce the desired behavior.

Feminist Theory

Feminist theory views inequity in terms of gender with females as victims of an almost universal patriarchal model in which the sociopolitical, family, and religious institutions are dominated by males. Proponents of feminist theory focus on areas of interest to females, including social and economic inequality, power structures, gender discrimination, racial discrimination, and gender oppression. Feminists often point to the exclusion of women in the development of theories about human behavior, research, and other academic matters. Some feminists believe that oppression of women is inherent to capitalism, where females are often paid less than males, but others believe that it is inherent in all forms of government because they are all based on patriarchal models. Feminists recognize that gender, social class, and race are all sources of oppression with ethnic minorities and those in the lower social classes often suffering the most oppression. Feminists note that the idea that families headed by women are dysfunctional is based on patriarchal ideals.

Carol Gilligan's Morality of Care

Carol Gilligan's morality of care is the feminist response to Kohlberg's moral development theory. Kohlberg's theory was based on research only on men. Gilligan purports that a morality of care reflects women's experience more accurately than one emphasizing justice and rights. Key concepts include the following:

- **Morality of care** reflects caring, responsibility, and non-violence, while **morality of justice and rights** emphasizes equality.
- The two types of moralities give two distinct charges, to not treat others unfairly (justice/rights) and to not turn away from someone in need (care). Care stresses interconnectedness and nurturing. Emphasizing justice stems from a focus on individualism.
- **Aspects of attachment**: Justice/rights requires individuation and separation from the parent, which leads to awareness of power differences. Care emphasizes a continuing attachment to parent and less awareness of inequalities, not a primary focus on fairness.

Older Adulthood

How the Elderly Deal with Life Transitions

Typically, the elderly population seeks to cope with whatever problem comes their way without the benefit of mental health care. In 1991, Butler and Lewis developed a definition for **loss** in relation to the elderly. Elderly can experience a range of emotions whenever loss or death occurs. Examples of loss could be loss of friends, loss of significant others or spouse, a loss of social roles within the community, a loss of work or career, a loss of a prestigious role, a loss of income, a loss of physical vigor, or a loss of health. Some may experience personality changes or changes in sexual appetites. Elderly people may have a situational crisis that puts a strain on their resources. The resiliency of this population is evident by the large number of seniors who live independently with only a little support. Only 4-6% live in nursing homes or assisted living facilities, and 10-15% receive homecare.

FACTORS PREVENTING THE ELDERLY FROM RECEIVING MENTAL HEALTH SERVICES

While mental illness is often overestimated in the elderly population, it is still prevalent, with one in five elderly individuals experiencing some sort of mental illness. The most significant **mental illnesses** experienced by the elderly are anxiety, severe cognitive impairment, and mood disorders. Anxiety is the most prevalent of these problems. These numbers may be skewed by the fact that the elderly may not be seeking help when needed. Sadly, suicide rates are higher in this population than in any other population. The older a person gets, the higher the rate of suicide. Anxiety and depression cause much suffering in the elderly.

There are a number of factors that **prevent the elderly from receiving mental health services**. Part of the problem lies in the strong values which guide the elderly to solve their own problems. Other seniors feel they should keep quiet about private issues. Still others feel a negative connotation from past stigmas attached to those who needed mental health care. Baby boomers approaching old age have been bombarded with literature on psychology and healthy lifestyles. Therefore, the baby boomer generation may take on a healthier attitude about receiving the appropriate mental health care for their needs. A limited number of counselors, social workers and therapists are trained in geriatric care. Providers for the elderly have difficulties working with payment policies and insurance companies. In addition, seeing the client's aging problems may cause unpleasant personal issues about aging to surface for the provider.

Human Behavior in the Social Environment

Person-in-Environment Theory

The **person-in-environment** theory considers the influence the client has on their environment and the influence that multiple environments (social, economic, family, political, cultural, religious, work, ethnic, life events) have on the client. This is an interactive model that is central to many professional helping relationships and recognizes the impact of oppression and discrimination on the client. The person-in-environment theory supports the goals of providing personal care for the client and furthering the cause of social justice. The person-in-environment theory is the basis for the strengths-based perspective in which the initial focus is placed on the personal strengths of the client and the strengths within the client's environment. It involves utilizing psychosocial interventions and assessing behavior on the basis of interactions between the client and the environment because the client's life situation results from the relationship between the client and the environment.

Hildegard Peplau's Theory of Interpersonal Relations

Hildegard Peplau developed the theory of interpersonal relations in 1952, applying Sullivan's theory of anxiety to nursing practice, developing a framework for psychiatric nursing. The model, however, can be applied to other helping disciplines. The relationship comprises the helping professional (counselor, social worker, or nurse) who has expertise and the individual (client or patient) who wants relief from suffering/problems.

According to Peplau, the professional-individual relationship evolves through 4 phases:

Phase	Details
Preorientation	The helping professional prepares, anticipating possible reactions and interventions.
Orientation	Roles and responsibilities are clarified in the initial interview.
Working	The professional and individual explore together and promote the individual's problem-solving skills.
Termination	The final phase consists of summarizing and reviewing.

The helping professional uses process recording, which includes observing, interpreting, and intervening to help the client, but also self-observation to increase self-awareness. Peplau believed that individuals deserved human care by educated helpers and should be treated with dignity and respect. She also believed that the environment (social, psychosocial, and physical) could affect the individual in a positive or negative manner. The helping professional can focus on the way in which clients react to their problems and can help them to use those problems as an opportunity for learning and maturing.

Systems Theory

Systems theory derives its theoretical orientation from general systems theory and includes elements of organizational theory, family theory, group behavior theory, and a variety of sociological constructs. Key **principles** include the following:

- Systems theory endeavors to provide a methodological view of the world by synthesizing key principles from its theoretical roots.
- A fundamental premise is that key sociological aspects of clients, families, and groups cannot be separated from the whole (i.e., aspects that are systemic in nature).
- All systems are interrelated, and change in one will produce change in the others.

- Systems are either open or closed: Open systems accept outside input and accommodate, while closed systems resist outside input due to rigid and impenetrable barriers and boundaries.
- Boundaries are lines of demarcation identifying the outer margins of the system being examined.
- Entropy refers to the process of system dissolution or disorganization.
- Homeostatic balance refers to the propensity of systems to reestablish and maintain stability.

Ecosystems Theory

Ecosystems (or life model) theory derives its theoretical orientation from ecology, systems theory, psychodynamic theory, behavioral theory, and cognitive theory. Key principles include the following:

- There is an interactive relationship between all living organisms and their environment (both social and physical).
- The process of adaptation is universal and is a reciprocal process by individuals and environments mutually accommodating each other to obtain a "goodness of fit."
- Changes in individuals, their environments, or both can be disruptive and produce dysfunction.
- This theory works to optimize goodness of fit by modifying perceptions, thoughts, responsiveness, and exchanges between clients and their environments.
- On a larger (community) level, treatment interventions by the ecosystems approach are drawn from direct practice and include educating, identifying and expanding resources, developing needed policies and programs, and engaging governmental systems to support requisite change.

Impact of Family on Human Behavior

Family Types

A **family** consists of a group of people that are connected by marriage, blood relationship, or emotions. There are many different variations when referring to the concept of family.

- The **nuclear family** is one in which two or more people are related by blood, marriage, or adoption. This type of family is typically parents and their children.
- The **extended family** is one in which several nuclear families related by blood or marriage function as one group.
- In a **single-parent structure**, there is only one parent caring for the children in the household.
- In a **blended family** a parent marries or remarries after he or she has already had children. Blended families are often referred to as stepfamilies because they consist of a parent, a stepparent, and one or more children.

A **household** consists of an individual or group of people residing together under one roof. The practitioner will often interact with families on many different levels. This may involve meeting the family once during treatment or establishing a long-term relationship with the family over the course of long-term treatment.

Functional Family

A functional family will be able to change roles, responsibilities, and interactions during a stressful event. This type of family can experience **nonfunctional behaviors** if placed in an acute stressful event; however, they should be able to reestablish their family balance over a period of time. The functional family will have the ability to deal with **conflict and change** in order to deal with negative situations without causing long-term dysfunction or dissolution of the family. They will have completed vital life cycle tasks, keep emotional contact between family members and across generations, over-closeness is avoided, and distance is used to resolve issues. When two members of the family have a conflict, they are expected to **resolve** this conflict between themselves and there is **open communication** between all family members. Children of a functional family are expected to achieve age-appropriate functioning and are given age-appropriate privileges.

Family Life Cycle

The family life cycle comprises the states typical individuals go through from childhood to old age. Stages include:

Stage	Details
Independence	Individuals begin to separate from the family unit and develop a sense of their place in the world. Individuals may begin to explore careers and become increasingly independent in providing for self needs. Individuals often develop close peer relationships outside of the family.
Coupling	Individuals develop intimate relationships with others and may live together or marry, moving toward interdependence, joint goal setting and problem-solving. Individuals learn new communication skills and may have to adjust expectations.
Parenting	Individuals make the decision to have or adopt children and adjust their lives and roles accordingly. Relationships may change and be tested, and parents may shift focus from themselves to their children.
Empty nest	Individuals may feel profound loss and stress at this change, especially since this is also the time when health problems of age and the need to care for parents arise. Relationships with children evolve.
Retirement	Individuals may undergo many changes and challenges and must deal with deaths of family and friends and their own mortality.

Change in Family Roles of Men and Women in United States

The family roles of men and women in the United States have changed drastically over the past several decades. Women were traditionally the primary caretakers of children, so they were expected to maintain the household while the men worked to provide for the family. However, this is no longer the case, as there has been a drastic increase in the number of women entering the work force in the recent years. This change is partially due to the fact that it has become more difficult for families to live off of one income. It can be extremely difficult for a family to find the time and money to care for a child, especially if that child has a disability, because both parents are typically required to work.

How a Family Aids the Development, Education, and Function of its Members

A family can aid the development, education, and function of its members in two major ways. First, parents and grandparents typically pass their heritage down to their children and teach them what is considered acceptable through their actions, customs, and traditions. In other words, a person typically acquires culture through his or her family, and that culture helps the person function in society and interact socially with other people. Second, a person's family can act as an effective support network in many situations. A family may be able to provide some of the emotional, financial, or other types of support a person needs.

Effects of Mental Illness on Family

Families with a member that has a **chronic mental illness** will provide several functions that those without mentally ill members may not need. These functions can include providing support and information for care and treatment options. They will also monitor the services provided the family member and address concerns with these services. Many times, the family is the biggest **advocate** for additional availability of services for mental health clients. There can often be disagreements between the care providers and the family members concerning the dependence of the client within the family. Parents can often be viewed as overprotective when attempting to encourage a client's independence and self-reliant functioning. They will need support and reassurance if the client leaves home. On the other hand, many parents will provide for their child for as long as they live. Once the primary care provider dies, the client may be left with no one to care for them and they may experience traumatic disruptions.

Incongruous Hierarchy

An incongruous hierarchy is a family relationship in which a minor figure controls the family dynamic. The control engine may be the exhibition of inappropriate behavior at crucial times. It is a "tail wags the dog" type of scenario. A child throws an entire family into turmoil by ranting and throwing a fit each evening at bedtime. The child's father reacts by attempting to soothe her, offering her candy and letting her stay up late. The child's mother is angry with the father for doing so, and begins shouting at him and withholding affection. An older brother loses sleep because of the daily hysterics, and subsequently performs poorly in school. This type of family dysfunction is called incongruous hierarchy.

Family Violence

Family violence can include physical, emotional, sexual, or verbal behaviors that occur between members of the same family or others living within the home. This behavior can include both abuse and neglect and involve the elderly, spouses, and children. Family violence is often kept a secret and may be the main issue with many family problems. Many times, actions that would be considered unacceptable to strangers or friends are often the norm between family members. Violence and abuse occur due to the unique interactions between the family members based upon personality differences, situational variations, and sociocultural influences.

Characteristics of Violent Families

Violent families will often share many of the same characteristics. Many times, the abusive family member will have suffered abuse from their family while growing up. This type of abuse is a **multigenerational transmission** and is a cycle of violence. These abusers have learned to believe that violent behavior is a way to solve problems. Violent families are also usually socially isolated so that others such as friends, teachers, neighbors, or law enforcement officials do not become aware that the abuse is occurring. The abuser will also use and abuse power to **control** the victim. They may be considered a person of authority, such as a parent would be to a child. Power is a very important factor with abuse of an intimate partner. The abuser is often very controlling of their partner and will attempt to dominate every aspect of their life. Another commonality among abusers is **substance abuse**; however, one is not dependent upon the other. Many times, the use of alcohol or drugs may escalate violent behaviors by decreasing inhibitions.

Family Life Education

Family life education, which can include parenting and financial management classes, aims to give people the information and tools they need in order to strengthen family life. Approaches to family life education include:

- **Strength-based**: Assisting clients to identify their strengths and those of their environment in order to increase their sense of personal power and engagement.
- **Cultural**: Focusing on cultural norms and the diverse needs of different populations as well as utilizing communication and activities that correspond to different cultures.
- **Selective**: Aiming at specific groups, such as LGBTQ parents or grandparents, in order to ascertain their unique needs and to provide appropriate education. Some programs may be designed for at-risk groups, such as those in court-ordered education programs because of abuse or neglect.
- **Universal**: Universal education focuses on all members of a particular population, such as all parents, despite differences among the parents. These programs often focus on general information, such as growth and development, and cover a range of topics.

Developmental Model of Couples Therapy

The developmental model of couples therapy (Bader & Pearson) accepts the inevitable change in relationships and focuses on both individual and couple growth and development. The goal is to assist the couple to recognize their stage of development and to gain the skills and insight needed to progress to the next stage. Problems may especially arise if members of the couple are at different stages. Stages include:

Stage	Details
Bonding	Couples meet, develop a romantic relationship, and fall in love, focusing on similarities rather than differences. Sexual intimacy is an important component.
Differentiating	Conflicts and differences begin to arise, and couples must learn to work together to resolve their problems.
Practicing	Couples become more independent from each other, establish outside friendships, and develop outside interests.
Rapprochement	Couples move apart and then together again, often increasing intimacy and feeling more satisfied with the relationship.
Synergy	Couples become more intimate and recognize the strength of their union.

Anna Freud's Defense Mechanisms

According to Anna Freud, defense mechanisms are an unconscious process in which the ego attempts to expel anxiety-provoking sexual and aggressive impulses from consciousness. Defense mechanisms are attempts to protect the self from painful anxiety and are used universally. In themselves they are not an indication of pathology, but rather an indication of disturbance when their cost outweighs their protective value. Anna Freud proposed that defense mechanisms serve to protect the ego and to reduce angst, fear, and distress through irrational distortion, denial, and/or obscuring reality. Defense mechanisms are deployed when the ego senses the threat of harm from thoughts or acts incongruent with rational behavior or conduct demanded by the super-ego.

The following are terms that pertain to **Anna Freud's defense mechanisms**:

Compensation	Protection against feelings of inferiority and inadequacy stemming from real or imagined personal defects or weaknesses.
Conversion	Somatic changes conveyed in symbolic body language; psychic pain is felt in a part of the body.
Denial	Avoidance of awareness of some painful aspect of reality.
Displacement	Investing repressed feelings in a substitute object.
Association	Altruism; acquiring gratification through connection with and helping another person who is satisfying the same instincts.
Identification	Manner by which one becomes like another person in one or more respects; a more elaborate process than introjection.
Identification with the Aggressor	A child's introjection of some characteristic of an anxiety evoking object and assimilation of an anxiety experience just lived through. In this, the child can transform from the threatened person into the one making the threat.
Introjection	Absorbing an idea or image so that it becomes part of oneself.
Inversion	Turning against the self; object of aggressive drive is changed from another to the self, especially in depression and masochism.
Isolation of Affect	Separation of ideas from the feelings originally associated with them. Remaining idea is deprived of motivational force; action is impeded and guilt avoided.
Intellectualization	Psychological binding of instinctual drives in intellectual activities, for example the adolescent's preoccupation with philosophy and religion.
Projection	Ascribing a painful idea or impulse to the external world.
Rationalization	Effort to give a logical explanation for painful unconscious material to avoid guilt and shame.
Reaction Formation	Replacing in conscious awareness a painful idea or feeling with its opposite.
Regression	Withdrawal to an earlier phase of psychosexual development.
Repression	The act of obliterating material from conscious awareness. This is capable of mastering powerful impulses.
Reversal	Type of reaction formation aimed at protection from painful thoughts/feelings.
Splitting	Seeing external objects as either all good or all bad. Feelings may rapidly shift from one category to the other.
Sublimation	Redirecting energies of instinctual drives to generally positive goals that are more acceptable to the ego and superego.
Substitution	Trading of one affect for another (e.g., rage that masks fear)
Undoing	Ritualistically performing the opposite of an act one has recently carried out in order to cancel out or balance the evil that may have been present in the act.

Biological Theories

Color Vision and Color Blindness Theories

There are two basic **theories of color vision.**

- Young-Helmholtz proposed a **trichromatic theory**, stating that there are color receptors for the three primary colors (red, green, blue). According to this theory, all other colors are based on variations and combinations of these three.
- The **opponent-process theory** of Ewald Hering proposed that there are three receptors, but they are red-green, yellow-blue, and white-black. Cells in these receptors are stimulated one way or the other, and the overall pattern in their stimulation creates differences in color perception.

Neither trichromatic nor opponent-process theory adequately explains color perception, so the current consensus is that at the retinal level trichromatic theory holds, while the thalamus operates on an opponent-process model.

Color blindness occurs when an individual has a recessive trait on the X chromosome. Males are more likely than females to be colorblind.

Weber's Law, Fechner's Law, and Stevens' Power Law

Weber's law states that the more intense a stimulus, the greater will be the increase in stimulus intensity necessary for the stimulus to be perceived over time.

Fechner built on Weber's law and was able to determine the exact relationship between the magnitude of a stimulus and the magnitude of the reaction. **Fechner's law** states that stimulus changes are logarithmically related to psychological sensations.

Stevens determined that the work of Weber and Fechner was only good for studying stimuli of moderate intensity. In order to examine extreme stimuli, Stevens had to develop his **Power law**, which describes sensation as an exponential function of stimulus intensity. Stevens' work depended on a system of magnitude estimation, in which subjects assigned numerical values to the intensities of various stimuli.

Synesthesia and Psychophysics

Synesthesia is when the stimulation of one sensory modality triggers the stimulation of another sensory modality. Synesthetic individuals report being able to see the color of words or taste shapes. There is no clear understanding of the etiology of **synesthesia**, although many researchers believe that it is caused by "cross-wiring" in the brain.

The study of the relationship between physical stimulus magnitudes and their corresponding psychological sensations is called **psychophysics.** An important part of psychophysics is the determination of absolute thresholds (minimum stimulation needed to produce a sensation) and difference thresholds (smallest unit of stimulus intensity needed to recognize a difference in stimulus intensity).

Assessment Process

Importance of Individual Assessment in Counseling

Counselors hold the belief that the individual has a specific blueprint of behaviors, genetic characteristics, and life circumstances that make them a unique person. The **individual assessment** is the first step in both the counselor and the client gaining insight into the individual. Counseling is designed to help the client gain a perspective on how he or she behaves through the following:

- The counselor works to establish a **rapport** with the client and to develop the client's positive self-esteem.
- The client is made to understand how **genetics** can influence a person's characteristics and behaviors and is encouraged to gain perspective about negative circumstances in early life.
- **Self-knowledge** is used to help the client learn how to make better decisions and to take responsibility for his or her own actions.
- The client learns **coping strategies** to deal with unpleasant circumstances or memories.

The Role of Observation in Assessment

Levels of Observation

One form of assessment involves nonstandard procedures that are used to provide individualized assessments. Nonstandard assessment procedures include observations of client behaviors and performance. There are three **levels of observation** techniques that can be applied:

- The first level is **casual informational observation**, where the counselor gleans information by watching the client during unstructured activities throughout the day.
- The second level is **guided observation**, an intentional style of direct observation accomplished with a checklist or rating scale to evaluate the performance or behavior seen.
- The third level is the **clinical level**, where observation is done in a controlled setting for a lengthy period of time. This is most often accomplished on the doctoral level with applied instrumentation. Clinical predictions are then based on the intuition and experience of the observing clinician.

Instruments Used During the Observation Process

The following **instruments** can be used in an observation:

- The **checklist** is used to check off behaviors or performance levels with a plus or minus sign to indicate that the behavior was observed or absent. The observer can converse with the client as they mark the checklist.
- The **rating scale** is a more complex checklist that notes the strength, frequency, or degree of an exhibited behavior. Likert scales are applied using the following ratings: 1. Never; 2. Rarely; 3. Sometimes; 4. Usually; and 5. Always. The evaluator of the behavior makes a judgment about whatever question has been asked on the rating scale.
- The **anecdotal report** is used to record subjective notes describing the client's behavior during a specified time or in a specified setting, and is often applied to evaluate a suspected pattern.

Structured interviews, questionnaires, and personal essays or journals may also be useful in the observation process, depending on the client's ability to participate in these exercises.

Review Video: Basic Skills of a Counselor
Visit mometrix.com/academy and enter code: 965456

Assessing Children

In order to obtain a useful interview from a child, the clinician must establish a good **rapport** and maintain the cooperation of the child. Establish rapport by:

- Using **descriptive** statements to encourage the child (e.g., "You're doing well.")
- Using **reflective** statements that encourage the child to think about what he or she has said (e.g., "You sound very angry about that.")
- **Praising** the child specifically for those things that contribute to a good interview
- Avoiding criticism
- When relevant, using **play**, such as anatomically correct dolls to help children discuss issues of sexual function and abuse or medical issues and interventions

Thematic Assessment

Thematic assessment appraises major themes that have happened over the lifetime of a client. As the client discusses or describes the life events, the therapist makes notes of the themes or predominant topics that create a pattern. The predominant themes are then related to the assessment, which attempts to bring into focus a better understanding of what these themes mean. The assessment can be in the form of a pencil-and-paper test, a behavioral assessment, or a clinical interview.

- One type of paper-and-pencil test is the **Minnesota Multiphasic Personality Inventory (MMPI)**, with the most recent version updated in 2020, the MMPI-3.
- **Behavioral chart assessments** can be used to document a person's habitual, explosive, angry episodes.
- **Clinical interviews** are used for cognitive imagery assessments.

Review Video: Life Stages in Client Assessment
Visit mometrix.com/academy and enter code: 535888

Spheres of Influence in Terms of Client Assessment

The spheres of influence of a client progress outward from the self and should be carefully assessed by the counselor:

- **Self**: Personal beliefs, values, thoughts, and behaviors influence the client's response to therapy and willingness to interact with the counselor.
- **Family**: Family values, expectations, and behavioral norms that may affect the client's thought processes and behavior. Parents, children, and partners having the strongest effect (positive or negative), although extended family may also affect the client.
- **Friends/Neighbors**: The influence may vary widely, depending on the closeness of the relationship, the client's response to peer pressure, and the need or desire to conform to norms.
- **School/Work**: Clients may feel pressured to attain certain goals and conflicted about doing so. These conflicts and pressures may influence the goals that clients set for themselves.

- **Community/Government**: Community organizations, government assistance, laws and regulations may all affect a client's understanding of themselves, their rights, and their belief systems.
- **Country/World**: Broad cultural norms bring expectations that may affect the client.

Assessing a Client's Readiness to Change

The counselor must assess the client's readiness to change in order to determine the best therapeutic approach. If, for example, a client is in court-ordered therapy or in therapy because of family intervention, the client may lack motivation to change and is not likely to actively engage in therapy. Clients may state directly that they have no problem or may simply fail to follow through. Some may feel that they need to change but don't yet have the will to do so. These clients often state an intent to work on the problem at a future time, "I'm going to cut down on my drinking after I change jobs." Some clients may recognize a problem and have a clear plan, while others actively begin to make changes. The counselor should begin by asking clients if they believe they have a problem and, if so, when they intend to take action to change. The goal of therapy for most clients should be to help the client to move toward an acceptance of the need for change and to making plans, as most clients entering therapy are not yet ready to take action.

Assessing Members of Culturally Diverse Populations

Guidelines that psychologists should remember when assessing members of culturally diverse populations include the following:

- Clarify the purpose of the evaluation for the examinee.
- Be sensitive to any test material that unfairly discriminates against individuals of a particular culture.
- Use an alternate method of assessment that is more appropriate to the individual, if necessary. Consider an interpreter or a professionally translated paper-and-pencil test if the client's primary language is not English.
- Before beginning an assessment, become familiar with the norms and values of the examinee's culture.
- Recognize that the job is to establish a good rapport with the examinee and call a replacement psychologist if good rapport is not possible.

Assessing Intelligence

Theoretical Approaches to Intelligence

There are various theoretical approaches to intelligence:

- **Spearman** proposed the existence of a general intelligence factor (G) and any number of specific intelligence factors (S) unique to a task.
- **Horn and Cattell** adjusted this model by dividing (G) into two categories:
  - *Crystallized intelligence (Gc):* The knowledge and skills acquired through education and experience
  - *Fluid intelligence (Gf)*: The ability to solve new problems
- **Sternberg** asserted that successful intelligence is composed of analytical, practical, and creative elements, and argued that standardized tests focus almost exclusively on analytical elements.
- **Gardner** proposed eight different kinds of intelligence: Linguistic, musical, logical-mathematical, spatial, bodily-kinesthetic, interpersonal, intrapersonal, and naturalistic.

Intelligence Throughout the Lifespan

Research efforts have been interested in the growth and decline of intelligence over the lifespan, and how that correlates with the same measures of one's IQ. **The Seattle Longitudinal Study** was conducted by Schaie et al. at seven-year intervals from 1956 to 2005. The study concluded that "there is no uniform pattern of age-related changes across all intellectual abilities, and that studies of an overall index of intellectual ability (IQ) therefore do not suffice to monitor age changes and age differences in intellectual functioning for either individuals or groups." Subsequent research in this line indicates perceptual speed is the only area in which the elderly experience significant decline.

Research conducted by Horn indicated that while **crystallized intelligence** will continue to increase throughout life, **fluid intelligence** will peak in adolescence and decline thereafter. Decline in fluid intelligence has been linked to diminished processing speed, stemming from reductions in working memory.

Effects of Heredity and Environment on Intelligence

Research has shown that individuals with a genetic similarity have similar levels of intelligence. Heritability estimates for intelligence range from about 0.6 to 0.8, meaning that 32-64% of the variability in intelligence comes from **genetic factors**.

Other research has sought to describe the link between environment and intelligence. One environmental factor that has been consistently linked to performance on intelligence tests is **socioeconomic status**.

The **Flynn effect** describes the gradual increase in IQ test scores that has occurred worldwide over time, as nations become more industrialized. The Flynn effect does not seem to involve genetic factors and therefore is solely based on the environment and evolving resources.

Evaluation and Decision Making in the Assessment Process

Evaluation is the process of analyzing accumulated data in order to improve a counselor's ability to make a decision based on reliable standards. The accumulated data is given careful consideration and appraisal by the evaluator (the counselor) to ensure that it is complete and accurate. The evaluator must make some kind of interpretation or inference about the data that has been collected. This inference is known as a **value judgment** and is a common task for the counselor. The counselor uses a methodical and well-organized system to help make these value judgments.

Decision making is a process in which the collected data has been weighed against possible consequences and test results. Decisions must be made regarding prioritization of interventions, risk or danger the client may be in that must be addressed, identification of approaches that are failing and succeeding, and the creation of a counseling plan specific to the client's personality, life experiences, and problem(s) at hand.

Client Interviews

Obtaining a Client History and Data from Multiple Sources

During the admissions assessment, information about the **client's history** should be gathered. The interview should occur in a space that allows for privacy, but it should not be isolated in case the client becomes violent or threatening. Asking open-ended questions in a nonjudgmental manner (e.g., What problem brings you here today?) is more effective than asking yes or no questions. Questions should focus on one problem or symptom at a time (e.g., Tell me about your sleeping habits.). Depending on the client's condition, information may be obtained by:

- Directly interviewing the client
- Observing the client's behavior and interactions with others
- Reviewing previous hospitalization and discharge records
- Interviewing family or caregivers, ideally without the client present so caregivers can speak freely (Care should be taken not to violate the client's right to privacy and the client should be asked for their permission to speak with others.)
- Interviewing police (if involved) and requesting a copy of police reports
- Interviewing EMS personnel and reviewing their written reports

Subjective and Objective Information

There are two types of information that medical providers will receive from clients: subjective and objective. Information obtained through these means is what the health care provider will utilize in documentation.

- **Subjective information** includes what the client tells the provider. This information is based on their description or opinion and is usually received verbally or through writing.
- **Objective information** is what the health care provider actually observes. This includes client behaviors as well as any findings during physical assessment.

Interviewing Pre-School Aged Clients

In most cases, it is better to interview the parent and child **separately**, though this may occur in the company of one another before the child is of school-age. Children can usually give better information about what they are feeling, and parents give better information on their external behavior. When talking with young children, speak in simple terms and short sentences. Convey a neutral attitude. Most children between the ages of 1-4 understand more than they can communicate. Children may not be able to communicate **absolute ideas**. Assessing the child during **play** may give insight into real world experiences that the child cannot verbalize through questions alone. Play will often allow for evaluation of physical and cognitive development, adaptability, social and moral development, and coping abilities. It may give great insight into the child's perceptions of social relationships and family. Play may include drawing, dolls, puppets, dress up clothes, or modeling clay.

Interviewing School-Aged Clients

The interview of the school-aged client usually takes place with the client sitting on a couch or in a chair. Talking with the client is the best way to build rapport. At this age, children are gaining more **independence** and it is important to respect that. Starting the interview with a casual conversation about school and their interests, such as their friends or video games, can help to lighten the mood. Asking about their favorite subjects in school and what they like the most and least about school can open the door to gaining some insight on their school performance. Most school-aged clients can provide their own medical history, depending upon the severity of their illness. At this age, the parent or guardian of the client should be present to confirm or clarify any medical history to ensure it is accurate. The client's history of academic performance, including any disciplinary issues at school, should be confirmed with the parent or guardian.

Interviewing Adolescent Clients

Establishing a healthy rapport with the adolescent client is essential in order to obtain an open, honest history. Regardless of where the client sits, the interviewer should sit to place themselves at the **same level** as the client. Initially, **client confidentiality** should be explained to the adolescent client and specifically what can and cannot be kept confidential. Any statements about wanting to hurt themselves or someone else cannot be kept confidential. The majority of the visit with an adolescent client should be done without the parent or guardian present unless it is necessary. The interview should contain open-ended questions that cover their home life, education or employment, activities alone and with friends, any drug use or dieting habits, sexuality, suicide and depression, and safety issues. When discussing any drug use with the adolescent client, make sure to ask about their friends' habits, also.

Interviewing Adult Clients

Within the first few minutes of the interview of the adult client, it is important that introductions are completed and are clear. Try to sit during the interview to not seem to be towering over the client and place yourself at the **same level** as them. Provide **active listening** to the client's concerns, empathy for these concerns, and concern for the client as an individual. When a client knows that that their concerns are taken seriously, they are more likely to be more active in their healthcare. Ask about job satisfaction, involvement in community activities, and social support to evaluate for possible signs of depression. Providing reassuring touch or a shared silence with the client may put them more at ease and let them know that their problems matter. It is important to not be quick to move onto the next question, and rather, let the client fully answer a question without interrupting them. Finally, while some of the problems expressed by the client may not seem medically significant, they should still be addressed to some degree to validate them.

Interviewing Elderly Clients

The interview of the elderly client differs from that of the adult client because the interviewer is trying to identify what the client can do versus what they should be able to do or would like to be able to do. In order to gather this information, it is important to spend the time necessary with the client and provide patience in listening to their **complete history**. Hearing loss, vision changes, and dementia can affect communication with the client, so more **time** may need to be spent with these clients and/or their family members. Important elements to consider in the interview process are the general health status of the client, their mental health status, the activities of daily living, their social support system, the future outlook, and any family concerns they may have. Identifying their reliance on community services that are available can help to identify the client's ability to care for themselves. There is a high incidence of depression and dementia amongst the elderly, and identification of these symptoms can help to determine in which area of living they need assistance.

Medication Reconciliation

When obtaining an in-home medication list, known as a medication reconciliation, the first step is to ask if the client has a list of medications or has brought current medications. If so, the health care provider should review each medication, including the **dose and frequency**. If the medicine is available, the **date** should be checked on the medicine bottle as clients often keep medications for long periods of time and should assess the amount of remaining medication in relation to the dispensing date. If necessary, the client, family, or caregivers should be asked to provide information about their medication(s), asking detailed questions about the drugs. Other questions can include the duration of treatment, reasons for taking the drugs, names of prescribing physicians, and the dispensing pharmacies. Specific questions should be asked about any complementary treatments (e.g., vitamins, probiotics) and over-the-counter medications, and specific categories of drugs (e.g., pain medicines, antacids, laxatives, stool softeners, antihistamines) used both frequently and infrequently.

Assessment Tests and Tools

Psychological Assessment Terminology

A **standardized test** is one in which the questions and potential responses from all tests can be compared with one another. Every aspect of the test must remain consistent.

A **behavioral assessment** assumes that an individual can only be evaluated in relation to his or her environment. Behavioral assessments must include a stimulus, organism, response, and consequences (SORC).

A **dynamic assessment** involves systematic deviation from the standardized test to determine whether the individual benefits from aid. This includes the process called "testing the limits," in which an examinee is provided with a sequence of extra clues.

Domain-referenced testing breaks evaluation into specific domains of ability—for instance, reading or math ability.

Measurement and Tests in the Assessment Process

The mental health care provider develops a representation of the client through the collection of facts. Psychometric instruments are used to collect pertinent data on the client. **Measurement** is a numerical value that has been allocated to a mannerism, attribute, or characteristic on the instrument. The measurement used must be one that is commonly understood by the general population.

A **test** is a task or series of tasks used to examine a psychomotor behavior or action that is indicative of a state of being. The state of being can be cognitively based or affective in nature. Answering written questions is a typical test scenario. The student goes through the task of answering academically based questions to indicate that cognitive learning has been accomplished in an academic class. The teacher grades the test and makes the inference that the student has learned on a cognitive or affective level.

Test Selection and Administration

The primary concern in test selection should be the client's needs and wants. Out of this consideration, the mental health care provider makes an informed decision about which **tests and psychometric techniques** to apply. A provider should suggest testing if there is a need to gain further information, but testing is not necessarily required. The client may perceive the testing to be some kind of threat or manipulative tool. In that case, the client should be reassured and educated about the real purpose of the test. **Competency level** should also be considered when selecting, administering, measuring, and evaluating the test results, including legal issues involving a particular assessment, and any **ethical issues** that may be associated with an assessment. The mental health care provider may require additional training in test procedures before giving and assessing a particular test.

Using the Internet for Test Selection

The internet provides an excellent search tool for the mental health provider. The internet can be used to locate specific tests that are applicable to the client's needs and wants. The **decision-making model** presented by Drummond in 1996 can be used to help select the most appropriate test. Any tests being considered should be evaluated for dimension, traits, and attributes. The decision should be based on what kind of information is anticipated to be the most useful. This involves a thorough perusal of the information already available at hand. The internet can also be used to search through objective evaluations given by others. Prospective tests should also be appraised for validity and reliability. The test and its results must provide the mental health care provider and the client with a practical use.

Issues Impacting Test Selection

The test-related issues that may impact the selection of a test include validity, reliability, and norm standards.

- The issue of **validity** in a test involves an effective examination that gives the desired results. Tests used within the mental health profession should have well founded, criterion-based content that measures what it is supposed to measure.
- Before using a test, make sure it has received an independent appraisal from established sources, and is considered **reliable**, meaning that the test results should be able to stand up over a period of time. The test should give a precise and accurate score. The entire test should be evaluated for its *reliability coefficient* and *standard of error measurement*. The test may present a split-half reliability that measures internal consistency among other assessment instruments.
- The test should follow the **norm-referenced criteria** for the client's age, sex, ethnic origin, culture, and socioeconomic status.

Paper-and-Pencil Tests vs. Performance Tests

Another choice in test selection is that between administering a paper-and-pencil test vs. a performance test.

- **Paper-and-pencil tests** are used by a variety of test takers. One drawback is found when the client cannot read at the same level at which the test is written.
- **Performance tests** are given with a verbal request. The verbal request elicits a response that measures whether the client can follow the instruction given.

Paper-and-pencil and performance tests can either be applied in group settings or in individual treatments. Group-administered tests may be given by untrained proctors in a variety of settings. Typically, the group completes a paper-and-pencil test. Individuals may take the test under the supervision of an administrator. The administrator understands the complexities involved in giving the test, scoring the test, and interpreting the test results. Paper-and-pencil tests or performance tests are used to collect data about an exhibited behavior. The data is then evaluated. Paper-and-pencil tests are used to provide a fast, inexpensive, and objective grade. Test publishers develop most of the commercial grade paper-and-pencil assessment tests available. The administrator or proctor of the paper-and-pencil test will distribute materials, read the directions to the group, time the test, and collect the test.

Using Computers in Psychological Assessments

The computer has gained popularity over paper-and-pencil tests and has changed the field of assessment through a wide range of mechanically based scoring mechanisms. The analog computer has been incorporated in tallying the score of the Strong Vocational Interest Blank, now called the Strong Interest Inventory, developed by Edward Kellog Strong in 1946. Computer software capabilities have given way to school-based vocational preference instruments. National testing organizations like the Educational Testing Service (ETS) uses computers to administer multiple college-admissions tests like the GRE and to score them. The computer is also used to administer and interpret some psychological instruments like the Rorschach and the MMPI tests.

NORM-REFERENCED VS. CRITERION-REFERENCED TESTS

Tests can be **norm-referenced** or **criterion-referenced**. Both require that the test is graded with a raw score. The raw score indicates the number of right answers or a pattern found. The client's raw score is then compared to a group score. The raw score in a criterion-related test is compared to a criterion that can determine mastery or minimum competency levels within a subject.

STRUCTURED VS. UNSTRUCTURED TESTS

The difference found between a **structured** and an **unstructured test** is the range or degree of structure applied. For instance, the Strong Interest Inventory is a structured vocational preference test that only allows the client to give one of six possible answers. The Rorschach inkblot test allows the client to answer with any response that comes to mind.

STANDARDIZED ASSESSMENT TOOLS USED IN EVALUATION PROCESS

The five standardized assessment tools or tests are the achievement test, the aptitude test, the intelligence test, the vocational preference instrument, and the personality test:

- The **achievement test** is used to measure what has been learned in academics, vocation, or other life experience.
- The **aptitude test** is used to make a prediction on the subject's future performance in a given field of study.
- The **intelligence test** predicts a person's academic performance in the future by determining the person's mental potential.
- The **vocational preference instrument** is used to discover a pattern of characteristics that describe the individual's preferences or inclination to do something in leisure, work, and educational settings.
- The **personality test** describes the person's behavior, attitudes, beliefs, and values, and is used to diagnose psychopathology or in relationship counseling.

ASSESSING TRAITS, STRENGTHS, AND WEAKNESSES

An assortment of tests is available to **delineate capabilities, tendencies, and personalities**:

- The selection category can include tests like the Graduate Record Exam (GRE) or the Law School Admissions Tests (LSAT). **Selection tests** may also include vocational preference tests or personality tests used in educational and occupational counseling.
- **Placement tests** are used to determine where a client belongs in a program. Colleges may use these tests to determine in which class a student should start a program of study.
- **Diagnostic tests** use a combination of psychometric techniques and tests to evaluate human performance levels, and incorporate the DSM diagnostic labels to determine a remediation program for a client. Many insurance carriers also require this DSM label before payment is released for services rendered. Individual progress is also typically measured using psychometric instruments to help evaluate progress toward a goal.

Intelligence Tests

Stanford-Binet Intelligence Scales

The Stanford-Binet intelligence scales (SB5) measure cognitive ability, assist in psychoeducational evaluation, diagnose developmental disabilities, and perform various assessments for individuals 2 to 85+. The SB5 test measures five **categories of intelligence**:

- Fluid reasoning
- Knowledge
- Quantitative reasoning
- Visual-spatial processing
- Working memory

SB5 measures each of these domains through both verbal and nonverbal activities. Subtests indicate which components of the SB5 are appropriate for the examinee. These subtest scores are combined to give four kinds of **composite score**:

- Factor index
- Domain
- Abbreviated battery
- Full-scale IQ

The standardization sample of the SB5 was based on 4,800 participants of various ages, socioeconomic statuses, geographic regions, and races.

WAIS-IV

Main Index Scores of WAIS-IV

The fourth edition of the **Wechsler Adult Intelligence Scale (WAIS-IV, 2008)** is used to measure the intellectual ability of late-adolescents and adults. The newest edition, WAIS-V, is currently under the clinical validation phase and has not yet been released. Wechsler considered intelligence to be a global ability made up of a number of interrelated functions. This interrelationship between the various types of intelligence is described in the current test in terms of four index scores:

- Verbal Comprehension Index (VCI)
- Perceptual Reasoning Index (PRI)
- Working Memory Index (WMI)
- Processing Speed Index (PSI)

Core Subtests of WAIS-IV

There are **ten core subtests** on the WAIS-IV:

- VCI: Similarities (abstract reasoning)
- VCI: Vocabulary (semantic knowledge)
- VCI: Information (general knowledge)
- PRI: Block Design (spatial processing)
- PRI: Matrix Reasoning (inductive reasoning)
- PRI: Visual Puzzles (spatial reasoning)
- WMI: Digit Span (working memory)
- WMI: Arithmetic (quantitative reasoning)
- PSI: Symbol Search (processing speed)
- PSI: Coding (associative memory)

Administration and Scoring of WAIS-IV

There are 2 **broad scores** in the WAIS-IV.

- **Full Scale IQ (FSIQ)**: Based on the combined scores for the ten VCI, PRI, WMI and PSI subtests
- **General Ability Index (GAI)**: Based only on the six subtests that test VCI and PRI

The **administration** of the test begins with picture completion and then a series of alternating verbal and nonverbal subtests. The only exception to this is that the digit span and information subtests are administered together. Some tests will be timed, while others will be allowed to go on until the examinee has finished. The raw **scores** for each subtest are converted into scaled scores with a standard conversion table. In the subtests, the mean score is 10 and the standard deviation is 3. For the full-scale performance and verbal IQs and factor indices, the mean is 100 and the standard deviation is 15.

Supplemental Subtests of the Intelligence Scales of the Revised WAIS-IV

Additional supplemental subtests are included with each intelligence scale in the WAIS-IV:

- Verbal Comprehension (VCI) Supplemental Subtest: Comprehension
- Perceptual Reasoning (PRI) Supplemental Subtests: Picture Completion and Figure Weights
- Working Memory (WMI) Supplemental Subtest: Letter-Number Sequencing
- Processing Speed (PSI) Supplemental Subtest: Cancellation

Group Intelligence Tests

Many different organizations, from schools to the armed forces, administer **group intelligence tests**:

- The **Kuhlman-Anderson Test (KA)** is for children in grades K-12; it measures verbal and quantitative intelligence. This test is unique in that it relies less on language than do other individual and group tests.
- The **Woodcock Johnson IV** consists of a test of cognitive abilities and a test of achievement; the latter of which measures oral language and academic achievement.
- The **Wonderlic Personnel Test (WPT-R)** takes about 12 minutes to fill out with paper and pencil; it purports to measure the mental ability of adults. The Wonderlic is a good predictor of performance, but some critics maintain that it unfairly discriminates against some cultural groups in certain jobs.

Tests for Cognitive and Intellectual Development in Children

WISC-V and WPPSI-IV

The **WISC-V** is a variation of the WAIS made especially for children between the ages of 6 and 17. WISC-V is closely based on neurocognitive models of information processing, and gives scores through five indexes:

- Verbal comprehension
- Visual-spatial
- Fluid reasoning
- Working memory
- Processing speed

Highly asymmetrical scores on the subtests are used to diagnose autism, ADHD, and other learning disorders.

The **WPPSI-IV** (released in 2012) is made for children between the ages of 2.5 and 7.25. For children that are either 2 or 3 years old, the test can measure verbal comprehension, and perceptual organization; for older children, processing speed can also be measured.

Infant and Preschool Tests

Tests administered to children aged 2 or younger are good at screening for developmental delays and disabilities, but have poor predictive validity. **The Denver II** screens for developmental delays by observing a child's performance in four developmental domains:

- Personal-social
- Fine motor adaptive
- Language
- Gross motor

If a child fails an item that 90% of younger children pass, he or she is scored as having a **developmental delay**.

The **Bayley Scales of Infant Development (BSID-III)** assess the development of children 1 to 42 months old on mental, motor, and behavior rating scales.

The **Fagan Test of Intelligence** tries to gauge the information processing speed of an infant, in order to predict childhood IQ. It does this by introducing novel stimuli and observing the reaction time of the child.

Kaufman Test of Educational Achievement, Cognitive Assessment System, and Slosson Tests

The **Kaufman Test of Educational Achievement (KTEA-3)** measures academic ability in children grades 1-12. It provides scores in three core areas:

- Reading
- Math
- Written Language

Verbal instructions and responses should be minimized on these tests to make them fair for all cultures.

The **Cognitive Assessment System (CAS2)** is based on the *PASS* (planning, attention, simultaneous processing, and sequential processing) model of intelligence, and is appropriate for children between the ages of 5 and 18 of all cultures and ethnicities.

The **Slosson tests** were designed to be fast ways of estimating intelligence in order to identify children at risk of educational failure.

ASSESSMENT OF INTELLECTUAL DISABILITY

Intellectual disability is defined as limitations in mental functioning mirrored by significant limitations in everyday functioning that are present early in life and before the age of 18.

- The **Individuals with Disabilities Act** states that all disabled individuals under the age of 25 need to be evaluated, and an *individualized educational plan (IEP)* needs to be developed for each child in order to provide education in the least restrictive environment.
- The case **Larry P. vs. Riles** established that IQ tests can be *racially discriminatory* and should not be used to place African-Americans in special education classrooms.
- The **Vineland Behavior Scales** measure communication, daily living skills, and socialization, for the purpose of developing *special education programs.*
- The **AAIDD Adaptive Behavior Scales** assess personal self-sufficiency, community self-sufficiency, personal-social responsibility, social adjustment, and personal adjustment for individuals ages 4-21.

VANDERBILT ADHD

Vanderbilt ADHD is used to assess whether a child has attention deficit hyperactivity disorder. The tool has 3 parts:

- Assessment by a parent
- Assessment by a teacher
- Follow-up assessment by a parent

The parental assessment evaluates 47 symptoms that may be associated with ADHD and 8 performance measures. The teacher assessment evaluates 35 symptoms, 3 academic performances (reading, math, written expression), and 5 classroom performance behaviors. The follow-up parental assessment evaluates 18 symptoms, 8 performance measures, and 12 possible side effects.

ACADEMIC ABILITY TESTING

Ability tests measure current status and predict future academic achievement. Types of **ability testing** include:

- **Curriculum-based measurement** is any form of assessment that focuses on the student's ability to perform the work of the school curriculum. Usually, a teacher will set a minimum standard for performance and provide remedial attention for any student who performs below this level.
- **Performance-based assessment** evaluates students on their execution of a task or creation of a product. It is meant to be egalitarian and culture-fair.
- The **Scholastic Achievement Test (SAT)** measures verbal and mathematical reasoning skills; it is used to predict the college success of high school students. Studies show that the SAT is more effective as a predictor when it is combined with grade-point average.
- The **Graduate Record Exam (GRE)** measures general scholastic abilities and may be taken in lieu of a normal secondary course of study.

PERSONALITY TESTS

STRUCTURED PERSONALITY TESTS

A structured personality test (as opposed to a projective test) measures emotional, social, and personal traits and behaviors through a series of multiple-choice questions or other unambiguous stimuli. There are four common strategies for structured personality tests:

- **Logical content method** bases its questions on deductive logic and a systematic theory of personality.
- **Theoretical method** measures the prevalence of the personality structures identified by a particular theory of personality.
- **Empirical criterion keying** has questions that are administered to different criterion groups; there are items that distinguish between the groups in the test.
- **Factor analysis tests** administer a large number of items to a large group of examinees, and then analyze their answers for any correlations.

MMPI-3

VALIDITY SCALES

The **Minnesota Multiphasic Personality Inventory-3 (MMPI-3)** was originally developed to diagnose psychiatric patients. The attitude of the examinee towards the test is indicated by his or her scores on various validity measures. In general, the validity scales can be grouped into three measurements: those that detect inconsistent response or non-response, those that detect the exaggerated self-reporting of the prevalence/severity of psychological symptoms, and those meant to detect those under-reporting psychological symptoms. Validity scales include:

- **Inconsistent/Non-Response***:* CNS ("cannot say"), VRIN (Variable response inconsistency, TRIN (True response inconsistency).
- **Exaggerated Response**: F (Infrequency, or "faking bad" in the first half of the test); Fb (F Back; "faking bad" in the second half of the test); Fp (F-Psychopathology (frequency of presentation).
- **Downplayed Response:** L (Lie; "faking good"); K (Defensiveness, denial); S (Superlative Self-Presentation).

SCORING, INTERPRETATION, AND PROFILE ANALYSIS

The MMPI-3 takes raw scores and converts them into T-scores with a mean of 50 and a standard deviation of 10. If a person scores above a 65, it is considered to be clinically significant. The most common use of the MMPI-3 is as an assessment of personality and behavior through profile analysis. Most of the time, the code is simply the two highest scores on the various subtests. The validity scales are then used to ensure that the profile is the result of an honest attempt at the test. The standardization sample approximated the 2020 US census in age, gender, race, and social class.

RORSCHACH INKBLOT AND TAT PROJECTIVE PERSONALITY TESTS

Projective personality tests assume that unstructured and ambiguous stimuli can elicit meaningful responses from individuals, particularly about personality and underlying conflicts. Projective tests are typically open-ended and therefore less susceptible to faking. The most famous projective test is the **Rorschach Inkblot Test**, in which a person is presented with ten cards containing bilaterally symmetrical inkblots and asked to free associate on the design. Scoring the Rorschach is very complex, but relies on the following dimensions of the individual's response:

- Location (as in where the subject sees whatever he or she describes)
- Determinants (why the subjects saw what they saw)
- Form quality (resemblance of the response to the inkblot)
- Content
- Frequency of occurrence

The Rorschach may provide interesting results, but its use in clinical work is dubious.

Another projective test is the **Thematic Apperception Test (TAT),** in which the examinee is asked to make up a story based on a random presentation of picture cards.

EPPS, 16 PF-5, NEO-3

The **Edwards Personal Preference Schedule**, based on the personality theory of Murray, contains 225 items that present an either-or choice to the examinee. This test strives to prevent examinees from responding in ways that they know are socially desirable. The test provides ipsative scores, meaning that the strengths of the candidate are given comparative, rather than absolute, value.

The **Sixteen Personality Factor Questionnaire (16PF 5th Ed)** is a factor analysis-based exam that identifies 16 primary personality traits and 5 secondary traits.

The **NEO-Personality Inventory (NEO-PI-3)** attempts to gauge an individual's level of the Big Five personality traits (extraversion, agreeableness, conscientiousness, neuroticism, and openness to experience). These traits are then broken down into facets, for example, neuroticism contains anxiety and depression.

Tests for Dementia, Attention, and Delirium

MMSE

The mini-mental state exam (MMSE), also known as the **Folstein test**, is a commonly used assessment tool for evaluating cognition. It is typically used to evaluate for the presence and severity of **dementia**. The MMSE consists of a 30-point questionnaire that evaluates immediate and short-term memory recall, orientation, arithmetic, the ability to follow simple commands, language, and other functional abilities such as copying a drawing. In clinical settings, it is very useful to detect initial impairment or follow responses over the course of an illness and/or treatment. This tool establishes a score based on education level and age. This score can be placed on a scale to determine **functionality** of the individual. A total possible score of 30 can be achieved. A score of 24 or greater is considered a normal functioning level. The lower the score, the greater the degree of dementia or mental dysfunction. It is possible that simple physical limitations such as the inability to read or hear or decreased motor function may negatively affect the total score.

Trail Making Test

The Trail Making Test (Parts A and B) assesses brain function and indicates increasing dementia. It is useful for detecting early Alzheimer's disease, and those who do poorly on part B often need assistance with activities of daily living (ADLs). The individual is given a demonstration of each part before beginning:

- **Part A** has 25 sequentially-numbered scattered circles across the page, and the individual is advised to use a pencil/pen to draw a continuous line to connect in ascending order the circles (starting with 1 and ending with 25).
- **Part B** is slightly more complex and has circles with numbers (1-12) and circles with letters (A-L) scattered about the page. The individual is advised to draw a continuous line alternating between numbers and letters in ascending order (1-A-2-B....).

The test is scored according to the number of seconds required for completion:

- **A**: 29 seconds is average, and >78 indicates deficiency.
- **B**: 75 seconds is average, and >273 seconds indicates deficiency.

TIME AND CHANGE TEST

The Time and Change Test assesses **dementia** in adults and is effective in diverse populations. First, the individual is shown a clock face set at 11:10 and has one minute to make two attempts at stating the correct time. Next, the individual is given change (7 dimes, 7 nickels, and 3 quarters) and asked to give the clinician $1.00 from the coins. The individual has two minutes and two attempts to make the correct change. Failing either or both tests is indicative of dementia.

DIGIT REPETITION TEST

The Digit Repetition Test is used to assess **attention**. The individual is told to listen to numbers and then repeat them. The clinician starts with two random single-digit numbers. If the individual gets this sequence correct, the clinician then states three numbers and continues to add one number each time until the individual is unable to repeat the numbers correctly. People with normal intelligence (without intellectual disability or expressive aphasia) can usually repeat 5-7 numbers, so scores <5 indicate impaired attention.

CONFUSION ASSESSMENT METHOD

The Confusion Assessment Method is used to assess the **development of delirium** and is intended for those without psychiatric training. The tool covers 9 factors. Some factors have a range of possibilities and others are rated only as to whether the characteristic is present, not present, uncertain, or not applicable. The tool provides room to describe abnormal behavior. Factors indicative of delirium include:

- **Onset**: Acute change in mental status
- **Attention**: Inattentive, stable, or fluctuating
- **Thinking**: Disorganized, rambling conversation, switching topics, or illogical
- **Level of consciousness**: Altered, ranging from alert to coma
- **Orientation**: Disoriented (person, place, time)
- **Memory**: Impaired
- **Perceptual disturbances**: Hallucinations, illusions
- **Psychomotor abnormalities**: Agitation (tapping, picking, moving) or retardation (staring, not moving)
- **Sleep-wake cycle**: Awake at night and sleepy in the daytime

The tool indicates delirium if there is an acute onset with fluctuating inattention and disorganized thinking or altered level of consciousness.

Tests for Anxiety and Depression

Hamilton Anxiety Scale

The Hamilton Anxiety Scale (HAS or HAMA) is utilized to evaluate the anxiety related symptomatology that may present in adults as well as children. It provides an evaluation of overall **anxiety** and its degree of severity. This includes **somatic anxiety** (physical complaints) and **psychic anxiety** (mental agitation and distress). This scale consists of 14 items based on anxiety produced symptoms. Each item is ranked 0-4 with 0 indicating no symptoms present and 4 indicating severe symptoms present. This scale is frequently utilized in psychotropic drug evaluations. If performed before a particular medication has been started and then again at later visits, the HAS can be helpful in adjusting medication dosages based in part on the individual's score. It is often utilized as an outcome measure in clinical trials.

GAD-7

General Anxiety Disorder-7 (GAD-7) is used to assess the severity of an individual's anxiety and focuses on the previous 2 weeks. The questions are as follows:

1. Feeling nervous, anxious, on edge?
2. Unable to stop/control worrying?
3. Worrying excessively about different things?
4. Having trouble relaxing?
5. Being excessively restless?
6. Easily annoyed/irritated?
7. Fearful something terrible will occur?

Responses are scored as 0 (not at all), 1 (several days), 2 (more than half of days), or 3 (nearly every day). Scores and assessment:

- **5-9 mild anxiety**, requires monitoring.
- **10-14 moderate anxiety**, requires further diagnostic tests, including MMSE and referral to a professional.
- **15+ severe anxiety**, requires active treatment.

Beck Depression Inventory

The Beck Depression Inventory (BDI) is a widely utilized, self-reported, multiple-choice questionnaire consisting of 21 items, which measures the **degree of depression**. This tool is designed for use in adults between the ages of 17 and 80 years of age. It evaluates physical symptoms such as weight loss, loss of sleep, loss of interest in sex, and fatigue, along with attitudinal symptoms such as irritability, guilt, and hopelessness. The items rank in four possible answer choices based on an increasing severity of symptoms. The test is scored with the answers ranging in value from 0 to 3. The total score is utilized to determine the degree of depression. The usual ranges include: 0-9 no signs of depression, 10-18 mild depression, 19-29 moderate depression, and 30-63 severe depression.

Geriatric Depression Scale

The Geriatric Depression Scale (GDS) is a self-assessment tool to identify older adults with depression. The test can be used with those with normal cognition and those with mild to moderate impairment. The test poses 15 questions to which individuals answer "yes" or "no" and a point is assigned for each answer that indicates depression. A score of >5 points is indicative of depression:

1. Are you basically satisfied with your life?
2. Have you dropped many of your activities and interests?
3. Do you feel your life is empty?
4. Do you often get bored?
5. Are you in good spirits most of the time?
6. Are you afraid that something bad is going to happen to you?
7. Do you feel happy most of the time?
8. Do you often feel helpless?
9. Do you prefer to stay at home rather than going out and doing new things?
10. Do you feel you have more problems with memory than most?
11. Do you think it is wonderful to be alive now?
12. Do you feel pretty worthless the way you are now?
13. Do you feel full of energy?
14. Do you feel that your situation is hopeless?
15. Do you think that most people are better off than you are?

Children's Depression Rating Scale-Revised

The Children's Depression Rating Scale-Revised (CDRS-R) evaluates a child for depressive disorders and monitors treatment response. CDRS-R includes 17 items, 14 of which are assessed during an interview, and 3 of which are assessed by the clinician's interpretation of the individual's nonverbal cues. The CDRS-R is designed specifically for individuals aged 6-12 but may also be used during an interview with the individual's parents, caregivers, and teachers. The items included in the interview include the following: schoolwork, capacity to have fun, social withdrawal, sleep, appetite or eating patterns, excessive fatigue, physical complaints, irritability, guilt, self-esteem, depressed feelings, morbid ideation, suicidal ideation, weeping, depressed affect, tempo of speech, and hypoactivity.

PHQ-9

Patient Health Questionaire-9 (PHQ-9) is used to determine the severity of depression and focuses on answers to questions related to the previous 2 weeks. The questions are as follows:

1. Little interest/pleasure in activities?
2. Feelings of depression or hopelessness?
3. Sleeping difficulties?
4. Tiredness of lack of energy?
5. Poor appetite or excessive eating?
6. Feelings of being a failure or letting down self/others?
7. Difficulty concentrating?
8. Speaking/moving slowly or fidgeting?
9. Suicidal ideation?

Responses are scored as 0 (not at all), 1 (several days), 2 (more than half of days), or 3 (nearly every day). Scores and assessment:

- **0-4: minimal or no depression**—monitor but likely does not need treatment
- **5-9: mild depression**—may need treatment
- **10-15: moderate depression**—may need treatment
- **15-19: moderately severe depression**—treatment required
- **20-27: severe depression**—treatment required

Suicide risk assessment should be carried out for any individuals indicating suicidal ideation.

Multiple Aptitude Test Batteries and Special Batteries

Multiple aptitude test batteries measure ability in a number of different areas; one of their weaknesses is that they often lack adequate differential validity, meaning that the various parts of the test do not have different validities for different categories.

- **Differential aptitude tests (DAT)** identify job-related abilities and are used for career counseling and employee selection.
- The **general aptitude test battery (GATB)** was developed by the US Employment Service for vocational counseling and job placement. There are other tests used to measure special aptitudes.
- **Psychomotor tests** are used to assess speed, coordination, and general movement responses. These typically have low validity coefficients because they are highly specific and susceptible to practice effects.
- **Mechanical aptitude tests** are used to assess dexterity, perceptual and spatial skills, and mechanical reasoning. The different skills that fall within this category are relatively independent.

Assessment of Individuals with Physical Disabilities

The **Americans with Disabilities Act of 1990** declares that any test administered to a disabled job applicant or employee should reflect only the person's ability on the test, and not his or her disability. Employers are also required to make reasonable accommodations for disabled employees.

- The **Columbia Mental Maturity Scale (CMMS)** is a test of general reasoning ability that does not require fine motor skills or verbal responses. It is useful for assessing students with cerebral palsy, brain damage, intellectual disability, and speech impediments.
- The **Peabody Picture Vocabulary Test (PPVT-5)** measures receptive vocabulary without requiring verbal responses.
- The **Haptic Intelligence Scale (HIS)** uses tactile stimuli, so it is good for assessing blind and partially-sighted individuals.
- The **Hiskey-Nebraska Test of Learning Aptitude (H-NTLA)** contains twelve nonverbal subtests which can be administered verbally or in pantomime; it is good for assessing children with hearing impairments.

World Health Organization Disability Assessment Schedule 2.0

The World Health Organization Disability Assessment Schedule 2.0 (WHODAS 2.0), is the DSM-5 recommended tool for assessing **global impairment and functioning**. It is based on ICD and ICF classifications. In previous versions of the DSM, global disability was assessed by the Global Assessment of Functioning (GAF) scale. WHODAS comes as a self-report tool with either 12 or 36 questions, taking around 7-15 minutes to administer. These questions help to assess the individual's performance in 6 domains over the last 30 days. The **six domains** are: cognition, participation, mobility, self-care, life activities, and interacting with other people. Using the questionnaire, the tool produces a score that represents the individual's global disability. Pros of the tool include that it is reliable and valid, even across cultures. Cons include that due to the self-report nature of the tool, there is no way to check the validity of the individual's responses to the questions.

Neuropsychological Assessments

The **Benton Visual Retention Test (BVRT)** assesses visual memory, spatial perception, and visual-motor skills in order to diagnose brain damage. The subject is asked to reproduce from memory the geometric patterns on a series of ten cards.

The **Beery Developmental Test of Visual-Motor Integration (Beery-VMI-6)** assesses visual-motor skills in children; like the BVRT, it involves the reproduction of geometric shapes.

The **Wisconsin Card Sorting Test (WSCT)** is a screening test that assesses the ability to form abstract concepts and shift cognitive strategies; the subject is required to sort a group cards in an order that is not disclosed to him or her.

The **Stroop Color-Word Association Test (SCWT)** is a measure of cognitive flexibility; it tests an individual's ability to suppress a habitual reaction to stimulus.

The **Halstead-Reitan Neuropsychological Battery (HRNB)** is a group of tests that are effective at differentiating between normal people and those with brain damage. The clinician has control over which exams to administer, though he or she is likely to assess sensorimotor, perceptual, and language functioning. A score higher than 0.60 indicates brain pathology.

The **Luria-Nebraska Neuropsychological Battery (LNNB)** contains 11 subtests that assess areas like rhythm, visual function, and writing. The examinee is given a score between 0 and 2, with 0 indicating normal function and 2 indicating brain damage.

The **Bender Visual-Motor Gestalt Test (Bender-Gestalt II)** is a brief examination that involves responding to 16 stimulus cards containing geometric figures, which the examinee must either copy or recall.

AIMS

The abnormal involuntary movement scale (AIMS) is an assessment tool that can be utilized to assess **abnormal physical movements**. These movements can often be the resulting side-effects of certain antipsychotic medications and can be associated with tardive dyskinesia or chronic akathisia. These motor abnormalities can also be associated with particular illnesses. Based on a five-point scale, the movements of three specific physical areas are evaluated to determine a total score. These areas are the face and mouth, trunk area, and the extremities. The AIMS has been established as a reliable assessment tool and also has a very simple design that provides a short assessment time. This allows it to be easily utilized in an inpatient or outpatient setting to provide an objective record of any abnormal physical movements that can change over the course of time.

Brief Psychiatric Rating Scale for Children

The Brief Psychiatric Rating Scale for Children (BPRS-C) is designed to identify presenting symptoms and annotate the severity of each symptom, on a scale ranging from "not present" to "extremely severe." BPRS-C is used to diagnose psychiatric disorders for both children and adolescents through an interview with the child and parent(s).

Symptoms evaluated on the scale include:

- **Behavioral symptoms**, such as uncooperativeness and hostility
- **Mood symptoms**, such as depressive mood and anxiety
- **Sensory symptoms**, such as hallucinations, delusions, and speech characteristics
- **Symptoms of awareness and alertness**, such as disorientation, hyperactivity, distractibility, and others
- **Symptoms of affect**, such as emotional withdrawal and blunted affect

The BPRS-C assessment tool is a cursory look at many symptoms typically displayed with mental disorders.

Yale-Brown Obsessive-Compulsive Scale

The Yale-Brown Obsessive-Compulsive Scale (Y-BOCS) is a useful tool for identifying and diagnosing obsessive-compulsive disorders. Y-BOCS aims to identify obsessions, including: aggressive, contamination, sexual, hoarding/saving, religious, need for symmetry, somatic, and miscellaneous obsessions such as cleaning/washing, checking, repeating, and counting. Y-BOCS asks the individual to rate the time he or she spends on obsessions and compulsions during the week prior to the clinician's interview. It asks the individual how much control he or she has over the compulsion/obsession, and how much distress it causes him or her. Y-BOCS has questions about resistance and interference. The clinician can ask for clarification and if the individual volunteers information, it is included in the assessment. The final rating is based on the clinician's judgment.

Communicating Test Results

Test results must be communicated to the client in an ethical manner that will be of benefit to the client. This information should not add to the client's sense of bewilderment, embarrassment, unworthiness, or be perceived as critical in nature. The mental health care provider should provide significant results to the client out of a sincere desire to help. The client should understand the reason for giving the test and what information will be gleaned from its results. Then, the results and the scores should be discussed in relation to the questions asked on the test. The client should be encouraged to make his or her own interpretation of the results discussed. This can alleviate an attitude of passive acceptance or a more defensive rejection concerning the outcome of the test. The client should be affirmed by the communication efforts of the provider.

Diagnostic Tests

PET Scan

Positron-emission tomography (PET) involves injecting the individual with a radioactive glucose tracer that is taken up by active brain cells. By analyzing images of brains that have been injected with radioactive glucose, doctors can gauge regional cerebral blood flow, glucose metabolism, and oxygen consumption, all of which correlate with the brain's level of activity. PET scans are often used by clinicians to assess the cerebral damage that has been done by cerebrovascular disease, major neurocognitive disorder (formerly dementia), schizophrenia, Alzheimer's disease, and other disorders. Researchers often use PET scans to determine which areas of the brain are active during certain functions.

CT Scan

The procedure known as **neuroimaging** has vastly improved scientists' ability to assess the structure and function of living brains. The two most common techniques of neuroimaging are computed axial tomography (CT or CAT) and magnetic resonance imaging (MRI). In **CT scans**, an x-ray is taken of various horizontal cross-sections of the brain. CT scans are good for diagnosing pathological conditions like tumors, blood clots, and multiple sclerosis.

Head CT for an Individual with Altered Mental Status

The **CT scan** is a common imaging technique used to diagnose individuals who present with altered mental status. The CT scan can identify **traumatic brain injury** and **mass lesions**, such as brain tumors or hematomas, as well as cerebral edema, so it may be invaluable for neurological disorders, but it is primarily used to **rule out differential diagnoses** rather than to diagnose mental health disorders. CT scans may also be used in addition to other tests to help confirm a possible diagnosis. For example, individuals with schizophrenia tend to have enlarged ventricles with increased CSF and a concomitant reduction in brain volume with sulci that are more widened than in a non-schizophrenic brain. Despite these findings, the CT alone cannot be used for diagnosis, and no specific pattern of abnormality has been noted with depression or bipolar disorder, although there is evidence that the frontal cortex shrinks in size with uncontrolled bipolar disease and depression and increases with treatment, so long-term monitoring may show differences.

MRI

An MRI uses magnetic fields and radio waves to produce cross-sectional images. MRIs are able to produce more detailed images than CT scans, and MRIs can produce images from any angle, not just horizontally. MRIs are able to construct three-dimensional representations of brains.

EEG Testing in an Individual with Altered Level of Consciousness

The **electroencephalogram (EEG)** is sometimes used to test individuals with altered level of consciousness in order to evaluate the individuals' **electrical impulses** (brain waves). EEG is indicated for suspected seizure activity, encephalopathies, infarcts, and altered consciousness. The purpose is to identify abnormal electrical activity, which may be noted as slowing, which occurs where there has been injury or an infarct. Waves include delta (1-4 Hz), alpha (8-13 Hz), theta (4-7

Hz), beta (12-40 Hz), sleep spindles (12-14 Hz), and spikes and waves (variable frequency). Spikes and waves indicate that tissue is irritated. Findings indicate:

- **Metabolic encephalopathy**: Intermittent slowing with triphasic waves
- **Cerebral anoxic damage**: Generalized slowing in delta and theta range
- **Coma state**: Prognosis poor if EEG shows unchanging alpha waves with stimulation
- **CNS depressant overdose**: Transient periods of absence of electrical activity
- **Epilepsy**: Unusual electrical activity within the brain, partial seizures evident from only some of the electrodes while generalized seizures evident from all electrodes
- **ADHD**: A 20-minute EEG procedure FDA-approved to diagnose children with ADHD

Testing for Delirium

Appropriate testing for an individual presenting with delirium, transient confusion and alterations in consciousness depends on the age and circumstances. **Delirium** is most common in older adults in response to illness or surgery but can occur at any age. **Hyperactive delirium** may be associated with alcohol withdrawal or drug toxicity. **Hypoactive delirium** may result from disease processes, such as hepatic encephalopathy. Some have mixed symptoms, becoming more agitated during the evening and night. Testing includes:

- **Confusion Assessment Method (CAM) or CAM-ICU** helps to differentiate confusion from other causes of altered consciousness.
- The **CAM-S** form of the CAM test is used to determine the severity of delirium.
- A **Delirium Symptom Interview** also helps to identify delirium.
- **Laboratory tests**: If the cause of the individual's confusion is not evident, numerous tests may be done to rule out other causes, including CBC, blood glucose, renal and liver function tests, drug and alcohol screening, sed-rate, thyroid function tests, HIV, and thiamine and vitamin B_{12} levels.

Laboratory Tests for Psychiatric Illnesses

At the current time, diagnosis of psychiatric illnesses is based almost completely on symptoms and history, and no laboratory tests have been FDA approved for diagnosis; however, **biochemical markers** have been identified for some psychiatric disorders, including schizophrenia, bipolar disorder, and depression. Some companies have collected data and applied for FDA approval for these tests and are now marketing tests. This testing is not in common use because its use is not yet reimbursed by Medicare/Medicaid or insurance companies. Some researchers believe that genetic testing and imaging (PET, MRI) may also have larger roles in diagnosis in the future. Currently, **laboratory tests** are used for primarily two reasons:

- Rule out differential diagnoses and identify concomitant disorders. Many different tests may be used, but in many cases the results of tests don't alter the original diagnosis, so testing is done selectively, based on individual's age, history, and physical exam.
- Monitor serum levels of drugs during therapy, such as lithium levels.

Laboratory Tests for Individuals Presenting with New Onset Psychiatric Issue

When individuals present with a new onset psychiatric issue, a series of **laboratory tests** may be conducted to determine potential causes, rule out differential diagnoses, and identify concomitant disorders:

- **Blood alcohol level and urine drug screening** to determine if the individual is experiencing overdosing, withdrawal symptoms, or toxic reaction
- **Blood glucose level** to determine if the individual has hypoglycemia or hyperglycemia that may be affecting mental status
- **Urinalysis and urine culture** to determine if an infection is present (may result in confusion in older adults)
- **Pregnancy testing** to determine if females are pregnant before initiating treatment.
- **Liver and kidney function tests** to evaluate for hepatic and renal encephalopathy
- **CBC** to assess for anemia, infection, or other abnormalities
- **HIV antibodies** to rule out HIV/AIDS
- **Lyme antibodies** to rule out neuropsychological symptoms related to Lyme disease
- **Lumbar puncture** to examine cerebrospinal fluid for suspected infection

Indicators for Risk to Self or Others

Components of a Risk Assessment

A risk assessment evaluates the client's condition and their particular situation for the presence of certain risk factors. These risks can be influenced by age, ethnicity, spirituality, or social beliefs. They can include risk for suicide, harming others, exacerbation of symptoms, development of new mental health issues, falls, seizures, allergic reactions, or elopement. This assessment should occur within the first interview and then continue to be an ongoing process. The client's specific risks should be prioritized and documented, and then interventions should be put into place to protect this client from these risks.

Suicidal Ideation

Danger to the self or suicidal ideation occurs frequently in clients with mood disorders or depression. While females are more likely to attempt suicide, males actually successfully commit suicide 3 times more than females, primarily because females tend to take overdoses from which they can be revived, while males choose more violent means, such as jumping from a high place, shooting, or hanging. Risk factors include psychiatric disorders (schizophrenia, bipolar disorder, PTSD, substance abuse, and borderline personality disorder), physical disorders (HIV/AIDS, diabetes, stroke, traumatic brain injury, and spinal cord injury), and a previous violent suicide attempt. Passive suicidal ideation involves wishing to be dead or thinking about dying without making plans while active suicidal ideation involves making plans. Those with active suicidal ideation are most at risk. People with suicidal ideation often give signals, direct or indirect, to indicate they are considering suicide because many people have some ambivalence and want help. Others may act impulsively or effectively hide their distress.

Suicide Risk Assessment

A suicide risk assessment should be completed and documented upon initial interview, with each subsequent visit, and any time suicidal ideations are suggested by the client. This risk assessment should evaluate and score the following criteria:

- Would the client sign a contract for safety?
- Is there a suicide plan, and if so, how lethal is the plan?
- What is the elopement risk?
- How often are the suicidal thoughts?
- Have they attempted suicide before?

Any associated symptoms of hopelessness, guilt, anger, helplessness, impulsive behaviors, nightmares, obsessions with death, or altered judgment should also be assessed and documented. A higher score indicates a higher the risk for suicide.

Warning Signs of Suicide

The warning signs of suicide include the following:

- Depression
- Prior suicide attempts
- Family suicide history
- Abrupt increase in substance abuse
- Reckless and impulsive behavior
- Isolation
- Poor coping
- Support system loss
- Recent or anticipated loss of someone special
- Verbal expression of feeling out of control
- Preoccupation with death
- Behavioral changes not otherwise explained (a sudden changed mood from depressed to happy, the giving away of one's personal belongings, etc.)

Where **risk of suicide is suspected**, the client should be questioned directly about any thoughts of self-harm. This should be followed by a full assessment and history (particularly family history of suicide). Where the threat of suicide is not imminent, one commonly used intervention is the no-suicide contract, in which the client signs a written agreement promising to contact the suicide hotline or a counselor, social worker, or other specified professional rather than carry out an act of suicide. While commonly used, these contracts have not been proven to reduce suicide attempts and therefore should not be used in isolation as an intervention for suicide risk, nor should they be used when threat of suicide is high. When a client already has a plan for suicide, or has multiple risk factors, hospitalization must be arranged. If any immediate attempt has already been made, a medical evaluation must occur immediately.

Signs and Risk Factors of Client's Danger to Others

Violence and aggression are not uncommon among clients and pose a danger to others. Risk factors include mental health disorders, access to weapons, history of personal or family violence, abuse, animal cruelty, fire setting, and substance abuse. Violence and aggression should be handled as follows:

- **Violence** is a physical act perpetrated against an inanimate object, animal, or other person with the intent to cause harm. Violence often results from anger, frustration, or fear and occurs because the perpetrators believe that they are threatened or that their opinion is right and the victim is wrong. It may occur suddenly without warning or following aggressive behavior. Violence can result in death or severe injury if the individual attacks, so anyone in the presence of an actively violent client should back away and seek safety.
- **Aggression** is the communication of a threat or intended act of violence and will often occur before an act of violence. This communication can occur verbally or nonverbally. Gestures, shouting, speaking increasingly loudly, invasion of personal space, or prolonged eye contact are examples of aggression requiring the client be redirected or removed from the situation.

Five-Phase Aggression Cycle

The five-phase aggression cycle is as follows:

Triggering	Client responds to a triggering event with anger or hostility. Client may exhibit anxiety, restlessness, and muscle tension. Other signs include rapid breathing, perspiration, loud angry voice, and pacing.
Escalation	Client's responses show movement toward lack of control. Client's face flushes and he or she becomes increasingly agitated, demanding, and threatening, often swearing, clenching fists, and making threatening gestures. Client is unable to think clearly or resolve problems.
Crisis	Client loses emotional and physical control. Client throws objects, hits, kicks, punches, spits, bites, scratches, screams, shrieks, and cannot communicate clearly.
Recovery	Client regains control. Client's voice lowers, muscle tension relaxes, and client is able to communicate more rationally.
Post-crisis	Client may attempt reconciliation. Client may feel remorse, apologize, cry, or become quiet or withdrawn. Client is now able to respond appropriately.

Managing Active Threats of Homicidality by Clients

A client may be deemed a threat to others if:

- Client makes a serious threat of physical violence.
- The threat is made against one or more specifically named individuals.

When a threat meeting these criteria is made, even in the context of a privileged-communication relationship, a duty to protect is generated. In such a situation, the professional is required not only to notify appropriate authorities and agencies charged to protect the citizenry, but also to make a good-faith effort to warn the intended victim or, failing that, someone who is reasonably believed to be able to warn the intended victim.

The duty to warn stems from the 1976 legal case *Tarasoff v. Regents of the University of California,* where a therapist heard a credible threat and called only law enforcement authorities, failing to notify the intended victim. The murder occurred, and the case was appealed to the California Supreme Court, from which the rubric of duty to protect an intended victim has been established.

Intake, Assessment, and Diagnosis Chapter Quiz

1. Which of the following is NOT an unconscious element that influences behavior according to Freud?

a. Covert desires
b. Taboos
c. Dreams
d. Defenses

2. Which of the following developmental stages occurs between ages 6-11 according to Erikson?

a. Trust vs. Mistrust
b. Autonomy vs. Shame
c. Initiative vs. Guilt
d. Industry vs. Inferiority

3. Who of the following developed the empty organism concept?

a. Skinner
b. Kohlberg
c. Peplau
d. Pavlov

4. The __________ contains 11 subtests that assess areas like rhythm, visual function, and writing.

a. HRNB
b. SCWT
c. LNNB
d. BVRT

5. The fourth edition of the Wechsler Adult Intelligence Scale has which four indexes?

a. VCI, PLI, WMI, PSI
b. TSM, PRI, VHS, PSI
c. VCI, PRI, WMI, PSI
d. WMI, VCI, PSI, NMI

6. Bader and Pearson are known for which of the following?

a. Theory of moral development
b. Developmental model of couples therapy
c. Person-in-environment theory
d. Theory of interpersonal relations

7. Seeing external objects as either all good or all bad refers to which of the following defense mechanisms?

a. Identification
b. Sublimation
c. Splitting
d. Displacement

8. Which of the following describes the defense mechanism of introjection?

a. Replacing in conscious awareness a painful idea or feeling with its opposite.
b. Somatic changes conveyed in symbolic body language; psychic pain is felt in a part of the body.
c. Turning against the self; object of aggressive drive is changed from another to the self, especially in depression and masochism.
d. Absorbing an idea or image so that it becomes part of oneself.

9. The third level of observation where observation is done in a controlled setting for a lengthy period of time is known as

a. Casual informational observation
b. Clinical level observation
c. Truman level observation
d. Guided observation

10. Which of the following is NOT a group intelligence test?

a. Denver II
b. Kuhlman-Anderson Test
c. Woodcock Johnson IV
d. Wonderlic Personnel Test

Areas of Clinical Focus

Note: If you've noticed that the NCMHCE does not include any questions from the Areas of Clinical Focus domain, you might be tempted to skip over this chapter. We recommend that you do NOT do this, for two reasons. First, it is unquestionably better for your clients if you as the counselor have a better understanding of the disorders and difficulties your clients are experiencing. Second, even though no questions are technically included from this domain, the concepts reviewed here will still provide insight for the questions from other domains. Please study this section with the same level of care that you would the rest of the book.

Psychiatric Disorders and Diagnosis

DSM-5 Classifications

The major DSM-5 classifications are as follows:

- Neurodevelopmental disorders
- Schizophrenia spectrum and other psychotic disorders
- Bipolar and related disorders
- Depressive disorders
- Anxiety disorders
- Obsessive-compulsive and related disorders
- Trauma- and stressor-related disorders
- Dissociative disorders
- Somatic symptom and related disorders
- Feeding and eating disorders
- Elimination disorders
- Sleep-wake disorders
- Sexual dysfunctions
- Gender dysphoria
- Disruptive, impulse-control, and conduct disorders
- Substance-related and addictive disorders
- Neurocognitive disorders
- Personality disorders
- Paraphilic disorders
- Other mental disorders
- Medication-induced movement disorders
- Other conditions that may be a focus of clinical attention

Intellectual Disabilities

Very few (approximately 5%) cases of intellectual disability are **hereditary**. Hereditary forms of intellectual disability include Tay-Sachs, fragile X syndrome, and phenylketonuria. Most cases of intellectual disability (about 30%) are due to **mutations in the embryo** during the first trimester of pregnancy. Babies born with Down syndrome or those exposed to environmental toxins while in the uterus fall into this category. About 10% of cases of intellectual disability are due to **pregnancy or perinatal problems**, like fetal malnutrition, anoxia, and HIV. About 5% of those with intellectual disability have **general medical conditions** (like lead poisoning, encephalitis, or malnutrition) suffered during infancy or childhood. Approximately 20% are intellectually disabled because of either **environmental factors** or **other mental disorders** (e.g., sensory deprivation or autism). In the remaining 30%, etiology is **unknown.**

PKU

Phenylketonuria (PKU) is one cause of intellectual disability. It occurs when an infant lacks the enzyme to metabolize the amino acid phenylalanine, found in high-protein foods and aspartame sweetener. PKU is a rare recessive genetic disorder diagnosed at birth by a simple blood test. It affects mostly blue-eyed, fair babies. Expectant mothers can reduce the hazard of PKU by maintaining a diet low in phenylalanine. Untreated PKU typically leads to some form of intellectual disability. Some of the symptoms common to individuals with PKU are impaired motor and language development and volatile, erratic behavior. PKU can be treated if it is diagnosed in a timely fashion. Individuals must monitor their diet to keep phenylalanine blood levels at 2-10 mg/dL. Some phenylalanine is required for growth.

Down Syndrome

Down syndrome (Trisomy 21) occurs when a person has three #21 chromosomes instead of two. **Down syndrome** causes 20-30% of all cases of moderate and severe intellectual disability (1:800 births). Around 80% of Trisomy 21 pregnancies end in miscarriage. Classic physical characteristics associated with Down syndrome are slanted, almond-shaped eyes with epicanthic folds; a large, protruding tongue; a short, bent fifth finger; and a simian fold across the palm. Individuals with Down syndrome age rapidly. Medical conditions that often accompany Down syndrome and cause individuals to have a shorter life expectancy than normal, or poor quality of life, include heart lesions, leukemia, respiratory and digestive problems, cataracts, and Alzheimer's disease.

Communication Disorders

A number of disorders are lumped together under the heading of **communication disorders**:

- Language disorders
- Speech sound disorders
- Childhood-onset fluency disorders (stuttering)
- Social communications disorders

Childhood-onset fluency disorder (stuttering) typically begins between the ages of 2 and 7, and is more common in males than females. Research shows stuttering can be controlled through the removal of psychological stress in the home. Children who are constantly told not to stutter tend to stutter all the more. Many children find success through controlled and regular breathing exercises, accompanied by positive encouragement. In most cases, though, the child will spontaneously stop stuttering before the age of 16.

Many conditions that previously fell under the DSM-IV category of **pervasive developmental disorders** meet the criteria for **communication disorders** in DSM-5. Because autism spectrum disorder has social and communication deficits as part of its defining characteristics, it is important to note that communication disorders should not be diagnosed when there are repetitive behaviors or narrowed interests or activities.

Learning Disorders and Associated Conditions

A specific learning disorder is diagnosed as learning and academic difficulty, as evidenced by at least one of the following for at least six months (after interventions have been tried):

- Incorrect spelling
- Problems with math reasoning
- Problems with math calculation and number sense
- Difficulty reading
- Problems understanding what is read
- Difficulty using grammar and syntax

A child will be diagnosed with a learning disorder when he or she scores substantially lower than expected on a standardized achievement test and confirmed by a clinical assessment. The expectation for the child's score should be based on age, schooling, and intelligence, and the definition of "substantially lower" is a difference of two or more standard deviations. Learning disorders are frequently attended by delays in language development or motor coordination, attention and memory deficits, and low self-esteem. Learning disorders can be graded by severity as mild, moderate, or severe.

Prognosis and Etiology of Learning Disorders

Specific learning disorders include specific learning disorder with **impairment in reading**, specific learning disorder with **impairment in mathematics**, and specific learning disorder with **impairment in written expression**. Research has shown that boys are more likely to develop specific learning disorders with impairment in reading than girls. Although learning disorders are typically diagnosed during childhood or adolescence, they do not go away without treatment, and indeed may become more severe with time. Children who have a learning disorder with impairment in reading are far more likely than others to display antisocial behavior as an adult. At present, many researchers believe that reading disorders derive from problems with **phonological processing**.

Proposed **causes of learning disorders** include:

- Incomplete dominance and other hemispheric abnormalities
- Cerebellar-vestibular dysfunction
- Exposure to toxins, like lead

Autism Spectrum Disorder

Symptoms

There are two categories of symptoms necessary for a diagnosis of autism spectrum disorder. The first category is **deficits in social interaction and social communication**, which includes:

- Absence of developmentally appropriate peer relationships
- Lack of social or emotional reciprocity
- Marked impairment in nonverbal behavior
- Delay or lack of development in spoken language
- Marked impairment in the ability to initiate or sustain conversation
- Stereotyped or repetitive use of language or idiosyncratic language
- Lack of developmentally appropriate play

The other category of symptoms necessary for diagnosis of autism spectrum disorder is **restricted, repetitive patterns of behavior (RRBs), interests, and activities**. These include:

- Preoccupation with one or more stereotyped and restricted patterns of interest
- Inflexible adherence to nonfunctional routines or rituals
- Stereotyped and repetitive motor mannerisms
- Persistent preoccupation with the parts of objects

Diagnosis

Both categories of symptoms will be present in the ASD diagnosis. **Severity levels** are: **Level 1** (requiring support), **Level 2** (requiring substantial support), and **Level 3** (requiring very substantial support). Of note, ASD encompasses four disorders that were previously separate under DSM-IV: autistic disorder, Asperger's disorder, childhood integrative disorder, and pervasive developmental disorder. Individuals with ASD associated with other known conditions or environmental factors should have the diagnosis written: autism spectrum disorder associated with (name of condition).

Prognosis

Autism spectrum disorder (ASD) is frequently first suspected when an infant does not respond to his or her caregiver in an age-appropriate manner. Babies with ASD are not interested in cuddling, do not smile, and do not respond to a familiar voice. They are often misdiagnosed as profoundly deaf. The current scientific consensus is that four different disorders previously believed to be separate are actually just different **degrees** on the autism spectrum. Many children with ASD severity level 1 may escape diagnosis until a much later age. At the higher end of the spectrum (which was once referred to as Asperger's syndrome), individuals have impairment in social interactions and a limited repertoire of behaviors, interests, and activities, but they do not display other significant delays in language, self-help skills, cognitive development, or curiosity about the environment. They are extremely sensitive to touch, sounds, sights, and tastes, and have strong clothing preferences. The prognosis of the individual with ASD will largely depend on where they are on the spectrum. Unfortunately, even a small degree of improvement in ASD takes a great deal of work. Only one-third of children with autism will achieve some **independence** as adults. Those with ASD who have developed the ability to communicate verbally by age 5-6 and have an IQ over 70 have the best chance for future independence.

Characteristic Behavior Patterns

Some very noticeable, specific behavior patterns characteristic of autism spectrum disorder include:

- Lack of eye contact and disinterest in the presence of others
- Infants who rarely reach out to a caregiver
- Hand-flapping
- Rocking
- Spinning
- Echolalia (the imitating and repeating the words of others)
- Obsessive interest in a very narrow subject, like astronomy or basketball scores
- Heavy emphasis on routine and consistency, and violent reactions to changes in their normal environment

One half of people with autism remain mute for their entire lives. The speech that does develop may be abnormal. The majority of people with autism have an IQ in the intellectual disability range.

Etiology and Treatment

There are a few structural abnormalities in the brain that have been linked to autism spectrum disorders. These include a **reduced cerebellum** and **enlarged ventricles**. Research has also suggested that there is a link between autism and abnormal levels of **norepinephrine**, **serotonin**, and **dopamine**. The support for a genetic etiology of ASD has been increased by studies indicating that siblings of children with autism are much more likely have autism themselves. As for treatment, the most successful interventions focus on teaching individuals with autism the practical skills they will need to survive independently. Therapy should also include development of social skills and the reduction of undesirable behavior. Individuals with autism who reach a moderate level of functioning can be given direct vocational training.

Review Video: Autism
Visit mometrix.com/academy and enter code: 395410

ADHD

Diagnosis

Attention-deficit/hyperactivity disorder, commonly known as ADHD, can be diagnosed only if a child displays at least six symptoms of inattention or hyperactivity-impulsivity. Their onset must be before the age of 12, and they must have persisted for at least 6 months. The symptoms must not be motivated by anger or the wish to displease or spite others.

Inattentiveness Symptoms (must have 6 for diagnosis for children)	Impulsivity/Hyperactivity Symptoms (must have 6 for diagnosis for children)
• Forgetful in everyday activity • Easily distracted (often) • Makes careless mistakes and doesn't give attention to detail • Difficulty focusing attention • Does not appear to listen, even when directly spoken to • Starts tasks but does not follow through • Frequently loses essential items • Finds organizing difficult • Avoids activities that require prolonged mental exertion	• Frequently gets out of chair • Runs or climbs at inappropriate times • Frequently talks more than peer • Often moves hands and feet, or shifts position in seat • Frequently interrupts others • Frequently has difficulty waiting on turn • Frequently unable to enjoy leisure activities silently • Frequently "on the go" and seen by others as restless • Often finishes other's sentences before they can

Associated Features

Even though they are found to have **average or above-average intelligence**, children with ADHD typically score lower than average on **IQ tests**. Almost every child with ADHD will have some trouble in school, with about a quarter having major problems in **reading**. Also, **social adjustment** can be difficult for children with ADHD. Various reports give the co-diagnosis of Conduct Disorder with ADHD occurring 30-90% of the time. Other common co-diagnoses include **Oppositional Defiant Disorder**, **Anxiety Disorder**, and **Major Depression**. About half of all children who are diagnosed with ADHD are also suffering from a learning disorder.

Subtypes

There are three subtypes of ADHD:

- **Predominantly Inattentive Type** is diagnosed when a child has six or more symptoms of inattention and fewer than six symptoms of hyperactivity-impulsivity.
- **Predominantly Hyperactive-Impulsive Type** is diagnosed when there are six or more symptoms of hyperactivity-impulsivity and fewer than six of inattention.
- **Combined Type** is diagnosed when there are six or more symptoms of both hyperactivity-impulsivity and inattention.

ADHD is 4-9 times more likely to occur in boys than in girls, although the gender split is about half and half for Predominantly Inattentive Type. The rates of ADHD among adults appear to be about equal for both males and females.

Etiology

The theory that ADHD is a **genetic disorder** is supported by data that shows slightly higher rates of the disorder occur among biological relatives than among the general population, and there are higher rates among identical twins, rather than fraternal twins. ADHD is associated with structural abnormalities in the brain, like subnormal activity in the frontal cortex and basal ganglia, and a relatively small caudate nucleus, globus pallidus, and prefrontal cortex. Symptoms of ADHD vary widely, depending on the child's environment. Repetitive or boring environments encourage symptoms, as do those in which the child is given no chance to interact. One theory of ADHD asserts that it is the result of an inability to distinguish between important and unimportant **stimuli** in the environment.

Prognosis

The behavior of children with ADHD is likely to remain consistent until **early adolescence**, when they may experience diminished overactivity, but continue to suffer from attention and concentration problems. ADHD adolescents are much more likely to participate in antisocial behaviors and to abuse drugs. More than half of all children who are diagnosed with ADHD will continue to suffer from it as **adults**. These adults are more susceptible to divorce, work-related trouble, accidents, depression, substance abuse, and antisocial behavior. Children with ADHD who are co-diagnosed with Conduct Disorder are especially likely to have these problems later in life.

Treatment

Somewhat counterintuitively, central nervous system stimulants like **methylphenidate (Ritalin)** and **amphetamine (Dexedrine)** control the symptoms of ADHD. Side effects include headaches, gastrointestinal upset, anorexia, sleep difficulty, anxiety, depression, blood sugar and blood pressure increase, tics, and seizures. Research has consistently shown that **pharmacotherapy** works best when it is combined with **psychosocial intervention**. Many teachers have used the basic elements of **classroom management** to control the symptoms of ADHD. This involves laying out clear guidelines and contingencies for behavior, so that students do not have to speculate on what will happen in class or what they should be doing. Therapy that tries to increase the child's ability to **self-regulate behavior** has been shown to be less successful. It is always helpful when **parents** are involved in the treatment program.

Conduct Disorder

Diagnosis

Conduct disorder criteria are as follows:

Criteria A	Persistent pattern of behavior in which significant age-appropriate rules or societal norms are ignored, and others' rights and property are violated (theft, deceitfulness); aggression to people and animals and destruction of property are common. To meet diagnosis criteria individuals will display three of the fifteen possible symptoms over the course of a year. All the symptoms can be categorized as belonging to one of the four categories below: • Aggression to people or animals • Destruction of property • Deceitfulness or theft • Serious violations of rules
Criteria B	The patterns of behavior cause academic, social, or other impairments.
Criteria C	The behaviors couldn't better be classified as antisocial personality disorder.

Individuals with conduct disorder persistently violate either the rights of others or age-appropriate rules. They have little remorse about their behavior, and in ambiguous situations, they are likely to interpret the behavior of other people as hostile or threatening.

Etiology

According to Moffitt, there are two basic **types** of conduct disorder:

- **Life-course-persistent type** begins early in life and gets progressively worse over time. This kind of conduct disorder may be a result of neurological impairments, a difficult temperament, or adverse circumstances.
- **Adolescence-limited type** is usually the result of a temporary disparity between the adolescent's biological maturity and freedom. Adolescents with this form of conduct disorder may commit antisocial acts with friends. It is quite common for children with adolescence-limited conduct disorder to display antisocial behavior persistently in one area of life and not at all in others.

Treatment for Conduct Disorder and Oppositional Defiant Disorder

Research suggests that conduct disorder **interventions** are most successful when they are administered to preadolescents and include the immediate family members. Some therapists have developed programs of **parent therapy** to help adults manage the antisocial behavior of their children, as this has been demonstrated to have good success. Most programs advise rewarding good behavior and consistently punishing bad behavior.

Oppositional Defiant Disorder is similar to conduct disorder and is characterized by:

- Patterns of negative or hostile behavior towards authority figures
- Frequent outbreaks of temper and rages
- Deliberately annoying people
- Blaming others
- Spite and vindictiveness

This pattern of negative, hostile, defiant behavior, and vindictiveness however, is less serious violations of the basic rights of others that characterize conduct disorders. Behavior is motivated by interpersonal reactivity or resentful power struggle with adults.

Motor Disorders

Motor disorders are a type of neurodevelopmental disorder. **Motor disorders** can be classified as developmental coordination disorders, stereotypic movement disorders, and tic disorders. **Tic disorders** are further classified as Tourette's disorder, persistent motor or vocal tic disorder, and provisional tic disorder. **Tics** are defined in the DSM as "sudden, rapid, recurrent, nonrhythmic, stereotyped motor movements or vocalizations that feel irresistible yet can be suppressed for varying lengths of time."

Tourette's Syndrome

Tourette's syndrome is a neurological disorder characterized by at least one vocal tic and multiple motor tics that appear simultaneously or at different times, and appears before the age of 18. Those with **Tourette's syndrome** typically have multiple motor tics and one or more vocal tics. Those with chronic motor or vocal tic disorder have either motor or vocal tics. Individuals with Tourette's syndrome are likely to have obsessions and compulsions, high levels of hyperactivity, impulsivity, and distractibility.

Treatment

Most successful treatments for Tourette's syndrome include **pharmacotherapy**. The antipsychotics **haloperidol (Haldol)** and **pimozide (Orap)** are successful in relieving the symptoms of Tourette's syndrome because they inhibit the flow of dopamine in the brain; their success has led many scientists to speculate that Tourette's Disorder is caused by an excess of dopamine. In some cases, psychostimulant drugs amplify the tics displayed by the individual. In these cases, a doctor may treat the hyperactivity and inattention of Tourette's with **clonidine** or **desipramine**. The former of these is a drug usually used to treat hypertension, while the latter is typically used as an antidepressant.

Enuresis and Encopresis

Encopresis and enuresis make up the two major categories of elimination disorders. **Enuresis** is repeated urinating during the day or night into the bed or clothes at least twice a week for three or more months. Most of the time this urination is involuntary. Enuresis is diagnosed only when the child has reached an age at which continence can be reasonably expected (at least age five for DSM-5 criteria), and he or she does not have some other medical condition that could be to blame, like a urinary tract infection. Enuresis is treated with a night alarm, which makes a loud noise when the child urinates while sleeping. This is effective about 80% of the time, especially when it is combined with techniques like behavioral reversal and overcorrection. Desmopressin acetate (DDAVP) nasal spray, imipramine, and oxybutynin chloride (Ditropan) may help control symptoms. **Encopresis** is the involuntary fecal soiling in children who have already been toilet trained. Encopresis diagnosis cannot be made until the child is at least 4 years of age per DSM-5 criteria.

Pica and Rumination Disorder

Pica is the persistent eating of non-food substances such as paint, hair, sand, cloth, pebbles, etc. Those with **pica** do not show an aversion to food. In order to be diagnosed, the symptoms must persist for at least a month without the child losing an interest in regular food. Also, the behavior must be independent and not a part of any culturally acceptable process. Pica is most often manifested between the ages of 12 and 24 months. Pica has been observed in developmentally disabled children, pregnant women, and people with anemia.

Rumination disorder is the regurgitation and re-chewing of food.

Avoidant/Restrictive Food Intake Disorder

Diagnosis

The **criteria for avoidant/restrictive food intake disorder** are as follows:

Criteria A	A disruption in eating evidenced by not meeting nutritional needs and failure to gain expected weight or weight loss, nutritional deficiency requiring nutritional supplementation, or interpersonal interference.
Criteria B	This disruption is not due to lack of food or culture.
Criteria C	There does not appear to be a problem with the individual's body perception.
Criteria D	The disturbance can't be explained by another medical condition.

Anorexia Nervosa

Diagnosis

The characteristics of **anorexia nervosa** are:

Criteria A	Extreme restriction of food, lower than requirements, leading to low body weight
Criteria B	An irrational fear of gaining weight or behaviors that prevent weight gain, despite being at low weight
Criteria C	Distorted body image or a lack of acknowledgement of severity of current weight

A general standard used to determine the minimum healthy body weight is that it should be at least 85% of the norm for the individual's height and weight. People with restricting type anorexia lose weight through fasting, dieting, and excessive exercise. People with binging/purging type anorexia lose weight by eating a great deal and then either vomiting it or inducing immediate defecation with laxatives. People with anorexia are preoccupied with food. The physical symptoms of **starvation** are constipation, cold intolerance, lethargy, and bradycardia. The physical problems associated with **purging** are anemia, impaired renal function, cardiac abnormalities, dental problems, and osteoporosis.

Gender, Age, Etiology, and Treatment

The vast majority of people with anorexia are **female**, and the onset of anorexia is usually in **mid-to-late adolescence**. Onset may be associated with a stressful life event. Some studies associated anorexia with middle- and upper-class families that have a tendency towards competition and success. Girls with anorexia are likely to be introverted, nonassertive, and conscientious. Their mothers are likely to also be very concerned about food intake and weight. The immediate goal of any treatment program is to help the individual gain weight. Sometimes this requires hospitalization. **Cognitive therapy** is also often employed to correct the individual's misconceptions about healthy weight and nutrition.

BULIMIA NERVOSA

DIAGNOSIS

The characteristics of **bulimia nervosa** are:

Criteria A	Cyclical periods of binge eating characterized by discretely consuming an amount of food that is larger than most individuals would eat in the same time period and situation. The individual feels a lack of control over the eating.
Criteria B	Characterized by binge eating followed by purging via self-induced vomiting/laxatives/fasting/vigorous exercise in order to prevent weight gain
Criteria C	At least one binge eating episode per week for three months
Criteria D	It is marked by a persistent over-concern with body shape and weight.
Criteria E	The eating and compensatory behaviors do not only occur during periods of anorexia nervosa.

Binges are often caused by interpersonal stress and may entail a staggering caloric intake. The **medical complications** associated with bulimia are fluid and electrolyte disturbances, metabolic alkalosis, metabolic acidosis, dental problems, and menstrual abnormalities.

GENDER, AGE, ETIOLOGY, AND TREATMENT

As with anorexia, the vast majority of people with bulimia are **female**. The onset is typically in **late adolescence** or **early adulthood**, and may follow a period of dieting. There are indications of a **genetic etiology** for bulimia. Also, there are links between bulimia and low levels of the endogenous opioid beta-endorphin, as well as low levels of serotonin and norepinephrine. The main point of any treatment for bulimia is encouraging the individual to get control of eating, and modifying unhealthy beliefs about body shape and nutrition. Treatment often involves **cognitive-behavioral techniques** like self-monitoring, stimulus control, cognitive restructuring, problem-solving, and self-distraction. Some antidepressants, like imipramine, have been effective at reducing instances of binging and purging.

Anxiety Disorders

Types of anxiety disorders include the following:

Panic disorder	Recurrent brief but intense fear in the form of panic attacks with physiological or psychological symptoms
Specific phobia	Fear of specific situations or objects
Generalized anxiety disorder	Chronic psychological and cognitive symptoms of distress and excessive worry lasting at least 6 months
Separation anxiety disorder	Excessive anxiety related to being separated from someone the individual is attached to
Selective mutism	Inability to speak in social settings (when it would seem appropriate) though normally able to speak
Social anxiety disorder	Anxiety about social situations
Agoraphobia	Anxiety about being outside of the home or in open places

Review Video: Anxiety Disorders
Visit mometrix.com/academy and enter code: 366760

Panic Disorder

Diagnosis

An individual may be diagnosed with **panic disorder** if he or she suffers recurrent unexpected panic attacks, and one of the attacks is followed by one month of either persistent concern regarding the possibility of another attack or a significant change in behavior related to the attack. **Panic attacks** are brief, defined periods of intense apprehension, fear, or terror. They develop quickly, and usually reach their greatest intensity after about ten minutes. Attacks must include at least 4 characteristic **symptoms**, which include:

- Palpitations or accelerated heart rate (tachycardia)
- Sweating
- Chest pain
- Nausea
- Dizziness
- Derealization
- Paresthesia (pins and needles or numbness)
- Shaking
- Shortness of breath
- Fear of losing control
- Fear of dying
- Chills or heat sensation
- Feeling of choking

Prevalence and Gender Issues

The consensus of research is that 1-2% of the population will suffer panic disorder at some point during their lives, and 30-50% of these individuals will also suffer **agoraphobia**. Panic disorder has a higher rate of diagnostic comorbidity when it is accompanied by agoraphobia. Panic disorder is far more likely to occur in **females** than males, and females with a panic disorder have a 75% chance of also having agoraphobia. There is a great deal of variation in the age of onset, but the most frequent ages of occurrence are in adolescence and the mid-30s. Children can experience the physical symptoms of a panic attack, but are unlikely to be diagnosed with panic disorder because they do not have the wherewithal to associate their symptoms with catastrophic feelings. The individual can be diagnosed with agoraphobia even if they are not diagnosed with panic disorder, but the two are commonly diagnosed together.

Treatment and Differential Diagnosis

The most effective treatment for panic attacks appears to be controlled in vivo exposure with response prevention, known as **flooding**. Flooding is typically accompanied by cognitive therapy, relaxation, breathing training, or pharmacotherapy. **Antidepressant medications** are often prescribed to relieve the symptoms of panic disorder. If stand-alone drug treatment is used, the risk of relapse is very high. Differential diagnoses for panic disorder include social phobia, and medical conditions like hyperthyroidism, hypoglycemia, cardiac arrhythmia, and mitral valve prolapse. Panic disorder can be distinguished from social phobia by the fact that attacks will sometimes occur while the individual is alone or sleeping.

Phobias

Diagnosis

A specific phobia is a marked and persistent fear of a particular object or situation, other than those associated with social phobia or agoraphobia. When an individual with a phobia is exposed to the feared object or event, he or she will have a panic attack or some other anxiety response. Adults with a specific phobia should be able to recognize that their fear is irrational and excessive. The onset of a specific phobia is typically in childhood or in the mid-20s. According to the DSM-5, there are five **subtypes** of specific phobia:

- Animal
- Natural environment
- Situational
- Blood-injection-injury
- Other

The blood-injection-injury subtype has different physical symptoms than the others. Individuals with blood-injection-injury phobia have a brief increase in heart rate and blood pressure, followed by a drop in both, often ending in a brief loss of consciousness (fainting). Other phobic reactions just entail the increase in heart rate and blood pressure, without loss of consciousness.

Distinguishing Symptoms of Agoraphobia

Symptoms that distinguish panic disorder from **agoraphobia** include the fear of being in a situation or place from which it could be difficult or embarrassing to escape, or of being in a place where help might not be available in the event of a panic attack. Agoraphobia usually manifests when the individual is alone outside of the home, is in a crowd, or is traveling in a train or automobile. Those who suffer from agoraphobia will typically go to great lengths to avoid problematic situations, or they will only be able to enter certain situations with a companion and under heavy distress. One of the main problems with agoraphobia is that it causes the individual to severely limit the places they are willing to go. These individuals often become reclusive.

Etiology and Treatment

The **two-factor theory** proposed by Mower asserts that phobias are the result of avoidance conditioning, when an individual associates a neutral or controlled stimulus with an anxiety-causing, unconditioned stimulus. The phobia reinforces a strategy of avoidance because it prevents anxiety (even though the neutral stimulus was not to blame for the anxiety in the first place). Another theory for the etiology of phobias is offered by **social learning theorists**, who state that phobic behaviors are learned by watching avoidance strategies used by one's parents. As with panic disorder, **in vivo exposure** is considered the best treatment for a specific phobia. **Relaxation and breathing techniques** are also helpful in dispelling fear and controlling physical response.

Generalized Anxiety Disorder

Individuals may be diagnosed with generalized anxiety disorder (GAD) if they have excessive anxiety about multiple events or activities. This anxiety must have existed for at least six months and must be difficult for the individual to control. The anxiety must be disproportionate to the feared event. Anxiety must include at least three of the following:

- Restlessness
- Fatigue on exertion
- Difficulty concentrating
- Irritability
- Muscle tension
- Sleep disturbance

The treatment for GAD usually entails a **multicomponent cognitive-behavioral therapy**, occasionally accompanied by pharmacotherapy. **SSRI** antidepressants and the anxiolytic buspirone have both demonstrated success in diminishing the symptoms of GAD.

Separation Anxiety Disorder

Onset

Many children who suffer from separation anxiety disorder will refuse to go to school, and may claim physical ailments to avoid having to leave the home. In some cases, the child will actually develop a headache or stomachache as a result of anxiety about separation from the home or from an individual to whom they are attached. The refusal to go to school may begin as early as 5 or as late as 12. If the separation anxiety occurs after the age of 10, however, it is quite possibly the result of depression or some more severe disorder. There are various treatment plans for separation anxiety disorder, all of which recommend that the child immediately resume going to school on a normal schedule.

Symptoms

Separation anxiety disorder is characterized by age-inappropriate and excessive anxiety that occurs when an individual is separated or threatened with separation from his or her home or family unit. In order to be diagnosed with separation anxiety disorder, the child must exhibit **symptoms** for at least four weeks and onset must be before the age of 18. Individuals with separation anxiety disorder will manifest some of the following symptoms:

- Excessive distress when separated from home or attachment figures
- Persistent fear of being alone
- Frequent physical complaints during separation

Children with separation anxiety tend to be from loving, stable homes. For many, the disorder begins to manifest after the child has suffered some personal loss.

Social Anxiety Disorder

The characteristics of social anxiety disorder or **social phobia** are a marked and persistent fear of social situations or situations in which the individual may be called upon to perform. Typically, the individual fears criticism and evaluation by others. The response to the feared situation is an immediate panic attack. Those with social phobia either avoid the feared situation or endure it with much distress. The fear and anxiety regarding these social situations have a negative impact on the individual's life, and is present for at least six months. Adults should be able to recognize that their fear is excessive and irrational. As with other phobias, social phobia is best treated with **exposure** in combination with **social skills and cognitive therapy**. Antidepressants and the beta-blocker propranolol are helpful for treating social phobia.

Obsessive-Compulsive Disorder

The following are the **criteria for obsessive-compulsive disorders:**

Criteria A	The individual exhibits obsessions, compulsions, or both. **Obsession**: continuous, repetitive thoughts, compulsions, or things imagined that are unwanted and cause distress. The individual will try to suppress thoughts, ignore them, or do a compulsive behavior. **Compulsion**: recurrent behavior or thought the individual feels obliged to perform after an obsession to decrease anxiety; however, the compulsion is usually not connected in an understandable way to an observer.
Criteria B	The obsessions and compulsions take at least one hour per day and cause distress.
Criteria C	The behavior is not caused by a substance.
Criteria D	The behavior could not better be explained by a different mental disorder.

Note if the criteria are met with good insight (individual realizes OCD beliefs are not true), poor insight (individual thinks the OCD beliefs are true), or absent insight (individual is delusional, truly believing OCD beliefs are true). Note if the individual has ever had tic disorder.

Other obsessive-compulsive and related disorders include:

- Body dysmorphic disorder
- Hoarding disorder
- Trichotillomania (hair-pulling disorder)
- Excoriation (skin-picking disorder)

Gender Issues, Etiology, and Treatment

OCD is equally likely to occur in adult males and adult females. The average age of onset is lower for males, so the rates of OCD among male children and adolescents are slightly higher than among females. Evidence suggests that OCD is caused by low levels of **serotonin**. Structurally, OCD seems to be linked to overactivity in the **right caudate nucleus**. The most effective treatment for OCD is exposure with response prevention in tandem with medication, usually either the tricyclic clomipramine or an SSRI. Therapies that provide help with stopping thought patterns seem to be especially successful in battling OCD. When drugs are used alone, there remains a high risk of relapse.

Review Video: Obsessive-Compulsive Disorder (OCD)
Visit mometrix.com/academy and enter code: 499790

PTSD

Diagnosis

An individual may be diagnosed with post-traumatic stress disorder (PTSD) if he or she develops symptoms after exposure to an extreme trauma. Examples of extreme trauma include: witnessing the death or injury of another person, experiencing injury to self, learning about the unexpected or violent death or injury of a family member or friend, or repeatedly being exposed to trauma (such as first responders or military soldiers). The traumatic event must elicit a reaction of intense fear, helplessness, or horror. The **characteristic symptoms** of PTSD are:

- Persistent re-experiencing of the event
- Persistent avoidance of stimuli associated with the trauma
- Persistent symptoms of increased arousal (difficulty concentrating, staying awake, or falling asleep)

These symptoms must have been present for at least a month; symptoms may not begin until three or more months after the event.

Treatment

The preferred treatment for PTSD is a **comprehensive cognitive-behavioral approach** that includes:

- Exposure
- Cognitive restructuring
- Anxiety management
- SSRIs to relieve symptoms of PTSD and comorbid conditions

Some psychologists criticize single-session psychological debriefings, because they believe one session amplifies the effects of a traumatic event. Another controversial therapy used to treat PTSD is eye movement desensitization and reprocessing; the positive benefits of this therapy may be more to do with the exposure that goes along with it than with the eye movements themselves.

Acute Stress Disorder

Acute stress disorder has symptoms similar to those of post-traumatic stress disorder. Acute stress disorder is distinguished by symptoms that occur for more than 3 days and but less than one month. An individual is diagnosed with acute stress disorder when he or she has 9 or more **symptoms** from any of the following 5 categories, which begin after the trauma:

- Intrusion
- Negative mood
- Avoidance symptoms
- Dissociative symptoms
- Arousal symptoms

An individual with acute stress disorder persistently relives the traumatic event, to the point where he or she takes steps to avoid contact with stimuli that bring the event to mind, and experiences severe anxiety when reminiscing about the event.

Review Video: What is Acute Stress Disorder?
Visit mometrix.com/academy and enter code: 538946

Additional Trauma- and Stressor-Related Disorders

Additional trauma- and stress-related disorders include:

Reactive attachment disorder	Child rarely seeks or responds to comfort when upset, usually due to neglect of emotional needs by caregiver (e.g., children who are institutionalized or in foster care). Reactive attachment disorder is characterized by a markedly disturbed or developmentally-inappropriate social relatedness in most settings. This condition typically begins before the age of five. In order to definitively diagnose this disorder, there must be evidence of pathogenic care, which may include neglect or a constant change of caregivers that made it difficult for the child to form normal attachments.
Disinhibited social engagement disorder	Child has decreased hesitations regarding interacting with unfamiliar adults. Does not question leaving normal caregiver to go off with a stranger.
Adjustment disorder	The individual has behavioral or emotional changes occurring within 3 months of a stressor. These changes cause distress for the individual and are disproportional to the actual stressor.

Somatoform Disorders

Conversion Disorder

Conversion disorder is a somatoform disorder characterized by either loss of bodily functions or symptoms of a serious physical disease. The individual becomes blind, mute, or paralyzed in response to an acute stressor. Occasionally, individuals develop hyperesthesia, analgesia, tics, belching, vomiting, or coughing spells. These symptoms do not conform to physiological mechanisms, and testing reveals no underlying physical disease. The sensory loss, movement loss, or repetitive physical symptoms are not intentional. The individual is not malingering to avoid work, or factitiously seeking attention. The symptoms of a conversion disorder can often be removed with **hypnosis** or **Amytal interview**. Some researchers believe that simply suggesting that these symptoms will go away is the best way to relieve them. The individual can develop complications, like seizures, from disuse of body parts.

Primary Gain, Secondary Gain, and Differential Diagnoses

The **etiology of conversion disorder** is explained in terms of two psychological mechanisms:

- A conversion disorder may be used for **primary gain** when the symptoms keep an internal conflict or need out of the consciousness.
- A conversion disorder is used for **secondary gain** when the symptoms help the individual avoid an unpleasant activity or obtain support from the environment.

In order to diagnose a conversion disorder, there must be evidence of *involuntary* psychological factors. Conversion disorder is occasionally confused with factitious disorder and malingering, both of which are voluntary.

Somatic Symptom Disorder

Somatic symptom disorder is a somatoform disorder, meaning that it suggests a medical condition but is not fully explainable by the medical condition, substance abuse, or other medical disorder. Individuals with somatic symptom disorder often describe their problems in dramatic, overstated, and ambiguous terms. They excessively worry or think about the symptoms and spend much time and energy worrying about health issues. Somatic symptom disorders cause clinically significant distress or impairment, and are not produced intentionally. A somatic symptom disorder involves recurrent multiple somatic complaints and though no one symptom has to be continuous, some symptoms are present for at least six months. Medical attention has been sought, but no physical explanation has been found.

Illness Anxiety Disorder

Individuals with illness anxiety disorder (formerly hypochondriasis) have an unrealistic preoccupation with having or getting a serious illness that is based on a misappraisal of bodily symptoms. This preoccupation is disproportional to symptoms or medical evidence. Individuals with illness anxiety disorder likely know a great deal about their condition, and frequently go to a number of different doctors searching for a professional opinion that confirms their own. They likely either experience frequent health related checks (either by doctors or by self-checks) or avoidance of doctors and healthcare facilities. The symptoms of this disorder have been present for at least six months, however the specific illness that the individual fears may change.

Delirium

Delirium is characterized by a clinically significant deficit in cognition or memory as compared to previous functioning. In order for delirium to be diagnosed, the individual must have disturbances in consciousness and either a change in personality or the development of perceptual abnormalities. These changes in cognition may appear as losses of memory, disorientation in space and time, and impaired language. The perceptual abnormalities associated with delirium include hallucinations and illusions. Delirium usually develops over a few hours or days, and may vary in intensity over the course of the days and weeks. If the cause of the delirium is alleviated, it may disappear for an extended period of time.

The **criteria** for delirium are as follows:

Criteria A	A disturbance in consciousness or attention
Criteria B	Develops over a short period of time, and fluctuates throughout the day
Criteria C	Accompanied by changes in cognition
Criteria D	Not better explained by another condition
Criteria E	Caused by a medical condition or is substance related

Five groups of people at **high risk** for delirium:

- Elderly people
- Those who have a diminished cerebral reserve due to major neurocognitive disorder (formerly dementia), stroke, or some other medical condition
- Those who have recently undergone cardiotomy
- Burn victims
- Individuals who are drug-dependent and in withdrawal

Delirium can also be **caused** by:

- Systemic infections
- Metabolic disorders
- Fluid and electrolyte imbalances
- Postoperative states
- Head trauma
- Long hospital stays, such as those in the intensive care unit

The **treatment** for delirium usually aims at curing the underlying cause of the disorder and reducing the agitated behavior. Antipsychotic drugs can be good for reducing agitation, delusions, and hallucinations, while providing a calm environment can decrease the appearance of agitation.

Neurocognitive Disorders

Major and minor neurocognitive disorders (NCD) may be due to any of the following: Alzheimer's disease, Frontotemporal lobar degeneration, Lewy body disease, vascular disease, traumatic brain injury, substance or medication use, HIV Infection, prion disease, Parkinson's disease, Huntington's disease, another medical condition, and multiple etiologies. **Criteria** are as follows:

Criteria A	A change in cognitive ability from baseline. This information can be determined by the individual, a well-informed significant other, family member, or caretaker, or it can be determined by neuropsychology testing.
Criteria B	For a major neurocognitive disorder, the cognitive change interferes with ADLs and independence. For a minor neurocognitive disorder, the cognitive change doesn't interfere with normal ADLS and independence, if accommodations are used.
Criteria C	The cognitive change cannot be defined as delirium only.
Criteria D	The cognitive change is not better described as another mental disorder.

Differential Diagnosis

Some of the cognitive symptoms of major depressive disorder are very similar to those of **neurocognitive disorders**. Indeed, this kind of depression is frequently referred to as pseudodementia. One difference is that the **cognitive deficits** typical of neurocognitive disorders will get progressively worse, and the individual is unlikely to admit that he or she has impaired cognition.

Pseudodementia, on the other hand, typically has a very rapid onset and usually causes the individual to become concerned about his or her own health. There are also differences in the quality of memory impairment in these two conditions: Individuals with **neurocognitive disorders** have deficits in both recall and recognition memory, while individuals who are **depressed** only have deficits in recall memory.

Diagnosis

Individuals who suffer from neurocognitive disorders are likely to manifest a few **cognitive deficits**, most notably memory impairment, aphasia, apraxia, agnosia, or impaired executive functioning. Depending on the etiology of the neurocognitive disorders, these deficits may get progressively worse or may be stable.

These individuals could have both **anterograde** and **retrograde amnesia**, meaning that they find it difficult both to learn new information and to recall previously learned information. There may be a decrease in language skill, specifically manifested in an inability to recall the names of people or things. Individuals may also have a hard time performing routine motor programs, and may be unable to recognize familiar people and places. Abstract thinking, planning, and initiating complex behaviors are difficult.

NEUROCOGNITIVE DISORDER DUE TO ALZHEIMER'S DISEASE

Particular kinds of **Alzheimer's disease** have been linked with specific genetic abnormalities. For instance, those with early-onset familial Alzheimer's often have abnormalities on **chromosome 21**, while individuals whose onset is later are likely to have irregularities on **chromosome 19**. Those with Alzheimer's disease have also been shown to have significant **aluminum deposits** in brain tissues, a malfunctioning **immune system**, and a low level of **acetylcholine**. Some of the drugs used to treat Alzheimer's increase the cholinergic activity in the brain. These drugs, which include the trade names **Cognex** and **Aricept**, can temporarily reverse cognitive impairment, though these improvements are not sustained when the drugs are removed.

STAGES OF ALZHEIMER'S DISEASE

Over half of all cases of neurocognitive disorder are caused by Alzheimer's disease. Alzheimer's begins slowly and may take a long time to become noticeable. Researchers have outlined **three stages** of Alzheimer's disease:

- **Stage 1** usually comprises the first 1-3 years of the condition. The individual suffers from **mild anterograde amnesia**, especially for declarative memories. He or she is likely to have **diminished visuospatial skill**, which often manifests itself in wandering aimlessly. Also common to this stage are indifference, irritability, sadness, and anomia.
- **Stage 2** can stretch between the second and tenth years of the illness. The individual suffers increasing **retrograde amnesia**, restlessness, delusions, aphasia, acalculia, ideomotor apraxia (the inability to translate an idea into movement), and a generally flat mood.
- In **Stage 3** of Alzheimer's disease, the individual suffers **severely impaired intellectual functioning**, apathy, limb rigidity, and urinary and fecal incontinence. This last stage usually occurs between the eighth and twelfth years of the condition.

Alzheimer's disease is quite difficult to diagnose directly, so it is usually only diagnosed once all the other possible causes of major neurocognitive disorder (formerly dementia) have been eliminated. A brain biopsy that indicates extensive neuron loss, amyloid plaques, and neurofibrillary tangles can give solid evidence of Alzheimer's disease. Individuals who develop Alzheimer's disease usually only live about ten years after onset. The disease is more common in females than males, and is more likely to occur after the age of 65.

TREATMENT

Though Alzheimer's disease is a degenerative condition with no known cure, there are a number of different **treatments** that can provide help to those who suffer from the disease:

- Group therapy that focuses on orienting the individual in reality and encourages him or her to reminisce about past experiences
- Antidepressants, antipsychotics, and other pharmacotherapy
- Behavioral techniques to fight the agitation associated with Alzheimer's
- Environmental manipulation to improve memory and cognitive function
- Involving the individual's family in interventions

Neurocognitive Disorder Due to HIV Infection

Individuals with AIDS develop a particular form of neurocognitive disorder. In its early stages, the **Human Immunodeficiency Virus** causes major neurocognitive disorder (formerly dementia), which appears as forgetfulness, impaired attention, and generally decelerated mental processes. **Neurocognitive disorders** due to HIV progresses include poor concentration, apathy, social withdrawal, loss of initiative, tremor, clumsiness, trouble with problem-solving, and saccadic eye movements. One of the ways that neurocognitive disorders due to HIV is distinguished is by motor slowness, the lack of aphasia, and more severe forms of depression and anxiety. It shares these features with neurocognitive disorders due to Parkinson's and Huntington's diseases.

Neurocognitive Disorder Due to Vascular Disease

In order to be diagnosed with neurocognitive disorder due to **vascular disease**, the individual must have **cognitive impairment** and either **focal neurological signs** or **laboratory evidence of cerebrovascular disease**. Neurocognitive disorder has varying symptoms, depending on where the brain damage lies. Focal neurological signs may include exaggerated reflexes, weaknesses in the extremities, and abnormalities in gait. Symptoms gradually increase in severity. Risk factors for vascular neurocognitive disorder are hypertension, diabetes, tobacco smoking, and atrial fibrillation. In some cases, an individual may be able to recover from neurocognitive disorder due to vascular disease. Stroke victims, for instance, will notice a great deal of improvement in the first six months after the cerebrovascular accident. Most of this improvement will be in their physical, rather than cognitive, symptoms.

Neurocognitive Disorder Due to Huntington's Disease

Individuals with **Huntington's disease** suffer degeneration of the GABA-producing cells in their substantia nigra, basal ganglia, and cortex. This inherited disease typically appears between the ages of 30 and 40. The **affective symptoms** of Huntington's disease include irritability, depression, and apathy. After a while, these individuals display **cognitive symptoms** as well, including forgetfulness and dementia. Later, **motor symptoms** emerge, including fidgeting, clumsiness, athetosis (slow, writhing movements), and chorea (involuntary quick jerks). Because the affective symptoms appear in advance of the cognitive and motor symptoms, many people with Huntington's are misdiagnosed with depression. Individuals in the early stages of Huntington's are at risk for suicide, as they are aware of their impending deterioration, and will have the loss of impulse control associated with the disease.

Neurocognitive Disorder Due to Parkinson's Disease

The following symptoms are commonly associated with neurocognitive disorder due to **Parkinson's disease**:

- Bradykinesia (general slowness of movement)
- Resting tremor
- Stoic and unmoving facial expression
- Loss of coordination or balance
- Involuntary pill-rolling movement of the thumb and forefinger
- Akathisia (violent restlessness)

Most people with Parkinson's will suffer from **depression** at some point during their illness, and 20-60% will develop major neurocognitive disorder (formerly dementia). Research indicates that those with Parkinson's have a deficiency of **dopamine-producing cells** and the presence of **Lewy bodies** in their substantia nigra. Many doctors now believe that there is some **environmental cause** for Parkinson's, though the etiology is not yet clear. The medication L-dopa (Dopar,

Larodopa) alleviates the symptoms of Parkinson's by increasing the amount of dopamine in the brain.

Schizophrenia

Diagnosis

Schizophrenia is a psychotic disorder. Psychotic disorders are those that feature one or more of the following: delusions, hallucinations, disorganized speech or thought, or disorganized or catatonic behavior. Schizophrenia **diagnostic criteria** are as follows:

Criteria A	Diagnosis requires at least two of the following symptoms, one being a core positive symptom: • Hallucinations (core positive symptom) • Delusions (core positive symptom) • Disorganized speech (core positive symptom) • Severely disorganized or catatonic behavior • Negative symptoms (i.e., avolition, diminished expression)
Criteria B	Individual's level of functioning is significantly below level prior to onset.
Criteria C	If the individual has not had successful treatment there are continual signs of schizophrenia for more than six months.
Criteria D	Depressive disorder, bipolar disorder, and schizoaffective disorder have been ruled out.
Criteria E	The symptoms cannot be attributed to another medical condition or a substance.
Criteria F	If the individual has had a communication disorder or Autism since childhood, a diagnosis of schizophrenia is only made if the individual has hallucinations or delusions.

Etiology

Both twin and adoption studies have suggested that there is a **genetic component** to the etiology of schizophrenia. The rates of instance (concordance) among first-degree biological relatives of people with schizophrenia are greater than among the general population. **Structural abnormalities** in the brain linked to schizophrenia are enlarged ventricles and diminished hippocampus, amygdala, and globus pallidus. **Functional abnormalities** in the brain linked to schizophrenia are hypofrontality and diminished activity in the prefrontal cortex. An abnormally large number of the people with schizophrenia in the Northern Hemisphere were born in the late winter or early spring. There is speculation that this may be because of a link between prenatal exposure to influenza and schizophrenia.

Schizophrenia and Dopamine

For many years, the professional consensus was that schizophrenia was caused by either an excess of the neurotransmitter **dopamine** or oversensitive **dopamine receptors**. The **dopamine hypothesis** was supported by the fact that antipsychotic medications that block dopamine receptors had some success in treating schizophrenia, and by the fact that dopamine-elevating amphetamines amplified the frequency of delusions. The dopamine hypothesis has been somewhat undermined, however, by research that found elevated levels of norepinephrine and serotonin, as well as low levels of GABA and glutamate in schizophrenics. Some studies have shown that clozapine and other atypical antipsychotics are effective in treating schizophrenia, even though they block serotonin rather than dopamine receptors.

Positive Symptoms

The symptoms of schizophrenia may be **positive, negative,** or **disorganized.** Positive symptoms are **delusions** and **hallucinations**. Delusions are false beliefs that are held despite clear evidence to the contrary. The delusions suffered by a schizophrenic usually fall into one of three categories:

- **Persecutory**, in which the person believes that someone or something is out to get him or her.
- **Referential**, in which the person believes that messages in the public domain (like song lyrics or newspaper articles) are specifically directed at him or her.
- **Bizarre**, in which the person imagines that something impossible has happened.

The most common sensory mode for hallucinations is sound, specifically the audition of voices.

Disorganized and Negative Symptoms

For many psychologists, the classic characteristic of schizophrenia is **disorganized speech.** Disorganized speech manifests as:

- Incoherence
- Free associations that make little sense
- Random responses to direct questions

Disorganized behavior manifests as:

- Shabby or unkempt appearance
- Inappropriate sexual behavior
- Unpredictable agitation
- Catatonia and decreased motor activity

Negative symptoms of schizophrenia include:

- Restricted range of emotions
- Reduced body language
- Lack of facial expression
- Lack of coherent thoughts
- Inability to make conversation
- Avolition (the inability to set goals or to work in a rational, programmatic manner)

Catatonia

Criteria for catatonia includes at least three of the following:

- Catalepsy
- Defying or refusing to acknowledge instruction
- Echolalia
- Echopraxia
- Little to no verbal response
- Grimacing
- Agitation
- Semi-consciousness
- Waxy flexibility
- Posturing
- Mannerism
- Stereotypy

Associated Features

Features commonly associated with schizophrenia are:

- Inappropriate affect
- Anhedonia (loss of pleasure)
- Dysphoric mood
- Abnormalities in motor behavior
- Somatic complaints

One of the more troublesome aspects of schizophrenia is that the afflicted individual rarely has any insight into his or her own condition and so is unlikely to **comply** with treatment. People with schizophrenia often develop substance dependencies, especially to nicotine. Though many people believe that those with schizophrenia are more likely to be violent or aggressive than individuals in the general population, there is no statistical information to support this assertion. The onset of schizophrenia is typically during the ages of 18-25 for males and 25-35 for females. Males are slightly more likely to develop the disorder.

Prognosis and Differential Diagnosis

Individuals typically develop schizophrenia as a **chronic condition**, with very little chance of full remission. Positive symptoms of schizophrenia tend to decrease in later life, though the negative symptoms may remain. The following factors tend to **improve prognosis**:

- Good premorbid adjustment
- Acute and late onset
- Female gender
- Presence of a precipitating event
- Brief duration of active-phase symptoms
- Insight into the illness
- Family history of mood disorder
- No family history of schizophrenia

Differential diagnoses for schizophrenia include bipolar and depressive disorders with psychotic features, schizoaffective disorder, and the effects of prolonged and large-scale use of amphetamines or cocaine.

TREATMENT

Treatment for schizophrenia begins with the administration of **antipsychotic medication**. Antipsychotics are very effective at diminishing the positive symptoms of schizophrenia, though their results vary from person to person. Antipsychotics have strong side effects, however, including tardive dyskinesia. Medication is more effective when it is taken in combination with psychosocial intervention. Many people with schizophrenia are prone to relapse if they receive a great deal of criticism from family members, so it may be a good idea to initiate **family therapy** in which the level of expressed emotion in the family is discussed. Those who are recovering from schizophrenia also benefit from **social skills training** and **help with employment**.

SCHIZOAFFECTIVE DISORDER

The **criteria** for schizoaffective disorder are as follows:

Criteria A	For diagnosis the individual must have at least two of the following symptoms, one being a core positive symptom. The individual will experience the symptoms during a continuous period of illness during which there will also be a significant manic or depressive mood episode. • Hallucinations (known as a core positive symptom) • Delusions (known as a core positive symptom) • Disorganized speech (known as a core positive symptom) • Severely disorganized or catatonic behavior • Negative Symptoms (such as avolition or diminished expression)
Criteria B	Individual experiences hallucinations or delusions for at least two weeks during illness that do not occur during a significant depressive or manic mood episode.
Criteria C	The individual experiences significant depressive or manic mood symptoms for most of the time of the illness.
Criteria D	The symptoms cannot be attributed to another medical condition or a substance.

SCHIZOPHRENIFORM DISORDER

The **criteria** for schizophreniform disorder are as follows:

Criteria A	Diagnosis requires at least two of the following symptoms, one being a core positive symptom: • Hallucinations (known as a core positive symptom) • Delusions (known as a core positive symptom) • Disorganized speech (known as a core positive symptom) • Severely disorganized or catatonic behavior • Negative Symptoms (such as avolition or diminished expression)
Criteria B	An illness of at least one month but less than six months duration.
Criteria C	Depressive disorder, bipolar disorder, and schizoaffective disorder have been ruled out.
Criteria D	The symptoms cannot be attributed to another medical condition or a substance.

Brief Psychotic Disorder

Brief psychotic disorder is characterized as a delusion that has sudden onset and lasts less than one month. Brief psychotic disorder is a classification of the schizophrenia spectrum and other psychotic disorders.

Criteria A	At least one of the following symptoms: delusions, hallucinations, disorganized speech, or catatonic behavior.
Criteria B	The symptoms last more than one day but less than one month. The individual does eventually return to baseline functioning.
Criteria C	The disorder cannot be attributed to another psychotic or depressive disorder.

Delusional Disorder

Delusional disorder is typified by the presence of a persistent delusion. Delusion may be persecutory type, jealous type, erotomanic type (that someone is in love with delusional person), somatic type (that one has physical defect or disease), grandiose type, or mixed.

The following are the **criteria** for delusional disorder:

Criteria A	The individual experiences at least one delusion for at least one month or longer.
Criteria B	The individual does not meet criteria for schizophrenia.
Criteria C	Functioning is not significantly impaired, and behavior except dealing specifically with delusion is not bizarre.
Criteria D	Any manic or depressive episodes are brief.
Criteria E	The symptoms cannot be attributed to another medical condition or a substance.

It should be specified if the delusions are bizarre. Severity is rated by the quantitative assessment measure "Clinician-Rated Dimensions of Psychosis Symptom Severity."

Bipolar Disorders

Documentation and Gender Influences

Bipolar disorders should be documented with current (or most recent) features, whether manic, hypomanic, or major depressive episode noted. The current severity of mild, moderate, or severe should also be noted as well as any applicable specifiers. Partial or full remission should be noted when applicable. Example: bipolar I disorder, current episode manic, moderate severity, with anxious distress. Bipolar **specifiers** include:

- With anxious distress
- With melancholic features
- With peripartum onset
- With seasonal pattern
- With psychotic features
- With catatonia
- With atypical features
- With mixed features
- With rapid cycling

Bipolar II is distinguished from Bipolar I by the fact that the individual has never had either a manic or a mixed episode. Males and females develop Bipolar I disorder equally, but Bipolar II is much more common for females. On average, the age of onset for the first manic episode is the early 20s.

Etiology and Treatment

Among all mental disorders, Bipolar I and II disorders are the most clearly linked to **genetic factors**. Identical twins are overwhelmingly more likely to develop the disease than are fraternal twins. Research suggests a traumatic event may precipitate the first manic episode, although later manic episodes do not need to be preceded by a stressful episode. The most effective treatment for Bipolar I and II is **lithium**. Lithium reduces manic symptoms and eliminates mood swings for more than 50% of individuals. One major problem with lithium is that it works so well, many individuals consider themselves cured and stop taking it, causing a relapse. Pharmacotherapy is most effective when combined with psychotherapy. Individuals who do not respond to lithium treatment are given **anticonvulsants** like carbamazepine or divalproex sodium. Anticonvulsants are also used in lieu of lithium for individuals who have rapid cycling or dysphoric mania.

Bipolar I Disorders

The **criteria** for bipolar I disorder are as follows:

Criteria A	The individual must meet the criteria (listed below) for at least one manic episode. The manic episode is usually either proceeded or followed by an episode of major depression or hypomania.
Criteria B	The episode cannot be explained by schizophrenia spectrum and other psychotic disorders criteria.

The manic episode **criteria** are as follows:

Criteria A	An episode of significantly elevated, demonstrative, or irritable mood. There is significant goal-directed behaviors, activities, and an increase in the amount of energy the individual normally has. These symptoms are present for most of the day and last at least one week.
Criteria B	During the period described in criteria A, the individual will experience 3 of the following symptoms (if the individual presents with only an irritable mood, 4 of the following symptoms need to be present for diagnosis): • Less need for sleep • Excessive talking • Inflated self-esteem • Easily distracted • Flight of ideas • Engages in activities that have negative consequences • Engages in either goal directed activity or purposeless activity
Criteria C	The episode causes significant impairment socially.
Criteria D	The symptoms cannot be attributed to a substance.

Bipolar II Disorders

The **criteria** for bipolar II disorder are as follows:

Criteria A	The individual has had one or more major depressive episodes and one or more hypomanic episodes.
Criteria B	The individual has never experienced a manic episode.
Criteria C	The episode doesn't meet criteria for schizophrenia spectrum or other psychotic disorder.
Criteria D	The depressive episodes or alterations between the two moods cause significant impairment socially or functionally.

A **hypomanic episode** is severe enough to be a clear departure from normal mood and functioning, but not severe enough to cause a marked impairment in functioning, or to require hospitalization. The **criteria** for hypomania are as follows:

Criteria A	An episode of significantly elevated, demonstrative, or irritable mood. There are significant goal-directed behaviors, activities, and an increase in the amount of energy the individual normally has. These symptoms are present for most of the day and last at least 4 days.
Criteria B	During the period described in criteria A, the individual experiences 3 of the following symptoms (if the individual presents with only an irritable mood, 4 of the following symptoms need to be present for diagnosis): • Less need for sleep • Excessive talking • Inflated self-esteem • Easily distracted • Flight of ideas • Engages in activities that have negative consequences • Engages in goal directed activity or purposeless activity
Criteria C	The episode causes a change in the functioning of the individual.
Criteria D	The episode causes changes noticeable by others.
Criteria E	The episode does not cause social impairments.
Criteria F	The symptoms cannot be attributed to a substance.

Cyclothymic Disorder

Cyclothymic disorder is characterized by chronic, fluctuating mood with many hypomanic and depressive symptoms, which are not as severe as either bipolar I or bipolar II. The **criteria** are as follows:

Criteria A	The individual experiences a considerable number of hypomania symptoms without meeting all the criteria for hypomanic episodes and experiences depressive symptoms that do not meet the criteria for major depressive episode for two years or more (can be for one year or more in <18 years of age).
Criteria B	During the above time period, the individual exhibits the symptoms more than half of the time and they are never symptom free for more than two months at a time.
Criteria C	The individual has not met the criteria for manic, hypomanic, or major depressive episodes.
Criteria D	The episode doesn't meet criteria for schizophrenia spectrum or other psychotic disorder.
Criteria E	The symptoms cannot be attributed to a substance.
Criteria F	The episodes cause significant impairment socially or functionally.

Major Depressive Disorder

Major Depressive Episode

The **criteria** for a major depressive episode are as follows:

Criteria A	The individual experiences 5 or more of the following symptoms during 2 consecutive weeks. These symptoms are associated with a change in their normal functioning. (Note: Of the presenting symptoms, either depressed mood or loss of ability to feel pleasure must be included to make this diagnosis.): • Depressed mood • Loss of ability to feel pleasure or have interest in normal activities • Decreased aptitude for thinking • Thoughts of death • Fatigue (daily) • Inappropriate guilt or feelings of worthlessness • Observable motor agitation or psychomotor retardation • Weight loss or gain of more than 5% in one month • Hypersomnia or Insomnia (almost daily)
Criteria B	The episode causes distress or social or functional impairment.
Criteria C	The symptoms cannot be attributed to a substance or another condition or disease.
Criteria D	The episode does not meet the criteria for schizophrenia spectrum or other psychotic disorder.
Criteria E	The individual does not meet criteria for manic episode or a hypomanic episode.

Diagnosis and Gender

Major depressive disorder is diagnosed when an individual has one or more major depressive episodes without having a history of manic, hypomanic, or mixed episodes. There are a few different **specifiers** (categories of associated features) for major depressive disorder issued by the DSM-5:

- With anxious distress
- With melancholic features
- With peripartum onset
- With seasonal pattern
- With psychotic features
- With catatonia
- With atypical features
- With mixed features

Some studies estimate that 20% of women will have symptoms worthy of a diagnosis of major depressive disorder after giving birth.

From the beginning of adolescence on, the rate of major depressive disorder is about twice as great for females as for males. Before adolescence, the rates are about the same. Most major depressive disorders occur in the mid-twenties.

Cognitive-Behavioral Etiologies

Three major cognitive-behavioral etiologies have been offered for major depressive disorder:

- The **learned helplessness model** proposed by Seligman suggests afflicted individuals have been exposed to uncontrollable negative events in the past and have a tendency to attribute negative events to internal, stable, and global factors.
- **Rehm's self-control model** suggests depression occurs in individuals who obsess over negative outcomes, set extremely high standards for themselves, blame all of their problems on internal failures, and have low rates of self-reinforcement coupled with high rates of self-punishment.
- **Beck's cognitive theory** suggests depression is the result of negative and irrational thought and beliefs about the depressive cognitive triad (the self, the world, and the future).

Prognosis and Catecholamine Hypothesis

The severity and duration of a major depressive episode varies from case to case, but symptoms usually last about six months before remission to full function. 20-30% of individuals have lingering symptoms for months or years. About 50% of individuals experience more than one episode of major depression. Oftentimes, multiple episodes are precipitated by some severe psychological trauma. The **catecholamine hypothesis** suggests major depressive episodes are due to a deficiency of the neurotransmitter norepinephrine. The **indolamine hypothesis** proposes that depression is caused by inferior levels of serotonin.

Etiology

Besides the catecholamine and indolamine hypotheses, there are a few other proposed ideas for the etiology of major depressive disorder. Some researchers speculate depression is caused by **hormonal disturbances**, like an increased level of cortisol. Cortisol is one of the stress hormones secreted by the adrenal cortex. Other researchers speculate there is a connection between depression and diminished new cell growth in certain regions of the brain, particularly the subgenual prefrontal cortex and hippocampus. The **subgenual prefrontal cortex** is the part of the brain associated with the formation of positive emotions. Many antidepressant drugs seem to stimulate new growth in the **hippocampus**.

Symptoms

Symptoms of major depressive disorder vary with age. For **children**, common symptoms are:

- Somatic complaints
- Irritability
- Social withdrawal

Male preadolescents often display aggressive and destructive behavior. When **elderly** individuals develop a major depressive disorder, it manifests as memory loss, distractibility, disorientation, and other cognitive problems. Many major depressive episodes are misdiagnosed as major neurocognitive disorder (formerly dementia). It is very common in non-Anglo cultures for the symptoms of depression to be described solely in terms of their somatic content. Latinos, for instance, frequently complain of jitteriness or headaches, while Asians commonly complain of tiredness or weakness.

Treatment

The typical treatment program for major depressive disorder combines antidepressant drugs and psychotherapy. Three classes of **antidepressant medication** are commonly prescribed:

- **Selective serotonin reuptake inhibitors (SSRIs)** are prescribed for melancholic depressives; they have a lower incidence of serious adverse side effects than do tricyclics.
- **Tricyclics (TCAs)**, are prescribed for classic depression, involving vegetative bodily symptoms, a worsening of symptoms in the morning, acute onset, and short duration of moderate symptoms.
- **Monoamine oxidase inhibitors** are prescribed as a last resort for individuals who have an unorthodox depression that includes phobias, panic attacks, increased appetite, hypersomnia, and a mood that worsens as the day goes on.

Review Video: What is Major Depression?
Visit mometrix.com/academy and enter code: 632694

Depressive Disorder with Seasonal Pattern

Depressive disorder with seasonal pattern, formerly called seasonal affective disorder (SAD), is a depressive disorder that afflicts people in the Northern Hemisphere from October to April. Symptoms of this disorder are hypersomnia, increased appetite, weight gain, and an increased desire for carbohydrates. Research suggests this disorder is caused by circadian and seasonal increases in the level of melatonin production by the pineal gland from lack of sunlight. Affected individuals are treated with phototherapy (exposure to full-spectrum white light for several hours each day), aerobic exercise, and SSRIs.

Persistent Depressive Disorder

The **criteria** for persistent depressive disorder are the following:

Criteria A	For at least two years, the individual experiences for most of a day, more days than they don't experience it, a depressed mood.
Criteria B	The individual experiences 2 or more of the following when depressed: • Low self-esteem • Decreased appetite or overeating • A feeling of hopelessness • Fatigue • Difficulty concentrating • Insomnia or hypersomnia
Criteria C	During the episode the individual has not had relief from symptoms for longer than 2 months at once.
Criteria D	The individual may have met the criteria for a major depressive disorder.
Criteria E	The individual does not meet criteria for cyclothymic disorder, manic episode, or hypomanic episode.
Criteria F	The episode does not meet the criteria for schizophrenia spectrum or other psychotic disorder.
Criteria G	The symptoms cannot be attributed to a substance.
Criteria H	The symptoms cause distress or impairment socially or functionally.

Of those with persistent depressive disorder, 25-50% of individuals show sleep EEG abnormalities. Women are 2-3 times more likely to suffer from persistent depressive disorder than men. Around 75% of individuals with persistent depressive disorder develop major depressive disorder within 5 years. First degree relatives are likely to also suffer major depression or persistent depressive disorder. Treatment programs for persistent depressive disorder usually include a combination of **antidepressant drugs** (especially fluoxetine) and either **cognitive-behavioral therapy or interpersonal therapy**.

Review Video: Persistent Depressive Disorder
Visit mometrix.com/academy and enter code: 361077

Suicide Statistics and Correlates

Gender, Race, and Marital Status

Statistics indicate that 4-5 times as many males as females successfully commit **suicide**. However, females attempt suicide about 3 times as often as males. The reason for this disparity is that men tend to employ more violent means of self-destruction, including guns, hanging, and carbon monoxide poisoning. Among racial and ethnic groups, the suicide rate is highest among whites. The exception is **American Indian** and **Alaskan Natives** aged 15-34, for whom suicide is the second leading cause of death. As for **marital status**, the highest rates of suicide are among divorced, separated, or widowed people. The suicide rate for single people trails that of those groups, but it remains higher than the suicide rate for married people.

History, Age, and Drugs of Choice

Suicide is the eighth leading cause of death for **males** in the United States, and sixteenth for **females**. Indicators that a person is at risk for a suicide attempt include:

- Previous suicide attempt in 60-80% of cases
- Warning issued by the prospective suicide in 80% of cases

Drug suicides are the most common (>70% annually). In order of preference, suicides use: Sedatives (especially benzodiazepines), antidepressants, opiates, prescription analgesics, and carbon monoxide from car exhaust. The most likely persona to commit a successful suicide is a male, Caucasian, 45-49 years of age. Women are more likely to be saved from an attempted suicide through treatment at an Emergency Department. The average age of those saved is 15-19. A sharp increase in suicides aged 10-19 may be due to the increased use of antidepressants, which now carry an FDA black box warning. Around 25% of suicide attempts by seniors over age 65 are successful.

Psychiatric Disorders and Biological Correlates

Most of those who commit suicide are suffering from some mental disorder, most commonly **major depressive disorder** or **bipolar disorder**. Suicide associated with depression is most likely to occur within three months after the symptoms of depression have begun to improve. The risk of suicide among adolescents with depression increases greatly if the adolescent also has conduct disorder, ADHD, or is a substance abuser, particularly of inhaled solvents. As for biological correlates, people who commit suicide have been found to have low levels of **serotonin** and **5HIAA** (a serotonin metabolite). Individuals at risk for suicide need immediate psychological intervention and a 24-hour suicide watch.

Cognitive Correlates and Life Stress

Research into suicide has indicated that **hopelessness** is the most common predictor of an inclination to self-destruction. It is a more accurate predictor even than the intensity of depressive symptoms. **Self-assigned or society-assigned perfectionism** has also been blamed for suicide. Many suicides are preceded by some **traumatic life event**, like the end of a romantic relationship or the death of a loved one. For adolescents, the most common precipitant of suicide is an **argument with a parent or rejection by a boyfriend or girlfriend**. Among adolescents, the common warning signs of suicide are talking about death, giving away possessions, and talking about a reunion with a deceased individual.

Factitious Disorder

An individual diagnosed with factitious disorder (FD) intentionally manifests physical or psychological symptoms to satisfy an intrapsychic need to fill the role of a sick person. The individual with FD presents the illness in an exaggerated manner and avoids interrogation that might expose the falsity. These individuals may undergo multiple surgeries and invasive medical procedures. They often hide insurance claims and hospital discharge forms. A disturbing variation of FD is **factitious disorder imposed on another** (sometimes referred to as Munchausen's syndrome by proxy), in which a caregiver intentionally produces symptoms in another individual. Usually, a mother makes her young child ill.

Malingering vs. Factitious Disorder

Malingering is feigning physical symptoms to avoid something specific, like going to work, or to gain a specific reward. Consider malingering as a possibility when:

- A person obtains a medical evaluation for legal reasons or to apply for insurance compensation.
- There is marked inconsistency between the individual's complaint and the objective findings, or if the individual does not cooperate with a diagnostic evaluation or prescribed treatment.
- The individual has an antisocial personality disorder.

Malingering contrasts with factitious disorder because in FD the individual does not feign physical symptoms for personal gain or to avoid an adverse event, but does it with no obvious external rewards.

Dissociative Disorders

Dissociative disorders are a disruption in consciousness, identity, memory, or perception of the environment that is not due to the effects of a substance or a general medical condition. These are all characterized by a disturbance in the normally integrative functions of identity, memory, consciousness, or environmental perception.

Dissociative identity disorder (previously multiple personality disorder)	Two or more personalities exist within one person, with each personality dominant at a particular time.
Dissociative amnesia	Inability to recall important personal data, more than forgetfulness. It is not due to organic causes and comes on suddenly.
Depersonalization/derealization disorder	Feeling detached from one's mental processes or body, as if one is an observer.

Cultural influences can cause or amplify some of the symptoms of dissociative disorders, so take these into account when making a diagnosis. For instance, many religious ceremonies try to foster a dissociative psychological experience; individuals participating in such a ceremony may display symptoms of dissociative disorder without requiring treatment.

Dissociative Amnesia

Individuals may be diagnosed with dissociative amnesia if they have more than one episode in which they are unable to remember important personal information, and this memory loss cannot be attributed to ordinary forgetfulness. The gaps in the individual's memory are likely to be related to a traumatic event. The three most common patterns of dissociative amnesia are:

- **Localized**, in which the individual is unable to remember all events around a defined period
- **Selective**, in which the individual cannot recall some events pertaining to a circumscribed period
- **Generalized**, in which memory loss spans the individual's entire life

It should be specified if this is with dissociative fugue, a subtype of dissociative amnesia, which is a purposeful travel that is associated with amnesia.

Dissociative Fugue and Depersonalization Disorder

A **dissociative fugue** is a subtype of dissociative amnesia and is an abrupt, unexpected, purposeful flight from home, or another stressful location, coupled with an inability to remember the past. The individual is unable to remember his or her identity and assumes a new identity. Fugues are psychological protection against extreme stressors like bankruptcy, divorce, separation, suicidal or homicidal ideation, and rejection. Fugues happen in wars, natural disasters, and severe accidents. Fugues affect 2 in every 1,000 Americans. There will be no recollection of events that occur during the fugue. Individuals in a fugue state may seem normal to strangers. Dissociative fugue is a specifier that can be used with dissociative amnesia.

Depersonalization/derealization disorder is diagnosed when an individual has recurrent episodes in which he or she feels detached from his or her own mental processes or body or to the surroundings. In order to be diagnosed, this condition must be intense enough to cause significant distress or functional impairment.

Sexual Dysfunctions

A sexual dysfunction is any condition in which the sexual response cycle is disturbed or there is pain during sexual intercourse, and this causes distress or interpersonal difficulty. **Types** of sexual dysfunctions:

- Delayed ejaculation
- Erectile disorder
- Female orgasmic disorder
- Female sexual interest/arousal disorder
- Genito-pelvic pain/penetration disorder
- Male hypoactive sexual desire disorder
- Premature ejaculation
- Substance-induced sexual dysfunction

Male erectile disorder is the inability to attain or maintain an erection. This condition is linked to diabetes, liver and kidney disease, multiple sclerosis, and the use of antipsychotic, antidepressant, and hypertensive drugs. **Orgasmic disorders** are any delay or absence of orgasm after the normal sexual excitement phase. Premature ejaculation is orgasm that occurs with a minimum of stimulation and before the person desires it. Premature ejaculation may be in part due to deficiencies in serotonin.

Physical and Psychological Components and Treatments

Any individual with sexual dysfunction should be given a medical evaluation for diabetes, pelvic scars, kidney disease, hypertension, and drug interactions. Use sleep studies to determine if an impotent male gets an erection at night, and determine whether the cause of impotence is physical or psychological. **Psychological impotence** can be treated with cognitive-behavioral therapy. Sex therapy is most helpful in treating premature ejaculation. Sensate focus is used to reduce performance anxiety and increase sexual excitement. Kegel exercises, which strengthen the pubococcygeus muscle, can improve sexual pleasure. As for pharmacotherapy, Viagra is helpful in attaining and maintaining erections.

Genito-Pelvic Pain/Penetration Disorder and Categories of Sexual Dysfunctions

Genito-pelvic pain/penetration disorder is persistent difficulty with genital pain associated with sexual intercourse or involuntary spasms in the pubococcygeus muscle in the vagina, which make it difficult to have sexual intercourse, or fear or anxiety related to anticipation of pain during intercourse. Sexual dysfunctions are categorized as lifelong or acquired, and generalized or situational, depending on their cause. **Generalized dysfunctions** occur with every sexual partner in all circumstances. **Situational dysfunctions** only occur under certain circumstances. The cause may be psychological, physical, or both.

Paraphilic Disorders

Paraphilic disorders are intense, recurrent sexual urges or behaviors involving either nonhuman objects, non-consenting partners (including children), or the suffering or humiliation of oneself or one's partner. **Common paraphilias** include:

- Fetishistic disorder
- Transvestic disorder
- Pedophilic disorder
- Exhibitionistic disorder
- Voyeuristic disorder
- Sexual masochism disorder
- Sexual sadism disorder
- Frotteuristic disorder (rubbing against a non-consenting person)

The most common **treatment** for paraphilia was previously in vivo aversion therapy, but now it is more common for treatment to include covert sensitization, in which the imagination is given aversion therapy. The medication Depo-Provera has been found to relieve paraphiliac symptoms for many men, although this relief ceases as soon as the man stops taking the drug.

Gender Dysphoria

DSM-5 defines gender dysphoria (formerly gender identity disorder) as a marked incongruence between one's expressed gender and assigned gender that causes significant distress or impairment over a period of at least 6 months. Informally, gender dysphoria is used to describe a person's persistent discomfort and disagreement with their assigned gender. DSM-5 criteria for diagnosis in **children** include:

- Strong desire to be of the other gender or insistence that one is the other gender
- Strong preference for clothing typically associated with the other gender
- Strong preference for playing cross-gender roles
- Strong preference for activities stereotypical of the other gender and rejection of those activities stereotypical of one's assigned gender
- Strong preference for playmates of the other gender
- Strong dislike of one's own sexual anatomy
- Strong desire for the sex characteristics that match one's expressed gender

DSM-5 criteria for diagnosis in **adolescents and adults** include:

- Marked incongruence between expressed gender and one's existing primary and secondary sex characteristics
- Strong desire to rid oneself of these sex characteristics for this reason
- Strong desire for the sex characteristics of the other gender
- Strong desire to be of the other gender and to be treated as such
- Strong conviction that one's feelings and reactions are typical of the other gender

Sleep-Wake Disorders

Sleep-wake disorders include the following:

Insomnia disorders	Difficulty falling asleep, staying asleep, or early rising without being able to go back to sleep.
Hypersomnolence disorder	Sleepiness despite getting at least 7 hours with difficulty feeling awake when suddenly awoke, lapses of sleep in the day, feeling unrested after long periods of sleep.
Narcolepsy	Uncontrollable lapses into sleep, occurring at least three times each week for at least 3 months.
Obstructive sleep apnea hypopnea	Breathing related sleep disorder with obstructive apneas or hypopneas.
Central sleep apnea	Breathing related sleep disorder with central apnea.
Sleep-related hypoventilation	Breathing related sleep disorder with evidence of decreased respiratory rate and increased CO_2 level.
Circadian rhythm sleep-wake disorder	Sleep wake disorder caused by a mismatch between the circadian rhythm and sleep required by person.
Non-rapid eye movement sleep arousal disorder	Awakening during the first third of the night associated with sleep walking or sleep terrors.
Nightmare disorder	Recurring distressing dreams that are well remembered and cause distress.
Rapid eye movement sleep behavior disorder	Arousal during REM sleep associated with motor movements and vocalizing.
Restless legs syndrome	The need to move legs due to uncomfortable sensations, usually relieved by activity.

Review Video: Chronic Insomnia
Visit mometrix.com/academy and enter code: 293232

Review Video: Sedative and Hypnotic Drugs
Visit mometrix.com/academy and enter code: 666132

Adjustment Disorders

Adjustment disorders appear as maladaptive reactions to one or more identifiable psychosocial stressors. In order to make the diagnosis, the onset of symptoms must be within three months of the stressor, and the condition must cause impairments in social, occupational, or academic performance. The symptoms do not align with normal grief or bereavement. Symptoms remit within six months after the termination of the stressor or its consequences. The adjustment disorder should be specified with at least one of the following:

- Depressed mood
- Anxiety
- Mixed anxiety and depressed mood
- Disturbance of conduct
- Mixed disturbance of emotions and conduct

Personality Disorders

Personality disorders occur when an individual has developed personality traits so maladaptive and entrenched that they cause personal distress or interfere significantly with functioning.

The DSM-5 lists five **traits** involved in personality disorders:

- Neuroticism
- Extraversion/introversion
- Openness to experience
- Agreeableness/antagonism
- Conscientiousness

The following are the **criteria** for personality disorders:

Criteria A	Long-term pattern of maladaptive personality traits and behaviors that do not align with the individual's culture. These traits and behaviors will be found in at least two areas: • Impulse control • Inappropriate emotional intensity or responses • Inappropriately interpreting people, events, and self • Inappropriate social functioning
Criteria B	The traits and behaviors are inflexible and exist despite changing social situations.
Criteria C	The traits and behaviors cause distress and impair functioning.
Criteria D	Onset was adolescence or early adulthood and has been enduring.
Criteria E	The behaviors and traits are not due to another mental disorder.
Criteria F	The behaviors and traits are not due to a substance.

Cluster A, B, and C Personality Disorders

Personality disorders are **clustered** into three groups:

Cluster A (eccentric or odd disorders)	**Cluster B** (dramatic or excessively emotional disorders)	**Cluster C** (fear- or anxiety-based disorders)
Paranoid	Antisocial	Avoidant
Schizoid	Borderline	Dependent
Schizotypal	Histrionic	Obsessive-Compulsive
	Narcissistic	

Paranoid Personality Disorder

Paranoid personality disorder is a pervasive pattern of distrust and suspiciousness that involves believing the actions and thoughts of other people to be directed antagonistically against oneself. In order to make the diagnosis, the individual must have at least four of the following **symptoms**:

- Suspects that others are somehow harming him or her
- Doubts the trustworthiness of others
- Reluctant to confide in others
- Suspicious without justification about fidelity of one's partner
- Reads hidden meaning into remarks or events
- Consistently has grudges
- Believes there are attacks on his or her character that others present do not perceive

Schizoid Personality Disorder

Schizoid personality disorder is characterized by a pervasive lack of interest in relationships with others and limited range of emotional expression in contacts with others. Four of these **symptoms** must be present:

- Avoidance of or displeasure in close relationships
- Always chooses solitude
- Little interest in sexual relationships
- Takes pleasure in few activities
- Indifference to praise or criticism
- Emotional coldness or detachment
- Lacks close friends except first-degree relatives

Schizotypal Personality Disorder

Schizotypal personality disorder is characterized by pervasive social deficits, oddities of cognition, perception, or behavior. Diagnosis requires five of the following:

- Ideas of reference
- Odd beliefs or magical thinking
- Lack of close friends except first-degree relatives
- Bodily illusions
- Suspiciousness
- Social anxiety (excessive)
- Inappropriate or constricted affect
- Peculiarities in behavior or appearance

Antisocial Personality Disorder

Antisocial personality disorder is a general lack of concern for the rights and feelings of others. In order to receive a diagnosis of antisocial personality disorder, the individual must:

- Be at least 18
- Have had a history of conduct disorder before age 15
- Have shown *at least three* of the following symptoms before the age of 15:
  - Failure to conform to social laws and norms
  - Deceitfulness
  - Impulsivity
  - Reckless disregard for the safety of self and others
  - Consistent irresponsibility
  - Lack of remorse
  - Irritability or aggressiveness

Antisocial personality disorder may also include an inflated opinion of self, superficial charm, and a lack of empathy for others.

Borderline Personality Disorder

Borderline personality disorder is a pervasive pattern of instability in social relationships, self-image, and affect, coupled with marked impulsivity. A diagnosis of borderline personality disorder requires five of the following **symptoms**:

- Frantic efforts to avoid being abandoned
- A pattern of unstable and intense personal relationships, in which there is alternation between idealization and devaluation
- Instability of self-image
- Potentially self-destructive impulsivity in at least two areas
- Recurrent suicide threats or gestures
- Affective instability
- Chronic feelings of emptiness
- Inappropriate anger
- Paranoid ideation or dissociative symptoms

The changes in self-identity may manifest as shifts in career goals and sexual identity; impulsivity may manifest as unsafe sex, reckless driving practices, and substance abuse.

Borderline personality disorder is most common in people between the ages of 19 and 34. Most individuals see substantial improvement over a period of 15 years. Impulsive symptoms are the first to recede.

Review Video: Borderline Personality Disorder
Visit mometrix.com/academy and enter code: 550801

Dialectical behavior therapy (DBT) is often used to treat borderline personality disorder; it combines cognitive-behavioral therapy with the assumption of Rogers that the individual must accept his or her problem before any progress can be made. There are three basic strategies associated with dialectical behavior therapy:

- Group skills training
- Individual outpatient therapy
- Telephone consultations

Regular DBT has reduced the number of suicides and violent acts committed by individuals with borderline personality disorder.

Histrionic Personality Disorder

Histrionic personality disorder is excessive emotionality and attention-seeking behavior. Five **symptoms** from the following list must be present:

- Annoyance or discomfort when not receiving attention
- Inappropriate sexual provocation
- Rapidly shifting and shallow emotions
- Vague and impressionistic speech
- Exaggerated expression of emotion
- Easily influenced by others
- Believes relationships are more intimate than they actually are
- Uses physical appearance to draw attention to self

Narcissistic Personality Disorder

Narcissistic personality disorder is grandiose behavior along with a lack of empathy and a need for admiration. The individual must exhibit five of these **symptoms** for diagnosis:

- Grandiose sense of self-importance
- Fantasies of own power and beauty
- Belief in personal uniqueness
- Need for excessive admiration
- Sense of entitlement
- Exploitation of others
- Lack of empathy
- Envious of others or believes other envy him or her
- Arrogant behaviors

Avoidant Personality Disorder

Avoidant personality disorder is a pervasive pattern of social inhibition, feelings of inadequacy, and hypersensitivity to negative evaluation. A person with avoidant personality disorder exhibits at least four of these **symptoms**:

- Avoiding work or school activities that involve interpersonal contact
- Unwillingness to associate with any person who may withhold approval
- Preoccupation with concerns about being criticized or rejected
- Conception of self as socially inept, inferior, or unappealing to others
- General reluctance to take personal risks or engage in dangerous behavior
- Does not reveal self in intimate relationships, due to fear of shame
- Not able to excel in new situations due to fear of inadequacy

Dependent Personality Disorder

Dependent personality disorder is excessive reliance on others. A diagnosis of dependent personality disorder requires five of these **symptoms**:

- Difficulty making decisions without advice
- Need for others to assume responsibility for one's actions
- Fear of disagreeing with others
- Difficulty self-initiating projects
- Feelings of helplessness or discomfort when alone
- Goes to great lengths to get support from others
- Seeks new relationships when an old one ends
- Preoccupied with the thought of having to care for self

Obsessive-Compulsive Personality Disorder

Obsessive-compulsive personality disorder is a persistent preoccupation with organization and mental or interpersonal control. Four of these **symptoms** are required for the diagnosis of obsessive-compulsive personality disorder:

- Preoccupation with rules and details
- Perfectionism that interferes with progress
- Excessive devotion to work
- Counterproductive rigidity about beliefs and morality
- Inability to throw away old objects
- Reluctance to delegate authority to others
- Rigid or stubborn
- Hoards money without spending

Behavioral Pediatrics

Disclosure

Behavioral pediatrics, otherwise known as pediatric psychology, has become a more popular field because research revealed that many psychological disorders originate in childhood. For the most part, a pediatric mental health provider should be open with the child about his or her condition. Children may need some psychological help if they are to undergo any major medical procedures. Providers must relay any information related to the mental or medical condition in language the child can understand. **Multicomponent cognitive-behavioral interventions**, in which the child is given information about his or her condition and armed with some coping strategies, are especially helpful.

Hospitalization, Compliance, and School Adjustment

Children who need to be **hospitalized** for a significant period of time are especially at risk of developing psychological problems, in large part because they have been separated from their families. Children and adolescents are generally less **compliant** with medical regimens. This may be because of poor communication, parent-child problems, or a general lack of skill. For adolescents, peer pressure and the desire for social acceptance may motivate noncompliance with potentially embarrassing medical programs. Children with serious medical conditions are more likely to have trouble **adjusting to school**. Problems may be caused by the illness itself, by the frequent absences it necessitates, or by the social stigma of illness. Some treatments, like chemotherapy, are associated with deficits in neurocognitive functioning and greater risk of learning disabilities.

Substance Abuse

History of Substance Use and Abuse in the United States

Scope of Addictions Associated with Drug and Alcohol Use

According to the National Institute of Alcohol Abuse and Alcoholism, 85.6% of Americans reported drinking alcohol at some point in their life, almost 70% reporting that they drank in the last year (2019). Around 50% of Americans drink **alcohol** as part of their daily routine; 10% of these routine drinkers will fall into addictive, habitual use. Statistics show that approximately 2% of the American population is addicted to **illegal drugs**, despite the *Harrison Narcotic Act of 1914,* the first legislation to ban the use of illegal drugs. Emergency rooms have exponentially increased their caseloads of patients who are drug abusers that accidentally overdose, take poisonous drug substitutes, or try to commit suicide. ER caseloads of drug casualties have also increased to include date-rape victims, drug mules whose ingested containers of smuggled drugs broke, drunk or impaired driving victims, and children who are accidentally poisoned by eating their parents' stash or absorbing toxins from growing operations. Alcohol and drugs are linked to thefts and domestic violence. Children who observe their intoxicated parents may come to accept addiction and suffer similar problems later in life.

Review Video: Addictions
Visit mometrix.com/academy and enter code: 460412

Evolution of Drug Use in the US from 1960's to Present

In the 1960's, recreational drug use became more widespread in the US, and Americans turned to drugs like **marijuana, hallucinogens**, and **LSD**, which became more accessible at this time. Society witnessed the use of drugs first on college campuses, then in high schools, in the workplace, and even within the military. Vietnam War veterans returned with addictions to heroin. By the 1980's, cocaine use mushroomed to include much of middle-class America. Texas and New York gave convicted criminals a life sentence for possession of marijuana. Hardcore drugs like heroin are still popular. However, designer drugs like China White, Ecstasy, Cat, Aminorex, and gamma-Butyrolactone are more prevalent than heroin now because they are very cheap to produce but can be sold at an astronomical profit. Currently in the US, the most common **drugs of abuse** are amphetamines, cocaine, codeine, heroin, and other opioids (morphine, hydromorphone, fentanyl, and methadone), hypnotics (meprobamate, methaqualone), PCP, sedatives (barbiturates and benzodiazepine), and THC.

Historical Cocaine Use in the US

The first recorded use of **cocaine** was as a medicinal tea in 1596 by the Spaniards. France exported cocaine-laced wine to the US in 1863. Surgeons and psychiatrists touted cocaine as a cure-all and anesthetic in the 1880's. John Stith Pemberton patented Coca-Cola in 1886 as a commercial tonic for the elderly and debilitated. Many over-the-counter products contained cocaine until the *Harrison Narcotic Act of 1914* limited it for medical use only. *1970's Controlled Substances Act* also prohibited cocaine manufacturing, production, and distribution except for medical use as a Schedule II drug.

Prohibition

Temperance and religious groups tried to stop the sale, manufacturing, transportation, and distribution of alcoholic drinks during **prohibition** from 1920-1933 through the 18th Constitutional Amendment of 1919. Crime syndicates flourished. In 1933, the 21st Amendment was passed to repeal the 18th Amendment. This was the only time in America's history that an amendment was rescinded.

Theoretical Approaches to Addiction

Object-Relations Theory

The object-relations theory holds that the alcoholic or drug addict is trying to deal with negative feelings about failed relationships. Resulting from these failures, the addict may experience depression, anxiety, anger, aggression, insularity, negativity, atypicality, and/or post-traumatic stress disorder (PTSD). Victims of child sexual abuse (CSA), neglect, or physical abuse as a child often turn to alcohol or drugs to deal with the memories of abuse that were suppressed as a survival mechanism and festered untreated in the person's mind. The addict may also have residual physical damage, such as improper development from malnutrition that leads to poor academic and intellectual functioning. The addict tries to assuage the pain with a chemical that blunts it temporarily. Alcohol, legally prescribed drugs, toxic herbs, or street drugs are methods of self-medication to decrease the pain by obscuring memories and altering consciousness.

Psychoanalytic Model of Addiction

The psychoanalytic model of addiction states the use of alcohol or drugs is the way a person has chosen to cope with anxiety or unconscious conflicts within his or her mind. The psychoanalytic model is directly related to the work of Sigmund Freud, who coined the term id to describe instinctual urgings. He believed that id instincts are seen in the libido and in aggressive acts. The superego tries to control the instinctive urges of the id. This is where internal conflict develops and is displayed in the ego, which exhibits states of anxiety. Defense mechanisms take the form of denial, projection, or redirecting the unacceptable impulses. Conflicted people use drugs and alcohol to disguise emotions that are too painful to confront. Addiction is a form of self-medication.

Review Video: Psychoanalytic Approach
Visit mometrix.com/academy and enter code: 162594

Social Learning Theory and Addiction

In 1977, Albert Bandura developed the social learning theory to describe the relationship of a person to his or her environment. Bandura theorized that people learn from watching other people. He believed people self-regulate and manage their behaviors based on their established principles and inner values (standards). Inner values are not influenced unduly by external rewards or retributions. An inner value that does not oppose drinking to excess contributes to a person's alcoholic behavior. An inner value that opposes drinking to excess means the person has a restrictive view of drinking and will self-regulate by stopping before he or she is intoxicated. The person who experiences a distinct difference between values and behaviors finds it necessary to change one or the other so that the values win out over the undesired behavior. This leads to a change of behavior that befits the person's set of values.

Classical Conditioning and Operant Conditioning Theory Models

Classical conditioning theory was developed by Russian Ivan Pavlov in the 1890's. Pavlov's experiments were based on the reflexive reactions of dogs that had been conditioned to salivate (the conditioned response) at the sound of a bell (the conditioned stimulus) that meant they would be fed soon. Addicts have a conditioned response associated with circumstances where drugs or alcohol were used. The conditioned response can be psychological (craving the drug or alcohol), or physical. The circumstance or environment is the conditioned stimulus.

Operant conditioning was developed by American B.F. Skinner in the 1930's using rats and pigeons. It describes responses of the conditioned individual to negative or positive reinforcers. Negative reinforcers are the addict's withdrawal signs and symptoms. The positive reinforcer is relieving the withdrawal symptoms by taking the drug or alcohol. Addictive behaviors can be switched off by removing the reinforcers.

Disease Model of Alcoholism

The disease model is accepted by self-help organizations such as Alcoholics Anonymous (AA). The **disease model** contends that alcoholism is chronic (an unremitting, gradual disease that becomes more severe over time) and requires treatment. Alcoholism likely has a genetic root. Persons predisposed to the disease of alcoholism have genetic markers for lowered levels of platelet MAO activity, serotonin function, prolactin, adenylate cyclase, and ALDH2. Other theorists believe alcoholism is a learned behavior, rather than genetic. Research in this area is inconclusive. In 1956, E. M. Jellinek endorsed the American Medical Association's adoption of alcoholism as a disease. He described alcoholism as an infirmity with four stages of progression: Pre-alcoholic, prodromal, crucial, and chronic. Jellinek believed that alcoholics suffered from chemical dependencies that became relentless cravings for alcohol.

Stages of Progression in Drug and Alcohol Use

Not everyone who has used drugs or alcohol has a problem with addiction. The counselor must determine if the client has a pathological addiction or just engages in experimental use. The first step is to grade the client on the continuum of drug use, based on a five-stage progression.

Stage 1: Abstinence	The client who is abstinent or involved in self-denial of use. Abstinence may allow for an occasional glass of wine. However, the person who chooses this route probably was heavily addicted to alcohol in the past, and completely abstains now to keep from falling back into old, addictive ways. Twelve step programs like AA and Narcotics Anonymous advocate complete abstinence. Self-help groups like these are complementary reinforcement for formal therapy because meetings are held daily in most metropolitan areas, and peer pressure can prevent a relapse. The therapeutic role in cases of past addictions is to help them stay "on the wagon" of abstinence. Even one drink can be detrimental to an alcoholic because it can trigger a drinking binge.
Stage 2: Experimental Use	Teens and young adults partake of a chemical to find out what it feels like. It is an expected rite of passage for many segments of our culture. Problems with experimentation include drunk driving and date rape. GHB is dissolved in alcohol at raves because it enhances the libido and lowers inhibitions. Victims enter a dream state and act drunk. They relax, sometimes to the point of unconsciousness, have problems seeing clearly, are confused, and have no recall of events or the passage of time while drugged.
Stage 3: Social Use	The test to determine if a person is a social user or addicted is whether or not the person can stop drug use. For example, a social drinker can drink a controlled amount and doesn't need it to function as a normal human being. But if a person needs alcohol or a drug to satisfy cravings, prevent unpleasant withdrawal symptoms, or as a means of coping with daily life, then it is considered an addiction. Counseling involves an educational group to develop coping skills and relationship skills with peers.

Stage 4: Abuse	The client's problem can be physiological or psychological in nature, or both. The addiction is detrimental to personal safety, family relationships, academic life, and work functions. Spousal and child abuse often coincide with drug abuse. Drunk driving and theft to support a habit are societal problems resulting from addictive behavior. Friends and associates are probably uncomfortable around the abuser by the time the addiction is visibly evident. At this point, the employer can insist the abuser get help on a professional level through employee assistance or public programs as a condition of continued employment. Abusers benefit from psychological counseling on a weekly basis and an intervention program to stop the alcohol or drug abuse. Antabuse (disulfiram), methadone, levo-alpha-acetylmethadol (LAAM), buprenorphine, and naltrexone are useful adjuncts to counseling to wean the abuser off the drug. Intensive outpatient programs may be sufficient for recovery.
Stage 5: Chemical Dependency	The addict experiences withdrawal symptoms when the drug or alcohol is not available for consumption. The addict builds up a tolerance to the drug to the point that more and more is needed just to keep from experiencing physical withdrawal. The high is harder and harder to reach. The addict is now at increased risk for unintentional overdose, because street drugs have inconsistent strengths. The addict is also on the verge of failing in marriage, academics, and work. The addict experiences serious medical issues like ventricular tachycardia and atrial fibrillation, and more powerful drugs like clonidine (Catapres patches or tablets) are used to prevent death. Permanent damage from Korsakoff's syndrome or Wernicke's encephalopathy may result from a poor diet lacking in vitamins. Long-term, inpatient rehabilitation programs are crucial in most cases. Intensive outpatient programs may be sufficient for a minority.

SCREENING AND ASSESSMENT

QUESTIONS ASKED IN A CLINICAL INTERVIEW

12 questions to ask a client in a clinical interview as a means of screening for drug/alcohol abuse include the following:

- **Question 1**: Find out the client's motivation for getting a mental health referral.
- **Question 2**: Obtain historical background about the beginning and severity of the client's drug and alcohol use. Discuss changes or deterioration in the client's behavior from the alcohol and drug use.
- **Question 3**: Determine the longest length of time that the client has stayed sober. Delve into the reasons why this period of sobriety ended.
- **Question 4**: Ask about the intoxication level that the client reaches when drinking or using drugs. Are there blackouts? Violent incidents? Is it harder to get a high now than when the client first started using drugs?
- **Question 5**: Find out the arrest record of the client. Pay particular attention to impaired driving (DUI) and domestic violence charges resulting from chemical abuse.
- **Question 6**: Find out about military service where drug or alcohol use was part of the client's service time.
- **Question 7**: Discuss addictive cycles of abuse found in the client's family. Note psychological disorders in family members and dysfunctional family relationships.
- **Question 8**: Find out the psychiatric history of the client.

- **Question 9**: Ask the client about his or her educational and work experience, including any drug or alcohol activities at school or in the workplace.
- **Question 10**: Get the medical and substance use history of the client. Note chronic pain treated with OxyContin or other pain relievers, which subsequently led to addiction.
- **Question 11**: Ask about prior drug and alcohol abuse treatment programs in which the client participated. Is the client a recidivist? If so, use a different treatment technique.
- **Question 12**: Discuss drug and/or alcohol levels revealed by the client's latest toxicology screen.

The answers gleaned in the clinical interview should correspond with other data collected from various sources. If there is a discrepancy, determine the truth of the situation.

MAST AND DAST ASSESSMENT TOOLS

The **Michigan Alcohol Screening Test (MAST)** was developed in 1971. The original assessment consisted of 25 yes or no questions with a complex grading system in which each question carried different weight when scoring. In the most recently revised version of this screening tool, the client must answer yes or no to 22 questions, which are then scored with a 0 or 1 based on the answer. Clients who score 0-2 have no alcohol problem. Clients who score 3-5 are early to middle problem drinkers. Clients who score 6 or more are problem drinkers. This test is accurate with a 0.05 level of confidence, according to the National Council on Alcoholism and Drug Dependence. Some research indicates that the 6-point cut-off for labeling an alcoholic should be raised to 10 points.

The **Drug Abuse Screening Test (DAST)** is the non-alcoholic counterpart to the MAST. If either the MAST or DAST is positive for addiction, then use the **Addiction Severity Index (ASI)** to determine in what areas the drug use has been the most invasive. The areas assessed include medical, legal, familial, social, employment, psychological, and psychiatric. The ASI test is longer, covering 180 items.

SASSI

The **Substance Abuse Subtle Screening Inventory (SASSI-4)** was first developed in 1988 to help identify covert abusers. Multiple revisions have occurred since. Typically, abusers hide their drug problems with lies, subterfuge, and defensive responses because they are:

- Unwilling to accept responsibility
- Hesitant to confront bad feelings and pain
- Afraid of the consequences (incarceration or rehabilitation programs)
- Conflicted (have mixed feelings) about quitting use of the chemical

The counselor uses the SASSI-4 to determine the truth, produce profiles useful for treatment planning, and understand the client. It can be administered as a one-page paper and pencil test, a computerized test with automated scoring, or an audio tape test. SASSI-4 takes 15 minutes to complete and 5 minutes to score. The adult version has an overall accuracy of 93%. The Adolescent SASSI-A3 has an overall accuracy of 94%. They both contain face-valid and subtle items, which do not tackle drug abuse in a directly apparent way.

TREATMENT

SUBSTANCE USE TREATMENT PROGRAMS

Substance abusers do best when they abstain from drug and alcohol use entirely during their **treatment**. Relapses in the client's use interfere with treatment. Try not to conduct a session with an intoxicated client. Encourage the client to reschedule his or her session should intoxication be suspected. Make travel arrangements to ensure the client does not operate a vehicle on the way home while in an intoxicated state. Encourage the client to stay out of old hangouts where alcohol or drugs were used, and to discard drug paraphernalia and t-shirts associated with drugs or alcohol because they can evoke a conditioned response. Teach clients relaxation and imagery exercises to help them curb their urges and anxiety. Use operant conditioning to help clients tone down euphoric memories. Clients need reminders of negative consequences of addiction such as divorce, arrest, hangover, loss of income, or loss of health.

Methadone Therapy for Opiate Addiction

Methadone, an opioid itself, is used as pharmacotherapy to treat opioid use disorder, most commonly in the case of heroin addiction. Because it acts as an opioid agonist, it binds to the same mu-receptors as heroin (and other narcotics), but has less dangerous side-effects and can be administered orally, essentially eliminating the risks associated with intravenous opioid administration commonly experienced by opioid abusers. Methadone is commonly prescribed to help individuals addicted to opiates through their initial withdrawal from the addictive substance, and then the dose is tapered to help the individual achieve a drug-free state. In addition to preventing withdrawal symptoms, methadone also decreases cravings for opioids and mutes the high that was achieved by the addictive substance by building the individual's tolerance to opioids. Methadone therapy has proven particularly helpful in treating pregnant women with opioid addiction due to its ability to prevent cravings while having a less damaging impact on the fetus. It also helps the mother attain a more sober state, which facilitates healthier decision-making and a higher likelihood of participation in recommended prenatal care.

Methadone therapy may only be prescribed by a physician who has been specifically approved by the FDA to prescribe methadone treatments. While it is outside of the scope of the counselor to prescribe methadone therapy, the counselor must be aware of the possibility that a client with opioid use disorder is on methadone therapy, or be prepared to refer clients with opioid addiction to a physician that may be able to oversee this therapy if it is indicated.

Alcoholics Anonymous

Alcoholics Anonymous (AA) is a 12-step self-help program that relies on comradery and accountability, with many locations throughout the United States. Meetings are held in church halls, libraries, and clubs. AA should be offered along with appropriate counseling by a therapist, because the meetings are not considered psychological therapy. The benefit of an AA meeting to the client is the reinforcement of the coping skills taught in counseling sessions and access to a peer group that is supportive. The group provides a sponsor (usually of the same sex) to help the client have a role model who has enjoyed a long period of sobriety. The alcoholic develops a more positive outlook of the self and a sense of unity with the group, so feelings of isolation are removed. The client gains a sense of hope about his or her future and comes to recognize that the substance use is out of control. Alcoholics are encouraged to seek God or a higher power of authority for outside help.

AA Relapse Prevention Card and Other Coping Strategies

The alcoholic participating in AA carries an AA relapse prevention card. The client is given this card to help him or her find alternative activities that do not include drugs or alcohol. The card contains instructions to communicate his or her feelings to a trusted AA member and phone numbers for the sponsor and the client's spouse or parents. The card may also instruct the client in relaxation techniques or imagery to get through the cravings. A client may find it beneficial to write down his or her feelings in a journal and bring it to the counseling sessions. Teach the client assertiveness techniques to stand up to his or her AA peers if they make inappropriate suggestions.

Strategies to Prevent Relapse

Strategies to prevent relapse include the following:

- Clients find it beneficial to get a reward when they have abstained from drugs or alcohol successfully, as a positive reinforcement. This strategy is known as a **contingency management or contractual agreement**. The reward should be one that the client wants, otherwise it will be an ineffective reward.
- **Cognitive therapy** is marked by replacing negative thought patterns with positive self-talk. Thought patterns that are automatically negative may trigger the client to relapse. When negative thought patterns happen, the client should replace them with a more functional action. Some techniques for reducing negative self-talk include free association, dream interpretation, and memory techniques. The client may rely on drugs to replace relationships.
- A new approach, called **motivational enhancement therapy**, uses role playing to teach the client how to communicate goals and feelings.

Indicators of Substance Abuse

General Indicators of Substance Abuse

Many people with substance abuse (alcohol or drugs) are reluctant to disclose this information, but there are a number of indicators that are suggestive of substance abuse:

Physical signs include:

- Burns on fingers or lips
- Pupils abnormally dilated or constricted; eyes watery
- Slurring of speech or slow speech
- Lack of coordination, instability of gait, or tremors
- Sniffing repeatedly, nasal irritation, persistent cough
- Weight loss
- Dysrhythmias
- Pallor, puffiness of face
- Needle tracks on arms or legs

Behavioral signs include:

- Odor of alcohol or marijuana on clothing or breath
- Labile emotions, including mood swings, agitation, and anger
- Inappropriate, impulsive, or risky behavior
- Missing appointments
- Difficulty concentrating, short term memory loss, blackouts
- Insomnia or excessive sleeping
- Disorientation or confusion
- Lack of personal hygiene

Alcohol

Alcohol is described as follows:

- A liquid distilled product of fermented fruits, grains, and vegetables
- Can be used as a solvent, an antiseptic, and a sedative
- Has a high potential for abuse
- Small-to-moderate amounts taken over extended periods of time may have positive effects on health

Possible Effects of Alcohol

The following are **possible effects of alcohol use**:

- Intoxication
- Sensory alteration
- Reduction in anxiety

PARTICULAR CHALLENGES OF DIAGNOSIS AND TREATMENT OF ALCOHOL ABUSE

Challenges in **diagnostics and treatment of alcohol abuse** include the following:

- Alcohol is the most available and widely used substance.
- Progression of alcohol dependence often occurs over an extended period of time, unlike some other substances whose progression can be quite rapid. Because of this slow progression, individuals can deny their dependence and hide it from employers for long periods.
- Most alcohol-dependent individuals have gainful employment, live with families, and are given little attention until their dependence crosses a threshold, at which time the individual fails in their familial, social, or employment roles.
- Misuse of alcohol represents a difficult diagnostic problem as it is a legal substance. Clients, their families, and even clinicians can claim that the client's alcohol use is normative.
- After friends, family members, or employers tire of maintaining the fiction that the individual's alcohol use is normative, the individual will be more motivated to begin the process of accepting treatment.

ALCOHOL USE ASSESSMENT TOOLS

The **CAGE tool** is used as a quick assessment to identify problem drinkers. Moderate drinking, (1-2 drinks daily or one drink a day for older adults) is usually not harmful to people in the absence of other medical conditions. However, drinking more can lead to serious psychosocial and physical problems. One drink is defined as 12 ounces of beer/wine cooler, 5 ounces of wine, or 1.5 ounces of liquor.

- **C** – *Cutting down*: "Do you think about trying to cut down on drinking?"
- **A** – *Annoyed at criticism*: Are people starting to criticize your drinking?
- **G** – *Guilty feeling*: "Do you feel guilty or try to hide your drinking?"
- **E** – *Eye opener*: "Do you increasingly need a drink earlier in the day?

"Yes" on one question suggests the possibility of a drinking problem. "Yes" on ≥2 indicates a drinking problem.

The **Clinical Instrument for Withdrawal for Alcohol (CIWA)** is a tool used to assess the severity of alcohol withdrawal. Each category is scored 0-7 points based on the severity of symptoms, except #10, which is scored 0-4. A score <5 indicates mild withdrawal without need for medications; for scores ranging 5-15, benzodiazepines are indicated to manage symptoms. A score >15 indicates severe withdrawal and the need for admission to the unit.

1. Nausea/Vomiting
2. Tremor
3. Paroxysmal Sweats
4. Anxiety
5. Agitation
6. Tactile Disturbances
7. Auditory Disturbances
8. Visual Disturbances
9. Headache
10. Disorientation or Clouding of Sensorium

Alcohol Overdose

Symptoms of alcohol overdose include the following:

- Staggering
- Odor of alcohol on breath
- Loss of coordination
- Dilated pupils
- Slurred speech
- Coma
- Respiratory failure
- Nerve damage
- Liver damage
- Fetal alcohol syndrome (in babies born to alcohol abusers)

Alcohol Withdrawal and Treatment

Chronic abuse of ethanol (alcoholism) can lead to physical dependency. Sudden cessation of drinking, which often happens in the inpatient setting, is associated with **alcohol withdrawal syndrome**. It may be precipitated by trauma or infection and has a high mortality rate, 5-15% with treatment and 35% without treatment.

Signs and symptoms: Anxiety, tachycardia, headache, diaphoresis, progressing to severe agitation, hallucinations, auditory/tactile disturbances, and psychotic behavior (delirium tremens).

Diagnosis: Physical assessment, blood alcohol levels (on admission).

Treatment includes:

- **Medication**: IV benzodiazepines to manage symptoms; electrolyte and nutritional replacement, especially magnesium and thiamine.
- Use the **CIWA scale** to measure symptoms of withdrawal; treat as indicated.
- Provide an **environment** with minimal sensory stimulus (lower lights, close blinds) and implement fall and seizure precautions.
- **Prevention**: Screen all clients for alcohol/substance abuse, using CAGE or other assessment tool. Remember to express support and comfort to client; wait until withdrawal symptoms are subsiding to educate about alcohol use and moderation.

Psychosocial Treatments for Alcohol Abuse

The following are psychosocial treatments for alcohol abuse:

- Cognitive behavioral therapies
- Behavioral therapies
- Psychodynamic/interpersonal therapies
- Group and family therapies
- Participation in self-help groups

Cannabis

Cannabis is the hemp plant from which marijuana (a tobacco-like substance) and hashish (resinous secretions of the cannabis plant) are produced.

Possible Effects

Effects of cannabis include:

- Euphoria followed by relaxation
- Impaired memory, concentration, and knowledge retention
- Loss of coordination
- Increased sense of taste, sight, smell, hearing
- Irritation to lungs and respiratory system
- Cancer
- With stronger doses: Fluctuating emotions, fragmentary thoughts, disoriented behavior

Overdose and Misuse

Symptoms of cannabis **overdose** include:

- Fatigue
- Lack of coordination
- Paranoia

Cannabis **misuse** indications are as follows:

- Animated behavior and loud talking, followed by sleepiness
- Dilated pupils
- Bloodshot eyes
- Distortions in perception
- Hallucinations
- Distortions in depth and time perception
- Loss of coordination

Narcotics

Narcotics are drugs used medicinally to relieve pain. They have a high potential for abuse because they cause relaxation with an immediate rush. Possible effects include restlessness, nausea, euphoria, drowsiness, respiratory depression, and constricted pupils.

Misuse and Symptoms of Overdose

Indications of possible **misuse** are as follows:

- Scars (tracks) caused by injections
- Constricted pupils
- Loss of appetite
- Sniffles
- Watery eyes
- Cough
- Nausea
- Lethargy
- Drowsiness
- Nodding
- Syringes, bent spoons, needles, etc.
- Weight loss or anorexia

Symptoms of narcotic **overdose** include:

- Slow, shallow breathing
- Clammy skin
- Convulsions, coma, and possible death

Withdrawal Syndrome for Narcotics

The symptoms of narcotic **withdrawal** are as follows:

- Watery eyes
- Runny nose
- Yawning
- Cramps
- Loss of appetite
- Irritability
- Nausea
- Tremors
- Panic
- Chills
- Sweating

Depressants

Depressants are described below:

- Drugs used medicinally to relieve anxiety, irritability, or tension.
- They have a high potential for abuse and development of tolerance.
- They produce a state of intoxication similar to that of alcohol.
- When combined with alcohol, their effects increase and their risks are multiplied.

Possible Effects

Possible effects of depressant use are as follows:

- Sensory alteration, reduction in anxiety, intoxication
- In small amounts, relaxed muscles, and calmness
- In larger amounts, slurred speech, impaired judgment, loss of motor coordination
- In very large doses, respiratory depression, coma, death

Newborn babies of abusers may exhibit dependence, withdrawal symptoms, behavioral problems, and birth defects.

Misuse, Overdose, and Withdrawal

The following are indications of possible depressant **misuse**:

- Behavior similar to alcohol intoxication (without the odor of alcohol)
- Staggering, stumbling, lack of coordination
- Slurred speech
- Falling asleep while at work
- Difficulty concentrating
- Dilated pupils

Symptoms of an **overdose** of depressants include:

- Shallow respiration
- Clammy skin
- Dilated pupils
- Weak and rapid pulse
- Coma or death

Withdrawal syndrome may include the following:

- Anxiety
- Insomnia
- Muscle tremors
- Loss of appetite

Abrupt cessation or a greatly reduced dosage may cause convulsions, delirium, or death.

STIMULANTS

Stimulants are drugs used to increase alertness, relieve fatigue, feel stronger and more decisive, achieve feelings of euphoria, or counteract the down feeling of depressants or alcohol.

POSSIBLE EFFECTS

Possible effects include:

- Increased heart rate
- Increased respiratory rate
- Elevated blood pressure
- Dilated pupils
- Decreased appetite

Effects with high doses include:

- Rapid or irregular heartbeat
- Loss of coordination
- Collapse
- Perspiration
- Blurred vision
- Dizziness
- Feelings of restlessness, anxiety, delusions

MISUSE, OVERDOSE, AND WITHDRAWAL

Stimulant **misuse** is indicated by the following:

- Excessive activity, talkativeness, irritability, argumentativeness, nervousness
- Increased blood pressure or pulse rate, dilated pupils
- Long periods without sleeping or eating
- Euphoria

Symptoms of stimulant **overdose** include:

- Agitated behavior
- Increase in body temperature
- Hallucinations
- Convulsions
- Possible death

Withdrawal from stimulants may cause:

- Apathy
- Long periods of sleep
- Irritability
- Depression
- Disorientation

HALLUCINOGENS

Hallucinogens are described below:

- Drugs that cause behavioral changes that are often multiple and dramatic.
- No known medical use, but some block sensation to pain and their use may result in self-inflicted injuries.
- "Designer drugs," which are made to imitate certain illegal drugs, can be many times stronger than the drugs they imitate.

POSSIBLE EFFECTS

Possible effects of use:

- Rapidly changing mood or feelings, both immediately and long after use
- Hallucinations, illusions, dizziness, confusion, suspicion, anxiety, loss of control
- **Chronic use**: Depression, violent behavior, anxiety, distorted perception of time
- **Large doses**: convulsions, coma, heart/lung failure, ruptured blood vessels in the brain
- **Delayed effects**: flashbacks occurring long after use
- **Designer drugs**: possible irreversible brain damage

MISUSE AND OVERDOSE

The following are indications of hallucinogen **misuse**:

- Extreme changes in behavior and mood
- Sitting or reclining in a trance-like state
- Individual may appear fearful
- Chills, irregular breathing, sweating, trembling hands
- Changes in sensitivity to light, hearing, touch, smell, and time
- Increased blood pressure, heart rate, blood sugar

Symptoms of hallucinogen **overdose** include:

- Longer, more intense episodes
- Psychosis
- Coma
- Death

Steroids

Steroids are synthetic compounds closely related to the male sex hormone testosterone and are available both legally and illegally. They have a moderate potential for abuse, particularly among young males.

Possible Effects

Effects include:

- Increase in body weight
- Increase in muscle mass and strength
- Improved athletic performance
- Improved physical endurance

Misuse and Overdose

The following are indications of possible **misuse** of steroids:

- Rapid gains in weight and muscle
- Extremely aggressive behavior
- Severe skin rashes
- Impotence, reduced sexual drive
- In female users, development of irreversible masculine traits

Overdose of steroids includes the following:

- Increased aggressiveness
- Increased combativeness
- Jaundice
- Purple or red spots on the body
- Unexplained darkness of skin
- Unpleasant and persistent breath odor
- Swelling of feet, lower legs

Withdrawal Syndrome

Withdrawal syndrome may include the following:

- Considerable weight loss
- Depression
- Behavioral changes
- Trembling

Discrimination

Systemic/Institutionalized Discrimination

Systemic or institutionalized discrimination is the unfair and unjust treatment of populations because of race, gender, sexual orientation, religion, disability, or any other perceived difference by society in general and by the institutions of society.

Institution	Evidence of racism, sexism, or ageism
Healthcare	Provision and access to care may be unequal. People often lack insurance or depend on Medicaid, which limits access. Lack of prenatal care results in higher rates of infant morbidity/mortality. People often develop chronic illnesses because of poor preventive care.
Employment	Discriminatory hiring practices limit employment and advancement opportunities, resulting in unemployment or low income, which can result in homelessness, substance abuse, or criminal activity.
Finances/Housing	People may be denied loans or face high interest rates, limiting their ability to buy homes, pay for education, and start businesses or resulting in high rates of debt. Low-cost housing is often in areas of high crime and gang activity, which is especially a risk for adolescents and the elderly.
Education	Children may attend substandard schools with few enrichment programs, putting them at a disadvantage as they progress through school and into job market or advanced education programs. Many students graduate without adequate skills or drop out.
Criminal justice	People of color are more likely to be arrested and to receive longer sentences for crimes.

Effects of Discrimination on Behavior

Discrimination can result in significant effects, primarily negative, on its subjects:

- **Health problems**: Individuals may suffer from increased stress, anxiety, sadness, and depression. Individuals may develop stress-related disorders, such as hypertension or eating disorders. Individuals may not have access to adequate healthcare or insurance and often delay seeking medical help.
- **Substance abuse**: Individuals may seek relief from the stress of discriminatory actions by resorting to the use of alcohol or drugs in order to dull their feelings.
- **Violence/Conflict/Antisocial behavior**: Individuals may respond with anger and seek vengeance against perpetrators of discrimination (or entire groups representing these perpetrators). Adolescents, for example, may join gangs so that they feel accepted. Some individuals may resort to criminal activity, such as robbery.
- **Withdrawal**: Some individuals begin to pull inward and withdraw from social activities or engagement in work or school, leading to increasing failure and even further discrimination. Discrimination in employment and housing may lead to high rates of unemployment and homelessness.
- **Disenfranchisement**: Individuals may feel that they have no voice and may avoid voting or face obstacles to voting, such as lack of proper identification or transportation.

Ageism and Stereotypes of the Elderly

Ageism is an attitude toward the capabilities and experiences of old age which leads to devaluation and disenfranchisement. Some **stereotypes of the elderly** include the assumptions that all elderly individuals are:

- Asexual
- Rigid
- Impaired (psychologically)
- Incapable of change

Implications of Bias in Human Service Clinical Work

Health and mental health services express the ideology of the culture at large (dominant culture). This may cause harm to clients or reinforce **cultural stereotypes**. Examples of this include:

- **Minorities and women** often receive more severe diagnoses and some diagnoses are associated with gender.
- **African-Americans** are at greater risk for involuntary commitment.
- **Gay and lesbian people** are sometimes treated with ethically questionable techniques in attempts to reorient their sexuality.

Immigrant Clients

Stresses Associated with Immigration

The process of **immigration introduces many stresses** that must be managed. They include the following:

- Gaining entry into and understanding a foreign culture
- Difficulties with language acquisition
- Immigrants who are educated often cannot find equivalent employment
- Distance from family, friends, and familiar surroundings

Consideration When Assessing Immigrant Clients' Needs

The following are considerations when assessing an immigrant's needs:

- Why and how did the client immigrate?
- Social supports the client has or lacks (community/relatives)
- The client's education/literacy in language of origin and in English
- Economic and housing resources (including number of people in home, availability of utilities)
- Employment history and the ability to find/obtain work
- The client's ability to find and use institutional/governmental supports
- Health status/resources (pre- and post-immigration)
- Social networks (pre- and post-immigration)
- Life control: Degree to which the individual experiences personal power and the ability to make choices

Key Concepts of Diversity and Discrimination

Key concepts of diversity and discrimination include the following:

Race	The concept of race first appeared in the English language just 300 years ago. Race has great social and political significance. It can be defined as a subgroup that possesses a definite combination of characteristics of a genetic origin.
Ethnicity	Ethnicity is a group classification in which members share a unique social and cultural heritage that is passed on from one generation to the next. It is not the same as race, though the two terms are used interchangeably at times.
Worldview	Worldview is an integral concept in the assessment of the client's experience. This can be defined as a way that individuals perceive their relationship to nature, institutions, and other people and objects. This comprises a psychological orientation to life as seen in how individuals think, behave, make decisions, and understand phenomena. It provides crucial information in the assessment of mental health status, assisting in assessment and diagnosis, and in designing treatment programs.
Acculturation	Acculturation is the process of learning and adopting the dominant culture through adaptation and assimilation.
Ethnic identity	Ethnic identity is a sense of belonging to an identifiable group and having historical continuity, in addition to a sense of common customs and mores transmitted over generations.
Social identity	Social identity describes how the dominant culture establishes criteria for categorizing individuals and the normal and ordinary characteristics believed to be natural and usual for members of the society.
Virtual/actual social identity	Virtual social identity is the set of attributes ascribed to persons based on appearances, dialect, social setting, and material features. Actual social identity is the set of characteristics a person actually demonstrates.
Stigma	Stigma is a characteristic that makes an individual different from the group, and is perceived to be an intensely discreditable trait.
Normalization	Normalization describes treating the stigmatized person as if he or she does not have a stigma.
Socioeconomic status	Socioeconomic status is determined by occupation, education, and income of the head of a household.
Prejudice	Prejudice is bias or judgment based on value judgment, personal history, inferences about others, and application of normative judgments.
Discrimination	Discrimination is the act of expressing prejudice with immediate and serious social and economic consequences.
Stereotypes	Stereotypes are amplified distorted beliefs about an ethnicity, gender, or other group, often employed to justify discriminatory conduct.
Oppressed minority	A group differentiated from others in society because of physical or cultural characteristics. The group receives unequal treatment and views itself as an object of collective discrimination.
Privilege	Advantages or benefits that the dominant group has. These have been given unintentionally, unconsciously, and automatically.
Racism	Generalizations, institutionalization, and assignment of values to real or imaginary differences between individuals to justify privilege, aggression, or violence. These societal patterns have the cumulative effect of inflicting oppressive or other negative conditions against identifiable groups based on race or ethnicity.

Exploitation

Characteristics of Perpetrators of Exploitation

Characteristics of perpetrators of exploitation may vary widely, depending on the type of exploitation, making them difficult to identify.

- Many of those that are involved in **sex trafficking** are part of large criminal enterprises or have a history of criminal acts and antisocial behavior. The perpetrator may exhibit a domineering attitude, speaking for the victims and never leaving the victim unattended.
- Perpetrators of **elder exploitation** are usually family members or caregivers who take advantage of the victims financially. These perpetrators may appear as loving and caring or sometimes abusive. Business people may take advantage of the elderly by overcharging for goods and services, and some people use scams to get victims to pay or invest money.
- Those involved in **exploitation of child labor** are often in agriculture, working children (most often immigrants) for long hours in the fields at low wages.
- Perpetrators of **slavery/involuntary servitude** may come from cultures with different values, or may be individuals with personal values that allow them to take advantage of others.

Sexual Trafficking

Risk factors for sexual trafficking include being homeless or a runaway, being part of the LGBTQ community, being African American or Latino, having involvement in the child welfare system, having a substance use disorder, and being an illegal immigrant. **Sexual trafficking** may include the following:

- **Children**: Children may be bought or sold for sexual use or forced by family members, even parents, into sex trafficking. Runaways are often picked up on the street and offered shelter, and some children are lured through internet postings. Children who resist may be beaten or even killed. Young girls especially may serve in prostitution rings or be forced to participate in pornography. Many turn to substance abuse.
- **Adults**: Many adult victims begin as victims of sexual trafficking during childhood and continue into adulthood as part of prostitution rings or the pornography industry which they are afraid of or too dependent on to try to escape. Substance abuse is common, often used to self-treat depression or other mental health conditions. Physical abuse is common, as are high rates of STDs and HIV. Forced abortions are also common.

Financial Exploitation

Individuals (especially the elderly and disabled) who become unable to manage their own financial affairs become increasingly vulnerable to **financial exploitation**, especially if they have cognitive impairment or physical impairments that impair their mobility. Financial exploitation includes any of the following:

- Outright stealing of property or persuading individuals to give away possessions
- Forcing individuals to sign away property
- Emptying bank and savings accounts
- Using stolen credit cards
- Convincing the individual to invest money in fraudulent schemes
- Taking money for home renovations that are not done

Indications of financial abuse may be unpaid bills, unusual activity at ATMs or with credit cards, inadequate funds to meet needs, disappearance of items in the home, change in the provision of a will, and deferring to caregivers regarding financial affairs. Family or caregivers may move permanently into the client's home and take over without sharing costs. Clients may be unable to recoup losses and forced to live with reduced means and may exhibit shame or confusion about loss.

Exploitation of Immigration Status

People whose immigration status is illegal are especially at risk of exploitation because they have little recourse to legal assistance that doesn't increase the risk of deportation. Many have paid a high price to "coyotes" to smuggle them into the country and may have been robbed or sexually abused with impunity. Once in the United States, they are often hired at substandard wages and without benefits, including insurance. Many have little access to health care and may suffer from dental and health problems. Housing is often inadequate, and children may drop out of school or have poor attendance because parents move from place to place. Immigrants are often fearful of authorities. Mental health problems, such as depression and substance abuse, are common, but little treatment is available, and many immigrants come from cultures that consider mental illness a cause for shame. Legal immigrants who qualify for assistance may face similar problems, especially related to employment and housing, because of poor language skills and societal discrimination.

Globalization and Institutionalism

GLOBALIZATION

Globalization refers to the international integration and interaction of multiple systems, such as economics, communications, and trade. Considerations include the following:

- **International integration**: This term most often refers to financial and business affairs related to trade and investments. For example, one company may manufacture in the United States, Europe, and China and do business throughout the world. International integration is most successful when tariffs and quotas are eliminated or restricted in order to allow the free flow of goods. International integration may affect the cost of items to the client and may affect job opportunities.
- **Financial crisis**: Because of international integration, a financial crisis (devaluing currency, recession, inflation) in one country can have a profound effect on other countries. For example, the financial crisis that occurred in 2008-2009 resulted in high rates of unemployment and increased homelessness worldwide. The unemployed were unable to afford goods, causing businesses to fold or suffer losses, increasing unemployment, and increasing prices to the consumer.
- **Interrelatedness of systems**: Something that affects one system is likely to have an effect on other systems. For example, if a person works in a US factory that manufacturers equipment and a disaster occurs in the country from which the factory obtains materials, production may slow down and profits decrease, making it difficult for the company to obtain loans needed to finance operations, and the client may be laid off. Because the person has little or no income, they may be unable to make mortgage payments, resulting in the bank foreclosing, and the person becoming homeless.
- **Technology**: Knowledge flows with technology, and those countries with the most technological progress tend to have stronger economies and higher standards of living. Technology transfers have facilitated international integration and allowed instant sharing of information around the world, making inventory control, manufacturing, and delivery (shipping, ground, and air transport) more efficient.

IMPACT OF GLOBALIZATION ON ENVIRONMENTAL CRISES AND EPIDEMICS

Globalization may have a profound effect on the following crises:

- **Environmental crises**: As industrialization moves into developing countries, pollution and stripping of natural resources follows. The increased worldwide demand for goods means that countries are motivated more by monetary gain than environmental concerns. Forests are decimated, water and air polluted, but the global community has been unable to reach a worldwide agreement on environmental planning, resulting in increasingly common environmental problems.
- **Pandemics**: Because of the rapid increase in international marketing and travel, it is now almost impossible to completely contain an outbreak that at one time may have been local, such as Ebola (which has killed over 11,000 people), HIV (which has killed over 35 million people), and most recently, the COVID-19 pandemic which is still active worldwide, killing half a million Americans in its first year. Additionally, health laws and practices vary widely, so not all populations have adequate preventive care or treatment. Thus, any outbreak can pose a worldwide threat. Viruses especially pose a grave threat because they readily mutate and treatment may be unavailable or inadequate.

Problems of Globalization Created by Modernization

Based on the idea that agrarian and impoverished countries would be improved by industrialization, **modernization** has been criticized for contributing to the problems of globalization. In globalization, multinational corporations have relocated their operations and jobs to less-developed regions where poverty remains the norm and average wages are extremely low. These corporations make higher profits, whereas workers in more-developed countries lose their jobs to workers in less-developed countries. Although the merits of this process in regard to workers in the less-developed countries can be debated, the effects on the previously employed workers in the more-developed countries are undeniably negative.

Institutionalism

Institutionalism is the idea that social interventions should be state run, and planning should be centralized in government. Reform is initiated through the electoral process, and a benevolent state would oversee reform efforts. Social services would be provided by the state as well. Critiques would include the assumption of a paternalistic and helpful state, run by individuals uninterested in personal power and gain at the expense of others. However, a counterargument may be the success of countries of northern Europe (e.g., Sweden, Denmark, and Norway) where institutionalism provides citizens with health care, free education, employment, childcare, and housing benefits.

Social and Economic Justice

CHILDREN

CHILDREN IN POVERTY IN THE US

The following are basic facts/statistics relating to children in poverty in the US:

- Almost **one in six** children lives in poverty.
- **Minority** children under age six are much more likely than white children of the same age to live in poverty.
- Many of these children in poverty are **homeless** or are in the **child welfare system**.
- Fewer than one-third of all poor children below age six live solely on **welfare**.
- More than half of children in poverty have at least one **working parent**.
- Children of **single mothers** are more likely to live in poverty.
- Poor children have increased risk of **health impairment**.

CHILDREN IN THE FOSTER CARE SYSTEM

The following are some barriers that children in the foster care system face in this country:

- Children in foster care often go through frequent **relocations** due to rejection by foster families, changes in the family situation, returns to biological families and later returns to foster care, agency procedures, and decisions of the court. Additionally, many foster children experience **sexual and physical abuse** within the foster care system.
- Due to frequent changes in their situation, children in foster care may **change schools** multiple times, which can have an adverse impact on their academic achievement.
- Many youths age out of the foster care system at age 18; this can abruptly **end the relationships** with foster families and other supportive structures.
- Compared with children raised with their own families, children who have been through the foster care system have a higher incidence of **behavioral problems**, increased **substance abuse**, and greater probability of entering the **criminal justice system**.

SOCIAL WELFARE ORGANIZATIONS

APPROACHES TO SOCIAL WELFARE POLICY MAKING

The **rational approach to social welfare policy making** is an idealized and structured approach. It includes identifying and understanding a social problem, identifying alternative solutions and their consequences for consumers and society, and rationally choosing the best alternatives. The rational approach minimizes ideological issues.

The political approach recognizes the importance of compromise, power, competing interests, and partial solutions. Those who are most affected by social policies often have the least amount of political power to promote change. Those who have political power are often influenced by interests that are seeking to protect their own position. Policy makers are often concerned with retaining privilege and power. Without aggressive advocacy, the needs of the disadvantaged can become marginalized.

Administrative Challenges

Administrative challenges unique to social welfare organizations include the following:

- Clinical services can be difficult to assess objectively.
- It is difficult to evaluate prevention programs, as few techniques are able to measure events that have not occurred.
- Staff turnover is high due to low salary and burnout.
- Programs are often dependent on the political environment for funding.
- It can be difficult to implement systematization or routine work due to the flexibility often required when dealing with human problems.

Lesser Eligibility

This concept of lesser eligibility asserts that welfare payments should not be higher than the lowest paying job in society and derives from Elizabethan Poor Law. It suggests that economic and wage issues underlie the size of benefits and the availability of welfare. Some believe it is a way to control labor and maintain incentives for workers to accept low-paying or undesirable jobs that they might otherwise reject.

Challenges for Programs for Poor and Homeless People

One criticism of program development supposedly targeting homeless and poor people is that whereas programs affecting the middle class, such as Individual Development Accounts (IDAs), are put into operation upon conception, programs for poor people are first put through testing phases, with implementation taking years, if it happens at all. In program development for the poor, policies at the level of government may be at odds with actually implementing and carrying out a program.

Criminal Justice System

The criminal justice system includes agencies and processes involved in apprehending, prosecuting and defending, reaching a verdict, sentencing, and punishing offenders:

- **Law enforcement agencies**: These may include police, sheriffs, highway patrol, US Marshal service, FBI, DEA, ICE, and ATF. Law enforcement agencies may be local, state, or federal. Their purpose is to investigate and apprehend criminals.
- **Court system**: Prosecutors provide evidence against an individual, and defense attorneys attempt to discredit the evidence or otherwise provide a defense against the charges brought. Judges preside over court cases and may, in some cases, determine the verdict and sentence. In some states, judges determine if probable cause for arrest exists (preliminary hearing). A grand jury may meet in other state and federal cases to determine whether the evidence indicates probable cause.
- **Jail/prison systems**: Individuals may be incarcerated in local jails or state or federal prisons for varying duration of sentences.
- **Probation system**: Some individuals may receive probation instead of jail or prison time but must report regularly to probation officers and may have other requirements, such as attending rehab programs. Individuals released from jail or prison on parole may also enter the probation system for a specified period of time.

Criminal Justice Process

The criminal justice process includes the following:

- **Investigation** of a crime by law enforcement officers.
- **Probable cause** of a crime must be established in order to obtain a search warrant unless exigent circumstances exist.
- **Interrogation** may be carried out to obtain information on the suspect after the suspect receives the Miranda warning.
- An **arrest** may be made with or without a warrant in public places and with a warrant in private. After an arrest, the person must be charged or released within 24-48 hours (state laws vary).
- With federal cases and in some states, a grand jury decides whether **evidence supports probable cause**. In some states, this decision is made by a judge in a preliminary hearing.
- **Arraignment** involves presenting the charge in court and reading the charges to the individual.
- **Bail** may be set to allow the individual to remain out of jail.
- The case may be resolved by a **plea bargain or a trial** in which the evidence is presented, a **verdict** reached, and sentence determined.
- The individual may be eligible for **appeal** if found guilty.

Impact of Early Experience Within the Criminal Justice System

Early experience within the criminal justice system depends to some degree on the action taken. For example, an adolescent arrested for delinquent acts is more likely to reoffend if the sentence is punitive than if it is more lenient. Additionally, the child or adolescent may develop negative attitudes toward law enforcement and authority in general, and is more likely to commit crimes as an adult. Those who are incarcerated in juvenile facilities may suffer bullying and abuse from others, resulting in emotional and physical problems, and may receive inadequate education, limiting future educational and employment opportunities. Children in the juvenile justice system have high rates of depression, but mental health care and rehabilitation programs are often very limited. Children charged as adults may spend many years in juvenile facilities and then prison, and youth incarceration is one of the highest predictors of recidivism. Many youths are in juvenile detention because of non-violent offenses (such as drug use) but may be exposed to and influenced by more serious offenders.

Out-of-Home Placement and Displacement

Out-of-Home Displacement

Out-of-home displacement may have varying effects on clients and client systems:

- **Natural disasters***:* Some clients may develop PTSD and have recurring nightmares or fears regarding the disaster, especially if it was particularly frightening or the individual or family members experienced injuries. Some may experience depression and withdrawal. Living situations may change if the home was damaged or destroyed, sometimes forcing clients into sharing homes with others, living in substandard housing, or being homeless. Some may have to move away from schools, neighborhoods, and friends.
- **Homelessness**: Many clients that are homeless develop depression and low self-esteem and may engage in substance abuse. Children may attend school irregularly, have difficulty studying, and lack adequate clothing and nutrition. They may be bullied by other children aware of their circumstances. Families may be separated and children placed in separate shelters or foster care. Risk of injuries and chronic disease increases.

Out-of-Home Placement

Out-of-home placements may have varying effects on clients and client systems, depending on the age, duration, and reason:

- **Hospitalization**: Both children and adults may feel fearful and anxious. Children, especially, may feel abandoned or rejected and may regress (bed wetting, thumb sucking). Children may be compliant out of fear when alone but cry and express feelings when parents or other caregivers are present. Adolescents may resent the lack of privacy, isolation, and loss of control. Adults may be concerned about the family unit and loss of income.
- **Foster care**: Children may have difficulty attaching and may become depressed or exhibit behavioral issues (anger or aggression). Developmental delays are common, and children often have poor educational backgrounds, resist studying, get low grades, or must repeat grades. Children may act out or become withdrawn after family visits.
- **Residential care**: Those in residential care may suffer from abuse or molestation because of inadequate supervision. Adults may have an increased risk of falls and injuries. Clients of all ages may become withdrawn and regress because of a lack of personal attention and caring. Small children, especially, may exhibit growth and developmental delays.

Follow-up After Placing Child in Out-of-Home Placement

Follow-up after placing a child in out-of-home placement may vary according to the state regulations, age of the child, type of placement, and the child's specific plan of care, but common **follow-up activities** include:

- Making regularly scheduled visits to observe the child and caregivers in the home environment
- Ensuring that the child's special needs, such as for medical care or counseling, are met
- Assessing the caregiver's communication with the child, disciplinary actions, and attention to special needs, such as giving medications and providing a special diet
- Recording compliance with court ordered actions required of the child (such as rehabilitation for an adolescent drug abuser) or the parents (such as attendance at child development or anger management classes or testing free of alcohol and drugs)
- Monitoring health and education, including school records of grades and attendance
- Ensuring that support services are provided to the caregivers as needed
- Sending periodic reports to the court

Permanency Planning

Permanency planning for permanent placement should begin when the child is admitted to the care of child protective services (CPS) and the initial plan of care is developed. Permanent placement may include reunification, foster care, kinship placement, adoption, residential care facility, group home, or transition to adult living. **Elements of permanency planning** include:

- Assessing the child and the child's needs as well as those of the potential caregivers
- Reviewing any previous CPS records
- Noting any previous history with the juvenile justice system and reviewing records
- Preparing the child by engaging them in the process as appropriate for their age through explaining options, showing photographs, and asking for the child's input
- Reviewing health and education records (including lists of schools attended and grades) to ascertain the child's needs and the need for interventions or support services
- Establishing permanency goals and target dates
- Attending permanency hearings and providing justification for termination of parental rights when appropriate

Sexual Orientation

Sexuality

Sexuality is an integral part of each individual's personality and refers to all aspects of being a sexual human. It is more than just the act of physical intercourse. A person's sexuality is often apparent in what they do, in their appearance, and in how they interact with others. There are four main aspects of sexuality:

- **Genetic identity** or one's chromosomal gender
- **Gender identification** or how one perceives oneself with regard to male or female
- **Gender role** or the attributes of one's cultural role
- **Sexual orientation** or the gender to which one is attracted

Assessing and attempting to conceptualize a person's sexuality will lead to a broader understanding of the client's beliefs and allow for a more holistic approach to providing care.

Gender Identity

Gender identity is the gender to which the individual identifies, which may or may not be the gender of birth (natal gender). Most children begin to express identification and behaviors associated with gender between ages 2 and 4. The degree to which this identification is influenced by genetics and environment is an ongoing debate because, for example, female children are often socialized toward female roles (dresses, dolls, pink items). Societal pressure to conform to gender stereotypes is strong, so gender dysphoria, which is less common in early childhood than later, may be suppressed. At the onset of puberty, sexual attraction may further complicate gender identity although those with gender dysphoria most often have sexual attraction to those of the same natal gender, so a natal boy who identifies as a girl is more likely to be sexually attracted to boys than to girls. Later in adolescence, individuals generally experiment with sexual behavior and solidify their gender identity.

Influence of Sexual Orientation on Behaviors

The degree to which sexual orientation influences behavior may vary widely depending on the individual. For example, some gay males may be indistinguishable in appearance and general behavior from heterosexual males while others may behave in a stereotypically flamboyant manner. The same holds true for lesbians, with some typically feminine in appearance and behavior and others preferring a more masculine appearance. The typical heterosexual model (two people in a stable relationship) is increasingly practiced by homosexual couples while others prefer less traditional practices. Depending on the degree of acceptance that LGBTQ individuals encounter, they may hide their sexual orientation or maintain a heterosexual relationship in order to appear straight. LGBTQ individuals are at higher risk of depression and suicide, especially if they experience rejection because of their sexual orientation or have been taught that it is sinful. LGBTQ individuals with multiple sexual partners (especially males) are at increased risk for STDs, including HIV/AIDS.

Coming Out Process

The coming out process is the act of revealing LGBTQ sexual orientation to family and friends. This generally occurs during adolescence or early adulthood although some may delay coming out for decades or never do so. Individuals may come out to select groups of people. For example, friends may be aware of an individual's orientation but not family or co-workers. Coming out can be frightening for many people, especially if they have reason to fear rejection or fear for their safety. Stages in coming out typically progress in the following order:

Stage	Actions and feelings involved
Confusion	The individual may be unsure of feelings or be in denial.
Exploration	The individual begins to question orientation and wonder about LGBTQ people.
Breakthrough	The individual accepts the likelihood of being LGBTQ and seeks others of the same orientation.
Acceptance	The individual accepts orientation and begins to explore and read about the LGBTQ culture.
Pride	The individual begins to exhibit pride in orientation and may reject straight culture or exhibit stereotypically LGBTQ behaviors.
Synthesis	The individual comes to terms with the reality of the LGBTQ orientation, is at peace with their identity, and is generally out to family, friends, and co-workers.

Practice Issues When Working with LGBTQ Clients

Possible practice issues with LGBTQ clients include, but are not limited to, the following:

- Stigmatization and violence
- Internalized homophobia
- Coming out
- AIDS
- Limited civil rights
- Orientation vs. preference (biology vs. choice)

Problematic treatment models for treating gay and lesbian people include the following:

- The moral model for treatment is religiously oriented and views homosexuality as sinful.
- Reparative or conversion psychotherapy focuses on changing a person's sexual orientation to heterosexual. Traditional mental health disciplines view this type of treatment as unethical and as having no empirical base.

Self-Image

Factors Influencing Self-Image

Factors influencing self-image include the following:

- **Spirituality**: Religious or spiritual beliefs may affect how individuals see their place in the world and their self-confidence. Individuals may gain self-esteem through secure beliefs and membership in a like group, but belief systems with a strong emphasis on sin may impair self-image.
- **Culture**: Individuals are affected (negatively and positively) by cultural expectations, especially if they feel outside of the norm.
- **Ethnicity**: Whether or not the individual is part of the dominant ethnic group may have a profound effect on self-image. Minority groups often suffer discrimination that reinforces the idea that they are less valuable than others.
- **Education**: Those with higher levels of education tend to have a better self-image than those without, sometimes because of greater unemployment and fewer opportunities associated with low education.
- **Gender**: Society often reinforces the value of males (straight) over females and LGBTQ individuals.
- **Abuse**: Those who are abused may often develop a poor self-image, believing they are deserving of abuse.
- **Media**: The media reinforces stereotypes and presents unrealistic (and unattainable) images, affecting self-image.

Body Image

Body image is the perception individuals have of their own bodies, positive or negative. An altered body image may result in a number of responses, most often beginning during adolescence but sometimes during childhood:

- **Obesity**: Some may be unhappy with their body image and overeat as a response, often increasing their discontent.
- **Eating disorders**: Some may react to being overweight or to the cultural ideal by developing anorexia or bulimia in an attempt to achieve the idealized body image they seek. They may persist even though they put their lives at risk. Their body image may be so distorted that they believe they are fat even when emaciated.
- **Body dysmorphic disorder**: Some may develop a preoccupation with perceived defects in their body image, such as a nose that is too big or breasts or penis that is too small. Individuals may become obsessed to the point that they avoid social contact with others, stop participating in sports, get poor grades, stop working, or seek repeated plastic surgery.

Grief

Impact of Grief on the Individual

Grief is an emotional response to loss that begins at the time a loss is anticipated and continues on an individual timetable. While there are identifiable stages of grief, it is not an orderly and predictable process. It involves overcoming anger, disbelief, guilt, and a myriad of related emotions. The grieving individual may move back and forth between stages or experience several emotions at any given time. Each person's grief response is unique to their own coping patterns, stress levels, age, gender, belief system, and previous experiences with loss.

Kubler-Ross's Five Stages of Grief

Kubler-Ross taught the medical community that the dying person and their family welcome open, honest discussion of the dying process. She believed that there were certain stages that people go through while experiencing grief. The stages may not occur in order; they may occur out of order, some may be skipped, and some may occur more than once. **Kubler Ross's stages of grief** include the following:

- **Denial**: The person denies the loss and tries to pretend it isn't true. During this time, the person may seek a second opinion or alternative therapies (in the case of a terminal diagnosis) or act as though the loss never occurred. They may use denial until they are better able to emotionally cope with the reality of the loss or changes that need to be made.
- **Anger**: The person is angry about the situation and may focus that rage on anyone or anything.
- **Bargaining**: The person attempts to make deals with a higher power to secure a better outcome to their situation.
- **Depression**: The person anticipates the loss and the changes it will bring with a sense of sadness and grief.
- **Acceptance**: The person accepts the loss and is ready to face it. They may begin to withdraw from interests and family.

Review Video: The Five Stages of Grief
Visit mometrix.com/academy and enter code: 648794

Anticipatory Grief

Anticipatory grief is the mental, social, and somatic reactions of an individual as they prepare themselves for a perceived future loss. The individual experiences a process of intellectual, emotional, and behavioral responses in order to modify their self-concept, based on their perception of what the potential loss will mean in their life. This process often takes place ahead of the actual loss, from the time the loss is first perceived until it is resolved as a reality for the individual. This process can also blend with past loss experiences. It is associated with the individual's perception of how life will be affected by the particular diagnosis as well as the impending death. Acknowledging this anticipatory grief allows family members to begin looking toward a changed future. Suppressing this anticipatory process may inhibit relationships with the ill individual and contribute to a more difficult grieving process at a later time. However, appropriate anticipatory grieving does not take the place of grief during the actual time of death.

Disenfranchised Grief

Disenfranchised grief occurs when the loss being experienced cannot be openly acknowledged, publicly mourned, or socially supported. Society and culture are partly responsible for an individual's response to a loss. There is a social context to grief. If a person incurring the loss will be putting himself or herself at risk by expressing grief, disenfranchised grief occurs. The risk for disenfranchised grief is greatest among those whose relationship with the thing they lost was not known or regarded as significant. This is also the situation found among bereaved persons who are not recognized by society as capable of grief, such as young children, or needing to mourn, such as an ex-spouse or secret lover.

Grief vs. Depression

Normal grief is self-limiting to the loss itself. Emotional responses will vary and may include open expressions of anger. The individual may experience difficulty sleeping or vivid dreams, a lack of energy, and weight loss. Crying is evident and provides some relief of extreme emotions. The individual remains socially responsive and seeks reassurance from others.

By contrast, **depression** is marked by extensive periods of sadness and preoccupation often extending beyond two months. It is not limited to the single event. There is an absence of pleasure or anger and isolation from previous social support systems. The individual can experience extreme lethargy, weight loss, insomnia, or hypersomnia. Crying is absent or persistent and provides no relief of emotions. Professional intervention is often required to relieve depression.

Domestic Violence

Abusive Behaviors Associated with Domestic Violence

Abusive behaviors often occur in a series of escalating degrees.

1. The series begins with **verbal abuse** in the form of mocking comments, put-downs, name-calling, or abusive language.
2. The next degree is **emotional abuse** in the form of rejecting, degrading, terrorizing, isolating, corrupting, financially exploiting, and denying emotional responsiveness.
3. **Physical abuse** is next on the continuum in the form of restraining, slapping, beating, biting, burning, striking with an object, strangulation, and the use of weapons with the intent of wounding or causing death.

According to the CDC, 1 in 4 women and 1 in 10 men have experienced some form of intimate partner violence.

Review Video: Domestic Abuse
Visit mometrix.com/academy and enter code: 530581

Societal Cost of Abuse

Abuse costs Americans over $4 billion dollars per year for:

- Physical injuries treated by medical practitioners
- Psychological injuries treated by mental health professionals
- Violence prevention campaigns
- Police and judiciary costs
- Emergency housing
- Social services costs

There are also hidden costs from **eroded social capital** like:

- Increased morbidity from stress
- Lost pay from work absences
- Low productivity from worry at work and painful movement
- Lower earnings and savings
- Increased mortality from suicide through depression
- Poor school performance by traumatized children
- Increased mortality from murder

Victims can be either a member of an intimate relationship, or children in violent homes, which are often neglected or abused. Victims of childhood abuse often become the perpetrators of violence in later life. Many suffer from poor self-esteem that undermines their job choices and social interactions.

Violence Against Women Act of 1994

President Bill Clinton signed the Violence Against Women Act of 1994, a law based on zero tolerance for violence. **Zero tolerance** means no reported abuse will be ignored; the perpetrator always faces stiff penalties. The Violence Against Women Act was not a productive deterrent from abuse because the stiff penalties caused women to withdraw from legal protection. Abused women feared:

- Police would take their children away from the violence
- Their husbands or significant others would retaliate after release from jail
- They would be unable to cope financially without their husband's or significant other's income to help support the family
- Taking on the fees charged by lawyers, bondsmen, and the courts

Women are frequent targets for abuse because they are often:

- Untrained in self-defense
- Small enough to wound and intimidate easily
- Socialized not to leave a relationship except under extreme duress

Women in Abusive Relationships

Women tend to stay in abusive relationships for many reasons, including:

- Abuse being normalized from watching their parents participate in similarly dysfunctional relationships
- Being concerned that their children will have no traditional nurturer if they leave
- Feeling a social responsibility to keep up the facade of a happy home
- Early training from childhood that they are inferior and deserve abuse

Abuse screening tools have been implemented in doctors' and mental health providers' offices in an effort to identify abused women who do not spontaneously disclose. The woman is asked:

- Whether or not she has been physically struck over the last year
- About the safety of her present relationship
- About past relationships that may threaten her present safety

Common Problems That Children of Abuse May Develop

Physical and mental issues often develop in a **child from an abusive home** that follows him or her into adulthood. Some common behavior and social problems include:

- Deficient social skills
- Inadequate problem-solving skills; aggressiveness
- Delinquency
- Oppositional behaviors
- Attention deficit/hyperactivity disorder (ADHD)
- Obsessive-compulsive disorders (OCD)
- Suicidal tendencies
- Drug and alcohol abuse
- Social disengagement
- Denial
- Anxiety and depression
- Social withdrawal
- Avoidance of problems
- Excessive self-criticism

These social, behavioral, and intimacy problems are very prevalent and costly to our society, and degrade the children's quality of life.

Characteristics of Abusers

Abusers of either sex have various unmet psychological needs or motivations. Common **types of abusers** include the following:

- A person who assaults his or her victims in the **home setting** and has a strong need to dominate relationships with his or her intimate partners.
- The abuser who is suffering from significant **psychological issues**, like antisocial personality disorder, who is a convicted criminal, or who has past assault and battery charges (often dropped by intimidated victims).
- The person who works through a **continuum of abusive behaviors**. These often begin with verbal and emotional abuses, which lead to throwing objects at the victim, intimidation, and an effort to dominate the relationship by withholding money or restraining movement and social access. Violence can escalate, followed by feelings of remorse. The pattern can become part of a never-ending cycle of behavior.

Male Abusers

Male abusers were usually abused as children, watched their mothers being abused, or saw abuse perpetrated by male friends (e.g., gang rapes as initiation rites). The **male abuser** often displays one or several of the following qualities:

- He has a **disproportionate sense of entitlement** that he has the right to hurt others, especially females. He truly believes he has the right to hit a woman if she is unfaithful or withholding sex from him.
- He usually **does not have a good opinion of women** because that is the way he has been socialized.
- He often justifies his behavior by stating he was **drunk or high on drugs** at the time of an attack.
- He may have a **psychological problem** such as post-traumatic stress disorder (PTSD), a delayed reaction caused by trauma or witnessing an event that caused him a great deal of suffering. Other psychological problems common to abusers are depression, poor self-esteem, personality disorders, and psychopathy.

Male abusers may have been abandoned as children. **Abandonment** leads to a state of rage in the adult male. Be alert to three states of child abuse that commonly have detrimental effects on the future adult male:

- The father or an adult male authority figure inflicts physical abuse on a male child.
- The father inflicts emotional abuse by rejecting and humiliating his son.
- The mother does not form a maternal bond with her son.

Anger is part of the attachment process. The attachment object may be the victim of the violence as the male abuser takes out his feelings of jealousy or rejection. The male's veneer of icy indifference conceals a strong emotional dependency on the significant other or wife.

Recommended Treatment Appropriate for Abusers

The first step is to determine if abuse actually exists and to diagnose the type of abuser. Rule out addiction to drugs or alcohol. If the abuser is an addict, refer the abuser to a separate drug or alcohol intervention program, in conjunction with treatment. Next, determine the severity of past abuse perpetrated on the abuser when he or she was a child. The abuse need not have been directed at the child. It is sufficient that he or she witnessed violence being perpetrated on other family members. Evaluate the abuser for borderline personality disorder and post-traumatic stress disorder. Provide the abuser with anger management training in a group setting. Anger management involves discussions of dominant and controlling behaviors, and the development of personal responsibility. The abuser needs to control his own or her own behavior.

The male abuser should be **counseled** regarding the abuse that was perpetrated on him as a child. The male adult should understand that he was a victim himself, and is not to be blamed for the past abuse perpetrated upon him as a child. He is not the one that caused others to hurt him. Bring to light his wrong assumptions. Try to develop his understanding of the root of his self-esteem issues. The male needs to develop a healthier self-view and learn thought patterns that lead to appropriate behavior. Encourage him to discuss and deal with internal conflicts and the internalized pain of his past. Use a motivational approach to help the male client gain a healthy perspective on his behavior. Base the approach on cognitive, emotional, and behavioral conflicts in the client's life.

Avoid **jointly counseling** a couple in an abusive relationship, as this can lead to further abuse. Assess the clients individually, followed by group therapy. The small group of 6-8 members should be led either by a sole male counselor, or male and female co-counselors to help the clients see positive interaction between a male and female. The co-leader relationship must be evenly balanced in power and control of the group. The focus of the group is self-improvement. Each individual in the group examines his or her emotional responses that are reflected in angry behaviors. The **emotions** behind the anger are usually sadness, pain, rejection, and humiliation. Turn angry behavior to the appropriate expression of emotion. Discuss families and relationships. Relate childhood experiences to present attitudes and behaviors.

Components of a 20-Week Anger Management Group Outline

Anger management group therapy can be accomplished in 20 weeks with one session per week. The anger management treatment group should consist of 6-8 male members. Here is a suggested outline for discussion topics:

- **Week 1**: The group makes a participation agreement. Each individual shares their personal violence statement.
- **Week 2**: Clients learn to take a time-out from anger. Discuss other anger management principles. Provide some stress management skill instructions.
- **Week 3**: Each client participates in a discussion on issues they face in their daily life that they can or cannot control. Follow this discussion with another discussion on conflict, emotions, and actions. Encourage clients to practice the use of "I" messages to communicate their feelings. Help clients to gain insight into assertive requests and refusals.
- **Week 4**: Involve clients in an examination of values and discuss the clients' reactions.
- **Week 5**: Discuss the continuum of abuse and the power wheel.
- **Week 6**: Discuss childhood experiences, especially the parental relationship that the child witnessed, and parenting styles.
- **Week 7**: Discuss how abuse of the child is reflected in the life of the adult. The resulting conversation will deal with emotions that this discussion conjures up.
- **Week 8**: Clients discuss the difference between punishment and discipline.
- **Week 9**: Clients discuss praise and respect.
- **Week 10**: Discuss self-talk and its impact, and examine scripts.
- **Week 11**: Discuss the abuse cycle along with a conversation regarding communication.
- **Week 12**: Incorporate empathy, listening, and reflection.
- **Week 13**: Discuss assertiveness.
- **Week 14**: Summarize and consolidate the communication skills taught in the first 13 weeks.
- **Week 15**: Review the power wheel and include a practice exercise.
- **Week 16**: Discuss intimacy.
- **Week 17**: Give empathy exercises.
- **Week 18**: Follow-up on the empathy exercises.
- **Week 19**: Outline a relapse prevention plan.
- **Week 20**: Summarize and reinforce what was learned in the previous 19 weeks. In ending conversation, discuss ways to implement the relapse prevention plan in case a problem develops.

Possible Issues Resulting from Treatment

Treatment that involves discussing the client's abusive relationship with others may unearth feelings that are uncomfortable for both the client and the counselor. The client may want to place the blame for his or her violent actions on the client's spouse or significant other. Help the client to understand the motivations behind those actions and the desire to place the blame elsewhere. Understanding helps the client to establish a closer relationship with his or her spouse. Do not force the client to take responsibility for his or her behavior, or criticize the client, as this will likely cause the client to become defensive. Do not force a confrontation that could turn into an aggressive act. Confrontations increase the sense of humiliation the client is feeling. Humiliation will lead the client to express feelings of blame and anger.

Stress, Crisis, and Trauma

Stress

Relationship Between Stress and Disease

Stress causes a number of physical and psychological changes within the body, including the following:

- Cortisol levels increase
- Digestion is hindered and the colon stimulated
- Heart rate increases
- Perspiration increases
- Anxiety and depression occur and can result in insomnia, anorexia or weight gain, and suicide
- Immune response decreases, making the person more vulnerable to infections
- Autoimmune reaction may increase, leading to autoimmune diseases

The body's **compensatory mechanisms** try to restore homeostasis. When these mechanisms are overwhelmed, pathophysiological injury to the cells of the body result. When this injury begins to interfere with the function of the organs or systems in the body, symptoms of dysfunction will occur. If the conditions are not corrected, the body changes the structure or function of the affected organs or systems.

Psychological Response to Stress

When stress is encountered, a person responds according to the threat perceived in order to compensate. The threat is evaluated as to the amount of harm or loss that has occurred or is possible. If the stress is benign (typical day-to-day burdens or life transitions) then a challenge is present that demands change. Once the threat or challenge is defined, the person can gather information, resources, and support to make the changes needed to resolve the stress to the greatest degree possible. Immediate psychological response to stress may include shock, anger, fear, or excitement. Over time, people may develop chronic anxiety, depression, flashbacks, thought disturbances, and sleep disturbances. Changes may occur in emotions and thinking, in behavior, or in the person's environment. People may be more able to adapt to stress if they have many varied experiences, good self-esteem, and a support network to help as needed. A healthy lifestyle and philosophical beliefs, including religion, may give a person more reserve to cope with stress.

Impact of Different Kinds of Stress

Everyone encounters stress in life and it impacts each person differently. There are the small daily hassles, major traumatic events, and the periodic stressful events of marriage, birth, divorce, and death. Of these stressors, the daily stress that a person encounters is the one that changes the health status over time. Stressors that occur suddenly are the hardest to overcome and result in the greatest tension. The length of time that a stressor is present also affects its impact, with long-term, relentless stress, such as that generated by poverty or disability, resulting in disease more often. If there is **ineffective coping**, a person will suffer greater changes resulting in even more stress. The solution is to help clients to recognize those things that induce stress in their lives, find ways to reduce stress when possible, and teach effective coping skills and problem-management.

Crisis

Characteristics of a Crisis

A crisis occurs when a person is faced with a highly stressful event and their usual problem solving and coping skills fail to be effective in resolving the situation. This event usually leads to increased levels of anxiety and can bring about a physical and psychological response. The problem is usually an acute event that can be identified. It may have occurred a few weeks or even months before or immediately prior to the crisis and can be an actual event or a potential event. The crisis state usually lasts less than six weeks with the individual then becoming able to utilize problem solving skills to cope effectively. A person in crisis mode does not always have a mental disorder. However, during the acute crisis their social functioning and decision-making abilities may be impaired.

Types of Crises

Developmental

There are basically two different types of crises. These types include developmental or maturational crisis and situational crisis. A **developmental crisis** can occur during maturation when an individual must take on a new life role. This crisis can be a normal part of the developmental process. A youth may need to face and resolve crisis to be able to move on to the next developmental stage. This may occur during the process of moving from adolescence to adulthood. Examples of situations that could lead to this type of crisis include graduating from school, going away to college, or moving out on their own. These situations would cause the individual to face a maturing event that requires the development of new coping skills.

Situational

The second type of crisis is the **situational crisis**. This type of crisis can occur at any time in life. There is usually an event or problem that occurs, which leads to a disruption in normal psychological functioning. These types of events are often unplanned and can occur with or without warning. Some examples that may lead to a situational crisis include the death of a loved one, divorce, unplanned or unwanted pregnancy, onset or change in a physical disease process, job loss, or being the victim of a violent act. Events that affect an entire community can also cause an individual situational crisis. Terrorist attacks or weather-related disasters are examples of events that can affect an entire community.

Collecting a Trauma History

A trauma history should be collected from any client with a known history of physical/emotional abuse, accident involvement, or signs/symptoms of PTSD from known or unknown events. There are several methods of trauma history collection:

- **Trauma History Screen (THS)**: The client self-reports (via questionnaire) by responding with "Yes" or "No" to 14 event types and includes the number of times the event occurred. These events include abuse, accidents/natural disasters, military service, loss of loved ones, and life crises/transitions. Next, the client is prompted to respond to the question, "Did any of these things really bother you emotionally?" If the client responds with "Yes," they are then instructed to provide details about every event that bothered them.
- **Trauma History Questionnaire (THQ)**: Similar to the THS, this questionnaire requires the client to self-report experiences with 24 potentially traumatic events, and then to provide the frequency and details of each experience.

Terrorism and Natural Disasters

Impact of Terrorism on the American Population

The **September 11 attacks** are the most prominent example of foreign terrorism against the United States in recent decades. On 9/11/2001, Al-Qaeda terrorists used hijacked passenger aircraft to attack the World Trade Center buildings in New York City and the Pentagon, and were believed to be targeting the US Capitol building with another hijacked plane that was brought down in Pennsylvania before reaching its intended destination. Around 3,000 people were killed in the attacks. Media coverage was extensive and continuous, which was unusual at that time, and it contributed to varying degrees of psychological trauma for people across the nation.

In more recent years, the United States has experienced **domestic terrorism** and **independent acts of violence** that have also pervaded the American psyche. Mass shootings occurring in public places previously thought of as places of safety (e.g., schools, churches, shopping centers) have led to efforts to prepare children and adults alike for future attacks in their schools or workplaces through the use of mandatory drills and efforts such as the Run-Hide-Fight campaign. These practices, combined with the now-standard extensive media coverage of any mass casualty incident, can create an underlying and pervasive fear that impacts the worldview of Americans today.

Impact of Terrorism on Victims

Terrorism can lead victims to lose the safe assumptions they made about the world around them. Loss of assumption means the **terror victim** loses their trust in mankind's ability to perform good or charitable acts. The terror victim may question the significance and meaning of humanity's existence. Loss of assumption leads to a form of post-traumatic stress disorder (PTSD) in terror victims. Terrorists typically use bombs, acts of violence, or intimidation. The **psychological problem** occurs when the victim is faced with the motivations and antisocial logic that cause the actions of the terrorist. A severe, violent terrorism event can cause temporary mental disturbance, such as in Stockholm syndrome, where the victims bond with their captors and defend them against police. Other terms for Stockholm syndrome are Bonding-to-the-Perpetrator and Trauma-Bonding, seen in domestic abuse where the battered spouse and children refuse to leave their abuser.

Impact of Terrorism on the Psychological State of the Victim

There are multiple immediate and long-term **psychological effects** of terrorism on its victims:

- The terror victim loses positive assumptions about the world by experiencing great fear and loss of his or her sense of personal invulnerability.
- The victim may lose sight of meaningful interpretations of mankind's position in the world.
- The victim may lose confidence in that which was previously within his or her control.
- The victim may be overwrought and afraid of future possible acts of terrorism.
- Fear invades the victim's daily life and routines, causing a state of incapacitating and irrational apprehension.
- The victim finds that his or her self-image has changed from confident to unsure and is full of self-doubts.

Vicarious Impact of Terrorism on Victim's Loved Ones and Community Members

Terrorism has a vicarious effect on those associated with the victim. **Vicarious traumatization** is experienced by members of a community that has been subject to bombings or deliberate acts of terrorism. Many in the United States experienced vicarious trauma after the fall of the World Trade Center buildings and the Oklahoma City bombing. Members of the media added to the vicarious trauma by broadcasting these events to the general public. The unintended effect of this exposure caused adults and children to suffer from post-traumatic stress disorder. PTSD clients suffer depression, apprehension, and are more susceptible to alcohol or substance abuse.

Stages Experienced in Aftermath of Disaster

The survivors of a disaster go through a series of emotional and psychological stages.

- In the first stage, the survivor sees himself or herself as a **hero** and acts out these heroic thoughts by helping to save someone else or their property.
- These altruistic feelings of individual heroism are followed by a **honeymoon period,** in which the whole neighborhood joins together to work as one unit to save others.
- The honeymoon period is followed by the **disillusionment stage**, which comes as a result of the postponement of help from others. The person feels let down by others.
- The final stage involves the **reconstruction period**. The survivor no longer looks for help from others, but instead takes control and responsibility for his or her situation, and works to resolve the problem.

Cognitive Appraisal of Terrorism

The person who adopts a **positive cognitive appraisal** of the terrorist act develops coping styles to deal with the event. Those who take on a **negative cognitive appraisal** find they feel out of control of the situation and that there is nothing they can do to prevent future acts of terror from being directed against them. This feeling of helplessness is especially concentrated in members of the community who lived or worked near the disaster site. The negative individual may have sustained injuries as a result of the terrorists' actions, or lost people they knew and cared about, and is extremely likely to suffer from PTSD.

Role of Mental Health Provider in Aftermath of Traumatic Events

An act of terror or a natural disaster will likely increase demand on the mental health provider to provide services in the field.

- As a **first responder**, provide psychological first aid by letting victims know they have reached safety.
- The **secondary response** should be one of direction by setting up triage. Provide workers and bereaved priority care. Stabilize the survivors.
- The **third response** should be one of connection. Rescue workers need to be connected to support systems that give them the psychoeducational support they need to complete the tasks at hand. Follow up with acute care treatment.
- The **final response** is consultation or referral to other specialized service providers.

Mental Health Interventions to Establish in a Disaster

Mental health interventions are critical responsibilities of the counselor in times of crisis. Help the victim to cope by re-establishing feelings of well-being, predictability, and stability. Let the victim see that social support is available and that the counselors assigned are caring and kind. Next, help the victim grasp the meaning of the traumatic event and adapt to changes in worldview and loss of assumption. This can involve the development of an appreciation for life. The victim may find that his or her priorities have changed as a result of the trauma and require direction in order to formulate new priorities and positive expectations. Help the victim find outlets that can produce feelings of good will and help build confidence. Suggest that the victim help others to partake in the heroic actions of the community.

THREE-PHASE FRAMEWORK OF CRISIS INTERVENTION

The three-phase framework of intervention for a crisis are as follows:

- In the **pre-attack phase**, threat assessment and prevention are performed by law enforcement, military, and the intelligence resources available. The therapist gives pre-incident resiliency training to emergency response teams.
- In the **acute event management phase**, the mental health therapist provides continuing psychological support and encouragement to the emergency response teams and seeks to provide the victims and the community with factual, age-appropriate information.
- In the **reconstruction phase**, the counselor instructs people on coping strategies and communication skills, reassures the victims, and helps them feel safe by reconnecting them to their normal routines and schedules. Specifically, the counselor tries to help the victim adjust to a loss of assumption and change in worldview.

FIVE-PHASE FRAMEWORK OF CRISIS INTERVENTION

The five-phase framework of crisis intervention is as follows:

- The **pre-incident phase** entails the preparation involved in anticipation of an incident, often applicable in the case of forecasted natural disasters, but also in training efforts.
- The **impact phase** lasts for the first 48 hours following the crisis. Basic needs are the priority. The counselor tends to the psychological first aid required in this period.
- The **rescue phase** lasts from after the first 48 hours through the first week. A needs assessment is performed, crisis counseling is initiated, and information is disseminated.
- The **recovery phase** lasts from the end of week 1 through week 4, during which crisis counseling is ongoing and the recovery status is monitored.
- The **return to life phase** lasts for the next 2 years. More long-term counseling may be required for some victims as they are supported to a return to life (career, family life, mental health) after the trauma.

PRE-INCIDENT PHASE OF INTERVENTION

The goals of the pre-incident phase include preparation, set-up, and improving coping skills by training first responders. The counselor works in partnership to shape policy and inform others. The counselor sets up and organizes structures that are capable of providing swift assistance.

IMPACT PHASE OF INTERVENTION

The goals of the impact phase include survival and communication techniques during the 48 hours following the event. The survivor may be in denial at this point, or may display fight-or-flight reactions. They may appear unable to respond, as if frozen in an admission of defeat. The first responder's job is to rescue and protect the victim. The counselor seeks to provide four types of services to the victim and first responders:

- Basic needs
- Psychological first aid
- Assessment of the impact on the environment
- Technical assistance, consultation, and training opportunities

During the impact phase of disaster intervention, the counselor uses keen observation to triage the victims with the most severe symptoms for priority treatment. The counselor keeps check on factors that may introduce further stress to the situation. The counselor also provides technical assistance, consultation, and training to the victims and the first responders to re-establish community structures. Families may require some grief counseling and training on how to cope with their feelings that are a result of the disaster. Organizations may need the counselor's help to connect the appropriate service to the caregivers, first responders, and leaders within the community. The counselor can improve the organization's ability to provide care to survivors.

Immediate Post-Impact Stage

The immediate post-impact stage lasts **up to 48 hours after a traumatic event**. This is the stage where mental health providers give psychological first aid to the victims to stabilize them. The Critical Incident Stress Management (CISM) system is designed to reduce negative psychological reactions to trauma. Disaster survivors and rescue workers are given the opportunity to discuss the trauma and its resulting conditions by defusing in one-hour long conversations with a counselor. During this phase, the counselor must support and encourage the participants to calm them. Debriefing is a two-hour long meeting to provide information to the rescue workers about the survivors and how to best meet their needs. Psychoeducational debriefings are designed to provide assistance and direction to those suffering from post-traumatic stress disorder (PTSD).

Debriefings After Disasters

The **communal debriefing** is given to victims who have endured an experience that caused them to feel marked as socially unacceptable in some manner. Do not conduct a communal debriefing before giving pre- and post-intervention assessments to the group members individually. The victims have experienced an emotional shock, producing extreme, acute traumatic symptoms, such as suicidal ideation, severe disassociations, and substance abuse. Survivors with any of these symptoms should be referred for specialized, higher level treatments as soon as they become available. Exclude victims who are acutely bereaved by the death of a loved one from psychological debriefing, because research indicates that debriefing is a leading contributor to PTSD in some survivors. The American Red Cross and the Federal Emergency Management Agency (FEMA) both employ debriefing practices as part of their standard intervention procedures.

Rescue Phase of Intervention

The rescue phase occurs within the **first week of the disaster**. This stage has adjustment goals. The survivor may be resilient or exhausted in this stage. The first responders are assisted by other helpers who seek to orient the survivors and provide secondary assistance. The counselor's role in the rescue stage is to perform a needs assessment to determine the status of the survivor and to ensure that his or her needs are being met. The counselor establishes a recovery environment, where he or she can assess the needs of various groups and individuals. The counselor performs a walk-through to determine if everyone has gained the assistance that is needed, because some are unwilling or unable to seek out help on their own. A clinical assessment is performed in the triage stage. Survivors may be referred to other specialists, or hospitalized. High risk individuals are targeted for immediate treatment.

Outreach and Information Element of Intervention

In the outreach and information distribution element of the rescue phase of disaster intervention, the counselor seeks to inform those in need of the services that are available. Information can be shared through websites, community structures, bulletin boards, runners, word of mouth, or fliers. The counselor works to re-establish social interaction. The survivor may need instruction in coping strategies, and the caregivers need education about stress responses found in survivors, including triggers that can cause the victim to experience traumatic flashbacks. Caregivers should be aware of risk factors, services that are available, and the difference between normal and abnormal functioning levels. The counselor also provides family and group support systems and spiritual support. The counselor fosters natural social supports and helps care for those suffering with bereavement. The counselor participates in debriefings as part of the rescue operations.

Recovery and Return to Life Phases of Intervention

The recovery stage extends from **one to four weeks after the disaster**. The recovery phase goals involve planning and appraisal. Survivors are grieving, and some have intrusive memories. Teach caregivers to be sensitive in response to the survivors. Monitor the recovery process and the environment. Watch and listen to traumatized survivors. Look for toxins or physical dangers that could be present at the site. Watch for potential threats that may become an issue. Examine and observe the services that are provided to the surviving community.

The return-to-work phase occurs from **two weeks to two years following the disaster**, and its goal is regeneration. Try to reduce or alleviate psychological symptoms by offering more long-term psychotherapy to individuals, families, or groups. If the client's trauma is still not responding to psychotherapy, refer him or her to a psychiatrist for pharmacotherapy, and perhaps hospitalization.

Cognitive-Behavioral Intervention in Later Phase Treatments

Cognitive-behavioral intervention (CBI) is for those victims who have shattered basic assumptions. Class size should ideally be 8-10 people but definitely no more than 15. Deliver 15 lessons, 2-3 times per week, for 90 minutes each. Two instructors are required to address stress and anxiety in traumatized victims. Teach victims how to identify and modify disturbing thoughts and how to independently employ relaxation techniques when anxious or stressful reactions are triggered.

The survivors that should **not** use this technique include the following:

- The bereaved
- Survivors who suffer from intense, intrusive fear or panic attacks
- Survivors with an IQ below 80
- Those who cannot engage in abstract reasoning
- Those adults who do not have at least a 5th grade education
- Clients with cardiovascular disease, such as uncontrolled arrhythmias
- Survivors who disassociate should not perform deep relaxation strategies that could produce trance-like states. Instead, incorporate breathing exercises into their treatment therapy.

Exposure Strategies and Eye Movement Desensitization and Reprocessing (EMDR)

Exposure strategies are part of the cognitive-behavioral intervention (CBI) for treating survivors of traumatic events. The survivor re-exposes himself or herself to an imaginary traumatic place that resembles the initial trauma scene. Alternatively, the survivor may choose to revisit the actual trauma scene.

Eye Movement Desensitization and Reprocessing (EMDR) is a treatment successfully used with Vietnam War veterans who suffer from post-traumatic stress disorder (PTSD) from wartime assignments. EMDR joins two interventions, exposure strategies and cognitive-restructuring, into one procedure. Doctors Silver and Rogers support EMDR in their Humanitarian Assistance Program that helps victims around the world.

Grief Counseling

Bereavement is the physical, psychological, social, and spiritual grief response of family members and close friends to a loved one's death. In 1991, William Worden distinguished grief counseling from grief therapy:

- **Grief counseling** facilitates the normal, uncomplicated response to death in a reasonable amount of time.
- **Grief therapy** uses special techniques to end abnormal, complicated grief that is prolonged, produces somatic symptoms or behavioral derangement, or is exaggerated.

Worden said the counselor should attempt to change the subjective experience and behavior of the bereaved and provide symptomatic relief. Treat the bereaved in a private area. Conduct one-hour sessions for individuals, and 90-minute sessions for groups. Sessions can be closed (registration is required, and the number of treatment sessions is limited), or open (no registration is required, and treatment sessions are ongoing). Get referrals from crisis intervention hotlines. Utilize the "empty chair" Gestalt technique, art and music therapy, journaling, meditation, role playing, and reviewing photos or personal possessions of the dead to relieve grief.

Constructivist Intervention

Constructivist intervention is underpinned by the ideas that the loss of one human being affects us all, and every human needs to express grief when they experience loss. Grievers may find meaning through allegorical reflections that allow them the opportunity to carefully consider the traumatic events that resulted in loss. Many people find comfort in formal rituals, like memorial services, which bring survivors together to act as a single entity. Community-wide memorial services help affected neighborhoods to reconstruct meaning and redefine their life roles for the future. Informal family rituals help the survivors to honor the loved one who died, privately. Verbal expression of grief is also therapeutic. Additionally, both local and national communities can be comforted and supplied with hope by watching or reading about the humanitarian efforts of rescuers and donors.

Trauma's Effect on Children

Children who are subjected to trauma and terrorism are either not psychologically mature enough to cope with the event or have not reached the developmental age to understand what has actually happened. Assess for the following **signs and symptoms of trauma in children**:

- Depression
- Anxiety
- Behavioral changes
- Aggression
- Dissociative responses
- Helplessness
- Generalized fear
- Heightened arousal
- Nightmares or sleep disturbances
- Acting out the trauma in a repetitive play scenario
- School avoidance
- Preoccupation with danger and the parents' concerns and fears
- Rebelliousness
- Social withdrawal and attempts to distance themselves from others
- Recklessness and excessive risk-taking

Needs of Children After Trauma

The child has specific counseling needs after a traumatic event:

- Make conversations age-appropriate and talk to the child in a language that he or she understands well.
- Present opportunities for the child to demonstrate tenderness and love for the surviving parent (in the case of losing a parent/loved one) and continue to develop their relationship.
- Ensure surroundings are safe and healthy to restore feelings of security and place in the world.
- Plan opportunities for play and enjoyable activities to build his or her confidence.
- Find a way for the child to contribute to the solutions of problems.
- Tell the child the truth, but omit unnecessary details, because they may overwhelm the child.
- Allow the child to express concerns about the traumatic event in ways that help him or her develop understanding.

Role of Counselor in Helping a Child After Traumatic Event

The counselor plays a specific role in supporting a child through a traumatic event. The following are important considerations:

- Do not provide cognitive-based interventions (CBI) to children under 7, because they do not develop self-talk until age 5 or 6, and have not yet mastered it.
- Do not minimize the danger that caused the trauma, or encourage the child to delve too deeply into negative emotions. Instead, help the child to develop a story that relates the factual events of what happened.
- Many young children are not equipped to express their emotions because they lack the correct vocabulary. Nonverbal communications help children who cannot accurately express their emotions.
- Play therapy helps the child deal with anxiety over a traumatic event. Try re-enactments, role-plays, or art forms.
- If the child has obsessive thoughts, sleep disturbances or bedwetting, or behavioral problems for more than a few days after the traumatic incident, then refer the child to a psychiatrist for further assessment. The child may require drug therapy or more intensive psychotherapy.

Play Therapy Treatments

Play helps children communicate and understand traumatic events, even if they do not have good language skills. For example, child survivors of 9/11 re-enacted the crash using blocks and toy planes, and role-played firemen and other helpers in this scenario. Role-play allows the child to attach a deeper meaning to tragic events. Creative art therapists use an art form as a play therapy intervention. Art provides the child with a safe environment to explore feelings about the traumatic event. **Play therapy** for children impacted by 9/11 related to the following:

- The concept of immediate death
- Disability from inhaled particles
- Victims' bodies that could not be recovered from the rubble of the twin towers
- Loss of privacy through media attention
- Disenfranchised grief, because certain deaths were trumpeted as heroic, while others went unacknowledged

- Botched efforts to break the news to children who lost a parent
- Doubts over the memorial service, because victims' status depended on whether they were civilians or public service members
- Loss of control over the memorial service
- Intrusive media presence at the memorial service

Play therapy was also utilized after the mass shooting at Sandy Hook Elementary School in Connecticut in 2012, resulting in the deaths of 20 children and 6 adults. Crisis intervention involved the use of play therapy, along with music and art therapy, to help the children to feel safe within the walls of their school again.

Impact of Trauma on the Counselor

Secondary traumatic stress disorder (STSD) appears when a counselor ignores his or her physical and emotional symptoms of distress and burnout. Sometimes, **countertransference** reactions occur in mental health providers, making their reactions appear under-responsive or over-responsive.

- **Under-responsive reactions** indicate that the counselor has ceased to be affected by the pain and suffering of the survivor.
- **Over-responsive reactions** indicate that the counselor has lost the ability to remain emotionally detached from the survivor's pain.

Either reaction is inappropriate and can lead to a serious problem for both the counselor and the survivor. Counselors should be able to access help for themselves from other mental health providers. Counselors require adequate rest, physical and mental breaks or vacations, relaxation and recreation, and social support systems. Use these strategies to help maintain a balanced state.

Vicarious Traumatization, Compassion Fatigue, and Burnout

Disaster and terrorism counselors must constantly evaluate self-care areas. The counselor must not become so caught up in the victim's suffering that **vicarious traumatization** occurs, in which the counselor absorbs the negative psychological consequences of the trauma that occurred to their client. The counselor must also avoid reaching a state of **compassion fatigue**. These two conditions are a direct result of a long-term commitment to care. The counselor becomes so caught up in the pain that he or she witnesses in the survivors that prolonged stress leads to **burnout**. Burnout appears as a variety of disturbances, including the following:

- Sleep disturbances
- Backaches
- Fatigue
- Headaches
- Irritability
- Mental confusion
- Cynicism
- Depression
- Intense vulnerability

American Red Cross Response System

The American Red Cross founded a system that organized volunteers to respond to disasters systematically.

- The Red Cross first responds with the **damage assessment team**, who evaluate what is needed.
- The **disaster action team** then provides food and medical supplies to the first responders and survivors.
- **Disaster response human resources** includes **disaster mental health (DMH) services**, consisting of licensed and trained volunteers who provide psychological assistance to the survivors. DMH services delivers an organized response and assures quality control during a disaster.

The Red Cross requires their mental health counselors obtain Red Cross licensed training. Psychologists, psychiatrists, social workers, marriage and family therapists, and psychiatric nurses are eligible to receive DMHS-certified training.

ARC Certification for Mental Health Providers Working in Disaster Relief Situations

The American Red Cross (ARC) has developed a **certification procedure** to ensure that mental health providers are trained to be **disaster responders**. Mental health providers who wish to receive ARC-certified training can find it from the Red Cross's website. The events of 9/11 caused many anxious moments and a great deal of unorganized response. Counselors who responded to the 9/11 crisis found out after the fact that they were ill-prepared to meet the needs of the survivors. This awareness resulted in a substantial increase in responders taking **Red Cross DMH training courses** in 2002. 9/11 responders wanted to be adequately prepared for the next disaster and to prevent future problems in caring for survivors. Before seeking DMH certification, the mental health provider must have these prerequisites:

- A Master's degree in the mental health field
- Work experience in the mental health field
- Licensure by applicable boards

After receiving their DMH certification, counselors should become standing members of the Red Cross chapter nearest to their homes, and make prior arrangements with their employers allowing them to take necessary time off from work to assist in a disaster.

Red Cross Service Delivery Given to Survivors at Disaster Sites

The professionals working in **Red Cross' disaster mental health (DMH) services** provide psychological assistance to the survivors at the **disaster site**. Service given is in an interventional format. The client may be seeking food, medical care, or information. Confidentiality is difficult in this setting. The counselor either gives interventions to a small collection of survivors, or to a large group of people, such as family and friends awaiting casualty lists. The counselor may supply information to the media to reach a wide audience. Many interventions are based on a single point of contact where the counselor tries to keep survivors occupied or entertained (e.g., the counselor asks clients to help with clean up and issues cleaning supplies or distributes reading material, coloring books, and toys to children). Counselors assess survivors for sound mental health and stability during casual conversation and observation.

Resources

NCCEV, NACCT, and NMHA

The **National Center for Children Exposed to Violence (NCCEV)** is located at Yale University's Child Studies Center. NCCEV publishes materials for mental health providers working with children who have been subjected to acts of terror or natural disasters. The center makes a strong distinction between how to respond to natural disasters versus how to respond to acts of terror.

The **National Advisory Committee on Children and Terrorism (NACCT)** suggests that early intervention is critical in helping a child develop resiliency after a traumatic event. NACCT's material makes distinctions between age groups and cultural diversities for counselors.

Mental Health America (MHA) also produces materials that can be found on their website.

The Family Readiness Kit

The Family Readiness Kit is a tool that parents can use to prepare their families for emergency situations. This disaster plan was created by the American Academy of Pediatrics. The plan involves listing emergency contacts and other pertinent information. Children are taught to keep their identification and cards listing medical needs with them in an emergency. The family designates meeting points in case of a disaster. These meeting points include a destination nearby home, a family member's or trusted friend's home in another town, and the children's school plan and meeting location. Families who evacuate their homes must shut off all utility, fuel, and water supplies, circumstances permitting. It is recommended that the family also leave a note stating their destination. The **Family Readiness Kit** can be found on the AAP's website.

NASP Resources and ARC

The **National Association of School Psychologists (NASP)** has prepared a publication that adults can use with children subjected to terrorism. The leaflet, *A National Tragedy, Helping Children Cope: Tips for Parents and Teachers* is available on the NASP website. A trusted adult uses it as a guideline to help the child regain feelings of safety and security, and to cope with the changes in his or her world following a catastrophic event.

The **American Red Cross (ARC)** recommends that families create a four-step Family Disaster Plan before an impending natural disaster or if Homeland Security anticipates terrorism. ARC states that making children part of disaster planning relieves their anxiety and feelings of helplessness during an actual event. ARC also offers a financial plan for emergency preparedness, explains how to stock an emergency supplies kit, and explains how to take care of pets in a disaster.

Career Counseling

Historical Development of Career Counseling from Post WWI

After World War I, the works of Frank Parson were incorporated into **career counseling efforts**. Interest inventories, such as those created by E. K. Strong in 1927, became more popular. In 1939, G. Frederick Kuder created his own version of interest inventories. In 1962, many counselors adopted the popular Myers-Briggs Type Indicator (MBTI) inventory. In 1973, John Holland developed a theory that led to the establishment of the Self-Directed Search, the Harrington-O'Shea Career Decision-Making System, and the Interest Finder. In 1990, Donald Super expanded the narrow ideas found in interest inventories by adding a values-based approach and an examination of personality types. The Strong Interest Inventory was revised in 1994 and 2004. Resultingly, modern and comprehensive career counseling includes the consideration of personality types, values, and interests.

Values-Based Approach Found in Career Counseling

The value-based career theory (Brown, 2002) posited that central to career counseling is an understanding of the client's underlying values. According to this model, goal-directed behavior is stimulated by values. Values are an incentive. Therefore, the client gains satisfaction when he or she reaches a value-based goal. When the client does not reach a value-based goal successfully, disappointment and dejection are the likely outcome. Value-based goals can be well defined or based on a crystallized priority ranking. According to Brown's model, the three types of values are **cultural**, **work**, and **life values**.

Cultural values are further divided into social relations, time, and relationship to nature, activity, and self-control. Social relations are then further divided into individualism, collateralism, and hierarchy. (Collateralism's motto is: "Over and above one's basic needs, to each one according to one's needs, and from each one proportionate to one's collateral.") The values-based approach attempts to define motivating factors in order to develop a holistic lifestyle plan for the client.

Cultural Values

Self-Control and Time

Self-control is derived from cultural values and is defined as the client's control over his or her thought patterns, emotions, and actions. The client may have some reservations, especially if the client is of certain cultures where this characteristic is prevalent (Asian American or American Indian descent). Do not alienate the reserved client by asking questions that are too personal.

Time perspectives are cultural values separated into future, past-future, present, and circular.

- **Future perspective clients** are unconcerned with past events.
- **Past-future perspective clients** use past events as background to learn from while developing future plans.
- **Present perspective clients** are not worried about the future and live only in the now.
- **Circular perspective clients** see time as part of nature and are unconcerned with time schedules.

Problems occur when future time perspective employers hire workers with circular time or present time perspectives, who do not understand stringent emphasis on deadlines, timeliness, and punctuality.

Social Relations

Social relations are derived from cultural values. **Social relations** are divided into individualism, collateralism, and hierarchy.

- Persons who prioritize **individualism** place a high level of importance on making independent decisions.
- Persons who prioritize **collateralism** place a high level of importance on making decisions that reflect positively on their peers or family members.
- Persons who prioritize **hierarchy** place a high level of importance on making a decision that will be approved of by the leader of their peer group or family. This is the alpha male in the patriarchal family and the alpha female in the matriarchal family.

Understanding the underlying influences that affect a client's career decision may change the delivery of career counseling to include a member of the client's social relations group.

Activity Values

Activity values are derived from cultural values, and are the client's response to a dilemma that necessitates an action of some kind. In Western European cultures, the response is to do something to alleviate the problem, which is termed a **doing activity**. Persons who hold this stance may act for personal gain. Some cultures respond by waiting to see what happens next, which is termed a **being activity**. Others respond with a **being-in-becoming activity**, which is deliberating in a controlled manner before commencing action in a calm and regulated manner. Activity values define how the client may respond to a work problem. Therefore, a career counselor must determine the client's activity value to find a good job fit.

Relationship to Nature Values and Life Values

Typically, persons with a strong belief in the **controlling power of nature** also hold fatalistic viewpoints. Fatalistic viewpoints define problem solving as a useless task. Some cultures hold that **people have controlling power** over nature and their environments and believe that there is every reason to problem solve.

Life values are classified into two groups: work and leisure. Three scales can be used to determine a client's work satisfaction. These three scales are the Values Scale, the Minnesota Importance Questionnaire, and the Life Values Inventory. The values and relationships involved in each are measured to determine levels of satisfaction felt by the client.

Work Values

Twenty-one work values were defined under the **Values Scale (VS)** published by Super and Nevill in 1986 as part of the Work Importance Study (WIS). These include: Ability utilization, achievement, advancement, prestige, economic security, autonomy, working conditions, authority, economic rewards, aesthetics, creativity, physical activity, social interaction, variety, social relations, altruism, cultural identity, physical prowess, personal development, risk, and lifestyle. In 1975, Weiss, Dawis, and Lofquist presented a list of needs that can be combined with the Values Scale to help determine a client's work values.

There are twenty values listed under the **MIQ or Minnesota Importance Questionnaire**, including ability utilization, achievement, social status, security, independence, working conditions, authority, activity, coworkers, compensation, creativity, variety, social service, responsibility, recognition, supervision-technical, supervision-human relationships, advancement, moral values, and company policies and practices. Clients expect fulfillment in these areas for work satisfaction.

Life Values

The **Life Values Inventory (LVI)** was created in 1996 by Crace and Brown. They categorized values under five life spectra: Work, leisure, spirituality, citizen, and relationships to significant others. Career planning cannot be made without regard to all spectra if the client is to reach fulfillment. The client is asked to grade value statements on a scale of 1-5 based on how strongly each value guides their behavior. The values can be contained within the following categories:

- **Achievement** contains social status, advancement, and authority.
- **Belonging** contains co-workers, social interaction, and working conditions.
- **Concern for the environment** contains altruism.
- **Concern for others** contains altruism and social service.
- **Creativity** contains aesthetics.
- **Financial prosperity** contains compensation, economic rewards, security, and prestige.
- **Humility, Objective Analysis, and Interdependence** stand-alone and are not further categorized.
- **Health and activity** contain activity and physical prowess.
- **Independence** contains autonomy, variety, cultural identity, and ability utilization.
- **Responsibility** contains supervision-technical, supervision-human relationships, and composing policies and practices.
- **Privacy** contains absence of co-workers.
- **Scientific Understanding** contains knowledge of science and scientific progress.
- **Spirituality** contains moral values and altruism.

Career Counseling Process

The career counselor's role is one of **facilitator** who assists the client in coming to a decision on his or her occupational choices and in making other role choices. Collateral and hierarchical social values are of primary concern to some clients. Food and shelter are high priority for individuals who cannot find positions that meet their qualifications. This client may be forced to take on a pot-boiler job (low-paying, difficult hours, or hard labor positions taken on in order to provide life's necessities for oneself and the family). The career counselor should consider working for necessities as a short-term solution only, and encourage the client to keep looking for a long-term solution. Geography, family obligations, and disabilities affect a person's ability to gain a desired position that is satisfying. When this happens, the counselor should seek to help the client determine life roles that can bring satisfaction.

Priorities

The career counselor can understand the **client's priorities** through the following considerations:

- The career counselor must take note of the **activity values** of a client. Clients who have a future or past-future perspective on time with a doing activity value should find the decision-making process easy.
- A client who has a very strong preference for either a **collateral or hierarchical social value** may have more difficulty deciding which career or life role to take on, as opposed to the client who prioritizes individualism.
- Use an additional list of priorities to determine **job satisfaction**. Persons who value their individualism also find it important to gain direct feedback in order to feel satisfaction. Persons who have a collateral value thrive on indirect, positive feedback from family and social groups.
- The career counselor should also make note of **job requirements** as determined by the prospective supervisor, such as job-related skills, aptitude for the work, interpersonal skills, and good work habits. The client will be evaluated against the job requirements, so these should be a prominent component of the client assessment.
- Identify the **client's values as distinct** from interested family members' who attend the counseling session. Some families make known exactly what is required of the person making a career choice, and other families are less clear about the choice that should be made. This can make it difficult to define the expectations of the family or leader of the family. Regardless, the client's values and interests should be investigated as independently as possible.

Client Cultural Identification

The first step of client cultural identification is determining through a series of questions if collateral social relations exist that will play a part in the client's decision-making process. These questions will help the counselor to avoid a stance that may seem culturally insensitive or biased towards individualism. The client should be the one to determine who is involved in his or her choice. It is not up to the counselor to make this determination. Adhere to verbal and nonverbal communications in accordance with cultural expectations. The following elements of communication mean different things to different cultures and should be used with care:

- Eye contact
- Interpersonal space
- Handshakes
- Facial expressions
- Verbal expressions that involve self-disclosure
- Volume
- Rapid speech
- Interruptions of others' speech
- Pauses
- Direct communications

Avoid elevated levels of self-disclosure. Avoid probing questions that might be perceived as rude.

First Stage of Assessment

The first stage of a career counseling assessment requires the counselor to assess the client for mental health problems that have not been previously identified and treated. Record problems already being treated in the client's profile. Persons with multiple disabilities may need a specialist in vocational assessment, so it may be appropriate to refer the client on to a specialist. Assess clients who do not have mental health issues according to their culture, work, and life values. The goal in this assessment is to help the client reveal his or her core values and to sort out those values according to priorities. Educate the client about how his or her values influence motivation. Help the client to understand the process involved in goal setting and self-evaluation. The client can expect to be apprised of life roles that do not directly involve an occupational choice, but may provide satisfaction and fulfillment in agreement with the client's life plan.

Goal Setting and Assessment

Goal setting and assessment should occur after the client states his or her expectations, desired outcomes, and motivation. The client's **goal**:

- Does not need to be obtainable at this point
- May or may not confirm previous choice decisions
- May not meet the client's needs for life's necessities
- May not be compatible with the client's current relationships
- May require the client to change jobs
- May not meet the geographical criteria
- May not be the final product

However, if following the assessment regulations according to Brown's values-based career theory, the refinements will make the client's goal obtainable and fitting for the client's lifestyle plan.

End Results of Assessment

The end result of the assessment process will likely produce multiple employment options for the client. Use a balance sheet tool, such as that developed by Janis and Mann in 1977, to help the client narrow down the options further. Originally, this tool was intended to help students select a college. However, the counselor can adapt the balance sheet for career occupational choices. Instruct the client on how to check O*NET (the Occupational Information Network) for up-to-date occupational data. Encourage the client to seek out professionals who are experienced in their field of interest and request informational interviews. Clients must develop employment skills, a resume, job search skills, and job interview skills. The culmination is the review of the expected outcomes discussed in the first session. Inform the client that he or she can return for further assistance.

Areas of Clinical Focus Chapter Quiz

1. Which of the following chromosome pairs are affected in cases of Down syndrome?

a. 12
b. 13
c. 19
d. 21

2. Which of the following is NOT a type of value according to Brown's value-based career theory (2002)?

a. Moral
b. Cultural
c. Work
d. Life

3. Which of the following medicines would you NOT expect to be involved in treatment for a patient with Tourette's syndrome?

a. Methylphenidate
b. Haloperidol
c. Pimozide
d. Clonidine

4. What is the earliest a child can be diagnosed with encopresis per DSM-5 criteria?

a. 7 years old
b. 6 years old
c. 5 years old
d. 4 years old

5. Which of the following is NOT a subtype of specific phobia?

a. Animal
b. Natural environment
c. Irrational
d. Blood-injection-injury

6. Which of the following is considered the best treatment for a specific phobia?

a. Psychopharmacology
b. In vivo exposure
c. Multicomponent cognitive-behavioral therapy
d. Hypnosis

7. An Amytal interview would have most likely been used to treat which of the following disorders?

a. Motor disorder
b. Conduct disorder
c. Conversion disorder
d. Adjustment disorder

8. Which of the following is considered a Cluster C personality disorder?

a. Obsessive-compulsive
b. Schizoid
c. Antisocial
d. Histrionic

9. According to the National Institute of Alcohol Abuse and Alcoholism, what percentage of Americans drink alcohol as part of their daily routine?

a. 35%
b. 50%
c. 75%
d. 85%

10. All of the following are stages experienced by survivors in the aftermath of a disaster EXCEPT?

a. Villain stage
b. Honeymoon period
c. Disillusionment stage
d. Reconstruction period

Treatment Planning

Theoretical Frameworks

THEORIES OF CARL JUNG

Jung's archetypes are the images and concepts that develop the collective unconscious of humanity. The main archetypes are:

- **The Way**: The image of a journey or voyage through life
- **The Self**: The aspect of the mind that unifies and orders experience
- **Animus and Anima**: The image of gender
- **Rebirth**: The concept of being reborn, resurrected or reincarnated
- **Persona**: The role or mask one shows to others
- **Shadow**: The dark side of one's personality
- **Stock characters**: Dramatic roles that appear over and over in folktales
- **The Hero**: The character who vanquishes evil and rescues the downtrodden
- **The Trickster**: The character who plays pranks or works magic spells
- **The Sage**: The wise old person
- **Power**: A symbol such as the eagle or the sword
- **Number**: Certain numbers appear throughout history and across cultures

The two **attitudinal types** according to Jung are:

- **Introvert**: One oriented toward the inner, subjective world
- **Extrovert**: One oriented toward the outer, external world

The four **functional types** according to Jung are:

- **Thinking**: An intellectual process involving ideas
- **Feeling**: An evaluative function involving value or worth
- **Sensing**: A function involving recognition that something exists, without categorizing or evaluating it
- **Intuiting**: A function involving creative inspiration without having all the facts

THEORIES OF SIGMUND FREUD

PSYCHOANALYTIC/PSYCHODYNAMIC PERSONALITY THEORY

Sigmund Freud, commonly known as the father of psychoanalysis, based his practice on **psychoanalytic and psychodynamic personality theories**. The foundations of these theories are based on the following concepts.

Levels of awareness:

- **Conscious**: Thoughts, feelings, desires of which a person is aware and able to control.
- **Preconscious**: Thoughts, feelings, desires not in immediate awareness but can be recalled to consciousness.
- **Unconscious**: Thoughts, feelings, desires not available to the conscious mind

Stages of development: Each person passes through stages of psychosexual development (can become trapped in any stage):

- **Oral**: Focus on sucking and swallowing
- **Anal**: Focus on spontaneous bowel movements or control over impulses
- **Phallic**: Focus on genital region, and identification with parent of same gender
- **Latency**: Sexual impulses are dormant, focus on coping with the environment
- **Genital**: Focus on erotic and genital behavior, leading to development of mature sexual and emotional relationships

Personality structure: The personality has three main components:

- **Id**: Unconscious pleasure principle, manifest by a desire for immediate and complete satisfaction with disregard for others
- **Ego**: Rational and conscious reality principle, which weighs actions and consequences
- **Superego**: Conscious and unconscious censoring force of the personality, which evaluates and judges behavior

Common **Freudian psychiatric terms** include:

- **Oedipus Complex or Electra Conflict**: At the age of four or five, the child falls in love with the parent of the opposite sex and feels hostility toward the parent of the same sex.
- **Defense mechanisms**: Conscious or unconscious actions or thoughts designed to protect the ego from anxiety.
- **Freudian slips**: Also known as parapraxes, these are overt actions with unconscious meanings.
- **Free association**: A method designed to discover the contents of the unconscious by associating words with other words or emotions.
- **Transference**: Transference takes place when feelings, attitudes and/or wishes linked with a significant figure in one's early life, which are projected onto others in one's current life.
- **Counter-transference**: This happens when the feelings and attitudes of the therapist that are projected onto the client inappropriately.
- **Resistance**: Resistance is anything that prohibits a person from retrieving information from the unconscious.
- **Fixation**: Someone who is bogged-down in one stage of development has a fixation.

Review Video: Who was Sigmund Freud?
Visit mometrix.com/academy and enter code: 473747

Freud's Concept of Superego

Freud coined the word *superego* to make sense out of the rules imposed upon us by our parents. Rules involving parents, family, religion, and culture contribute to our sense of right and wrong. The problem arises whenever a rule has been imposed that is unrelenting and harsh. Freud linked this to his interview of female clients. Victorian women had difficulty accepting their sexual urges as a natural occurrence. This conflict of right and wrong caused the females to experience hysterical paralysis and other notable anxiety disorders. However, symptoms were alleviated when the clients gained insight and emotional release from their inner turmoil. **Free association** is the client's expression concerning secretive and painful thoughts, feelings, and memories in a non-judgmental therapy session. The therapeutic bond or relationship is imperative in this technique. Free association used in this way can still be beneficial today.

Review Video: How do the Id, Ego, and Superego Interact?
Visit mometrix.com/academy and enter code: 690435

Freud's Concept of Transference

Freud's concept of **transference** can be applied to the exchanges that take place between the modern client and the mental health care provider. The client's propensity is to behave toward the provider as one would a key authority figure. The provider can help the client understand this propensity and work to help the client alter this unconscious transference to other people. Awareness of transference must become a part of the client's conscious thought. The client must be aware when this has happened and seek to change the behavior on a conscious level. Cognitive rethinking techniques and behavioristic role plays enable the provider's efforts to get the client to work through a maladaptive behavior. The provider can also use a variety of techniques to help the client internalize positive feelings and thought patterns.

Unconscious Mind in Conjunction with Psychodynamic Theories

Sigmund Freud's theories involve getting at **unconscious thoughts** that cause behaviors. The client must come to terms with unconscious thoughts rather than bottle up those feelings, and thus deal with issues in a more functional manner. **Psychodynamic theorists** of today try to help the client make a connection between the past and existing problems. However, a cognitive-behavioral approach may need to be supplemented with in-depth counseling. Some topics that may require further investigation are the client's family and parental interactions, unresolved issues, unconscious practices, and defensive mechanisms. Freud believed pathological thinking was at odds with the id instincts of Eros and Thanatos. Eros stands for the life processes involving love and relationships. Thanatos stands for death processes involving negative emotions and the fighting response. The mind is trying to manage these forces, which causes anxiety and the client forms phobias or conversion disorders.

Object-Relations School

The **Object-Relations School** looks at the primary caregiver relationship in a child's early years of growth. A positive parental relationship leads the infant to understand about safety, security, self-worth, nurturance, and caring. The infant grows into a child with a positive self-identity and is better able to form healthy relationships with others. Those infants that have a negative parental relationship feel unloved, detested, valueless, insignificant, inferior, and shamed. These images form the person's personality and behaviors. The inner belief system is referred to as the schema in the cognitive therapy model. It is known as the **incorporated object relation** in the psychodynamic model. Object-relations take into account the Freudian theories regarding instinctive urges. These urges are the driving force to form either loving or destructive relationships. The client explores the repressed feelings in front of a provider who has created a safe and trusted setting.

Alfred Adler's Theory of Individual Psychology

Alder's **key concepts** include:

- Inferiority feelings are the source of all human striving.
- Personal growth results from one's attempts to compensate for this inferiority.

Two types of **complexes** exist:

- **Inferiority**: An inability to solve life's problems
- **Superiority**: An exaggerated opinion of one's abilities and accomplishments in an attempt to compensate for an inferiority complex

The goal of life is to strive for superiority. Lifestyle is the unique set of behaviors created to compensate for inferiority and to achieve superiority.

Alder also theorized that **birth order** affects personality:

- **First born**: Happy, secure, and the center of attention until dethroned by the second child; interested in authority and organization
- **Second born**: Born into a more relaxed atmosphere and has the first-born as a model; interested in competition
- **Youngest child**: Pet of the family and may retain a sense of dependency

Fritz Perls' Gestalt Therapy

The removal of masks and facades is the goal of Gestalt therapy, according to Perls. A creative interaction needs to be developed so the client can gain an ongoing awareness of what is being felt, sensed, and thought. **Boundary disturbances** (lack of awareness of the immediate environment) may occur:

- **Projection**: Fantasy of what another person is experiencing
- **Introjection**: Accepting the beliefs and opinions of others without question
- **Retroflection**: Turning back on oneself that which is meant for someone else
- **Confluence**: Merging with the environment
- **Deflection**: Interfering with contact, used by receivers and senders of messages

Goal of therapy is integration of self and world awareness. **Techniques** of therapy include:

- **Playing the projection**: Taking on and experiencing the role of another person
- **Making the rounds**: Speaking or doing something to other group members to experiment with new behavior
- **Sentence completion**: "I take responsibility for…"
- **Exaggeration** of a feeling or action to clarify the purpose or intent
- **Empty chair dialogue**: Having an interaction with an imaginary provocateur
- **Dream world**: Explored by describing and playing parts of a dream

Carl Rogers' Client Centered Theory

Key concepts in **Carl Rogers' client centered theory** include:

- The **attributes** of the therapist
- **Congruence**: inner feelings match outer actions
- **Unconditional positive regard**: therapist sees the client as a person of intrinsic worth and treats the client non-judgmentally
- **Empathic understanding**: therapist is a sensitive listener

The **goal of therapy** is helping the client become a fully functioning person, achieving this goal by:

- Relinquishing facades
- Banishing "oughts"
- Becoming a non-conformist by moving away from cultural expectations
- Becoming self-directed as opposed to pleasing others
- Dropping defenses
- Trusting one's own intuition
- Accepting others

Neurolinguistic Programming

The major concepts of **neurolinguistic programming (NLP)** according to Bandler and Grinder include:

- **Representational Systems**: Sensory models through which people access information, such as audio, visual and kinesthetic models. Cues to representational systems are patterns which can be heard or observed.
    - Preferred predicates: a "view" that suggests a visual system
    - Eye-Accessing cues: looking upward suggests a visual system
    - Hand movements: pointing toward the ear suggests an auditory system
    - Breathing patterns: suggest a kinesthetic system
    - Speech pattern/tone: suggests an auditory system
- **Language structure**:
    - Surface structure: sentences that native speakers of a language speak and write
    - Deep structure: the linguistic representations from which the surface structures of a language are derived
    - Ambiguity: a surface language may represent more than one deep structure
- **Human modeling**: The process of representing something through language
    - Generalization: specific experiences that come to represent the entire category of which they are a member
    - Deletion: selected portions of the world are excluded from the representation created by an individual
    - Distortion: the relationship among the parts of the model which differ from the relationships they were supposed to represent

John Hattie's Theory of Self Concept

The major concepts of **Hattie's theory of self-concept** include:

- A cognitive appraisal consisting of beliefs about the self
- Expectations from self and others: High expectations can lead to low self-esteem and vice versa

Descriptions of oneself are:

- **Hierarchical**: From a description of simple or isolated characteristics to an all-inclusive description of the self
- **Multifaceted**: Having numerous dimensions

Methods of **integration** across dimensions include:

- **Self-verification**: Soliciting feedback to confirm the anticipated view of the self
- **Self-consistency**: Internal harmony among opinions, attitudes, and values
- **Self-complexity**: Viewing the self as complex and multifaceted
- **Self-enhancement**: Viewing the self's positive qualities as more important than the self's negative qualities

Neurobiological Theories

The general features and findings foundational to **neurobiological theories** include:

- Cognitive and emotional dysfunctions may result from any insult that affects the brain's neurotransmitters, such as genetic anomalies, infection, and nutrition.
- Neurotransmitters, such as acetylcholine, are chemical substances found in the nervous system that carry messages from the axon of one neuron to the receptor site on another. In the brain, these neurotransmitters may affect cognitive, emotional, and behavioral functioning. After utilization, neurotransmitters are either inactivated by enzymatic degradation (such as a cholinesterase) or are drawn back into the presynaptic neuron.
- Psychotherapeutic drugs are prescribed to influence the process of neurotransmitter production and absorption in an attempt to establish a "normal" neurochemical balance.

Theories of Emotion

Cross-cultural research has distinguished six basic **universal human emotions**: Fear, anger, happiness, disgust, surprise, and sadness. The **James-Lange theory** of emotion asserts that emotions are the body's reaction to changes in the autonomic nervous system caused by external stimuli. This theory is supported by the fact that quadriplegics report feeling less-intense emotions. The **Cannon-Bard theory** of emotion proposes that the body and emotions react to stimuli based on thalamic stimulation of the cortex and peripheral nervous system. The **two-factor theory of Schachter and Singer** proposes that emotions are the result of arousal, the cognitive interpretation of that arousal, and the environment in which the arousal occurs.

Change Theories

Transtheoretical Model

The **transtheoretical model** focuses on changes in behavior based on the individual's decisions (not on society's decisions or others' decisions) and is used to develop strategies to promote changes in health behavior. This model outlines stages people go through when changing problem behavior and trying to have a positive attitude about change. Stages of change include the following:

- **Precontemplation**: The person is either unaware or under-informed about consequences of a problem behavior and has no intention of changing behavior within the next 6 months.
- **Contemplation**: The person is aware of costs and benefits of changing behavior and intends to change within the next 6 months but is procrastinating and not ready for action.
- **Preparation**: The person has a plan and intends to initiate change in the near future (≤1 month) and is ready for action plans.
- **Action**: The person is modifying behavior change occurs only if behavior meets a set criterion (such as complete abstinence from drinking).
- **Maintenance**: The person works to maintain changes and gains confidence that he or she will not relapse.

Motivational Interviewing

Motivational interviewing (Miller, 1983) aims to help people identify and resolve issues regarding ambivalence about change and focuses on the role of motivation to bring about change. MI is a collaborative approach in which the interviewer assesses the individual's readiness to accept change and identifies strategies that may be effective with the individual.

Elements	Principles	Strategies
Collaboration rather than confrontation in resolving issues **Evocation** (drawing out) of the individual's ideas about change rather than imposition of the interviewer's ideas **Autonomy** of the individual in making changes	**Expression of empathy**: Showing understanding of individual's perceptions **Support of self-efficacy**: Helping individuals realize they are capable of change **Acceptance of resistance**: Avoiding struggles/conflicts with client **Examination of discrepancies**: Helping individuals see discrepancy between their behavior and goals	**Avoiding Yes/No questions**: Asking informational questions **Providing affirmations**: Indicating areas of strength **Providing reflective listening**: Responding to statements **Providing summaries**: Recapping important points of discussion **Encouraging change talk**: Including desire, ability, reason, and need

Resistance to Organizational Change

Performance improvement processes cannot occur without organizational change, and **resistance to change** is common for many people, so coordinating collaborative processes requires anticipating resistance and taking steps to achieve cooperation. Resistance often relates to concerns about job loss, increased responsibilities, and general denial or lack of understanding and frustration. Leaders can prepare others involved in the process of change by taking these steps:

- Be honest, informative, and tactful, giving people thorough information about anticipated changes and how the changes will affect them, including positives.
- Be patient in allowing people the time they need to contemplate changes and express anger or disagreement.
- Be empathetic in listening carefully to the concerns of others.
- Encourage participation, allowing staff to propose methods of implementing change so they feel some sense of ownership.
- Establish a climate in which all staff members are encouraged to identify the need for change on an ongoing basis.
- Present further ideas for change to management.

Theory Development

Philosophical Foundations of Counseling

The philosophical foundations of counseling are based on various theoretical approaches to human nature, behavior, and interactions:

- **Immanuel Kant** held the assumption that reality is based on subjective observations drawn from a person's objective reality or environmental events. Kant's theories are based on interactionism.
- **Sigmund Freud** found Kant's interactionism offered a starting point for his psychoanalytical work.
- **Gottfried Leibniz** was a philosopher who believed in personology, which states that a person can change when his or her perceptual awareness is changed. Leibniz's **theory of mind** is based on subjective reality—how a person perceives things to be within his or her own mind. Leibniz's **theory of personology** evolved into humanistic psychology, resulting in a counseling model known as **Rogers' person-centered psychotherapy**.
- **John Locke** held a more empiricist viewpoint, believing the human brain absorbs environmental events and sensory inputs from its surroundings in an effort to form meaning and knowledge, so studying only nature and the environment unlocks a person's mental health needs. Locke's empiric theories evolved into behavior therapy and behavioral counseling.

Despite the differences in philosophies, the goal of each of these psychotherapy models is the same. Each works to transform a person's thought patterns to affect the way that person handles emotional responses and behaves.

Stages of Theory Development

The stages of theory development can be divided into five paradigms:

Stage	Paradigm	Theorists
1	Original Paradigm	Freud's psychoanalysis, client-centered therapy, and behavior therapy
2	Paradigm Modification	Jung, Adler, Patterson, Bandura
3	Paradigm Specificity	Berne, Jourard, Genlin, Bech, and Krumboltz
4	Paradigm Experimentation	Strupp, Mitchell and Aron, Ellis, Beutler, Wexler, and Lazarus
5	Paradigm Consolidation	Lazarus, Seay, and Beutler

In the **paradigm modification stage**, Jung, Adler, Patterson, and Bandura adapted Freud's **original paradigm** (which was the foundation for psychoanalysis, client-centered therapy, and behavior therapy). Adaptation was necessary because the original paradigm of development theory did not adequately answer all of the questions these theorists raised. Jung had a more restrained viewpoint regarding Freud's bisexual theories. Adler had a more social viewpoint regarding Freud's theories. Modification stage theorists worked to add to the developing paradigm without making revolutionary changes.

In the **paradigm specificity stage**, changes to counseling tactics were initiated by theorists Berne, Jourard, Genlin, Beck, and Krumboltz. Berne replaced Freud's superego, id, and ego with adapted terms referring to the parent, child, and adult. Berne's new nomenclature allowed Freud's work to remain intact, except for minor alterations in terminology.

In the **paradigm experimentation stage**, Strupp, Mitchell, Aron, Ellis, Beutler, Wexler, and Lazarus initiated changes to the rules for conducting counseling sessions. Experimentation stage theorists began making abstract structures, practices, and paradigm-linked procedures. Stages 1-3 of theory development were greatly altered. Old parameters were disregarded by radical behaviorists who accepted more humanistic, cognitive processing theories. Humanists adopted relaxation techniques common to the behaviorist theories. The models found in stage 4 are inconsistent, without the foundational supports of previous paradigms, and are not reconciled with a philosophy.

Stage 5, **paradigm consolidation**, is in its infancy, started by the continued exploration of Lazarus, Seay, and Beutler. There are more developments along its horizon.

Motives For Psychotherapy

According to Joseph Rychlak, psychotherapy can be broken down into three basic motives that correspond with learning, ethics, and healing.

- **Scholarly motive** corresponds with learning. Rychlak believed this rationale for performing psychotherapy was best characterized in the works of Freud, where the psychotherapist is a scientist who records the inner workings of the mind, instinctive drives, and actions, and then analyzes the data collected.
- **Ethical motive** refers to the counselor's desire to help the client grow and express strong feelings and opinions about his or her life problems.
- **Curative motive** is when the psychotherapist wants to initiate the healing process for the client by engaging in such a way as to help modify those behaviors detrimental to the client's success in society.

Theories That Violate Paradigm Parameters

There are various theories that violate basic paradigm parameters. Examples include the following:

- Cognitive-behavioral theory operates on a person's interaction with his or her surroundings. Environmental interaction is based on the person's cognitive abilities to organize information. Cognitive-behavioral theory violates the paradigm parameters found in Lockean philosophy.
- Robert Carkhuff violated Leibniz' theories in his affective-behavioral approach therapy that reinterpreted Carl Rogers' work.

Non-conformity or violation is known as **technical eclecticism**. Technical eclecticism is designed to improve the therapist's ability to select the best treatment for the client, based on validated procedures, strategies, and applied techniques. Therapists choose a treatment focus and specific strategies that are consistent with the client's coping style, resistance level, and emotional arousal.

De-Emphasis on Theoretical Dependency

Thomas Kuhn (1962) suggested that psychotherapists adopt a single paradigm instead of the many paradigms already in place. Kuhn's suggestion was embraced in Lazarus' technical eclecticism, which allows more freedom of selection in choosing preferred or best theoretical models. Eclectic approaches allow for a mixture of different models. One example is to mix Freud's psychoanalytic approaches with Beck's cognitive theory. Another example is models that are founded on phenomenological knowledge structures, which incorporate Rogers' person-centered therapy. Some combine Wolpe's behavior therapy and behavior modification strategies. Model lines become indistinguishable when combinations of theoretical models cease to follow more structured guidelines. Abbreviations that demonstrate this blending are as follows: CB is a mixture of cognitive and behavioral standards, CA is a mixture of information processing structures with affective models, AB is a mixture of affective models with behavioral standards, and CAB is a combination of all three.

Treatment Planning Chapter Quiz

1. Stage 2 of theory development is:

a. The original paradigm
b. Paradigm modification
c. Paradigm experimentation
d. Paradigm consolidation

2. The unconscious motivation ruled by the pleasure principle is known as the:

a. Ego
b. Id
c. Superego
d. Shadow

3. Which of the following is one of Jung's archetypes?

a. The World
b. The King
c. The Hero
d. The Villain

4. Who developed Gestalt therapy?

a. Alder
b. Rogers
c. Perls
d. Hattie

5. Which of the following is NOT a basic universal emotion?

a. Fear
b. Anger
c. Surprise
d. Guilt

6. Which of the following lists the stages of change of the transtheoretical model from FIRST to LAST?

a. Precontemplation, Contemplation, Preparation, Action, Maintenance
b. Preparation, Precontemplation, Contemplation, Action, Maintenance
c. Precontemplation, Contemplation, Maintenance, Preparation, Action
d. Preparation, Action, Maintenance, Precontemplation, Contemplation

7. Who developed the theory of personology?

a. Leibniz
b. Rogers
c. Locke
d. Kant

8. Which of the following is NOT one of Rychlak's three basic motives?

a. Scholarly motive
b. Ethical motive
c. Curative motive
d. Carnal motive

9. Which of the following is NOT a strategy employed in motivational interviewing?

a. Providing affirmations
b. Avoiding Yes/No questions
c. Providing reflective listening
d. Discouraging change talk

10. Freudian slips are overt actions with unconscious meanings, also known as which of the following?

a. Dormant impulses
b. Parapraxes
c. Cathexis
d. Anti-cathexis

Counseling Skills and Interventions

Therapeutic Frameworks

Historical Impact on Therapeutic Interventions

Therapeutic interventions require the use of foundational models incorporating philosophy, theory, and practice methodologies. The disadvantage of applying past solutions is their tendency to hinder the application of unconventional solutions not found in old psychotherapy treatment manuals. Unconventional solutions may work for the individual who has not had success with a conventional method, though it may have previously worked for another client. Mental health care has undergone a progressive development throughout time. Therapeutic trends have become part of the accepted model for mental health care. Institutions of the past have been replaced with community treatment centers that have had an innovative impact on mental health. Treatments have become more **psychologically based** as clients' surroundings have become a factor. Psychologically-trained and educationally-trained counselors have begun to specialize.

Counseling vs. Psychotherapy

Some practitioners use the terms counseling and psychotherapy interchangeably to indicate the same service. However, those practitioners who believe these terms are not identical state the difference lies in the class of client that receives treatment. Other substantive differences in terminology include: the kind of therapy received, degree and nature of illness, clinical work setting or environment in which treatment is received, and the training received by the therapist. **Counseling** is a treatment that allows the client to express emotions while the therapist provides support, education, and feedback. However, **psychotherapy** is a remediation process that involves getting to the root cause of the problem. Neither counselor nor psychotherapist can make these divisions in treatment, as there is a distinctive overlap when talking with the client.

Cognitive-Behavioral Therapy

Cognitive-behavioral therapy (CBT) focuses on the impact that thoughts have on behavior and feelings and encourages the individual to use the power of **rational thought** to alter perceptions and behavior. This approach to counseling is usually short-term, about twelve to twenty sessions, with the first sessions used to obtain a history, the middle sessions used to focus on problems, and last sessions used to review and reinforce. Individuals are assigned "homework" during the sessions to practice new ways of thinking and to develop new coping strategies. The therapist helps the individual identify **goals** and then find ways to achieve those goals. CBT acknowledges that all problems cannot be resolved, but one can deal differently with problems. The therapist asks many questions to determine the individual's areas of concern and encourages the individual to question his or her own motivations and needs. CBT is goal-centered so each counseling session is structured toward a particular goal, such as coping techniques. CBT centers on the concept of unlearning previous behaviors and learning new ones, questioning behaviors, and doing homework. Different approaches to CBT include Aaron Beck's cognitive therapy, rational emotive behavior therapy, and dialectic behavior therapy.

Cognitive-Behavioral Group Therapy for Social Phobias

Cognitive-behavioral group therapy (CBGT) for social phobias is a form of **exposure therapy** done in a group environment, usually limited to about six clients with one or (preferably) two therapists to monitor and guide group exercises. Having an equal mix of men and women is preferred because social phobias often involve male-female interactions. Clients with different types of fears are appropriate for the group because they complement each other during therapy. The initial sessions involve psychoeducation about phobias and basic instruction in cognitive restructuring, including identifying automatic thoughts and discussing how they are errors in thinking. During exercises, such as speaking in front of the group, clients are asked to express their automatic thoughts and discuss them. The **subjective units of distress rating scale** (0–10 scale of distress) is used throughout exercises with clients giving their score every minute. Each client is provided with individualized homework. Sessions are usually weekly for 2–3 hours for 12–24 weeks.

Personal Science

Personal Science was developed in 1977 by Michael Mahoney, based on the cognitive-behavioral (CB) approach. The acronym SCIENCE is used to explain the sequential steps through which the therapist guides the client to solve a problem:

- **S** for *specification* of the problem
- **C** for *collection* of data or facts
- **I** for *identification* of patterns or reasons for existing behaviors
- **E** for *examination* of choices that can be used to modify behavior
- **N** for *narrowing* the options and experimenting with possible modifications
- **C** for *comparing* data or facts
- **E** for *expanding*, modifying, or substituting unwanted behaviors

Psychobehavioral Therapy and Cognitive-Client Therapy

Psychobehavioral therapy was developed in 1971 by George E. Woody. This is simply a combination of two psychoanalytic and behavioral techniques with a variety of eclectic approaches. Psychobehavioral therapy is based on the cognitive-behavioral (CB) approach.

Cognitive-client therapy was a cognitive-affective (CA) model designed by David Wexler in 1974. He used **information processing theory** as the foundation for his beliefs concerning cognitive roles. Wexler postulated that client-centered therapy was better established by combining affective experience with cognitive thoughts. Wexler's belief was similar to those of the cognitive-behaviorists. He believed that the client could gain control over his or her behavior through cognitive deliberations. Wexler also believed that emotional experiencing could not be accomplished without a forerunner of cognitive thought processes.

Acceptance Commitment Therapy

Acceptance commitment therapy (ACT) approaches behavioral change from a different perspective than conventional CBT. Clients are encouraged to examine their thought processes (**cognitive defusion**) when undergoing episodes of anxiety or depression. They identify a thought, such as "People think I am ugly," and then analyze whether or not this is true, listing evidence, and then evaluating whether or not the anxiety is decreased after this evaluation process. Eventually, this process becomes automatic, eliminating the need to write everything down. Mindfulness is a basic concept of ACT, and clients are encouraged to examine their values and control those things that are under their control, such as their facial expression or actions. ACT represents:

- **A**: Accepting reactions
- **C**: Choosing a direction
- **T**: Taking action to effect change.

Aaron Beck's Cognitive Therapy

Aaron Beck discovered that during psychotherapy clients often had a second set of thoughts while undergoing "free association." Beck called these **automatic thoughts**, which were labeled and interpreted, according to a personal set of rules. Beck called dysfunctional automatic thoughts **cognitive disorders**. Beck identified a triad of negative thoughts regarding the self, the environment, and the world. The key concepts in **Aaron Beck's cognitive therapy** include the following:

- **Therapist/client relationship**: Therapy is a collaborative partnership. The goal of therapy is determined together. The therapist encourages the client to disagree when appropriate.
- **Process of therapy**: The therapist explains the following: the perception of reality is not reality. The interpretation of sensory input depends on cognitive processes. The client is taught to recognize maladaptive ideation, identifying observable behavior, underlying motivation, and his or her thoughts and beliefs. The client practices distancing the maladaptive thoughts, explores his or her conclusions, and tests them against reality.
- **Conclusions**: The client makes the rules less extreme and absolute, drops false rules, and substitutes adaptive rules.

Eric Berne's Transactional Analysis

The major concepts of **transactional analysis** according to Eric Berne are:

- **Ego State**: One's personal frame of mind
- **Parent**: Parents who exhibit feelings/behaviors learned from their parents, which may be nurturing or critical
- **Adult**: An individual who exhibits feelings/behaviors of a mature adult
- **Child**: An individual who exhibits feelings/behaviors natural to children under seven years old
- **Transaction**: Verbal and nonverbal communication between two people
- **Complementary transactions**: A message sent from the ego state of Person A which is responded to in that same ego state, or a message sent to the ego state of Person B which is responded to in that same ego state
- **Crossed transactions**: A message sent from the ego state of Person A which is responded to in another ego state, or a message sent to the ego state of Person B which is responded to from another ego state
- **Ulterior transactions**: messages that occur on two levels, the social or overt level and the hidden or psychological level

Behaviorism

Behaviorists anticipate that the client can unlearn dysfunctional behaviors. Pavlov cultivated his theories from experiments where he conditioned dogs to salivate to different stimuli. Watson and Rayner experimented on a young boy by conditioning his response to white, furry animals, causing the boy to develop a phobia. This can be related to a person's development of a phobia after a negative experience. Some people become afraid of the water after a near drowning experience. Addictive cravings, anxieties, insomnia, and pain management may be improved with relaxation training and methodical desensitization techniques. B. F. Skinner's experiments involved operant conditioning, where he proposed that feelings and actions are reinforced and rewarded. Therefore, the way to stop a behavior is to take away the reinforcement. For example, a child who exhibits misbehaviors in school may be doing so to gain the teacher's attention.

Operant Conditioning

Operant conditioning is based on feelings and actions that are reinforced and rewarded. The way to stop the behavior is to take away the reinforcement. An explanation for a client's pathological behavior is that it was reinforced. Behaviorists look for rewards that may cause their client to act out inappropriately. For example, a person who feels isolated may experience health problems out of a need to gain attention from hospital staff and or family. Token economy and contingency contractual agreements are the result of operant conditioning. Albert Bandura created **social learning theory** in 1969, based on people learning from watching others. Violence on television has been linked to real life violent acts by social learning theory. Proponents say a more functional TV model should be presented to replace the pathological behavior. Behaviorists use relaxation techniques, imagery, systematic desensitization, reinforcement contingencies, positive role modeling, and token economies.

Albert Ellis's Rational Emotive Therapy

Key concepts of **Albert Ellis's rational emotive therapy** include the idea that people control their own destinies and interpret events, according to their own values and beliefs.

Forms of irrational beliefs include:

- Something is awful or terrible
- One cannot tolerate something
- Something or someone is damned or cursed

"**Musturbatory" ideologies** have three forms:

- I must do well and win approval or I am a rotten person.
- You must act kindly toward me or you are a rotten person.
- My life must remain comfortable or life hardly seems worth living.

Therapy consists of detecting and eradicating irrational beliefs, as follows:

- **Disputing**: Detecting irrationalities, debating them, discriminating between logical and illogical thinking, and defining what helps create new beliefs
- **Debating**: Questioning and disputing the irrational beliefs
- **Discriminating**: Distinguishing between wants and needs, desires and demands, and rational and irrational ideas
- **Defining**: Defining words and redefining beliefs

Rational Behavior Therapy

Rational behavior therapy was developed in 1977 by Maxie C. Maultsby, Jr. It is a more direct method of dealing with a client's emotional state than Ellis' rational emotive therapy from the mid-1950's. Maultsby was Albert Ellis' student. Rational behavior is based on the cognitive-behavioral (CB) approach and has five steps, known as **emotional re-education**:

1. **Self-analysis** using rational thought helps the client to gain intellectual insights.
2. **Changing actions** or behaviors to reflect newly gained intellectual insights.
3. **Cognitive emotive dissonance** is a refocus of attention that helps the client bring feelings and thought patterns into alignment with each other.
4. **Rationalized feelings** promote cohesive thought patterns through consistent emotional insights.
5. **Habitual practice** of newly gained insights develops new personality traits in the client.

MULTIMODAL BEHAVIOR THERAPY

Multimodal Behavior Therapy was invented in 1971 by Arnold Lazarus. This is a complex system that mingles client-conceptualization theories into all the human modalities of cognition, affect, and behavior that cannot be excluded from a client's everyday life. Lazarus believed that there were exactly seven modalities. He used the acronym **BASIC ID** to explain each one:

- **B** for *behavior*
- **A** for *affect*
- **S** for *sensory*
- **I** for *imagery*
- **C** for *cognition*
- **I** for *intrapersonal*
- **D** for *drugs*

Multimodal Behavior Therapy has no guide for which technique to choose for treatment, no set therapy process, or sequential steps to take. Multimodal Behavior Therapy identifies a theme, and then the therapist utilizes the BASIC ID techniques for treating the client.

Review Video: Multimodal Behavior Therapy
Visit mometrix.com/academy and enter code: 813824

RECOVERY MODEL

The recovery model approach to mental health **shifts control** of treatment options to the client rather than the provider deciding the plan of care. This has been effective in those clients who have the capacity to make decisions to allow them to be more independent and take a more active role in the decision-making regarding their treatment plan. The goal of this model is to allow the client to be more **autonomous** so that they may achieve the ultimate goals of finding employment and housing and living independently. The more independent the client can become, the more they progress to making independent decisions about the treatment of their mental health issues. This model is not appropriate for those clients who are so incapacitated by their illness that they do not understand they are ill. The amount of independence and decision-making that is turned over to the client should increase as they become more stable.

PHYSIOLOGICAL FOUNDATION FOR PSYCHOTHERAPY

The **physiological foundation for psychotherapy** is gaining momentum as research in this area advances. Biopsychological research is based on the notion that biological systems in the body are linked to human behaviors. Prescription drugs are used to alter brain chemistry to help the client cope with imbalances in their biological systems. An alternative or supplement to drug therapy is exercise that releases endorphins and helps the client to decrease feelings of depression. In the past, the person receiving psychological treatment was treated more like a casualty who was responsible for his or her own injured state. The mental health provider held to the belief that the client's mental state, shortfalls involving relationships, and maladaptive behaviors were at the root of the client's mental disorder.

Organizational Models for Psychoecological Delivery

The **organizational models for psychoecological delivery** were identified by Seay in 1983. Care can be delivered through direct preventive interventions, remedial, or aftercare systems.

- **Direct preventive interventions** are the primary delivery target.
- **Remedial care** is the secondary delivery target.
- **Aftercare** is tertiary prevention.

These five areas are addressed:

- Residential
- Community
- Educational
- Business and political arenas
- The private sector

Services offered include:

- Individual psychotherapy
- Group psychotherapy
- Family psychotherapy
- Educational courses
- Synchronization of services
- Restructuring the client's surroundings
- Making contacts within the community
- Advocacy
- Referral
- Ongoing professional instruction and training
- Psychodiagnostics
- Research and assessment
- Financial support

The model contains:

- Counseling/psychotherapy
- Marriage counseling services
- Family counseling services
- Drug and alcohol therapy
- Environmental restructuring
- Funding
- Community health centers
- Other approaches

This model should correct some of the organization deficiencies that are currently part of the mental health provider system.

Trauma-Informed Care

Trauma-informed care acts on the premise that many individuals have experienced some sort of trauma, and therefore every client should be approached with sensitivity and care. Traumatic events are deeply individualized, and what may have been traumatic to one individual, may not be to the next. Withholding judgment of what qualifies as trauma is imperative for the psychiatric-mental health professional.

The five elements of trauma-informed care include the following:

- **Safety**: Ensuring that the client feels emotionally and physically safe must be the first priority in order to create a conducive environment for treatment.
- **Choice**: Treatment cannot be forced and must honor the individual's right to choose.
- **Collaboration**: The client and the provider must work collaboratively through shared decision-making.
- **Trustworthiness**: The client must trust the provider in order for treatment to be effective. Trustworthiness can be established by communicating what is happening and what will happen next to the client.
- **Empowerment**: Empower the client with tools to cope on their own so that their recovery extends outside the walls of treatment.

Parent-Child Interaction Therapy

Parent-child interaction therapy (PCIT) is designed for preschool children with conduct disorder or oppositional defiant disorder. Sessions are usually 1 hour a week for 10–16 weeks. The therapist observes the parent-child interaction from outside the room (usually with a two-way mirror) and provides feedback. PCIT has two phases:

- **Child-directed interaction:** Parents learn specific skills to use when engaging children in free play, including reflecting a child's statements and describing and praising appropriate behavior while ignoring undesirable behavior. The goal is to strengthen the parent–child bond and eliminate undesirable behavior.
- **Parent-directed interaction:** During this phase, positive behaviors are increased and undesirable behaviors are decreased. Parents learn to give clear commands, provide consistent reinforcement, and use time out for noncompliance.

Incredible Years Program

The **Incredible Years program** for conduct disorder and oppositional defiant disorder has both a child (ages 4–7) and a parent component:

- **Child**: "Dinosaur school" is a group of children (about six children) who attend 2-hour weekly sessions for about 17 weeks. Videos and life-sized puppets are used to demonstrate ways of dealing with interpersonal problems, such as making friends, empathizing, coping with teasing, and resolving conflicts. Children practice social skills and are rewarded for positive social skills. Parents receive weekly updates and are asked to reward children for positive social skills.
- **Parent**: Parents meet in groups (about ten parents) for 2-hour sessions for 22 weeks. Parents view seventeen videos modeling appropriate methods for dealing with problem behavior and discuss them in the group. Parents learn to initiate nonthreatening play sessions, use positive reinforcement and consistent limit-setting, and learn strategies for dealing with problem behavior, such as time-outs.

PSST and PMT

Problem-solving skills training (PSST) is designed for children 7-13 years old to address antisocial behavior, conduct disorder, and oppositional defiant disorder. Parents of these children can take a **parent management training (PMT)** course simultaneously.

- **PSST**: Children attend 50-minute individual weekly sessions for 25 weeks. The therapist presents problem situations similar to those faced by the child and then helps the child to evaluate the situation, develop goals, and alternate goals for dealing with these situations. As homework, children are assigned "super solver" tasks in which they use skills learned in therapy in real-life situations. Parents learn to assist the child in using new strategies.
- **PMT**: Parents attend a total of 16 sessions of 2 hours each over a period of 6-8 months. Parents learn techniques for managing their child's behavior, such as reinforcement, shaping, and time-outs. The therapist uses a variety of teaching methods, including instruction, modeling, and role-playing.

Condition-Specific Therapeutic Approaches

Habit Reversal Therapy for Impulse Control Disorders

Habit reversal therapy (HRT), a form of cognitive-behavioral therapy, is used to help people with tic disorders and for those with impulse control disorders, such as trichotillomania. A number of steps are involved, which are listed below.

- **Awareness**: The client must pay attention, as behaviors are often unconscious. This often involves keeping a detailed log of the behavior, including time, duration, activity during the episode, and emotional state before, during, and after these behaviors.
- **Identification of Triggers**: The log and client interviews help to identify triggers to help clients understand when they are at risk of the behavior and how to use stimulus control to prevent the behavior or to avoid triggers.
- **Assessment**: The client begins to identify feelings (negative or positive) associated with the behavior and the reason for it.
- **Competitive response**: The client carries out another action to compete with the urge to carry out the behavior, thereby preventing it.
- **Assessment of Rationalizations**: The client must confront the rationalizations used to allow the behavior to continue.
- **Mindfulness**: The client learns that it is not necessary to give in to the urge to carry out the behavior as urges often are of short duration.

Therapy Options for Obsessive-Compulsive Disorder

Therapy for obsessive-compulsive disorder aims to develop expression of thoughts and impulses in a manner that is appropriate:

Behavioral therapy (most successful):

- Combined exposure with training to delay obsessive responses; best used in conjunction with pharmacotherapy
- Steady decrease of rituals by exposure to anxiety-producing situations until client has learned to control the related obsessive compulsion
- Reduction of obsessive thoughts by the use of reminders or noxious stimuli to stop chain-of-thought patterns, such as snapping a rubber band on the wrist when obsessive thoughts occur

Family therapy (primary issues):

- Helping the family to avoid situations that trigger OCD response
- Pointing out the tendency of family members to reassure the client, which is apt to support the obsession
- Introducing family strategies, which involve the following:
    - Remaining neutral and not reinforcing through encouragement
    - Avoiding trying to reason logically with the client

Pharmacologic therapy (FDA-approved medications for OCD):

- Clomipramine (Anafranil)
- Sertraline (Zoloft)
- Paroxetine (Paxil)
- Fluoxetine (Prozac)
- Fluvoxamine (Luvox)

EXPOSURE AND RESPONSE/RITUAL PREVENTION

Exposure and response/ritual prevention (ERP) is a type of therapy used to treat obsessive-compulsive disorder (OCD). ERP helps the client learn to reduce anxiety by not performing ritualistic behavior. The goal is to habituate the person to the anxiety associated with an act so that it lessens and the ritual stops. Steps include the following:

1. **Psychoeducation**: ERP begins with education about the nature of OCD and ritualistic behavior.
2. **Ritual/fear analysis**: Fact-finding may be carried out in one or two sessions, during which a fear hierarchy is outlined regarding obsessional material starting with those that cause low anxiety and building to those that cause extremely high anxiety.
3. **Exposure and response/ritual prevention**: Exposure begins with small steps. For example, if a person is obsessed with germs, a first step might be to touch a tissue that touched a toothpick that touched a dirty tissue. The response/ritual prevention part is to avoid washing hands after touching the tissue. This may be done repeatedly to desensitize the person before moving to a high-anxiety item on the fear hierarchy.

THERAPY FOR PTSD

Individuals with **post-traumatic stress disorder (PTSD)** are usually treated with antidepressants, mood stabilizers, or antipsychotic drugs, depending on their symptoms, but one of the following therapies is essential:

- **Cognitive-behavioral therapy (CBT)**: Individuals learn to confront trauma through psychoeducation, breathing, imaginary reliving, and writing; they are taught to recognize thoughts related to their trauma and attempt a method of coping, such as distraction and self-soothing.
- **Eye-movement desensitization and reprocessing**: This form of CBT requires the individual to talk about the experience of trauma while keeping the eyes and attention focused on the therapist's rapidly moving finger. (There is no clear evidence this is more effective than standard CBT.)

- **Family therapy**: PTSD impacts the entire family, so counseling and classes in anger management, parenting, and conflict resolution may help reduce family conflict related to the PTSD.
- **Sleep therapy**: Individuals may fear sleeping because of severe nightmares. Sleep therapy teaches methods to cope with nightmares through imagery rehearsal therapy and relaxation techniques.

Psychoeducation for Bipolar Disorder and Schizophrenia

Psychoeducation, often part of cognitive-behavioral therapy, involves teaching individuals about their disease to help them manage symptoms and behavior.

- **Bipolar disorder**: Individuals are taught to understand the patterns of their disease and the triggers of mood changes so they can seek appropriate medical help. Additionally, they are taught to use self-monitoring tools, such as a daily record, to determine patterns of activity, such as sleeping, so they can maintain as consistent a schedule of eating, sleeping, and engaging in physical activities as possible; consistency tends to reduce unstable mood swings.
- **Schizophrenia**: Individuals must be taught about their disease and the effects of medications. Because medication may not eliminate all symptoms, such as hearing voices, individuals are taught methods to test reality to determine if their perceptions are correct.

Dialectical Behavioral Therapy for Borderline Personality Disorder

Dialectical behavioral therapy was developed for the treatment of clients with **borderline personality disorder (BPD)**. In therapy, the mental health professional helps clients to change behavior by replacing **dichotomous thinking** that paints the world as black or white with rational (dialectical) thinking. This therapy is based on the premise that clients with BPD lack the ability to self-regulate, have a low tolerance for stress, and encounter social and environmental factors that impact their behavioral skills. Therapy includes the following:

- **Cognitive-behavioral therapy** (once a week) focuses on adaptive behaviors that help the client to deal with stress or trauma. Therapy focuses on a prioritized list of problems: suicidal behavior, behavior that interferes with therapy, quality of life issues, post-traumatic stress response, respect for self, acquisition of behavioral skills, and client goals.
- **Group therapy** (2.5 hours a week) helps the client learn behavioral skills, such as self-distracting and soothing.

Motivational Enhancement Therapy for Substance Abuse

Motivational enhancement therapy (MET) is a nonconfrontational, structured approach to treatment for substance abuse that is usually done in four sessions. MET helps motivate the client to change, accept responsibility for change, and remain committed to change. The MET therapist guides the client through different stages of change:

1. **Pre-contemplation**: Client does not wish to change behavior.
2. **Contemplation**: Client considers positive and negative aspects of drug or alcohol use.
3. **Determination**: Client makes a decision to change.
4. **Action**: Client begins to modify behavior over time (2–6 months).
5. **Maintenance**: Client remains abstinent.
6. **Relapse**: Client begins the cycle again. Relapses are common.

The therapist questions, compliments, and supports the client but avoids criticizing, labeling, or directly advising the client. Clients, especially those who have failed previous attempts to stop using, require much encouragement. A pretreatment assessment is completed, and the client is provided with a written report at the first meeting. The therapist uses eight strategies during sessions:

- Eliciting statements of self-motivation
- Listening empathetically
- Questioning
- Providing feedback
- Providing affirmation
- Handling or preventing resistance by reflecting, amplifying, or changing focus
- Reframing
- Summarizing

Visualization to Treat Anxiety Disorders

Visualization (therapeutic imagery) is used to treat **anxiety disorders** primarily for relaxation, stress reduction, and performance improvement. Visualization may be used in conjunction with many other types of therapy, such as exposure therapy, which can be very stressful for some people. Visualization strives to create a visual image of a desired outcome in the mind of the client when he or she imagines himself or herself in that place or situation. Intense concentration helps to block feelings of anxiety. For example, if the focus is on reducing anxiety, the mind focuses on that goal of therapy. All of the senses (e.g., looks, smells, feelings, sounds) may be used to imagine the feeling of relaxation in a certain place.

Single-Session Therapy

Single-session therapy is the **most frequent form of counseling** because individuals often attend only one session for various reasons even if more are advised. Individuals may not have insurance or believe that one session is sufficient. Sessions typically last 1 hour. The goal is to identify a problem and reach a solution in one session. The therapist serves as a facilitator to motivate the individual to view the problem as part of a pattern that can be changed and to identify a solution. The therapist may use a wide range of techniques that culminates in a **plan for the individual** (e.g., homework exercises) so the individual can begin to make changes.

Solution-Focused Therapy

Solution-focused therapy aims to differentiate methods that are effective from those that are not, and to identify areas of strengths so they can be used in problem solving. The premise of solution-focused therapy is that change is possible but that the individual must identify problems and deal with them in the real world. This therapy is based on questioning to help the individual establish goals and find solutions to problems:

- **Pre-session**: The client is asked about any differences he or she noted after making the appointment and coming to the first session.
- **Miracle**: The client is asked if any "miracles" occurred or if any problems were solved, including what, if anything, was different and how this difference affected relationships.
- **Exception**: The client is asked if any small changes were noted and if there were any problems that no longer seemed problematic and how that manifested.
- **Scaling**: The client is asked to evaluate the problem on a 1-10 scale and then to determine how to increase the rating.
- **Coping**: The client is asked about how he or she is managing.

Counseling Techniques

Open vs. Closed Questioning in Counseling

Open questioning asks for general information about a topic ("Can you tell me about your childhood?") and cannot be answered with a simple "yes" or "no." Open questioning is used to encourage the client to talk about issues and is often used at the beginning of a discussion to help put the client at ease and to gain information that the counselor expects the client knows about and can share. Open questions are less threatening than closed (more specific) questions because the client can choose how much to disclose.

Closed questions ask for specific factual information ("Did your father physically abuse you?") and are often asked as follow-up questions to the initial open questions. Because closed questions often require a short answer ("yes" or "no"), the closed question is often followed by another open question to allow the client to expound ("Can you tell me more about that?").

Proxemics

Proxemics is the study of personal space and the distance between individuals at which people feel comfortable or uncomfortable. **Proxemics** vary according to culture, and the counselor should assess the client's personal space of comfort and avoid violating that space or communicating the wrong message. In the United States, distances are classified as the following:

- **Intimate** (0-2 feet): Reserved for those in very close relationships, such as mother-child, person-partner, spouse-spouse. However, some clients, such as some with autism, may feel uncomfortable at intimate distance with anyone.
- **Personal** (2-4 feet): This distance ("arm's length") is commonly used for conversations with friends and associates. Generally, the closer the relationship, the closer the distance.
- **Social** (4-12 feet): A broader distance is maintained between strangers and acquaintances, especially in public spaces such as a store or at formal social gatherings.
- **Public** (greater than 12 feet): Interactions in public, such as a public speaking event, are often at a far distance, and people may feel comfortable moving about and avoiding eye contact.

Enhancing the Client's Coping Methods

Professional counselors help their clients adjust and function in their everyday surroundings. Environments consist of work, school, home, and neighborhood communities. Professional counselors help individual clients gain better awareness of personal growth and self-development. The progression of this awareness is directed in care that helps the client cope with crises and issues in everyday life situations. The client is directed to develop appropriate **coping methods**. The client may also be referred for other health care services when the client has more complex needs or stresses that are not handled within the professional counselor's scope. The counselor educates the client in coping strategies for particular situations.

Utilizing the Developmental Preventive Model

The mental health counselor helps the client handle life stresses by applying developed skills. The counselor also helps the client to evaluate his or her own character strengths. The counselor operates on a **developmental preventive model**. This positive approach model concentrates on the client's normalcy and the client's ability to obtain wellness. The counselor attempts to prevent relapses of the mental illness or disorder, and to keep new illnesses from developing. The model recognizes that each person will go through certain crises in life. The way a person deals with the crises constitutes normal development. The developmental preventive model allows for a more natural way to view and accept needed mental health services.

Applying Self-Awareness to the Counselor-Client Relationship

Self-awareness helps a counselor to provide foundational therapeutic benefits. The counselor comes with his or her own experiences that provide a good backdrop for relating to others. The counselor allows the client to explore his or her own thought patterns, wishes, wants, and goals in a session. The counselor may discuss his or her own comparative experiences in the session while giving the client feedback about an incident. This approach can be seen in the work of Carl Rogers, who believed in promoting an atmosphere of therapy that provided a sense of self-respect and honor for others. Roger's approach is contrary to the long-established, more analytical therapeutic method found in the works of Freud. Self-awareness is one attribute that put professional counselors in a distinctive class not commonly found in other vocations.

Prioritizing Counselor Self-Care

Important in the list of techniques utilized by the counselor is also the ability to conduct **self-care**. The mental health counselor should take care of his or her own needs, to ensure an ongoing ability to do the job. Self-care should be attended to on a daily basis. The counselor should seek out psychotherapy, coaching, exercise, meditation, hobbies, and healthy relationships with others.

- **Psychotherapy** is useful in helping the counselor realize areas in which he or she may be deficient. Training may be needed in a specific area. Psychotherapy can help the counselor to target character issues that can have a negative impact on virtue ethics.
- **Coaching** is useful in helping the counselor target career or family goals. Coaching can be achieved via the phone or secure internet connections.
- **Exercise programs** are beneficial but should be scheduled as a fun and rewarding part of the day.
- **Meditation** can be utilized, in the form of transcendental meditation, yoga, or breathing exercises.

The counselor should develop **hobbies** and **healthy relationships** with others. Hobbies and a wide range of interests help the counselor to remain stimulated on an intellectual and emotional level. These activities can give the counselor a zest for life and help them to refocus their attention. Family and friends provide the counselor with social and emotional outlets. These outlets can help the counselor reduce feelings of isolation that can lead to burnout. Peers or colleagues can be supportive in the work environment. These supportive groups can provide needed opportunities for socialization in the work setting. Overall, the counselor should approach self-care needs as priorities in their daily life.

Family Therapy

Goals of Family Therapy

Family therapy is a therapeutic modality theorizing that a client's psychiatric symptoms are a result of **pathology within the client's family unit**. This dysfunction is due to problems within the system, usually arising from conflict between marital partners. Psychiatric problems result from these behaviors. This conflict is expressed by:

- **Triangulation**, which manifests itself by the attempt of using another family member to stabilize the emotional process
- **Scapegoating**, which occurs when blaming is used to shift focus to another family member

The **goals** of family therapy are:

- To allow family members to recognize and **communicate their feelings**
- To determine the **reasons for problems** between marital partners and to **resolve** them
- To assist parents in **working together** and to strengthen their **parental authority**
- To help define and clarify **family expectations and roles**
- To learn more and different **positive techniques for interacting**
- To achieve **positive homeostasis** within the family
    - Homeostasis means remaining the same, or maintaining a functional balance. Homeostasis can occur to maintain a dysfunctional status as well.
- To enhance the family's **adaptability**
    - Adaptability is maintaining a balanced, positive stability in the family. A prerequisite for balanced stability, and a basic goal of family therapy, is to help the client family develop strategies for dealing with life's inevitable changes. Morphogenesis is the medical term often applied to a family's ability to react functionally and appropriately to changes.

Theoretical Approaches to Family Therapy

Four theoretical approaches to family therapy are **strategic**, **behavioral**, **psychodynamic**, and **object relations** theories:

- A **strategic approach** to family therapy was proposed by Jay Haley. Haley tried to map out a different strategic plan for each type of psychological issue addressed. With this approach, there is a special treatment strategy for each malady.
- A **behavioral approach** uses traditional behavior-modification techniques to address issues. This approach relies heavily on reinforcement strategies. B.F. Skinner is perhaps the most famous behaviorist. This approach relies on conditioning and often desensitizing as well.
- The **psychodynamic approach** attempts to create understanding and insight on the part of the client. Strategies may be diverse, but in all of them the therapist acts as an emotional guide, leading the client to a better understanding of mental and emotional mechanisms. One common example is Gestalt therapy.
- **Object relations theory** asserts that the ego develops attachment relationships with external and internal objects. A person's early relationships to objects (which can include people) may result in frustration or rejection, which forms the basis of personality.

STRATEGIC FAMILY THERAPY

Strategic family therapy (Haley, 1976) is based on the following concepts:

- This therapy seeks to learn what **function** the symptom serves in the family (i.e., what payoff is there for the system in allowing the symptom to continue?).
- **Focuses**: Problem-focused behavioral change, emphasis of parental power and hierarchical family relationships, and the role of symptoms as an attribute of the family's organization.
- Helplessness, incompetence, and illness all provide **power positions** within the family. The child uses symptoms to change the behavior of parents.

Jay Haley tried to develop a strategy for each issue faced by a client. Problems are isolated and treated in different ways. A family plagued by alcoholism might require a different treatment strategy than a family undermined by sexual infidelity. Haley was unusual in that he held degrees in the arts and communication rather than in psychology. Haley's strategies involved the use of directives (direct instructions). After outlining a problem, Haley would tell the family members exactly what to do. If John would bang his head against the wall when he was made to do his homework, Haley might tell a parent to work with him and to be there while he did his homework.

VIRGINIA SATIR AND THE ESALEN INSTITUTE'S EXPERIENTIAL FAMILY THERAPY

Virginia Satir and the Esalen Institute's experiential family therapy draws on sociology, ego concepts, and communication theory to form **role theory concepts**. Satir examined the roles of "rescuer" and "placatory" that constrain relationships and interactions in families. This perspective seeks to increase intimacy in the family and improve the self-esteem of family members by using awareness and the communication of feelings. Emphasis is on individual growth in order to change family members and deal with developmental delays. Particular importance is given to marital partners and on changing verbal and nonverbal communication patterns that lower self-esteem.

SATIR'S COMMUNICATION IMPEDIMENTS

Satir described four issues that impede communication between family members under stress. Placating, blaming, being overly reasonable, and being irrelevant are the **four issues which blocked family communication**, according to Virginia Satir:

- **Placating** is the role played by some people in reaction to threat or stress in the family. The placating person reacts to internal stresses by trying to please others, often in irrational ways. A mother might try to placate her disobedient and rude child by offering food, candy, or other presents on the condition that he stop a certain behavior.
- **Blaming** is the act of pointing outwards when an issue creates stress. The blamer thinks, "I'm very angry, but it's your fault. If I've wrecked the car, it's because you made me upset when I left home this morning."
- **Irrelevance** is a behavior wherein a person displaces the potential problem and substitutes another unrelated activity. A mother who engages in too much social drinking frequently discusses her split ends whenever the topic of alcoholism is brought up by her spouse.
- Being overly reasonable, also known as being a **responsible analyzer** is when a person keeps his or her emotions in check and functions with the precision and monotony of a machine.

Murray Bowen's Family Systems Theory

Bowen's family systems theory focuses on the following concepts:

- The role of **thinking versus feeling/reactivity** in relationship/family systems.
- Role of **emotional triangles**: The three-person system or triangle is viewed as the smallest stable relationship system and forms when a two-person system experiences tension.
- **Generationally repeating family issues***:* Parents transmit emotional problems to a child. (Example: The parents fear something is wrong with a child and treat the child as if something is wrong, interpreting the child's behavior as confirmation.)
- **Undifferentiated family ego mass**: This refers to a family's lack of separateness. There is a fixed cluster of egos of individual family members as if all have a common ego boundary.
- **Emotional cutoff**: A way of managing emotional issues with family members (cutting off emotional contact).
- Consideration of thoughts and feelings of **each individual family member** as well as seeking to understand the family network.

Review Video: Bowen Family Systems
Visit mometrix.com/academy and enter code: 591496

Family System Theory Assumptions About Human Behavior

Family systems theory makes several basic assumptions:

- Change in one part of the family system brings about change in other parts of the system.
- The family provides the following to its members: unity, individuation, security, comfort, nurturance, warmth, affection, and reciprocal need satisfaction.
- Where family pathology is present, the individual is socially and individually disadvantaged.
- Behavioral problems are a reflection of communication problems in the family system.
- Treatment focuses on the family unity; changing family interactions is the key to behavioral change.

Motivations for Change and Means Through Which Change Occurs

The **motivations for change** according to Bowen's family systems theory are as follows:

- **Disequilibrium** of the normal family homeostasis is the primary motivation for change according to this perspective.
- The family system is made up of three subsystems: the marital relationship, the parent-child relationship, and the sibling relationship. **Dysfunction** that occurs in any of these subsystems will likely cause dysfunction in the others.

The **means for change** in the family systems theory approach is the family as an interactional system.

Contributions to Family Systems Theory

The **psychodynamic theory** emphasizes multi-generational family history. Earlier family relations and patterns determine current ones. Distorted relations in childhood lead to patterns of miscommunication and behavioral problems. Interpersonal and intrapersonal conflict beneath apparent family unity results in psychopathology. Social role functioning is influenced by heredity and environment.

Don Jackson, a major contributor to family therapy, focuses on **power relationships**. He developed a theory of double-bind communication in families. Double-bind communication occurs when two conflicting messages communicated simultaneously create or maintain a no-win pathological symptom.

Assessment and Treatment Planning in the Family Systems Theory

Assessment in family systems theory includes the following:

- Acknowledgement of **dysfunction** in the family system
- **Family hierarchy**: Who is in charge? Who has responsibility? Who has authority? Who has power?
- Evaluation of **boundaries** (around subsystems, between family and larger environment): Are they permeable or impermeable? Flexible or rigid?
- How does the **symptom** function in the family system?

Treatment planning is as follows:

- The therapist creates a mutually satisfactory contract with the family to establish service boundaries.
- Bowenian family therapy's goal is the differentiation of the individual from the strong influence of the family.

Sal Minuchin's Structural Family Therapy

Sal Minuchin's structural family therapy seeks to strengthen boundaries when family subsystems are enmeshed, or seeks to increase flexibility when these systems are overly rigid. Minuchin emphasizes that the family structure should be hierarchical and that the parents should be at the top of the hierarchy.

Joining, enactment, boundary making, and mimesis are four techniques used by Salvador Minuchin in structural family therapy:

- **Joining** is the therapist's attempt at greeting and bonding with members of the family. Bonding is important when obtaining cooperation and input.
- Minuchin often had his clients enact the various scenarios which led to disagreements and conflicts within families. The **enactment** of an unhealthy family dynamic would allow the therapist to better understand the behavior and allow the family members to gain insight.
- **Boundary making** is important to structural family therapies administered by Salvador Minuchin, because many family conflicts arise from confusion about each person's role. Minuchin believed that family harmony was best achieved when people were free to be themselves yet knew that they must not invade the areas of other family members.
- **Mimesis** is a process in which the therapist mimics the positive and negative behavior patterns of different family members.

Therapeutic Methods Employed by Carl Whitaker

Carl Whitaker, known as the dean of family therapy, developed **experiential symbolic family therapy**. Whitaker would freely interact with other family members and often played the part of family members who were important to the dynamic. He felt that experience, not information and education, had the power to change family dynamics.

Whitaker believed that in family therapy, theory was also less important than experience and that co-therapists were a great aid to successful counseling. Co-therapists freed one of the counselors to participate more fully in the counseling sessions. One counselor might direct the flow of activity while the other participated in role playing. The "psychotherapy of the absurd" is a Whitaker innovation which was influenced by the "theatre of the absurd," a popular existential art form at the time. In this context, the absurd is the unreasonable exaggeration of an idea, to the point of underscoring the underlying meaninglessness of much of human interaction. A person who repeated a neurotic or destructive behavior, for example, was being absurd. The **psychotherapy of the absurd**, as Whitaker saw it, was a method for bringing out repeated and meaningless absurdities. A person pushing against an immovable brick wall, for example, might eventually understand the psychological analogy to some problem behavior.

Theories of Causality

Multiple theories of causality exist in the interpretation of family dynamics, which are then applied to the selection of therapeutic interventions. While linear causality (the concept that one cause equals one effect) uses a direct line of reasoning and is commonly used in individual counseling, **circular/reciprocal causality** is often used in family therapy and refers to the dynamic interactions between family members. Think of a situation in which one member of a family (a father, perhaps) has a severe emotional problem accompanied by violent and angry outbursts. The father periodically assaults his teenage son. Reciprocal or circular causality would apply in this family situation, since the father's angry behavior resonates throughout the family, causing different problems for each person. The spouse might feel inadequate to protect her son and sink into a depression. The other children would suffer, too, from anxiety and fear that the same treatment would befall them. Owing to circular causality, a single cause can have many effects.

Paradoxical Intervention Strategies

Paradoxical intervention strategies involve the use of the client's disruptive behavior as a treatment itself, requiring the client to put the behavior in the spotlight to then motivate change. This technique tries to accomplish the opposite of what it suggests on the surface. Interventions include the following:

- **Restraining** is advising that a negative behavior not be changed or be changed only slightly or slowly. This can be effectively used in the context of couples therapy when a couple is struggling with intimacy issues. The therapist may challenge the couple to refrain from sexual intimacy for a period of time, thus removing certain stressors from that dynamic, possibly resulting in a positive intimate experience that occurs naturally and spontaneously.
- **Positioning** is characterizing a negative behavior in an even more negative light through the use of exaggeration. "David, do you feel you are not terrifying your family enough with your reckless driving or that you ought to drive faster in order to make them worry more about your wellbeing? Perhaps that way you will know that they care about you," says the therapist using positioning as a technique. It is important that this technique be used only with great care, as it can be harmful to clients with a negative self-image. It is generally used in situations where the client is behaving in a certain negative way in order to seek affirmation or attention.
- **Prescribing the symptom** is another paradoxical technique used by therapists to obtain an enlightened reaction from a client. A therapist using this technique directs the client to activate the negative behavior in terms that are absurd and clearly objectionable. 'John, I want you to go out to that sidewalk overpass above the freeway and yell as loud as you can at the cars passing below you. Do it for at least four hours." The therapist prescribes this activity to cure his client's dangerous tendency toward road rage.

- **Relabeling** is recasting a negative behavior in a positive light in order to get an emotional response from the client. "Perhaps your wife yells at you when you drink because she finds this behavior attractive and wants your attention," the therapist might say. The therapist might even support that obviously illogical and paradoxical argument by pointing out invented statistics, which support the ridiculous assertion.

Extinction, Time Out, and Thought Stopping

Behavior modification is a term used in facilities like schools and jails to bring behavior into line with societal or family rules:

- **Extinction** is the process of causing a behavior to disappear by providing little or no reinforcement. It is different from punishment, which is negative reinforcement rather than no reinforcement at all. Very often, a student will be removed from the general population and made to sit alone in a quiet room. In schools, this goes by various names, but is often called in-school suspension (ISS). It is hoped that, through lack of reinforcement and response from outside, the offensive behavior will become extinct.
- **Time out** is another extinction technique, generally applied to very young children. A disobedient child will be isolated for a specified, usually short time whenever he or she misbehaves. The method's operant mechanism assumes that we are all social animals and require the reinforcement of the outside world. Deprived of this, we adapt by altering our behavior.
- **Thought stopping** is a learned response which requires the participation and cooperation of the client to change a negative behavior. When it is successful, the client actively forbids negative thoughts from entering his or her mind.

Specific Family Therapy Interventions

Family Therapy Interventions Used with OCD

Family therapy interventions used to treat individuals with **obsessive-compulsive disorder (OCD)** include therapy oriented to develop expression of thoughts and impulses in a manner that is appropriate. This approach assumes that family members often:

- Attempt to avoid situations that trigger OCD responses
- Constantly reassure the individual (which often enables the obsession)

Family therapy to address these issues involves:

- Remaining neutral and not reinforcing through encouragement
- Avoiding attempts to reason logically with individual

Family Therapy Interventions for Panic Disorders

Family dynamics and therapy interventions for **panic disorders** include:

- Individuals with agoraphobia may require the presence of family members to be constantly in close proximity, resulting in marital stress and over-reliance on the children.
- Altered role performance of the afflicted member results in family and social situations that increase the responsibility of other family members.
- The family must be educated about the source and treatment of the disorder.
- The goal of family therapy is to reorganize responsibilities to support family change.

Functional Family Therapy for Adolescents with Antisocial Behavior

Functional family therapy (FFT) is designed for adolescents (11–17 years of age) with **antisocial behavior**. FFT uses the principles of family systems theory and cognitive-behavioral therapy and provides intervention and prevention services. While the therapy has changed somewhat over the past 30 years, current FTT usually includes three phases:

1. **Engagement/motivation**: The therapist works with the family to identify maladaptive beliefs to increase expectations for change, reduce negativity and blaming, and increase respect for differences. Goals are to reduce dropout rates and establish alliances.
2. **Behavior change**: The therapist guides the parents in using behavioral interventions to improve family functioning, parenting, and conflict management. Goals are to prevent delinquent behavior and build better communication and interpersonal skills.
3. **Generalization**: The family learns to use new skills to influence the systems in which they are involved, such as school, church, or the juvenile justice system. Community resources are mobilized to prevent relapses.

Multisystemic Therapy for Adolescents with Antisocial Behavior

Multisystemic therapy (MST) is a **family-focused program** designed for adolescents (11–17 years of age) with antisocial and delinquent behaviors. The primary goal is **collaboration** with the family to develop strategies for dealing with the child's behavioral problems. Services are delivered in the family's natural environment rather than at a clinic or office with frequent home visits, usually totaling 40–60 hours over the course of treatment. Sessions are daily initially and then decrease in frequency. A variety of different therapies may be used, including family therapy, parent training, and individual therapy. Therapists use different approaches but adhere to basic principles, including focusing on the strength of the systems, delivering appropriate treatment for developmental level, and improving family functioning. The goals of therapy are to improve family relations and parenting skills, to engage the child in activities with nondelinquent peers, and to improve the child's grades and participation in activities, such as sports.

Therapeutic Methods for Counseling an Adolescent With Behavioral Problems

When an **adolescent's behavior** is a problem, some parents have him or her sign an agreement to perform in a specified manner. The agreement may state that a reward will be provided to the adolescent so long as the contract is upheld. The therapist can help parents and children write an effective contract. Another time-honored method of behavior conditioning is the withholding of leisure activity until chores are done. In a family therapy session, the therapist might advise stating the case like this: "Your television has a parental guide lock which will not be turned on unless you can demonstrate that all your homework is complete."

Role of the Therapist

The role of the therapist in family therapy is to interact in the here and now with the family in relation to current problems. The therapist is a consultant to the family. Some aspects of the therapist's role differ according to school of thought:

- **Structural**: The therapist actively challenges dysfunctional interaction.
- **Strategic and Systemic**: The therapist is very active.
- **Milan School**: Male/female clinicians are co-therapists; a team observes from behind a one-way mirror and consults and directs the co-therapists with the clients.
- **Psychodynamic**: The therapist facilitates self-reflection and understanding of multi-generational dynamics and conflicts.
- **Satir**: The therapist models caring, acceptance, love, compassion, nurturance in order to help clients face fears and increase openness.

Key Concepts of Family Therapy

Key **concepts of family therapy** include the following:

Behavior modeling	The manner in which a child bases his or her own behavior on the behavior of his or her parents and other people. In other words, a child will usually learn to identify acceptable behaviors by mimicking the behavior of others. Some children may have more difficulty with behavior modeling than others.
Boundaries	The means of organization through which system parts can be differentiated both from their environment and from each other. They protect and improve the differentiation and integrity of the family, subsystems, and individual family members.
Collaborative therapy	Therapy in which a different therapist sees each spouse or member of the family.
Complementary family interaction	A type of family relationship in which members present opposite behaviors that supply needs or lacks in the other family member.
Complementarity of needs	Circular support system of a family, in which reciprocity is found in meeting needs; can be adaptive or maladaptive.
Double-bind communication	Communication in which two contradictory messages are conveyed concurrently, leading to a no-win situation.
Family of origin	The family into which one is born.
Family of procreation	The family which one forms with a mate and one's own children.
Enmeshment	Obscuring of boundaries in which differentiation of family subsystems and individual autonomy are lost. Similar to Bowen's "undifferentiated family ego mass." Characterized by "mind reading" (partners speak for each other, complete each other's sentences).
Heritage	The set of customs, traditions, physical characteristics, and other cultural artifacts that a person inherits from his or her ancestors.
Homeostasis	A state of systemic balance (of relationships, alliances, power, authority).
Identified patient	The "symptom bearer" in the family.
Multiple family therapy	Therapy in which three or more families form a group with one or more clinicians to discuss common problems. Group support is given and problems are universalized.
Scapegoating	Unconscious, irrational election of one family member for a negative, demeaned, or outsider role.

Group Work

Counseling Values in Group Practice

The underlying values of group counseling include:

- Every individual has dignity and worth.
- All people have a right and a need to realize their full potential.
- Every individual has basic rights and responsibilities.
- The group acts out democratic values and promotes shared decision-making.
- Every individual has the right of self-determination in both setting and achieving goals.
- Positive change is made possible by honest, open, and meaningful interaction.

Purposes and Goals of Group Practice

Group practice takes a multiple-goal perspective to solving individual and social problems and is based on the recognition that group experiences have many important functions and can be designed to achieve any or all of the following:

- Provide restorative, remedial, or rehabilitative experiences
- Help prevent personal and social distress or breakdown
- Facilitate normal growth and development, especially during stressful times in the life cycle
- Achieve a greater degree of self-fulfillment and personal enhancement
- Help individuals become active, responsible participants in society through group associations

Advantages of Group Work

Advantages of group work include the following:

- Members can help and identify with others dealing with similar issues and situations.
- Sometimes people can more easily accept help from peers than from professionals.
- Through consensual validation, members feel less violated and more reassured as they discover that their problems are similar to those of others.
- Groups give opportunities to members to experiment with and test new social identities and roles.
- Group practice is not a replacement for individual treatment. Group work is an essential tool for many counselors and can be the method of choice for some problems.
- Group practice can complement other practice techniques.

Review Video: Group Work and its Benefits
Visit mometrix.com/academy and enter code: 375134

Importance of Relationships in Group Work

Establishing meaningful, effective relationships in group work is essential, and its importance cannot be overemphasized. The counselor will form multiple changing relationships with individual group members, with sub-groups, and with the group as a whole. There are multiple other parties who have a stake in members' experiences, such as colleagues of the counselor, agency representatives, relatives, friends, and others. The counselor will relate differentially to all of those individuals.

Types of Counseling Groups

The different types of counseling groups are as follows:

- **Educational groups**, which focus on helping members learn new information and skills.
- **Growth groups**, which provide opportunities for members to develop a deeper awareness of their own thoughts, feelings, and behavior, as well as develop their individual potentialities (i.e., values clarification, consciousness-raising, etc.).
- **Therapy groups**, which are designed to help members change their behavior by learning to cope with and improve personal problems and to deal with physical, psychological, or social trauma.
- **Socialization groups**, which help members learn social skills and socially acceptable behaviors and help members function more effectively in the community.
- **Task groups**, which are formed to meet organizational, client, and community needs and functions.

Group Structure and Group Properties

Group structure refers to the patterned interactions, network of roles and statuses, communications, leadership, and power relationships that distinguish a group at any point in time.

Group properties are attributes that characterize a group at any point in time. They include:

- Formal vs. informal structure
- Primary group (tight-knit family, friends, neighbor)
- Secondary relationships (task centered)
- Open vs. closed
- Duration of membership
- Autonomy
- Acceptance-rejection ties
- Social differentiation and degrees of stratification
- Morale, conformity, cohesion, contagion, etc.

Closed Groups vs. Open Groups

Groups can be either closed or open, serving different functions and purposes:

Closed Groups	Open Groups
• Convened by counselors. • Members begin the experience together, navigate it together, and end it together at a predetermined time (set number of sessions). • Closed groups afford better opportunities than open groups for members to identify with each other. • Closed groups provide greater stability to the helping situation, and they allow the stages of group development progress more powerfully. • Closed groups provide a greater amount and intensity of commitment due to the same participants being counted on for their presence.	• Open groups allow participants to enter and leave according to their choice. • A continuous group can exist, depending on the frequency and rate of membership changes. • The focus shifts somewhat from the whole group process to individual members' processes. • With membership shifts, opportunities to use the group's social forces to help individuals may be reduced. The group will be less cohesive, and therefore less available as a therapeutic instrument. • The counselor is kept in a highly central position throughout the life of the group, as he or she provides continuity in an open structure.

Short-Term Groups and Formed Groups

Some circumstances call for the formation of short-term and/or formed groups:

Short-Term Groups	Formed Groups
• Short-term groups are formed around a particular theme or in order to deal with a crisis. • Limitations of time preclude working through complex needs or adapting to a variety of themes or issues. • The counselor is in the central position in a short-term group.	• Deliberately developed to support mutually agreed-upon purposes. • Organization of the group begins with the realization of a need for group services. • The purpose is established by an identification of common needs among individuals in an agency or counselor caseload. • The group is counselor-guided in interventions and timing by an understanding of individual and interpersonal behavior related to the group's purpose. • It is advisable to have screening, assessment, and preparation of group members in formed groups. • Different practice requirements for voluntary and non-voluntary groups exist, as members will respond differently to each.

Small Group Theory

System Analysis and Interactional Theory of Small Groups

The system analysis and interactional theory of small groups is a broadly used framework for understanding small groups. In this framework, small groups are living systems that consist of interacting elements that function as a whole. In this framework, a social system is a structure of relationships or a set of patterned interactions. System concepts help maintain a focus on the whole group, and explain how a group and its sub-groups relate functionally to larger environments. This framework describes how interaction affects status, roles, group emotions, power, and values.

Social System Concepts and General Systems Concepts

The following are **social system concepts** used in the system analysis and interactional theory of small group work:

- **Boundary maintenance**: Maintaining group identities and separateness
- **System linkages**: Two or more elements combine to act as one
- **Equilibrium**: Maintaining a balance of forces within the group

General systems concepts used in the system analysis and interactional theory of small group work are as follows:

- **Steady state**: The tendency of an open system to remain constant but in continuous exchange
- **Equifinality**: The final state of a system that can be reached from different initial conditions
- **Entropy**: The tendency of a system to wear down and move toward disorder

Symbolic Interactionism

Symbolic interactionism is characterized by the following:

- Emphasizes the **symbolic nature** of people's relationships with others and the external world versus a social system analysis that emphasizes form, structures, and functions.
- Group members play a part in determining their own actions by recognizing symbols and **interpreting meaning**.
- Human action is accomplished mainly through the process of **defining and interpreting situations** in which people act. The counselor uses such concepts to explain how individuals interact with others, and to understand the following:
  - The role of the individual as the primary resource in causing change
  - The significance of social relationships
  - The importance of self-concept, identification, and role identity in group behavior
  - The meanings and symbols attributed to group interactions

Gestalt Orientations and Field Theory

Gestalt psychology played a major part in the development of group dynamics. Contrasting with earlier psychologies that stressed elementary sensations and associations, Gestalt theorists viewed experiences not in isolation, but as perpetually organized and part of a **field** comprised of a system of co-existing, interdependent factors. Group dynamics produced a plethora of concepts and variables:

- Goal formation
- Cohesion
- Group identification and uniformity
- Mutual dependency
- Influences and power
- Cooperation and competition
- Productivity

Group dynamics (or group processes) provide a helpful framework of carefully defined and operationalized relevant group concepts.

Sociometry

Sociometry, inspired by the work of J. L. Moreno, is both a general theory of human relations and a specific set of practice techniques (psychodrama, sociodrama, role playing).

- Sociometric tests are devised to measure the affectivity factor in groups.
- Quality of interpersonal attraction in groups is a powerful force in rallying group members, creating feelings of belonging, and making groups sensitive to member needs.

Cognitive Consistency Theory and Balance Theory

The basic assumption of **cognitive consistency theory** is that individuals need to organize their perceptions in ways that are consistent and comfortable. Beliefs and attitudes are not randomly distributed but rather reflect an underlying coherent system within the individual that governs conscious processes and maintains internal and psychosocial consistency.

According to the balance theory, processes are balanced when they are consistent with the individual's beliefs and perceptions. Inconsistency causes imbalance, tension, and stress, and leads to changing perceptions and judgments which restore consistency and balance. The counselor incorporates varying ideas from these orientations. Some stress the need for the group to be self-conscious and to study its own processes, emphasizing that cognition is apparent in contracting, building group consciousness, pinpointing or eliminating obstacles, and sharing data.

Social Reinforcement and Exchange Theory

The **social reinforcement and exchange theory** in regard to group work is summarized as follows:

- Social exchange theorists propose that members of groups are motivated to seek **profit** in their interactions with others (i.e., to maximize rewards and minimize costs).
- Analysis of interactions within groups is done in terms of a series of **exchanges or tradeoffs** group members make with each other.
- The individual member is the **primary unit of analysis**. Many of the core concepts of this theory are merely transferred to the group situation and do not further the understanding of group processes.

Group Formation

Elements in the Group Formation Process

The key elements in the group formation process include the following:

- The counselor makes a clear and uncomplicated statement of purpose that includes both the members' stakes in coming together and the agency's (and others') stakes in serving them.
- The counselor's part should be described in as simple terms as possible.
- Identify the members' reactions to the counselor's statement of purpose and how the counselor's statement connects to the members' expectations.
- The counselor helps members do the work necessary to develop a working consensus about the contract.
- Recognize goals and motivations, both manifested and latent, stated and unstated.
- Recontract as needed.

Counselor's Role in Group Member Selection

The counselor's process of selecting members for a group is as follows:

- The counselor explains **reasons** for meeting with group applicants.
- The counselor elicits applicants' **reactions** to group participation.
- The counselor assesses applicants' **situations** by engaging them in expressing their views of the situation and goals in joining the group.
- The counselor determines **appropriateness** of applicants for the group, accepts their rights to refuse membership, and provides orientation upon acceptance into the group.

Heterogeneity vs. Homogeneity in Group Formation

Issues of heterogeneous vs. homogenous group formation include the following:

- A group ought to have sufficient homogeneity to provide stability and generate vitality.
- Groups that focus on socialization and developmental issues or on learning new tasks are more likely to be homogeneous.
- Groups that focus on disciplinary issues or deviance are more likely to be heterogeneous.
- The composition and purposes of groups are ultimately influenced or determined by agency goals.

Beginning Phase of Group Process

Intervention Skills

Intervention skills of the counselor that are used in the **beginning phase** of group process include the following:

- The counselor must tune into the needs and concerns of the members. Member cues may be subtle and difficult to detect.
- The counselor must seek members' commitment to participate through engagement with members.
- The counselor must continually assess the following:
  - Members' needs/concerns
  - Any ambivalence/resistance to work
  - Group processes
  - Emerging group structures
  - Individual patterns of interaction
- The counselor must facilitate the group's work.

Facilitating the Group's Work

The counselor's role in facilitating group process is as follows:

- Promote **member participation and interaction**.
- Bring up **real concerns** in order to begin the work.
- Help the group keep its **focus**.
- Reinforce observance of **rules** of the group.
- Facilitate **cohesiveness** and focus the work by **identifying emerging themes.**
- Establish counselor **identity** in relation to group's readiness.
- **Listen** empathically, **support** initial structure and rules of the group, and **evaluate** initial group achievements.
- Suggest **ongoing tasks or themes** for the subsequent meeting.

Stressors

The following are stressors that the counselor might experience in the beginning phase of group process:

- Anxiety regarding gaining acceptance by the group
- Integrating group self-determination with an active leadership role
- Fear of creating dependency and self-consciousness in group members which would deter spontaneity
- Difficulty observing and relating to multiple interactions
- Uncertainty about the counselor's own role

Middle Phase of Group Process

Intervention skills of the counselor used in the **middle phase** of group process include the following:

- Judge when work is being avoided
- Reach for opposites, ambiguities, and what is happening in the group when good and bad feelings are expressed
- Support different ways in which members help each other
- Partialize larger problems into more manageable parts
- Generalize and find connections between small pieces of group expression and experience
- Facilitate purposeful communication that is invested with feelings
- Identify and communicate the need to work and recognize when work is being accomplished by the group

Ongoing Group Development

Group development refers to the ongoing group processes that influence the progress of a group, or any of its sub-groups, over time. Group development typically involves changing structures and group properties that alter the quality of relationships as groups achieve their goals. Understanding group development gives counselors a blueprint for interventions that aid the group's progression toward attaining goals. A danger in using development models is in the counselor forcing the group to fit the model, rather than adapting interventions for what is occurring in the group. A complex set of properties, structures, and ongoing processes influence group development. Through processes that are repeated, fused with others, modified, and reinforced, movement occurs.

Models of Group Practice

Linear Stage Models of Group Development

There are many models of group development, often describing the group's process through a series of **linear stages** in which the group progresses predictably from one to another.

Tuckman's five stages of group development are as follows:

1. **Form**: Group comes together, rules are established and agreed upon, and members are relatively subdued and hesitant.
2. **Storm**: Expression of feelings begins by the members who still feel individual versus members of the group; there may be resistance to cues by the counselor or signs of cynicism.

3. **Norm**: A sense of unity and teamwork prevails; members begin to interact with and encourage one another.
4. **Perform**: A sense of hierarchy dissipates as the member take control of the group process and feel empowered in an open and trusting team environment.
5. **Adjourn**: The team recognizes time for closure, some members may mourn the loss of the group and need guidance and support for next steps, and reflection on progress and celebration of accomplishments occur.

The **Boston Model** (Garland, Jones, & Kolodny) of group development is as follows:

1. **Preaffiliation stage**: Consists of regulation by the counselor, expressions of concern or anxiety, heavy dependence on the counselor, hesitant disclosure of personal goals, clarification of purpose, timeline, and roles
2. **Power and control stage**: Consists of limit setting, clarification, and the use of the program
3. **Intimacy stage**: Consists of handling transference, rivalries, and a degree of uncovering
4. **Differentiation stages**: Consist of clarification of differential and cohesive processes, and group autonomy
5. **Separation**: Consists of a focus on evaluation, handling ambivalence, and incorporating new resources

The **Relational Model**, developed by Schiller, in regard to group development in groups of women, is as follows:

- Preaffiliation
- Establishing a relational base
- Mutuality and interpersonal empathy
- Challenge and change
- Separation and termination

Social Goals Model

The social goals model of group practice is as follows:

- The primary focus is to influence a wide range of small group experiences, to facilitate members' identifying and achieving of their own goals, and to increase social consciousness and social responsibility.
- It assumes a rough unity between involvement in social action and the psychological health of the individual. Early group work was concerned with immigrant socialization and emphasized principles of democratic decision making, in addition to tolerance for difference.
- The methodology is focused on establishing positive relationships with groups and members, using group processes in doing with the group rather than for the group, identification of common needs and group goals, stimulation of democratic group participation, and providing authentic group programs stemming from natural types of group living.

REMEDIAL/REHABILITATIVE MODEL

The remedial/rehabilitative model of group practice is as follows:

- It uses a medical model and the counselor is focused primarily on **individual change**.
- This model includes **structured** program activities and exercises.
- It is more commonly found in organizations concerned with **socialization**, such as schools, and in those concerned with treatment and social control (inpatient mental health treatment, etc.).
- Practice techniques in this model focus on **stages** of treatment.
    - **Beginning**: Intake, group selection, diagnosis of each member, and setting specific goals.
    - **Middle**: Planned interventions. Counselor is central figure and uses direct means to influence group and members. Counselor is spokesperson for group values and emotions. Counselor motivates and stimulates members to achieve goals.
    - **Ending**: Group members have achieved maximum gains. Counselor helps clients deal with feelings about ending. Evaluation of work, possible renegotiation of contract.

RECIPROCAL INTERACTIONAL OR MEDIATING MODEL

The reciprocal interactional or mediating model of group practice can be summarized as follows:

- The counselor is referred to as a **mediator** and participates in a network of reciprocal relationships. Goals are developed mutually through contracting process. The interaction and insight of group members is the primary force for change in what is seen as a "mutual aid" society.
- **Counselor's task**: Help search for common ground between group members and the social demands they experience, help clients in their relationships with their own social systems, detect and challenge obstacles to clients' work, and contribute data.
- **Phases** of intervention:
    - **Tuning in or preparation for entry**: The counselor helps the group envision future work, but makes no diagnosis. The counselor is also sensitive to members' feelings.
    - **Beginning**: The counselor engages group in contracting process, and the group establishes clear expectations.
    - **Middle**: The middle phase consists of searching for common ground, discovering/challenging obstacles, data contribution, sharing work visions, and defining limits/requirements
    - **Ending**: Finally, the counselor is sensitive to his or her own reactions and members' reactions and helps members evaluate the experience and consider new beginnings.

FREUDIAN/NEO-FREUDIAN APPROACH

The Freudian/Neo-Freudian approach to group practice is as follows:

- Groups consist of 8-10 members.
- Interaction is mainly through discussion.
- Group members explore feelings and behavior, and interpret unconscious processes.
- The counselor uses interpretation, dream analysis, free association, transference relations, and working through.
- This approach aims to help group members re-experience early family relationships, uncover deep-rooted feelings, and gain insight into the origins of faulty psychological development.

TAVISTICK GROUP-CENTERED MODELS

The Tavistick "group as a whole" group-centered model for group practice is as follows:

- This approach derives from Wilfred Bion's work with leaderless groups. Bion developed analytic approaches that focused on the **group as a whole**.
- Latent group feelings are represented through the group's prevailing emotional states or **basic assumption cultures**.
- The therapist is referred to as a **consultant**. The consultant does not suggest an agenda, establishes no rules and procedures, but instead acts as an observer. A major role of the consultant is to alert members to ongoing group processes and to encourage study of these processes.
- The consultant encourages members to explore their experiences as group members through **interaction**.

GROUP THERAPY METHODS

PROCESS GROUPS

Irvin Yalom's "here-and-now" or process groups are characterized by the following:

- Yalom stressed using clients' **immediate reactions** and discussing members' **affective experiences** in the group.
- Process groups have relatively unstructured and spontaneous sessions.
- Process groups emphasize **therapeutic activities**, like imparting information, or instilling hope, universality, and altruism.
- The group can provide a **rehabilitative narrative** of primary family group development, offer socializing techniques, provide behavior models to imitate, offer interpersonal learning, and offer an example of group cohesiveness and catharsis.

MORENO'S PSYCHODRAMA GROUP THERAPY

Moreno's psychodrama group therapy is summarized as follows:

- **Spontaneous drama techniques** contribute to powerful therapy to aid in the release of pent-up feelings and to provide insight and catharsis to help participants develop new and more effective behaviors.
- The five **primary instruments** used are the stage, the client or protagonist, the director or therapist, the staff of therapeutic aides or auxiliary egos, and the audience.
- Psychodrama group therapy can begin with a **warm-up**. The warm-up uses an assortment of techniques such as self-presentations, interviews, interaction in the role of the self and others, soliloquies, role reversals, doubling techniques, auxiliary egos, mirroring, multiple doubles, life rehearsals, and exercises.

Behavioral Group Therapies

Behavioral group therapies are characterized by the following:

- The **main goals** are to help group members eliminate maladaptive behaviors and learn new behaviors that are more effective. Behavioral groups are not focused on gaining insight into the past, but rather on current interactions with the environment.
- It is one of the few research-based approaches.
- The counselor utilizes **directive techniques**, provides information, and teaches coping skills and methods of changing behavior.
- The counselor arranges **structured activities**. The primary techniques used include restructuring, systematic desensitization, implosive therapies, assertion training, aversion techniques, operant-conditioning, self-help reinforcement and support, behavioral research, coaching, modeling, feedback, and procedures for challenging and changing conditions.

Influencing the Group Process

Influencing group process in group work methodology can be done through the following:

- The counselor's ability to recognize, analyze, understand, and influence group process is necessary and vital. The group is a system of relationships rather than a collection of individuals. This system is formed through associations with a unique and changing quality and character (this is known as group structures and processes).
- Processes that the counselor will be dealing with include understanding group structures, value systems, group emotions, decision-making, communication/interaction, and group development (formation, movement, termination).

Externalizing

The counselor must be prepared to help individual members profit from their experiences in and through the group. Ultimately, what happens to group members and how they are influenced by the group's processes determines the success of any group experience, not how the group itself functions as an entity. The counselor should give attention to helping members relate beyond the group (**externalizing**), to encouraging active participation and involvement with others in increasingly wider spheres of social living. This should occur even when the group is relatively autonomous.

Programming

The importance of programming in group work methodology is as follows:

- The counselor uses activities, discussion topics, task-centered activities, exercises, and games as a part of a planned, conscious process to address individual and group needs while achieving group purposes and goals.
- Programming should build on the needs, interests, and abilities of group members and should not necessitate a search for the unusual, esoteric, or melodramatic.
- Counseling skills used in implementing programs include the following: initiating and modifying program plans to respond to group interests, self-direction, responsibility, drawing creatively upon program resources in the agency and environment, and developing sequences of activities with specific long-range goals.
- Using program activities is an important feature of group practice.

Contracting Working Agreements in Group Work

Only if group members are involved in clarifying and setting their own personal and common group goals can they be expected to be active participants on their own behalf. **Working agreements** consider not only counselor-member relationships, but also others with a direct or indirect stake in the group's process. Examples would be agency sponsorship, collaborating staff, referral and funding sources, families, caretakers, and other interested parties in the public at large.

The following are the **counselor's role in contracting**:

- Setting goals
- Determining membership
- Establishing initial group structures and formats

All three of these elements require skillful management by the counselor.

Analyzing Group Processes

The following are categories for analyzing group work:

- Communication processes
- Power and influence
- Leadership
- Group norms and values
- Group emotion
- Group deliberation and problem solving

Group Practice with Special Populations

Groups for Serious Mental Illness

Group work with clients who have serious mental illness should include the following elements:

- **Clearly defined programs** that use psychosocial rehabilitation approaches (not psychotherapeutic).
- Focus on making each group session **productive and rewarding** for group members.
- **Themes** addressed include dealing with stigma, coping with symptoms, adjusting to medication side effects, dealing with problems (family, relationships, housing, employment, education, etc.), and real and imagined complaints about mental health treatment organizations.
- Many groups in community-based settings focus on helping members learn **social skills** for individuals with limited or ineffective coping strategies.
- Mandated groups in **forensic settings** are highly structured and focus on basic topics such as respect for others, responsibility for one's behavior, or staying focused.

Chemical Dependency Groups

Group work for chemical dependency focuses on the following:

- Group work is the treatment of choice for **substance use disorder**.
- Guidelines for these groups include maintaining confidentiality, using "I" statements, speaking directly to others, never speaking for others, awareness of one's own thoughts and feelings, honesty about thoughts and feelings, and taking responsibility for one's own behavior.
- Types of groups used include:
  - **Orientation groups** that give information regarding treatment philosophy/protocols.
  - **Spiritual groups** that incorporate spirituality into recovery.
  - **Relapse prevention groups** that focus on understanding and dealing with behaviors and situations that trigger relapse.
  - **AA and NA self-help groups** utilize the principles and philosophies of 12-step programs. For family and friends, **Nar-Anon** and **Al-Anon groups** provide support.

Parent Education Groups

Parent education groups are used in social agencies, hospitals, and clinics. They are often labeled as psycho-ed groups or parent training groups and use a cognitive-behavioral approach to improve the parent-child relationship. Parent education groups are often structured to follow manuals or curricula. Their main focus is helping parents improve parent-child interactions, parent attitudes, and child behaviors.

Abused Women's Groups

Abused women's groups can be described as follows:

- Provide a warm, accepting, and caring environment in which members can feel secure.
- Structured for consciousness raising, dispelling false perceptions, and resource information.
- Common themes these groups explore include the use of power which derives from the freedom to choose, the need for safety, the exploration of resources, the right to protection under the law, and the need for mutual aid.
- Basic principles of these groups include respect for women, active listening and validation of members' stories, ensuring self-determination and individualization, and promoting group programs that members can use to demonstrate their own strength and achieve empowerment.
- For post-group support, groups typically seek to utilize natural supports in the community.

Groups for Spouse Abusers

Groups for spouse abusers (perpetrators of domestic violence) are explained below:

- Work with this population is typified by resistance and denial.
- Clients have difficulty processing guilt, shame, or abandonment anxiety and tend to convert these feelings into anger.
- These clients have difficulties with intimacy, trust, mutuality, and struggle with fear of abandonment and diminished self-worth.
- Mandatory group treatment is structured. It is designed to challenge male bonding that often occurs in such groups.
- Including spouses/victims in these groups is quite controversial in clinical literature.

Groups for Sex Offenders

Groups for sex offenders are summarized below:

- Typically, membership in these groups is ordered by the court. There is no assurance of confidentiality, as counselors may have to provide reports to the courts, parole officers, or other officials.
- Clients typically deny wrongdoing, test counselors, and are often resistant.
- In groups with voluntary membership, confidentiality is extremely important, as group members often express extreme fear of exposure.
- Prominent themes include denial, victim-blaming, blaming behavior on substances, blaming behavior on uncontrollable sex drives/needs.
- Treatment emphasizes the importance of conscious control over drives/needs, regardless of their strength or if they are natural.
- A culture of victimization is strongly discouraged.

Groups for Children of Alcoholics

Groups for children of alcoholics are discussed below:

- Individuals who grow up with parents who abuse alcohol and/or drugs often learn to distrust others as a survival strategy. They become used to living with chaos and uncertainty and with shame and hopelessness.
- These individuals commonly experience denial, secrecy, and embarrassment.
- They may have a general sense of fearfulness, especially if they faced threats of violence, and tend to have rigid role attachment.
- Treatment in these groups requires careful planning, programming, and mutual aid in the form of alliances with parental figures and other related parties in order to create a healthy environment that increases the individual's safety and ability to rely on self and others.

Groups for Sexually Abused Children

Groups for sexually abused children are summarized below:

- The counselor must pay particular attention to her or his own attitudes toward sexuality and the sexual abuse of children.
- Important in these groups are contracting, consistent attendance, and clearly defined rules and expectations.
- Clients may display control issues and may challenge the counselor's authority.
- Confidentiality is not guaranteed.
- Termination can be a particularly difficult process.
- Common themes that come up include fear, anger, guilt, depression, anxiety, inability to trust, and delayed developmental/socialization skills.
- Programming can include ice breaking games, art, body drawings, letter writing, and role playing.

Termination of Group Process

Group members' experience of termination and the counselor's role in helping group members to cope with the ending of the group are discussed below:

- Group members may have feelings of loss and may desire to minimize the painful feelings they are experiencing.
- Members may experience ambivalence about ending.
- The counselor will:
  - Examine her or his own feelings about termination
  - Focus the group on discussing ending
  - Help individuals express their feelings of loss, relief, ambivalence, etc.
  - Review achievements of the group and members
  - Help members prepare to cope with next steps
  - Assess members' and group's needs for continued services
  - Help members with transition to other services

Methods of Forestalling or Dealing with Termination

The following are group members' methods of forestalling or dealing with termination:

- **Simple denial**: A member may forget ending, act surprised, or feel "tricked" by termination.
- **Clustering**: Members may physically draw together, also called super-cohesion.
- **Regression**: Reaction can be simple-to-complex. Earlier responses reemerge, outbursts of anger, recurrence of previous conflicts, fantasies of wanting to begin again, attempts to coerce the leader to remain, etc.
- **Nihilistic flight**: Members may reject and perform rejection-provoking behavior.
- **Reenactment and review**: Members begin recounting or reviewing earlier experiences in detail or actually repeating those experiences.
- **Evaluation**: Members assess meaning and worth of former experiences.
- **Positive flight**: There is a constructive movement toward self-weaning. Members find new groups, etc.

Using Humor in the Counseling Process

Therapeutic Humor

The American Association of Therapeutic Humor defines **therapeutic humor** as an intervention. An intervention is an action that seeks to stop something from happening that may be undesirable. The intervention of therapeutic humor can be an expression of laughter that can stimulate playful discovery about a problem that the client may be experiencing. Some therapeutic benefits are found in humorous expressions or in the appreciation of such expressions. Humor can help people deal with absurd, bizarre, or out of the ordinary life events in a healthy manner. This therapeutic result can lead to an increase in work performance. Likewise, humor can be used to reinforce learning. Another benefit can be found in improving the person's sense of well-being. Humor can help treat persons with an illness of emotional, cognitive, spiritual, social, or physical origin.

Historical Use of Humor in Psychotherapy

In 1951, Carl Rogers promoted the **therapeutic relationship** that could be gained through bonding between the counselor and the client. Humor can be used to improve this bond, promote trust, make important interpersonal connections, and help the clients deal with subjects that make them anxious. Social interaction can increase dialogue. Studies indicate people are more likely to trust someone who is amusing over someone who appears sober-minded. Humor may indicate to the client that the counselor shares his or her world view. Freud proposed that humor indicates the client and counselor have reached an agreement of some kind.

Correlates of Humor

The correlates of humor are what make it successful in producing an amusing result. There are three **correlates of humor**:

- The **suddenness** of the punch line or surprising conclusion gives the audience the opportunity to laugh at the unexpected twist.
- **Optimal arousal** is derived from an appropriate level of intellectual, emotional, or physical stimulation (e.g., adults find it difficult to laugh at childish jokes that have ceased to be of interest).
- **Play frame** is setting up the joke or story to be non-threatening for the listener. Some jokes may be too intense for the individual's comfort level. Play frame involves cueing the listener through facial expressions or vocal tones that intend a time for play.

Categories of Humor

Humor can be separated into three categories:

- **Incongruity** is depicted in humorous jokes, stories, or scenes that create one set of expectations for an outcome, which are altered in the punch line to produce a totally different outcome than first expected.
- **Release** is a humorous way to let off pent-up, negative emotions that have aggressive or sexual undertones. Sarcasm is a form of release. Sometimes, pent-up emotions are released after a physical event that was particularly stressful.
- **Superiority** is humor exercised at the expense of another, as in slapstick humor.

Physical Symptoms That Can Be Relieved Using Humor

Physical symptoms that may be relieved through the use of humor include the following:

- Reduction of pain
- An increased immune system response, particularly immunoglobin A, a disease-fighting antibody found in mucous membranes that repels attacks by viruses and bacteria.
- Improved mental functions
- Muscle exercise and relaxation
- Improved respiration
- Stimulated circulation
- Decreased stress hormones
- Decreased blood pressure

Psychotherapeutic Benefits of Humor

Tensions, aggression, and negative feelings can be released by humor. This translated into **psychotherapeutic studies and applications of humor**:

- In 1942, Obrdlik studied a group of citizens who used humor to relieve the tensions of being in a town occupied by Nazi soldiers.
- In 1959, Coser studied patients using humor during their hospital confinements.
- In 1960, Frankl proposed exaggerating to make the patient laugh at absurd solutions to a problem.
- In 1977, Albert Ellis explored expressive therapy.
- In 1985, Murstein and Brust explored humor linking romantic couples.
- In 1994, Minden used humor to treat military veterans suffering with depression. Six sessions produced a reduction in their anxieties.
- In 2004, Berk declared humor helps the client to gain a new perspective on problems.

The counselor should apply these perspectives to the counseling relationship by encouraging the client to express his or her negative feelings and explaining that expression is much healthier than repression, which leads to physical health problems.

Possible Harmful Effects of Humor

In 1994, Brooks warned counselors to ensure that their relationships with clients are stable and conducive before making attempts to incorporate humor. Without a foundation of trust, the use of humor may have counterproductive results. Brooks outlined the following areas of sensitivity to be considered when using humor:

- Do not make the client the target of humor or ridicule the client.
- Do not fall back on humor to relieve one's own inner tensions about a subject. The session is not for the counselor's benefit. The client's needs are paramount.
- Avoid humor when there is any hint of negative personal feelings about the client.
- Do not allow the client to use humor as a defense mechanism to avoid painful topics.
- Only apply humor when a substantial time has passed after a crisis.

Counseling Skills and Interventions Chapter Quiz

1. Morphogenesis is:

a. An adaptability skill a family may use in handling change.
b. An adaptability skill a family may use in balancing stability.
c. An adaptability skill a family may use when having a new child.
d. An adaptability skill a family may use when experiencing extreme stress.

2. Mahoney developed which acronym based on the cognitive behavioral approach?

a. NARROW
b. SCIENCE
c. EXAMINE
d. BRAIN

3. The idea that people control their own destinies and interpret events according to their own values and beliefs is a key concept of which of the following?

a. Acceptance commitment therapy
b. Rational emotive therapy
c. Rational behavior therapy
d. Solution-focused therapy

4. Yalom's process groups are characterized by all of the following EXCEPT?

a. Utilizing delayed and thoughtful responses
b. Emphasizing therapeutic activities
c. Providing a rehabilitative narrative of primary family group development
d. Discussing members' affective experiences

5. Which of the following is the study of personal space and the distance between individuals at which people feel comfortable or uncomfortable?

a. Proxemics
b. Contiguity
c. Juxtapology
d. Vicinics

6. Using blame to shift focus to another family member is known as:

a. Intellectualization
b. Justification
c. Rationalization
d. Scapegoating

7. Which of the following is NOT one of the four communication impediments described by Satir?

a. Placating
b. Unresponsive
c. Irrelevance
d. Being overly reasonable

8. The idea that one cause equals one effect is called

a. Reciprocal determinism
b. Linear causality
c. Circular causality
d. Relational causality

9. Which of the following theories posits that members of groups are motivated to seek profit in their interactions with others?

a. Assimilation-contrast theory
b. Balance theory
c. Social exchange theory
d. Transactional analysis theory

10. How many correlates of humor are there?

a. Six
b. Five
c. Four
d. Three

Core Counseling Attributes

Therapeutic Environment

Therapeutic Milieu

The **therapeutic milieu** is a stable environment provided by an organization to assist in a **treatment plan**. The main purposes of a milieu are to teach individuals certain social skills and to provide a **structured environment** that promotes interactions and personal growth along with attempting to control many types of deviant or destructive behaviors. There are **five main components** that the milieu should include in therapy. These components include containment, structure, support, involvement, and validation. Through the use of these components, the therapeutic milieu can help the individuals achieve their highest level of functioning.

Containment Component

The **containment component** in a milieu involves the actual **physical safety** of the participants. It provides a **safe clean physical environment** as well as providing food and some medical care. The actual environment will often be very comfortable with colorful walls, pictures, and comfortable chairs and couches. Participants are allowed a certain freedom of movement throughout this environment. Many times, the participants will work to help maintain a clean and functioning environment. They may perform certain tasks or chores to help with the upkeep of the milieu. This containment will provide a feeling of safety and trust for the individual.

Structured Component

The **structured component** in the milieu lies hand in hand with **consistency**. The milieu provides a place with consistent staff members, consistent physical surroundings, and limits on behavior. This predictability allows the participants to feel safe and secure and to know what to expect. This environment also provides **structure** through providing an environment where the participants can interact with a purpose. These purposes can range from daily tasks and chores to the different roles they may assume within various meetings. Through acceptance of this consistent and structured environment, the individual can begin to achieve some level of self-responsibility and consequences for their actions.

Support Component

The **support component** in a milieu comes directly from the staff members involved in the milieu. Their goal is to help the participants have increased **self-esteem** through creating an environment of acceptance for all individuals. They provide a safe and comfortable atmosphere, therefore decreasing anxiety levels. Encouragement, empathy, nurturing, reassurance, and providing physical wellbeing for participants will help increase their feelings of self-worth. Consistency in attitudes and actions by all staff members are very important in the success of this setting. By providing this type of environment, the milieu will assist clients in their abilities to gain new healthy relationships and appropriate interactions with others.

Involvement Component

The **involvement component** of the milieu is the development of a sense of **open involvement** for each client from the staff members. The staff should convey their desire to be personally involved with each client through both their actions and attitudes. They should encourage the clients to **communicate** with them openly about feelings and experiences. This sense of individual interest and involvement will help to increase the client's sense of self-worth and self-esteem. The staff members should encourage client involvement through encouraging client-lead group sessions and activities. By becoming involved, the clients have opportunities to practice new social skills, such as working together with others, learning to compromise, and dealing with conflict. The hope of involvement is to achieve the goal of appropriate social interactions for each client.

VALIDATION COMPONENT

The **validation component** of the milieu is the recognition of each client as an **individual**. The staff members should convey **respect and consideration** for each and every client. This respect and consideration should be shown through acts of kindness, empathy, nonjudgmental attitude, and acceptance of each individual for who they are. In a milieu, each client contributes through responsibilities and involvement in many decision-making processes. Through these actions, the clients should begin to feel some self-responsibility and with this new sense of responsibility comes validation for their individuality and humanity.

CHARACTERISTICS OF A SUCCESSFUL MILIEU

The characteristics of a **successful milieu** include:

- Successful communication between and among staff and clients
- Standards that provide consistency and security
- Client government using the democratic process
- Client responsibility for his or her own treatment
- Encouraging self-perception and change
- Acknowledging and positively dealing with destructive behavior and poor judgment

CONFLICT RESOLUTION

When attempting to **resolve conflict** between two or more individuals, the desired outcome is a feeling by each party of getting what they wanted out of the situation. Resolving conflict should include the following steps:

1. **Problem Identification**: The parties are each allowed their opportunity to discuss what they think is wrong. This portion of the resolution process may become emotional and involve angry outbursts.
2. **Ascertain Expectations**: Each party identifies exactly what they want. With the disclosure of these expectations, a sense of trust can begin to evolve. The mental health professional will need to remain objective and respectful to everyone involved during this phase.
3. **Identify Special Interest**: Determine if anyone has unspoken objectives or interests that could slow down the resolution progress. Everyone needs to be honest about what they want and need.
4. **Brainstorm Resolution Ideas**: Assist the parties with creating ideas to help resolve the conflict.
5. **Reach a Resolution**: Assist the parties in bringing together a situation where everyone can feel happy about the outcome.

CLIENT-PROVIDER RELATIONSHIP

INTRODUCTORY PHASE

The first thing the mental health care provider should do when meeting a client is to find out **why** they are there. This **initial phase** provides a time for the provider and client to get to know each other. There is no definite time frame and this phase can last for a few minutes to a few months. There are certain goals that should be accomplished during this time. The provider and client should develop a mutual sense of trust, acceptance, and understanding. They may enter into a contract with each other. They will need to determine expectations, goals, boundaries, and ending criteria for the contract. This initial phase often involves obtaining the client's history, his or her account of the problems, and developing a general understanding of the client.

Working Phase

The second phase of the client-provider relationship is the **working phase**. During this time the client will identify and evaluate specific problems through the development of insight and learn ways to effectively **adapt their behaviors**. The provider will assist the client in working through feelings of fear and anxiety. They will also foster new levels of self-responsibility and coping mechanisms. The development of new and successful ways of approaching problems is the goal of this phase. The provider may often face resistance by the client to move through this phase, and by utilizing different communication techniques may help to assist the client in moving forward.

Termination Phase

The final stage of the client-provider relationship is the **termination or resolution phase**. This phase begins from the time the problems are actually solved to the actual **ending of the relationship**. This phase can be very difficult for both the client and the provider. The client must now focus on continuing without the guiding assistance of the therapy. The client will need to utilize their newfound approaches and behaviors. This time may be one of varying emotions for the client and they may be reluctant to end the relationship. They may experience anxiety, anger, or sadness. The provider may need to guide the client in utilizing their newfound strategies in dealing with their feelings about the termination of the relationship. Focus should be placed on the future.

Therapeutic Communication

Verbal Communication

Verbal communication is achieved through spoken or written words. This form of communication represents a very small fraction of communication as a whole. Much information achieved verbally may be **factual** in nature. Communication occurs along a two-way path between the client and the provider. One limitation of verbal communication can be **different meanings of words** in different ethnic and cultural populations. The meanings may differ in denotative, actual meaning, and/or connotative, implied meaning, of the words. The use of words may differ depending upon personal experiences. The client may assume the provider understands their particular meaning of the word.

Empathy

Empathy is perhaps one of the most important concepts in establishing a therapeutic relationship with a client, and it is associated with **positive client outcomes**. It is the ability of one person to put themselves in the shoes of another. Empathy is more than just knowing what the other person means. The provider should seek to imagine the **feelings** associated with the other person's experience without having had this experience themselves and then communicate this understanding to the client. Empathy should not be confused with sympathy, which is feeling sorry for someone. The provider should also be aware of any social or cultural differences that could inhibit the conveyance of empathy.

Open-Ended Statements and Reflection

Broad **open-ended statements** allow the client the opportunity to expand on an idea or select a topic for discussion. This type of communication allows the client to feel like the provider is actually listening and interested in what they have to say. It also helps the client gain insight into his or her emotions or situations.

Reflection conveys interest and understanding to the client. It can also allow for a time of validation so the provider can show that they are actually listening and understanding the shared information. It involves some minimal repetition of ideas or summing up a situation. These ideas or summaries are directed back to the client often in the form of a question.

Restating and Clarification

Restating and clarification are verbal communication techniques that the provider may use as part of therapeutic communication. **Restating** involves the repetition of the main points of what the client expressed. Many times, the provider will not restate everything but narrow the focus to the main point. This technique can achieve both clarification of a point and confirmation that what the client said was heard.

Clarification involves the provider attempting to understand and verbalize a vague situation. Many times, a client's emotional explanations can be difficult to clearly understand and the provider must try to narrow down what the client is trying to say.

Silence and Listening

Silence and listening are very effective during verbal communication.

- **Silence** allows the client time to think and formulate ideas and responses. It is an intentional lull in the conversation to give the client time to reflect.
- **Listening** is more active in nature. When listening, the provider lends attention to what the client is communicating. There are two different types of listening.
  - **Passive listening** allows the client to speak without direction or guidance from the provider. This form of listening does not usually advance the client's therapy.
  - **Active listening** occurs when the provider focuses on what is said in order to respond and then encourage a response from the client.

Rapport and Validation

Communication between the mental health care provider and the client can be improved by establishing rapport and validating certain information. **Establishing rapport** with a client involves achieving a certain level of harmony between the provider and the client. This is often achieved through the establishment of trust through conveying respect, nonbiased views, and understanding. By establishing rapport, the provider helps the client feel more comfortable about sharing information.

Validation requires the provider to use the word "I" when talking with the client. It evaluates one's own thoughts or observations against another person's and often requires feedback in the form of confirmation.

Use of Therapeutic Communication with Groups

A **group** is a gathering of interactive individuals who have commonalities. Interventions through **group sessions** can provide an effective treatment opportunity to allow for growth and self-development of the client. This setting allows the clients to interact with each other. This allows the clients to see the emotions of others, such as joy, sorrow, or anger, and to receive as well as participate in feedback from others in the group. The group can be very supportive and thrive in both inpatient and outpatient settings. The one thing the group cannot lack is definite **leadership and guidance** from the health care provider. The provider must guide the members of the group in facilitating therapeutic communications.

Nonverbal Communication in the Therapeutic Relationship

Nonverbal communication occurs in the form of expressions, gestures, body positioning or movement, voice levels, and information gathered from the five senses. The **nonverbal message** is usually more accurate in conveying the client's feeling than the **verbal message**. Many clients will say something quite different than what their nonverbal communication indicates. Nonverbal communication may also vary by cultural influences. The mental health care provider must be aware of these cultural differences and respect their place within the therapy. The provider should utilize positive, respectful, non-threatening body language. A relaxed, slightly forward posture with uncrossed arms and legs may encourage communication.

Vocal Cues, Action Cues, and Object Cues as Forms of Nonverbal Behaviors

There are many different types of nonverbal behaviors. There are five main areas of **nonverbal communication**. They include vocal cues, action cues, object cues, space, and touch.

- **Vocal cues** can involve the qualities of speech, such as tone and rate. Laughing, groaning, or sounds of hesitation can also convey important communication.
- **Action cues** involve bodily movements. They can include things such as mannerisms, gestures, facial expressions, or any body movements. These types of movements can be good indicators of mood or emotion.
- **Object cues** include the use of objects. The client may not even be aware that they are moving these objects. Other times the client may choose a particular object to indicate a specific communication. This intentional use of an object can be less valuable than other forms of nonverbal communication.

Space and touch as nonverbal forms of communication can vary greatly depending upon social or cultural norms.

- **Space** can provide information about a relationship between the client and someone else. Most people living in the United States have four different areas of space. **Intimate space** is less than 1.5 feet, **personal space** is 1.5-4 feet, **social-consultative space** is 9-12 feet, and **public space** is 12 feet or more. Observations concerning space and the client's physical placement in a setting can give a great deal of insight into different interpersonal relationships.
- **Touch** includes personal or intimate space with an action involved. This fundamental form of communication can send very personal information and communicate feelings such as concern or caring.

Non-Therapeutic Communication

Techniques that are detrimental to establishing a trusting therapeutic relationship include giving advice, challenging the client's communications, or indicating disapproval. **Giving advice** includes telling the client what they should do in a particular situation. This does not allow the client to develop the ability to solve their own problems and may not always be the right answer. **Challenging** occurs when the client's thoughts are disputed by the provider. This communication only serves to lower the client's self-esteem and create an environment of distrust between the client and the mental health care provider. **Disapproval** occurs when the provider negatively judges the client's beliefs or actions. This again serves to lower client self-esteem and does not foster their ability to solve their own problems or create new coping abilities.

Client Safety Issues

Professional Assault Response

A protocol for a **professional assault response** should be established at all mental health facilities because statistics show that 75% of mental health staff experience a **physical assault**. Most injuries are incurred by nursing staff caring for violent clients. Assaults may occur in both psychiatric units and emergency departments, where security staff may also be assaulted. Additionally, clients may be victims. Common injuries include fractures, lacerations, contusions, and unconsciousness from head injuries. Victims are at risk for psychological distress and post-traumatic stress syndrome, so a prompt response is critical. The assault response should include the following:

- Routine assessment of clients for violent or aggressive tendencies
- Protocol for managing violent or aggressive clients
- Physical assessment and medical treatment as needed for injuries
- Completion of an incident report by those who were involved or who observed the incident

Psychological intervention, including individual counseling sessions and critical incident stress management, require a response team that includes staff members who are trained to deal with crisis intervention (e.g., psychologists, psychiatrists, nurses, peer counselors, social workers).

Contraband and Unsafe Items

State regulations identify **contraband and unsafe items** that are prohibited from mental health and correctional facilities; however, each facility must develop site-specific restrictions and protocols for responding to contraband and unsafe items. **Contraband** may include the following:

- Alcohol or products (mouthwash) that contain alcohol
- Drugs, including prescription, over-the-counter, and illicit drugs
- Poisonous and toxic substances
- Pornographic or sexually explicit material
- Food (hoarded or excessive)

Depending on the type of facility or clients, a wide range of items may be considered **unsafe**. These often include the following:

- Knives, scissors, sharp instruments, and razor blades
- Flammable materials, such as lighter fluid and matches
- Breakable items, such as glass and mirrors
- Dangerous materials (which might be used for a suicide attempt), such as belts (over 2 in wide), large buckles, rope, electrical cords (i.e., over 6 feet in length), and wire
- Potential weapons, such as pens (except felt point), pencils, and plastic bags
- Electrical equipment, such as fans and recording devices

Therapeutic Relationships and Communication

Conditions Required for a Positive Therapeutic Relationship

In order for a counselor to establish a positive therapeutic relationship, he or she must express non-possessive warmth and concern, genuineness, appropriate empathy, nonjudgmental acceptance, optimism regarding prospects for change, objectivity, professional competence, ability to communicate with a client, and self-awareness. Self-disclosure should be used only purposefully and for the client's benefit.

For clients to contribute to a positive therapeutic environment, they must have hope and courage to undertake change processes, be motivated to change, and trust in the counselor's interest and skill. They must also be dealt with as an individual and not a case, personality type, or category. Clients must be able to express themselves, to make their own choices, and to change at their own pace.

Professional Objectivity in Counselor-Client Relationship

Objectivity requires remaining neutral when making judgements. Because of the nature of counseling, a large part of evaluation tends to be subjective and not easily quantified, but these evaluations can then reflect the counselor and the counselor's biases. The goal should be to make objective observations as much as possible—reporting what is seen and heard rather than the subjective opinion about those things. In order to ensure that opinions are objective, specific parameters should be developed for decision making. For example, when evaluating a client's socioeconomic status, judging by language and appearance may produce one opinion while judging according to occupation and income may produce another (and probably more accurate) opinion. The way a counselor measures may also reflect biases. For example, measuring gender by male and female only suggests a subjective rejection of other choices, such as non-binary or transgender.

Principles of Communication

Communication involves the conveying of information, whether verbally or nonverbally, between individuals and has two key aspects: sending and receiving information. Each of these requires unique skills, and effective communication requires proficiency in both. **Essential principles of communication** include:

- All aspects of communication must be considered and interpreted in any exchange.
- Communication may be written, verbally spoken, or nonverbally delivered via body language, gestures, and expressions.
- Not all communication is intentional, as unintentional information may also be conveyed.
- All forms of communication have limits, further imposed by issues of perception, unique experiences, and interpretation.
- Quality communication accounts for issues of age, gender, ethnicity/culture, intellect, education, primary language, emotional state, and belief systems.
- Optimum communication is active (or reflective), using strategies such as furthering responses (nodding, etc.), paraphrasing, rephrasing, clarification, encouragement ("tell me more"), partialization (reducing long ideas into manageable parts), summarization, feelings reflection, exploring silence, and nonverbal support (eye contact, warm tone, neutral but warm expressions, etc.).

Quality Communication with Clients

The following are key rules for quality communication with clients:

- Don't speak for the client; instead allow the client to fully express him or herself.
- Listen carefully and try diligently to understand.
- Don't talk when the client is speaking.
- Don't embellish; digest what the client has actually said, not what was presumed to be said.
- Don't interrupt, even if the process is slow or interspersed with long pauses.
- Don't judge, criticize, or intimidate when communicating.
- Facilitate communication with open-ended questions and a responsive and receptive posture.
- Avoid asking "why" questions, which can be perceived as judgmental.
- Communicate using orderly, well-planned ideas, as opposed to rushed statements.
- Moderate the pace of speech and adjust expressions to fit the client's education, intellect, and other unique features.
- Ask clarifying questions to enhance understanding.
- Attend to nonverbal communication (expression, body language, gestures, etc.).
- Limit closed-ended and leading questions.
- Avoid "stacked" (multi-part) questions that can be confusing.

Congruence in Communication

Congruence in communication is consistently communicating the same message verbally and nonverbally. The individual's words, body language, and tone of voice should all convey the same message. If they do not, then the communication is incongruent, and the receiver cannot trust the communication. For example, if a person says, "I really want to help you," in a very harsh tone of voice and with an angry affect, the communication is incongruent, and the message may actually be perceived as the exact opposite of the words spoken. Communication is also incongruent if the individual gives a series of conflicting messages: "I'm going to get a job," "Why should I work?" "I know I need to work," "There's no point in taking a low-paying job." The counselor must be alert to the congruence of client communication in order to more accurately assess the client as well as be aware of personal congruence of communication when interacting with client. This helps to ensure that the counselor can cultivate a relationship built on trust.

Active Listening

Active listening techniques include the use of paraphrasing in response, clarification of what was said by the client, encouragement ("tell me more"), etc. Key **overarching guidelines** include the following:

- Don't become preoccupied with specific active listening strategies; rather, concentrate on reducing client resistance to sharing, building trust, aiding the client in expanding his or her thoughts, and ensuring mutual understanding.
- The greatest success occurs when a variety of active listening techniques are used during any given client meeting.
- Focus on listening and finding ways to help the client to keep talking. Active listening skills will aid the client in expanding and clarifying his or her thoughts.
- Remember that asking questions can often mean interrupting. Avoid questioning the client when he or she is midstream in thought and is sharing, unless the questions will further expand the sharing process.

Allowing Clients Uninterrupted Opportunities to Speak

There are many reasons to limit a client's opportunities to speak. Time may be inadequate, the workload may be impacted, the client may seem distracted or uninterested in sharing, etc. However, only by **allowing the client to divulge his or her true feelings** can the counselor actually know and understand what the client believes, thinks, feels, and desires.

Barriers to client sharing include the following:

- **Frequent interruptions**: Instead, the counselor might jot a short note to prompt a question later.
- **Supplying client words**: A client may seem to have great difficulty finding words to express his or her feelings and the counselor may be tempted to assist. However, this may entirely circumvent true expression, as the client may simply say, "Yes, that's it," rather than working harder to find his or her true feelings.
- **Filling silence**: Long pauses can be awkward. The counselor may wish to fill the silence, but in doing so, he or she may prevent the client from finding thoughts to share.

Utilizing Nonverbal Communication

To facilitate the sharing process it is important for a counselor to present as warm, receptive, caring, and accepting of the client. However, the counselor should also endeavor not to bias, lead, or repress client expressions by an inappropriate use of **nonverbal** cues. Frowning, smiling, vigorous nodding, etc., may all lead clients to respond to the counselor's reactions rather than to disclose their genuine feelings and thoughts. To this end, a counselor will endeavor to make good eye contact, use a soft tone of voice, present as interested and engaged, etc., but without marked expressions that can influence the dialogue process. Sitting and facing the client (ideally without a desk or other obstruction in between), being professionally dressed and groomed, sitting close enough to be engaging without invading the client's space, and using an open posture (arms comfortable in the lap or by the sides, rather than crossed over the chest) can all facilitate the communication process.

Leading Questions

Leading questions are those that predispose a particular response. For example, saying, "You know that it is okay to ask questions, don't you?" is a strongly leading question. While it may seem an innocuous way to ensure that someone feels free to ask questions, it may not succeed in actually eliciting questions. Instead, ask the client directly, "What questions do you have?" This way of asking not only reveals that questions are acceptable, but is much more likely to encourage the client to openly share any confusion he or she is having.

Even less forceful leading questions can induce a bias. For example, when a couple comes in for counseling, the counselor asking, "Would you like to sit over here?" could prevent the counselor from seeing how they elect to arrange themselves in relation to the counselor and to each other (a very revealing element in the relationship). Instead, the counselor might simply say, "Feel free to sit anywhere you'd like." Avoiding leading questions is an important skill in the communication process.

Obtaining Sensitive Information from Clients

Sensitive information includes that involving sexual activity, abuse, intimate partner violence, substance abuse, and mental health issues. Clients are more likely to answer questions truthfully if they have developed a relationship of trust with the questioner. **Methods of obtaining sensitive information** include the following:

- Embedding the questions in a series of questions in context: "Do you spend time with your friends?" "Are your friends sexually active?" "Do you think you are more or less sexually active than your friends?" "How many sexual partners have you had?"
- Asking for facts and not opinions
- Using familiar language and terminology
- Asking for permission to question, "Do you mind if I ask you about..." and explaining the reason for questioning, "In order to plan for your medical care, I need to ask you about..."
- Using a scale (1 to 10) rather than asking for detailed information
- Explaining what kinds of information can remain confidential and what kinds cannot (such as child abuse)

Multicultural Counseling

Diversity in the United States

In recent years, the African American population has grown and many individuals in that population have moved to suburban areas and established more lucrative socioeconomic positions. The Latino population has also grown drastically, now outnumbering the African American population (18.5% to 13.4% according to the US Census of 2019). This growth has elevated the Latino population to the largest minority group in America. Native Americans (referred to as American Indians by the US Census) are one of the smallest minority groups in America (1.3%). However, this small group has had a lucrative experience in the operation of reservation-based casinos and other service-oriented businesses. The Native American population has also made economic gains from construction and retail. The counselor must be aware and cognizant of the **diverse mental health needs of the minority groups in America**. Competence in these areas include the following:

- Self-awareness about one's own prejudices and cultural backgrounds
- Knowledge about diverse populations
- Skills in treating diverse populations

History of Multicultural Counseling

The United States has a populace derived from a variety of different countries and cultures. The Association for Multicultural Counseling and Development publishes a guide to the culture, ethnicity, and race of individual groups of people served by mental health providers. The foundation for the association was laid by civil rights groups of the 1950s-1960s, renowned for their social justice reforms that addressed racial problems, discrimination issues, subtle biases, and segregation in schools and public places. **Multicultural counseling** promotes cultural competence as an ongoing training effort for counselors working in other disciplines. Cultural awareness outlines are used during multicultural counseling. Multicultural counselors must receive appropriate training and preparation that includes preventive care.

Essential Elements of Multicultural Counseling

In 1990, Don C. Locke defined these **four elements** of the ever-changing role of multicultural counseling:

1. Multicultural counseling is aware of the cultural background, values, and world view of the client and the therapist.
2. Multicultural counseling makes note of socialization aspects in regard to race, ethnicity, and culture of the client.
3. Multicultural counseling makes every effort to see the individual within the group of people that he or she belongs.
4. Multicultural counseling does not label the person as deficient, but acknowledges that there can be a difference between the person as an individual and his or her group.

The differences in a person may need to be addressed to help the person come to terms with his or her own self-identity. The individual is also encouraged to value the racial or ethnic group of which he or she is a member.

Review Video: Multicultural Counseling
Visit mometrix.com/academy and enter code: 965442

Framework for Cultural Understanding

The framework for cultural understanding is based on the diverse cultural backgrounds that exist between a client and a counselor. Personal experiences shape the counselor's and the client's worldview and impact behaviors of both. Areas in which different points of view surface include historical perspectives, social perspectives, economical perspectives, and political perspectives. Likewise, socialization and life experiences change the client's and counselor's worldviews and behaviors. Counseling sessions are impacted by differences between the counselor and the client because they can cause a lack of empathy and understanding in the client/counselor relationship. Prejudices and biases are detrimental to the counselor/client relationship. If one is considering becoming a counselor, they should expect to have their own belief system scrutinized, and to establish an operations framework where commonalities are first identified to achieve empathy and understanding.

Multicultural Awareness Continuum

The linear tool used to help a counselor gain cultural competence is the **Multicultural Awareness Continuum**. The counselor cannot expect to achieve mastery, as the continuum is designed to be ongoing and revisited throughout the career of the counselor. Progression allows the counselor to go on to the next level, but if the counselor is confronted by a deficiency in his or her awareness when treating a culturally diverse person, then the counselor returns to the previous level for insight into that aspect of the culture. Levels of cultural competence within the Multicultural Awareness Continuum include the following:

1. Self-awareness
2. Awareness of one's cultural groupings
3. Awareness of racism, sexism, and poverty in relation to cultural problems
4. Awareness of individual differences
5. Awareness of other groups of people and cultures
6. Awareness of diversity
7. Skills and techniques related to the multicultural counselor

Levels of the Multicultural Awareness Continuum

The first level of the Multicultural Awareness Continuum is a **high level of self-awareness**. This component is essential for the counselor to understand why he or she feels a certain way and to identify biases in his or her own thinking. It is imperative for a counselor to understand how he or she interacts with others. Likewise, the counselor needs to examine his or her beliefs, attitudes, opinions, and values. A multicultural counselor must spend time in introspection to determine areas in which he or she may have cultural biases.

The second level has to do with an **awareness of one's own culture**. Certain cultures may place values upon a person's name, its origin and cultural significance. Other cultures may place values upon birth order. Some cultures have naming ceremonies for infants. Language and its use can also play a significant part in the values placed upon a person through his or her culture.

The third level on the Multicultural Awareness Continuum is **awareness of racism, sexism, and poverty bias**. Counselors discover this awareness by looking closely at their own personal belief system. Sexism and racism are an entrenched part of cultural beliefs. Some counselors and clients may not have biases against token minority individuals whom they know personally, but may think of smaller cultures folded into the American melting pot as subtly inferior. Poverty touches everyone to some extent. Many have either experienced poverty directly, or have simply seen shocking evidence of its existence. The counselor must determine his or her own bias before helping others gain insights into a cultural belief system.

The counselor must not overgeneralize any culture. This lends itself to the fourth and fifth levels of multicultural awareness. The fourth level is an **awareness of individual differences**. Overgeneralization leads to misconceptions founded on observations of only a few members of a culture. To avoid misconceptions, treat the client first and foremost as an individual with his or her own set of unique needs and then as a member of his or her specific culture. Understand that the individual has to function both as a member of their own culture and in American society at large. Avoid projecting personal cultural beliefs on the client.

The fifth level is an **awareness of other cultures**. This begins with the client's language. A multicultural counselor does not need to learn a foreign language in its entirety, but just certain words that have significant meanings. In 1980, Hofstede researched 40 countries to determine identifiable differentiations in their various cultures. He determined the following characteristics are the most identifiable:

- Power distance
- Uncertainty avoidance
- Masculinity/femininity
- Individualism/collectivism

In 1961, Kluckhorn and Strodtbect determined the following characteristics are the most identifiable:

- Time
- View of human nature
- Importance of relationships
- Human activity
- View of the supernatural

In 2001, Gelso and Fretz exhibited a series of dimensions to describe the differences they found between ethnic groups within American society. Gelso and Fretz described five areas:

- Family relationships, and how the person perceived oneself in relation to family
- Value of self over value of family
- Value of individual success or value of combined success of the family
- Importance of the past versus importance of the present or future
- Concepts regarding focus of control over one's life choices and events

In each of these areas, the counselor must be able to understand and identify exactly what viewpoint the client holds. Out of this understanding, the counselor can provide explanations regarding the nature of the client's stress that will initiate a more trusted, shared view.

The sixth level of awareness is the **awareness of diversity**, which begins with a grasp of just how erroneous the idea is that America's cultures have joined to become one super-culture. There are marked differences in the cultures of various races, ethnicities, religious groups, and sexual orientations. In the melting pot theory, the differences in these cultures went undervalued and unrecognized. Immigrants and the poor were encouraged to buy into the values, beliefs, and attitudes of mainstream America. The melting pot theory is being replaced by the mosaic theory, and the terms "salad bowl" or "rainbow coalition." The salad bowl concept suggests a mix of ingredients that are best when the flavors are allowed to stand out and complement each other.

The final level on the Multicultural Awareness Continuum is the **necessary skills and techniques required to counsel diverse populations**. A prerequisite for beginning the multicultural process is the counselor's general competence in counseling. The counselor is required to complete each level of study successfully and satisfy internship requirements in order to achieve general competency. The counselor should be thoroughly educated in counseling theories, standards, and applications. The historical significance of the theory must be understood in context of the time period in which the theory was framed. The theorist's own cultural belief system should be noted, in conjunction with the theory he or she developed. By studying the theory in context, the counselor can better understand how to maintain the integrity of the theory when applying it to cultural groups. A counselor should perform within his or her own cultural sub-group before attempting to perform those same duties with clients of other cultural groups. There is no replacement for basic counseling skills.

Preparations Involved in Training Multicultural Counselors

Since concepts of globalization are ever widening, it is imperative that a counselor maintains constant vigilance to **maintaining cultural competency**. The counselor should assume that training and education will be a life-long venture. Preparation methods should involve an all-inclusive educational program that takes into account the client's developmental capacities and a wide range of psychological theories and content available in colleges and institutions. The American Mental Health Counselors Association (AMHCA) stresses the importance of the counselor exploring his or her own cultural, ethnic, racial, and religious identity as the groundwork for this training. The counselor puts the client's needs first. To abide by AMHCA's code of ethics regarding diversity, the counselor must refer a client whenever an irresolvable conflict arises in the areas of culture, ethnicity, race, or religion.

The Multicultural Counseling Framework

The **content of the framework** for multicultural counseling is communicative, collaborative, open to alteration or exchange, and open to quality improvement according to the client's needs. Consider the client's existing issues and incorporate up-to-date research that impacts these issues. Some core structures are required to provide consistency of care, including the following:

- Communication styles that involve an exchange of ideas and information
- Beliefs, opinions, and attitudes about psychological problems or issues
- Strategies or devised plans of action for handling and solving problems
- Counseling expectations of conduct and performance levels
- Racial identity development (the way someone absorbs cultural behavior and societal thinking from birth)
- The way the counselor sees people, events, and happenings in relation to their world view

Following this framework will help the counselor meet the needs of the client.

Prevention as Part of Multicultural Counseling Model

Prevention is any practice that eliminates potential client suffering from psychological, emotional, and social distress. The Surgeon General reports one out of five Americans has a mental disorder but only a small portion seek out mental health services. *Mental Health: Culture, Race, and Ethnicity* (2001) is a supplement to the U.S. Department of Health and Human Services report on mental health, and addresses the issue that persons of diverse ethnic and racial backgrounds are highly unlikely to access needed mental health services. Statistics would improve if **multicultural counseling** was available in areas not currently serviced. Ideally, at-risk groups should receive preventive care through schools, employers, social policy, vocational programs, and women and infant medical facilities. Communities can promote preventive care models through advocacy, outreach, psychoeducational interventions, and self-help groups.

PRIMARY PREVENTION AND SYSTEMS APPROACH USED IN MULTICULTURAL COUNSELING MODELS

The multicultural mental health counselor uses his or her progressive insights and creativity to produce a positive result in helping clients. Different systems are incorporated within this task. Social justice and equity issues are a part of the lifestyle of the counselor. The counselor is willing to take preventive actions to make a difference for the client. The counselor works hard to gain cultural awareness and understanding by learning through experience, study, and training to acquire needed skills. A **systems approach** makes note of the following parameters:

- The client and existing issues
- Societal surroundings attributed to the existing issues
- The way that the person relates to issues within his or her surroundings

The counselor makes an initial assessment to determine the client's overall mental health status and how that is impacted by the issues at hand.

SOCIAL JUSTICE AS PART OF THE MULTICULTURAL COUNSELING MODEL

Social justice is equated with problematic issues in racial conflicts, sexism, and sexual preferences. Discrimination and prejudice negatively impact quality of life for both individuals and groups. Changing discriminatory practices and prejudicial viewpoints is part of preventive mental health practices. Domestic violence, sexual attacks, child abuse, discriminatory educational and suspension practices, discriminatory employment and promotion procedures, and culturally insensitive managers and coworkers are just some possible areas where social justice should be applied. The counselor instructs the client in coping or empowerment skills that assist the client to overcome the detrimental effects of social injustice. The multicultural counselor works to change organizational, institutional, and societal thought patterns and actions of social injustice which have an adverse impact on a client's mental health status and general feeling of wellbeing.

COMPONENTS THAT CAN IMPROVE MULTICULTURAL EDUCATIONAL COURSES

Multicultural educational courses can be improved with a broader scope on diverse populations. The United States has a diverse populace and the world at large is becoming one of mixed culture. The counselor should be apprised of issues that might arise in multiracial or multiethnic families. **Educational courses** include those that inform the counselor about religious factors, spiritual factors, gender factors, sexual orientation, disability issues, socioeconomic statures, age factors, and immigrant issues. The multicultural element may also be introduced across the curriculum in all areas of study. Counselor educators can promote multicultural competencies in educational courses. These competencies will influence the care the minority client receives by ensuring that the counselor is skilled in consultation, outreach, and advocacy.

DETERMINING PERSONAL PREJUDICES AND ORGANIZATIONAL PREJUDICES

The danger of projecting a specific trait onto a whole group lies in a misconception about the client and leads to pathological labels that can be discriminatory. Contrarily, these misconceptions can produce guilt in the counselor who is trying to make up for the client's feeling of oppression. These misconceptions can get in the way of the counseling session. The counselor may choose to use a systems approach in exploring differences between **personal prejudices** that determine how an individual acts, and **organizational prejudices** that determine how an organization or institution acts. For example, discrepancies in behavior result when:

- The worker's personal beliefs conflict with official policies in the workplace.
- The congregation's beliefs do not follow the church's official policy.
- The electorate does not agree with government policy.

Therefore, the counselor must determine what beliefs and attitudes are promoted by those organizations in which the counselor is a member. A counselor may wish to apply a systems approach to his or her place of employment to find out if there are institutional prejudices present within.

Core Counseling Attributes Chapter Quiz

1. The stable environment provided by an organization to assist in a treatment plan is known as which of the following?

a. Safe space
b. Therapeutic milieu
c. Structural equanimity
d. Integral environment

2. How many main areas of nonverbal communication are there?

a. Six
b. Five
c. Four
d. Three

3. If someone is 10 feet away from someone else, they are in which category of space?

a. Intimate space
b. Personal space
c. Social-consultative space
d. Public space

4. What percentage of mental health staff experience physical assault at work?

a. 40%
b. 50%
c. 60%
d. 75%

5. All of the following are methods for obtaining sensitive information EXCEPT:

a. Embedding the questions in a series of questions in context
b. Utilizing hypothetical questions instead of asking directly
c. Using familiar rather than clinical language
d. Using a scale (1 to 10) rather than asking for detailed information

6. The melting pot theory of diversity in America is being replaced by which of the following theories?

a. River theory
b. Mosaic theory
c. Mainstream theory
d. Demarcation theory

7. The Surgeon General reports that roughly how many Americans have a mental disorder?

a. 1 in 20 (5%)
b. 1 in 15 (7%)
c. 1 in 10 (10%)
d. 1 in 5 (20%)

8. All of the following are non-therapeutic communication techniques EXCEPT:

a. Clarification
b. Challenging
c. Disapproval
d. Giving advice

9. Which of the following would NOT be considered unsafe or contraband items in a mental health facility?

a. Alcohol
b. Over-the-counter medicine
c. Matches
d. Felt point pen

10. Which of the following refers to consistently communicating the same message verbally and nonverbally?

a. Rehearsed
b. Congruence
c. Moderation
d. Orchestration

Chapter Quiz Answer Key

Professional Practice and Ethics

1. A: Content validity, which can also be called rational validity or logical validity, is the reflection of the subject matter in the content of the test; for example, a math test will contain material covered in the specific math course.

2. C: Concurrent validity is the immediate comparison of test results with the results from other sources that measure the same factors in the same short time span.

3. A: There are nine steps used in the problem-solving model for ethical dilemmas designed by Koocher and Keith-Spiegel in 1998:

- Step 1: Determine the ethical problem.
- Step 2: Review the ethical guidelines available that pertain to the problem at hand, including possible solutions that have previously worked with other clients.
- Step 3: Peruse the impact that other sources may have on the decisions that should be made to resolve the problem.
- Step 4: Consult with trusted professionals about the problem and possible solutions.
- Step 5: Assess the human rights and civil liberties of the client, which may be impacted by the solution to the problem, and consider possible consequences of the solution for the problem at hand.
- Step 6: Create a number of avenues that may be explored in the solution to the problem.
- Step 7: Evaluate the possible consequences that can be the result of each solution applied to the problem at hand.
- Step 8: Make a decision about one solution to be implemented.
- Step 9: Follow through with the decision that was made.

4. D: Immanuel Kant is most commonly associated with the deontological view of ethics. One foundational philosophy developed by Kant was his categorical imperative. Deontological perspectives deal in universal truths, where everyone receives equal treatment. Therefore, when a counselor believes that privacy should be part of their service, then that privacy is applied to all clients in every situation. There is no room for exceptions to the rule. Likewise, there is no need to consider consequences in this philosophy, as all people are treated equally. The Golden Rule is at the heart of deontology ("Do unto others as you would have them do unto you").

5. B: John Stuart Mill proposed that the utilitarian should break confidentiality when it benefited the majority of the people. In 1976, a lawsuit was brought to the California Supreme Court to contest the deontological perspective against the utilitarian perspective. In the case of *Tarasoff versus the Board of Regents of the University of California*, the courts supported the utilitarian perspective on breaking confidentiality for the good of the majority. The court allowed that keeping confidentiality in this case could have caused injury to others. However, some counselors do tend to believe that confidentiality should be an absolute right of the client.

6. B: The most basic single system design is the A-B design. The baseline phase (A) has no intervention, followed by the intervention phase (B) with data collection. Typically, data are collected continuously through the intervention phase. Advantages of this design include the following:

- Versatility
- Adaptability to many settings, program styles, and problems
- Clear comparative information between phases

A significant limitation, however, is that causation cannot be demonstrated.

7. C: The key steps in the research process are as follows:

1. Problem or issue identification: Includes a literature review to further define the problem and to ensure that the problem has not already been studied
2. Hypothesis formulation: Creating a clear statement of the problem or concern, worded in a way that it can be operationalized and measured
3. Operationalization: Creating measurable variables that fully address the hypothesis
4. Study design selection: Choosing a study design that will allow for the proper analysis of the data to be collected

8. B: The three common study designs used in the research process include the following:

- An exploratory research design is common when little is known about a particular problem or issue. Its key feature is flexibility. The results comprise detailed descriptions of all observations made, arranged in some kind of order. Conclusions drawn include educated guesses or hypotheses.
- When the variables chosen have already been studied (e.g., in an exploratory study), further research requires a descriptive survey design. In this design, the variables are controlled partly by the situation and partly by the investigator, who chooses the sample. Proof of causality cannot be established, but the evidence may support causality.
- Experimental studies are highly controlled. Intervening and extraneous variables are eliminated, and independent variables are manipulated to measure effects in dependent variables (e.g., variables of interest)—either in the field or in a laboratory setting.

9. C: A population is the total set of subjects sought for measurement by a researcher.

10. A: Correlation refers to the strength of relatedness when a relationship exists between two or more numerical values, which, when assigned a numerical value, is the correlation coefficient (*r*). A perfect (1:1) correlation has an *r* value of 1.0, with decimal values indicating a lesser correlation as the correlation coefficient moves away from 1.0. The correlation may be either positive (with the values increasing or decreasing together) or negative (if the values are inverse and move opposite to each other).

Intake, Assessment, and Diagnosis

1. B: Freud's psychoanalytic theory postulates that behavior is influenced not only by environmental stimuli (i.e., physical influences) and external social constrains and constructs (i.e., taboos, rules, social expectations), but also by four specific unconscious elements as well. These elements exist only in the unconscious mind, and individuals remain substantively unaware of all the forces, motivations, and drives that shape their thoughts and behavioral decisions. The four elements are:

- Covert desires
- Defenses needed to protect, facilitate, and moderate behaviors
- Dreams
- Unconscious wishes

2. D: The Industry vs. inferiority stage occurs between 6 to 11 years of age:

- Same as Freud's latency stage.
- The need of the child is to make things well, to be a worker, and a potential provider.
- Developmental task is mastery over physical objects, self, social transaction, ideas, and concepts.
- School and peer groups are necessary for gaining and testing mastery.
- Psychological dangers include a sense of inferiority, incompetence, self-restraint, and conformity.

3. A: B. F. Skinner developed the empty organism concept, which proposes that an infant has the capacity for action built into his or her physical makeup. The infant also has reflexes and motivations that will set this capacity in random motion. Skinner asserted that the law of effect governs development. Behavior of children is shaped largely by adults. Behaviors that result in satisfying consequences are likely to be repeated under similar circumstances. Halting or discontinuing behavior is accomplished by denying satisfying rewards or through punishment.

4. C: The Luria-Nebraska neuropsychological battery (LNNB) contains 11 subtests that assess areas like rhythm, visual function, and writing. The examinee is given a score between 0 and 2, with 0 indicating normal function and 2 indicating brain damage.

5. C: The fourth edition of the Wechsler Adult Intelligence Scale (WAIS-IV, 2008) is used to measure the intellectual ability of late-adolescents and adults. This interrelationship between the various types of intelligence is described in the current test in terms of four index scores:

- Verbal Comprehension Index (VCI)
- Perceptual Reasoning Index (PRI)
- Working Memory Index (WMI)
- Processing Speed Index (PSI)

6. B: The developmental model of couples therapy (Bader & Pearson) accepts the inevitable change in relationships and focuses on both individual and couple growth and development. The goal is to assist the couple to recognize their stage of development and to gain the skills and insight needed to progress to the next stage. Problems may especially arise if members of the couple are at different stages.

7. C: The following are terms that pertain to Anna Freud's defense mechanisms:

- Splitting—Seeing external objects as either all good or all bad. Feelings may rapidly shift from one category to the other.

8. D: The following are terms that pertain to Anna Freud's defense mechanisms:

- Introjection—Absorbing an idea or image so that it becomes part of oneself.

9. B: One form of assessment involves nonstandard procedures that are used to provide individualized assessments. Nonstandard assessment procedures include observations of client behaviors and performance. There are three levels of observation techniques that can be applied:

- The first level is casual informational observation, where the counselor gleans information by watching the client during unstructured activities throughout the day.
- The second level is guided observation, an intentional style of direct observation accomplished with a checklist or rating scale to evaluate the performance or behavior seen.
- The third level is the clinical level, where observation is done in a controlled setting for a lengthy period of time. This is most often accomplished on the doctoral level with applied instrumentation. Clinical predictions are then based on the intuition and experience of the observing clinician.

10. A: Many different organizations, from schools to the armed forces, administer group intelligence tests:

- The Kuhlman-Anderson Test (KA) is for children in grades K-12; it measures verbal and quantitative intelligence. This test is unique in that it relies less on language than do other individual and group tests.
- The Woodcock Johnson IV consists of a test of cognitive abilities and a test of achievement; the latter of which measures oral language and academic achievement.
- The Wonderlic Personnel Test (WPT-R) takes about 12 minutes to fill out with paper and pencil; it purports to measure the mental ability of adults. The Wonderlic is a good predictor of performance, but some critics maintain that it unfairly discriminates against some cultural groups in certain jobs.

Areas of Clinical Focus

1. D: Down syndrome (Trisomy 21) occurs when a person has three #21 chromosomes instead of two. Down syndrome causes 20-30% of all cases of moderate and severe intellectual disability (1:800 births). Around 80% of Trisomy 21 pregnancies end in miscarriage. Classic physical characteristics associated with Down syndrome are slanted, almond-shaped eyes with epicanthic folds; a large, protruding tongue; a short, bent fifth finger; and a simian fold across the palm.

2. A: The value-based career theory (Brown, 2002) posited that central to career counseling is an understanding of the client's underlying values. According to this model, goal-directed behavior is stimulated by values. Values are an incentive. Therefore, the client gains satisfaction when he or she reaches a value-based goal. When the client does not reach a value-based goal successfully, disappointment and dejection are the likely outcome. Value-based goals can be well defined or based on a crystallized priority ranking. According to Brown's model, the three types of values are cultural, work, and life values.

3. A: Most successful treatments for Tourette's syndrome include pharmacotherapy. The antipsychotics haloperidol (Haldol) and pimozide (Orap) are successful in relieving the symptoms of Tourette's syndrome because they inhibit the flow of dopamine in the brain; their success has led many scientists to speculate that Tourette's Disorder is caused by an excess of dopamine. In some cases, psychostimulant drugs amplify the tics displayed by the individual. In these cases, a doctor may treat the hyperactivity and inattention of Tourette's with clonidine or desipramine. The former of these is a drug usually used to treat hypertension, while the latter is typically used as an antidepressant.

4. D: Encopresis is the involuntary fecal soiling in children who have already been toilet trained. Encopresis diagnosis cannot be made until the child is at least 4 years of age per DSM-5 criteria.

5. C: Adults with a specific phobia should be able to recognize that their fear is irrational and excessive. The onset of a specific phobia is typically in childhood or in the mid-20s. According to the DSM-5, there are five subtypes of specific phobia:

- Animal
- Natural environment
- Situational
- Blood-injection-injury
- Other

6. B: As with panic disorder, in vivo exposure is considered the best treatment for a specific phobia. Relaxation and breathing techniques are also helpful in dispelling fear and controlling physical response.

7. C: The symptoms of a conversion disorder can often be removed with hypnosis or Amytal interview. Some researchers believe that simply suggesting that these symptoms will go away is the best way to relieve them. The individual can develop complications, like seizures, from disuse of body parts.

8. A: Personality disorders are clustered into three groups:

Cluster A (eccentric or odd disorders)	**Cluster B** (dramatic or excessively emotional disorders)	**Cluster C** (fear- or anxiety-based disorders)
Paranoid	Antisocial	Avoidant
Schizoid	Borderline	Dependent
Schizotypal	Histrionic	Obsessive-Compulsive
	Narcissistic	

9. B: According to the National Institute of Alcohol Abuse and Alcoholism, 85.6% of Americans reported drinking alcohol at some point in their life, almost 70% reporting that they drank in the last year (2019). Around 50% of Americans drink alcohol as part of their daily routine; 10% of these routine drinkers will fall into addictive, habitual use.

10. A: The survivors of a disaster go through a series of emotional and psychological stages.

- In the first stage, the survivor sees himself or herself as a hero and acts out these heroic thoughts by helping to save someone else or their property.
- These altruistic feelings of individual heroism are followed by a honeymoon period, in which the whole neighborhood joins together to work as one unit to save others.
- The honeymoon period is followed by the disillusionment stage, which comes as a result of the postponement of help from others. The person feels let down by others.
- The final stage involves the reconstruction period. The survivor no longer looks for help from others, but instead takes control and responsibility for his or her situation, and works to resolve the problem.

Treatment Planning

1. B: Stage 2 of theory development is paradigm modification by Jung, Adler, Patterson, and Bandura.

2. B: Personality structure: The personality has three main components:

- Id: Unconscious pleasure principle, manifest by a desire for immediate and complete satisfaction with disregard for others
- Ego: Rational and conscious reality principle, which weighs actions and consequences
- Superego: Conscious and unconscious censoring force of the personality, which evaluates and judges behavior

3. C: Jung's archetypes are the images and concepts that develop the collective unconscious of humanity. The main archetypes are:

- The Way: The image of a journey or voyage through life
- The Self: The aspect of the mind that unifies and orders experience
- Animus and Anima: The image of gender
- Rebirth: The concept of being reborn, resurrected or reincarnated
- Persona: The role or mask one shows to others
- Shadow: The dark side of one's personality
- Stock characters: Dramatic roles that appear over and over in folktales
- The Hero: The character who vanquishes evil and rescues the downtrodden
- The Trickster: The character who plays pranks or works magic spells
- The Sage: The wise old person
- Power: A symbol such as the eagle or the sword
- Number: Certain numbers appear throughout history and across cultures

4. C: The removal of masks and facades is the goal of Gestalt therapy, according to Perls. A creative interaction needs to be developed so the client can gain an ongoing awareness of what is being felt, sensed, and thought.

5. D: Cross-cultural research has distinguished six basic universal human emotions: Fear, anger, happiness, disgust, surprise, and sadness. The James-Lange theory of emotion asserts that emotions are the body's reaction to changes in the autonomic nervous system caused by external stimuli. This theory is supported by the fact that quadriplegics report feeling less-intense emotions.

6. A: The transtheoretical model focuses on changes in behavior based on the individual's decisions (not on society's decisions or others' decisions) and is used to develop strategies to promote changes in health behavior. This model outlines stages people go through when changing problem behavior and trying to have a positive attitude about change. Stages of change include the following:

- Precontemplation: The person is either unaware or under-informed about consequences of a problem behavior and has no intention of changing behavior within the next 6 months.
- Contemplation: The person is aware of costs and benefits of changing behavior and intends to change within the next 6 months but is procrastinating and not ready for action.
- Preparation: The person has a plan and intends to initiate change in the near future (≤1 month) and is ready for action plans.

- Action: The person is modifying behavior change occurs only if behavior meets a set criterion (such as complete abstinence from drinking).
- Maintenance: The person works to maintain changes and gains confidence that he or she will not relapse.

7. A: Gottfried Leibniz was a philosopher who believed in personology, which states that a person can change when his or her perceptual awareness is changed. Leibniz's theory of mind is based on subjective reality—how a person perceives things to be within his or her own mind. Leibniz's theory of personology evolved into humanistic psychology, resulting in a counseling model known as Rogers' person-centered psychotherapy.

8. D: According to Joseph Rychlak, psychotherapy can be broken down into three basic motives that correspond with learning, ethics, and healing.

- Scholarly motive corresponds with learning. Rychlak believed this rationale for performing psychotherapy was best characterized in the works of Freud, where the psychotherapist is a scientist who records the inner workings of the mind, instinctive drives, and actions, and then analyzes the data collected.
- Ethical motive refers to the counselor's desire to help the client grow and express strong feelings and opinions about his or her life problems.
- Curative motive is when the psychotherapist wants to initiate the healing process for the client by engaging in such a way as to help modify those behaviors detrimental to the client's success in society.

9. D: Motivational interviewing (Miller, 1983) aims to help people identify and resolve issues regarding ambivalence about change and focuses on the role of motivation to bring about change. MI is a collaborative approach in which the interviewer assesses the individual's readiness to accept change and identifies strategies that may be effective with the individual.

Elements	Principles	Strategies
Collaboration rather than confrontation in resolving issues Evocation (drawing out) of the individual's ideas about change rather than imposition of the interviewer's ideas Autonomy of the individual in making changes	Expression of empathy: Showing understanding of individual's perceptions Support of self-efficacy: Helping individuals realize they are capable of change Acceptance of resistance: Avoiding struggles/conflicts with client Examination of discrepancies: Helping individuals see discrepancy between their behavior and goals	Avoiding Yes/No questions: Asking informational questions Providing affirmations: Indicating areas of strength Providing reflective listening: Responding to statements Providing summaries: Recapping important points of discussion Encouraging change talk: Including desire, ability, reason, and need

10. B: Common Freudian psychiatric terms include:

- Freudian slips: Also known as parapraxes, these are overt actions with unconscious meanings.

Counseling Skills and Interventions

1. A: Adaptability is maintaining a balanced, positive stability in the family. A prerequisite for balanced stability, and a basic goal of family therapy, is to help the client family develop strategies for dealing with life's inevitable changes. Morphogenesis is the medical term often applied to a family's ability to react functionally and appropriately to changes.

2. B: Personal Science was developed in 1977 by Michael Mahoney, based on the cognitive-behavioral (CB) approach. The acronym SCIENCE is used to explain the sequential steps through which the therapist guides the client to solve a problem:

- S for *specification* of the problem
- C for *collection* of data or facts
- I for *identification* of patterns or reasons for existing behaviors
- E for *examination* of choices that can be used to modify behavior
- N for *narrowing* the options and experimenting with possible modifications
- C for *comparing* data or facts
- E for *expanding*, modifying, or substituting unwanted behaviors

3. B: Key concepts of Albert Ellis's rational emotive therapy include the idea that people control their own destinies and interpret events, according to their own values and beliefs.

4. A: Irvin Yalom's "here-and-now" or process groups are characterized by the following:

- Yalom stressed using clients' immediate reactions and discussing members' affective experiences in the group.
- Process groups have relatively unstructured and spontaneous sessions.
- Process groups emphasize therapeutic activities, like imparting information, or instilling hope, universality, and altruism.
- The group can provide a rehabilitative narrative of primary family group development, offer socializing techniques, provide behavior models to imitate, offer interpersonal learning, and offer an example of group cohesiveness and catharsis.

5. A: Proxemics is the study of personal space and the distance between individuals at which people feel comfortable or uncomfortable. Proxemics vary according to culture, and the counselor should assess the client's personal space of comfort and avoid violating that space or communicating the wrong message.

6. D: Family therapy is a therapeutic modality theorizing that a client's psychiatric symptoms are a result of pathology within the client's family unit. This dysfunction is due to problems within the system, usually arising from conflict between marital partners. Psychiatric problems result from these behaviors. This conflict is expressed by:

- Triangulation, which manifests itself by the attempt of using another family member to stabilize the emotional process
- Scapegoating, which occurs when blaming is used to shift focus to another family member.

7. B: Satir described four issues that impede communication between family members under stress. Placating, blaming, being overly reasonable, and being irrelevant are the four issues which blocked family communication, according to Virginia Satir:

- Placating is the role played by some people in reaction to threat or stress in the family. The placating person reacts to internal stresses by trying to please others, often in irrational ways. A mother might try to placate her disobedient and rude child by offering food, candy, or other presents on the condition that he stop a certain behavior.
- Blaming is the act of pointing outwards when an issue creates stress. The blamer thinks, "I'm very angry, but it's your fault. If I've wrecked the car, it's because you made me upset when I left home this morning."
- Irrelevance is a behavior wherein a person displaces the potential problem and substitutes another unrelated activity. A mother who engages in too much social drinking frequently discusses her split ends whenever the topic of alcoholism is brought up by her spouse.
- Being overly reasonable, also known as being a responsible analyzer is when a person keeps his or her emotions in check and functions with the precision and monotony of a machine.

8. B: Multiple theories of causality exist in the interpretation of family dynamics, which are then applied to the selection of therapeutic interventions. While linear causality (the concept that one cause equals one effect) uses a direct line of reasoning and is commonly used in individual counseling, circular/reciprocal causality is often used in family therapy and refers to the dynamic interactions between family members.

9. C: The social reinforcement and exchange theory in regard to group work is summarized as follows:

- Social exchange theorists propose that members of groups are motivated to seek profit in their interactions with others (i.e., to maximize rewards and minimize costs).
- Analysis of interactions within groups is done in terms of a series of exchanges or tradeoffs group members make with each other.
- The individual member is the primary unit of analysis. Many of the core concepts of this theory are merely transferred to the group situation and do not further the understanding of group processes.

10. D: The correlates of humor are what make it successful in producing an amusing result. There are three correlates of humor:

- The suddenness of the punch line or surprising conclusion gives the audience the opportunity to laugh at the unexpected twist.
- Optimal arousal is derived from an appropriate level of intellectual, emotional, or physical stimulation (e.g., adults find it difficult to laugh at childish jokes that have ceased to be of interest).
- Play frame is setting up the joke or story to be non-threatening for the listener. Some jokes may be too intense for the individual's comfort level. Play frame involves cueing the listener through facial expressions or vocal tones that intend a time for play.

Core Counseling Attributes

1. B: The therapeutic milieu is a stable environment provided by an organization to assist in a treatment plan. The main purposes of a milieu are to teach individuals certain social skills and to provide a structured environment that promotes interactions and personal growth along with attempting to control many types of deviant or destructive behaviors. There are five main components that the milieu should include in therapy. These components include containment, structure, support, involvement, and validation. Through the use of these components, the therapeutic milieu can help the individuals achieve their highest level of functioning.

2. B: There are many different types of nonverbal behaviors. There are five main areas of nonverbal communication. They include vocal cues, action cues, object cues, space, and touch.

3. C: Space can provide information about a relationship between the client and someone else. Most people living in the United States have four different areas of space. Intimate space is less than 1.5 feet, personal space is 1.5-4 feet, social-consultative space is 9-12 feet, and public space is 12 feet or more. Observations concerning space and the client's physical placement in a setting can give a great deal of insight into different interpersonal relationships.

4. D: A protocol for a professional assault response should be established at all mental health facilities because statistics show that 75% of mental health staff experience a physical assault. Most injuries are incurred by nursing staff caring for violent clients. Assaults may occur in both psychiatric units and emergency departments, where security staff may also be assaulted. Additionally, clients may be victims. Common injuries include fractures, lacerations, contusions, and unconsciousness from head injuries.

5. B: Sensitive information includes that involving sexual activity, abuse, intimate partner violence, substance abuse, and mental health issues. Clients are more likely to answer questions truthfully if they have developed a relationship of trust with the questioner. Methods of obtaining sensitive information include the following:

- Embedding the questions in a series of questions in context: "Do you spend time with your friends?" "Are your friends sexually active?" "Do you think you are more or less sexually active than your friends?" "How many sexual partners have you had?"
- Asking for facts and not opinions
- Using familiar language and terminology
- Asking for permission to question, "Do you mind if I ask you about..." and explaining the reason for questioning, "In order to plan for your medical care, I need to ask you about..."
- Using a scale (1 to 10) rather than asking for detailed information
- Explaining what kinds of information can remain confidential and what kinds cannot (such as child abuse)

6. B: The sixth level of awareness is the awareness of diversity, which begins with a grasp of just how erroneous the idea is that America's cultures have joined to become one super-culture. There are marked differences in the cultures of various races, ethnicities, religious groups, and sexual orientations. In the melting pot theory, the differences in these cultures went undervalued and unrecognized. Immigrants and the poor were encouraged to buy into the values, beliefs, and attitudes of mainstream America. The melting pot theory is being replaced by the mosaic theory, and the terms "salad bowl" or "rainbow coalition." The salad bowl concept suggests a mix of ingredients that are best when the flavors are allowed to stand out and complement each other.

7. D: The Surgeon General reports that approximately one out of five Americans has a mental disorder but only a small portion seek out mental health services. *Mental Health: Culture, Race, and Ethnicity* (2001) is a supplement to the U.S. Department of Health and Human Services report on mental health, and addresses the issue that persons of diverse ethnic and racial backgrounds are highly unlikely to access needed mental health services.

8. A: Techniques that are detrimental to establishing a trusting therapeutic relationship include giving advice, challenging the client's communications, or indicating disapproval. Giving advice includes telling the client what they should do in a particular situation. This does not allow the client to develop the ability to solve their own problems and may not always be the right answer. Challenging occurs when the client's thoughts are disputed by the provider. This communication only serves to lower the client's self-esteem and create an environment of distrust between the client and the mental health care provider. Disapproval occurs when the provider negatively judges the client's beliefs or actions. This again serves to lower client self-esteem and does not foster their ability to solve their own problems or create new coping abilities.

9. D: Depending on the type of facility or clients, a wide range of items may be considered unsafe. These often include the following:

- Potential weapons, such as pens (except felt point), pencils, and plastic bags

10. B: Congruence in communication is consistently communicating the same message verbally and nonverbally. The individual's words, body language, and tone of voice should all convey the same message. If they do not, then the communication is incongruent, and the receiver cannot trust the communication. For example, if a person says, "I really want to help you," in a very harsh tone of voice and with an angry affect, the communication is incongruent, and the message may actually be perceived as the exact opposite of the words spoken. Communication is also incongruent if the individual gives a series of conflicting messages: "I'm going to get a job," "Why should I work?" "I know I need to work," "There's no point in taking a low-paying job." Being alert to the congruence of client communication makes it possible to more accurately assess the client.

NCMHCE Practice Test #1

Case Study 1

PART ONE

INTAKE

CLIENT

Age: 9

Sex: Male

Gender: Male

Sexuality: Unknown

Ethnicity: Caucasian

Relationship Status: Not Applicable

Counseling Setting: School

Type of Counseling: Individual

Presenting Problem: Severe Temper Outbursts

Diagnosis: Disruptive Mood Dysregulation Disorder (DMDD), Provisional (F34.81)

PRESENTING PROBLEM:

You are a school-based mental health clinical counselor conducting an initial intake evaluation. A 9-year-old 3rd-grade male is accompanied by his mother, who reports that the client has been in several school and neighborhood altercations. She states she is at her "wit's end" with him and is about to lose her job due to constant calls from his school. The client's teacher reports that the client has daily temper outbursts, and his mother says that his mood is irritable for most of the day, every day. The client was recently suspended from school for flipping over his desk when his teacher told him he lost recess privileges. The mother first noticed these behaviors when her son was in kindergarten. The client recently kicked a hole in his wall after losing a video game. His grades are poor, and the school is currently evaluating him for special education services. The client was reluctant to take part in the intake. He shrugged his shoulders when asked if he would agree to participate in counseling.

MENTAL STATUS EXAM:

The client's affect is irritable and angry. He sits with his arms crossed and exhibits poor eye contact. His appearance is somewhat disheveled. Mother reprimands the client multiple times, requesting that he "sit up straight" and "answer the lady's questions." The client mumbles responses at his mother's prompting and is otherwise minimally engaged. The client reports that he "gets mad" daily and feels unjustly "blamed for everything." His motor activity is somewhat fidgety. Speech and language skills are developmentally appropriate. The client states he "sometimes" feels sad and denies feeling worried or scared. His appetite is good and his sleep is poor. The mother attributes his sleep difficulties to the client staying up late playing video games.

HISTORY OF CONDITION:

The client's milestones were all developmentally appropriate; he was walking at ten months, toilet trained by 24 months, and speaking in complete sentences at almost 30 months. The mother describes the client as "moody" beginning in kindergarten. His temper outbursts began to escalate in intensity and duration within the last few years. During this time, there were no known associated stressors. The mother reports that the client has always had a hard time following directions and difficulty complying with authority figures.

FAMILY HISTORY:

The client has two maternal half-brothers, ages 18 and 20, and has positive relationships with both of them. His parents divorced when the client was three years old, and the mother has physical custody of the child. Before the divorce, the client witnessed verbal and physical altercations between his parents. The client's father visits periodically, and he has been in and out of substance abuse treatment centers for most of the client's life. When angry with his mother, the client tells her he wishes he could live with his father. The client's maternal grandmother is diagnosed with bipolar disorder, and the client's mother states she struggles "off and on" with depression. Aside from the father's substance use disorder, a paternal history of mental illness is unknown.

1. In addition to severe temper outbursts, which information is most indicative of the diagnosis of Disruptive Mood Dysregulation Disorder (DMDD)?

a. Irritability
b. Defiance towards authority
c. Social-emotional difficulties
d. Impulsivity

2. The child is unwilling to agree to participate in counseling. Which of the following best illustrates what is required for counseling services to begin?

a. A consent form signed by both parents
b. An assent form signed by the child
c. A consent form signed by both parents and an assent form signed by the child
d. A consent form signed by a custodial parent and an effort to obtain assent from the child

3. Which of the following would best help create a therapeutic alliance with this client?

a. Helping the client master coping skills he can successfully apply when feeling angry
b. Sharing the treatment plan with the client to establish clear expectations
c. Using core facilitative conditions, such as reflection and validation
d. Demonstrating universality to minimize transference and instill hope

4. What information would best guide the initial development of the client's treatment plan?

a. Collateral information from the client's teacher
b. Classroom observation
c. Consultation with an interdisciplinary team
d. The client's motivation to change

PART TWO

FIRST SESSION, THREE WEEKS AFTER THE INITIAL INTAKE

The client is seen for the first time since the initial intake due to being suspended the previous week. He displays an angry affect, sits with his arms closed, and faces the wall. You begin to establish rapport by engaging the client in a game. The client starts to open up and discloses that he feels angry every day and attributes this to his mom "always bothering" him and "everybody always picking" on him. He believes that his teacher doesn't like him, and he is unhappy that his desk is no longer with the other students but instead right next to the teacher. He states that when he feels angry, his heart races, he clenches his fists, and he feels a tightness in his chest.

5. Given the client's ability to describe what happens when he feels angry, how would you proceed?

a. Refer the client for a psychiatric medication evaluation.
b. Teach the client relaxation techniques to use when experiencing associated physiological symptoms.
c. Have the client keep a journal and record the relationship between behavioral symptoms and negative self-talk.
d. Request that the client's teacher move the client's desk back with the other students.

6. The client has recently become eligible for special education services, including an Individualized Education Program (IEP). Which one of the following federal laws mandates that an IEP must be completed within 30 days of eligibility?

a. Section 504 of the Rehabilitation Act of 1973
b. Individuals with Disabilities Education Act (IDEA)
c. Title II of the Americans with Disabilities Act (ADA)
d. Title VII of the Civil Rights Act of 1964

7. Which assessment tool should you use to evaluate the client's executive functioning, attention, and cognitive processing?

a. Denver Developmental Screening Test II (DDST-II)
b. Cognitive Assessment System (CAS2)
c. The NEO-Personality Inventory (NEO-3)
d. The Children's Systemizing Quotient (SQ-C)

8. What is the logical error demonstrated when the client is asked to identify anger triggers?

a. Personalization
b. Polarized thinking
c. Emotional reasoning
d. Overgeneralization

9. You and the client's mother develop an incentive chart for the client. The mother uses a token system to reward skills learned in family therapy, and she uses planned ignoring when the client displays maladaptive behaviors. This is an example of which one of the following?

a. Motivational interviewing (MI)
b. Contingency management (CM)
c. Exposure and response prevention (ERP)
d. Habit reversal training (HRT)

Part Three

Second Session, Four Weeks After the Initial Intake

You have attempted to arrange a family session with the mother, but she is unable to take off work to attend. The client arrives for his second session eager to share that he is "on green" this morning, which means the client's behavior for the day has been good. You praise him for staying in his seat and keeping his hands and feet to himself. The client responds well to your praise. When engaging in a feelings identification activity, the client identifies feeling unhappy and worried when his father doesn't show up for scheduled visitation. The client explains that his parents frequently argue about "how to take care of me" and "sometimes push each other." He quickly abandons the feelings activity and asks if he can go back to class. You deny the client's request to leave and instead give him the option of selecting another activity. The client refuses to do so and begins to kick your file cabinet repeatedly. He proceeds to knock papers off your desk. When redirected, the client's behavior escalates. He quickly becomes inconsolable as he cries and yells, "I hate counseling, this school, and everyone in it!"

10. Given the severity of the client's emotional and behavioral difficulties, as well as the disruptive behavior displayed during this session, what would be your next best step?

a. Initiate an immediate psychiatric medication evaluation.
b. Conduct a crisis risk assessment.
c. Arrange for an alternative school placement.
d. Refer the family for intensive in-home family therapy services.

11. During the feelings identification activity, you respond to your client's disclosure by stating, "You're feeling sad and miss your dad. And on top of worrying about him, it sounds like you feel responsible for some of your parents' grown-up problems. Am I getting this right?" This is an example of a(n):

a. Complex reflection
b. Additive encourager
c. Clarification
d. Advanced paraphrase

12. You arrive at school one morning and find the child's father in the main office. He is requesting to talk to you about his son. What is the best way for you to proceed?

a. State that you cannot disclose whether or not the child is your client and cannot meet with him.
b. Explain to the father that you can only see him if the client's mother provides written consent.
c. Tell the father you only work by appointment and arrange to see him the following week.
d. Tell the father that you can listen to his concerns but cannot disclose any information.

13. Your client could benefit from a referral for in-home counseling, but the client's insurance does not cover the services. Your supervisor asks you to find an in-network provider for the client. In doing so, you adhere to which one of the following ethical principles?

a. Veracity
b. Justice
c. Autonomy
d. Fidelity

Case Study 2

PART ONE

INTAKE

CLIENT

Age: 48

Sex: Female

Gender: Female

Sexuality: Heterosexual

Ethnicity: Caucasian

Relationship Status: Separated

Counseling Setting: Private practice

Type of Counseling: Individual

Presenting Problem: Alcohol use

Diagnosis: Alcohol Use Disorder, Moderate, Provisional (F10.20)

PRESENTING PROBLEM:

You are a counselor working in private practice evaluating a 48-year-old female with a history of alcohol misuse. Three weeks ago, the client was hospitalized due to alcohol poisoning. She explains that she was in a blackout before waking up in the hospital and was told her BAC was 0.26, just over three times the legal limit. This occurred on the evening she discovered that her husband was having an affair. The client briefly attended a drug and alcohol intensive outpatient program (IOP) but felt she was not improving with group therapy and would like to try individual therapy instead. She admits that there are times in her life when she has abused alcohol but does not believe she is an alcoholic. The client experiences frequent anxiety and admits to using alcohol "just to take the edge off" and to help her fall asleep. Her alcohol intake increased nearly six months ago when her youngest child left for college. During this time, her husband of 25 years announced he was leaving and filing for divorce. She struggles with being an "empty nester" and is mourning the loss of the life she and her husband built together.

MENTAL STATUS EXAM:

The client's hands tremble, and she becomes tearful on several occasions. There is mild perspiration on her forehead. She endorses feeling hopeless about the future but denies suicidal ideation. The client shows no signs of intoxication or impairment. She presents as well-dressed with good hygiene. Both affect and mood are dysphoric. She apologizes several times for crying and states she has been "a mess" lately due to not sleeping for the last several days. Her demeanor becomes somewhat defensive when asked about her drinking, and she appears to minimize the impact this has had on her life.

FAMILY AND WORK HISTORY:

The client worked briefly as an office manager but became a stay-at-home mom once she had kids. As a devout Catholic, she reports feeling heartbroken and ashamed that her husband is filing for divorce. The couple frequently entertained guests at their home, which abruptly stopped after their separation. Her oldest daughter is not speaking to her and is "taking her father's side," which has caused her great sadness and resentment. Her middle child, who lives locally, is married with children but does not allow the client to visit her grandchildren unsupervised. She believes her children's father has spread lies about her alcohol use and feels he "drinks just as much" but appears to do so with impunity. The client's mother was addicted to pain pills, and her father was diagnosed with bipolar disorder. The client witnessed interpersonal violence between her parents as a child and often felt unsafe growing up.

HISTORY OF SUBSTANCE USE AND ADDICTIVE BEHAVIOR:

The client first started drinking at the age of 14. Her drinking increased significantly while in college and in her early 20's. The client was able to stop drinking through her three pregnancies but began to drink daily when her children became school-aged. She acknowledges that drinking during the day first started while waiting in the school's carpool line and increased when her husband returned home from work. She has received three DUIs and had the third offense expunged. After the third DUI, she was court-ordered to attend Alcoholics Anonymous. She stated she resented having to "get a piece of paper signed" and being asked to attend 90 meetings in 90 days. The client denies substance use beyond experimenting with marijuana in college. She concedes that alcohol has been problematic in the past but feels she can successfully control her intake.

1. Which instrument would you use to assess this client for both problematic alcohol use and related psychological and emotional adjustment?

a. The Alcohol Use Disorders Identification Test (AUDIT)
b. Cut Down, Annoyed, Guilty, and Eye-Opener (CAGE)
c. The Adult Substance Use Survey (ASUS)
d. The Drug Abuse Screening Test (DAST)

2. You ask your client the following: "On a 1-10 scale, with 10 being the highest, How confident are you that you can stop drinking altogether?" The client states, "I would say a 6." Using motivational Interviewing, which response would best elicit change talk?

a. "Why are you not a 10?"
b. "Why are you a 6 and not a 0?"
c. "Tell me more about how you decided you are a 6."
d. "What would your life look like if you were at a 7?"

3. Given the client's treatment history, which one of the following would provide you with a multidimensional biopsychosocial assessment to determine if outpatient counseling is an appropriate level of care?

a. Prevention and Early Intervention (PEI) criteria
b. Early Periodic Screening, Diagnosis, and Treatment (EPSDT) standards
c. American Society of Addiction Medication (ASAM) guidelines
d. National Institute on Drug Abuse (NIDA) screening tool

4. What information provided by the client is most indicative of the DSM-5 diagnosis of Alcohol Use Disorder?

a. The client sees or hears things that others do not.
b. Adverse consequences associated with alcohol consumption have increased in severity within the last 6 months.
c. On more than one occasion, the client has been arrested or had other legal problems because of alcohol use.
d. The client has continued to consume alcohol, even though it causes difficulties with her family or friends.

5. You are nearing the end of your initial intake session. Which of the following actions would best help improve treatment compliance for this client?

a. Provide the client with information for online and in-person 12-step recovery meetings.
b. Summarize the client's presenting problem, barriers to treatment, and associated risks of prolonged alcohol use.
c. Teach basic relaxation and mindfulness techniques to help improve insomnia.
d. Facilitate the negotiation of agreed-upon treatment goals.

6. You think you may know the client's husband. To ensure that there are no boundary violations, you search for your client online and look through her public social media postings. Is your behavior consistent with ethical standards of practice?

a. Yes, the information is public and you have an ethical responsibility to maintain boundaries.
b. No, you have an ethical responsibility to respect the client's privacy of her presence on social media.
c. Yes, your informed consent includes the risks and benefits of engaging in technology and social media.
d. No, in doing so, you are violating client confidentiality.

PART TWO

FIRST SESSION, THREE WEEKS AFTER THE INITIAL INTAKE

The client has arrived 15 minutes late for your scheduled session. When you approach the waiting room, you find her loudly talking on her cell phone. She abruptly ends the call and follows you back to your office. She is visibly shaken and angry. She explains that her soon-to-be ex-husband is a "master manipulator" and is "ruining my life." She remains confident that she can stop drinking but states she can only do so once her family situation is under control. After all, she states, "You would drink too if you had my problems." She begins to de-escalate as the session progresses, and she is able to identify and prioritize treatment issues. Her sleep continues to be a concern. Upon further exploration, she indicates she is having nightmares and has been for quite some time. The two of you work together to prioritize treatment plan goals. Her mood and demeanor brighten as the session concludes.

7. When discussing treatment issues, you ask, "How does drinking align or not align with your goal of improving relationships with your family?" What is the value of posing this question?

a. It allows for the focus to be kept on the client's alcohol misuse.
b. It helps create a discrepancy between the client's actions and personal values.
c. It assists with providing baseline measures for treatment plan goals.
d. It helps create incentive-based interventions used in contingency management.

8. Given the client's history of childhood trauma and continued alcohol use, how would you deliver trauma-informed care for this client in the early stages of treatment?

a. Process the details of the client's trauma experience or trauma narrative.
b. Help the client understand symptoms of their trauma and offer appropriate outside supports.
c. Provide education on the physiological dangers of treating trauma amid alcohol misuse.
d. Address the trauma if the client agrees to concurrent, short-term psychopharmacological treatment.

9. Your client states she is currently not ready to stop drinking. You respond, "It's up to you to decide if and when you are ready. No one can make that choice for you." Which core principle of professional ethical behavior is best reflected in this response?

a. Veracity
b. Fidelity
c. Autonomy
d. Justice

10. In addition to helping her sleep, the client states that drinking helps her feel more connected to others. How would an Adlerian therapist address these thoughts with the client?

a. Introduce the concept of social interest and authenticity as replacements for the false sense of security she currently experiences when drinking with others.
b. Support the client by showing empathy, unconditional positive regard, and nonjudgmental acceptance.
c. Help the client learn new social skills and gain confidence through role play and corrective feedback.
d. Instruct the client to identify the irrational belief associated with the activating event of drinking with others.

Part Three

Second Session, 9 Weeks After the Initial Intake:

During the previous session, the client committed to controlled drinking and agreed on a limit of two drinks per night. She admits to having limited success with this goal and concedes to over-indulging when feeling "stressed out." You learn she ran into a woman from her church who she discovered was a recovering alcoholic. She agreed to meet the woman at an AA meeting, and the client was surprised she could relate to other alcoholics. The client's affect brightened as she reported that she has had seven days of continuous sobriety. She continues to have a strained relationship with her now ex-husband. Her youngest child is home on spring break, which has helped improve her mood and kept her accountable for staying sober. She is able to use relaxation and mindfulness techniques for insomnia, which have been effective at times at improving her sleep pattern.

11. According to the Transtheoretical Stages of Change model, in which stage would you classify this client?

a. Precontemplation
b. Preparation
c. Action
d. Contemplation

12. You continue your discussion with the client, stating, "You've mentioned your ex-husband knows how to push your buttons, and you feel he has caused you to increase your alcohol consumption in the past. Can you tell me more about what your mood is like right after those interactions?" What is the value in asking this question within the context of cognitive-behavioral therapy?

a. To help guide the development of a functional analysis
b. To convey genuineness and unconditional positive regard
c. To uncover unconscious forces that drive behavior
d. To help create a subjective units of disturbance (SUD) scale

13. Your client states, "I can't do anything right anymore; I've failed as a parent." Using Rational-Emotive Behavioral Therapy (REBT), you respond with the following:

a. "You felt criticized by your ex-husband and your automatic thought was that you can't do anything right, including parenting."
b. "All parents feel like that every so often. It's just part of the human condition."
c. "You told me you were a stay-at-home mother. Would a failed parent make that sacrifice?"
d. "What evidence is there that indicates you haven't failed but instead succeeded as a parent?"

Case Study 3

Part One

Intake

Client

Age: 22

Sex: Male

Gender: Male

Sexuality: Homosexual

Ethnicity: Latino American

Relationship Status: Single

Counseling Setting: Community Mental Health Center

Type of Counseling: Individual

Presenting Problem: Depression

Diagnosis: Major Depressive Disorder, Moderate

Presenting Problem:

You are providing counseling services at a Community Mental Health Center. A 22-year-old Latino male, accompanied by his aunt, presents with symptoms of depression. The aunt is concerned about the client's social isolation, feelings of hopelessness, and excessive daytime sleeping. Four months ago, the client's parents kicked him out of their home after discovering a suggestive social media post of him with another male. He is close with his aunt and uncle, who have allowed him to stay in their basement. The client's father refuses to speak to him and has told him he is "less than a man" and an embarrassment to the family. The client's symptoms worsened last month when he was laid off from his job as a server.

Mental Status Exam:

The client is pleasant and dressed in age-appropriate attire. He is tearful when discussing his family and states this has been difficult for him. The client has had no previous suicide attempts. He is observed biting his nails. He describes feeling sad daily and states he sleeps during the day because he cannot sleep at night. He is slightly underweight but denied any difficulties with appetite. The client's speech is coherent and clear. He denies suicidal ideation but often questions his worth and purpose.

Family and Work History:

The client was recently laid off from his job as a server at an upscale restaurant in the downtown area. He misses the sense of family he had with his previous co-workers and feels "stuck" and "unable to move forward." The client is a third-generation Cuban American whose paternal grandparents immigrated to the United States during Castro's regime. His parents worked hard to put him and his siblings through Catholic school and instilled in him traditional heteronormative religious values and "familism" (i.e., the belief that the family unit is more important than individual needs). The client also has a strong work ethic but states he is poorly motivated to seek another job because he doesn't want to be "shot down."

History of Condition:

The client reports that he has struggled with bouts of depression from a very early age. He explains that he never felt like he fit in. In middle school, he was bullied and harassed. He remembers locking himself in his room, crying, and asking God for help during this time. He continued to ask for forgiveness and bargain with God as he grew older. In his mid- to late-teens, he began drinking and vaping, "because I couldn't keep my end of the bargain," he explains. Despite finding acceptance in the community, he still feels guilty for disappointing his parents. The client reports feeling "defective" and carries a significant amount of shame related to his sexual orientation.

1. Which screening instrument would you choose to determine the severity of the client's depression?

a. Bender-Gestalt Test
b. Patient Health Questionnaire (PHQ-9)
c. Brief Psychiatric Rating Scale (BPRS)
d. Achenbach System of Empirically Based Assessment (ASEBA)

2. You are devoutly religious, and homosexuality goes against your personal beliefs. How should you handle personal values that conflict with those belonging to the client?

a. Refer the client to another provider whose values are more aligned with the client's.
b. Ask the client to call your attention to any unintentional microaggressions that may occur during your clinical encounters.
c. Seek training to help you avoid imposing your beliefs onto clients.
d. Continue to work with the client as long your values are not openly discriminatory.

3. What information gathered during the assessment is most indicative of the diagnosis of Major Depressive Disorder (MDD)?

a. Strained relationships with family members
b. Excessive guilt
c. Poor coping skills
d. Emotional dysregulation

4. Your client is unmotivated to seek employment because he doesn't want to be "shot down." According to person-centered theory, what is the root of your client's maladaptive behavior?

a. The client has developed a failure identity as the result of not taking responsibility for change.
b. The client has an underlying irrational belief that he must be capable in all areas of life or else he is worthless.
c. The client has developed incongruence between the value of being employed and the behavior of not seeking employment.
d. The client has adopted the unhealthy life position of "I'm not okay. You're not okay."

5. Given the client's background, all of the following factors may place him at higher risk for suicide EXCEPT:

a. Job loss
b. Social isolation
c. Sexual orientation
d. Previous suicide attempt

Part Two

First Session, Four Weeks After the Intake Session

The client displays a blunted affect and remains pleasant and cooperative. He reports that he did apply for a few jobs, but it has been difficult due to his past experiences of workplace harassment and discrimination. He is socializing more frequently, primarily at LGBTQ-friendly bars and clubs. The client states he used to go to the gym daily and has recently started going some on the weekends. He explains that he has felt less depressed but remains poorly motivated. He denies suicidal ideation. The client is unsure how to prioritize goals for treatment.

6. You conduct a DSM-5 Cultural Formulation Interview (CFI) with the client. What is the primary purpose of this instrument?

a. To establish a means for incorporating cultural considerations and clinical symptoms as the sole basis for making an accurate DSM-5 clinical diagnosis
b. To provide culturally specific guidelines to assist with determining the client's readiness and motivation to change
c. To help determine if the client is open to working with a culturally different counselor
d. To enhance clinical understanding of the client's cultural identity and the cultural definition of the identified problem

7. Which are the most effective means for understanding the client's experiences of prejudice, discrimination, and inclusion?

a. Examine the client's contextual manifestations through the lens of intersectionality.
b. Understand the complexity of the client's gender identity, sexual orientation, and gender expression.
c. Explore one's own internalized biases regarding sex, sexual orientation, gender, and related behavioral and cultural norms.
d. Address misinformation and disinformation surrounding issues of diversity, sexuality, and cultural sensitivity.

8. To help the client identify treatment plan goals, you ask him to envision what it would be like if he woke up one day and a miracle had occurred—a miracle that caused his problem to cease to exist. Which therapy approach does this reflect?

a. Gestalt therapy
b. Client-centered therapy
c. Solution-focused brief therapy
d. Motivational enhancement therapy

9. The client states he is tired of the obstacles he faces due to his sexual orientation. He no longer wants to be attracted to men and believes being gay is a sin. He has heard of conversion/reparative therapy and would like to pursue this treatment option. How do you respond?

a. Consult a therapist who provides this treatment prior to determining whether a referral is appropriate.
b. Discuss the benefits and harms and refer the client to a therapist who provides this treatment.
c. Encourage the client to seek religious guidance and continue to treat the client.
d. Discuss the harms of this treatment and continue to treat the client.

10. The client reports feeling "defective" and carries a significant amount of shame related to his sexual orientation. Using a constructionist approach, how would you assist the client with these feelings?

a. Improve the client's sense of self-worth by showing unconditional positive regard.
b. Construct an authentic sense of self by examining the consequences of overgeneralization.
c. Create a strengths-based narrative emphasizing affirming community experiences.
d. Teach new skills by increasing environmental rewards and positive reinforcement to mitigate avoidance and shame.

Part Three

Second Session, Twelve Weeks After the Intake Session

The client reports fewer symptoms of hopelessness and depression. He discloses that he has been seeing a guy he met at his previous job. He is happy with this new relationship but says he's still "fighting against" feelings of guilt and shame surrounding his sexual orientation and his parents continued rejection of him. The client says he has attended Metropolitan Community Church (MCC) with his boyfriend and was surprised to hear their messages of acceptance and inclusion. He has stopped going to bars and nightclubs since dating and reports less substance and alcohol misuse. The client states it has been quite some time since he felt like he had no purpose in life.

11. You have selected acceptance and commitment therapy (ACT) and mindfulness to best address which of the following?

a. Negative self-talk
b. Sexual desire
c. Shame and guilt
d. Social isolation

12. How should the client's disclosures about dating and attending church affect the direction of therapy?

a. It determines the need for you to help the client establish his own LGBTQIA+ identity.
b. It helps connect these events to the client's management of his hopelessness, depression, and social isolation.
c. It allows you to explore if the client has the ego-strength required for dating and finding a new church.
d. It causes you to re-evaluate potential risks associated with the client being "out" in the community.

13. When the client shares recent developments, you find yourself tearing up as you tell him you are happy that he is starting to experience a level of peace in his life. Which core counseling attribute does this represent?

a. Genuineness
b. Empathetic responding
c. Metacommunication
d. Cultural attunement

Case Study 4

Part One

Intake

Client

Age: 18

Sex: Male

Gender: Male

Sexuality: Heterosexual

Ethnicity: Caucasian

Relationship Status: Single

Counseling Setting: University Counseling Center

Type of Counseling: Individual and Group

Presenting Problem: Interpersonal relationships

Diagnosis: Autism Spectrum Disorder. 299.00 (F84.0)

Presenting Problem:

You are a counselor a university counseling center. The university has a program providing limited assistance to students diagnosed with Autism Spectrum Disorder (ASD). The ASD program director has referred an 18-year-old white male enrolled in the program. She is concerned over his recent run-in with campus police. The client arrives to his scheduled counseling session today and explained that he has a girlfriend who "now apparently wants nothing to do with me." Campus security has been involved due to the client showing up at his girlfriend's dorm, yelling and creating a disturbance. The client explains that his peers told him he would have sex in college once he got a girlfriend. When his girlfriend refused to have sex, he said he didn't understand and only wanted to talk. The client continues to express a desire to have sex now that he is in college by stating matter-of-factly, "I haven't had much luck, but I'm going to keep trying." When asked about interests, the client spoke at length about his love for snakes and knowledge of all 300 worldwide species.

Mental Status Exam:

The client is sloppily dressed and appears his stated age. He exhibits pressured speech at times; otherwise, he speaks in a monotonous tone. The client becomes irritable when discussing the incident with campus police, and brightens when expressing his passion for snakes. He displays poor eye contact and there is difficulty with normal back-and-forth conversation. The client denies suicidal or homicidal ideation. He lives on campus in sober student housing and denies drug or alcohol use.

History of the Presenting Problem:

The client provides written consent for you to speak to his mother. His mother explains that the client was originally diagnosed with Asperger's disorder and ADHD in early childhood. She acknowledges that the client has difficulty tolerating frustration, primarily when encountering changes in routine. She further explains that she worries "constantly" about him having clean clothes, staying organized, and waking up for class on time. She states she calls the client at 8:00 am every morning to help him wake up and stay on track. The mother also says the client finds noise in the cafeteria overstimulating, so he often skips meals.

FAMILY AND WORK HISTORY

The client is a first-year student majoring in architectural engineering with a 3.6 GPA. He held a part-time job at a local grocery store while in high school. The client's parents have been married for 15 years, and he has one younger sibling living at home. The mother takes an SSRI for depression and anxiety. The client's father struggled with similar issues as the client growing up, but he was never formally diagnosed. His family's home is 45 minutes from campus, and the client's mother visits most weekends to check on the client and help him clean his room.

RELATIONSHIPS:

The mother states the client has always had difficulty with peer relationships. She explains that he has always wanted a girlfriend, but he could never find someone who appreciated his differences. However, the client did have a small group of friends in high school who all played Dungeons and Dragons together. She thanks you for calling and states she will encourage the client to return to you for counseling services.

1. What information provided by the client and his mother is required for the diagnosis of autism spectrum disorder?

a. Sleep-wake disturbances
b. Extreme mood lability
c. Sensory hyper-reactivity
d. Impulsive outbursts

2. The client readily provides consent for you to speak to his mother; however, he tells you he will just meet with you for the intake and does not wish to sign an informed consent. How should you proceed?

a. Do not move forward with the intake due to the client's limited capacity to provide consent.
b. Do not move forward with the intake due to the need to honor the client's autonomy.
c. Move forward with the intake without signed consent due to the need to assess safety and risk.
d. Move forward with the intake after obtaining the mother's written consent.

3. You discuss the case with your supervisor, who encourages you to use a structural family therapy approach to examine the relationship between the client and his mother. Which statement best reflects this approach?

a. The client and the mother are highly emotionally fused and undifferentiated.
b. The client and the mother belong to an enmeshed family subsystem.
c. The client and the mother's maladaptive behavior is the result of misunderstandings and a lack of loyalty and trust.
d. The client and the mother's dysfunctional communication is the result of a reinforced circular feedback loop.

4. You meet with the client's parents and sibling for family therapy to establish a strong working relationship. How would a structural family therapist best accomplish this task?

a. Engage in the process of joining.
b. Teach problem-free talk.
c. Demonstrate an enactment.
d. Use triangulation to reduce anxiety.

5. Which statement would best help enhance the client's motivation to change?

a. "You're disappointed your girlfriend is not having sex with you, but just like building a building, intimate relationships are constructed one brick at a time."
b. "You were told having a girlfriend in college would lead to sex, and you're disappointed that's not happening for you."
c. "You're disappointed that your girlfriend doesn't want to have sex with you. I believe I can help, but the ball is in your court."
d. "Your girlfriend declined to have sex with you, but you've decided to keep trying."

Part Two

First Session, Four Weeks After the Initial Intake

The client arrives twenty minutes late for his appointment today. He explains that Mondays are the days he does laundry, and he cannot come again on a Monday. You review the required components of informed consent with the client. He expresses an understanding of the counseling process and provides written consent. The client states he has re-considered counseling because he believes you can help him find another girlfriend who will have sex with him. You tell him about a small group you run with other neurodiverse men, most of whom are on the autism spectrum. He expresses an interest in joining after hearing that sexual intimacy would be part of the curriculum. He provides a more solid commitment when you tell him the group is not held on Mondays.

6. What are the advantages of group therapy for individuals with autism spectrum disorder?

a. Social skills training can be used to improve social-emotional reciprocity.
b. Emotional bonds can be created when group members share similar goals and interests.
c. Group cohesion can help promote deeper expressions of emotional intimacy.
d. Groups members can establish group-specific social norms that are shaped and reinforced in real-time.

7. Applied behavior analysis (ABA), an evidence-based practice for individuals with ASD, relies on the principles of social learning theory. Which of the following best illustrates the four steps of social learning?

a. The group discusses appropriate sexual behavior, the client correctly recalls behavioral skills, the client applies the skills to a consensual relationship, and the client has sex.
b. The group discusses appropriate sexual behavior, the client correctly recalls behavioral skills, the client applies the skills to a consensual relationship, and the client does not have sex.
c. The group watches a video on appropriate sexual behavior, the client correctly recalls appropriate behavioral skills, the client applies the skills to a consensual relationship, and the client has sex.
d. The group watches a video on appropriate sexual behavior, the client correctly recalls the behavioral skills, the client applies the skills to a consensual relationship, and the client does not have sex.

8. Because of his history with the campus police, you focus on helping the client regulate angry emotional outbursts using which one of the following techniques?

a. Systematic desensitization
b. Cognitive reappraisal
c. Rolling with resistance
d. Mapping

9. You arrive to your client's group to find members on their cell phones sharing pictures of you and your family from your private social media account. How should you respond?

a. Use it as a teachable moment to educate members on respecting the privacy of others.
b. Use it as a basis to explain the importance of group-specific parameters regarding confidentiality.
c. Redirect the members to group tasks and personally seek technological knowledge and skills required for the ethical and legal use of social media.
d. Use it to explain the benefits, limitations, and boundaries included in your social media policy.

PART THREE

SECOND SESSION, TWELVE WEEKS AFTER THE INITIAL INTAKE SESSION

The client has attended and actively participated in all group therapy sessions. You are preparing the group for termination and discussing a "graduation" ceremony. The client has taken on a leadership role in the group, and you have asked him if he would be your "assistant" for the next group of neurodiverse men. The client approaches you, shakes your hand, and uses eye contact as he politely thanks you for the offer. You state you are pleased he has accepted. He then says, in a matter-of-fact tone, "Absolutely, I see that you really need help with offering better refreshments and teaching certain skills."

10. Your client's treatment plan goals address socio-emotional communication skills required for the diagnosis of ASD. Based your last exchange, has the client made progress on his treatment plan goals?

a. No, he did not consider your emotional welfare when responding to your offer.
b. Yes, he exhibited improvement in reciprocal social engagement.
c. No, he exhibits an intrusive social approach.
d. Yes, he has made emotional connections with peers and is motivated to help others.

11. In part, attitudes stemming from ableism prevent many young adults with ASD from receiving adequate education on intimacy and sexuality. Which statement best describes ableism?

a. Ableism is he intentional discrimination and marginalization of individuals with ASD resulting from prejudicial beliefs that they are less capable or worthy.
b. Ableism is the intentional discrimination and marginalization of individuals with ASD supported by prejudicial actions that they are less capable and worthy.
c. Ableism is the intentional and unintentional discrimination and marginalization of individuals with ASD resulting from prejudicial beliefs that they are less capable or worthy.
d. Ableism is the intentional and unintentional discrimination and marginalization of individuals with ASD resulting from an unwillingness to acknowledge and address deficits among individuals suffering with ASD.

12. During the last group session, a member stated, "I didn't know there were other people on campus that viewed things in the same way that I do." This is an example of which one of the following?

a. Catharsis
b. Transference
c. Altruism
d. Universality

13. You conduct a pre-test and post-test measuring each group member's social skills and conclude that the group was ineffective. If COVID-19 occurred between the pre-test and post-test, which factor likely served as a threat to the study's internal validity?

a. Statistical regression
b. Maturation
c. Attrition
d. History

Case Study 5

PART ONE

INTAKE

CLIENT

Age: 38

Sex: Male

Gender: Male

Sexuality: Heterosexual

Ethnicity: Caucasian

Relationship Status: Married

Counseling Setting: Private Practice

Type of Counseling: Individual

Presenting Problem: Marital Difficulties

Diagnosis: Obsessive-Compulsive Personality Disorder 301.4 (F 60.5)

PRESENTING PROBLEM:

You are a counselor working in private practice and meeting your client for the first time today. The client is here at his wife's insistence, who has threatened divorce if he does not seek and comply with therapy. The client explains that he is swamped at work and has already lost an hour of productivity traveling to your office. He discloses that he has been married just over four years and has a daughter who is 3½. The couple dated briefly and married when the client's wife discovered she was pregnant. The client believes that if he didn't leave his wife a schedule and checklist, "things would never get done." He states that they would be in "so much debt" if it weren't for his detailed household budget. In his estimation, conflict occurs each time his wife tried to do things "her way" because "it is never the right way." You paraphrase and clarify the client's concerns.

MENTAL STATUS EXAM:

The client is meticulously dressed and immaculately groomed. He frequently checks his watch and states he has owned his watch since adolescence and it "still works like new." His speech is even, and his affect is blunted. At times, he is defensive and attempts to talk over you. He exhibits poor insight into his marital problems and is excessively preoccupied with perfectionism, structure, and order.

FAMILY AND WORK HISTORY:

The client works as a web designer and developer. He allows you to obtain collateral information from his wife. You reach his wife by phone, who explains that the client has "an explosive temper when I don't do things exactly how he asks." The client's wife states he can be controlling, overly critical, and irrational at times. This is the client's first marriage. The client's wife wants to participate in couples counseling but says the client is adamant about her not joining.

1. What attitudes and behaviors would a client diagnosed with obsessive-compulsive personality disorder display (OCPD)?

a. Persistent, unwanted thoughts and repetitive rituals
b. Frequent fears of being alone
c. Excessive drive to attain financial success
d. Inflexibility regarding morals and values

2. Which diagnostic feature of OCPD tends to cause difficulties with close relationships?

a. They are oblivious to the fact that others are annoyed by their inflexibility and perfectionism.
b. They possess ego-dystonic personality traits that are pervasive and less amenable to change.
c. They must constantly adjust their expectations when perfectionistic standards are not met.
d. They disregard family activities and believe leisure time should be an individual pursuit.

3. Using the personality trait model defined in Section III of the DSM-5, entitled the "Alternative DSM-5 Model for Personality Disorders," what assumptions can be made about the client's negative affectivity domain?

a. It manifests in deceitfulness and impulsivity.
b. It originates from future-oriented feelings of hopelessness and pessimism.
c. It is marked by an inefficient persistence at tasks.
d. It is characterized by separation and insecurity.

4. What is the value in clarifying and paraphrasing the client's presenting problem?

a. It helps promote an egalitarian relationship.
b. It enables expressions of immediacy.
c. It assists in clarifying values.
d. It fosters the creation of discrepancy.

5. You are use using acceptance and commitment therapy (ACT) with the client, which involves combining behavioral therapy with which one of the following?

a. Mindfulness
b. Shaping
c. Unbalancing
d. Developing discrepancy

Part Two

First Session, Four Weeks After the Intake Session

The client states that his wife now refuses to follow the client's to-do lists, and he is growing more frustrated with her defiance. Their daughter turned four this past week, and he felt like he made it clear to his wife that throwing a party for a four-year-old was costly and unnecessary. After working all weekend, he returned home and found that his wife had thrown a party anyway. He stated he "hit the roof" and expressed feeling disrespected despite all the effort he makes towards establishing a detailed budget "with no room for error." The conversation turns to his upbringing, and he discloses that he was placed in therapeutic foster care in early childhood and remained there until he turned 18. You discuss the implications of early childhood attachment with the client.

6. What are you trying to accomplish by discussing the implications of early childhood attachment with the client?

a. Show the association between unmet childhood needs and maladaptive schemas.
b. Establish the connection between adverse childhood experiences and risk level for perpetration.
c. Illustrate the relationship between temperament and unrelenting standards.
d. Demonstrate the connection between biopsychosocial factors and symptom severity.

7. Which cognitive distortion operates from the premise that his wife's refusal to conform to the client's high standards is associated with ineptitude and defiance?

a. Overgeneralization
b. Black and white thinking
c. Personalization
d. Mind reading

8. While in session with the couple, you state, "You're telling me that you value your marriage and family, yet you remain unwilling to change behaviors that are causing you to lose them." This is an example of which one of the following?

a. Interpretation
b. Confrontation
c. Reframing
d. Empathetic attunement

9. Based on the information provided thus far, what is the best strategy for engaging the client in treatment planning?

a. Determine his motivation to change.
b. Appeal to his goal-oriented personality.
c. Prioritize his diagnostic symptoms.
d. Enlist the help of his wife.

Part Three

Second Session, Ten Weeks After the Intake Session

The client arrives with his wife for his scheduled individual session today. You have yet to meet his wife in person. Before you can obtain an accurate appraisal of the situation, you find yourself mediating a conflict that has quickly intensified. The wife has given the client an ultimatum—to either stop the "endless manipulation, control, and sharp criticism" or she will take their daughter and go live with her mother, who resides in another state. The wife states that she has shown up today in a last-ditch effort to save their marriage. The client expresses a desire to remain with his wife and daughter.

10. What are the ethical implications for seeing both the client and his wife during the scheduled therapy session with the client?

a. An ethical violation was not committed because there is implied consent due to the client being present with his wife.
b. An ethical violation was not committed since safely de-escalating conflict creates an exception and allows confidentiality to be breached.
c. An ethical violation was committed because the client is the identified patient and has not waived his right to confidentiality.
d. An ethical violation was committed because you did not clarify the nature of your relationship with both participants at the outset of counseling.

11. The client discloses that he has recently taken up boxing to release pent-up energy. This is an example of which one of the following?

a. Rationalization
b. Reaction formation
c. Regression
d. Sublimation

12. If the client and his wife were to pursue couples counseling, which approach would best address attachment needs and bonding?

a. Systematic desensitization
b. Solution-focused therapy
c. Emotionally focused therapy
d. Rational-emotive behavioral therapy

13. How would a client with OCPD most likely approach termination?

a. Feel threatened, experience symptom regression, and become emotionally dysregulated in the counselor's presence
b. Attempt to delay termination and desperately cling to the counselor
c. Have a measured external reaction, is self-congratulatory, is indifferent toward the counselor
d. Terminate too early, deny emotional reactions, and act dismissively toward the counselor

Case Study 6

PART ONE

INTAKE

CLIENT

Age: 14

Sex: Male

Gender: Male

Sexuality: Heterosexual

Ethnicity: Asian-American (Karen)

Grade: 8th

Counseling Setting: Child and Family Services Agency

Type of Counseling: Individual and Family

Presenting Problem: Substance Misuse and Acculturation Difficulties

Diagnosis: Substance Use Disorder, Moderate (F2.911); Acculturation difficulty (V62.4 Z60.3)

PRESENTING PROBLEM:

You are working as a counselor in a child and family mental health agency. A 14-year-old Asian-American male presents with family members who are concerned about the client's drug use. The family is part of an ethnic population from Southeast Asia who resettled in the United States just under two years ago. The client is fluent in English and interprets for the family. The client goes to a public school specifically designed to improve English proficiency and has, until recently, done well academically. The parents have limited English proficiency (LEP). The parents provide a letter from his school stating the client was suspended after administrators found marijuana and amphetamines in the client's locker. The client expresses remorse and says he became highly anxious and fearful when the school resource officer became involved. He explains, "Where I come from, the police are not there to protect or help." The client willingly completes a substance use screening assessment, and the results indicate he is at risk for meeting the diagnostic criteria for substance use disorder.

MENTAL STATUS EXAM:

The client is polite and cooperative. He is neatly dressed and is the only member of his family who is not wearing traditional Karen clothing. His affect is restricted, and his eye contact is poor. The client denies suicidal and homicidal ideation. He reports feeling anxious and sad frequently. He expresses that he is particularly worried at school and has had a difficult time adjusting. The client states that he lived in outdoor homes and buildings before coming to the United States. He explains, "Here, I feel like I'm trapped in a cage."

FAMILY HISTORY:

As part of the Karen community in Southeast Asia, the client and his family lived in a refugee camp near the Thai-Burma border before coming to the United States. His family fled to an internal displacement camp (IDC) to escape ethnic violence and torture. The family arrived in the refugee camp when the client was two years old and stayed for nearly a decade before coming to the United

States. He reports that his parents do not drink or use drugs; however, he states that drugs and alcohol were prevalent in the IDC. His family is Christian and is involved with a local church that sponsors individuals from the Karen community and helps with resettlement.

1. Which screening tool assesses substance use disorder among youth between the ages of 12-17?

a. Drug Abuse Screen Test (DAST-10)
b. Delinquent Activities Scale (DAS)
c. Screening to Brief Intervention (S2BI)
d. Brief Addiction Monitor (BAM)

2. What is the primary ethical risk of allowing the client to interpret for his family?

a. It might cause the client to experience secondary trauma when discussing his parent's torture.
b. It might reinforce unhealthy boundaries and contribute to parental inadequacy.
c. There is the potential for misdiagnosis if the client chooses to interpret selectively.
d. It might violate the principles of self-determination and autonomy inherent in informed consent.

3. You would like to use a screening instrument to determine the severity of your client's depression and anxiety. Which one of the following screening instruments has a standardized modification for adolescents?

a. Cut down, annoyed, guilty, and eye-opener (CAGE)
b. EQ-5D
c. Patient Health Questionnaire (PHQ-9)
d. Alcohol Use Disorders Identification Test (AUDIT)

4. What other information would you need to substantiate the diagnosis of substance use disorder (SUD)?

a. Additional consequences involving law enforcement
b. Levels of dependence and use for both substances
c. Strong desire or urge to use the substance
d. The effects of acculturation on substance use

5. Which one of the following is a technique of person-centered theory?

a. Acting as if there is not a problem
b. Showing unconditional positive regard
c. Challenging irrational beliefs
d. Using free association

6. Which of the substance abuse interventions offers a parent training component to reinforce drug-incompatible behaviors at home?

a. Motivational enhancement therapy (MET)
b. Cognitive-behavioral therapy (CBT)
c. Multi-systemic therapy (MST)
d. Contingency management therapy (CM)

Part Two

First Session, 4 Weeks After the Intake Session

The client continues to be compliant with therapy but is having difficulty discontinuing his drug use. He states he uses because it changes his mood and helps him forget about not fitting in at home or school. He explains that when he speaks English or dresses in non-traditional clothing, his family says they feel like, "I'll forget where I came from. But when I leave the house, all I hear is, 'Go back to where you came from.'"

The client states he began using at the end of 7th grade and started using daily approximately four months ago. He admits to feeling guilty about how his use affects his family but claims, "It's not like I'm an addict or anything." His parents arrive today with an interpreter and attend a concurrent parenting group with a psychoeducational component that addresses adolescent substance abuse.

7. Using a motivational interviewing (MI) approach, how would you respond to the client's uncertainty regarding his problematic drug use?

a. "Your screening assessment tells a different story. What role is denial playing for you in this present moment?"
b. "You may not be ready to stop. What is it about using that you really need to hold onto?"
c. "Your disease affects your rational thinking. Can you identify and challenge those thoughts?"
d. "Your addiction continues to harm your parents. What is the payoff for you today?"

8. According to the DSM-5, what aspects of the client's clinical presentation qualifies as "acculturation difficulty"?

a. Difficulty adapting to cultural expectations due to demands from the dominant culture impacting treatment or prognosis
b. Difficulty adapting to cultural expectations due to an inability to balance demands from the dominant culture with the demands from the minority culture
c. Rejection, exclusion, and discrimination by those who hold social power in the dominant culture
d. Rejection, exclusion, and discrimination by those lacking social power in the minority culture

9. At the end of today's session, you respond, "While on the one hand you really enjoy using and don't want to give it up, on the other hand you feel guilty about how your drug use affects your family." How would you classify this response?

a. Reframing
b. Summarization
c. Empathetic reflection
d. Encourager

Part Three

Second Session, 12 Weeks After the Intake Session

The client is now attending family therapy with his parents and has made progress. His last four drug screens have been negative, and the client is beginning to show insight into his problem. The parents have improved with limit setting and are learning how to help the client achieve a healthy sense of identity. The parents are becoming better acclimated to the United States and have developed stronger connections within their church and community.

10. According to the transtheoretical, or stages of change (SOC), model, in which stage would you currently classify this client?

a. Precontemplation
b. Maintenance
c. Contemplation
d. Action

11. Which graphical depiction would you use to represent the client's family dynamics, including cross-generational coalitions, subsystems, and other significant interactions?

a. Genogram
b. Family map
c. Ecomap
d. Sculpting

12. Which family systems approach would best help the client's parents regain control by examining hierarchical positioning, challenge shifting boundaries, assigning tasks, and reframing?

a. Multi-generational therapy
b. Strategic family systems therapy
c. Structural family therapy
d. Contextual family therapy

13. The client has met his treatment plan goals, is pleased with his progress, and is ready to end therapy. The client and his parents have also made therapeutic gains in family therapy; however, his parents are not prepared to end treatment and would like to keep seeing you without the client. After providing pretermination counseling, how should you proceed?

a. Terminate with all parties.
b. Terminate with the client and continue working with the parents.
c. Encourage the client to continue therapy and continue working with all parties.
d. Terminate with all parties after referring the parents to another provider.

Case Study 7

PART ONE

INTAKE

CLIENT

Age: 32

Sex: Female

Gender: Female

Sexuality: Heterosexual

Ethnicity: Caucasian

Counseling Setting: Community Mental Health Agency

Type of Counseling: Individual

Presenting Problem: Depressed Mood

Diagnosis: Bipolar II 296.89 (F31.81), current episode depressed

PRESENTING PROBLEM:

You work at a community mental health agency providing outpatient services to adults. Today, you are meeting with a 32-year-old female who presents with her husband for an initial intake session. The client's husband is concerned about his wife's depressive symptoms. She is experiencing sadness, decreased appetite, and hypersomnolence. The client also expresses hopelessness and has lost interest in doing the things she once enjoyed. Until recently, the client worked at an art gallery. When employed, she reports that she, "just couldn't get out of bed" and was eventually let go due to excessive absences. After her employment ended, her depressive symptoms worsened. The client was able to recall a time nearly one year ago when she felt "almost the opposite" of how she feels now. During this time, she experienced increased energy and felt more inspired and creative. The client explains that she and her husband used to travel selling their art at juried art exhibitions most weekends, but it has been awhile since she has joined him.

MENTAL STATUS EXAM:

The client is dressed casually and is somewhat disheveled. She avoids eye contact and displays a flat affect. The client admits to having suicidal thoughts in the past but currently denies both suicidal and homicidal ideations. Her speech is soft in volume and tone. She tends to provide one-word responses but is cooperative when asked to elaborate. The client denies audio-visual hallucinations, and her thought content is coherent. The client's mood is depressed, and her affect is flat. She appears tired and reports she has insomnia at night and is sleeping most of the day. The client has experienced depression off-and-on, beginning in late adolescence.

FAMILY HISTORY:

The client is married and has a 10-year-old daughter from a previous marriage. The client explains that her father was "distant and quiet unless he was drinking." She remembers hearing that her paternal grandfather declared bankruptcy "at least once" due to gambling losses. The client's mother has been diagnosed with bipolar disorder, with acute episodes requiring hospitalization.

The client indicates that a former therapist also diagnosed her with bipolar disorder, but she rejects the diagnosis stating her symptoms are "nothing like my mother's."

1. How does the DSM-5 differentiate between Bipolar II disorder and Bipolar I disorder?

a. Bipolar II disorder is a milder form of bipolar I disorder.
b. Bipolar II disorder is a more severe form of bipolar I disorder.
c. Bipolar II disorder requires at least one episode of major depression; bipolar I does not.
d. Bipolar II disorder requires at least one episode of mania; bipolar I requires more than one episode of mania.

2. Based on the client's diagnosis, which assessment instrument would you use to obtain baseline data on the client's current level of functioning?

a. DSM-5 Level 1 Cross-Cutting Symptom Measures
b. Stages of Change Readiness and Treatment Eagerness Scale (SOCRATES)
c. Level of Care Utilization System (LOCUS)
d. Brief Psychiatric Rating Scale (BPRS)

3. How would you engage the client during the initial phase of treatment?

a. Tell her about your theoretical orientation and experience.
b. Explore factors she believes maintains her depression.
c. Determine the expectations she has regarding the length of time in treatment.
d. Encourage her to keep a thought log to track maladaptive cognitions.

4. Which intervention would you select to help the client process grief related to her job loss?

a. Reality therapy (RT)
b. Solution-focused brief therapy (SFBT)
c. Acceptance and commitment therapy (ACT)
d. Interpersonal psychotherapy (IPT)

Part Two

First Session, 6 Weeks After the Initial Intake Session

The client reports that she has been feeling less depressed. Her affect is full-range and appropriate to the situation. She continues to have sleeping difficulties that seem to worsen when experiencing unexpected stressors. The client explains that she has been arguing with her daughter's father about financial matters, which developed after the client lost her job. The client believes her depressive symptoms are exacerbated after spending significant periods of time on social media. The client remarks, "My husband's patience with me is growing thin. I don't think I can ever live up to his expectations."

5. Given the client's current clinical presentation, which approach would best address the client's concerns?

a. Mindfulness based relaxation and stress reduction (MBSR)
b. Interpersonal social rhythm (IPSRT)
c. Behavioral modification (BMOD)
d. Rational-emotive behavioral theory (REBT)

6. After your discussion with the client about her social media use, she sends you a Facebook friend request. What is your ethical obligation regarding the use of social media, distance counseling, and other related technology?

a. To have written procedures in place and reviewed before or during the client's initial session
b. To include in the client's record all electronic communication, except clerical information (e.g., appointment scheduling)
c. To recognize the potential harm and benefits of developing an informal virtual relationship with clients, former clients, and their families and personal friends
d. To disclose that you maintain a professional and personal online presence, and it may be difficult for the client to distinguish between the two

7. Counselors practicing the ethical use of distance counseling, technology, and social media disclose to clients all of the following EXCEPT:

a. There are some individuals who may have unauthorized access to their electronic health records.
b. The lack of visual cues and voice intonations used with electronic communication may affect the counseling process.
c. Informed consent for distance counseling, technology, and social media is no different than the protocol used with face-to-face counseling.
d. The need to identify alternative methods of service delivery may occur, because of the possibility of technology failure.

8. How would a client-centered therapist view this remark by the client?

"My husband's patience with me is growing thin. I don't think I can ever live up to his expectations."

a. As a mistaken style of life resulting from inferiority feelings
b. As incongruence stemming from a discrepancy between self-image and one's ideal self
c. As a failure identity resulting from irresponsibly meeting the need for love
d. As sadness resulting from the "I'm not OK," "You're OK" life position

9. How would an Adlerian therapist address the client's depressive symptoms resulting from significant time spent on social media?

a. Examine the client's unhealthy life position of "I'm not okay; you're okay."
b. Transform a failure identity into a success identity.
c. Identify the activating event, beliefs, and consequences (i.e., the ABC model).
d. Emphasize the importance of social interest and a purposeful, goal-oriented "lifestyle."

Part Three

Second Session, 12 Weeks After the Initial Intake Session

The client continues to benefit from counseling and presents today with a euthymic mood. She has met her treatment plan goals related to depressive symptoms and reports a better understanding of her illness. The client has begun painting again and accompanied her husband to an art show this past weekend. She expresses gratitude for your work together and is especially thankful that you have helped her get back into doing what she likes to do. At the end of the session, she gives you an original painting as a token of appreciation. She explains that the abstract painting conveys the emotional transformation she has experienced in counseling. You let the client know you would be joining a private practice in a few weeks. You explain you would be happy to see her again if needed and gave her your new business card with the address and contact information for the practice.

10. How would you navigate gift giving with the client?

a. You decline the gift because she is a talented artist and the painting is high in monetary value.
b. You decline the gift because to do so would not be culturally offensive to this client.
c. You accept the gift but explain that agency policy prohibits you from reciprocating.
d. You accept the gift because rejecting the gift would hurt the client.

11. What are the ethical guidelines for self-referring clients to private practice?

a. It is prohibited for five years following the last professional contact.
b. It is prohibited unless provided pro bono.
c. It is prohibited unless your agency makes explicit provisions.
d. It is prohibited under all circumstances.

12. The client's husband calls and requests the client's records. You are hesitant to comply because there are documented conversations concerning marital discord. According to the HIPAA Privacy Rule, how should you respond?

a. You cannot provide the record to the husband because there is a potential for harm to the client.
b. You cannot provide the record to the husband without first asserting counselor-client privilege.
c. You cannot provide the record to the husband unless the client is aware of the request and does not object.
d. You cannot provide the record to the husband unless requested by a third-party payor.

13. You smile and tell the client, "You've done a lot of hard work to get to this place. I'm so pleased with how far you've come." This is an example of which one of the following?

a. Empathy
b. Congruence
c. An encourager
d. Summarization

Case Study 8

PART ONE

INTAKE

CLIENT

Age: 32

Gender: Female

Sexuality: Bisexual

Ethnicity: Caucasian

Counseling Setting: Agency

Type of Counseling: Individual

Presenting Problem: Binge-eating

Diagnosis: Binge-Eating Disorder 307.51 (F50.8), Moderate

PRESENTING PROBLEM:

You are working at an agency serving clients from the metropolitan area. Your client is a 32-year-old bisexual female presenting with feelings of sadness, frustration, and shame due to increased episodes of binge eating. The client explains that she has tried unsuccessfully to manage her weight and control her eating. She states she is secretive when bingeing and feels "disgusted" afterward but "completely unable" to stop the compulsion. The client reports binge eating six times per week, with episodes worsening in the last two years. She identifies as bisexual and reports her binge eating increased after coming out to her family. She continues to struggle with depressive symptoms, including feelings of hopelessness, depressed mood, and anhedonia. The client's weight places her in the category of obese, and she has recently been diagnosed with borderline diabetes. Towards the end of the session, the client states, "This is starting to affect my health. If I could change anything in my life, it would be to stop binge eating."

MENTAL STATUS EXAM:

The client presents as polite and cooperative. She was well-groomed and dressed appropriately for the situation. Her affect is blunted, and she is tearful when discussing episodes of binge eating. The client has poor eye contact and periodically bites her fingernails. Her thought content is clear. She does not endorse audiovisual hallucinations, and she is oriented to person, place, time, and situation. The client denies suicidal and homicidal ideations. She denies previous suicidal attempts but states that she used to engage in cutting when she was an adolescent.

FAMILY AND HISTORY:

The client is an only child and has never been married. She describes her relationship with her parents as "close until recently." She and her family belong to a Christian evangelical church, and her family does not accept the client's sexual orientation. Her father is an accountant without any known mental illness. The client's mother has been diagnosed with depression and anxiety. When growing up, the client states her parents placed a strong emphasis on how things looked on the outside. She feels she has failed her parents and carries shame and guilt over her body weight and sexual orientation.

1. Which is included in the DSM-5 criteria for binge-eating disorder (BED)?

a. Recurrent compensatory behavior (e.g., purging)
b. Dietary restrictions between binging to influence body shape
c. Marked distress associated with binge eating
d. Dissociation during or following binge eating episodes

2. Of the following diagnoses, which is highly comorbid with BED?

a. Borderline personality disorder
b. Post-traumatic stress disorder
c. Generalized anxiety disorder
d. Obsessive-compulsive disorder

3. Based on the client's clinical presentation, what topic should be discussed to help develop initial treatment plan goals?

a. The effects of internalized biphobia
b. Behaviors maintaining maladaptive eating
c. Cognitions associated with depressed mood
d. Social isolation and other interpersonal deficits

4. Of the following, which one is NOT an accurate depiction of the use of motivational interviewing (MI)?

a. Counselors leave the decision up to the client to change.
b. Counselors take a direct approach during the initial phases of MI.
c. Counselors use strategies to elicit change talk.
d. Counselors support the client's self-efficacy.

5. You consider yourself evangelical and uphold values consistent with church teachings. How should you handle your opposing values?

a. Seek guidance and consultation from the client.
b. Seek professional training in that area and continue to work with the client.
c. Speak to your supervisor about referring the client.
d. Tell your supervisor about the issue and agree to follow-up if it becomes problematic.

PART TWO

FIRST SESSION TWO WEEKS AFTER THE INITIAL INTAKE

The client reports that she started her week doing well but had a setback a few days ago, causing her to lose confidence in her ability to change. Despite her progress in reducing binge-eating episodes, the client remarks, "I'll never control my eating." She says she is frustrated and feels hopeless and unmotivated. You address her ambivalence to change, as well as obstacles she has experienced in the past. When discussing exercise, the client states, "You don't understand! I've tried exercise, and it never works." You provide the client with self-monitoring sheets to record the following in real-time: daily food intake, maladaptive eating patterns, and thoughts and feelings that accompany binge eating. She is hesitant but agrees to give it a try for one week.

6. Using motivational interviewing to respond to the client's attitude towards exercise, which statement represents an amplified reflection?

a. "You've tried exercise and don't think it will ever work for you."
b. "You're frustrated at my suggestion, so much so that it seems like you've reached a boiling point."
c. "You're done with taking suggestions; there are no options left for you."
d. "You feel like nothing works, but you remain persistent. Making this change must be really important to you."

7. After her setback, the client states, "I'll never control my eating." Which of the following maladaptive styles of thinking is reflected in the client's statement?

a. Catastrophizing
b. Overgeneralization
c. Dichotomous thinking
d. Self-fulfilling prophecy

8. You are using self-monitoring to obtain baseline data and wish to use the SMART framework for constructing treatment plan goals and objectives. Which of the following accurately depicts the five SMART criteria?

a. Strengths-based, measurable, appropriate, rational, timeless
b. Specific, measurable, achievable, realistic, and timely
c. Strengths-based, measurable, appropriate, rational, and timely
d. Specific, measurable, achievable, realistic, and timeless

Part Three

Second Session, Ten Weeks After the Initial Intake

The client has made steady progress toward reducing maladaptive eating. After several weeks of collecting self-monitoring data, you and the client successfully identify patterns that maintain the problem of binge eating. The client's depressive symptoms have improved, and she is seeking interpersonal connections. She has set appropriate boundaries with her family and distanced herself from their church. The client briefly attended a more liberal church, experienced biphobia, and did not return. She explains, "In my parent's church, I'm not straight enough. In the LGBTQ community, I'm not gay enough." You have introduced her to dialectical behavioral therapy, and she attributes mindfulness to improved depressive symptoms.

9. The client reports being told, "There's no way I'd go out with someone who is bisexual. They'd eventually leave me for someone from the opposite sex." Which form of microaggression is represented by this statement?

a. Microinsult
b. Microinvalidation
c. Microassault
d. Microinjury

10. The client's depression has lifted, and she is seeking interpersonal connections. Which one of the following theorizes that the client's intrinsic desire for connection is driven by competence, relatedness, and autonomy?

a. Self-actualization process
b. Self-determination theory
c. Self-reflection method
d. Self-fulfilling prophecy

11. Which Dialectical Behavior Therapy (DBT) module teaches radical acceptance using alternative coping skills (e.g., self-soothing)?

a. Core mindfulness
b. Interpersonal effectiveness
c. Emotional regulation
d. Distress tolerance

12. Using the Transtheoretical Model (TTM) of the Stages of Change Model (SOC), which technique helps move the client from the contemplation stage to the preparation stage?

a. Commitment and activation
b. Rolling with resistance
c. Tipping the decisional balance
d. Flexible pacing

13. Your agency collects client satisfaction surveys that include a 5-point Likert rating scale. You notice that the client selected only neutral (i.e., all 3s) answers. This is most likely the result of which one of the following?

a. The halo effect
b. Leniency bias
c. Central tendency bias
d. Primacy bias

Case Study 9

PART ONE

INTAKE

CLIENT

Age: 26

Sex: Male

Gender: Male

Sexuality: Heterosexual

Ethnicity: Caucasian

Relationship Status: Single

Counseling Setting: Community Mental Health Agency

Type of Counseling: Individual

Presenting Problem: Hallucinations and Delusions

Diagnosis: Schizophrenia 295.90 (F20.9)

PRESENTING PROBLEM:

You are a counselor working in an outpatient community mental health center serving clients with severe psychiatric disorders. A 26-year-old male, accompanied by his caseworker, presents for counseling due to symptoms of schizophrenia. The caseworker reports that the client was doing well until he stopped taking his prescription medication. He resides in assisted living, where he was placed after being discharged from the hospital last month. The client claims someone he calls "the shadow man" is following him and putting poison in his food. The caseworker reports that the client has been more agitated recently and has engaged in verbal altercations with other residents. The client is refusing to take his medication because of the side effects. He had an initial therapeutic response to Haldol, an antipsychotic, but stopped taking it because it made him restless and nervous. He explains, "I felt like I constantly had to keep moving." The client is adamant about his desire to stay off medication and becomes angry when his caseworker mentions the possibility of going back into the hospital.

MENTAL STATUS EXAM:

The client displays an angry affect, and his mood is irritable. His speech is disorganized and pressured. He is oriented to person, place, time, and situation. He reports audiovisual hallucinations, which include seeing "the shadow man" and hearing voices others cannot hear. The client exhibits tangential and disconnected thinking. He is firm in his conviction that he is being poisoned and says he is exhausted from constantly trying to maintain vigilance. The client's insight and judgment are poor. He denies suicidal ideation, homicidal ideation, and command hallucinations. The client first experienced symptoms of schizophrenia in his late teens but was misdiagnosed with bipolar disorder until recently.

FAMILY HISTORY:

The client has an older brother who transports the client to appointments and periodically checks in with the client. Hospital records indicate that the client becomes increasingly agitated during visits with his parents. The hospital social worker noted that his father was critical and dismissive toward the client during family therapy. The client's mother is diagnosed with generalized anxiety disorder and had to quit her job due to the overwhelming burden of the client's care. The father blames the client for the excessive toll his illness has placed on the family.

1. How would you classify the type of delusion the client is experiencing?

a. Persecutory
b. Nihilistic
c. Grandiose
d. Somatic

2. You administer the Scale for the Assessment of Positive Symptoms (SAPS) to determine the severity of which of the following?

a. Avolition
b. Diminished speech
c. Agitation
d. Social withdrawal

3. Which of the following medication side effects is the client experiencing?

a. Dystonia
b. Akathisia
c. Tardive dyskinesia
d. Parkinsonism

4. How should you respond to the client's desire to stay off medication and out of the hospital?

a. Tell him you will work with him to avoid rehospitalization if he agrees to take his medication.
b. Tell him you will work with him to avoid rehospitalization if he agrees to be evaluated for a different medication.
c. Tell him you will work with him to avoid rehospitalization, and he is not obligated to take medication.
d. Tell him you will grant an extended trial period off medication and re-assess at his next visit.

Part Two

First Session, Six Weeks After the Initial Intake

The client is attending group therapy and reports it helps him feel less isolated and alone. He has learned from the group leader and group participants that other medications (i.e., second-generation atypical antipsychotics) have fewer side effects, and he has requested a psychiatric medication evaluation. The client states he is constantly worrying about "the shadow man," which has taken its toll physically. He recounts a recent visit with his parents where his father blamed him for his mother's anxiety. During the same visit, his father criticized the client's poor choices in life and, according to the client, "He guilt-tripped me for not being more like my brother." The client believes his parents are to blame for his current situation because they ignored his needs once he reached adolescence and refused to help when he was struggling.

5. Which of Yalom's curative factors does the client experience when saying he feels less isolated and alone?

a. Cohesiveness
b. Universality
c. Instillation of hope
d. Catharsis

6. You colead the client's process-oriented group with a trained counselor. Which one of the following is LEAST indicative of a process-oriented group?

a. Teaching the importance of medication compliance
b. Assessing intragroup interactions
c. Allowing for the use of silence
d. Identifying and discussing group themes and patterns

7. Which of the following best explains the parents' emotional expression (e.g., criticism, anger) when interacting with the client?

a. Self-serving bias
b. External locus of control
c. The Dunning-Kruger effect
d. Fundamental attribution error

8. Which one of the following is a leadership skill used to connect members and facilitate cohesion and universality?

a. Chaining
b. Pacing
c. Sculpting
d. Linking

9. Which concept would a gestalt therapist use to explain the client's tendency to blame his parents for his current situation?

a. Projection
b. Introjection
c. Retroflection
d. Confluence

PART THREE

SECOND SESSION, EIGHT WEEKS AFTER THE INITIAL INTAKE

The client began a new medication, which has helped with his delusional thinking. He continues to hear voices but reiterates that he does not hear command hallucinations. The client is able to focus on interpersonal relationships and has shown interest in obtaining part-time employment. He reports that he continues to benefit from group therapy. He has identified decreasing maladaptive thoughts and improving social skills as long-term treatment plan goals.

10. Which of the following rational-emotive behavioral therapy (REBT) techniques is used to help identify the salient aspects of the client's delusional belief system?

a. Inference chaining
b. Normalizing
c. Linking
d. Emotion-based reasoning

11. Which cognitive-behavioral technique (CBT) can be used to investigate alternative explanations for the client's delusions?

a. Scaling questions
b. Unified detachment
c. Peripheral questioning
d. Symptom analysis

12. You co-lead the client's group and use social skills training to help the client with his long-term treatment goals. Which principle of operant conditioning underlies the use of cueing, coaching, and prompting?

a. Social modeling
b. Discriminative stimuli
c. Environmental restructuring
d. Behavioral practice

13. The client blames his parents for his problems. You ask the client to add the phrase "... and I take responsibility for it" at the end of his statements to create present-moment awareness and help him assume responsibility for his current difficulties. This is a technique of which one of the following?

a. Gestalt therapy
b. Transactional analysis
c. Acceptance and commitment therapy (ACT)
d. MI

Case Study 10

PART ONE

INTAKE

CLIENT

Age: 8

Sex: Female

Gender: Female

Grade: 3rd

Ethnicity: African American

Counseling Setting: School-based

Type of Counseling: Individual and Family

Presenting Problem: Defiance

Diagnosis: Oppositional Defiant Disorder 313.81 (F91.3)

PRESENTING PROBLEM:

You are a school-based mental health counselor conducting an initial intake with an 8-year-old African American female in the 3rd grade. The client presents today with her paternal grandmother (PGM), the client's legal guardian. The PGM states that the client is argumentative, refuses to take responsibility for her actions, and has a tantrum when she receives a consequence for her behavior. She reports that the client is restricted from "every single privilege indefinitely." The client has been told she can regain privileges once she "learns to act her age." The client states she is treated unfairly and "blamed for everything" at home and school. The client's teacher reports that she has difficulty following directions, is easily annoyed by her classmates, and frequently loses her temper. The client's grades are poor, and she is below grade level in reading. However, she enjoys art and proudly reports that one of her pictures came in 1st place and is hanging in the library.

MENTAL STATUS EXAM:

The client displays an angry affect and sits with her arms crossed. She is well dressed and well groomed. The client's PGM repeatedly prompts her to say, "yes ma'am" and "no ma'am" when answering questions. The client sits slumped in her chair. She agrees to color in a feelings thermometer that reflects increased anger, sadness, and fear. Her insight is poor. The client often refuses to eat school lunch, and the PGM reports that the client is a picky eater.

FAMILY HISTORY:

The client's paternal grandmother received legal guardianship when the client was in 1st grade due to parental neglect. The client's mother and father have had ongoing issues with substance abuse. The client's father is currently incarcerated for drug-related offenses. The PGM reports that the client's mother continues to "run the streets" and shows up periodically asking for money. The PGM states that the client's mother abused drugs while pregnant and that the client was born prematurely. In addition, the client's father had similar school difficulties and dropped out of high school in the 10th grade.

HISTORY OF CONDITION:

The client's disruptive behavior began in early childhood. When the client was four years old, her tantrums were so severe that she disrupted two daycare placements and was not allowed to return. In kindergarten, the client was given a stimulant by her primary care provider to assist with symptoms of ADHD. The PGM says she is no longer on the medication and believes the client chooses to misbehave, explaining, "she is strong-willed, just like her father." The client's school records show she has an individualized education plan (IEP) and receives limited services for developmental delays in reading and written expression.

1. Using the DSM-5 criteria, how would you differentiate oppositional defiant disorder (ODD) from conduct disorder (CD)?

a. ODD includes emotional dysregulation, while CD does not.
b. ODD includes conflict with authority, while CD does not.
c. ODD includes destruction of property, while CD does not.
d. ODD includes cruelty to animals, while CD does not.

2. In the DSM-5, ODD is classified under which of the following?

a. Neurodevelopmental disorders
b. Disruptive, impulse-control, and conduct disorders
c. Bipolar and related disorders
d. Trauma and stressor related disorders

3. Which alternative behavior best targets the PGM's needs based on her current parenting approach?

a. Ignore negative behavior.
b. Provide clear expectations.
c. Use consistent follow through.
d. Give directives in a calm, matter-of-fact manner.

4. You meet with the client and her grandmother to create a genogram so you can assess the family's multigenerational transmission process. Which one of the following family theorists is known for this technique?

a. Salvador Minuchin
b. Jay Haley
c. Virginia Satir
d. Murray Bowen

5. Given the client's clinical presentation, how would you structure the first individual session with the client?

a. Identify maladaptive cognitions.
b. Establish treatment plan goals.
c. Process grief and loss issues.
d. Engage her in a therapeutic art activity.

6. You tell the client, "Imagine waking up one morning and a miracle had occurred. You notice that your problems ceased to exist. What would this look like for you?" This technique is associated with which one of the following?

a. SFBT
b. Person-centered therapy
c. REBT
d. DBT

PART TWO

FIRST SESSION, FOUR WEEKS AFTER THE INTAKE SESSION

You are meeting with the client individually and providing parenting training with the client's PGM. The client's teacher has implemented a behavioral chart for the classroom, and you ensure the client is receiving appropriate reinforcement for targeted behaviors. The teacher believes the client's behavior indicates ADHD, and you have agreed to conduct classroom observations. During the observation, you note that the client gets out of her seat multiple times to sharpen her pencil. While doing so, she glares at other students and is observed balling up her fists and threatening others. The teacher yells at the client to sit down and stop disrupting the classroom, which has little effect on the client's behavior.

7. Which instrument would you select to further assess the client's social and emotional problems, including DSM-specific disorders such as ADHD, ODD, and other conduct problems?

a. The Achenbach Child Behavior Checklist (CBCL)
b. The Brief Symptoms Inventory-18 (BSI-18)
c. The Woodcock-Johnson IV (WJ IV)
d. The Conners' Third Edition (Conners 3)

8. The client receives a sticker from her teacher to positively reinforce predetermined operant behaviors. Which of the following is NOT a key principle of operant conditioning?

a. Extinction
b. Punishment
c. Stimulus control
d. Reproduction

9. Which one of the following accurately describes criterion-referenced measurements?

a. Measurements are ranked on a bell curve.
b. Measurements compare a person's knowledge or skills against a normed group.
c. Measurements compare a person's knowledge or skills against a predetermined standard.
d. Measurements determine how a person's knowledge or skills compare to someone with similar traits.

10. You are working collaboratively with the client's teacher and PGM to establish treatment plan goals. Which criterion-referenced method would you select to measure incremental behavioral changes for up to three targeted behaviors?

a. SMART goal setting
b. Behavior Intervention Plan (BIP)
c. Goal Attainment Scaling (GAS)
d. Functional Behavioral Assessment (FBA)

PART THREE

SECOND SESSION, TWELVE WEEKS AFTER THE INTAKE SESSION

The client's formal assessment, along with informal observations, warrants a psychiatric evaluation to assess for ADHD, and the PGM has agreed to this. The client has done well in therapy and has met her short-term counseling goals. She has processed grief and loss concerning separation from her parents and shows improvement with emotional regulation. The use of brief strategic family therapy (BSFT) has helped address patterns of interaction between the client and her PGM, and the client is having fewer tantrums. The PGM reports that the client continues to talk back, and she is not completing her chores. You plan to conduct a series of home visits to assist the PGM with parent management skills but receive word from your agency's office indicating the client has lost insurance coverage.

11. Brief Strategic Family Therapy (BSFT) uses which of the following?

a. Linking and pacing
b. Reframing and restructuring
c. Enactments and sculpting
d. Chaining and modeling

12. Which of the following aspects of parent management training (PMT) illustrates the concept of extinction?

a. The client refuses to do a chore and loses a portion of her allowance.
b. The PGM ignores temper tantrums that were previously reinforced with attention, causing the tantrums to discontinue.
c. The teacher progressively removes prompts that are no longer required for the client to stay in her seat.
d. The PGM's end goal of shaping the client's behavior (e.g., cleaning her room) is achieved by reinforcing successive approximations to the goal. (I.e., "I need you to pick your clothes up off the floor" or "I need you to pull the covers up to your pillow.").

13. Which is the best course of action upon discovering the client has lost insurance coverage?

a. Terminate the counseling relationship and offer appropriate referrals.
b. Initiate bartering with the client in exchange for the continuation of services.
c. Provide the remaining services pro bono to avoid client abandonment.
d. Suspend services indefinitely and resume when the client's insurance is reinstated.

Case Study 11

PART ONE

INTAKE

CLIENT

Age: 19

Sex: Male

Gender: Male

Sexuality: Heterosexual

Ethnicity: Caucasian

Relationship Status: Single

Counseling Setting: Private Practice

Type of Counseling: Individual

Presenting Problem: Suicidality related to body image

Diagnosis: Body Dysmorphic Disorder 300.7 (F45.22), with absent insight/delusional beliefs

PRESENTING PROBLEM:

You are working in private practice and conducting an initial intake session with a 19-year-old male who presents today with his mother. The client was recently admitted to a psychiatric hospital for suicidality and was discharged four days ago. His mother reports that the client tried to commit suicide by overdosing. The client reports feeling increasingly hopeless following a "failed" cosmetic surgery procedure. He explains that he had an otoplasty performed to change the proportion and position of his ears. He states he has always hated his ears and is convinced people are staring and laughing at his "deformity." His mother reports that she reluctantly consented to the surgery a year and a half ago, despite believing it was unnecessary. The client does not leave the house without wearing a beanie or hoodie. He has completed high school with no interest in attending college. He is unemployed due to shame and embarrassment over his "defective" appearance. Two weeks ago, the hospital psychiatrist changed his medication and placed him on a selective serotonin reuptake inhibitor (SSRI).

MENTAL STATUS EXAM:

The client's mood is sad and irritable. His speech is pressured when discussing his appearance but is otherwise normal. He is appropriately groomed and wears a beanie covering his ears. He admits to repetitively dissecting his face in the mirror several hours a day. The client offers that he cannot hide his ears with his hair because "it is too thin." He denies audio/visual hallucinations. The client's thought content is organized and coherent, but he shows poor insight and delusional thinking about how he and others regard his appearance. The client avoids social settings and reports that sometimes, an entire week goes by where he doesn't leave the house. He denies suicidality and currently does not have a plan or intent to harm himself or others. Appetite and sleep are fair. The client denies drug use and states he consumes alcohol occasionally. You provide an in-depth suicide assessment, and you and the client work together to create a suicide safety plan.

FAMILY HISTORY:

The client's parents are divorced and he lives with his mother and two younger siblings. There is a history of child protective services (CPS) involvement due to reports of domestic violence between his parents. The client witnessed these incidents between that ages of 10 and 12. His parents subsequently divorced and the client has had minimal contact with this father since. The client's maternal aunt is diagnosed with obsessive-compulsive disorder. His mother previously attended therapy for anxiety and other trauma-related symptoms. The client began experiencing symptoms of body dysmorphic disorder at age 13, with symptoms worsening after starting high school.

1. Which of the client's following symptoms is NOT listed as a DSM-5 diagnostic criterion for body dysmorphic disorder (BDD)?

a. Repetitive mirror checking in response to appearance concerns
b. Self-oriented perfectionism regarding performance, appearance, and routine
c. Occupational distress and impairment primarily due to BDD symptoms
d. Appearance-related preoccupation with flaws that others don't see

2. Which of the following instruments uses a 21-item self-report questionnaire to determine one's current intensity, frequency, and duration of suicidality?

a. The Beck Scale for Suicide Ideation (SSI)
b. Suicide Probability Scale (SPS)
c. Hamilton Depression Scale (HDS or HAM-D)
d. Columbia Suicide Severity Rating Scale (C-SSRS)

3. Which of the following is NOT is an established evidence-based component of a client's safety plan?

a. Identify early warning signs (e.g., body shaming, isolation).
b. Establish a "no suicide" safety contract.
c. Identify distractions to use when feeling suicidal (e.g., take a walk, call a friend).
d. Create an accessible list of emergency contacts and social supports to use when feeling suicidal.

4. With the overall goal of creating anxiety habituation, you instruct the client to gradually face feared social situations without performing ritualized tasks (e.g., mirror-checking). This is an example of which of the following?

a. Cognitive diffusion
b. Behavior activation
c. Distress tolerance
d. Exposure and response prevention

5. The client states, "When I leave the house, everyone is staring at my ears and laughing at my deformity." This is an example of which one of the following?

a. All-or-nothing thinking
b. Black-and-white thinking
c. Personalization
d. Emotional reasoning

Part Two

First Session, Two Weeks After the Intake Session

You and the client review his safety plan. The client believes the antidepressant has helped decrease his feelings of hopelessness and suicidality. Despite the hot and humid conditions, the client arrives at his counseling session in a hoodie. He explains that he has been getting out of the house "some" but continues to avoid social situations because of overwhelming thoughts of others staring at him and mocking his appearance. The client was a no-show for his appointment last week and has requested distance counseling to avoid anxiety experienced when leaving the house. You and the client work together to set appropriate treatment plan goals; however, this is difficult due to poor insight into his presenting problem. You provide psychoeducation about BDD and ask about his goals for the future.

6. You have discussed the client's request for distance counseling with your supervisor, considered the potential risks and benefits, and have determined that honoring the client's request is the best course of action. Before implementation, which of the following "test" questions would you ask yourself to help finalize this decision according to the American Counseling Association's (ACA) *Practitioner's Guide to Ethical Decision-Making*?

a. Are there legal implications to this decision?
b. Can I faithfully fulfill this obligation?
c. Would this decision harm the client?
d. Would I want my behavior reported in the press?

7. Which is of the following is an ethical expectation for certified counselors providing distance counseling and maintaining a social media presence?

a. Refrain from viewing a client's personal or public social media profile without permission; however, counselors must discuss professional limitations with maintaining confidential electronic communication.
b. Ensure that professional social media accounts are merged with personal accounts to avoid ambiguity and confusion.
c. Develop informed consent procedures covering issues such as the possibility of technology failure, emergencies, and the increased risk for harmful boundary violations.
d. Refrain from entering personal virtual relationships with clients for a period of 5 years following the last professional contact.

8. The client does not believe psychotherapy is the best solution to his problems. How should you respond to his lack of insight and motivation to change?

a. "When I look at you, I don't see the imperfections you point out."
b. "How does preoccupation with your appearance stop you from participating in life?"
c. "Can we examine how your distress is rooted in the core beliefs you developed as a child?"
d. "I'm wondering if you can keep a journal to record your thoughts and feelings when looking in the mirror"

Part Three

Second Session, Twelve Weeks After the Intake Session

The client has been free of suicidal ideation for four weeks now. Psychoeducation has helped him gain insight into BDD. Distance counseling has been effective in decreasing ritualistic behaviors, and you provide face-to-face sessions every other week to help decrease avoidance behaviors. The client has benefited from cognitive-behavioral therapy (CBT). He attended two social events this month and has decreased ritualistic "safety behaviors" once used to prevent a feared consequence. He would like to take two college courses in the fall and is nearing the termination stage of therapy.

9. During a CBT exercise, you discover that the client believes his "defective" appearance makes him unworthy of love. This is an example of which of the following?

a. Intermediate belief
b. Automatic thought
c. Core belief
d. Hot thought

10. Which one of the following is NOT a characteristic method of CBT?

a. The assignment of homework
b. Use of Socratic questioning
c. An emphasis on unconscious experiences
d. An approach that is structured and directive

11. To help with the client's avoidance of anxiety-provoking situations, you gradually and incrementally expose him to fears previously arranged on a fear hierarchy through a process known as which of the following?

a. Systematic desensitization
b. Graded exposure
c. Flooding
d. Subjective units of distress

12. Which one of the following would qualify as the client's ritualistic safety behaviors?

a. Complying with his selective serotonin reuptake inhibitor (SSRI) medication
b. Wearing a beanie or hoodie while away from home
c. Agreeing to contact the counselor if he experiences suicidal ideations
d. Identifying core beliefs that contribute to anxiety in social situations

13. As you near the termination phase with your client, you recommend which of the following to help assess progress, maintain learned skills, and prevent relapse?

a. Value-based living
b. Psychoeducation
c. Booster sessions
d. Mentorship

Answer Key and Explanations for Test #1

Case Study 1

1. A: Disruptive Mood Dysregulation Disorder (DMDD) is characterized by severe and recurrent temper outbursts and irritability. According to the DSM-5, irritability must be chronic and persistent (nearly every day, most of the day). Defiance to authority, a characteristic of Oppositional Defiant Disorder, is not a manifestation of DMDD. Socio-emotional difficulties characterize Autism Spectrum Disorder, and impulsivity is a symptom of ADHD, making both answer options incorrect. Further, if a client meets the criteria for both DMDD and ODD, they should be assigned the diagnosis of DMDD.

2. D: According to the NBCC Code of Ethics (2016), "When counseling minors, [...] counselors seek the assent of clients to services and include them in decision making as appropriate." Counselors recognize the need to balance the ethical rights of clients to make choices, their capacity to give consent or assent to receive services, and parental or familial legal rights and responsibilities to protect these clients and make decisions on their behalf. Answer D best illustrates this ethical commitment. Consent forms can be signed by either parent. Most state laws require parental consent, but it is unnecessary to obtain consent from both parents. Some states only require an assent form signed by the client but there are no states that allow this practice for children under the age of 12.

3. C: The use of humanistic, person-centered responses, including reflection and validation, significantly influence the therapeutic alliance. Helping the client to master coping skills to apply when he is feeling angry is an appropriate counseling intervention but is less likely to contribute to creating a therapeutic alliance. Including the client in the treatment planning process, rather than solely sharing the completed treatment plan, helps build and strengthen the therapeutic alliance. Presenting the client with a menu of goals and objectives is one way to include a child in developing a treatment plan. Universality and the installation of hope, part of Irvin Yalom's curative factors, are therapeutic experiences associated with group therapy; these factors are not associated with minimizing transference.

4. A: Remember, you are looking for the best option for creating an initial plan of care. Since you are school-based, collateral information obtained from the client's teacher would best guide this process. Collateral information from the teacher allows you to obtain measurable information about the client's presenting problem. In doing so, you can determine the frequency, duration, and severity of the client's angry outbursts. Classroom observations are useful, but only provide information for a moment in time and are subject to the Hawthorne effect. The Hawthorne effect occurs when a subject changes their behavior simply due to knowing they are being observed. An interdisciplinary approach is used when seeking to improve or enhance treatment outcomes but is not the best option for information gathering. Lastly, the client's motivation to change is an important consideration for adults but less so for children. For children, the therapeutic alliance and the family's treatment compliance greatly influence the client's motivation to change.

5. B: Evidence-based practices for DMDD include cognitive-behavioral therapy and mindfulness-based interventions. Relaxation skills training is a mindfulness-based intervention. Since the client can identify physiological symptoms associated with feeling angry (e.g., heart races, teeth clench, chest tightness), the next step would be to teach relaxation and other emotional regulation skills. Although medication can be prescribed to children with acute symptoms, this is generally initiated if therapy alone proves ineffective. Asking the client to keep a journal would not be appropriate for this client as there is currently no demonstration of insight or motivation. At present, requesting that the teacher move the client's desk back with his peers is not in the client's or the other students' best interest.

6. B: For students in institutions receiving federal funding, three federal laws protect the rights of students with disabilities: IDEA, Section 504 of the Rehabilitation Act of 1973, and Title II of the ADA. Of the three, IDEA is the only law that mandates an IEP (to be completed within 30 days of eligibility) to provide a free appropriate public education in the least restrictive environment. An IEP is a written document that identifies the specialized instruction and services that an individual receives. Section 504 of the Rehabilitation Act of 1973 is a civil rights law, as opposed to IDEA, which is a federal special education law. Section 504 offers accommodations for students with a mental or physical impairment that interferes with their learning. The ADA offers civil rights protections for all individuals with disabilities. Title VII of the ADA prohibits state and local governments from discrimination, which applies to federally funded public schools.

7. B: This question tests your knowledge of developmentally appropriate assessment instruments. The Cognitive Assessment System (CAS2) is based on the PASS (planning, attention, simultaneous processing, and sequential processing) model of intelligence and can be administered to children between the ages of 5 and 18. Testing results provide information on specific learning and intellectual disabilities. The CAS2 also provides insight into symptoms of ADHD, which is a comorbid condition of DMDD. The Developmental Screening Test II (DDST-II) is a screening tool used with children aged 1 month to 6 years of age, therefore is not indicated. The NEO-Personality Inventory measures personality traits of adults ages 21-91 (with an additional revised version for adolescents). The Children's Systemizing Quotient (SQ-C) is an assessment instrument for Autism Spectrum Disorder and is used with children ages 4-11.

8. D: The client attributes his angry feelings to his "mother always" bothering him and "everybody always" picking on him—both untrue statements. This is an example of overgeneralization. Overgeneralization is a faulty belief system that occurs when general assumptions are made based on one or two experiences. The words *always* and *never* are often a part of an overgeneralized statement. Personalization occurs when individuals erroneously attribute external events to their own actions. ("My behavior caused the entire class to lose recess; I ruined everyone's day!") Polarized thinking happens when one engages in black-and-white or dichotomous thinking. ("If I can't be the best, then I'm nothing.") Emotional reasoning is the result of believing that one's feelings are facts, despite conflicting evidence. ("I feel worthless, so I must be.")

9. B: CM is based on the principle of operant conditioning and involves shaping desired behaviors. CM uses "if, then" contingencies to provide or withhold rewards in response to predetermined behaviors (e.g., "if" the client stops playing video games after being asked the first time, "then" he can stay up 15 minutes past his bedtime). A token economy is a form of CM that uses positive reinforcement and extinction. Tokens serve as behavioral reinforcements and are administered when the targeted or desired behavior occurs. When the client displays maladaptive behavior, the mother ignores the behavior. Planned ignoring removes the desired response (e.g., attention) through extinction. MI is a collaborative approach used to help clients resolve ambivalence and increase motivation. ERP is used with children experiencing anxiety or panic disorder; it involves incrementally exposing the child to anxiety-related triggers in a safe setting to reduce or eliminate anxiety-related responses (e.g., rituals). HRT is an intervention used with children who have tics or Tourette's syndrome. HRT techniques include identifying sensations occurring directly before the tic to respond to that urge in a new way.

10. B: The client, who initially had a good morning, quickly becomes inconsolable and destructive when recalling his parents' domestic violence. Conducting a crisis risk assessment prioritizes safety concerns, making it an essential step in providing vital services to a client with multiple risk factors (e.g., bullying, trauma, attachment, poor school performance, hopelessness, and mood instability). A comprehensive risk assessment helps determine the intensity of treatment services required to meet the client's current needs. A referral to a psychiatrist or to an in-home treatment provider would likely be part of a crisis plan of care but are inadequate as stand-alone interventions. An appointment with a psychiatrist may take time to secure, and parental consent is required before placing a child on medication. Also, certain medications take time to build up in the client's system before symptom reduction occurs. As part of a crisis plan, a referral for intensive in-home therapy may be helpful as the mother's work schedule compromises her availability. However, wrap-around services, such as intensive-in-home treatment and a referral for case management, are likely to be identified and prioritized after analyzing the risk assessment results. The client is already in the process of being evaluated for special education; therefore, you cannot unilaterally arrange for an alternative school placement. Federal laws require the client to be placed in the least restrictive environment, with specific procedural standards outlined in PL 94-142 (the Individuals with Disabilities Education Act).

11. A: Complex reflections go beyond simple reflections and paraphrasing by addressing the client's underlying or implicit thoughts, feelings, and experiences. In this response, you validate the client's feelings (sad and worried), allude to additional feelings of being overwhelmed (and on top of worrying), and attempt to counter any personal responsibility for "grown-up problems." Since the client is still in the early stages of therapy, it is often helpful to ask if your interpretation is correct. ("Am I getting this right?") This response helps subtly shift the power dynamic from that of an authoritative adult to one who understands the child and the world around them. An encourager or lead is a prompt used to help the client continue expressing themselves. Encouragers can be both verbal ("Please, go on") or non-verbal (head nodding) and are used to convey interest in what the client is expressing. Additive empathy is a core counseling attribute (rather than an additive encourager). Clarification is used when the client's statement is vague or confusing. (Client: "I'm just done." Therapist: "Can you tell me what it means for you to be done?") Paraphrasing selectively focuses on the client's intended message or meaning. Paraphrases are different from reflections in that paraphrases solely concentrate on the content of the client's statement. Paraphrases do not involve reflecting the client's feelings.

12. C: You can arrange to meet with the father by appointment, which would not breach confidentiality as he is the client's biological father. Since this client's mother has physical custody, the father also has the right to participate in counseling when clinically appropriate. When determining applicable legal and ethical guidelines regarding confidentiality, it is essential for you to first differentiate between legal custody and physical custody. Parents with legal custody can make unilateral decisions regarding their child's treatment. In cases where the courts have established legal custody, you must obtain a copy of the court order before initiating counseling services. With physical custody, the issue of consent is irrelevant. That is, both parents can make treatment decisions on behalf of their child, and both parents have the right to request their child's mental health records. By making an appointment with the father, you establish professional boundaries and allow yourself time to seek supervision and consultation for this complex ethical matter. Although state laws vary, if there is a court order (i.e., an emergency protective order (EPO) or a domestic violence order (DVO) against the father, then he would be violating this order simply by being at the child's school. If you believe the father poses an imminent risk to the child at any point in therapy, you are mandated to make child protective services (CPS) report. You may also refuse to see the father if you feel that your safety is compromised or believe your contact with the father is detrimental to the client's treatment. In these complex cases, you must follow an ethical decision-making model and seek supervision and consultation to determine the best course of action.

13. B: Justice is an ethical principle, and social justice is a professional value associated with the ethical commitment to promote equal access to resources, rights, and opportunities for everyone. The ACA Code of Ethics (2014) defines justice as "treating individuals equitably and fostering fairness and equality." Equitable treatment includes having equal opportunities for accessible healthcare. Finding a provider that takes the client's insurance is one way to practice the principle of justice. Doing so helps to improve outcomes, instill trust, and provide equal opportunities for the client and his family. The principle of veracity calls on counselors to conduct themselves truthfully and professionally. Autonomy is expressed when counselors support the client's right to control the direction of their lives. Autonomy is the foundational principle of informed consent. Fidelity involves respecting commitments and honoring promises.

Case Study 2

1. C: The Adult Substance Use Survey (ASUS) is a 64-item questionnaire that assesses an individual's perceived alcohol or substance use. There are additional questions designed to evaluate emotional difficulties and other mood-related issues. The Alcohol Use Disorders Identification Test (AUDIT) is used to help identify alcohol consumption, alcohol-related health problems, and drinking behaviors. The CAGE is a four-item screening instrument measuring an individual's problematic alcohol use related to cutting down, others' annoyance with one's alcohol use, personal guilt over use, and alcohol use first thing in the morning. The Drug Abuse Screening Test (DAST) detects drug abuse and dependence and is not used to assess alcohol use or mood-related issues.

2. B: Motivational Interviewing (MI) and Motivational Enhancement Therapy (MET) are evidence-based treatment practices that employ a person-centered, strengths-based approach to reduce ambivalence and evoke lasting behavioral change. The confidence ruler is an MI strategy that uses scaling questions to determine the client's desire to change. By asking, "Why are you a 6 and not a 0?" the client may then respond by providing reasons why she feels confident in her ability to stop drinking, such as abstinence attained during her three pregnancies. This technique helps initiate a conversation about the client's perceived ability to change. Asking, "Why are you not a 10?" shifts the conversation to one that is problem-based rather than strengths-based. "Tell me more about how you decided to be a 6" may elicit some degree of change talk, but it is not as precise as the response produced when using the MI confidence ruler technique. Lastly, asking the client what her life would look like if she had greater confidence in her ability to stop drinking does not help reduce ambivalence in the same way answer B does.

3. C. ASAM guidelines can be used to assess a client's level of care and ensure that counselors are providing integrated, seamless, and ongoing service planning. The client began outpatient treatment after prematurely leaving inpatient therapy. ASAM uses a multidimensional approach that considers the biopsychosocial needs of each client, including substance dependency and withdrawal, to determine placement. PEI criteria are unrelated to substance use and instead provide placement for older adults at risk for developing severe mental disorders. EPSDT standards support the comprehensive health needs of children younger than age 21 who receive public health insurance. Finally, the NIDA screening instrument is used to determine an individual's level of risk associated with substance use. Depending on the risk level, the provider will advise the patient on their drug use, assess their readiness to change, arrange for a referral, or continue to offer support.

4. D: This question addresses the client's reported symptoms and the diagnostic criteria for Alcohol Use Disorder (AUD). AUD is diagnosed in individuals who meet at least 2 of 11 criteria in the same 12-month period, as outlined in the DSM-5. The client admitted to continuing to consume alcohol even though it was causing family difficulties (e.g., divorce, estrangement from her oldest child, and supervised visits with her grandchildren). This criterion is one out of the 11 criteria recognized in the DSM-5. Individuals who see, feel, or hear things that others don't are symptoms of alcohol-induced psychosis, which the client did not experience. The client did have negative consequences associated with alcohol consumption, and those consequences did increase in severity within the last 6 months; however, that is not a characteristic of AUD. The client's 3 DUIs would qualify as legal troubles; however, this criterion was recognized in the DSM-IV and not included in the DSM-5.

5. D: The therapeutic alliance is associated with instilling hope, optimism, and motivation—all of which are related to improved treatment compliance. One way to establish a therapeutic alliance is to negotiate agreed-upon treatment goals for therapy. This client-counselor collaborative relationship is also strengthened by having confidence in the methods used to attain these identified goals. Due to the client's previous dissatisfaction with Alcoholics Anonymous, providing the client with 12-step recovery information would not be beneficial at this time. The therapist's communication skills, including summarization, can positively affect the therapeutic alliance; however, summarizing the client's problems, barriers, and risks is problem-oriented rather than solution-oriented. Providing problem-focused feedback can prevent the client from joining with the therapist. Relaxation and mindfulness are evidence-based approaches for improving insomnia. Teaching these skills does not ensure successful mastery of the client's alcohol use, and the client may want to prioritize other issues.

6. B: According to the ACA Code of Ethics (2014), "Counselors respect the privacy of their clients' presence on social media unless given consent to view such information." As such, viewing the client's social media page is not consistent with ethical standards of practice. Because you have an ethical responsibility to maintain boundaries, it is unethical for you to search the client's social media page without permission. It is standard practice to include social media, technology, and distance counseling benefits and limitations in the process of informed consent. However, the client's permission to search their social media page must be attained regardless of specifications included in informed consent. Searching the client's social media page is not a violation of confidentiality because you are not disclosing personal information.

7. B: According to Miller & Rollnick (2013), developing discrepancy between the client's values and behaviors helps increase the client's motivation to change. The onus is on the client, rather than the counselor, to argue for change. In doing so, you help elicit intrinsic motivation by emphasizing the conflict between the client's drinking and the value she places on familial relationships. This question goes beyond simply focusing on the client's alcohol use, making answer A incorrect. Developing discrepancy helps the client narrow down treatment plan goals, but it does not provide baseline measures for the treatment plan. Contingency management is a treatment approach that involves presenting clients with tangible rewards for attaining and maintaining abstinence.

8. B: The principles of trauma-informed care (TIC) are emotional safety, collaboration, choice, empowerment, and transparency. Counselors using a TIC approach help the client understand symptoms of their trauma and offer appropriate outside supports (e.g., Seeking Safety groups). When treating AUD and addressing trauma, the goal in the early stages of therapy is to increase emotional safety by minimizing the risk of re-traumatization. Providing the client with an understanding of symptoms rather than exploring their trauma narrative (i.e., recalling details of the trauma), helps accomplish this goal. Processing trauma in the early stages of therapy can increase the client's risk of decompensation before developing adequate coping skills. While there are physiological risks associated with treating both trauma and AUD, the counselor must remain transparent by providing information on the risks, as well as the benefits, of concurrent treatment. Attaining short-term psychopharmacological treatment is not a TIC condition, as it does little to empower clients to make educated choices for their care.

9. C: According to the ACA's Code of Ethics (2014), there are six core principles of professional, ethical behavior: autonomy, nonmaleficence, beneficence, justice, fidelity, and veracity. This question asks you to identify the best match between your statement and an ethical principle. Conveying to the client that it is up to them to decide whether or not they stop drinking reflects the principle of autonomy. Autonomy, or "fostering the right to control the direction of one's life" (ACA, 2014), respects the client's independence, which supports and empowers self-determination. Veracity is truthfulness. Fidelity involves respecting commitments and honoring promises. Lastly, justice promotes fair and equitable treatment toward all clients.

10. A: Adlerian therapists would introduce the concept of social interest and authenticity as replacements for the false sense of security she currently experiences when drinking with others. Social interest emphasizes belonging and connection with others by valuing the "common good" over individual interests and endeavors. Individuals with substance use disorder often struggle with a sense of belonging and authenticity, making Adlerian therapy a best practice for alcohol use disorder. Humanistic, or person-centered, therapists demonstrate empathy, unconditional positive regard, and nonjudgmental acceptance. Social skills training is a behavioral approach that helps clients learn new social skills through instruction, behavioral rehearsal, corrective feedback, and positive reinforcement. Rational-emotive behavioral therapy (REBT) would be used to identify the irrational belief associated with an activating event (i.e., drinking with others).

11. B: The Transtheoretical Stages of Change (SOC) Model, developed by Miller & Rollnick (2013), outlines the following SOC: precontemplation, contemplation, preparation, action, and maintenance. This client has just entered the preparation stage. Individuals in the preparation stage consider making a change but are unsure exactly how to do so. Like others in this stage, this client has taken significant steps towards sobriety, but there is still unresolved ambivalence.

She has explored AA and is in early sobriety but will need specific behavioral goals and a more solid commitment to reach the action stage. Individuals in the precontemplation stage are not considering a change, while those in the contemplation stage are beginning to consider making a change. Those in the contemplation stage are still drinking but are weighing the pros and cons of cutting back or abstaining. This client was in the contemplation stage when she attempted to cut back to two drinks per night. Individuals in the action stage have a specific behavioral plan and are committed to the process of change. When individuals become more stable in their sobriety, they have reached the maintenance stage.

12. A: The value in posing this question is to help guide the development of a functional analysis. A functional analysis increases the effectiveness of cognitive-behavioral therapy (CBT) by using the ABC model to examine and understand the sequence of thought patterns and behaviors. The ABC model examines antecedents (A), or what comes before the behavior, the actual behavior (B), and the consequence of that behavior (C). Establishing what the client's mood is like right after interacting with her ex-husband helps connect the behavior, antecedents, and consequences. Person-centered therapy, rather than CBT, is characterized by genuineness and unconditional positive regard. Psychoanalytic theorists focus on uncovering unconscious forces that drive behavior. Counterconditioning, a form of classical conditioning, uses a subjective unit of disturbance scale (SUDs) to assess levels of distress so events with lower levels of arousal can counteract these events. Biofeedback is an example of counterconditioning that incorporates the use of SUDs.

13. D: Rational-Emotive Behavioral Therapy (REBT) takes the ABC model used in CBT and adds two more elements—D and E—with D representing disputing irrational thoughts and E representing the newly formed alternative thoughts. Counselors using the technique of forceful disputing ask the client to review evidence that supports or does not support the client's irrational thought. Answer A is an example of cognitive behavioral therapy rather than REBT. The activating event would be the ex-husbands criticism. The dysfunctional automatic thought is the statement about her inability to do anything right, including parenting. The potential consequences are frustration, hopelessness, depression. If you state that every parent feels like a failure every so often (Answer B), you might leave the client thinking their feelings are invalid. Answer C uses a closed-ended question and does not enable the client to engage in the forceful disputing of an irrational belief.

Case Study 3

1. B: The PHQ-9 is a 9-item self-report screening instrument used to assess the severity of depression. The test takes approximately 5 minutes to administer. It is one method used to help practitioners appropriately match interventions for the following levels of depression: none/minimum, mild, moderate, moderately severe, and severe. The Bender-Gestalt is used to help determine an individual's level of neuropsychological impairment. The Brief Psychiatric Rating Scale (BPRS) consists of 24 items used to assess symptoms of psychosis in those with psychotic disorders, including schizophrenia. The Achenbach System of Empirically Based Assessment (ASEBA) assesses adaptive functioning, as well as behavioral, emotional, and social competencies.

2. C: According to the ACA Code of Ethics (2014), "Counselors are aware of—and avoid imposing—their own values, attitudes, beliefs, and behaviors. Counselors respect the diversity of clients, trainees, and research participants and seek training in areas in which they are at risk of imposing their values onto clients, especially when the counselor's values are inconsistent with the client's goals or are discriminatory in nature." Answer C is the only answer option that reflects this ethical standard.

3. B: The client's diagnosis of Major Depressive disorder is confirmed by the following symptoms: excessive guilt, suicidal ideation, insomnia, persistent negative mood, and feelings of worthlessness. These symptoms must be present during a sustained period of 2 weeks, which is also confirmed in the assessment. Strained relationships with family members have exacerbated the client's symptoms, but this is not a clinical manifestation of MDD. Poor copings skills are not required for a diagnosis of MDD. Emotional dysregulation occurs when individuals exhibit emotional reactions that are disproportional to the actual event. Individuals diagnosed with Disruptive Mood Dysregulation Disorder, PTSD, and bipolar disorder, rather than MDD, tend to exhibit emotional dysregulation.

4. C: Person-centered therapy is a non-directive approach designed to help clients recognize incongruence between their personal values (i.e., the value of being employed) and behavior (not seeking employment). Core facilitative conditions used to help the client obtain this goal are empathy, genuineness, and unconditional positive regard. Glasser's reality therapy helps clients transform failure identities into success identities by encouraging personal responsibility. Rational-emotive behavioral therapy (REBT) would attribute the client's maladaptive behavior to the irrational belief that he must be capable in all areas of life or else he is worthless, leading to remaining stuck. Healthy and unhealthy life positions are characteristics of transactional analysis.

5. D: Job loss, social isolation, sexual orientation, and previous suicide attempts all place individuals at higher risk for suicide. The client has experienced job loss and social isolation. His depressive symptoms were further complicated by his family's response to his sexual orientation. However, the client denied suicidal ideation as well as previous suicide attempts in his mental status exam, so this factor would not place him at higher risk for suicide.

6. D: The benefits of using the DSM-5 CFI would be to enhance clinical understanding of the client's cultural identity and the cultural definition of the identified problem. The APA developed the CFI as a holistic, person-centered approach to better understand the influence of cultural identity on the client's clinical presentation and treatment. The CFI is a 16-question interview that "emphasizes four domains of assessment: cultural definition of the problem (questions 1–3); cultural perceptions of cause, context, and support (questions 4–10); cultural factors affecting self-coping and past help seeking (questions 11–13); and cultural factors affecting current help seeking (questions 14–16)" (APA, 2013). The CFI is not to be used as the sole basis for determining a diagnosis. Although use of the CFI may help determine the client's readiness and motivation to change, this is not the primary purpose of the interview. Determining if the client is open to working with a culturally different counselor is not the intended purpose of the CFI.

7. A: The most effective means for understanding this client's experiences of prejudice, discrimination, and inclusion is to examine the client's contextual manifestations through the lens of intersectionality. Intersectionality considers each individual's privileged and marginalized status in terms of all intersecting contexts. This client is a young, Catholic, Latino American who self-identifies as a gay male. Each construct serves as a foundation for his identity. The client's identity influences how he relates to the world and how he is affected by sociocultural values and norms. Since the client identifies as a gay male, his gender identity is not in question. Gender expression refers to how an individual's dress, behavior, or haircut reflects one's gender identity, making answer B incorrect. Culturally sensitive therapy involves recognizing one's personal biases; this is not an effective means for understanding this client's specific experiences of prejudice, discrimination, and inclusion. Counselors are ethically responsible for addressing misinformation and disinformation on an individual and institutionalized level. However, this alone will not assist you with understanding the client's marginalized experiences.

8. C: Solution-Focused Brief Therapy (SFBT) is a short-term, solution-oriented best practice used to help clients establish and reach goals by improving motivation and creating measurable behavioral change. The Miracle Question is an SFBT technique that encourages the client to envision a future without the problem. The client is then asked to provide details of what is pictured, enabling you to partner with the client to form manageable and attainable treatment planning goals. Gestalt therapy is based on developing a here-and-now awareness. Client-centered therapy emphasizes attaining congruence between one's ideal self and actual self. Motivational Enhancement Therapy emphasizes increasing change talk to reduce ambivalence.

9. D: The American Counseling Association (ACA) and several other professional organizations have determined that conversion therapy causes harm to patients, and since counselors have an ethical obligation to "do no harm," they should actively advise clients against it. Despite this, conversion therapy is still legal in most states. The ACA Code of Ethics (2014) requires that "counselors recognize historical and social prejudices in the misdiagnosis and pathologizing of certain individuals and groups and strive to become aware of and address such biases in themselves or others." Referring the client to someone who provides this treatment would be considered unethical in all circumstances, and therefore consulting that therapist to determine referral opportunities would also be inappropriate. Since conversion therapy is a religious-based practice the ACA would hold that encouraging the client to seek religious guidance is a vague suggestion and includes an element of risk. The best option is therefore answer choice D.

10. C: A constructionist approach would assist with creating a strengths-based narrative emphasizing affirming community experiences. Constructionists believe that individuals create personal meaning in their lives through social constructs (i.e., relationships with others). Theories that use a constructionist approach include object-relations theory, solution-focused therapy, emotionally focused therapy, and narrative therapy. Narrative therapy uses a strengths-based approach to help clients retell their stories and reauthor their lives. The client attests to finding acceptance in the LGBTQ community, which may help guide the client to an affirming sense of self. Showing unconditional positive regard is a person-centered technique rather than a constructivist approach. CBT would emphasize that the client is engaging in overgeneralization, a cognitive distortion used when taking one incident and using it as the only source of evidence for a general conclusion. Finally, behavioral therapists would teach new skills by increasing environmental rewards and positive reinforcement.

11. C: Acceptance and commitment therapy and mindfulness are evidence-based mental health interventions for various mental health disorders, including depression. The premise of ACT is that moving individuals toward acknowledging and accepting (rather than fighting) their thoughts and feelings in the present moment influence behavioral changes. The fact that the client is fighting against feelings of guilt and shame makes ACT and mindfulness an effective means for helping the client learn to gradually accept these feelings, as well as the thoughts that accompany them. Although some consider ACT a form of cognitive-behavioral therapy (CBT), ACT seeks to accept (rather than change) thoughts and feelings, whereas CBT aims to change thoughts so one's feelings can change. Sexual desire is a physiological concept rather than a thought or feeling. When appropriate, behavioral therapy best addresses sexual desire. Social isolation is a behavior. There are thoughts and feelings underlying social isolation, but social isolation as a behavior is better addressed through behavioral modification or other behavioral therapy techniques.

12. B: By connecting dating and attending church with the client's treatment plan goals, you and the client can best determine the direction of therapy. The client is in the mid to late stages of treatment. Evaluating these events in the context of his treatment plan goals will help clarify the client's readiness for termination. The client already has established his identity as a gay male, making answer A incorrect. Determining the client's ego-strength could undermine the client's confidence and self-efficacy, making this option incorrect. Re-evaluating the potential risks associated with being out in the community is also incorrect because the client is already well aware of the risks.

13. A: Counselors show genuineness by responding in a manner that is consistent with the client's and their own internal emotional experiences. Genuineness is about responding authentically, in the present moment, in a way that is verbally and emotionally congruent; i.e., there is consistency between the counselor's words and non-verbal behaviors. Empathetic responding occurs when counselors convey an understanding and non-judgmental acceptance of a client's expressed and underlying feelings. It consists of perceiving, understanding, experiencing, and responding. Empathetic responding differs from genuineness in that it refers to the counselor's response to the client's, not the counselor's, emotional expression. Metacommunication refers to the counseling process as it is unfolding. It is communication about communication, including verbal or non-verbal cues, that carry depth and meaning. Counselors who show cultural attunement skillfully communicate that they both know and do not know the cultural realities of those we treat. Cultural attunement is about remaining teachable and having the desire, humility, and curiosity to acknowledge things such as privilege and oppression, for example.

Case Study 4

1. C: Researchers indicate over three-quarters of those diagnosed with ASD show hypo or hyper-reactivity to sensory stimuli. The 5th edition of the Diagnostic and Statistical Manual of Mental Disorders (2013) lists sensory processing difficulties as one of four types of restricted, repetitive patterns representative of the diagnosis of ASD. The client's difficulty tolerating cafeteria noise is an example of sensory hyper-reactivity. It is common for individuals with ASD to have difficulties with sleep-wake disturbances, including insomnia, narcolepsy, and restless leg syndrome. However, the DSM-5 does not list sleep disturbance as a criterion for ASD. Mood lability is a comorbid symptom of ASD rather than a diagnostic criterion. For individuals with ASD, mood lability is often the result of sensory over-stimulation, difficulty tolerating a change in routine, or difficulty reading social cues. Impulsive outbursts are also commonly associated with ASD; however, the DSM-5 does not require this to diagnose ASD.

2. B: For this client, it is best to proceed by honoring the ethical principle of autonomy and permitting the client to decline services. The APA Code of Ethics (2014) defines informed consent as "a process of information sharing associated with possible actions clients may choose to take, aimed at assisting clients in acquiring a full appreciation and understanding of the facts and implications of a given action or actions." Clients must be deemed competent and have the capacity to provide voluntary consent. An assent is permissible when, "counseling minors, incapacitated adults, or other persons unable to give voluntary consent (APA, 2014)." The client has a 3.6 GPA and an unremarkable mental status exam, indicating competency. Allowing the mother to provide informed consent is incorrect due to the client's competency and the fact that he is now 18. Informed consent is not required in rare instances when there is a significant risk instead of a slight or remote risk. Considerations for determining significant risk include its frequency, type, severity, and duration. Additionally, there must be a determination that the behavior can or cannot be mitigated by reasonable interventions. The client created a disturbance that we assume was deemed concerning because of campus police involvement; however, with the information provided, we cannot ascertain that he posed a significant risk (i.e., he denied suicidal and homicidal ideation).

3. B: Developed by Salvador Minuchin, structural family therapy is based on the premise that family subsystems and boundaries are either disengaged or enmeshed. The mother and the client are an enmeshed subsystem due to being overly dependent and close. Multigenerational (Extended) Family Systems therapists use the term *undifferentiated family ego mass* to describe individuals in families with high levels of emotional fusion and low levels of differentiation. Contextual family therapists view maladaptive behavior as an imbalance in loyalty, trust, and mutual understanding. Strategic family therapists view maladaptive behavior as the result of circular communication. Circular communication occurs when a behaviorally reinforced feedback loop maintains the family's homeostasis and dysfunction.

4. A: Joining is a foundational component of structural family therapy. Counselors join with families through the processes of tracking (i.e., "following the facts" in content and interactions), mimesis (i.e., becoming like the family), confirmation (e.g., identifying the disconnect between verbal and nonverbal communication), and accommodation (i.e., making personal adjustments to the family's way of being). Each process is designed to strengthen the therapeutic alliance among all family members. SFBT treatment is known for teaching problem-free talk—a technique that is used to help all family members share aspects of their lives that are going well. Enactments are also used in structural family therapy as a way to actively demonstrate interactions and explore changes within the family dynamics. Unlike joining, the counselor requests that family members interact with one another rather than interacting directly with the counselor. The use of triangulation to reduce anxiety among family dyads is a Bowenian family therapy technique.

5. B: Of all answer options, increasing the client's motivation to change is best attained by stating, "You were told having a girlfriend in college would lead to sex, and you're disappointed that's not happening for you." The statement is an example of an empathetic reflection, a micro skill associated with strengthening the counselor-client relationship. The statement also sets the stage for establishing a discrepancy between the client's values or expectations and current behaviors. It is a natural lead to discussing what an intimate relationship looks like, the reality of exploring it, and the appropriateness of establishing it. The therapeutic alliance is strongly associated with increased motivation to change. Answer A attempts to engage the client by using his major in architectural design to create an analogy between the building blocks of an intimate relationship and building an actual building. This statement is likely to be misunderstood because individuals on the autism spectrum think concretely and not metaphorically. Telling the client that the ball is in his court is also a statement that, if taken literally, creates a misunderstanding. The statement, "Your girlfriend declined to have sex with you, but you've decided to keep trying," is a paraphrase. A paraphrase reflects the factual aspects of the client's statements. Paraphrases let clients know that they are being heard, but they are not as powerful as empathetic reflections.

6. A: Social skills training can be used to help improve social-emotional reciprocity. This question tests your knowledge of ASD and group dynamics. Applied Behavioral Analysis (ABA) is the gold standard for the treatment of ASD. ABA uses behavioral reinforcement to shape behaviors and enhance social skills. Answers A, B, and C describe a product-oriented group, or a behavioral group with pre-established goals and specific target behaviors. Answer D represents process-oriented groups. Process-oriented groups focus on the impact of the group process itself. Group cohesion, one of Yalom's curative factors, occurs when members create emotional bonds with shared interests and goals. Group cohesion is a process-oriented aspect of group therapy. Social norms can be established in real-time; however, this is best done when group leaders collaborate with group members to shape and reinforce appropriate social norms. Additionally, psychoeducation is a product-oriented group and a standard component for teaching social skills. Social norms primarily occur in process-oriented groups, making answer D incorrect.

7. C: Developed by Albert Bandura, social learning theory is based on the premise that individuals repeat behaviors when certain conditions are met. The theory asserts that individuals grow and learn when four conditions (in order) are met: attention, retention, reproduction, and motivation. In answer C, the client attends to a video (attention), he recalls the skill (retention), he applies the skills to a consensual relationship (reproduction), and has sex (a motivating reinforcer). A group discussion does not include an observed model, making answers A and B incorrect. In answer D, the client accurately recalled and retained the information and applied the skill. The client did not have sex, which did not create motivation to continue to apply learned skills.

8. B: Cognitive appraisal is a technique used to help with emotional regulation. The client's difficulties with emotional regulation led to the run-in with campus police. Cognitive reappraisal is a staged process beginning with the client examining his initial perception of the associated stressor, discerning if he has the skills and resources to cope with the stressor, and understanding if the solution lies in changing the situation or in his reaction to the situation. Systematic desensitization is used with anxiety and involves replacing a fear response with a relaxation response in counterconditioning. Reciprocal inhibition uses the new relaxation response to replace the fear response. MI uses "roll with resistance" as a nonconfrontational means for lessening opposition to change. The counselor is attempting to regulate outburst, rather than committing to a change. Mapping is a structural family technique used to creating a visual representation of family patterns of interaction, including family rules and family structures.

9. D: You should first use this as an opportunity to initiate a discussion or review your social media policy. According to the ACA Code of Ethics (2014), "Counselors clearly explain to their clients, as part of the informed consent procedure, the benefits, limitations, and boundaries of the use of social media." Using the event to teach members to respect the privacy of others does not explicitly address social media use. Using the event as a basis for discussing group confidentiality, privacy, and violations is helpful, but this does not expressly address the use of social media. The ACA Code of Ethics (2014) states, "Counselors who engage in the use of distance counseling, technology, and/or social media develop knowledge and skills regarding related technical, ethical, and legal considerations (e.g., special certifications, additional course work)." If counselors have a social media presence, they have an ethical and legal obligation to seek required technical knowledge and skills (e.g., use privacy settings). However, the primary course of action must include informing group members of their use of social media as part of the ongoing process of informed consent. Additionally, the NBCC Code of Ethics (2016) states that "After carefully considering all of the ethical implications, including confidentiality, privacy, and multiple relationships, [counselors] shall develop written practice procedures in regard to social media and digital technology, and these shall be incorporated with the information provided to clients before or during the initial session."

10. B: According to the DSM-5, social communication is characterized by "deficits in social-emotional reciprocity, ranging, for example, from abnormal social approach and failure of normal back-and-forth conversation; to reduced sharing of interests, emotions, or affect; to failure to initiate or respond to social interactions." When the client was offered a position as your assistant, he listened to your request and paused while awaiting a response. He also used eye contact. This illustrates social-emotional reciprocity. The client responded to the request by saying, "Absolutely, I see that you really need help with offering better refreshments and teaching certain skills." Since there is no evidence indicating that you found the comment to be derogatory, nor was there feedback provided indicating hurt feelings, answer A is incorrect. An intrusive social approach involves intrusive or inappropriate touching. Shaking someone's hand as an agreement and acceptance of an offer does not qualify as intrusive. Motivation to help others is not a diagnostic criterion for ASD and is therefore, incorrect. Additionally, it is unclear if he has motives to help others (e.g., rather than receive better refreshments or gain social prestige).

11. C: Ableism is the intentional and unintentional discrimination and marginalization of individuals with ASD resulting from prejudicial beliefs that they are less capable or worthy. Ableism is rooted in biases that can be either explicit (i.e., conscious or intentional) or implicit (i.e., unintentional or unconscious). Ableism grants privilege and favor to individuals who are healthy or non-disabled. Answers A and B refer solely to intentional discrimination, making those options incorrect. Answer D includes intentional and unintentional discrimination but is incorrect because it refers to an unwillingness to acknowledge and address deficits among individuals suffering from ASD. The medical model perpetuates stereotypes and biases by referring to individuals with ASD (and other disabilities) as having deficits (akin to being sick) that need an intervention to be cured from the suffering. Neurodiverse advocates maintain that barriers hinder those with ASD from reaching their full potential, and promote an integrative approach by valuing impairment as an integral part of diversity. In terms of sex education and ASD, ableism can lead to perceptions of individuals with ASD as asexual and childlike, leading to the overprotection of individuals expressing normal drives and interests. As a result, sexually active young adults with ASD encounter victimization, unwanted pregnancies, and sexually transmitted infections at higher rates than neurotypical individuals. Further, the ACA Code of Ethics (2014) calls for the promotion of social justice defined as, "treating individuals equitably and fostering fairness and equality."

12. D: This member's statement is an example of universality (one of Irvin Yalom's curative factors), which is the feeling that one receives when connecting with others. Group members learning that others who live on campus share similar viewpoints will likely reduce isolation, which is a by-product of universality. Catharsis is a psychodynamic term referring to the emotional release of previously repressed energy tied to a traumatic event. Transference is a Freudian concept that describes the redirection of a repressed emotion onto another person. Altruism is another one of Yalom's curative factors regarding group members learning to help others.

13. D: The One Group Pre-test Post-test design is a non-experimental design. Non-experimental designs do not have a control group and lack internal validity due to the possibility for an unaccounted third variable, known as a spurious variable. Internal validity measures the cause-and-effect relationship between the independent variable and the dependent variable. In this study, the independent variable is the group intervention. The dependent variable is the pre-test/post-test outcome measure associated with improved social skills. The spurious variable is known as history. History influences outcomes when an event occurs between the first and second outcome measure. COVID-19 is the event that likely affected outcome variables in this study, particularly one on social skills. Statistical regression occurs when subjects score extremely high (or low) on the pre-test and show improvement simply due to the passage of time between each measure. Maturation affects internal validity when subjects are impacted by the passage of time (i.e., in projects lasting several years). Attrition, or subjects dropping out of the study, also serves as a threat to internal validity.

Case Study 5

1. D: According to the DSM-5 (2013), "Individuals with obsessive-compulsive personality disorder may be excessively conscientious, scrupulous, and inflexible about matters of morality, ethics, or values. They may force themselves and others to follow rigid moral principles and very strict standards of performance." Persistent, unwanted thoughts and repetitive rituals characterize obsessive-compulsive disorder (OCD) rather than OCPD. OCPD is a Cluster C personality disorder. Anxious and fearful conditions are included in Cluster C personality disorders. Frequent fears of being alone are a symptom of dependent personality disorder. There is an excessive devotion to work and productivity for individuals with OCPD that is not otherwise accounted for or driven by financial success or necessity.

2. A: According to the DSM-5 (2013), "typical features of obsessive-compulsive personality disorder are difficulties in establishing and sustaining close relationships, associated with rigid perfectionism, inflexibility, and restricted emotional expression [...] they are oblivious to the fact that other people tend to become very annoyed at the delays and inconveniences that result from this behavior." Individuals with OCPD possess ego-syntonic traits rather than ego-dystonic traits. Individuals with ego-syntonic features are less amenable to change because there is little to no desire to change. Conversely, individuals with obsessive-compulsive disorder (OCD) have ego-dystonic traits, meaning they experience dissatisfaction with symptoms and desire change. Per the DSM-5, individuals with OCPD "are rigidly deferential to authority and rules and insist on quite literal compliance, with no rule bending for extenuating circumstances." Strict adherence to rules and authority persists despite personal distress while attempting to attain perfection. Leisurely activities are generally forfeited by prioritizing productivity and work. Solo vacations and vacations with others may be postponed, and when they do occur, they are highly structured in an effort to not waste time.

3. C: In a new section (Section III) of the DSM-5, a trait-specific approach to personality disorders is introduced. In the Alternative DSM-5 Model for Personality Disorders, characteristics of pathological personality traits are presented, along with impairments in functioning. Pathological personality traits are grouped into five domains: negative affectivity, detachment, antagonism, disinhibition, and psychoticism. Negative affectivity is defined as "frequent and intense experiences of high levels of a wide range of negative emotions (e.g., anxiety, depression, guilt/ shame, worry, and their behavioral (e.g., self-harm) and interpersonal (e.g., dependency) manifestations (DSM-5, 2013)." The negative affectivity of OCPD is perseveration. The DSM-5 (2013) defines this as "persistence at tasks long after the behavior has ceased to be functional or effective; continuance of the same behavior despite repeated failures." Deceitfulness and impulsivity, an aspect of negative affectivity, is associated with narcissistic personality disorder. Pessimism and hopelessness characterize the negative affectivity of anxiousness, which is associated with avoidant personality disorder. Lastly, separation and insecurity are aspects of the negative affectivity domain for borderline personality disorder.

4. A: By clarifying and paraphrasing the client's presenting problem, you allow the client to correct any inaccuracies and inconsistencies by rephrasing what the client has stated. A counselor's use of these skills can help promote a sense of partnership with the client, which can serve as a foundation for conceptualizing and creating treatment plan goals. Immediacy is grounded in the here-and-now experience of the counseling process and is generally facilitated by self-disclosure. The skill of immediacy is used to reflect a parallel experience or address what is going on between the counselor and client in real-time. Immediacy is best used after the counselor establishes a therapeutic alliance with the client. Values clarification differs from the communication skill of clarification. Counselors use values clarification to help clients recognize, understand, and prioritize personal ethical and moral values. Creating discrepancy is a motivational interviewing technique used to promote change talk by pointing out the disconnect between where the client is currently and where they would like to be.

5. A: ACT combines mindfulness and behavioral therapy to assist individuals with accepting distressing thoughts and feelings rather than fighting against them. ACT is an evidence-based practice for OCPD because of its focus on increasing psychological flexibility (i.e., reducing rigidity). The practice of mindfulness helps clients stay in the here-and-now and accept each thought and feeling without judgment. Shaping is used in operant conditioning and involves reinforcing successive approximations to a targeted behavior. Unbalancing is associated with structural family therapy and consists of the counselor aligning with a family member or subsystem to create disequilibrium. Developing discrepancy is used with MI to help the client explore the pros and cons of making a change.

6. A: The goal of discussing attachment with the client is to determine the association between unmet childhood needs and maladaptive schemas. Schema therapy is an integrative approach used to treat individuals with personality disorders. The theory integrates elements of attachment theory, cognitive-behavioral therapy, and object relations to address maladaptive schemas. A schema is an influential belief system acquired about oneself, others, and society at large. Maladaptive schemas originate from early childhood experiences and create emotional, cognitive, and behavioral impairments. Since there are no indications that the client's child is at risk for victimization, determining the client's risk level for perpetration is unnecessary. Temperament is inborn rather than environmental. While determining the role temperament plays in social and relational interactions is essential, the client's upbringing in foster care provides more insight into attachment and object relations. A biopsychosocial assessment uses a holistic approach to determine biological, social, and psychological influences on a client's presenting problem. The connection would need to be made between biopsychosocial factors and attachment rather than symptom severity.

7. B: Black and white thinking is the cognitive distortion associated with the belief that anyone who refuses to conform to the client's standards is seen as inept and defiant. Black and white thinking, also known as polarization or all or nothing thinking, is exhibited when shades of gray are not acknowledged. There is ridged inflexibility with others. If the wife agrees and conforms to the client's perfectionistic standards, all is well in the relationship. If the wife dissents and refuses to comply with the client's perfectionistic standards, she is inept and defiant. Something is either great or terrible; a person is either perfect or a failure. Overgeneralization, personalization, and mind-reading, generally result in self-blame, which is atypical for individuals with OCPD. Overgeneralization occurs when broad implications are based on one or two minor instances (e.g., "I let down a friend. Now everyone thinks I'm a total disaster!"). Personalization happens when one assigns themselves blame without solid logistical evidence. As the name implies, mind-reading occurs when one jumps to conclusions or negatively interprets another person's intentions, feelings, and actions.

8. B: This statement is an example of confrontation. Effective confrontation promotes greater awareness and insight by pointing out discrepancies in clients' thoughts, words, or actions. The goal of confrontation is to reduce resistance by calling attention to the incongruence between clients' expressed values and their behaviors. Counselors use interpretation to test a hypothesis or theory about a client's experiences or inner thoughts and feelings. Reframing is used when counselors rephrase a client's statement in a way that offers a different perspective or optimistic viewpoint. Counselors express empathetic attunement by becoming in sync with a client's inner feelings or emotional state.

9. B: Appealing to the client's goal-oriented personality helps provide a familiar foundation for the client and allows him to see how aspects of his personality can be useful. Determining the client's motivation to change is appropriate for individuals with ego-dystonic traits. Since the client has ego-syntonic traits, his motivation to change may be relatively non-existent. Prioritizing the client's diagnostic symptoms is less effective because it does not engage them in mutual collaboration. Enlisting the help of his wife would not appeal to the client since he does not believe the problem originates with him, nor does he believe she has accurate insight into the problem.

10. D: According to the ACA Code of Ethics (2014):

"When a counselor agrees to provide counseling services to two or more persons who have a relationship, the counselor clarifies at the outset which person or persons are clients and the nature of the relationships the counselor will have with each involved person. If it becomes apparent that the counselor may be called upon to perform potentially conflicting roles, the counselor will clarify, adjust, or withdraw from roles appropriately. [...] Counselors have an obligation to review in writing and verbally with clients the rights and responsibilities of both counselors and clients. [...] Counselors explicitly explain to clients the nature of all services provided. They inform clients about issues such as, but not limited to, the following: the purposes, goals, techniques, procedures, limitations, potential risks, and benefits of services; the counselor's qualifications, credentials, relevant experience, and approach to counseling; continuation of services upon the incapacitation or death of the counselor; the role of technology; and other pertinent information."

The issue of implied consent is valid for collateral contacts and may meet minimal ethical requirements; however, without a signed informed consent delineating your role and relationship with each participant, you may encounter ethical complications. The client initially allowed contact with his wife to obtain collateral information. The wife reported that she wanted to attend couples therapy, but the client was adamant that she did not participate. This brings into question the client's capacity to provide voluntary consent (i.e., it may be given under duress and thus invalid). Since conflict de-escalation in couples therapy is standard practice, this does not create an exception. The counselor did not commit an ethical violation due to the client not waiving his right to confidentiality. The issue lies with informed consent as a whole rather than one aspect of informed consent. Confidentiality is one aspect of informed consent.

11. D: Taking up boxing to release pent-up energy is an example of sublimation. Sublimation, rationalization, reaction formation, and regression are all defense mechanisms. Defense mechanisms are unconscious means for protecting a person from overwhelming feelings of anxiety. Sublimation occurs when a person redirects unacceptable urges in a socially acceptable way (e.g., boxing). Rationalization is when a person provides a logical reason for behaving or thinking instead of the actual reason or motive. Reaction formation occurs when a person expresses the opposite opinion, feeling, or action because their true belief causes great anxiety. Regression is the process of returning to an earlier stage of development when encountering overwhelming feelings of fear, anger, anxiety, or resentment.

12. C: Emotionally focused therapy (EFT) is based on John Bowlby's attachment theory. EFT acknowledges the role attachment plays in forming intimate bonds and lasting relationships. The goal is to tap into the couple's capacity and desire to attain a deeper connection with one another. Systemic desensitization is a behavioral intervention used with individuals experiencing anxiety, particularly with individuals experiencing phobias. Solution-focused therapy (SFT), or solution-focused brief therapy (SFBT), is future-oriented and limited in duration. SFT focuses on the couple's individual strengths rather than addressing more profound childhood experiences. Rational-emotive behavioral therapy (REBT) is a cognitive approach used to identify and dispute irrational thoughts.

13. D: Individuals with OCDP experience pathological personality traits marked by avoidance and detachment. Individuals with avoidant attachment styles would react to termination in the same way they react to close romantic partners or interpersonal relationships, which is to remain emotionally detached. Individuals with disorganized attachment styles feel threatened, experience symptom regression, and become emotionally dysregulated in the counselor's presence. Individuals with ambivalent attachment styles attempt to delay termination and desperately cling to the counselor. Lastly, individuals with varied attachment styles, particularly those associated with narcissistic personality disorder, are self-congratulatory and detached.

Case Study 6

1. C: In 2017, The National Institute on Drug Abuse (NIDA) released a two-minute assessment tool measuring substance use disorder risk for teens aged 12-17. The Drug Abuse Screen Test (DAST-10) is a 10-question self-screening tool for drug use in adults. The Delinquent Activities Scale (DAS) is a 36-question assessment instrument used with teens in the juvenile justice system. The Brief Addiction Monitor (BAM) is an assessment instrument for adults that assesses factors related to recovery, behavioral health, and substance use and risk.

2. D: The primary risk for allowing the client to interpret for his family is that it calls into question the validity of informed consent. The principles of self-determination and autonomy govern informed consent. While the adolescent is the identified client, he does not have the legal right to provide consent for treatment. According to the ACA Code of Ethics (2014), "Clients have the freedom to choose whether to enter into or remain in a counseling relationship and need adequate information about the counseling process and the counselor. [...] Counselors communicate information in ways that are both developmentally and culturally appropriate. When clients have difficulty understanding the language that counselors use, counselors provide necessary services (e.g., arranging for a qualified interpreter or translator) to ensure comprehension by clients." If counselors do not have immediate access to interpreters, remote options are available via phone or video. In certain instances, in some states, using nonprofessional interpreters is against the law. Experiencing secondary trauma is unlikely because there is an increased probability that the client is already aware of the torture or that the parents do not discuss it with anyone. Additional considerations include perpetuating the client's role as chief decision-maker, selective messaging, and intentional or unintentional miscommunication; however, these issues do not supersede the need to adhere to the principles of self-determination and autonomy.

3. C: PHQ-9 is a 9-item, self-administered screening instrument used to measure depression and anxiety. PHQ-9: Modified for Teens is adapted for use with adolescents. CAGE is a four-item screening instrument measuring an individual's problematic alcohol use related to cutting down, others' annoyance with one's alcohol use, personal guilt over use, and alcohol use first thing in the morning. EQ-5D measures health-related quality of life across five dimensions, including mobility, self-care, usual activities, pain/discomfort, and anxiety/depression. The EQ-5D-Y can be used with children and adolescents. Although measures are included for anxiety and depression, the instrument is not designed for the sole use of determining the severity of anxiety and depression. Finally, AUDIT is used to help identify alcohol consumption, alcohol-related health problems, and drinking behaviors

4. C: The DSM-5 added the criterion of craving, which was not included in the DSM-IV. Craving is described in the DSM-5 as a "strong desire or urge to use the substance." DSM-5 text further states that craving "makes it difficult to think of anything else" and "often results in the onset" of use. Criminal behavior and dependency are no longer criteria for SUD. The effects of acculturation on substance use are important to assess but would not help substantiate the diagnosis of SUD.

5. B: The technique associated with a person-centered therapy is showing unconditional positive regard. Counselors show this through warmth, care, and nonjudgmental acceptance. Acting as if there is not a problem is an Adlerian technique. Adlerians encourage clients to adopt an action-oriented mindset and use various techniques to help clients increase their level of functioning. REBT practitioners focus on challenging a client's irrational beliefs and replacing these beliefs with more realistic and logical ones. Free association is a Freudian concept used to tap into one's unconscious and gain insight. The process of free association involves the client verbalizing all of their thoughts without censorship.

6. D: Contingency management (CM) is an evidence-based practice with a parent training component. CM works by using behavioral modification strategies, including positive reinforcement, negative reinforcement, positive punishment, and negative punishment. The goal is to reinforce abstinence-related behaviors (e.g., negative drug screen) by offering low-cost vouchers or incentives. Motivational enhancement therapy is an evidence-based practice for substance abuse used to increase change talk by reducing ambivalence. Cognitive-behavioral theory is also an evidence-based practice that challenges distorting thinking and encourages healthy coping strategies. Multi-systemic therapy is a comprehensive in-home intervention for teens involved in the criminal justice system. It is a community-based, intensive intervention to assist families with collaboration with multiple systems, including schools, courts, and other community locations.

7. B: The use of MI is reflected in the following: "You may not be ready to stop. What is it about using that you really need to hold onto?" This statement stands apart from the other choices because it is non-confrontational, and the question appropriately addresses the client's ambivalence. MI is used to address ambivalence and promote change. One aspect of this approach is to avoid argumentation. Avoiding argumentation is accomplished by refraining from accusations of denial or using terms like disease or addict. The idea is to roll with resistance by allowing the client to discover discrepancies between where they see currently see themselves and where they'd like to be in the future.

8. A: According to the DSM-5 (2013), acculturation difficulty is a category that "should be used when difficulty in adjusting to a new culture (e.g., following migration) is the focus of clinical attention or has an impact on the individual's treatment or prognosis." Difficulty adapting to cultural expectations due to an inability to balance demands from the dominant culture with the demands from the minority culture does not fit the definition of acculturation difficulty. The category of Social Exclusion or Rejection V62.4 (Z60.4) should be used "when there is an imbalance of social power such that there is recurrent social exclusion or rejection by others. Examples of social rejection include bullying, teasing, and intimidation by others; being targeted by others for verbal abuse and humiliation; and being purposefully excluded from the activities of peers, workmates, or others in one's social environment" (APA, 2013).

9. C: This response is an example of an empathetic reflection, or more specifically, a double-sided empathetic reflection. A double-sided reflection is a motivational interviewing strategy used to help examine ambivalence and look at both sides of the client's discrepancies. Counselors use reframing to help clients view situations, feelings, and relationships in a more positive light. Summarization ties together multiple concepts, feelings, or ideas. Counselors can use summarization at the end of the session or throughout the session to narrow the focus or examine a particular theme. An encourager is also called a prompt or a furthering response and involves a word, phrase, or nod used to encourage the client to continue talking.

10. D: According to the SOC model, the client is in the action stage of change. This model, developed by Miller & Rollnick (2013), outlines the following stages: precontemplation, contemplation, preparation, action, and maintenance. This client has just entered the action stage. The client has been compliant with therapy and reports four negative drug screens. The SOC model is not always linear. The client has just entered the action phase and may regress toward earlier stages or may eventually reach the maintenance stage. Individuals in the precontemplation stage are not considering a change, whereas those in the contemplation stage are beginning to consider making a change. Those in the contemplation stage are still using substances but are weighing the pros and cons of cutting back or abstaining. Individuals in the action stage have a specific behavioral plan and are committed to the process of change. When individuals become more stable in their sobriety, they have reached the maintenance stage.

11. B: Salvador Minuchin, credited with developing structural family therapy, used family maps to graphically depict family dynamics, including cross-generational coalitions, subsystems, and differentiated intersectional boundaries. Family maps also show community supports and stressors, making it a good option for assessing protective factors and risk factors within the client's community. A genogram is also a visual depiction of family dynamics and is commonly associated with multigenerational (extended) family systems therapy, also known as Bowenian therapy. Family maps differ from genograms in that family maps show family dynamics and identify social supports and connections. Genograms depict family interactions and generational relationships to reduce inappropriate boundaries (e.g., triangulation) by increasing diffusion. An eco-map is similar to a family map, but the emphasis is on intrafamily dynamics within their current social context. For this client, identifying social relationships and connections within the community can help determine protective factors (e.g., church, school) and identify risk factors (e.g., social isolation, peers) for the parents and the client. Eco-maps differ from genograms and family maps by viewing family boundaries as either open or closed to their social environment. Virginia Satir used sculpting as a human validation process model technique. Sculpting is a nonverbal exercise in which counselors instruct family members to physically position themselves to represent certain aspects and patterns of family relationships and interactions.

12. C: Structural family therapy's primary purpose is to strengthen the boundaries within family systems. One objective of structural family therapy is to help parents regain control by assessing the family structure and assisting families with setting appropriate boundaries. Treatment phases include joining the family, reconceptualizing (diagnosing) the family, and applying restructuring techniques. Restructuring techniques include: assigning tasks, reframing, shifting boundaries (unbalancing), escalating stress, psychoeducation, blocking transactional patterns, and developing implicit conflict. Multigenerational (Bowenian or Extended) family therapy focuses on eight interconnected concepts. Bowenian family concepts include differentiation of self, emotional triangles, sibling positions, society emotional process, multigenerational transmission process, nuclear family emotional system, family projection process, and nuclear family emotional system. Strategic family therapy differs from structural family therapy in that strategic family therapy places much less emphasis on boundaries and instead focuses on patterns of communication and interactions. Some techniques of strategic family therapy include positive connotation (similar to reframing), paradoxical intervention, pretend techniques, and hypothesizing. Contextual family therapy emphasizes ethical elements of each family, including loyalty, trust, and relational principles.

13. A: After providing pretermination counseling, you should terminate with all parties. Per the ACA Code of Ethics (2014), "Counselors terminate a counseling relationship when it becomes reasonably apparent that the client no longer needs assistance, is not likely to benefit, or is being harmed by continued counseling." Termination with clients is an ongoing process that begins with informed consent at the outset of treatment. Since the client has met his treatment goals, he no longer needs assistance. Regarding multiple roles, the ACA Code of Ethics (2014) states, "When a counselor agrees to provide counseling services to two or more persons who have a relationship, the counselor clarifies at the outset which person or persons are clients and the nature of the relationships the counselor will have with each involved person. If it becomes apparent that the counselor may be called upon to perform potentially conflicting roles, the counselor will clarify, adjust, or withdraw from roles appropriately. [...] Counselors provide pretermination counseling and recommend other service providers when necessary." Since the identified client's goals have been met, the counselor should continue with pretermination counseling and go forward with the planned termination. The parents would not require an outside referral because treatment plan goals have been met. Church and community connections also serve as ongoing support for the family.

Case Study 7

1. C: Bipolar II disorder requires a major depressive episode; bipolar I does not. Specifically, "Bipolar II disorder, requiring the lifetime experience of at least one episode of major depression and at least one hypomanic episode, is no longer thought to be a milder condition than bipolar I disorder, largely because of the amount of time individuals with this condition spend in depression and because the instability of mood experienced by individuals with bipolar II disorder is typically accompanied by serious impairment in work and social functioning" (American Psychological Association, 2013). Further, bipolar I disorder no longer requires "the lifetime experience of a major depressive episode" (APA, 2013). Lastly, bipolar II no longer requires an episode of mania, but individuals must have a history of at least one hypomanic episode as a requirement for diagnoses.

2. A: The DSM-5 Level 1 Cross-Cutting Symptom Measures is "intended to help clinicians identify additional areas of inquiry that may have significant impact on the individual's treatment and prognosis. In addition, the measure may be used to track changes in the individual's symptom presentation over time (American Psychological Association, 2013)." There are 13 domains for adults, including depression and mania, making DSM-5 Level 1 Cross-Cutting Symptom Measures a solid choice for obtaining baseline data. The Stages of Change Readiness and Treatment Eagerness Scale (SOCRATES) is a self-administered instrument used to help determine an individual's motivation to change alcohol-related behaviors. Level of Care Utilization System (LOCUS) is an assessment instrument specifically designed to determine an appropriate level of care for individuals with addiction and psychiatric comorbidity. Finally, the Psychiatric Rating Scale (BPRS) measures psychosis and psychosis-related symptoms of schizophrenia or major psychotic disorders.

3. C: The best way to engage the client during the initial phase of counseling is to determine her expectations regarding the length of treatment. Strengthening the therapeutic alliance helps engage clients in therapy. The therapeutic alliance is enhanced when the client and therapist work collaboratively to determine agreed-upon tasks and treatment plan goals. The length of time in treatment is a part of informed consent and is documented on the client's treatment plan. Telling the client about your theoretical orientation and experience is incorrect because it does not actively engage the client. Counselors adopting a strengths-based approach are more likely to engage and motivate clients. Answers B and D are incorrect because the focus is on the problem rather than the solution.

4. D: Interpersonal psychotherapy (IPT) is an evidence-based practice for bipolar II disorder that addresses interpersonal deficits, including life transitions, conflict at home or in the work environment, and managing grief and loss. Grief and loss can pertain to losing another person or losing a healthy sense of self. IPT is beneficial for individuals with bipolar II disorder because psychosocial stressors can exacerbate diagnosis-specific symptoms. William Glasser is credited with developing reality therapy, which is based on the assumption that individuals are responsible for appropriately choosing behaviors to meet their goals, desires, and needs. Solution-focused therapy, or solution-focused brief therapy, is grounded in the assumption that individuals can make positive choices and can adopt workable solutions to problems. Acceptance and commitment therapy combines mindfulness and behavioral therapy elements to assist individuals with greater self-acceptance of uncomfortable feelings.

5. B: While all approaches can be used to address the client's concerns, interpersonal social rhythm therapy (IPSRT) would best address the client's level of functioning and clinical symptomatology. IPSRT is a best practice for bipolar disorder and is based on the premise that psychosocial stressors influence biological rhythms. When biological systems, such as the circadian rhythm, are disrupted, symptoms can be exacerbated for individuals experiencing bipolar disorder. The goal of IPST is to restore an individual's social rhythm by enhancing coping skills for stressful life events, regaining healthy routines, and determining how to best return to (or create) appropriate psychosocial and interpersonal rhythms. The client states that unexpected stressors have interrupted her sleep, making IPSRT the best approach for addressing the client's concerns. Mindfulness-based stress reduction (MBSR) uses meditation and relaxation practices to improve depression, anxiety, and pain. MBSR is an appropriate intervention for bipolar disorder but does not explicitly address social, interpersonal, and biological rhythms in the way IPSRT does. Because behavioral modification is a part of IPSRT, behavioral modification alone would not address concerns to the extent that IPSRT does. Rational-emotive behavioral theory is a cognitive theory based on the assumption that maladaptive thoughts contribute to emotional and behavioral difficulties and interfere with positive life experiences. When appropriate, this approach can help with depressive symptoms, however, IPSRT is just as effective for treated bipolar disorder and can address the client's interpersonal stressors, improve self-esteem, and enhance social support required for extended symptom abatement.

6. A: Your ethical obligation is to have written procedures in place and reviewed before or during the client's initial session. Answer B is incorrect. According to the NBCC Code of Ethics (2016), "NCCs shall include all electronic communications exchanged with clients and supervisees, including those through digital technology and social media methods, as a part of the record, even when strictly related to clerical issues such as change of contact information or scheduling appointments." Answer C is incorrect because it includes benefits and harms rather than only specifying harms. The NBCC Code of Ethics states, "NCCs shall recognize the potential harm of informal uses of social media and other related technology with clients, former clients and their families and personal friends." Lastly, the ethical guideline for an online virtual presence included in the ACA Code of Ethics (2014) states, "separate professional and personal web pages and profiles are created to clearly distinguish between the two kinds of virtual presence (ACA, 2014)."

7. C: According to the ACA Code of Ethics (2014), "In addition to the usual and customary protocol of informed consent between counselor and client for face-to-face counseling, [there are] issues, unique to the use of distance counseling, technology, and/or social media, [that] are addressed in the informed consent process." Specifically, counselors must explain that "individuals might have authorized or unauthorized access to such records or transmissions (e.g., colleagues, supervisors, employees, information technologists)" (ACA, 2014). Counselors acknowledge that the lack of visual cues and voice intonations used with electronic communication may affect the counseling process. Finally, counselors inform clients that there is a need to identify alternative methods of service delivery because of the possibility of technology failure.

8. B: Developed by Carl Rogers, client-centered therapy is based on the assumption that incongruence results from a discrepancy between one's self-image and ideal self. Conditions of worth are created when an individual takes on a significant other's condition of regard to the extent that self-experience is circumvented (or pursued). Alfred Adler adopted the belief that feelings of inferiority contribute to a mistaken style of life. According to William Glasser, credited with developing reality therapy, a failure identity occurs when the need for love is met in an irresponsible manner. Reality therapy, also known as control theory, emphasizes the importance of one's need for love and the need to feel worthwhile. Eric Berne, credited with developing transactional analysis, viewed depression and sadness as the result of adopting the "I'm not OK; you're OK" life position.

9. D: Adlerian therapists emphasize the importance of social connection, asserting that all individuals strive for "superiority," which is achieved through a purposeful, goal-oriented lifestyle. Adlerian therapists view maladjustment as the development of a mistaken style of life leading to feelings of inferiority. Transactional analysis uses positions such as "I'm not okay; you're okay" to describe how one views themselves and others. Reality therapists would work to transform a failure identity into a success identity by emphasizing personal choice and a commitment to change. REBT therapists identify the activating event, behavior, and consequences of the behavior (i.e., the ABC model) to help address irrational thinking.

10. D: You accept the gift because rejecting the gift would hurt the client. In weighing beneficence and malfeasance, it can be reasonably determined that rejecting the gift does more harm than accepting it. The gift represents the culmination of hard work and the return to enjoying things she loves. She credits the counselor for helping her through that journey. Therapy is coming to a close, and she has worked hard to achieve personal success. The ACA Code of Ethics (2014) states, "Counselors understand the challenges of accepting gifts from clients and recognize that in some cultures, small gifts are a token of respect and gratitude. When determining whether to accept a gift from clients, counselors take into account the therapeutic relationship, the monetary value of the gift, the client's motivation for giving the gift, and the counselor's motivation for wanting to accept or decline the gift." For this client, the gift's monetary value is of lesser significance than what it represents. The client's culture does not recognize small gifts as a token of respect and gratitude. Lastly, the policy for reciprocating is not necessarily a stipulation for receiving the client's gift.

11. C: The ACA Code of Ethics (2014) states, "Counselors working in an organization (e.g., school, agency, institution) that provides counseling services do not refer clients to their private practice unless the policies of a particular organization make explicit provisions for self-referrals. In such instances, the clients must be informed of other options open to them should they seek private counseling services." The 5-year period following the last professional contact refers to the ethical guideline for sexual or romantic relationships with former clients. Pro bono work is encouraged but generally applies to services to the public, such as speaking fees or sharing professional information.

12. C: The HIPAA Privacy Rule contains provisions about confidential information disclosures to family members. According to the HIPAA Privacy Rule, "Specifically, a covered entity is permitted to share information with a family member or other person involved in an individual's care or payment for care as long as the individual does not object." Specific state laws may differ. For answer A, the ACA Code of Ethics (2014) states, "Counselors limit the access of clients to their records or portions of their records, only when there is compelling evidence that such access would cause harm to the client." Since there is no indication that conversations about marital discord would create harm for the client, answer A is incorrect. However, some stipulations allow portions of a client's record to be removed if there are multiple clients. The ACA Code of Ethics (2014) further states, "in situations involving multiple clients, counselors provide individual clients with only those parts of records that relate directly to them and do not include confidential information related to any other client." Since there is no information indicating that you provided couples counseling, this stipulation does not apply. Counselors must assert counselor-client privilege if records are subpoenaed. Privilege is a legal requirement rather than a HIPAA Privacy Rule. The release of records to third-party payers is prohibited without the client's consent.

13. B: This is an example of congruence. Counselors demonstrate congruence through genuine and authentic feedback. Congruence is a person-centered technique communicated by counselors when their verbal and nonverbal messages are aligned. Along with congruence, empathy is a person-centered facilitative condition. Counselors display empathy when reflecting a client's feelings, thoughts, and perceptions from the client's point of view. An encourager is a verbal or nonverbal signal for the client to continue talking (e.g., saying "Please, go on"). Summarization ties together multiple concepts, feelings, or ideas.

Case Study 8

1. C: The DSM-5 criteria for BED include marked distress regarding binge eating. Dietary restrictions and recurrent compensatory behaviors are criteria associated with bulimia nervosa. Some individuals report dissociation during or immediately after binge eating, but this is not a criterion for BED. According to the DSM-5, "Binge-eating disorder has recurrent binge eating in common with bulimia nervosa but differs from the latter disorder in some fundamental respects. In terms of clinical presentation, the recurrent inappropriate compensatory behavior (e.g., purging, driven exercise) seen in bulimia nervosa is absent in binge-eating disorder. Unlike individuals with bulimia nervosa, individuals with BED typically do not show marked or sustained dietary restrictions designed to influence body weight and shape between binge-eating episodes. They may, however, report frequent attempts at dieting (APA, 2013)."

2. C: There is a high comorbidity rate with general anxiety disorder and BED. According to the DSM-5, "Binge-eating disorder is associated with significant psychiatric comorbidity that is comparable to that of bulimia nervosa and anorexia nervosa. The most common comorbid disorders are bipolar disorders, depressive disorders, anxiety disorders, and, to a lesser degree, substance use disorders. (APA, 2013)." Borderline personality disorder is a differential diagnosis rather than a comorbid condition. The DSM-5 includes binge eating in the impulsive behavior criterion as part of borderline personality disorder. Both diagnoses should be assigned if an individual meets full criteria for borderline personality disorder and binge-eating disorder. Post-traumatic stress disorder and obsessive-compulsive disorder are no longer classified as anxiety disorders as they were in previous versions of the DSM.

3. B: You would first identify behaviors maintaining maladaptive eating. Goals related to the client's maladaptive eating patterns are prioritized because binge-eating disorder is the client's primary diagnosis, and the client has expressed the desire to stop binge eating. There are several areas of exploration for this client, including depressive symptoms, her relationship with her family since coming out, her spirituality, and binge eating. The client prioritized the focus of treatment by stating, "This is starting to affect my health. If I could change anything in my life, it would be to stop binge eating." While treatment engagement is generally accomplished using a strengths-based approach, best practices for eating disorders suggest identifying and changing maladaptive eating first, followed by addressing any underlying issues.

4. B: Counselors do NOT take a direct approach during the initial phases of MI. MI is a person-centered, strengths-based approach used to reduce ambivalence and evoke lasting behavioral change. The counselor functions as a facilitator rather than an expert and guides the patient toward change. At no time is MI direct in nature, even in the initial phases. Counselors using MI emphasize autonomy, self-efficacy, and the use of evocation to elicit change talk.

5. B: The best way to handle your opposing values is to seek professional training in that area and continue to work with the client. Seeking professional training and supervision is designed to honor ethical counseling principles, specifically justice, nonmaleficence, and beneficence, and to preserve a safe counseling environment. According to the ACA Code of Ethics (2014), counselors avoid imposing "their own values, attitudes, beliefs, and behaviors" and "seek training in areas in which they are at risk of imposing their values onto clients, especially when the counselor's values are inconsistent with the client's goals or are discriminatory in nature." The primary focus of treatment must always be the client's goals and desired outcome. When opposing values are brought into the counseling process, the counselor is no longer impartial, and there is a danger of harming the client. Seeking guidance and consultation from the client is incorrect because of the power differential and the counselor's responsibility to obtain professional guidance. Referring the client to another provider is incorrect because "Counselors refrain from referring prospective and current clients based solely on the counselor's personally held values, attitudes, beliefs, and behaviors (ACA, 2014)."

6. C: The counselor's response representing an amplified reflection is: "You're done taking suggestions; it feels like there are no options left for you." Amplified reflections use the client's original statement and over-emphasize their point or intent. The purpose is to push the client past ambivalence and toward change. A simple reflection is represented in answer A: "You've tried exercise and don't think it will work." A simple reflection validates what the client has said and shows that you are listening to her concerns. Stating that it seems like the client may have reached a boiling point is not entirely accurate and illustrates a communication error, specifically a depth error. This occurs when the therapist reads too much into the client's statements. Answer B, which states: "You feel like nothing works, but you remain persistent. Making this change must be really important to you," is an example of reframing. Reframing is used to help the client see the problem from a different and generally more positive perspective.

7. B: Overgeneralization is a maladaptive thinking style that uses one event to create a sweeping rule for all other situations. This is reflected in the client's statement: "I'll never be able to control my eating." The setback is one event, and the general rule for the client is that this setback means the client will never succeed at controlling her eating. Catastrophizing occurs when a person embellishes a situation in such a way that the outcome is exaggerated. (E.g., "This setback means I'm a failure at life!") Dichotomous thinking, or black and white thinking, occurs when one engages in all-or-nothing beliefs. (E.g., "I binged after breakfast. My whole day is ruined.") Self-fulfilling prophecy is used when making future predictions and then acting in ways that guarantee the prediction comes true. (E.g., "I'll always be defined by my weight.")

8. B: SMART goals and objectives are specific, measurable, achievable, realistic, and timely. The counselor and the client construct specific goals and objectives by determining, in detail, what they would like to accomplish. Measurable goals consist of changes that are observable or quantifiable in terms of progress made within a pre-selected timeframe. Goals and objectives must be achievable. The client and counselor set achievable goals by examining the client's internal and external resources, such as personal characteristics and social support. Goals must be realistic or relevant to the client's diagnosis and overall plan for overcoming the presenting problem. Timely goals and objectives are an accurate reflection of the timeframe in which they can realistically be accomplished.

9. A: There are three types of microaggressions: microinsults, microinvalidations, and microassaults. Microinsults are behaviors or comments that are not meant to be discriminatory and generally stem from a lack of awareness and/or reliance on stereotypes. Researchers show that microaggressions are usually cumulative and detrimental to the health and well-being of those who experience them. It is not uncommon for individuals who identify as bisexual to experience biphobia within LGBTQ communities. Microinvalidations occur when comments or experiences are dismissed or seen as irrelevant. Microinvalidations often stem from heterosexism. An example of a microinvalidation would be to assume a married female has a husband. Microassaults are intentionally discriminatory and include purposeful acts of insensitivity, rudeness, and intolerance. Microinjury is not identified as a microaggression.

10. B: Self-determination theory is based on the assumption that people are motivated by competence, connection, and autonomy, which are all required to achieve psychological growth. Self-actualization is a term used by Abraham Maslow that refers to a person's highest level of personal fulfillment. Self-reflection is used in many approaches and is not specifically tied to a desire to have close personal relationships. A self-fulfilling prophecy is used when making future predictions and then acting in ways that guarantee that the prediction comes true.

11. D: Distress tolerance is one out of four DBT skills modules. Distress tolerance teaches clients to accept the present situation and employ coping or survival skills such as self-soothing, distraction, and weighing the pros and cons. Radical acceptance involves adopting a nonjudgmental stance and accepting or tolerating the outcome. The DBT module of core mindfulness is used to help the client remain fully aware and in the present moment. Interpersonal effectiveness uses assertiveness strategies and conflict resolution skills to help clients with interpersonal issues. Lastly, emotional regulation helps clients learn how to accurately label current feelings, decrease reactionary responses, and decrease the intensity of emotional experiences.

12. C: Tipping the decisional balance (DB) is essential for moving the client from the contemplation stage to the preparation stage of change. Prochaska and DiClemente (1984) developed the Transtheoretical Model (TTM) of the Stages of Change Model (SOC) that serves as the foundation for enhanced motivational interviewing (MI). The stages of change are precontemplation, contemplation, preparation, action, and maintenance. Tipping the decisional balance is used to move clients from ambivalence toward commitment and change. DB exercises include examining ambivalence and advocating for change talk. Commitment, activation, and taking steps (CAT) help move clients from preparation to action. Rolling with resistance is used to decrease sustain talk (i.e., what is keeping them in the problem) and is mainly used in the earlier SOC. Flexible pacing is an MI strategy used to help the counselor stay with the client and resist the urge to jump ahead or push the client forward rather than move at their own pace.

13. C: This is an example of central tendency bias. Central tendency bias occurs when a person rates items using only middle scores. This can happen when using a 5-point Likert scale and is prevented by instead using a 4-point Likert scale, which would force an individual's score to fall to the left or right of the center. Leniency bias is when raters use only favorable ratings even though they believe that there is room for improvement. The halo effect is the tendency for a rater to allow one good trait to overshadow others. Individuals engaged in the primacy bias allow information received early on to take precedence over information received later.

Case Study 9

1. A: The client's delusions are persecutory. The DSM-5 recognizes five types of schizophrenic delusions: persecutory, grandiose, somatic, erotomania, and jealousy. Subtypes are determined by the client's primary symptoms and can change over time. Persecutory delusions involve the fixed belief that someone intends to harm the individual. For this client, it is the shadow man. Nihilistic delusions are thoughts that center around the belief that complete devastation or catastrophe is soon approaching. Grandiose delusions occur when there is a preoccupation with believing that one is of great significance, is famous, or has other exceptional talents or traits. Somatic delusions are fixed beliefs concerning one's health or organ functioning.

2. C: The Scale for the Assessment of Positive Symptoms (SAPS) is a standardized testing instrument used to measure the severity of positive symptoms associated with schizophrenia. Positive symptoms include hallucinations, delusions, bizarre behavior, and positive formal thought disorder. Aggressive and agitated behaviors are considered bizarre behavior. Avolition, diminished speech, and social withdrawal are all negative symptoms of schizophrenia. The DSM-5 defines avolition as "An inability to initiate and persist in goal-directed activities. When severe enough to be considered pathological, avolition is pervasive and prevents the person from completing many different types of activities (e.g., work, intellectual pursuits, self-care) (APA, 2013)." Diminished speech, or alogia, involves reduced speech output and decreased verbal fluency. Social withdrawal, or asociality, includes limited social interactions or a lack of interest in socializing.

3. B: The client is experiencing akathisia. Akathisia manifests as nervousness, restlessness, tension, and creates the need for individuals to feel like they constantly need to move. First-generation antipsychotics, such as haloperidol (Haldol), are commonly associated with extrapyramidal side effects (EPS). There are several EPS associated with antipsychotic medications, such as phenothiazine neuroleptics and haloperidol, and many are painful and can be serious if not treated. Dystonia, tardive dyskinesia, and Parkinsonism are all examples of EPS. Dystonia involves involuntary muscle contractions and can occur in various body parts, including the neck, jaw, head, and back. Tardive dyskinesia affects individuals by causing involuntary movements of the tongue and may impede eating and swallowing. Parkinsonism is commonly expressed as unsteadiness and is characterized by a slow, shuffling gait.

4. C: The most ethically sound response is to tell him you will work with him to avoid rehospitalization, and he is not obligated to take medication. Counselors have the ethical obligation to abide by the principles outlined in the American Counseling Association Code of Ethics (2014). Answer C honors the principles of autonomy and justice. Autonomy involves allowing individuals to control the direction of their lives. Justice necessitates fair and equitable treatment. At this juncture, the client is oriented and is not a harm to himself or others. Trust is the cornerstone of counseling, and it is the counselor's responsibility to ensure the counseling environment is safe. All other answer options reflect the notion of a transactional relationship between taking medication and avoiding hospitalization, which creates a power imbalance between the client and counselor and can impede the client's growth and autonomy.

5. B: Universality helps members feel less isolated and alone by learning that others share some of the same issues and problems. Psychosocial interventions are included in best practices for individuals with schizophrenia. Treatment generally consists of psychoeducation and social skills training, with group therapy serving as the primary treatment modality. Cohesiveness is the *we* aspect of group therapy. It is different from universality in that cohesiveness reflects unified members, whereas universality is experienced when one realizes they are not alone. The installation of hope helps members have a positive outlook on the future. Catharsis is the release of feelings expressed in a safe group environment.

6. A: Teaching the importance of medication compliance is least indicative of a process-oriented group. Psychoeducational groups are content oriented and focus on teaching and conceptual learning. According to Yalom & Leszcz (2005), "While content involves looking at what specifically was said, process involves looking at the how and the why behind what was said." Trained counselors use process-oriented groups to assess interpersonal or intragroup interactions, introduce silence, and identify and discuss group themes and patterns. Although psychoeducation can be integrated into process groups, it is content oriented rather than process oriented.

7. D: Families high in emotional expression ascribe symptoms of mental disorders to internal attributes (e.g., personality, intentionality). The fundamental attribution error occurs when people overemphasize personality traits and disregard situational or external explanations for behavior. Psychoeducation for families high in emotional expression uses a revised attribution model to help families shift from attributing behavior to personality towards attributing behavior to illness. Self-serving bias occurs when individuals assume personal success related to internal attributes and personal failures are related to external attributes. Individuals with an external locus of control believe that luck, environment, or other external features serve as explanations for events or outcomes. The Dunning-Kruger effect occurs when there is an overestimation of personal knowledge and skills due to an inaccurate self-appraisal.

8. D: Linking is the leadership skill used to connect members and facilitate cohesion and universality. Leaders promote group cohesion or a group's sense of solidarity by creating a sense of belonging and connection. Universality involves learning that other people share similar thoughts, feelings, and experiences. Chaining is a behavioral intervention based on operant conditioning and is used to master complex sequences of behaviors. Chaining occurs through the association of responses such that each response acts as the stimulus for the following response. Pacing is a group leadership skill used to attend to the emotional intensity of a group. Sculpting is a human validation process family therapy technique used to position family members in a way that illustrates significant aspects of the family unit.

9. A: Gestalt therapists would use the concept of projection to explain the client's interaction with his parents. Projection is the tendency to discount one's role in an event and instead assign blame to others. Projection is common among individuals who, like the client, exhibit paranoia and suspicion. Introjection is the opposite of projection in that blame is assigned to oneself rather than the environment. Introjection involves psychologically swallowing information in the environment without proper analysis, judgment, or discernment. Introjection consists of doing what others would like one to do. Retroflection, which is translated into "turning back sharply against," is doing to oneself what one would do to others. Lastly, confluence occurs when there is no delineation between self and others. Confluence can manifest into resentment and intolerance of oneself and others.

10. A: Inference chaining is an REBT technique used to explore personal meanings associated with delusions. Inference chaining is used in rational-emotive therapy and is particularly effective for individuals experiencing delusions. The technique is used at the beginning of treatment to understand the underlying belief used to sustain the delusion. Linking is then used to gradually test reality by introducing other plausible explanations, with the overarching goal of decreasing distress created by the delusion. Normalizing is an effective cognitive-behavioral technique used to help process hallucinations. The stress-vulnerability model is used to normalize experiences associated with the onset of hallucinations and co-occurring stressors. Emotion-based reasoning was used by Aaron Beck, credited for developing cognitive-behavioral therapy. Emotional-based reasoning describes the maladaptive process in which delusions are categorized and involves believing that one's emotional experiences dictate reality.

11. C: Peripheral questioning is used to investigate alternative explanations for the client's delusions (e.g., "How do you know the shadow man is poisoning your food? What methods would he use to do this?"). This technique focuses on the client's specific symptoms to understand their origins and plausibility. Slowly, incremental reality testing is used to present hypotheses for alternative explanations. This technique helps reduce blame and enhances the therapeutic alliance. Scaling questions are associated with solution-focused brief therapy and are used to help clients track progress towards identified goals. For example, "Where are you on a 1-10 scale concerning the resolution of your problem?" Unified detachment is a technique used in integrative behavioral couple therapy (IBCT) involving communication in a detached and non-accusatory manner. Symptom analysis is a Jungian therapy technique used to help individuals achieve a state of individuation and self-realization.

12. B: The operant conditioning principle underlying cueing, coaching, and prompting is discriminative stimuli. Discriminative stimuli is based on the premise that certain behaviors were reliably reinforced in the past. These reinforced behaviors now serve as the antecedent stimulus that increases the probability of a response because of a history of reinforcing selected behavior (i.e., differential reinforcement). Modeling is a social learning concept, making it incorrect. Environmental restructuring influences behavior by permanently changing one's physical surroundings. Behavioral practice is a component of social skills training but is different than discriminative stimuli in that it involves repeating the learned skill until it reaches the point where it can be successfully generalized to real-life encounters.

13. A: Gestalt therapists use the technique of adding, "... and I take responsibility for it" at the end of client statements. Gestalt therapy is centered in the present moment and is designed to raise awareness of blocks to self-growth through the promotion of personal responsibility. Transactional analysis therapists use parent, adult, and child ego states to represent patterns of thinking, feeling, and acting. Techniques for transactional analysis include game and script analysis. ACT combines mindfulness and behavioral therapy to assist individuals with greater self-acceptance of uncomfortable feelings. ACT techniques include cognitive diffusion and creating a life compass. Finally, MI is a counseling approach that uses multiple strategies to evoke change, including developing discrepancy and rolling with resistance.

Case Study 10

1. A: Criteria for ODD include emotional dysregulation, while CD does not. Both ODD and CD include the criterion of conflict with authority. Only CD includes the destruction of property and cruelty to animals. It is important to distinguish between ODD and CD, and the DSM-5 makes that distinction in the differential diagnosis section. The differential diagnosis section can be found after the diagnostic criteria, along with additional text descriptions such as diagnostic features. According to the DSM-5, "Conduct disorder and oppositional defiant disorder are both related to conduct problems that bring the individual in conflict with adults and other authority figures (e.g., teachers, work supervisors). The behaviors of oppositional defiant disorder are typically of a less severe nature than those of conduct disorder and do not include aggression toward people or animals, destruction of property, or a pattern of theft or deceit. Furthermore, oppositional defiant disorder includes problems of emotional dysregulation (i.e., angry and irritable mood) that are not included in the definition of conduct disorder (APA, 2013)."

2. B: Oppositional defiant disorder is classified with disruptive, impulse control, and conduct disorder. Other diagnoses listed in this classification include intermittent explosive disorder, conduct disorder, antisocial personality disorder, pyromania, kleptomania, and other specified and unspecified disruptive, impulse-control, and conduct disorders. According to the DSM-5, "the disorders in this chapter are unique in that these problems are manifested in behaviors that violate the rights of others (e.g., aggression, destruction of property) and/or that bring the individual into significant conflict with societal norms or authority figures (APA, 2013)." While the diagnosis of ADHD is highly comorbid with ODD, ADHD belongs to the neurodevelopmental disorders category. Bipolar and related disorders include bipolar 1, bipolar 2, and cyclothymic disorder. Trauma and stressor related disorders include reactive attachment disorder, social engagement disorder, posttraumatic stress disorder, acute stress disorder, other specified trauma-and-stressor-related disorder, and unspecified trauma-and stressor-related disorder.

3. B: Providing clear expectations is reflective of the PGM's current learning needs. We gather from the intake session that the PGM has restricted the client from every single privilege indefinitely. The PGM has told the client that she can regain privileges once she learns to act her age. The best response targets the vague expectation for the client to act her age. You can provide effective parenting training by helping the PGM operationally define what it means for the client to act her age and how to state expectations in the affirmative (i.e., instruct the client on what she should do rather than what she shouldn't do). An example of a clear and positive directive is, "It's time for you to brush your teeth." rather than, "Stop playing. You know it's your bedtime." Further, by taking away privileges indefinitely, the PGM has no additional recourse for correcting subsequent misbehavior. While all other answer options are invaluable parenting strategies, insufficient information matches the alternative behaviors to the PGMs' needs. For example, we do not know if she is ignoring negative behavior, which appropriate behaviors she chooses to ignore, and when.

We also do not know if there is consistent follow through, nor do we know the manner in which she provides directives.

4. D: Murray Bowen is known for multigenerational (extended) family systems therapy. The multigenerational transmission process is a Bowenian technique used to assess how a family's dysfunctional interactions can be handed down from generation to generation. Bowen was the first to introduce the genogram, a visual depiction of a family's generational interactions, and significant patterns of relationships. Salvador Minuchin is associated with structural family therapy. Jay Haley is known for strategic family therapy. Finally, Virginia Satir pioneered the human validation process model of family therapy.

5. D: Given the client's clinical presentation, the best approach for your first session is to engage her in a therapeutic art activity. During the initial intake, the client proudly shared that her artwork came in 1st place. Focusing on the client's strengths rather than the client's clinical pathology helps establish a therapeutic alliance. The client has little to no contact with her parents, exhibits ODD behaviors at home and school, and is academically below grade level. Thus, the client's social, emotional, and academic needs likely contribute to strained relationships with authority and have a higher probability of eliciting negative feedback. Identifying maladaptive cognitions is incorrect due to the client's cognitive functioning. Establishing treatment plan goals is best accomplished after collecting relevant information from the client's teacher and grandmother. Processing grief and loss issues, as it pertains to separation from her parents, is important but will likely be more effective after establishing the therapeutic alliance.

6. A: SFBT is a short-term, solution-oriented approach used to help clients improve motivation and make measurable behavioral changes. The "miracle question" is a solution-focused technique that helps clients envision their future without the problem. Person-centered therapy uses the core facilitative conditions of unconditional positive regard, empathy, and genuineness. REBT is based on the assumption that irrational or self-defeating beliefs help the client stay "stuck" and serve as barriers to change. DBT is a type of CBT that involves teaching the skills of mindfulness, distress tolerance, interpersonal effectiveness, and emotional regulation.

7. A: The Achenbach Child Behavior Checklist (CBCL) helps detect social and emotional problems, including disorders such as ADHD, ODD, and other conduct problems. The CBCL detects DSM-specific symptoms in the following six categories: affective problems, anxiety problems, somatic problems, ADHD, oppositional defiant problems, and conduct problems. The CBCL also provides information on eight syndrome scales, including aggressive behavior, social issues, and rule-breaking behavior. The Brief Symptoms Inventory-18 (BSI-18) is an 18-item assessment that provides information on three subscales: somatization, depression, and anxiety. The Woodcock-Johnson IV (WJ IV) is an intelligence test that evaluates a wide range of cognitive functions with three batteries: the WJ IV Tests of Cognitive Abilities, the WJ IV Tests of Oral Language, and the WJ IV Tests of Achievement.

8. D: Reproduction is a social learning concept rather than a key principle of operant conditioning. There are four phases of social learning: (1) attention (i.e., noticing a particular behavior; (2) retention (i.e., remembering the information); (3) reproduction (i.e., imitating the behavior); and (4) motivation (i.e., the desire to imitate the behavior). Principles of operant conditioning include extinction, punishment, reinforcement, and stimulus control. For extinction to occur, there must first be a reinforced response. Extinction happens when the reinforcer for that response is stopped, which lessens the possibility of the behavior's recurrence. In operant conditioning, punishment is the presentation or removal of a circumstance or stimulus, resulting in the decreased probability of that response occurring. Finally, stimulus control is the process in which behavioral responses differentially happen in the presence or absence of particular stimuli.

9. C: Criterion-referenced measurements compare a person's knowledge of skills against a predetermined standard. For example, goal attainment scaling is a criterion-referenced measure because it measures the client's targeted behaviors, which is the predetermined standard or criterion. The client's progress is compared with previous scores. Criterion-referenced tests often use cut scores to categorize predetermined standards. For example, the goal attainment scaling scores can be used to determine minimum, moderate, and significant improvement. Norm-referenced measurements compare a person's knowledge or skills against a normed group, which can be ranked on a bell curve and compared with another person with similar traits. Examples of norm-referenced measures include pediatric growth charts or the SATs.

10. C: Goal Attainment Scaling (GAS) is a criterion-referenced, collaborative goal setting method that allows participants to measure three targeted behaviors. The targeted behaviors can be transferred to the client's treatment plan, with goals and objectives designed to measure incremental changes. For each targeted behavior, minimum, moderate, and significant improvement measures are used to determine the client's progress. SMART goal setting uses the SMART acronym to guide goal setting. SMART goals are specific, measurable, achievable, relevant, and time sensitive. A Behavior Intervention Plan (B.I.P.) is generally implemented as part of a student's Individualized Education Plan (I.E.P.) or 504 plan. The function of the B.I.P. is to identify problematic behaviors, determine their cause, and implement strategies that reward appropriate behavior. A Functional Behavioral Assessment (F.B.A.) entails identifying problematic behavior, measuring the behavior, and determining the function of the behavior.

11. B: Brief strategic family therapy (BSFT) uses reframing and restructuring after joining with the family and diagnosing the problem. BSFT is an evidence-based practice for ODD grounded in the here-and-now, emphasizes process over content, and includes techniques such as reframing and restructuring. Reframing, a form of restructuring, is used to help clients view situations, feelings, and relationships in a more positive light. Counselors use restructuring by instructing families to interact during the therapy session. This allows counselors to assess family dynamics (e.g., boundaries and alliances) and restructure family systems by providing alternative ways for members to behave and communicate. Linking is a group leadership skill used to help members relate to one another's challenges, solutions, and other shared experiences. Pacing occurs when counselors attend to the emotional intensity of a session. Brief strategic family therapists use enactments, while human validation process model family therapists use sculpting. Counselors use enactments by having family members talk to one another rather than the counselor. Enactments help illustrate relationship patterns and identify patterns and roles requiring modification. Sculpting is a non-verbal technique where the counselor physically arranges family members to help them envision aspects of emotional closeness or distance. Chaining, which refers to reinforcing the totality of a sequence of behaviors, is a behavioral therapy technique. Finally, modeling, which is necessary for imitation, is a component of social learning theory.

12. B: Extinction is demonstrated when the client's temper tantrums, which were previously reinforced with attention, are ignored and, as a result, discontinue. Ignoring the behavior does not automatically stop the behavior. For extinction to occur, the behavior must have previously been reinforced, and the behavior must stop after ignoring the same behavior. Punishment is illustrated when the client loses a portion of her allowance due to refusing to do a chore. One way to differentiate punishment from other aspects of PMT is that punishment refers to methods that decrease a specific behavior. Fading involves the progressive removal of prompts that were previously (and successfully) used when telling the client to stay in her seat. Fading is used after the response is consistently performed without prompts. Finally, the end goal of shaping is known as the terminal response.

13. A: The best course of action is to terminate the counseling relationship and offer appropriate referrals. The client has met her short-term goals and her treatment is nearing completion. Policies related to termination, payment, and insurance coverage are all part of informed consent. Informed consent is reviewed during the initial intake and continues throughout treatment. According to the American Mental Health Counselor Association (AMHCA) Code of Ethics (2020), "CMHCs may terminate a counseling relationship when clients do not pay fees charged or when insurance denies treatment. In such cases, appropriate referrals are offered to the clients." Bartering is unethical in this situation because it is initiated by the counselor. According to the American Counseling Association (ACA) code of ethics (2014), "Counselors may barter only if the bartering does not result in exploitation or harm, if the client requests it, and if such arrangements are an accepted practice among professionals in the community. Counselors consider the cultural implications of bartering and discuss relevant concerns with clients and document such agreements in a clear written contract." There is not a need to avoid client abandonment due to the conditions outlined in the informed consent. While providing pro bono services is encouraged, there are potential downfalls with providing services free or at a reduced cost. If you are not applying the same rate to all of your clients, this may be perceived as discrimination. Suspending services indefinitely is problematic simply because you may not know if or when the client's insurance will be reinstated. Additionally, medical necessity may be questioned because of the requirement to provide medically justifiable treatment (i.e., the right intensity, duration, and frequency) matching the client's current needs.

Case Study 11

1. B: Of the symptoms listed, self-oriented perfectionism regarding performance, appearance, and routine is not a diagnostic criterion of body dysmorphic disorder. Instead, this rigid perfectionism is a pathological personality trait associated with obsessive-compulsive personality disorder. While there is an element of perfectionism with BDD, it is limited to one's appearance rather than an aspect of extreme conscientiousness, which insists that all things must be perfect. According to the DSM-5, the diagnostic criteria for BDD include "A. Preoccupation with one or more perceived defects or flaws in physical appearance that are not observable or appear slight to others. B. At some point during the course of the disorder, the individual has performed repetitive behaviors (e.g., mirror checking, excessive grooming, skin picking, reassurance seeking) or mental acts (e.g., comparing his or her appearance with that of others) in response to the appearance concerns. C. The preoccupation causes clinically significant distress or impairment in social, occupational, or other important areas of functioning. D. The appearance preoccupation is not better explained by concerns with body fat or weight in an individual whose symptoms meet diagnostic criteria for an eating disorder (APA, 2013)."

2. A: The Beck Scale for Suicide Ideation (SSI) is a 21-item scale measuring the intensity, frequency, and duration of suicidal attitudes, plans, and behaviors in the last 7 days. Measurements include the number of previous suicide attempts, deterrents to suicide, and the amount of time spent preparing and contemplating the last attempt. In addition to determining a suicide probability score, the Suicidal Probability Scale (SPS) measures suicidal ideation, hopelessness, hostility, and negative self-evaluation. The SPS is a 36-item self-report inventory. The Hamilton Rating Scale for Depression (HRSD) is an interviewer-administered measure of depression and suicidality. Finally, the Columbia Suicide Severity Rating Scale (C-SSRS) calculates suicidal risk, assesses suicidal attitudes and behaviors, and determines risk and protective factors.

3. B: There is no empirical evidence supporting no-suicide contracts for safety. Historically, clinicians have asked clients to sign no-suicide contracts indicating that they would not act on suicidal thoughts or reach out for support when experiencing suicidality. Not only do no-suicide contracts lack empirical evidence, but critics believe there can be an implication of coercion from the counselor due to concerns over professional protection and liability. Instead, a collaborative, strengths-based approach to safety planning is thought to empower the client and enhance the therapeutic alliance. There are various evidence-based components to treatment planning, including but not limited to: identifying early warning signs, using distractions when feeling suicidal, identifying social and emergency supports, identifying coping strategies, and making the environment safe.

4. D: Instructing the client to gradually face feared social situations without performing ritualized tasks (e.g., mirror-checking) is known as exposure and response prevention (ERP). Exposure and response prevention, also known as ritual prevention, is an evidence-based practice for BDD treatment. ERP involves suggesting that the client remain in social situations until the urge to ask for reassurance or engage in mirror-checking decreases noticeably. Anxiety habituation occurs when the desire for the client to engage in mirror-checking discontinues indefinitely. Cognitive defusion, also called deliteralization, is used in acceptance and commitment therapy (ACT). The goal of cognitive defusion is to recognize and detach from thoughts that contribute to increased anxiety. Behavioral activation is a treatment for depression that involves identifying and initiating values-based activities to help lift depression rather than waiting for depression to lift before participating in values-based activities. Distress tolerance is a dialectical behavior therapy (DBT) technique that teaches radical acceptance of the present situation by using coping skills such as self-soothing and distraction.

5. C: This is an example of personalization. Personalization is a cognitive distortion that involves a person believing that they are being targeted by someone else's behavior (e.g., laughing) when it has nothing to do with that person. All-or-nothing thinking is synonymous with black-and-white thinking and polarized thinking (e.g., "If I'm not perfect, then I'm nothing"). Emotional reasoning results from believing that one's feelings are facts, despite contradictory evidence (e.g., "I feel deformed and worthless, so I must be that way").

6. D: Asking yourself if you want your behavior reported in the press (publicity) best helps finalize this decision. The American Counseling Association's (ACA) *Practitioner's Guide to Ethical Decision-Making* provides a framework emphasizing the following steps, "1. Identify the problem. 2. Apply the ACA Code of Ethics. 3. Determine the nature and dimensions of the dilemma. 4. Generate potential courses of action. 5. Consider the potential consequences of all options and determine a course of action. 6. Evaluate the selected course of action. 7. Implement the course of action (Forester-Miller & Davis, 2016)." When evaluating the selected course of action, there are three tests to help ensure the action is appropriate. The tests honor the principles of justice, publicity, and universality. According to the framework: "Justice: In applying the test of justice, assess your sense of fairness by determining whether you would treat others the same in this situation. Publicity: For the test of publicity, ask yourself whether you would want your behavior reported in the press. Universality: The test of universality asks you to assess whether you could recommend the same course of action to another counselor in the same situation (Forester-Miller & Davis, 2016)." Asking if there are legal implications to this decision is a consideration for step 1 of the decision-making model. The question regarding faithful fulfillment (fidelity) of this obligation is reviewed in step 3. According to the ACA's decision-making framework, step 3 uses the core principles of autonomy, justice, beneficence, nonmaleficence, and fidelity to examine the dimensions of the dilemma. Asking if this decision would harm the client applies the principle of nonmaleficence.

7. A: Distance counseling, technology, and social media use is covered in section H of the ACA Code of Ethics (2014). Concerning social media, counselors must refrain from viewing a client's personal or public social media profile without permission. Confidentiality and its limitations must be addressed in terms of potential unauthorized and authorized electronic records and their transmissions. Answer B is incorrect because counselors are encouraged to keep their personal and professional accounts separate. For answer C, developing informed consent procedures covering issues such as the possibility of technology failure and emergency policies is correct, but addressing the increased risk for harmful boundary violations (e.g., sexual relationships, exploitation) is incorrect because counselors are solely responsible for protecting clients from harm and eliminating risks. Boundary violations are not only unethical but may also have legal implications. Lastly, according to the ACA Code of Ethics, "counselors are prohibited from engaging in a personal virtual relationship with individuals with whom they have a current counseling relationship (e.g., through social and other media) (ACA, 2014)." The 5-year timeframe refers to sexual relationships. Specifically, "client interactions or relationships with former clients, their romantic partners, or their family members are prohibited for a period of 5 years following the last professional contact (ACA, 2014)."

8. B: The best response is: "How does preoccupation with your appearance stop you from participating in life?" Individuals with BDD often exhibit poor insight due to delusional beliefs about their appearance and delusions of reference. Experts suggest psychoeducation, coupled with empathy and a non-judgmental stance, can help improve insight and increase motivation to change. Experts advise against arguing or disagreeing with inaccurate perceptions, which makes answer A incorrect. Core beliefs and individual schemas can contribute to inaccurate perceptions, particularly when the perceptions are tied to poor self-worth; however, answer C is incorrect because an individual must first develop insight and motivation prior to tying cognitive distortions to core beliefs from childhood. Recording thoughts and feelings is helpful for examining cognitive distortions; however, this response is less likely to help improve insight and increase motivation to change.

9. C: This is an example of a core belief. Core beliefs are generally long-held, rigid, and pervasive beliefs that are often formed in childhood. The client equates his external attributes, which are distorted perceptions, with being unworthy or unloved. Cognitive restructuring is one mode of CBT used to address core beliefs. Intermediate beliefs occur between automatic thoughts and core beliefs. When an automatic thought (i.e., an immediate internal reaction) is generated, there is an intermediate process involving conditions and rules. For example, "If my appearance were not defective, I would be successful and worthy." Intermediate thoughts categorize these assumptions and are driven by core beliefs. Automatic thoughts are immediate, knee-jerk reactions to events or situations. Not all automatic thoughts are negative. It is the unhelpful automatic thoughts that counselors must help clients identify when using cognitive restructuring and other CBT techniques. Hot thoughts are automatic thoughts that happen along with an emotional change.

10. C: Unlike therapies such as psychoanalysis, CBT does not emphasize unconscious experiences. Completing homework is an expectation of CBT, which is necessary for applying what is learned in therapy to real-world experiences. CBT practitioners use Socratic questioning to help understand the client's underlying cognitions. CBT is a structured and directive approach, with the counselor working collaboratively with the client and functioning as a coach or teacher.

11. B: Graded exposure is a process that works by incrementally exposing the client to fears previously arranged on a fear hierarchy. Graded exposure is one component of exposure and response prevention (ERP). Graded exposure is used to gradually increase exposure to higher anxiety-provoking situations until the fear naturally subsides without the client performing ritualistic behaviors, such as mirror-checking. Systematic desensitization is a process that combines exposure with relaxation techniques. Flooding involves exposing the client to the highest level of anxiety-provoking stimuli from the beginning, rather than starting with the lower levels and building up. Subjective units of distress (SUD) measure perceived stress. SUDs are generally measured on a 0-100 scale and correspond to the client's individualized fear hierarchy. Graded exposure involves starting with exposure exercises with the lowest SUD measures first.

12. B: Wearing a beanie or hoodie while away from home is a safety behavior. Safety behaviors are used to prevent, diminish, or escape what is perceived as a feared catastrophe. Like other avoidance behaviors, safety behaviors create a positive feedback loop that reinforces anxiety due to cognitive misattributions of safety. Complying with his SSRI medication is not considered to be a safety behavior. Unlike fast-acting medications such as benzodiazepines, SSRIs do not provide immediate onset. Carrying a fast-acting medication such as a benzodiazepine would qualify as a safety behavior. Agreeing to contact the counselor if he is experiencing suicidal ideation is not classified as a ritualistic safety behavior. Core beliefs, which are generally long held, rigid, and pervasive, contribute to the client's anxiety rather than ensuring safety.

13. C: Booster sessions occur after treatment has ended and provide a way for clients to assess progress, maintain learned skills, and prevent relapse. Relapse prevention (RP) is an evidence-based practice for BDD. RP is a process in which skills are reviewed, potential challenges are addressed, and the idea of self-therapy is discussed. RP takes place prior to termination and during future pre-planned booster sessions. Value-based living is a component of acceptance and commitment therapy (ACT). Value-based living is an intervention that can help individuals with BDD de-emphasize the importance of attraction by focusing on other values in one's life. Psychoeducation is generally used at the beginning of treatment for individuals with BDD to help improve insight. Mentorship is not a component of relapse prevention.

NCMHCE Practice Test #2

Case Study 1

PART ONE

INTAKE

CLIENT

Age: 25

Sex: Male

Gender: Male

Sexuality: Heterosexual

Ethnicity: Caucasian

Relationship Status: Single

Counseling Setting: Counseling Clinic

Type of Counseling: Individual

Presenting Problem: Depression and Suicidal Ideation

Diagnosis: Major Depressive Disorder, Recurrent, Mild (F33.0)

PRESENTING PROBLEM:

You are a resident in counseling practicing in a private practice agency. During the initial counseling session, the 25-year-old single male client reports feeling depressed and hopeless. He has difficulty enjoying activities that he has enjoyed in the past and feels unsatisfied with most areas of his life. The client identifies that he is not happy at work and wants to make a career change. The client verbalizes feeling sad more often than not, and that this has been going on for about 2 years. The client decided to start counseling when he began experiencing suicidal thoughts. The client reports no plan or intent to attempt suicide but is concerned about his own well-being.

MENTAL STATUS EXAM:

The client appears to not have bathed recently because his hair is greasy and unkempt. The client has food stains on his clothing; however, he is dressed appropriately for the season. His motor movements are within normal limits. He is engaged in therapy, but he appears anxious as evidenced by hesitating before speaking and by his hand wringing. The client reports suicidal ideation with no plan or intent. The client reports a depressed mood more often than not and difficulty enjoying most activities. The client is oriented to person, place, time, and situation. The client reports that his appetite has increased lately and that he is experiencing hypersomnia.

FAMILY HISTORY:

The client reports that he has two younger brothers who are 19 and 22 years old. His parents divorced when he was 10 years old, and he grew up living with his mother but maintained a strong consistent relationship with his father. The client reports no history of trauma, neglect, physical abuse, sexual abuse, or emotional abuse. The client denies drug or alcohol use, although he reports that his father previously was an active alcoholic.

1. What would be the most appropriate short-term goal for management of depression symptoms?

a. Improve happiness
b. Improve hygiene
c. Change careers
d. Improve self-talk

2. Due to your observation of anxious behavior, you prompt the client to identify and rate his feelings at the start and end of the session. What would be the main purpose of this therapeutic intervention in the first session?

a. To facilitate discussion regarding goals for anxiety management
b. To determine the client's level of comfort
c. To facilitate the client's awareness of his anxious behavior
d. To determine if the counselor can meet the needs of the client

3. What area is most important for you to further assess to confirm a diagnosis of major depressive disorder, recurrent, mild?

a. The timeline of the depressive symptoms
b. The association of symptoms to drug and alcohol use
c. The presence or absence of social supports
d. Functioning at work, home, and socially

4. Due to the client's reported suicidal ideation, which of the following would be an appropriate intervention regarding management of suicide risk?

a. Coordinate for placement in a psychiatric hospital to safely address the crisis.
b. Create a safety plan.
c. Encourage the client to stay with his girlfriend so he is not alone.
d. Provide psychoeducation on cognitive reframing in order to manage depressive symptoms.

5. Which one of the following would be the most appropriate frequency for sessions based on the client's present suicidal ideation?

a. Weekly
b. Twice weekly
c. Fortnightly (every other week)
d. Daily

Part Two

First Session, 2 Weeks After the Initial Intake

The client reports that he has been sleeping more than usual and that this is affecting his ability to get to work on time. He reports that his boss started noticing his tardiness and has given him a verbal warning. Combined with the fear of losing his job, he expressed worry regarding increased conflict with his girlfriend and feeling more "on edge."

6. The client asks the clinician to call his girlfriend for some more insight into how depression is affecting his functioning. What is important to obtain in order to facilitate this collaboration?

a. Verbal consent from the client to collaborate with his girlfriend
b. A signed informed consent form
c. A signed release of protected health information (PHI)
d. A written and signed letter of consent from the client

7. Due to the client's difficulty with sleep, you provide psychoeducation on sleep hygiene. Sleep hygiene involves all of the following foci EXCEPT:

a. Room temperature
b. Time of initiation of sleep and time of waking
c. Maintaining 9 to 12 hours of sleep per 24 hours for a 25-year-old
d. Mindfulness activities prior to bed

8. You were a supervisor in a previous job and have experience supervising employees who are tardy. What should you do to support this client with improving his situation at work?

a. Tell the client about your experience as a supervisor and ways that you supported employees in improving attendance.
b. Reinforce the message that the client needs to improve his attendance or his job may be affected further.
c. Provide the client with psychoeducation on sleep hygiene.
d. Encourage the client to explain his struggle with managing sleep to his supervisor in order to increase the supervisor's empathetic response.

9. All of the following interventions are clinically appropriate therapeutic approaches to treating major depressive disorder, recurrent, mild EXCEPT:

a. Support groups
b. Cognitive behavioral therapy (CBT)
c. Referral for psychiatric medication management
d. Referral for electroconvulsive therapy

Part Three

Second Session, 3 Weeks After the Initial Intake

The client contacted you to reschedule a session sooner than the one you had originally scheduled. The client reported that he continues to have difficulty getting to work on time and was told that he needs to meet with his supervisor on Friday. The client expresses anxiety surrounding this because he worries about getting fired. The client began to cry during the session when talking about worry regarding being unemployed. The client came to the session in clothes that had stains on them, and his hair was messy and appeared greasy.

10. Due to increased anxiety and depressive symptoms, you choose to use CBT techniques. Which of the following would be an intervention used in CBT?

a. Cognitive restructuring or reframing
b. Reality acceptance
c. Assess for readiness for change
d. Operant conditioning

11. Which of the following is the least appropriate way to support a client who is crying during a therapy session?

a. Using empathy
b. Providing self-disclosure so the client does not feel alone
c. Using immediacy
d. Normalizing the client's emotions

12. Which assessment would be helpful in monitoring progress in this client's management of depressive symptoms?

a. Patient Health Questionnaire-9
b. Minnesota-Multiphasic Personality Inventory-2
c. Five Facet Mindfulness Questionnaire
d. Pittsburgh Sleep Quality Index

13. During the session, the client states, "Why should I even try to get to work on time? I'm just going to get fired anyway." Which one of the following would be the most accurate cognitive distortion to describe this statement?

a. Emotional reasoning
b. Overgeneralization
c. Labeling
d. Jumping to conclusions

Case Study 2

PART ONE

INTAKE

CLIENT

Age: 54

Sex: Male

Gender: Male

Sexuality: Heterosexual

Ethnicity: Multiracial

Relationship Status: Divorced

Counseling Setting: Local Government Mental Health Agency

Type of Counseling: Individual

Presenting Problem: Opioid Use

Diagnosis: Opioid Use Disorder, Severe (F11.20), Homelessness (Z59.0)

PRESENTING PROBLEM:

You are a mental health counselor working at a local government mental health agency, specializing in substance use counseling. An individual came in today to become a client for mental health case management and was encouraged to meet with a counselor to begin receiving therapy. The 54-year-old male client is currently living in a tent in the woods behind a local grocery store and reports that he lost his job a year ago following a divorce from his wife of 26 years. The client stated that about 3 years ago he had a back injury and following surgery was prescribed oxycodone. The client continued that he had difficulty stopping his use of the medication when the prescription ran out and connected with a friend to get fentanyl. He reports that he spends a lot of time on a street corner asking for money to get fentanyl and that he cannot seem to go a day without it. The client feels that he cannot sleep or function without the use of fentanyl and that this has affected his housing, marriage, employment, and social life. He acknowledges that fentanyl has negatively affected his life and that he is not sure if he wants to stop using it because he knows it would be hard to deal with life without it.

MENTAL STATUS EXAM:

The client has not maintained hygiene, as evidenced by him not smelling clean and wearing clothes that are visibly dirty. He appears to have bilateral tremors in his hands. The client is oriented to person, place, situation, and time. The client appears malnourished because he is very thin and frail.

FAMILY HISTORY:

The client got divorced about 1 year ago. He states that his wife left him because he lost his job and because of his fentanyl use. The client has two children that are 18 and 22 years old. The client no longer has contact with his ex-wife or children. The client reports no known mental health history or substance use history in his family.

1. If you did not specialize in working with individuals who struggle with opioid addiction, which of the following would be the most ethical decision to make with treatment planning?

a. Pursue further education on opioid addiction counseling.
b. Provide a referral for another counselor who specializes in opioid addiction counseling.
c. Use motivational interviewing techniques because these are effective with substance use disorders.
d. Refer the client to a Narcotics Anonymous group.

2. Because you do have experience counseling individuals with substance use, you decide to use a motivational interviewing approach for this client. Which of the following statements defines the focus of motivational interviewing?

a. Changing unhealthy behaviors in order to improve functioning
b. Challenging irrational thoughts and feelings in order to create more productive beliefs
c. Facilitating and creating an internal desire for change
d. Focusing on improving present situations and relationships, rather than examining past events

3. According to Abraham Maslow's hierarchy of needs, which of the following would be the most appropriate area of clinical focus at the start of therapy?

a. Begin substance use counseling to support the client in abstaining from fentanyl use.
b. Support the client by providing referrals to local soup kitchens and processing barriers to housing.
c. Assist the client with processing his feelings regarding cessation of fentanyl use.
d. Encourage the client to reach out to his children to develop a support system.

4. The client signs a release of protected health information (PHI) for his primary care physician (PCP). Which of the following would be the most ethical level of disclosure of PHI to provide to the PCP?

a. Provide minimal information regarding the client's mental health's effects on his physical health.
b. Provide information on treatment participation and progress.
c. Provide the client's progress notes and treatment plan.
d. Provide a biopsychosocial assessment so that the PCP has a well-rounded view of the client.

5. Which one of the following controlled substances is also an opioid?

a. Cocaine
b. Marijuana
c. Heroin
d. LSD

Part Two

First Session, 1 Week After the Initial Intake

The client discusses how his case manager has gotten him into a shelter and is currently working on securing housing for him. The client processes feelings surrounding the shelter and has begun a detox program for his fentanyl addiction. The client verbalizes that he is experiencing anxiety surrounding being at meetings with the case manager, talking with other residents, reintegrating into a "more normal life," and worrying about whether he can ever have a relationship with his kids or ex-wife if he gets sober. Through processing, you realize that this anxiety was present prior to drug use and that he has experienced anxiety throughout his life.

6. Due to the presence of anxiety symptoms, which would be the most probable second diagnosis to consider?

a. Agoraphobia
b. Social anxiety disorder
c. Substance/medication-induced anxiety disorder
d. Generalized anxiety disorder

7. All of the following criteria are associated with a diagnosis of generalized anxiety disorder EXCEPT:

a. Irritability
b. Being easily fatigued
c. Excess energy
d. Symptoms that occur for at least 6 months

8. During the session, the client states, "I don't see how things will improve because things have been bad for so long." Which of the following best defines this type of cognitive distortion?

a. Catastrophizing
b. Black-and-white thinking
c. Minimizing
d. Generalization

9. Based on the transtheoretical model of intentional behavior change, which stage would the client be in if he is beginning to analyze the pros and cons of his current behavior and situation?

a. Contemplation
b. Precontemplation
c. Action
d. Preparation

10. All of the following are considered short-term objectives for therapy EXCEPT:

a. Learning and implementing coping skills with a resulting decrease in anxiety and improved functioning
b. Identifying triggers for anxiety in order to understand the root of the anxious thoughts
c. Using the Generalized Anxiety Disorder-7 item (GAD-7) scale to determine the client's baseline anxiety and progressing toward reduction of anxiety symptoms
d. Learning and implementing strategies to delay the onset of anxiety following a trigger

PART THREE

EIGHTH SESSION, 10 WEEKS AFTER THE INITIAL INTAKE

Since the start of counseling and services with the local government mental health agency, the client has maintained sobriety from fentanyl and has been moved into stable housing via assistance from the agency. The client reports that the management of his anxiety has been better, but that he often feels lonely and unengaged. The client states that he is not sleeping well and thinks it is because he does not do much during the day. He continues to participate in Narcotics Anonymous daily in order to have interactions with other people. The client says that he tried to reach out to his children but they would not answer his phone call. You empathize with the client regarding his difficulty reaching out to his children. You and the client use this session in order to review progress and identify new goals.

11. Which of the following would be an appropriate goal to focus on based on this session?

a. Reconnect with family.
b. Explore reentering the workforce.
c. Continue the current focus.
d. Focus on improving hygiene and daily living skills.

12. Which of the following would be a helpful career aptitude tool for a client with limited resources?

a. O*Net Interest Profiler
b. Motivational Appraisal Personal Potential
c. Career Assessment Inventory
d. Criteria Cognitive Aptitude Test

13. Which of the following would be the most effective cognitive reframing of the statement "My kids hate me and don't want anything to do with me"?

a. "My kids don't like me right now, but eventually they will come around."
b. "My kids are done with me, and I should learn to move on."
c. "I hurt my kids, but I can take steps to rebuild my relationship with them."
d. "I hurt my kids, and I need to learn to be okay without them."

Case Study 3

PART ONE

INTAKE

CLIENT

Age: 8

Sex: Male

Gender: Male

Sexuality: Unknown

Ethnicity: Hispanic

Relationship Status: Single

Counseling Setting: Home Health Outpatient Therapy

Type of Counseling: Individual with Family Involvement

Presenting Problem: Behavioral Issues

Diagnosis: Oppositional Defiant Disorder, Severe (F91.3)

PRESENTING PROBLEM:

You are a home health outpatient therapist working with an 8-year-old male in the home setting. The client's parents will be actively involved in counseling due to the client's age. The client was referred to receive counseling by his school social worker. He has been having behavioral issues in school that have led to difficulty staying in the classroom and is resultantly falling behind in academics. During the first session, the client refuses to engage and leaves the room. The client's parents prompt him to return, and he calls them "jackasses" and leaves the room again. The parents finish the intake session with you and provide you with a report on their observations in the home and reports from the school social worker. The client reportedly often loses his temper and is generally easily annoyed or angered. The client has trouble taking direction from his teachers and parents. The client's parents also state that he often blames his younger sister for things that he does and often tries to annoy her. The parents have trouble identifying any of the client's friends and state that he does not get along with his peers.

MENTAL STATUS EXAM:

The client was argumentative and did not engage in the entire intake session. The client was oriented to person, place, situation, and time. He was dressed appropriately for the weather and appeared well groomed. The client appeared clean and had appropriate hygiene.

FAMILY HISTORY:

The client's parents are married, and he has a younger sister who is 6 years old. The client often deliberately annoys or angers his younger sister and has difficulty following directions from his parents.

1. All of the following are considered a differential diagnosis for oppositional defiant disorder EXCEPT:

a. Attention-deficit/hyperactivity disorder
b. Disruptive mood dysregulation disorder
c. Social anxiety disorder
d. Generalized anxiety disorder

2. After you finish talking with the client's parents, you decide to go to the living room where the client is. What would assist you in building rapport with this client?

a. Encourage the client to return to the home office where the session was taking place.
b. Engage the client in talking about the video game he is playing or play the game with him.
c. Continue the intake session in the living room with the client because he seems more comfortable here.
d. Initiate a conversation about sports with the client to find a common interest.

3. The client states, "My parents suck! They only care about my younger sister." Which one of the following statements would best be defined as a reflection of feeling by the counselor?

a. "You seem bothered by their attention at times, but do you wish you had a different kind of attention?"
b. "That sounds like it could feel very lonely or that maybe you feel overlooked."
c. "I can see how you might be frustrated or sad if you feel like they don't care about you."
d. "It sounds like you don't like your parents very much because you feel like they only care about your sister."

4. At this point in counseling, what referrals might be appropriate to consider in addition to individual/family therapy?

a. Applied behavior analysis
b. Psychiatry for medication management
c. Occupational therapy
d. Play therapy

5. Which of the following would be a clinically appropriate short-term goal at this point in therapy once rapport is built?

a. Improve grades and functioning in school.
b. Improve social interactions with peers and his sister.
c. Improve the client's awareness of the consequences of his actions.
d. Improve the client's ability to follow directions from his parents.

Part Two

First Session, 1 Week After the Initial Intake

You arrive at the client's house for the session, and he decides to meet with you in the family office and brings some toys with him. He sits on the floor, and you decide to sit on the floor with him and engage in play to continue building rapport. While playing, you begin to ask the client about what frustrates him about his parents, and, through processing, you identify that he desires some independence. You meet with the parents after the session and encourage them to give him some choices throughout his day so that he can have a sense of control. You state that they can be choices that may not be consequential, such as the order of the bedtime routine, so that the routine still happens but he has some control over the order of the process.

6. The client expresses frustration that his parents make him do homework when he gets home from school. Which of the following would be a supportive and empathetic response to the client?

a. "I can see how it might be frustrating to have to start homework right after school."
b. "Maybe it would be good to get the homework over with so you can play."
c. "When you listen to your parents, things seem to work out better for you."
d. "What if you asked your parents for a break before you start your homework, in order to take a break from schoolwork?"

7. During the session, the client requests that his parents bring him a snack, and they decline until the session is over, so the client begins to yell and throw a tantrum. Based on behavioral therapy, which of the following would be considered the function of this behavior?

a. Tangible
b. Sensory
c. Escape
d. Attention seeking

8. When addressing the client's behavioral response to the denial of a snack, which one of the following would be the most appropriate behavioral intervention?

a. The parents set a boundary that the client needs to wait until the session is over, so you support him in coping with the denial of his request.
b. Support the client in requesting the snack in a more appropriate manner and when he does, you provide the snack.
c. Support the client in calming down, and when he does, if he requests the snack in an appropriate manner, he may have it.
d. Maintain boundaries and allow the client time to accept the decision that was made about waiting until the end of the session for the snack.

9. Based on the client's developmental level, why is it important that his parents are engaged in his treatment?

a. The client is not self-aware enough to know when he needs to cope with strong emotions.
b. The presenting problem is centered around the client's difficulty with following directions from his parents and teachers.
c. The client does not want to participate in counseling, so his parents will be the ones participating in treatment.
d. The client is not developmentally able to deal with strong emotions, so his parents will need to support him.

PART THREE

FIFTH SESSION, 6 WEEKS AFTER THE INITIAL INTAKE

The client appears to be more comfortable with you as he greets you at the door and starts talking with you about his favorite TV show as you walk back to the office. The client talks about how his parents give different consequences to him than his younger sister and that they also give her more attention than they give him. You empathize with the client about this because it must be frustrating being treated differently. You assist the client with processing further, and he identifies feeling like he is "bad." But because he gets attention, he continues to push back against their authority. During this session, the client curses at his parents and they punish him by removing access to video games for the next week.

10. The client's parents have offered you dinner every week since you have started therapy with the client. All of the following are ethical considerations regarding gifts EXCEPT:

a. Accepting the meal may count as compensation to the clinician for services rendered
b. Declining a meal might be offensive due to the client's culture
c. The monetary impact of accepting the meal
d. The reason the parents are offering the meal

11. The parents are using punishment to alter behavior, and you want to educate them on positive reinforcement. Which would be an example of positive reinforcement to encourage appropriate behavior when the client is cursing?

a. The parents provide a time-out in the client's room to encourage more positive behavior.
b. The parents wait until the client calmly and quietly requests what he needs and they praise him for appropriate communication.
c. The parents walk away to demonstrate that they will not communicate with him when he curses at them.
d. The parents encourage him to request what he wants or needs in a more appropriate manner.

12. You are using the rational emotive behavior therapy ABC model with the client during this session. You want to challenge the client's belief that "my parents don't like me" following their punishment of him. All of the following statements would be a disputation of that belief EXCEPT:

a. "My parents do like me, and that is why they're punishing me."
b. "My parents don't like what I'm doing, so they punished me."
c. "My parents don't want me to be mean, so they made me take time to calm down."
d. "My parents don't like me right now, so they made me take time to calm down."

13. Which one of the following CBT terms most accurately defines the counselor's encouragement of the client to try to ask his parents for something in a calm, polite manner to see if there is a different outcome than when he yells and curses?

a. Behavioral experiment
b. Role play
c. Exposure therapy
d. Guided discovery

Case Study 4

Part One

Intake

Clients

Age:

Husband: 45

Wife: 43

Sex:

Husband: Male

Wife: Female

Gender:

Husband: Male

Wife: Female

Sexuality: Heterosexual

Ethnicity: Both Individuals Are Caucasian

Relationship Status: Married

Counseling Setting: Private Practice Counseling Clinic

Type of Counseling: Couples Counseling

Presenting Problem: Marital Distress

Diagnoses:

Couple Diagnosis: Adjustment Disorder with Anxiety (F43.22) and Relationship Distress with Spouse or Intimate Partner (Z62.898)

Individual Diagnosis (Wife): Generalized Anxiety Disorder (F41.1)

Presenting Problem:

You are a licensed therapist working at a private practice. The couple comes to counseling in order to work on their relationship following an infidelity. The wife has difficulty expressing what happened, and the husband interrupts her and expresses that his wife had an affair with a coworker 3 weeks ago. The couple states that they are currently talking very little aside from conversations that involve their children. The wife states that she is regretful of what she did and that she does want her marriage "to be saved." The husband explains that he is very hurt by her infidelity and that he is unsure if he can forgive her and continue being married to her. The couple has been married for 25 years and report that they both are in counseling to see if they can continue to be married following the affair. The husband expresses strong anxiety following the revelation of the affair and questions how he can be in a relationship with his wife following the infidelity. The wife is experiencing anxiety regarding her husband leaving her because she reports regretting the sexual interaction with her coworker and does not want to get divorced.

MENTAL STATUS EXAM:

The husband and wife were both oriented to person, place, time, and situation. Both individuals were dressed appropriately for the season and appeared clean. The husband presented as angry, and the wife presented as remorseful.

FAMILY HISTORY:

The couple has been married for 25 years. They have two children, a 14-year-old son and a 17-year-old daughter, and they report good relationships with their families of origin.

1. At this point in treatment, which of the following assessments would be clinically appropriate to use with the couple?

a. Dyadic Adjustment Scale
b. Beck Anxiety Inventory
c. Minnesota Multiphasic Personality Inventory
d. Family Environment Scale

2. All of the following are appropriate short-term treatment goals for the couple EXCEPT:

a. The couple will process events leading up to the affair in order to identify problem areas in the relationship.
b. The couple will learn and implement effective communication skills.
c. The couple will improve their quality time together in order to improve relationship satisfaction.
d. The couple will identify and process areas of resentment that led to the affair.

3. Which of the following would be important to discuss when reviewing informed consent that would be uniquely different for couples counseling?

a. Confidentiality
b. The risks of counseling that includes dealing with difficult topics during sessions
c. The nature of counseling
d. The clinician promoting the well-being of the individuals involved in counseling

4. The wife's anxiety appears to be clinically significant because it impacts the relationship. Which would be an appropriate first course of action regarding the wife's treatment for anxiety?

a. Provide individual counseling to the wife for anxiety.
b. Provide a referral for medication management.
c. Incorporate cognitive reframing and coping skills for anxiety in couples counseling sessions.
d. Provide a referral for individual counseling for anxiety.

5. Which one of the following is NOT a criterion for adjustment disorder?

a. Emotional and behavioral symptoms that start within 3 months of a stressor
b. Significant stress that impairs social, occupational, or other areas of functioning
c. The presence of psychotic features
d. Symptoms that are not based on a normative stress reaction

PART TWO

FIRST SESSION, 1 WEEK AFTER THE INITIAL INTAKE

The husband and wife come into the session and sit as far as they can from each other on the couch, and their individual body positions are oriented away from each other. You ask for any updates in the couple's relationship, and the husband states that they have not been talking about the affair and continue to only communicate regarding the kids. You attempt to process with the couple what the affair means for their relationship and what events led up to the affair. During the session, the husband stops talking and looks away from his wife when she talks about how she became frustrated that her husband did not spend quality time with her prior to the affair. She thinks that this led to her seeking attention from a man outside of the couple's relationship.

6. You want to explore the husband's feelings regarding the affair using the downward/vertical arrow technique. Which of the following questions demonstrates the use of this intervention in response to the statement "She cannot even remain faithful, so she clearly does not love me"?

a. "If that is the case, what does it mean for your future in this marriage?"
b. "How does this affect your hope for the marriage being successful?"
c. "How does that feeling affect your current relationship with your wife?"
d. "What would you need to see from your wife to be reassured that she loves you?"

7. Based on John and Julie Gottman's concept of the four horsemen of the apocalypse, which include criticism, defensiveness, contempt, and stonewalling, which one of the following terms describes the husband's communication style when he disengages from the session?

a. Criticism
b. Contempt
c. Stonewalling
d. Defensiveness

8. The Gottmans' four horsemen all have behavioral interventions that support the communication style. Which would be an appropriate intervention for stonewalling?

a. Use empathetic listening.
b. Take a break and then reconvene after the client is calmer.
c. Remember the partner's positive attributes.
d. Talk about feelings using "I" statements.

9. Which one of the following best defines mindful listening?

a. Focusing on listening when someone is speaking and focusing on what you are saying when you are talking
b. Trying to relate to the emotions expressed by others while listening
c. Repeating the message that you interpreted from what was said
d. Being able to summarize what is being said

Part Three

Third Session, 3 Weeks After the Initial Intake

You meet with the couple for the third session, and they report that they continue to have minimal communication. The couple continues to process feelings regarding the affair and begin to yell and curse at each other. The wife reports that she has tried to engage in quality time with her husband and that he has ignored these attempts. Around 10 minutes into the session, the husband leaves the session and walks out and proceeds to sit in the waiting area of your practice.

10. The husband left the session. What would be the most beneficial intervention for the couple?

a. Cancel the session in order to reconvene when the couple is willing to meet together because you are providing couples counseling.
b. Encourage the husband to return to the session.
c. Meet individually with both partners in order to process thoughts and feelings regarding the relationship.
d. Encourage both individuals to take responsibility for their contribution to the conflict.

11. You desire to support both individuals. Which is the most ethical intervention to support the couple?

a. Meet with the wife and then meet with the husband in the lobby because the practice door is closed and no one else is present in the practice setting.
b. Inform the husband of what the wife feels about him leaving because they are both clients and have access to information and no one else is present in the lobby.
c. Meet with the wife and then meet with the husband in a separate, empty office in the practice to maintain confidentiality.
d. Encourage the wife to come to the lobby to process the situation with the husband because the door is closed to the practice and no one else is present.

12. Which of the following cognitive distortions operates from the husband's premise that his "wife is always going to do what benefits her and not us because she is incapable of doing positive things for the relationship"?

a. Catastrophizing
b. Mental filter
c. Jumping to conclusions
d. "should" statements

13. Following this session, the couple decides to stop meeting with you together because they plan to separate. The husband states that he would like to continue working with you. According to the ACA Code of Ethics, which one of the following would be the most ethical decision in this scenario?

a. You cannot continue seeing him due to having a previous counseling relationship with his wife.
b. Provide a referral to another therapist due to your past counseling relationship with his wife.
c. You agree to provide individual counseling to him and offer to provide marital counseling if they end up wanting to stay together.
d. You agree to provide individual counseling and explain that if you start to counsel him independently, you cannot provide marital counseling for him and his wife should they decide to stay together.

Case Study 5

PART ONE

INTAKE

CLIENT

Age: 20

Sex: Female

Gender: Female

Sexuality: Heterosexual

Ethnicity: African American

Relationship Status: Single

Counseling Setting: College Campus Counseling Clinic

Type of Counseling: Individual Counseling

Presenting Problem: Depression and "Odd Behavior"

Diagnosis: Bipolar 1 Disorder, Current Episode Manic Without Psychotic Features, Moderate (F31.12)

PRESENTING PROBLEM:

You are a licensed therapist working on a college campus in the counseling center. A 20-year-old female client comes to counseling following 8 days of experiencing the following symptoms: little to no sleep most nights with the longest stretch of sleep being 2 hours, several middle-of-the-night shopping sprees, and distractibility. She reports that some of her college professors have called on her to stop talking during class and that she has not been doing very well in school this semester. The client identifies that she has felt this way before over the past 2 years and that this last time scared her because she was more aware of the negative impact it is having on her schooling. The client continues to relate that she also experiences depression at times and that she does not understand where it comes from but that it happens for a few weeks at a time every few months. When in a depressive episode, the client experiences a depressed mood more often than not, decreased enjoyment of activities, hypersomnia, fatigue, and a significant decrease in appetite.

MENTAL STATUS EXAM:

The client states that she slept for 4 hours the night before, which was the most she has slept in one night in the past week and that she now feels tired for the first time. The client had dark circles around her eyes and was wearing sweatpants and a t-shirt with stains on it. The client is oriented to person, place, time, and situation. The client's affect and speech are flat.

FAMILY HISTORY:

The client says that she and her family moved to the United States from Kenya when she was 5 years old. The client is the first member of her family to go to college, and she reports significant pressure from her parents to succeed. She feels that she has a good relationship with both of her parents. Her sister is 2 years younger than her, and they talk on the phone on a daily basis. The client identifies no other close family members because most are still living in Kenya.

1. Which of the following is the most effective form of treatment for bipolar disorders?

a. CBT
b. CBT and medication management
c. Medication management
d. Dialectical behavior therapy

2. All of the following are strengths that your client has that can be helpful in making progress toward her goals EXCEPT:

a. Energy
b. Desire to learn
c. Perseverance
d. Insight

3. All of the following would be appropriate short-term goals for the client following or during a manic episode EXCEPT:

a. Identify and learn to replace thoughts and behaviors that trigger or maintain manic symptoms.
b. Engage in good sleep hygiene.
c. Identify the thoughts and beliefs that support depression.
d. Improve impulse control.

4. Following the intake session, you determine that you have the experience and education to provide counseling, but because this is not your specialty, what would be an appropriate next step?

a. Refer to a therapist that specializes in bipolar disorder.
b. Refer to a psychiatrist for medication management and continued observation by another professional.
c. Continue to provide counseling, but seek peer supervision/consultation to ensure your interventions are clinically appropriate, and refer to a psychiatrist for medication management.
d. Seek continuing education regarding treatment of bipolar disorder.

5. Which one of the following is a possible symptom or criterion of a manic episode?

a. An inflated sense of self or grandiosity
b. Symptoms last at least 4 days
c. Symptoms are present but do not impair social or occupational functioning
d. Hallucinations

Part Two

First Session, 3 Days After the Initial Intake

The client comes to the counseling center during walk-in hours. The client is continuing to experience a manic episode. She reports that she went out to dance with friends the previous evening and ended up buying a gram of cocaine for $100 and reported doing several lines throughout the night. The client says that she has never used any drugs before and that it scared her that she would spend that much money on drugs and that she used drugs at all. You empathize with the client's frustration with her behavior and provide psychoeducation on impulse control to support her. The client appears tired as evidenced by her affect and slow movements, and she also appears to have poor hygiene because her clothes have visible stains and she has a slight body odor.

6. Based on the information presented, all of the following are behavioral triggers for impulsive behavior EXCEPT:

a. The client is awake late at night.
b. The client is out of the home late at night.
c. The client's routine is not maintained.
d. The client uses drugs.

7. Which one of the following assessments will assist you in monitoring the severity of the client's manic episode?

a. Minnesota Multiphasic Personality Inventory (MMPI-2)
b. General Behavior Inventory
c. Patient Health Questionnaire 9 (PHQ-9)
d. Brief Symptom Inventory

8. As an individual, you value hard work and were focused solely on school when you were in college; you think that the client is not prioritizing what is important for her. How can you balance your own values and support the client in working toward goals without letting your personal values affect treatment in a negative manner?

a. Self-disclosure can be beneficial, so you choose to share your own tactics in working toward goals.
b. You support the client's reflection on how her behavior is keeping her from her goals.
c. You are honest with the client about where your values lie in order to foster open discussion and create awareness of how personal biases affect the counseling process.
d. You ignore your own values because they should not have an impact on therapy, and you focus exclusively on the client's needs.

9. The client has not followed up with psychiatry referrals that you provided and is continuing to struggle with managing her manic symptoms. Which would be the most appropriate next step?

a. Evaluate cognitive barriers or reservations about medication.
b. Encourage or remind the client to follow up with the referrals.
c. Provide psychoeducation on the benefits of a combination of medicine and therapy for bipolar disorders.
d. Respect the client's personal decision not to follow up.

Part Three

Third Session, 1 Week After the Initial Intake

You meet with the client during your regularly scheduled session. The client says that the manic behavior has stopped and that she is starting to enter a depressive episode. The client identified mild depressive symptoms including a down mood, difficulty enjoying activities, and fatigue. The client states that she still has not contacted the psychiatrist because she does not know if she is ready for medication. You process this thought with the client and identify that she is worried about the side effects of the medication. You encourage the client to meet with the psychiatrist and be open about her worries in order to get more information on the medication options. The client expresses worry that her academic success has been affected by cycling moods. The client's grades are currently dropping, and she says that she does not have control over them. You empathize with the client and begin to talk about behavioral and cognitive interventions to improve functioning.

10. Based on the information that you already have, which of the following would be a clinically indicated behavioral intervention to manage increasing depressive symptoms?

a. Develop an exercise routine because exercise focuses on general well-being and can improve mood by releasing endorphins.
b. Encourage the client to plan out pleasurable activities that she has enjoyed in the past, and mention that she should do them even if she feels like she will not enjoy them.
c. Encourage the client to spend time with friends because this makes her happy.
d. Encourage the client to follow up with the psychiatrist in order to discuss medication for depression.

11. With which of the following would there be a beneficial collaboration that would require a release of PHI?

a. Disability resource center
b. Psychiatrist
c. Parents
d. PCP

12. All of the following demonstrate an open counseling stance EXCEPT:

a. Smiling
b. Arms are not crossed
c. Leaning forward
d. Mirroring

13. In order to solidify your diagnosis of bipolar I disorder, the criteria for a major depressive episode must be met. All of the following are included on the list of possible criteria for a major depressive episode EXCEPT:

a. Decreased interest or pleasure in all activities
b. Suicidal thoughts
c. Difficulty concentrating
d. Catatonia

Case Study 6

Part One

Intake

Client

Age: 12

Sex: Female

Gender: Female

Sexuality: Heterosexual

Ethnicity: Caucasian

Relationship Status: Single

Counseling Setting: Private Practice

Type of Counseling: Individual Counseling

Presenting Problem: Withdrawn and Avoidant Behavior

Diagnosis: Undetermined

Presenting Problem:

You are a licensed therapist working in private practice. A 12-year-old female client comes into your office for the intake session and is accompanied by her parents. The client's parents report that their daughter has been withdrawn and has refused to return to school for the past 6 school days. The client is avoiding eye contact with anyone and is slouching with her arms crossed. You try to engage the client in open questions to initiate the intake session with her, and she does not answer you or look at you. You ask her if privacy would make her more comfortable, and she nods, so you ask her parents if they would mind waiting in the lobby, and they agree. The client continues to refuse to talk about school, but she does engage in conversation with you about other topics.

Mental Status Exam:

The client appears oriented to person, place, time, and situation. The client is dressed appropriately for the weather and appears to be maintaining appropriate hygiene. The client was withdrawn for most of the session but was able to open up slightly about what was going on with her.

Family History:

The client says that she has a good relationship with her parents. She says that they are encouraging and supportive of her. The client says that she has a younger brother who is 6 years old and an older brother who is 16 years old. The client states that she has a good group of friends and spends time with them regularly.

1. You noted that the client is withdrawn and appears uncomfortable. All of the following approaches could build trust and comfort with the client EXCEPT:

a. Ask open-ended questions to provide the client with the opportunity to answer in a way that she chooses to.
b. Ask about the musical group depicted on the client's t-shirt.
c. Ask the client what she does for fun.
d. Ask the client to talk about anything she wants.

2. You continue to have trouble assisting the client with becoming more comfortable by talking about topics that may interest her. What else can you do in order to build a level of comfort with the client?

a. Explain the nature of therapy and how it can be helpful to her.
b. Play a board game with the client.
c. Use the silence skill to encourage the client to talk about what is happening.
d. Use the immediacy skill to address the client's feelings about the session and the therapist.

3. All of the following are appropriate short-term treatment goals EXCEPT:

a. Building trust so the client can feel comfortable enough to begin to identify and express feelings regarding her school attendance
b. Referring for psychological testing to determine the cause of the refusal to attend school
c. Assisting the client with identifying barriers to school attendance
d. Beginning to discuss increasing social connectedness due to withdrawn behavior

4. Following the session, the client's parents ask you for the details of your session with their daughter. What would be both the most ethical and clinically appropriate response?

a. The parents have a right to all information because the client is a minor, so you meet with them to discuss the details of the session.
b. You respect your client's right to privacy and tell the parents you do not think it would be best for treatment to share information without the client's consent.
c. First, you ask if you can talk with the client for permission and encourage the parents to provide their daughter with the space to speak freely during sessions.
d. You ask the client if you can talk with the parents, and she says "no," but you are able to talk with them anyway because she is a minor.

5. Which one of the following is an effective use of nonverbal attending?

a. Maintain eye contact to increase the closeness of the relationship because it demonstrates the desire to help.
b. Lean back in your chair in order to seem less threatening or less dominant.
c. Maintain an appropriate distance of approximately 4–8 feet.
d. Minimize the use of hand gestures and head nods.

PART TWO

FIRST SESSION, 4 DAYS AFTER THE INITIAL INTAKE

You and the client meet 4 days after the initial intake session due to truancy because she has missed several days of school. For about half of the session, the client seems to be withdrawn. She asks you what you are required to report, and you remind her of the limits of confidentiality. The client says that she understands, and then says she is going to talk about what happened anyway. She says that her volleyball coach asked to meet with her after practice about 7 months ago and when she entered his office, he asked to look at her right thigh following a fall during practice. She continues to state that when she showed him, he started to touch her genital area from the outside of her pants. She states that she ran out of the room and went home. She explains that after this event she quit the team and told her parents that she did not want to play anymore, but recently she has started to experience distressing memories of the sexual abuse; she refuses to go to school because she would see the man daily; she has difficulty feeling happiness; and she is experiencing feelings of shame, insomnia, and difficulty concentrating. You praise the client for disclosing this information and empathize with her about how hard it must have been to share this experience.

6. Which of the following would be the most appropriate next step due to the information provided during this session?

a. Invite the parents into the session to discuss the information provided.
b. You are a mandated reporter and will report this to the appropriate local government agency.
c. Invite the parents back into the session to discuss the information that was provided, and receive a release of PHI to report this to the school.
d. Invite the parents into the session to discuss the information provided, and report the information to the appropriate local government agency.

7. All of the following are appropriate short-term treatment goals following the new information presented during the session EXCEPT:

a. The client will process her feelings of shame associated with the sexual assault.
b. Identify and reduce the symptoms and effects of the sexual assault.
c. Process thoughts and feelings regarding the investigation process into the sexual assault.
d. Identify situations that could trigger a trauma response in order to reduce the impact of the sexual assault.

8. You are having difficulty disconnecting from the session today. What is the LEAST helpful self-care technique for you to actively manage your emotions?

a. Go to the gym and exercise for an hour.
b. Seek clinical supervision.
c. Spend time with friends after work.
d. Go home and go to sleep.

9. All of the following are general guidelines for mandated reporting EXCEPT:

a. To follow state regulations regarding time between learning of abuse or neglect and reporting the abuse or neglect
b. To consult with your agency prior to reporting
c. If your supervisor disagrees with reporting, report the abuse or neglect anyway
d. If you are unsure of whether the abuse or neglect is real or if anything will come of reporting, you must submit the report anyway

Part Three

Second Session, 1 Week After the Initial Intake

The client reports that a worker from the local child protective services office met with her and that she is worried about what the coach will do in response when he finds out that she reported him. The client says that she has not returned to school but that the school has provided the classwork and homework needed to keep up; she feels like the school is supporting her well enough to not fall behind. The client confirms that all of the symptoms that she described during her last session are still present.

10. Which of the following would be the most appropriate diagnosis based on the client's presenting symptoms?

a. Post-traumatic stress disorder, with delayed expression
b. Post-traumatic stress disorder, with depersonalization
c. Acute stress disorder, with depressed mood
d. Adjustment disorder, with depressed mood

11. If you are having trouble empathizing with a client, what would be the most beneficial tactic to understanding the client experience?

a. Accept that you cannot empathize with every client experience and that is fine.
b. Try to relate to the core feelings associated with the client's experience.
c. Research more about experiences that you do not relate to in order to try to understand the client's experience.
d. Be open with the client in that you do not understand what it was like for her to experience these circumstances.

12. Which of the following is LEAST likely to be a long-term effect of this client's trauma if left untreated?

a. Difficulty with intimacy
b. Difficulty with trust
c. Clinical depression or anxiety
d. Adjustment disorder

13. Which one of the following is an appropriate short-term goal for post-traumatic stress disorder?

a. Significantly reduce negative symptoms associated with the trauma.
b. Reduce avoidance of triggers for trauma symptoms.
c. Improve the client's ability to talk about her traumatic experience.
d. Use cognitive behavioral strategies to reduce the daily impact of the trauma.

Case Study 7

Part One

Intake

Client

Age: 60

Sex: Male

Gender: Male

Sexuality: Heterosexual

Ethnicity: Caucasian

Relationship Status: Married

Counseling Setting: Private Practice Clinic

Type of Counseling: Individual Counseling

Presenting Problem: Unemployment; Anxiety; Depressed Mood

Diagnosis: Adjustment Disorder with Mixed Anxiety and Depressed Mood (F43.23)

Presenting Problem:

You are a private practice therapist working in an outpatient clinic. Your 60-year-old male client comes into the intake session, sits down, and sighs deeply. You verbally acknowledge that the client looks as though he is carrying a big mental weight, and he nods. The client begins to talk about how he was let go from his job at an assembly plant a month prior due to budget cuts. The client says that he worked there for about 30 years and that he was most recently a plant manager for the past 10 years. The client states that the plant shut down because the automotive company moved their manufacturing to another country. The client expresses anxiety surrounding what he is going to do for work next. The client states that he worries that he does not have much to offer other employers due to the extent of time he spent at his last job and also that his age will make him unemployable. The client says that he has been isolating himself, feels down more often than not, and often worries about making ends meet. The client states that his wife is currently receiving cancer treatment and, because of this, they have significant, regular medical bills.

Mental Status Exam:

The client appears to have a depressed mood as evidenced by his affect, slow speech pattern, and body posture. The client is dressed appropriately for the season and is in clean clothing. The client is oriented to person, place, time, and situation.

Family History:

The client has been married for 25 years. He has three children, a 23-year-old son, a 21-year-old son, and an 18-year-old daughter. The client reports a strong relationship with his wife and children and states that they regularly spend quality time together.

1. All of the following statements are true regarding the informed consent process EXCEPT:

a. Informed consent includes a discussion of the risks of counseling.
b. Informed consent includes a discussion of copays, fees, and legal processes for nonpayment.
c. Informed consent only occurs during the intake session.
d. The client has the right to engage in or refuse counseling services.

2. Which of the following would be considered a positive attending trait for a therapist?

a. Speaking in a slow, soft, gentle tone
b. Using hand gestures to appear engaged
c. Turning your body 45 degrees away from the client to minimize a seemingly aggressive body posture
d. Saying "yes," "right," and "uh huh" or using head nods to show that you are listening

3. The client states, "I'm unemployable because I'm old and have nothing to offer. They were right to let me go and not move me to another plant." What kind of cognitive distortion does this represent?

a. Catastrophizing
b. Fortune-telling
c. Labeling
d. Mental filtering

4. The client does not currently have health insurance and says he will have difficulty continuing to pay for sessions at the current rate. Which of the following would be the most ethical method for determining your payment arrangement with this client?

a. You and the client set up a verbal agreement to trade the client's garden produce and woodworking in exchange for counseling services.
b. You maintain the self-pay rate with the client because it is important to be compensated for the service you are providing.
c. You consider the client's financial hardships and adjust your self-pay rate for the client.
d. You refer the client to another therapist who is willing to provide pro bono services.

5. The Age Discrimination in Employment Act of 1967 and its amendments include all of the following EXCEPT:

a. An employer should ensure that at least 20% of their workforce is older than 50 years of age.
b. Mandatory retirement of individuals in executive positions over age 65 years of age is permitted.
c. Employers may reduce benefits based on age only if the cost of reduced benefits is the same as the cost of providing full benefits to younger workers.
d. Preferences based on age are prohibited.

Part Two

First Session, 1 Week After the Initial Intake

The client comes into the session with a similar presentation as last week as he sits down and sighs deeply. You ask the client what he is thinking about, and he recounts an argument earlier in the day that he had with his wife when they were discussing finances. The client expresses frustration that they have had several arguments over the past week regarding finances. You empathize with the client and support him with further processing his anxiety about finances. The client expresses an immediate need to start working soon for financial reasons and because he is having a hard time "doing nothing" every day.

6. The client wants to work on the conflict that he and his wife are experiencing. Which of the following would be the most ethical and clinical decision based on the client's needs and current situation?

a. Offer to provide couples counseling in addition to continued individual counseling for your client after explaining the risks involved.
b. Refer the couple to a couples counselor.
c. Offer to have the client's wife in the session one time to focus on how they can support each other through this transition.
d. Continue individual counseling with the client and include methods on resolving conflicts with his wife during a single session.

7. You are conducting research for your part-time job at a university. All of the following are areas that your private practice client needs to know or consider as a participant EXCEPT:

a. That withdrawal from research can happen at any time
b. Any discomfort, power differentials, or risks that are involved in the research
c. The limitations of confidentiality
d. The payment he will receive for research

8. Which of the following would be an example of reflection skills when the client is talking about the need to start working soon because he feels like he is doing nothing every day?

a. "In addition to being frustrated and anxious about finances, it sounds like you might also feel bored and unengaged."
b. "It sounds like most days have been hard because you feel you are not doing much."
c. "I can see how hard it must be feeling the pressure of finding a new job and dealing with conflict at home."
d. "It sounds like we need to focus very intently on figuring out what you are going to do for work because this is causing you a lot of distress."

9. During the session, the client states, "I don't think I can provide for my family like I need to, so I'm worthless." Which one of the following areas needs to be explored following this statement?

a. Depression
b. Anxiety
c. Self-esteem
d. Work skills

Part Three

Fourth Session, 3 Weeks After the Initial Intake

The client comes into the session and reports that he and his wife have been getting along better since the last session following some conversations about what they can do to get through this situation together. The client says that he wants to work on figuring out what he is going to do for work next. You and the client discuss possible options, and he says a friend offered him a job at his restaurant. The client says that he is considering it just for the money but that he has never been a server before and has some reservations. You conduct a career interest assessment and discuss the results.

10. Which of the following assessments would be the most helpful in identifying possible career options for this client?

a. Myers-Briggs Type Indicator
b. Enneagram personality test
c. Work and Social Adjustment Scale
d. Motivational Appraisal of Personal Potential

11. The client has not been applying to jobs due to anxiety that he will not get a job due to his age. Which of the following would be an appropriate intervention to improve his motivation to apply to jobs?

a. Psychoeducation on relaxation techniques
b. Progressive muscle relaxation
c. Use of a CBT thought log to process during sessions
d. Role-playing

12. You encourage the client to use natural supports during this time because it can be helpful to have other people provide support. All of the following would be considered a natural support EXCEPT:

a. A childhood friend
b. A sibling who the client is close to
c. An acquaintance from the client's Bible study group
d. The therapist because you meet with the client regularly

13. The client expresses worry about being a server in a restaurant because he has never done it before. Which one of the following responses would be most helpful?

a. Process the client's experience in the automobile plant and compare it to being a server to demonstrate the overlap of skills between the two positions.
b. Encourage the client to continue looking for a position that more closely relates to his experience.
c. Encourage the client to take the position due to his financial needs.
d. Use your assessments to determine other positions that he might be a good match for.

Case Study 8

Part One

Intake

Client

Age: 4

Sex: Female

Gender: Female

Sexuality: Unknown

Ethnicity: Caucasian

Relationship Status: Not applicable

Counseling Setting: Private Practice Clinic

Type of Counseling: Family Therapy

Presenting Problem: Foster Care; Disengaged Child; Behavioral Problems

Diagnosis: Provisional Diagnosis of Reactive Attachment Disorder (F94.1)

Presenting Problem:

You are a private practice counselor specializing in working with children with developmental disorders. The 4-year-old female client is referred to you by her PCP and arrives with her foster parents, who join her in the first session. The client has been with her foster parents for the last 13 months after being removed from the care of her biological parents due to their incarceration for drug trafficking and attempted armed robbery. The foster parents are worried because the client exhibits minimal positive mood, irritability without an obvious trigger, and behaviors that appear to be clearly connected to attachment with caregivers. She experienced emotional and physical neglect from the birth parents and changes in primary caregivers. The foster parents also report that the client does not seek comfort when something happens that upsets her. The client did not engage very much in the intake session and was instead playing with the toys provided by the counselor. During the session, the client becomes upset with her foster parents when they prompt her to answer some questions. She hits the foster father, runs out to the lobby, and sits down with the toys. You leave the office and meet her in the lobby.

Mental Status Exam:

The client is disengaged, and when the foster parents prompt her to answer questions, she ignores them and continues playing. The client appears oriented to person, place, time, and situation because she answered questions about these topics. The client appeared more responsive to your questions than her foster parents.

Family History:

The client entered foster care 1 year ago when her parents were arrested on charges of drug trafficking and armed robbery. The client has been with the same foster parents for the past year. The client experienced emotional and physical neglect by her birth parents and was separated from her 5-year-old brother and 2-year-old sister when she entered foster care. The client appears to have had trouble with attachment to the foster parents per the foster parents' report.

1. Which of the following symptoms would be needed to make a diagnosis of reactive attachment disorder?

a. Minimal response to comfort when distressed
b. Frequent tantrums
c. Difficulty making friends
d. The disturbance is evident before the age of 10

2. Following the first session, the birth mother calls you from jail asking about her daughter's treatment, and you are able to verify that this is indeed the birth mother. Which of the following is true regarding the birth parents' right to access information regarding their biological daughter?

a. Only the foster parents have access to all of the information because they are the caregivers.
b. Because social services took over care of the child, they can decide if the birth parents have access to treatment information.
c. The birth parents still have a right to access information if their parental rights have not been terminated.
d. Regardless of whether the birth parents' rights have been terminated, they still have access to your client's information.

3. All of the following are appropriate treatment objectives for reactive attachment disorder EXCEPT:

a. Develop trust and comfort with the client.
b. Assist the foster parents with reframing the client's problem behaviors as opportunities to support and love their foster child.
c. Assist the foster parents with demonstrating expectations, feedback, and structure to demonstrate that they are in control.
d. Instruct the client on cognitive reframing on anxiety about being with the foster parents.

4. When the client leaves the room, which of the following is the most important to consider for an effective counseling intervention with your client?

a. Confidentiality when leaving the foster parents in your office
b. The manner in which you enter the lobby and approach the client
c. Discussing the need for safety and refraining from hitting
d. Encouraging the client to return to the office with the foster parents

5. Which one of the following is a differential diagnosis for reactive attachment disorder?

a. Oppositional defiant disorder
b. Conduct disorder
c. Autism spectrum disorders
d. Parent-child relational problems

PART TWO

FIRST SESSION, 2 WEEKS AFTER THE INITIAL INTAKE

You meet with the client 2 weeks after the initial intake because she refused to come for the session scheduled the past week. Because of the cancellation, you decide to change the focus of your session to meet the client's needs for comfort and security over the foster parents' need for guidance and skills. The client engages a little more in interacting with you, and you praise her for her involvement. At one point in the session, the client hits you and goes and sits down to continue playing. At the end of the session, you provide the foster parents with ways that they can increase attachment and positive interactions with your client. You empathize with the foster parents regarding their desire to help the client feel loved and cared for.

6. From a behavioral therapy perspective, which of the following interventions would demonstrate conflict tolerance in a manner that would meet the client's needs when she hits you?

a. You engage the client in cognitive reframing to manage her strong emotions.
b. You minimize your reaction and prompt the client to communicate her wants or needs.
c. You disengage from the client and provide no response so as to not reinforce the behavior.
d. You redirect the client to another activity in order to support her with managing her strong emotions.

7. The foster parents state, "we know that we are going to mess up, and she will be worse off." What kind of cognitive distortion is this?

a. Blaming
b. "should" statements
c. All-or-nothing thinking
d. Overgeneralization

8. All of the following can be beneficial in improving attachment between the foster parents and the client EXCEPT:

a. Engage in one-on-one play daily with the client.
b. Provide physical affection and verbal reinforcement daily to the client.
c. Encourage the parents to provide family activities focused on family cohesion.
d. Encourage the foster parents to bring the client to visit her birth parents to show that they affirm the client's past experiences and biological family.

9. Which one of the following therapeutic foci is most effective for a 4-year-old with attachment difficulties?

a. Rational emotive behavior therapy
b. Play therapy
c. Bibliotherapy
d. Psychodynamic therapy

Part Three

Fourth Session, 3 Weeks After the Initial Intake

At the start of the session, the foster parents ask the client if she would mind meeting alone with you; she agrees and asks to have access to the toy bin in your office. You and the client begin to play together, and you ask her if she talked to her birth parents. The client says "yeah, Mommy talked about coming home in a few years." You ask how she feels about living with her mother again, and she says she does not want to be with her because her mother does not want to be with her. You try to process this with the client, and she says that she likes her house and her school and does not want to leave. You meet with the foster parents and the client at the end of the session, and they report that spending quality time with the client on a daily basis has been helpful in improving their relationship. They state that they think they had been too afraid to overwhelm her and that at times they were trying to give her space, but they realize that the intentional time together has been helpful. You empathize with the foster parents and encourage them to continue to spend quality family time with her.

10. Which of the following terms describes the client's belief that "no one wants me"?

a. Schema
b. Automatic thought
c. Thought stopping
d. Transference

11. This is the first session in which the client expresses any significant thoughts or feelings. Which of the following demonstrates a clinically appropriate response to the client's expression of feelings regarding the statement "no one wants me" that keeps in mind the client's need for comfort in sessions?

a. Empathy
b. Cognitive reframing
c. Continue playing and do not provide a response to her expression of emotions
d. Use downward arrow questioning to find a deeper feeling behind this statement

12. The court provides a subpoena for an update on the counseling process. All of the following are appropriate considerations EXCEPT:

a. Obtaining legal counsel
b. Providing all progress notes and assessments
c. Providing only relevant material
d. Only sending information in an encrypted and secure manner

13. Which one of the following attachment styles best defines the client's relationship with her foster parents?

a. Secure
b. Avoidant/dismissive
c. Ambivalent/preoccupied
d. Disorganized/fearful

Case Study 9

Part One

Intake

Client

Age: 35

Sex: Male

Gender: Male

Sexuality: Heterosexual

Ethnicity: Hispanic

Relationship Status: Divorced

Counseling Setting: Private Practice Clinic

Type of Counseling: Individual Counseling

Presenting Problem: Anxiety; Depressed Mood, Difficulty with Changing Relationship Roles

Diagnosis: Adjustment Disorder with Mixed Anxiety and Depressed Mood (F43.23)

Presenting Problem:

You are a licensed counselor in Texas in a private practice. A 35-year-old male client comes to counseling for support during a recent divorce. The client says that he and his wife separated a year ago and had to wait a year for divorce per state law; therefore, they finalized the divorce recently. The client says that his wife decided she married him because she was lonely and that, after 8 years of being married, she wanted to find someone she loved. The client states that he still loves his ex-wife and that he has a hard time with his new relationship with her because he shares custody of his children and still has to communicate with her regularly. He continues saying that his wife often calls him for emotional support and he does not know how to respond when this happens because he loves her and wants to support her, but this is confusing for him. The client says that he knows he "shouldn't be with someone who doesn't want to be with him and that things won't go back to how they were." The client identifies that anxious and depressive symptoms are present and that they affect his ability to engage socially, engage with his children, and perform at work. The client wants to work on navigating his new relationship with his ex-wife, his relationship with his children, and being single again.

Mental Status Exam:

The client presents as oriented to person, place, time, and situation. The client appears anxious because he avoids eye contact often and expresses that he has never been in counseling and is nervous.

Family History:

The client was married for 8 years, has been separated for a year, and was divorced within the past month. The client reports a good relationship with his family of origin and with his ex-wife's family. He has two children, a 5-year-old son and a 6-year-old daughter. The client's children stay at his house every other week.

1. Which of the following would be considered a differential diagnosis for adjustment disorder?

a. Normal stress response
b. Generalized anxiety disorder
c. Bereavement
d. Disinhibited social engagement disorder

2. The client states that he still loves his ex-wife and that she often reaches out for support. Based on the information provided, which of the following would be an appropriate goal regarding his new relationship with his ex-wife?

a. The client will continue to engage in supporting his ex-wife because this is a positive interaction.
b. The client will explore boundaries to establish what his new role is with his ex-wife.
c. The client will stop engaging in supporting his ex-wife.
d. The client will continue to work toward reconciling his relationship with his ex-wife to see if they can make the relationship work.

3. The client requests to have a session with his children to support their continued transition to being children of divorced parents. The client's children live across state lines. Considering the location of the children, which of the following is the most ethical clinical decision?

a. Your main client, the father, is in your state; therefore, it is okay to have a family session.
b. You cannot provide a therapy session to the client's children because they are in a state in which you are not licensed.
c. You cannot provide counseling to the children while also counseling their father, so you provide referrals to a counselor licensed in both states.
d. You consult with the state boards of both states and follow their recommendations.

4. When considering cultural concepts of stress, ataque de nervios is a condition commonly described by clients of Latino descent. Which one of the following symptoms is NOT typical of ataque de nervios?

a. Irritability
b. Nausea
c. Vertigo
d. Sadness

5. When completing a mental status exam, which one of the following would be the most appropriate term to define this client's affect?

a. Flat
b. Blunted
c. Constricted
d. Congruent

Part Two

First Session, 1 Week After the Initial Intake

The client comes into your office and says hello in a quiet voice and then sits down, slumps his shoulders, and does not make eye contact. You inquire about what you see, and the client says that he has been feeling more depressed over the past week. The client says that he is experiencing low appetite, a down mood, fatigue, and irritability. You empathize with the client and discuss coping skills for depressive symptoms. The client expresses frustration with his church because he worked part-time in the church office until recently when they encouraged him to resign because he is divorced and he is now unable to work in the church because of this. You empathize with the client regarding his situation at church.

6. The client states, "I don't understand how a loving God would approve of disqualifying me from working at church because of a decision my wife made." The client then begins to cry. Which of the following responses would be considered an expression of validation?

a. "I can see how that would be frustrating for you because it might feel incongruent with your beliefs."
b. "It does sound frustrating to be encouraged to resign when the choice to divorce was not yours. I think it is perfectly understandable to be sad and frustrated about this."
c. "It sounds like you are frustrated that the church encouraged you to resign because of a situation that you do not have control over."
d. "If I am understanding you correctly, it sounds like you're feeling depressed and frustrated following the finalization of the divorce and the church encouraging you to resign."

7. You do not share the same religious views as the client. Which of the following would be the most helpful approach when considering the impact of your own beliefs in counseling?

a. You explain to your client that you do not share his beliefs; therefore, you may not be very helpful in supporting him.
b. You support the client's beliefs and do not impose your own values.
c. You continuously assess how your beliefs may affect the counseling process.
d. You encourage the client to assess his own beliefs and if he really does believe them because he is currently feeling that they are incongruent with those of the church.

8. Due to an increase in depressive symptoms, you explore major depressive disorder. All of the following are missing criteria for major depressive disorder EXCEPT:

a. A change of weight more than 5% in a month
b. A 2-week period of depressive symptoms
c. Decreased interest in preferred activities
d. Increased presence of risky behaviors

9. Which of the following would be the most appropriate clinical modality to treat depression?

a. Behavioral therapy
b. Cognitive behavioral therapy (CBT)
c. Dialectical behavior therapy
d. Exposure therapy

Part Three

Fourth Session, 3 Weeks After the Initial Intake

The client talks about when he went to see his daughter at a dance recital and how, afterward when he went to say hello to her, she ignored him. He called his ex-wife later that day, and she denied knowing what was wrong, but when he talked to his son, the boy said, "Mommy told us you didn't want to live with us anymore and that is why you left." The client expresses frustration and anger with his ex-wife because she chose to leave him, and he thinks that it is not fair that she is telling the children a lie and also that it is affecting his relationship with them. The client states that he wanted to talk to you before he confronted his wife about this. You and the client discuss conflict resolution skills.

10. The client provides you with a gas gift card, and he expresses that he is appreciative of your support. Which of the following would demonstrate the most appropriate response considering what you know about the client?

a. You consider accepting the gift due to cultural considerations.
b. You deny the gift because you do not want to cause economic hardship.
c. You consider what the client wants in return for the gift.
d. You consider why you want to accept the gift.

11. All of the following are appropriate conflict resolution strategies for the client and his ex-wife EXCEPT:

a. Identifying and establishing ground rules for conflict resolution
b. Identifying and establishing the co-parenting goals that benefit the children and parents most
c. Focusing on supporting your client in expressing himself effectively as the priority because he was the party that was hurt
d. Supporting the client in empathizing with his ex-wife for deeper understanding of how the situation occurred

12. You are supervising a counseling intern, who thinks that he is not a good match for this client. Which of the following would be an appropriate consideration for addressing this issue?

a. The impact of the client and the intern having different values on the counseling process
b. The fact that the intern has some experience with divorce, but might benefit from some education to improve his competency and therefore comfort with this client
c. The fact that the intern does not think that he has the skills to support the client; therefore, he should be guided in attempting to provide services within the skills that he has
d. The fact that the intern is not a Christian or Catholic and would not be able to support the client; therefore, a Christian counselor may be more appropriate for this client

13. The client asks if his ex-wife can come into the next session so they could work on co-parenting skills. Which one of the following is the most ethical course of action?

a. Explain your role with the client and provide a family therapy or couples counseling referral.
b. Explain that if you are going to work with the client and his wife, then you would not be able to revert back to individual counseling because you can only work with him in one modality to avoid a conflict of interest.
c. Explain that you are unable to meet with both of them because you are his individual counselor.
d. Explain guidelines for how you can provide individual therapy for him and his family or couples therapy for him and his ex-wife.

Case Study 10

PART ONE

INTAKE

CLIENTS

Age:

Client 1: age 12

Client 2: age 14

Client 3: age 14

Client 4: age 16

Client 5: age 13

Client 6: age 16

Sex: Males

Gender: Males

Sexuality: Varying

Ethnicity: Multiracial

Relationship Status: Single

Counseling Setting: Juvenile Justice Facility

Type of Counseling: Group Counseling

Presenting Problem: Involvement with the Justice System That Includes Various Mental Health Disorders and Crimes

Diagnosis: Imprisonment (Z65.1)

PRESENTING PROBLEM:

You are a licensed counselor working in a juvenile justice facility for teenage males. The group comprises six males that are required to attend as part of their incarceration with the expectation that it will shorten their sentences. The purpose of the group is to work on emotional regulation and to work together to share common experiences and identify goals that can be helpful in preventing reincarceration. During the intake session, you explained the purpose of the group and started with an ice-breaker activity. The clients participated in the ice-breaker activity that required you to redirect them back to the activity several times because they would joke and get off task. You attempt to go a little deeper by encouraging your clients to start talking about what happened to get them incarcerated, and they appear to be taking pride in the reasons they were in juvenile detention and making fun of those with lesser sentences. You redirect the clients to another topic.

Mental Status Exam:
All of the clients appear to maintain appropriate hygiene, and they are all oriented to person, place, time, and situation. They are all somewhat reserved with regard to going into deeper topics, but they participate fully.

Family History:
Several clients report coming from a single-parent home, whereas others are from a two-parent home. All clients report that they have siblings. Several clients reported having parents that were or are involved in the justice system.

1. Which of the following would be unethical for you regarding group counseling?

a. You are also the case manager for each individual; therefore, this is a dual relationship.
b. Confidentiality cannot be guaranteed because you cannot control what the clients share outside of sessions.
c. You do not have experience regarding incarceration, but you have been a therapist for 15 years and have experience in counseling.
d. You cannot force the clients to participate in sessions even though therapy is mandatory.

2. One goal of the first session is to set a positive tone for the group. Which of the following would support this goal?

a. Explain group rules to ensure structure so that everyone can participate equally.
b. With this specific group, speaking with authority to maintain control of the group and therefore ensuring that the group members know they do not have to fight for control.
c. Support the clients with feeling comfortable expressing frustration with the facility.
d. Get everyone to share.

3. All of the following are helpful in drawing out a group member EXCEPT:

a. Written activities
b. Cognitive reframing
c. Rounds
d. Dyads

4. Which of the following would be the most appropriate short-term goal in the next month for the group?

a. The group will build trust and cohesion.
b. The group will use assertive communication skills.
c. The group will demonstrate the effective use of anger management strategies.
d. The group will demonstrate empathy in the group setting.

5. The goal of your group is to prevent reincarceration through addressing the factors that brought these young people into the justice system. Which one of the following best defines this approach to group therapy?

a. Interpersonal group therapy
b. Cognitive-behavioral group therapy
c. Skill development group therapy
d. Support group therapy

Part Two

Third Session, 2 Weeks After the Initial Intake

You meet with the group, and they appear to be starting to become more comfortable with one another. You noticed that throughout the past week, when you saw your clients on their unit, they were spending more time together and that they are all talking when they come in for the session. During the session, you and the clients discuss past experiences that led to them engaging in the crimes that led to their incarceration. During this conversation, client 1 is talking about his father and how he killed a pedestrian while driving. Client 4 then asserts that client 1's father is going to hell for killing someone. You cut off client 4 and redirect the attention back to client 1.

6. Which of the following would demonstrate appropriate use of "cutting off" for client 4?

a. Engage with client 4 in conversation about the beliefs he holds and then return to client 1.
b. Ignore what was said by client 4 because you do not want to give it attention and reinforce his desire for conflict.
c. Tell the client that what he said was not helpful or supportive regarding the goals of the group and then encourage client 1 to continue.
d. Remind client 4 that what he said was against the goals of the group and that he might be asked to leave if he continues.

7. According to Tuckman's stages of group development, which stage is this group in?

a. Norming
b. Forming
c. Performing
d. Storming

8. You want to relate what client 1 is talking about with what client 3 has said earlier in the session. Which of the following terms identifies this intervention?

a. Linking
b. Coleading
c. Identifying allies
d. Reflection

9. Toward the end of this group session, you and the group talk about how being with peers who engage in antisocial behavior often leads to all members engaging in antisocial behavior. All of the following are mechanisms of peer group influence EXCEPT:

a. Reinforcement
b. Social comparison
c. Transmission of skills and values
d. Extinction

PART THREE

SIXTH SESSION, 5 WEEKS AFTER THE INITIAL INTAKE

You meet with the group for the sixth session, and they are focused and appear to be more respectful toward you because it appears that you can get their attention more easily to start the session. You separate the group into dyads at the start of the session and prompt the group members to talk about feelings related to the pros and cons of engaging in school. You overhear client 4 telling client 3 that it does not matter if client 3 does well in school because he is in juvenile detention for sexual assault and therefore he cannot redeem himself. You intervene and remind client 4 of the group rules about respecting others.

10. Client 4 continues to accuse other members of the group of engaging in sinful activities and continues to be disruptive to the group process. All of the following are important considerations EXCEPT:

a. Whether significant attempts have been made to redirect client 4 and to reinforce group rules
b. Having a conversation with client 4 about finding a more appropriate group during the session because it can be a good moment to teach other group members what is tolerable in the group, especially considering the detention setting
c. If client 4 is actively causing harm to others, you can ask him to leave the group immediately without a discussion
d. Considering to ask client 4 to sit silently or in the same room but not participate

11. Which of the following statements falls under a CBT approach to treatment?

a. An activating event occurs, and irrational or rational beliefs respond that affect the consequences of the event.
b. Identify and use client motivation in order to improve negative behaviors.
c. Behavior has a purpose, and what we do is intended to overcome a sense of inferiority.
d. The focus is on the client's present life rather than on past experiences and also on understanding the context of a person's present experience and taking ownership over it instead of placing blame.

12. You notice that one group member appears to be sexually attracted to another group member. Which of the following options would be the most likely to support the group goals?

a. Remind the group members that they cannot have a relationship with each other.
b. Discuss the relationship dynamics with the group because others may feel that the relationship is affecting group processes.
c. Continue to monitor how the relationship affects the group because individuals will do what they want regardless of the group rules.
d. Discuss with the involved individuals that an outside relationship could adversely affect the group process.

13. Many members of your group are diagnosed with conduct disorder. Which one of the following is a key characteristic of conduct disorder?

a. Opposition to authority and rules
b. Impulsive anger outbursts with rapid onset
c. Patterns of behavior in which the basic rights, rules, or norms of others are violated
d. Persistent failure to resist the urge to steal objects that are not needed from others

Case Study 11

PART ONE

INTAKE

CLIENT

Age: 25

Sex: Male

Gender: Male

Sexuality: Heterosexual

Ethnicity: Caucasian

Relationship Status: In a Relationship

Counseling Setting: Private Practice Clinic

Type of Counseling: Individual Counseling

Presenting Problem: Premature Ejaculation

Diagnosis: Provisional Diagnosis: Premature Ejaculation, Acquired, Generalized, Mild (F52.4)

PRESENTING PROBLEM:

You are a counseling resident at an outpatient clinic. Your 25-year-old male client reports he was in a bicycle accident a year ago and that, resultingly, he had reconstructive surgery to his penis. The client identifies that it takes approximately 30 seconds to a minute to ejaculate following vaginal penetration. The client reports that the symptoms occur every time he engages in sexual activities with his girlfriend. The client is a car salesman and also reports anxiety about performance at work and other areas of life. You suspect that the client may also have generalized anxiety disorder. The client reports that his girlfriend does not seem to mind that sex does not last long, but he feels bad because he also wants her to feel good during sex.

MENTAL STATUS EXAM:

The client is oriented to person, place, time, and situation. The client appears comfortable in the session as evidenced by his openness, congruent affect, and verbal expressions.

FAMILY HISTORY:

The client reports that he has been in a relationship with his girlfriend for 3 years. The client says that he is close with his parents and his younger brother.

1. According to the American Psychological Association (APA)'s *Diagnostic and Statistical Manual of Mental Disorders* (DSM-5), which of the following would be a differential diagnosis for premature ejaculation?

a. Generalized anxiety disorder
b. A specific phobia
c. Substance-induced sexual dysfunction
d. Medically induced sexual dysfunction

2. Which of the following would be the most helpful area to explore to determine the course of treatment for this client?

a. Determine if the premature ejaculation is based on medical limitations.
b. Identify the client's personal goals for treatment.
c. Explore the effects of sexual dysfunction on the client's relationship with his girlfriend.
d. Determine the effect of the client's anxiety's on daily functioning in all settings.

3. You are supervising an intern, and he is also your employee. Your intern reports that he recently experienced a breakup with a significant other, and this has made him late to several sessions; in turn, several clients have canceled upcoming sessions due to his unreliability. According to the ACA Code of Ethics, which of the following would be the best course of action as a clinical supervisor/manager in order to prevent harm to clients?

a. Support your intern through the breakup in order to prevent harm to current clients.
b. The intern is causing harm to clients; therefore, employment consequences must be enforced to remove the source of harm.
c. Sit in sessions with the intern and his clients to provide accountability.
d. Consider either reducing the intern's caseload or putting him on a short-term leave in order to reduce harm to clients.

4. You suspect that the client also has generalized anxiety disorder. All of the following would confirm this diagnosis EXCEPT:

a. Excessive anxiety experienced on more days than not for 6 months
b. Being easily fatigued
c. Having trouble falling asleep
d. Fear of panic attacks

5. Which one of the following would be the most beneficial collaborator(s) for holistic treatment planning in this scenario?

a. The client's PCP
b. A psychiatrist
c. The client's girlfriend
d. The client's friends

PART TWO

FIFTH SESSION, 4 WEEKS AFTER THE INITIAL INTAKE

The client comes to the session reporting that he and his girlfriend attempted to have sex the past week, and he wrote down some thoughts he was having on his CBT thought log. The client and the clinician reviewed his thoughts and engaged in cognitive reframing to support him in creating new scripts to use when engaging in sex. The client also wrote down physical responses to anxiety that he was experiencing before and during sex that included muscle tension and increased heart rate.

6. The client identified that one thought he had during sex was "I feel inadequate as a man; therefore, I must be inadequate because I can't fully satisfy my girlfriend." Which of the following cognitive distortions best defines this thought?

a. Emotional reasoning
b. All-or-nothing thinking
c. Fortune-telling
d. Overgeneralization

7. You ask the client what his life would be like if he did not feel that he can't satisfy his significant other, and he does not respond immediately. All of the following are important aspects of the use of silence EXCEPT:

a. Your client may provide a meaningful response as a result of the silence, so you maintain the silence.
b. The client is not responding to the silence, so you continue talking to try to elicit more information.
c. The client appears uncomfortable with the silence, so you provide him with a prompt to say whatever is coming to his mind.
d. After providing a period of silence, you use attending skills to let the client know it is his turn to speak.

8. The client states that he thinks that his girlfriend would be better off without him and that he should break up with her so she can find what she wants in a man. You decide to use the counseling skill of confrontation to challenge him. Which of the following would demonstrate the most beneficial use of confrontation based on what you know about the client?

a. You tell the client that this is not an appropriate response because he is using all-or-nothing thinking and extrapolating his thinking about his own worth as a man as equated to her feelings about him.
b. You tell the client that responding to these feelings by breaking up might be risky because the client's girlfriend has not shown that she is bothered by his sexual performance.
c. You tell the client that he would be making a big mistake by breaking up with his girlfriend because he might be able to improve their relationship.
d. You tell the client that he should continue to be with his girlfriend because although he has these thoughts it does not mean that they are the reality.

9. All of the following are effective behavioral techniques used to reduce premature ejaculation EXCEPT:

a. Pelvic floor exercises
b. Focus on foreplay
c. The use of condoms
d. The use of antidepressants

Part Three

Sixth Session, 5 Weeks After the Initial Intake

The client's girlfriend comes to the session to give input about what she experiences when they have sex. The client started by saying he wanted to share his self-talk from the thought log. The client's girlfriend denies any of the thoughts he thinks that she is having. You encourage the client to use her response as evidence for reframing his self-talk when he is nervous during sex. The client states, "the fact that she even has to say that means that I am inadequate." The client's girlfriend says she can tell that he is tense and "in his head" when they are having sex. She also notes that he appears sad after sex and often isolates himself for a while afterward. She also identifies that she feels tense when she notices that he is tense and that this makes her less likely to initiate sex. You empathize with the couple and provide psychoeducation regarding positive communication surrounding sex.

10. Based on the client's presenting problems, all of the following would be a beneficial intervention for the girlfriend to use to support the client during sex EXCEPT:

a. Immediacy behaviors
b. Positive affect
c. Comfort with silence
d. Eye contact

11. During this session, you identify that the client's girlfriend does not send any signals that sex is not pleasurable. Which of the following terms defines the use of focusing on the information available to manage thoughts and feelings?

a. Mindfulness
b. Cognitive reframing
c. Relaxation skills
d. Cognitive challenging

12. You have provided support for your counseling intern, and he continues to be late for and miss client sessions. Which of the following would meet ACA criteria for ethical considerations at this point?

a. You seek consultation and document your decision to terminate your supervisory relationship with the intern.
b. You see this as an opportunity to support the intern in balancing his personal life and his professional life.
c. You provide a corrective action plan to the intern in order to prevent further issues with his clients.
d. You encourage the intern to seek counseling in order to work through what he is going through.

13. The client asks to meet via online video for the next session. All of the following are practical and ethical problems with video sessions EXCEPT:

a. Provision of interventions for a CBT approach
b. Access to nonverbal cues
c. Increased ability for a client to misrepresent themselves
d. Limitations to confidentiality

Answer Key and Explanations for Test #2

Case Study 1

1. B: Improving hygiene is a good first step in managing depressive symptoms because it helps the patient show himself that he has value and promotes general well-being. Improving happiness and self-talk are usually more long term in nature because they require many things to change including behavior and cognition. Changing careers is a decision that the client will need to process and move toward, but it likely will not happen in the short term unless it is already in progress.

2. B: The client's level of comfort is assessed using this therapeutic intervention. This intervention involves the use of the counseling skill called "immediacy." Immediacy addresses emotional responses that are present in the counseling session and can facilitate deeper processing of emotions and building therapeutic rapport. Although the client's hesitation before speaking and him wringing his hands may indicate anxiety, it is common for clients to be nervous during their first therapy session. Creating awareness of anxious behavior alone may make the client feel judgment, which may make him more uncomfortable. This intervention will not, on its own, determine if the counselor is a good fit for the client.

3. D: All of these elements are important foci for treatment planning purposes. The timeline was already identified in the first session (2 years); therefore, it does not need to be assessed further to confirm this diagnosis. The client already relayed that he does not use drugs or alcohol; therefore, this has also already been addressed. The DSM-5 requires at least five depressive symptoms in order to meet the criteria for diagnosis of major depressive disorder, in addition to four additional criteria: the impact of symptoms on functioning in critical areas of the individual's life, the episodes are not attributed to substance use or other disorders, the episodes are not attributed to psychotic disorders, and the episodes are not also accompanied by alternating manic episodes. Enough symptoms were identified for the diagnosis; however, it is important for you to further assess the impact of these depressive symptoms on functioning across multiple areas of the client's life in order to confirm this diagnosis.

4. B: A safety plan would be the best first intervention because suicidal ideation is present, but without an intent or plan. A safety plan provides options for coping with negative thoughts and lists the people that the client can contact for support. Cognitive reframing will be beneficial in treating depression and at times suicidal thoughts, but this would not be taught quickly and effectively enough to assist the client in the first session. Encouragement to stay with his girlfriend may provide safety and/or be part of the safety plan, but it will not guide the client on how to manage his thoughts in the way that the safety plan would. Placement in a psychiatric hospital is not always necessary when someone has suicidal thoughts, and this may enhance the client's anxiety. Further questioning and assessments can be used to ensure that someone is at low risk for suicide and if they are lower risk, they can likely be stabilized in the community with a safety plan.

5. B: It is important to provide frequent sessions to this client at this point in treatment due to his reported suicidal ideation. Because the client's risk appears moderate due to the presence of suicidal ideation with no current intent or plan, seeing him twice weekly would be most appropriate. Weekly and fortnightly (every other week) sessions might not provide the oversight and guidance needed to stabilize the client. Daily sessions would be more appropriate in the presence of intent, and it would likely not be possible due to insurance not covering that frequency of sessions. Requiring daily sessions would also indicate severe risk and, therefore, the need for a higher level of care such as hospitalization.

6. C: The Healthcare Information Portability and Accountability Act of 1986 (HIPAA) Privacy Rule requires a signed release of PHI before a client's health information is shared with individuals internal and external to a facility (except for people directly involved in the client's care). The signed release of PHI identifies to whom the information can be provided, what information can be provided, what method of communication is permitted, and how long the communication can continue. Informed consent, although required in many circumstances, does not provide permission to release information and is more relevant to obtain from clients prior to performing procedures or interventions after the details, risks, and benefits have been thoroughly discussed. A written or verbal consent from the client would not be sufficient for this kind of contact.

7. C: At age 25, it is recommended to get at least 7 hours of sleep per night. The 9- to 12-hour range is more appropriate for the age range of 6 to 12 years old. Consistent times of sleep initiation and waking are important in improving sleep. The room temperature also impacts the quality of sleep, although temperature needs vary from person to person. Mindfulness and relaxation activities can help calm the body as a means to better prepare him for sleep.

8. C: Personal experience may be helpful in providing insight from the point of view of a supervisor; however, the main focus should be on sleep hygiene because this is the issue that is affecting the client's functioning. Encouragement to talk to their supervisor would not solve their problem with sleep, encourages the client to disregard the causative issue, and may cause more issues at work. A counselor should be aware of their own personal experiences and how they may affect objectivity.

9. A: CBT and electroconvulsive therapy are clinically proven, effective treatments for depressive disorders. Medications may be beneficial in the treatment of depression, and a referral to a psychiatrist or psychiatric nurse practitioner is required for that assessment and prescription because prescribing medications is outside of the scope of the counselor. Although support groups may be beneficial to a client, they are not clinical in nature. Therefore, support groups would not provide treatment; rather, they would provide a support system for a client.

10. A: CBT is based around cognitive restructuring and reframing, which can be a very effective intervention for anxiety or depression. Reality acceptance is part of dialectical behavior therapy and would not be as beneficial for this client because the anxiety is based around an unknown outcome. Assessing readiness for change is part of motivational interviewing, and it is not clear at this point whether the client is willing or able to change. Operant conditioning is a behavior therapy approach that involves positive/negative reinforcement and punishment.

11. B: Although self-disclosure may be appropriate at times in order to connect, it should only be used when it is relevant to the subject at hand. Because of the sensitivity and specificity required in using self-disclosure, it is the least appropriate way to support a client who is crying. Rather, this moment should be used to provide space for the client to experience their emotions and process their feelings. Empathy helps a client feel heard, and normalizing emotions assists clients with feeling that their feelings are valid. Immediacy focuses on inviting the client to evaluate what is happening internally in the moment when an emotion is experienced.

12. A: Focusing on mindfulness and sleep will be important in treatment; however, the Patient Health Questionnaire-9 is helpful in monitoring ongoing progress in depression symptoms and their effects on functioning. The Minnesota-Multiphasic Personality Inventory-2 is used to assess the client's mental state or the presence of psychiatric illness, and it does not specifically measure depressive symptoms or their effects on functioning.

13. D: This client is jumping to conclusions with this statement because he has deduced what is going to happen with little evidence. This cognitive distortion could negatively affect his work performance. Emotional reasoning involves using a feeling to determine reality, which would not characterize the thinking reflected in his statement. Labeling occurs when an individual makes an evaluation of value based on a situation. Overgeneralization is taking a single experience and applying it to other experiences.

Case Study 2

1. B: If a counselor does not have experience and education in providing counseling for certain diagnoses, then it is most ethical to refer the client to another counselor that specializes in that diagnosis (ACA Governing Council, 2014). It is also important to seek education on certain diagnoses prior to providing services (ACA Governing Council, 2014), although a referral would be more indicated in this scenario. Motivational interviewing is commonly viewed as beneficial for substance use disorders, but if the counselor is not competent in counseling these populations, then this would not be appropriate. Support groups can be helpful in working through a substance use disorder, but they are not a clinical service that can treat substance use disorders.

2. C: Focusing on internal desire for change is the core focus of motivational interviewing because it is centered on identifying and cultivating an individual's motivation for change and assisting the person with moving forward in therapy. Focusing on unhealthy behaviors alone is part of behavior therapy. Challenging irrational thoughts and feelings is the focus of rational emotive behavior therapy. Reality therapy focuses on improving present situations and not on the effects of past experiences on present functioning.

3. B: Maslow's hierarchy of needs has five levels that include, in order from bottom to top, physiological, safety, love/belonging, esteem, and, finally, self-actualization. The more basic needs starting with physiological must be met in order for an individual to begin working on the other areas. The client's housing and food situation are both physiological and safety needs and should be addressed and supported. Although working on cessation from fentanyl use and his feelings regarding stopping its use are important, the client is homeless and does not have resources, so this is the most important. The client's relationship with his children would be classified under the "love and belonging" level in the hierarchy and would not be the area of initial focus.

4. A: According to the ACA Code of Ethics, minimal provision of information is an important ethical consideration because you only want to disclose what is absolutely necessary (ACA, 2014). The PCP would only need to know what pertains to their specialty and their service provision, which would be the client's mental health and its impact on his physical health. Provision of progress notes, biopsychosocial assessment, treatment plan, and client treatment participation could be providing more than is necessary for coordination between services, exceeding the counselor's ethical obligations. If the provider were a psychiatrist prescribing mental health medication, the other areas would be more relevant for them to know.

5. C: Heroin is an opioid along with morphine, fentanyl, Oxycontin, oxycodone, and many more. Opioids are very effective in treating intense pain but are easily abused due to their effects. Cocaine is a stimulant, and stimulants increase the activity of the central nervous system. Marijuana is a psychoactive drug because it affects the functioning of the nervous system by altering consciousness, mood, perception, behavior, and cognition. LSD is a hallucinogenic drug that affects consciousness, thoughts, and emotions and oftentimes causes hallucinations and distortions in perception.

6. D: Generalized anxiety disorder appears to be the most probable diagnosis because the anxiety appears to cover many different areas of the client's life. Although some of the anxiety is related to social situations, social anxiety disorder is specifically about fear of judgment or scrutiny (American Psychiatric Association [APA], 2013). Although the client does use substances, the anxiety predates the substance use and it is possible that the substances helped the client feel a reduction in anxiety. Agoraphobia is the fear of being in public spaces alone, closed in with others, and it generally results in an individual being afraid to leave home (APA, 2013). Although the client does express anxiety about living in a shelter, that anxiety is likely less specific to his living situation than it is a generalized sense of being overwhelmed by all of the issues that he is currently confronting.

7. C: Excess energy is not associated with generalized anxiety disorder. This should not be confused with restlessness, which is a common symptom of generalized anxiety disorder, but it is associated with the inability to relax due to anxiety. Irritability, being easily fatigued, and having symptoms of anxiety lasting at least 6 months are the criteria for generalized anxiety disorder.

8. D: Generalization involves taking a situation, such as the client's recent history, and assuming that the future will be the same. Catastrophizing involves thinking the worst-case scenario will happen. Although the client thinks things will not improve, he isn't focused on the worst-case scenario. Rather, he is experiencing hopelessness that things will ever be different. Black-and-white thinking means thinking things have to be either perfect or a complete failure. Although the client worries about things being the same, he is not focused on two extreme outcomes, but on the continuation of his situation. Minimizing is reducing the actual impact of a situation by not thinking about a situation as being as intense or severe as it actually is.

9. A: This client is in the contemplation phase of the transtheoretical model of intentional behavior change because he is analyzing the risks and rewards of changing his current situation. The precontemplation phase involves little or no thought about changing current behaviors. The client is not in the stage of taking actions yet. The client has not made a commitment to change and is therefore not yet in the preparation phase.

10. A: Learning and implementing coping skills with a resulting increase in functioning would be considered a long-term goal for therapy because many steps need to occur prior to this result. Identifying triggers, monitoring the client's progress with the GAD-7, and teaching strategies to delay the onset of anxiety following a trigger are appropriate short-term goals that can generally be accomplished in the immediate weeks of initiating therapy.

11. B: The client is showing signs that he is prepared to explore reentering the workforce. The client has accomplished 10 weeks of sobriety, consistent participation in all services with the local government agency, and maintained housing for 7 weeks. Engaging in work can provide the client with a sense of purpose, meet some social needs for the client, and is part of adult life that the client will need in order to maintain consistent housing and meet his additional financial needs and desires. The client's family does not appear to be ready to reengage with him at this point because they do not respond to phone calls. The client's daily living skills were not mentioned in the session note and are therefore not indicated as an immediate or current need. The current focus of therapy should not be continued because the client's situation has improved significantly and he has maintained progress.

12. A: The O*Net Interest Profiler is a free online tool that is used to determine what abilities can lead to careers that match an individual's existing skills and abilities. The Motivational Appraisal Personal Potential, Career Assessment Inventory, and Criteria Cognitive Aptitude Test are all clinical counseling assessments that cost money. Although they would be helpful career assessments, they would not be accessible to the client with his current level of resources because he is currently financially reliant on the government. The O*Net Interest Profiler would give a good direction for the client to consider potential fields of work.

13. C: "I hurt my kids, but I can take steps to rebuild my relationship with them" is the most effective cognitive reframing statement. This reframing addresses the reality that the client hurt his children, and it provides the motivation to make changes to improve his relationship with them, but it does not promise an outcome because its focus is on taking steps. It is important to instill hope that the future can be better because a common cognitive distortion is that past experiences will be the same in the future. Expecting the children to "come around" does not acknowledge the work that is required on the part of the client for positive change to occur. Expressing the need to "learn to move on" or to "learn to be okay without them" does not provide the client with motivation to change.

Case Study 3

1. D: Generalized anxiety disorder would not be considered a differential diagnosis because anxiety about everyday situations does not generally lead to defiance to authority. Attention-deficit/hyperactivity disorder would be considered a differential diagnosis if failure to conform to requests of others occurs in situations that require sustained attention. Disruptive mood dysregulation disorder also presents as negative mood and temper outbursts, but these are often much more intense than in oppositional defiant disorder. Social anxiety disorder can be considered if the defiance occurs because of the fear of judgment and negative evaluation of others.

2. B: The client is resistant to the therapeutic process or is uninterested. The client may respond well to you showing interest in the game that he is playing because it is his preferred activity and topic. Although it may not feel therapeutic or clinical to talk about video games, this meets the client's developmental needs to talk about or engage in preferred activities or play. Sports may create further conversation, but it cannot be assumed that the client enjoys sports, nor is establishing common interests a priority in the therapeutic relationship. Encouraging the client to return to the office or to continue the session in the living room may not be fruitful because the client is clearly uninterested in therapy at this moment.

3. B: Expressing that the client might feel lonely or overlooked is a reflection of feeling, which is a method of deducing and acknowledging the emotions behind what the client has stated. Sometimes, this technique is beneficial because the client may not be aware of the roots of his feelings. Responding to the client's statement with a question about how he might be bothered by attention or may want different attention would be the use of clarification. Relating to the client's feelings by saying that you can understand how he might feel sad or frustrated is an expression of empathy. Identifying that you hear the client saying that he does not like his parents because they prefer his sister is an example of paraphrasing.

4. D: Play therapy may be beneficial because it can help children to improve communication and explore/express their emotions. Applied behavior analysis would not be indicated because the client is able to engage in cognitive counseling, which means talk therapy would be more beneficial. Medication management may be beneficial at some point, but there are no Food and Drug Administration-approved medications for oppositional defiant disorder, and therapy tends to be more effective than medication. Occupational therapy is not indicated because the individual appears to have no cognitive, physical, or sensory issues that would require skill development.

5. C: The client becoming more aware of the consequences of his actions would be an appropriate short-term goal at this point in the therapeutic relationship. This would be appropriate because it is prioritizing creating awareness more than a significant change in behavior and would assist the client in knowing what he is doing and how it affects himself and others. Assisting the client with awareness of his behavior can also help because if the client can find more effective ways of meeting his needs, he may be more motivated to make changes. Grades, functioning in school, social interactions, and ability to take directions are more long-term goals of therapy because they require incremental change and will take time to achieve.

6. D: It would be supportive to encourage the client to request what he needs, which is a break from schoolwork before starting his homework. It is also empathetic because it identifies and appreciates his unspoken desire for a break and makes the client feel understood and that his desires are valid. The statement identifying that it is frustrating to start schoolwork displays some empathy but does not provide an option for next steps to take and therefore is not the best response in this scenario. Telling the client to get his homework over with or encouraging him to listen to his parents does not provide empathy (because it reinforces the parents' request over his desire), nor does it assist the client with identifying actions that he can take to improve his situation.

7. A: These terms are often used as part of applied behavior analysis, and, in this situation, the function of behavior is for a tangible item. The client is seeking a snack and was denied one, so his behavior's function is to push his parents to get frustrated, give in to his behavior, and provide what he wants. The counselor's response to this would be to encourage more effective and appropriate manners of expressing his wants and needs. The behavior can be rewarded when he appropriately advocates for his wants and needs. It is possible that the request for a snack is to escape the session. However, the behavior was clearly escalated when he was denied the snack, so the behavior was more about being denied the item. The client is not requesting the snack for attention-seeking purposes, demonstrated by his strong reaction to not being able to have one at that moment. Generally, attention-seeking behavior is focused primarily on the attention, rather than the outcome of the request or behavior. In this scenario, the client is already the center of attention in the session.

8. A: The most appropriate behavioral intervention should address the problem behavior, which, in this case, is the reaction to being denied a snack immediately (and not the manner in which he requested the snack). When the client engages in inappropriate behavior in order to gain access to something (in this case, the snack immediately rather than after the session), you should support him in coping with the decision that was made if clear boundaries are set. If the client had inappropriately requested the snack, then you could support the client in requesting the snack more appropriately and provide the snack when he does. Simply allowing the client to accept the decision that was made by his parents is not enough because you want to empower him to cope with his strong emotions.

9. A: Developmentally, the client does not have the self-awareness to know when he needs to cope with strong emotions and thoughts; therefore, it will be important for his parents to prompt him to cope when he is experiencing these triggers. The client is able to deal with strong emotions at this age, but he may not always know when he needs to, so his parents' support will be very important. The presenting problem does involve a defiance in following directions from his parents, but this is not related to his developmental level. The client is currently resistant to therapy, but he has improved his engagement from the last session; therefore, it is possible that he will be able to fully participate at some point.

10. A: Compensation for services would fall under the ACA Code of Ethics section on bartering rather than ethical considerations for gifts (ACA, 2104). Bartering would involve further consideration and planning to include a written contract and is not being demonstrated in the offering of a meal. It is important to consider the cultural implications of declining a gift if it negatively affects the counseling relationship. Monetary impact is important because you would not want to regularly accept meals if it puts a financial strain on your client's family. It is also important to consider the motive for giving the gift because the parents may have expectations for a gift in return, which may complicate or strain the counseling relationship.

11. B: The parents praising appropriate behavior is positive reinforcement. Positive reinforcement involves adding something to increase desired behavior. The client desires attention from his parents, so providing positive praise would increase the likelihood of more appropriate communication. A time-out would be considered a punishment, which would focus on providing an adverse consequence to decrease a behavior. The parents walking away to demonstrate they do not approve of his behavior would not be positive reinforcement because they are not adding something to increase the target behavior. The parents' encouragement to request what he wants or needs is helpful, but it is not positive reinforcement.

12. D: The purpose of disrupting beliefs is to challenge thoughts that are harmful or unhelpful. The answer that states "my parents don't like me right now, so they made me take time to calm down" is still unhelpful because it validates that the client is not liked by his parents. The other options promote the idea that the parents care about him and want him to do and feel better.

13. A: A behavioral experiment is when the client engages in a behavior to see if it results in their expected outcomes or to see if the outcome changes. This can be helpful in treating anxiety because the client can see that their predicted outcomes are often worse than the actual outcomes. Role playing involves acting out different situations in order to prepare for a future situation. Exposure therapy is used for anxiety and phobias and involves exposing a client to their fears/phobias. This is done in small increments in order to increase the client's comfort and confidence in those situations and to show the client that the threat is not as extreme as anticipated. Guided discovery involves exploring different perspectives and providing evidence for and against certain beliefs.

Case Study 4

1. A: The Dyadic Adjustment Scale, a 32-question scale that assesses each individual's perception of the relationship and is used to assess for marital satisfaction, would be helpful for assessing each individual's satisfaction in the marriage and may prompt processing of what brought the couple to the point at which the wife had an affair. The wife has generalized anxiety disorder, which can be tracked using the Beck Anxiety Inventory; however, this would not be the focus of couples counseling. The Minnesota Multiphasic Personality Inventory may give insight into personality traits of both individuals; however, it would not be indicated at this point in counseling. The Family Environment Scale focuses more on the family system as a whole and not just the parental unit.

2. C: The couple is having difficulty with quality interaction at this point due to breakdowns in communication, so quality time would not be the focus for short-term goals. The couple does need to work on effective communication skills so they can work through what events led up to the affair and also so they can interact in a meaningful manner. The couple would also benefit from processing resentment because this is a common problem that leads to infidelity and is also a current barrier to the counseling process.

3. A: A unique limit to confidentiality is the clinician's inability to ensure that both individuals in couples counseling will not share information about the other. It is important to encourage both individuals to maintain confidentiality for each other in order to ensure a safe environment in the couples counseling session. The nature of counseling, the risks involved, and promotion of well-being are all common factors in the counseling setting.

4. D: The first course of action would be for the wife to receive individual outpatient therapy for her anxiety because it is clinically significant. You would not provide individual therapy for her because this would create bias in your provision of couples counseling. Medication management might be beneficial for the wife, but it would be helpful for the individual therapist to make this referral because they will be working specifically on her anxiety. Your focus with the couple is their relationship and not the wife's anxiety. Although cognitive reframing may be helpful for the couple, couples counseling should be focused on the couple's needs and not on the wife's individual diagnosis.

5. C: The presence of psychotic features is not a specifier for adjustment disorder, but the following specifiers might apply: with depressed mood, with anxiety, with mixed anxiety and depressed mood, with disturbance of conduct, with mixed disturbance of emotions or conduct, or unspecified. The specifier used for this couple is "with anxiety" because there is anxiety present about the future of their relationship. All of the other listed criteria (symptoms occurring within 3 months of the stressor, impaired functioning, and symptoms that are not based on a normative stress reaction) apply to adjustment disorder.

6. A: The downward or vertical arrow technique is a CBT intervention that assists in identifying core beliefs regarding thoughts or a situation. The counselor accepts the premise of what the person says and asks a projective question such as what it means for the future of the marriage (if the wife does not love her husband) and then further questioning based on the husband's response in order to narrow down what the husband's core belief is. The other questions are all helpful to ask and to explore, but the downward/vertical arrow question technique can help identify what the husband's deeper fear is regarding his wife's infidelity.

7. C: The husband's response is an example of stonewalling. Stonewalling occurs when a partner stops engaging in communication. Criticism involves attacking the partner for who they are and what they do. Contempt involves treating the partner with disrespect and ridicule. Finally, defensiveness involves making excuses for behavior and often deflects from addressing the partner's feelings. These often are sequential, going from criticism to contempt and subsequently from defensiveness to stonewalling (Lisitsa, 2021).

8. B: Taking a break and returning to the conversation when the partner is calmer would be an appropriate behavioral response to stonewalling. Using empathetic listening is beneficial, but it does not assist the client in calming down to return to a more communicative state. Remembering positive traits and using gratitude are helpful in managing feelings of contempt, but they do not address stonewalling. Using "I" statements is helpful, but it does not put the client in a state to process thoughts and feelings because he needs to return to a calm state to engage in effective communication.

9. A: Mindful listening is the act of being present when someone is speaking and when you are speaking. Relating to emotions would be better defined by empathy. Repeating the message heard is considered paraphrasing. Summarizing is only one element of mindful listening, and it does not necessarily reflect the act of being truly present as the sender and the receiver of the communication.

10. C: The most beneficial intervention at this point would be to separate the partners and meet with them individually. This may be helpful in creating a more comfortable environment for expression for both partners. You will gain insight into each person's perspective in a manner that is safer than the couples setting. It might be helpful to encourage the husband to return, but the couple is having trouble communicating, and getting each individual's unbiased perspectives could be very helpful. It is also helpful to get individuals to take responsibility for their own actions, but the couple is not capable of this at this point in therapy because they are just starting to explore their emotions regarding the wife's affair.

11. C: It would be most ethical to meet with the husband in a separate, empty office in the practice following the meeting with the wife. You want to protect both individuals' right to confidentiality, and you do not know whether the wife would be listening in on your conversation with the husband in the lobby. Because both individuals are clients, it is important to ensure that they each have a safe space to express themselves. You should provide this safety by using separate spaces for self-expression prior to returning to the joint session.

12. B: The client is focusing only on the negatives and ignoring positive interactions (such as when the wife tries to engage the husband in quality time and attempts to improve their relationship). This is an example of the cognitive distortion called mental filter, which is filtering out positive interactions and focusing on negative interactions. Catastrophizing is assuming that the worst will happen, which is not the focus of his thoughts. Jumping to conclusions involves coming to a conclusion without evidence. This client is not jumping to conclusions because his assumptions contradict the available evidence (assuming that his wife does not put her relationship first even with evidence that she is attempting to improve her relationship). "Should" statements involve expectations that are not met, but this does not apply because the client is not expressing an expectation of what the wife should do to alleviate the problem.

13. D: The ACA Code of Ethics allows for the counselor to change counseling modalities, but in these cases, the counselor must explain the possible consequences of the change, which may be financial, legal, personal, or therapeutic in nature. If you begin to provide individual counseling to the husband in this case, there is a possibility of becoming biased toward him, which would create a conflict of interest should you resume marital counseling with the couple. If you think the client's needs are out of your scope of practice, you can refer him to another counselor.

Case Study 5

1. B: The most effective form of treatment for bipolar disorders is a combination of medication management and psychotherapy (Mayo Foundation, 2021). Medication and CBT together are an effective treatment combination for this lifelong disorder that requires cognitive adjustments that can be supported by medication. Therapy alone, although it can be helpful, is more effective when combined with medication. Medication alone would address the behavioral and cognitive changes needed to create the lasting changes that are not impacted by medication. Dialectical behavior therapy is useful in treating mood disorders and substance use and is not proven to be beneficial for treatment of bipolar disorder.

2. A: Energy could be a strength for some clients, but due to the client's diagnosis, it is also the part of bipolar disorder that causes impulsivity and lack of sleep and in turn impairs functioning. Due to bipolar disorder, the client is also experiencing hypersomnia during major depressive episodes; therefore, energy is not a reliable or constant state for the client. The desire to learn is helpful to the client as a student who is willing to take in and apply new information. Perseverance is also a strength because the client is going through a difficult adjustment and perseverance is the ability to push through the situation despite these difficulties. Insight is a strength because it means that the client can look inwardly and gain a deeper understanding of her thoughts, feelings, and actions.

3. C: The client is still experiencing a manic episode; therefore, focusing on depression is not the main goal because it is not the most prevalent symptom. Focusing on cognitive processing skills and behaviors that trigger or maintain manic symptoms is important in order to work toward decreasing manic symptoms. Sleep hygiene is an important short-term goal because the client is currently not sleeping well and needs support with increasing her sleep. The client needs to work on impulse control because she is engaging in frequent late-night shopping sprees.

4. C: You have the experience and education for treatment of bipolar disorder; therefore, clinical supervision or consultation would be beneficial in ensuring that you are providing appropriate treatment. Therapists should seek supervision in areas of new specializations per the ACA Code of Ethics in order to ensure that the service provision is appropriate (2014, p. 8). That said, because evidence-based practice in the treatment of bipolar disorder supports the combination of counseling and medication management, a referral to psychiatry to oversee the medication management is also required because this is outside the scope of the counselor. A referral to another therapist would not be necessary because your education and experience are appropriate for effective treatment. It is always beneficial to seek ongoing education as a therapist, but if the client came to counseling and you did not already have the education in the area required to appropriately support her, you would refer her to another therapist.

5. A: An inflated sense of self and/or grandiose thinking are symptoms that often occur with manic episodes. Manic episodes have a criterion of 1 week of symptoms, whereas at least 4 days of symptoms is a criterion for a hypomanic episode. A hypomanic episode is not as severe as a manic episode and does not affect functioning in social or occupational settings. Hallucinations are not a symptom of a manic episode.

6. D: Managing behavioral triggers is a way to become more aware of when impulsive behavior may occur during a manic episode and provides activities that should be avoided or coped with in order to prevent impulsivity. Drug use is not a behavioral trigger for this client because the drug use was a result of impulsive behavior and did not lead to more impulsive behavior. For this client, being up late, going out with friends, and poor adherence to her usual routine increase the likelihood of impulsivity.

7. B: The General Behavior Inventory assesses the presence and severity of manic and depressive symptoms; therefore, it is the most appropriate tool for monitoring the severity of the client's symptoms. The MMPI-2 can support a bipolar I or II diagnosis, but it would not be beneficial in regularly measuring the severity of symptoms. The PHQ-9 is the major depressive disorder portion of the full PHQ that can help with the diagnosis and measurement of depressive symptom severity over time. The Brief Symptom Inventory measures many areas of symptomatology and may be useful in providing support for a bipolar diagnosis, but it does not provide measurement for the severity for manic episodes.

8. B: It is important to consider your own views and how they affect the counseling process with the client. With this client, it would benefit the therapeutic process to focus on assisting her with seeing how her behavior is keeping her from reaching her own goals. It may be helpful to share tactics that work for you, but self-disclosure should only be used if it will meaningfully impact the counseling process. Honesty about differences between the therapist and client is important at times, but in this case, it can be helpful for the client to see how her own behavior affects her progress. You should not ignore your own values, because they do impact therapy and the goal is to minimize the impact that they have.

9. A: The most appropriate answer is to evaluate the client's cognitive barriers and reservations about medication. This opens up a conversation about what makes it hard for the client to follow up and to address the anxiety or other barriers caused by manic behavior. The client's personal decision to not take medication is very important and should be respected; however, this is the second session and you have not fully processed the client's feelings about medication. It might help to provide psychoeducation about the benefits of medication and therapy, but this should have been done when you provided the referral, and it may feel like nagging to the client. You can encourage or remind the client to follow up, but this may not address what kept her from following up and therefore may not provide any practical solutions or support.

10. B: Based on the information provided, it would be most beneficial to encourage the client to plan activities that she knows she has enjoyed in the past. The cognitive distortion associated with assuming that she will not enjoy herself is called fortune-telling because she is assuming an outcome without knowledge to support the assumption, and she may in fact enjoy things more than she thinks, even if it is not to the extent that she used to. Exercise can improve mood and well-being, but the client has not expressed any interest in this activity. The client already spends time with friends and should continue to do so. The client reports not feeling ready to take medication, so this is an ongoing discussion.

11. A: The school's disability resource center would be helpful in seeking accommodations for the client in her classes. The Americans with Disabilities Act covers most mental health disorders and could assist the client with maintaining academic progress while she is working through starting to manage bipolar disorder. The client does not currently see a psychiatrist and also has not mentioned her PCP and does not appear to see them in any way that would require collaboration. Collaboration with the client's parents is not indicated because the client is currently living at school away from her parents.

12. C: Leaning forward can come across as aggressive or argumentative behavior if not reciprocated or as part of mirroring the client. It is best to sit back in the chair or, if standing, to lean on a wall. Smiling and keeping your arms open show that you are relaxed and not closed off to the client. Mirroring is helpful because it is about matching the emotions of the client and their posture, which shows attunement to the client's mental state.

13. D: Catatonia is characterized by abnormal movement—either through a complete lack of movement or through repetitive movements—and it is not characteristic, nor a criterion, of a major depressive episode. Decreased interest or pleasure in activities, suicidal thoughts, and difficulty concentrating are all included in the DSM-5 list of possible criteria for the diagnosis of a major depressive episode.

Case Study 6

1. A: Open-ended questions were not helpful during the intake session; therefore, you need to take a different approach. If you ask the client about the musical group depicted on her t-shirt or what she does for fun, you show interest in the client and what she values, which could lead to building rapport. It can be helpful to open things up and allow the client to identify whatever goals she wants or to start talking about whatever is easiest for her to start talking about. This gives the client control and lets her lead with what she is most comfortable talking about.

2. B: Because talking has not been beneficial, playing a game may help develop comfort because play is a nonthreatening activity that does not require disclosure. Play also helps some children lower their guard, and they may begin talking or be more willing to talk while you play. You have tried talking with her, and she is resistant to talking about what is happening; therefore, explaining the nature of therapy would not provide further benefit because you did this as part of informed consent. Immediacy has been attempted because you identified the client was not comfortable and tried to support her in this feeling. Silence may make the client feel pressured and even more uncomfortable, although it may be valuable later on in therapy because it does encourage reflection and communication.

3. B: Referral for psychological testing likely would not return much helpful information because the client is not comfortable enough to talk about what is happening. The goals should be achievable and should be relevant to the presenting situation. Building trust and identifying barriers to school attendance are important because this is the only obvious presenting problem even with minimal client participation. The focus on improving social connectedness is important due to withdrawn behavior.

4. C: You are balancing ethical and clinical concerns, and, in this situation, it is best for the client to be willing for you to talk with her parents and for the parents to accept a level of confidentiality for the client. If the client feels that she can talk with a level of confidentiality in the counseling sessions, then she is most likely to engage fully in treatment. The parents do have a right to all of the information, but this would not necessarily be clinically beneficial because the client may not trust you if you share all of the given information with her parents. If the client declines that you share information with the parents and the parents continue to request it, they do have a right to information, but it may not benefit treatment to do so. It is important to note that different states have different laws regarding the rights of minors in treatment.

5. A: Engaging with eye contact is an effective use of nonverbal attending because it demonstrates attention and interest, which supports the client in feeling comfortable. Leaning forward, using hand gestures, and nodding (vs. leaning back and minimizing the use of gestures and head nods) all demonstrate warm attending behaviors that will also increase the client's comfort. The most appropriate distance for personal conversation is 1.5–4 feet with approximately 3–4 feet being the most comfortable spacing for individuals.

6. D: As a therapist, you are a mandated reporter and must report all incidents of abuse or neglect to the local government agency that investigates those reports, such as the local child protective services office. It is also important to make the parents aware of what happened, and, although the client does not need to consent to this, you already know that she is okay with this because she said so earlier in the session. The client does not need to consent, but it is beneficial to the counseling relationship that she has consented to you breaking confidentiality. A release of PHI to talk with the school may be helpful but is not required to ensure the client's safety. It may be helpful to create a safety plan with the family to ensure that the client is not in a position to be sexually abused by this individual again at school. Reporting the incident to the local government agency and collaborating with the parents are the minimal steps needed at this point in therapy.

7. D: Identifying situations that may trigger a trauma response would likely come later in treatment from processing because the effects of the sexual assault are not fully understood at this point. It is important to begin processing the feeling of shame because this is a feeling the client is experiencing presently. One of the first steps in working through trauma is to process how it affects present functioning; therefore, it would be helpful to assist the client in reducing the sexual assault's effects on herself. It is also helpful to prepare the client for the investigation because this may be further triggering and occur quickly, and the client would be otherwise unprepared to emotionally manage the situation.

8. D: Going home and going to sleep may meet physical needs for sleep if work is overwhelming; however, it may not meet your self-care needs because you are having trouble refraining from thinking about your session today. Going to sleep does not deal with the emotions that are present and therefore would not be managing your reaction to the session. Exercise, clinical supervision, and socialization could all be beneficial acts of self-care to help you focus on the present and manage your thoughts regarding your client's situation.

9. B: Consulting with your agency might be the agency's protocol, but it is not required. It is up to each individual therapist to report suspected abuse or neglect. You should report the abuse or neglect even if your supervisor or agency disagrees with you because it is not your or your agency's responsibility to determine if a threat is credible. Each state has different regulations surrounding the amount of time that can pass between learning of abuse or neglect and reporting it, so it is important to know your state's regulations and adhere to them.

10. A: The symptomatology is consistent with post-traumatic stress disorder, with delayed expression due to presenting symptoms and the 6 months it took for symptoms to reach full post-traumatic stress disorder criteria. Post-traumatic stress disorder with depersonalization is the feeling of experiencing the trauma from the perspective of an outside observer, which is not consistent with reported symptoms. Acute stress disorder would require a time period of 30 days or less, so this would not be an appropriate diagnosis. Adjustment disorder presents as difficulty managing adjustment to life's stressors; this is not an appropriate diagnosis due to the presenting symptoms.

11. B: Although you will not always have shared life experiences with clients, you can try to understand the core feelings related to their experiences. Although you may have never experienced sexual assault, most people can understand the feelings of fear, violation, and possibly shame. Even though you cannot understand every client's experience the way the client does, you can still provide empathetic statements to the client based on your own experiences of those core feelings. Being open about your inexperience with the client situation can be helpful, but it does not promote an empathetic response. Research may provide more insight, but it would not help during this immediate session in terms of understanding the client's experience.

12. D: Adjustment disorders arise in reaction to major events or life changes that disrupt an individual's prior way of life. These events may be positive or negative in nature. Common causes include the divorce of parents, moving to a new home/state/school, marriage, having children, loss of a job, loss of a loved one, or retirement. Although an adjustment disorder may be peripherally linked to stress from trauma or retraumatization, it is the least likely of all of the options to result from sexual trauma (post-traumatic stress disorder would be more likely). Intimacy and trust might be difficult for the client in the future because they are directly related to the sexual assault. Depression and anxiety symptoms are already present and may progress to clinical levels if untreated.

13. D: Using cognitive behavioral strategies to reduce the daily impact of trauma is the most relevant short-term goal for this client because it is achievable in the most immediate future. Reducing negative symptoms in a significant manner is not likely to occur in the short term, nor is reducing the avoidance of triggers, because it takes time to process a traumatic event and implement the coping skills necessary to achieve these goals. Talking about a traumatic experience is not always beneficial for clients and may, in fact, cause more harm. In the early stages of treatment following a traumatic event, it is often more beneficial to manage the effects of the trauma than to force conversations about it.

Case Study 7

1. C: Informed consent occurs throughout the counseling relationship, not solely during the intake session, because you need to explain the changes in treatment and the risks involved throughout the counseling process. The risks of counseling, copays/fees, and the counselor's and client's rights and responsibilities are covered as part of this process.

2. A: Speaking in a slow, soft, gentle tone can encourage thought and engagement from the client and is a positive attending trait that can be used by the therapist (Sommers-Flanagan & Sommers-Flanagan, 2015, p. 64). Using hand gestures and frequently stating "yes" or "uh huh" along with head nods can interrupt the client by making them think that you have more to say, or it may make them avoid eye contact in order to avoid the distraction of seeing frequent head nodding (Sommers-Flanagan & Sommers-Flanagan, p. 65). Turning your body slightly away from the client may come across as being disengaged, whereas facing the client with an open body posture is more engaging.

3. C: This is an example of labeling because the client is making a generalized judgment about himself based on one event. The client is taking one bad experience and labeling himself as unemployable, which may not be an accurate assessment. The client is not catastrophizing because he is not exaggerating the impacts of the situation; rather, he is making a judgment about himself based on the situation. The client is not fortune-telling, and although identifying himself as unemployable may be a projective statement, it falls more under labeling because he is identifying himself based on one experience. Mental filtering occurs when an individual filters out the good and only focuses on the bad, and although this may also be happening, the statement does not present explicitly as mental filtering.

4. C: Based on the ACA Code of Ethics, the most ethical method in dealing with this dilemma is to consider the possible hardships imposed on the client and adjust your rate for the client (ACA Governing Council, 2014). Bartering for services is appropriate, but it requires a written contract that both parties agree on (ACA Governing Council, 2014). Maintaining the self-pay rate does not consider possible hardships for the client and would not be the most ethical consideration. Providing a referral might be appropriate, but it is most ethical to first consider an adjustment in the fee prior to referring him to another therapist.

5. A: The employer is not required to have a specific percentage of the workforce that must be above a certain age according to the Age Discrimination in Employment Act of 1967 and its amendments. However, employers do have guidelines about mandatory retirement for individuals in executive positions and reductions in benefits. It is also prohibited to have preferences based on age for a position.

6. C: The ACA Code of Ethics prohibits providing services to the client's family members because this affects objectivity in the counseling process (2014, p. 5). You can provide a counseling session for the client that involves his spouse if it focuses on supporting your client's well-being and is not an ongoing process because this would be a dual relationship and biases would affect efficacy. The couple should be referred to couples counseling; however, the client has concerns about paying for sessions and currently does not have health insurance, which would make this an untenable option.

7. D: The ACA Code of Ethics does not cover any payments for research because the clinician will still be providing therapy and the client will be paying for therapy (2014, p. 16). The client will be informed about how he can withdraw from the research at any time; of any discomfort, power differentials, or risks involved in the research; and also the limits of confidentiality in the research process (ACA Governing Council, p. 16).

8. A: Reflection is about identifying the underlying feelings that the client is experiencing based on what he says. Identifying that the client's statement about "doing nothing" every day might mean that he feels bored and unengaged identifies an unspoken feeling behind the statement and would be considered reflection. Stating that the client's days are hard because he is not doing much is a paraphrase because it restates the client's words in a different manner. Stating the difficulty of the pressure that the client is facing is an empathetic statement. Although it is important to focus on the client finding meaningful employment, this is not reflection. Paraphrasing, reflecting, empathizing, and defining goals all show the client that you are listening and are attuned with him.

9. C: As evidenced by his frustration with unemployment and feelings of worthlessness, the client's self-esteem is affected by his current situation. This would be important to investigate further. The client's depression and depressed mood have already been identified and are therefore not new symptoms. The client has demonstrated that he has work skills, and although it is within your role to support the client in finding new opportunities that match his skill set, the focus should be on the underlying root of the client's statement.

10. D: The Motivational Appraisal of Personal Potential career assessment identifies career options based on an individual's interests. The enneagram and the Myers-Briggs Type Indicator are personality tests, and, although they may identify traits about a person that may be helpful in processing options, they do not focus on career options. The Work and Social Adjustment Scale is an assessment that identifies how mental health functioning affects functioning in multiple areas of a client's life.

11. C: A CBT thought log can capture unhelpful thinking that is a barrier to applying to jobs and can be used in counseling sessions to process these thoughts in order to improve self-talk. It will be helpful to provide psychoeducation on relaxation techniques, such as progressive muscle relaxation, in order to manage anxiety when he is experiencing it; however, this would not improve motivation because it focuses on symptoms rather than on cognitive barriers. Role-playing might be helpful when it comes to interviewing, but it does not help the client with applying to jobs.

12. D: A natural support is a relationship that occurs naturally. Although the therapist is a regular support, they are not a naturally occurring support. A childhood friend and a sibling would be strong natural supports because these relationships have lasted for the long term. An acquaintance can also be a natural support. This one is an especially good support because he is in the client's Bible study and can provide further support for his spiritual needs.

13. A: Many job experiences have some level of overlap, with the skills required being applicable in other positions. Because the client has an immediate financial need to be employed, he should be supported in considering this position. His experience as a supervisor lends itself to helpful social skills, and his work in the automobile plant was hard labor. You should emphasize that these skills are relatable to being a server. Meanwhile, the client can continue to look for positions that might meet his financial needs better and/or interest him more; however, the client's financial needs are more urgent, and both of these things can be done while accepting the job that provides immediate work. It is not typically a therapeutic approach to recommend that someone make a life decision such as taking a job, leaving a job, staying with or leaving someone, etc. If these decisions do not end up in the client's favor, it could leave the counselor liable. Using assessments to find appropriate employment matches for your client is helpful, but the client has more pressing needs financially and has a more immediate employment need.

Case Study 8

1. A: The only symptom required to make the diagnosis of reactive attachment disorder would be noted minimal or rare response to comfort when the client is experiencing strong emotions. Frequent tantrums may be evident in reactive attachment disorder; however, it is can also be an indication of other disorders. Difficulty making friends is not a criterion for reactive attachment disorder. The age range for reactive attachment disorder is 9 months to 5 years old.

2. C: Unless parental rights are terminated, the birth parents have rights to PHI. The foster parents are able to provide reasonable medical and mental health care for the child that they are taking care of; therefore, because they are part of the therapeutic process, they also have access to this information.

3. D: The client is too young to have a cognitive focus in therapy because she will have trouble processing thoughts and feelings about her situation. Developing trust and comfort with the client is important because she is unengaged in therapy and may need help feeling comfortable with adults in order to engage in therapy. The foster parents would benefit from learning to reframe problem behaviors as opportunities to build their relationship with their foster child. They would also benefit from providing expectations, feedback, and structure on a consistent basis, which shows the client that her caregivers are in control and have her best interests in mind, which might help her manage strong emotions.

4. B: When considering effective counseling interventions for this client, you must first identify the underlying purpose of the behavior that must be addressed. In this case, while hitting is not an appropriate behavior, it was the client's method of communicating a feeling of insecurity. Effective counseling to address the feeling of insecurity must start with creating an environment that is comfortable and secure for the client, which is first communicated through the manner in which you enter the lobby and approach the client. Doing so calmly and without judgment will ensure that you are not there to reprimand, but to support. Only if the client feels secure, would discussing the need for safety and refraining from hitting be received and the possibility of the client returning to the office with her foster parents be realistic. Confidentiality when leaving the office is important (and can be enforced by locking your computer and/or taking your notebook so that neither are available to the parents), but this does not directly address an effective counseling intervention with the client.

5. C: Many features of reactive attachment disorder are also common in autism spectrum disorders; therefore, it is important to differentiate between the two diagnoses for the client. Oppositional defiant disorder and conduct disorder are not differential diagnoses for reactive attachment disorder because they are not based on the child's attachment to their caregivers; rather, they are based on behavioral problems. The existence of parent–child relational problems might be an appropriate description for this case, but it is not a formal diagnosis, and is rather a Z-code.

6. B: From a behavioral perspective, the function of the behavior would be to escape. In order to address this, you want to avoid reinforcing the behavior by providing a response, and you also want to prevent escape by encouraging her to communicate what she needs or wants. Encouragement to engage in cognitive reframing would not be developmentally appropriate because the client may not be able to use this skill and it is not a behavioral intervention. Choosing to disengage from the client and to not respond would not address the function of the behavior because when the function is "escape," you would be allowing the client to escape by disengaging and would reinforce the behavior. It may be helpful to redirect the client to calm down; however, this would not address the function of the behavior.

7. A: This kind of thinking places blame on the couple, and it may be helpful to focus on what the couple is doing well for the client in order to increase their confidence. "Should" statements focus on what the individual should do. The parents aren't focusing on what they should do; rather, they feel guilty for the client's potential future situation. This is not all-or-nothing thinking because the parents are not focusing on their actions as either extremely good or bad. Instead, they are blaming themselves for the client's situation. Overgeneralization focuses on creating an expectation based on an experience. The client's foster parents are not creating an expectation based on an experience because she is rather blaming them for the future outcome.

8. D: Encouragement to visit the client's birth parents should be a highly planned out event, should be coordinated with the foster care case manager, and should follow court recommendations. This kind of visit has the potential to cause harm to the client and also to the client's relationship with her caregivers. One-on-one play, physical affection, verbal reinforcement, and family cohesion activities can all foster a more appropriate attachment between the client and the foster parents.

9. B: Play therapy would be the most effective approach for this client because she is 4 years old and would benefit from playing out life circumstances instead of talking through them. Rational emotive behavior therapy would likely be above the cognitive level of the client because it requires the client to process rational and irrational thought processes. Bibliotherapy involves the use of books for therapy; the client is likely too young to benefit from this focus. Psychodynamic therapy focuses on identifying and processing one's emotions; the client is not at a cognitive level at which she can participate in this type of therapy.

10. A: A schema is a core belief that one has about themselves based on what has happened to them. Schemas may be irrational or unhelpful at times, but a healthy schema leads to a strong sense of self-worth and self-esteem. Although cognitive therapy approaches might not be directly helpful for the client, the parents can assist in adjusting schemas. Automatic thoughts occur when a situation triggers a thought that is unconscious and can be negative or positive. Thought stopping is a technique that focuses on stopping a negative or irrational thought. Transference is when an individual redirects feelings and emotions about one individual to an entirely different individual. Transference is likely happening from the birth parents to the foster parents.

11. A: Empathy would support the client in feeling heard and would assist you in connecting emotionally with the client's situation. Cognitive reframing may be developmentally difficult for the client and also might feel like you are pushing the client to move past her comfort level. It would not be helpful to continue playing and to refrain from acknowledging what the client said. Acknowledging the client's expression of emotions would reinforce her with expressing herself and would demonstrate care toward the client. The downward arrow technique would likely seem aggressive to the client, and she might refrain from further engagement in this session.

12. B: Even when information is subpoenaed, it is important to only provide relevant information, which means that you may not provide the client's entire file. The ACA Code of Ethics encourages only sharing information that is relevant to the entity receiving the information (ACA Governing

Council, 2014). It may be helpful to obtain legal counsel to navigate this situation because you want to ensure that you are providing what is legally appropriate. It is always important that information is sent in a manner that is compliant with HIPAA standards.

13. D: The client's behavior is characterized by heightened anxiety, increased irritability, and distance from others, which comprises a disorganized or fearful attachment style. A secure attachment style is when a child feels comfortable enough to communicate wants and needs, knows that their caregiver has their interest and safety in mind, is independent, and has good self-esteem. An avoidant, or dismissive, attachment style is characterized by insecurity, independence, a desire for intimacy but a fear of it, and the placement of distance between the self and others. An individual demonstrating an ambivalent or preoccupied attachment style focuses intensely on having relationships with others and feels very insecure when he or she does have a relationship because of a fear that the relationship will end.

Case Study 9

1. A: When bad things happen, it is normal that it affects the individual. A normal stress response is expected for situations that are difficult, but what distinguishes it as an adjustment disorder is when the stress affects functioning. Generalized anxiety disorder would involve anxiety surrounding general situations that affect functioning, but this would not be appropriate because the anxiety is surrounding his relationship with his wife and children. Although the client is experiencing the loss of a relationship, bereavement is not a consideration because the client is experiencing anxiety and depression surrounding the adjustment to a different way of life as opposed to just about the loss of a relationship. Disinhibited social engagement disorder is when children approach and engage with individuals with whom they are not familiar, but this does not define this individual's situation.

2. B: Exploring boundaries will be beneficial because the client does care about his ex-wife, which is part of who he is, and he also must maintain a relationship with her because they share custody of their children. Further engaging in supporting his ex-wife will continue to make the new roles confusing for the client and would not benefit him in identifying his new role in her life. The client reports that he continues to love his ex-wife, and, although not emotionally supporting her might be beneficial, he likely would not be ready to do this all at once. The client states that he "knows the relationship won't return to where it was"; therefore, it likely would put the client in a situation in which he could get hurt if you encourage him to try to reconcile.

3. D: Different states have varying rules for providing across-state counseling services. It is always important to consider state regulations regarding cross-border counseling services prior to providing counseling. Simply providing referrals may meet the family's needs; however, it would be more helpful to the client to find out more about the states' regulations. You cannot move forward with providing a session just because the father lives in the state you are licensed in.

4. D: Ataque de nervios, although not an official diagnosis, is a commonly used idiom in the Latin culture that describes certain symptoms. Translated directly into an "attack of nerves," sadness is not a common symptom of ataque de nervios because symptoms are more often based in anxiety. Irritability, nausea, and vertigo are symptoms commonly described by individuals complaining of these attacks.

5. D: The client's affect is best described as congruent because he is demonstrating anxious behavior, which is consistent with being in counseling for the first time. Congruence is demonstrated when a client's verbalized emotions match their body language and expressions.

People with constricted affect show evidence of restrained emotion, displaying much less explicit emotion than the typical person. A flat affect is defined by almost no emotional expression even in the presence of strong stimuli. A blunted affect is similar to a flat affect but involves mild expressions of emotion in the presence of strong stimuli.

6. B: Reflecting the emotion of being frustrated about the resignation and then moving to agreeing that the client's feelings are understandable is validation because it goes a step past reflection to normalizing his emotions. Understanding that a situation is frustrating aligns more with empathy. Simply acknowledging frustration regarding the situation would just be reflection because you are reflecting his emotion. Expressing understanding about frustration regarding the church situation and depressive symptoms is simply a summarization of what the client has said.

7. C: It would be most helpful to continuously assess how your own values and beliefs affect the counseling process. Although it is important to support your client's beliefs and not impose your own, there is a level of self-reflection that is important in the process of counseling to ensure that you are not unintentionally imposing your own beliefs. Although it might be helpful to explain that you do not share beliefs with the client, it also undermines your own ability to help him because it invalidates your ability to connect with him. It may also be helpful to support the client in assessing his own beliefs because it appears that he is feeling the conflict; however, your goal is to support his beliefs and values.

8. D: An increase in risky behaviors would align more with bipolar disorder, which does involve depressive episodes but is not required for major depressive disorder. The client needs at least five symptoms to meet the criteria for major depressive disorder that occur within a 2-week depressive episode, which include a change in weight of more than 5% in a month, and a decreased interest in preferred activities, among others.

9. B: CBT is a consistently accepted approach to treating depression because it focuses on addressing the unhelpful cognitive and behavioral processes that affect functioning. Behavioral therapy alone would not treat the cognitive needs of depression because depression is often affected by cognitive distortions and behavioral effects. Although dialectical behavior therapy is helpful with depression, it was created to treat borderline personality disorder, and CBT would be more generally accepted as helpful. Exposure therapy is primarily used to treat anxiety.

10. A: Based on what you know about this client, you consider the cultural reasons for the gift because it could be considered offensive in Hispanic cultures to decline a gift. It is also important to consider economic hardship, what the client may want or expect in exchange for the gift, and why you want the gift; however, with what you know thus far about the client, the most important aspect to consider is his culture.

11. C: With the focus of this session being conflict resolution, focusing only on one party would not be the most beneficial approach. The client does need to express himself effectively, but the individuals should take turns expressing themselves regarding the situation. Empathy toward his ex-wife would help the client understand what led her to talk with their children about the divorce in the manner that she did. The parents share custody of the children; therefore, they will need to work out what coparenting looks like and what their goals are as parents. Ground rules can add a framework for tough conversations and help the conversations stay on track toward resolution.

12. B: The intern would benefit from some education to improve competency because he does have some experience, which would make added education an appropriate option. Having different values or religious beliefs would not matter because the intern would not refer based on these differences because he should be focusing on supporting the client's worldview (ACA Governing Council, 2014, p. 6). The intern should not try to provide services the best that he can with the skills that he has if his skills do not meet the needs of the client.

13. A: You have had four sessions with this client and would likely already be too engaged, and therefore biased, to provide appropriate therapy to your client and his ex-wife at this point. It would be most ethical to refer the couple to another therapist if they would like to work on coparenting skills. Simply stating your inability to work with the couple without providing proper direction via a referral would not be the most ethical course of action because it does not support your client in seeking the additional help that he is requesting. If you provided individual and couples/family therapy, you would be risking bias toward this client because you work more directly with him and his needs.

Case Study 10

1. C: The most common unethical situation in the group setting is a counselor that does not have the knowledge or skills to lead the group. There are many positions that require a counselor to be a group counselor and to have another role with the client such as in this juvenile detention facility, in group homes, or in other community mental health roles. Often, dual relationships cannot be avoided in group counseling and at times are part of therapy such as dialectical behavior therapy, which is often a mixture of group and individual counseling. It is true that, when multiple clients are present such as in group, family, or couples counseling, you cannot guarantee confidentiality from all members, but you should encourage all clients to maintain confidentiality for the benefit of the group process. Although the clients may be forced to be in the group, you cannot force anyone to do anything against their will, which includes participation in mandatory therapy.

2. D: Getting everyone to share encourages participation and also makes everyone feel like they are part of the group. You would not want to do this in a forceful way because each client has the right to choose if they will participate, but getting everyone to participate would further the group process. Explaining group rules establishes that the group is about rules and boundaries and not about being open. Although rules are important, this is not a helpful way to start. You should be in control, and a level of control can help members feel more secure; however, speaking with authority would likely feel off-putting to this group due to their setting in the facility. Allowing space for your clients to discuss their frustrations regarding the facility might be helpful in the future, but this would not start the group off on a positive note.

3. B: Cognitive reframing might help manage anxiety in a group setting, but it does not specifically focus on encouraging participation and drawing out members. Written activities can be used to prompt responses and may be used in the context of rounds to promote the expectation that each member has a voice and is expected to provide a response. Dyads separate the members up into groups of two to discuss various topics and can ease some of the discomfort associated with larger group formats while promoting discussion in a smaller setting prior to returning to a group setting to report on what was discussed.

4. A: The group would most benefit from building trust and cohesion at this point in counseling because the correctional setting often encourages individuals to refrain from disclosure due to the fear of being targeted. Assertive communication skills, anger management strategies, and demonstrating affection will all be longer term goals as they work to develop these skills and implement them.

5. B: Incarceration in the juvenile population is due to a combination of thoughts and actions that result in illegal activity. Cognitive-behavioral group therapy is the most appropriate approach for this group because it focuses on the group identifying the thoughts and behaviors that affect them negatively and then changing those thoughts and behaviors to have a different outcome. Interpersonal group therapy works on several types of mental health issues by focusing on personal relationships with family, friends, or coworkers. Skill development group therapy focuses on teaching skills in multiple areas to improve functioning. Support groups are not typically led by a therapist and often involve people with similar struggles supporting each other. Although most of these modalities may provide secondary support for this therapy group, cognitive-behavioral therapy more comprehensively addresses the goal of changing thoughts and behaviors for a different outcome.

6. C: Cutting off would be telling client 4 that what he said was not acceptable in the group setting and then redirecting back to client 1. Engaging with client 4 about his beliefs would likely cause more harm, and this would not be a helpful intervention. You should not ignore client 4's statements because you want to support client 1 and set a precedent for what is acceptable in the group. Telling client 4 that what he said was against the group goals is helpful; however, threatening expulsion from the group does not support client 4 and might not be indicated at this point.

7. D: The storming phase focuses on group members establishing a hierarchy and often involves conflict even as group cohesion is developing. The forming stage is the initial stage in which the group comes together and becomes acquainted. The storming phase follows the forming stage. The norming phase is when the group members agree on how the group should be run and how individuals should interact. The performing stage is when the group is most productive and is working toward their goals.

8. A: This is an example of linking, which is the act of connecting individuals' experiences for the sake of bonding. Coleading involves two counselors leading a group to use their shared experiences for the benefit of the group. Identifying allies is helpful because it involves identifying group members who are helpful to the group process, but this does not equate to the use of linking. Reflection is restating the content of a message, and, although it is helpful, it is not the intervention you are using when linking a client's experience with another client's experience.

9. D: Extinction is a behavioral modification technique that focuses on removing reinforcement of a previously reinforced behavior with the hopes that it decreases and stops the behavior. This is not part of peer group influence. Reinforcement is present peer group influence, referring to the use of coercion, teasing, encouragement, criticism, and validation to dictate desired behavior. Social comparison is when an individual compares oneself to others in the group, which could lead to the individual changing their behavior to match the group's behavior. Transmission of skills and values happens when older or more experienced group members share values and skills with younger or less experienced group members.

10. B: The client has been causing significant disruptions that have affected other group members, and you need to address this after the group with the client. If you plan to address the client's disruptions and his need to be in another group provided by the facility, you do not want to do this in front of the other clients because this would present a power struggle in front of the others. It is important to consider your attempts at redirection and enforcing rules in order to assess and adjust your interventions. If the client is actively causing harm, you need to protect your other clients, which may involve ejecting the member from the group immediately or asking them to sit silently for the rest of the session. Although ejecting the client may affect his sentence, this was a decision that the client made, and attempts to refer to another group or problem-solve can be done after the group.

11. A: The concept that activating events lead to beliefs that affect consequences is in alignment with rational emotive behavior therapy, which is a subset of CBT. Motivational interviewing focuses on identifying client motivation and using that information to make changes regarding negative behaviors. The focus of overcoming a sense of inferiority is a focus of Adlerian therapy. Taking focus on the person's present life instead of past experience and responsibility on present experience is a gestalt therapy perspective.

12. D: It would be most helpful to talk with the involved individuals about their relationship and how it might adversely affect the group's process. Discussing the group rules, relationship dynamics, and monitoring the effects on the group will be helpful, but individuals will often proceed with the relationship anyway.

13. C: A key characteristic of conduct disorder is the violation of the rights, rules, or norms of others. This characteristic is also present with antisocial personality disorder; however, conduct disorder is often the more appropriate diagnosis for adolescents and children. Opposition to authority and rules is a characteristic of oppositional defiant disorder. Impulsive anger outbursts with rapid onset are characteristics of intermittent explosive disorder. The difficulty with refraining from taking others' items is characteristic of kleptomania.

Case Study 11

1. C: Substance-induced sexual dysfunction is a DSM-5 differential diagnosis because substance use can affect sexual functioning. Generalized anxiety disorder covers general anxiety about many topics, but it does not necessarily lead to sexual functioning impairment. Social phobia is about a very specific situation or trigger for anxiety, and, although the client does have anxiety about sex and work, this would not meet the criteria. Medically induced sexual dysfunction is not a DSM-5 diagnosis.

2. A: It is most important to determine what medical limitations the client might have because it is possible that the client's penis may be excessively sensitive and the premature ejaculation may not be improved through cognitive and behavioral interventions. Identifying the client's goals, exploring the sexual dysfunction's effects on his relationship, and identifying the effects that his anxiety has on his daily functioning are all important, but these factors do not matter if biological factors inhibit his progress.

3. D: The ACA Code of Ethics notes that if services to clients are impaired due to physical, mental, or emotional issues, then the termination of supervisory efforts may be considered. The code also states that the intern should seek assistance with these kinds of problems in order to prevent harm to clients. Therefore, a combination of supporting the intern (by reducing his caseload) combined with the consideration of employment or supervision consequences (such as a short-term leave) is the most appropriate course of action. Simply terminating supervision would not be indicated at this time because an effort needs to be made to support the intern. Sitting in the sessions might provide accountability for the intern to be on time; however, it does not address the root of his issues.

4. D: The fear of panic attacks meets the criteria for panic disorder, but it is not part of the required criteria for generalized anxiety disorder. Excessive anxiety that is present for more than 6 months, being easily fatigued, and trouble falling asleep are all criteria for generalized anxiety disorder.

5. A: The client's PCP would be the most beneficial contact for collaboration in a holistic approach because the concern includes the influence of a medical condition. A psychiatrist is an important collaborator for mental health needs, especially when psychopharmacy is required, but this would neglect the focus on the client's medical needs. The client's girlfriend and the client's friends also do not address the physical needs of the client's medical condition and therefore would not characterize the most holistic approach.

6. A: Emotional reasoning is the cognitive distortion displayed here because the client is accepting his emotion as a reality even though just feeling something does not make it true. The client is not experiencing all-or-nothing thinking because he is not experiencing polarized thinking. The client is not fortune-telling because he is not predicting future experiences based on present feelings. The client is not overgeneralizing because he is not applying his current feelings to other situations.

7. B: You should continue to maintain silence instead of continuing talking because you are missing the opportunity to use silence by continuing silence. Maintaining silence, providing a prompt to respond to the silence, and the use of attending skills to encourage silence are all helpful skills to prompt a response to the use of silence.

8. B: It would be most helpful to support the client with identifying that his feelings are risky because he does not have evidence to support his thoughts to break up. Telling the client that his thoughts are not an appropriate response is an aggressive response that has not been proven to be a helpful confrontation technique. Although the focus of improving the relationship is helpful, it would validate the client's thoughts and would not confront them. Telling the client that he should continue to be in this relationship just because he has thoughts about breaking up and how these may not be true would be more directive than confrontational.

9. D: The use of antidepressants is not a behavioral approach that would affect premature ejaculation; rather, it is a medical approach that helps delay the time to ejaculation. Pelvic floor exercises affect the client's ability to refrain from ejaculation and are an effective behavioral technique in delaying it. Foreplay in a sexual encounter can delay ejaculation and reduce anxiety prior to sexual intercourse. Condoms reduce sensitivity and can aid in delaying premature ejaculation.

10. C: Although comfort with silence can be a positive trait in a relationship, the client is still working through addressing negative self-talk and it would likely increase anxiety if silence is uncomfortable for him. Immediacy behaviors would involve the client's girlfriend responding to what she sees the client experiencing either through reassuring statements, questions, or behaviors. Positive affect promotes a more positive environment and would likely result in a more positive experience. Eye contact demonstrates that she is present with him and attentive to him and would also promote a positive experience.

11. A: Mindfulness is focusing on the present situation, which would be helpful in conjunction with using evidence to counteract cognitive distortions. Cognitive reframing and challenging are helpful techniques in managing cognitive distortions, but they do not directly focus on present evidence for beliefs. Relaxation skills are helpful, but they do not focus on cognitive functions.

12. A: At this point, documenting the consultation and terminating the relationship would be indicated because the intern is continuing to harm clients (ACA, 2014, p. 13). You have already tried to support the intern, and it was not helpful in preventing client harm or changing his behavior. At this point, a corrective action plan may not be helpful because the intern has not shown that he is willing to change. It may be helpful to encourage the intern to seek counseling; however, this does not address the potential for further client harm.

13. A: A CBT approach is still possible via telehealth; therefore, this is not a practical or ethical consideration. Access to nonverbal cues is inhibited when counseling is provided via telehealth. The client's ability to misrepresent themselves is heightened when services are accessed via telehealth because the client's identity can be manipulated in the case of audio-only sessions. Confidentiality is more difficult to guarantee when sessions are virtual because it cannot be guaranteed that the conversation is not being overheard on the client's end and because general privacy settings may be breached.

How to Overcome Test Anxiety

Just the thought of taking a test is enough to make most people a little nervous. A test is an important event that can have a long-term impact on your future, so it's important to take it seriously and it's natural to feel anxious about performing well. But just because anxiety is normal, that doesn't mean that it's helpful in test taking, or that you should simply accept it as part of your life. Anxiety can have a variety of effects. These effects can be mild, like making you feel slightly nervous, or severe, like blocking your ability to focus or remember even a simple detail.

If you experience test anxiety—whether severe or mild—it's important to know how to beat it. To discover this, first you need to understand what causes test anxiety.

Causes of Test Anxiety

While we often think of anxiety as an uncontrollable emotional state, it can actually be caused by simple, practical things. One of the most common causes of test anxiety is that a person does not feel adequately prepared for their test. This feeling can be the result of many different issues such as poor study habits or lack of organization, but the most common culprit is time management. Starting to study too late, failing to organize your study time to cover all of the material, or being distracted while you study will mean that you're not well prepared for the test. This may lead to cramming the night before, which will cause you to be physically and mentally exhausted for the test. Poor time management also contributes to feelings of stress, fear, and hopelessness as you realize you are not well prepared but don't know what to do about it.

Other times, test anxiety is not related to your preparation for the test but comes from unresolved fear. This may be a past failure on a test, or poor performance on tests in general. It may come from comparing yourself to others who seem to be performing better or from the stress of living up to expectations. Anxiety may be driven by fears of the future—how failure on this test would affect your educational and career goals. These fears are often completely irrational, but they can still negatively impact your test performance.

Review Video: 3 Reasons You Have Test Anxiety
Visit mometrix.com/academy and enter code: 428468

Elements of Test Anxiety

As mentioned earlier, test anxiety is considered to be an emotional state, but it has physical and mental components as well. Sometimes you may not even realize that you are suffering from test anxiety until you notice the physical symptoms. These can include trembling hands, rapid heartbeat, sweating, nausea, and tense muscles. Extreme anxiety may lead to fainting or vomiting. Obviously, any of these symptoms can have a negative impact on testing. It is important to recognize them as soon as they begin to occur so that you can address the problem before it damages your performance.

Review Video: 3 Ways to Tell You Have Test Anxiety
Visit mometrix.com/academy and enter code: 927847

The mental components of test anxiety include trouble focusing and inability to remember learned information. During a test, your mind is on high alert, which can help you recall information and stay focused for an extended period of time. However, anxiety interferes with your mind's natural processes, causing you to blank out, even on the questions you know well. The strain of testing during anxiety makes it difficult to stay focused, especially on a test that may take several hours. Extreme anxiety can take a huge mental toll, making it difficult not only to recall test information but even to understand the test questions or pull your thoughts together.

Review Video: How Test Anxiety Affects Memory
Visit mometrix.com/academy and enter code: 609003

Effects of Test Anxiety

Test anxiety is like a disease—if left untreated, it will get progressively worse. Anxiety leads to poor performance, and this reinforces the feelings of fear and failure, which in turn lead to poor performances on subsequent tests. It can grow from a mild nervousness to a crippling condition. If allowed to progress, test anxiety can have a big impact on your schooling, and consequently on your future.

Test anxiety can spread to other parts of your life. Anxiety on tests can become anxiety in any stressful situation, and blanking on a test can turn into panicking in a job situation. But fortunately, you don't have to let anxiety rule your testing and determine your grades. There are a number of relatively simple steps you can take to move past anxiety and function normally on a test and in the rest of life.

Review Video: How Test Anxiety Impacts Your Grades
Visit mometrix.com/academy and enter code: 939819

Physical Steps for Beating Test Anxiety

While test anxiety is a serious problem, the good news is that it can be overcome. It doesn't have to control your ability to think and remember information. While it may take time, you can begin taking steps today to beat anxiety.

Just as your first hint that you may be struggling with anxiety comes from the physical symptoms, the first step to treating it is also physical. Rest is crucial for having a clear, strong mind. If you are tired, it is much easier to give in to anxiety. But if you establish good sleep habits, your body and mind will be ready to perform optimally, without the strain of exhaustion. Additionally, sleeping well helps you to retain information better, so you're more likely to recall the answers when you see the test questions.

Getting good sleep means more than going to bed on time. It's important to allow your brain time to relax. Take study breaks from time to time so it doesn't get overworked, and don't study right before bed. Take time to rest your mind before trying to rest your body, or you may find it difficult to fall asleep.

Review Video: The Importance of Sleep for Your Brain
Visit mometrix.com/academy and enter code: 319338

Along with sleep, other aspects of physical health are important in preparing for a test. Good nutrition is vital for good brain function. Sugary foods and drinks may give a burst of energy but this burst is followed by a crash, both physically and emotionally. Instead, fuel your body with protein and vitamin-rich foods.

Also, drink plenty of water. Dehydration can lead to headaches and exhaustion, especially if your brain is already under stress from the rigors of the test. Particularly if your test is a long one, drink water during the breaks. And if possible, take an energy-boosting snack to eat between sections.

Review Video: How Diet Can Affect your Mood
Visit mometrix.com/academy and enter code: 624317

Along with sleep and diet, a third important part of physical health is exercise. Maintaining a steady workout schedule is helpful, but even taking 5-minute study breaks to walk can help get your blood pumping faster and clear your head. Exercise also releases endorphins, which contribute to a positive feeling and can help combat test anxiety.

When you nurture your physical health, you are also contributing to your mental health. If your body is healthy, your mind is much more likely to be healthy as well. So take time to rest, nourish your body with healthy food and water, and get moving as much as possible. Taking these physical steps will make you stronger and more able to take the mental steps necessary to overcome test anxiety.

Mental Steps for Beating Test Anxiety

Working on the mental side of test anxiety can be more challenging, but as with the physical side, there are clear steps you can take to overcome it. As mentioned earlier, test anxiety often stems from lack of preparation, so the obvious solution is to prepare for the test. Effective studying may be the most important weapon you have for beating test anxiety, but you can and should employ several other mental tools to combat fear.

First, boost your confidence by reminding yourself of past success—tests or projects that you aced. If you're putting as much effort into preparing for this test as you did for those, there's no reason you should expect to fail here. Work hard to prepare; then trust your preparation.

Second, surround yourself with encouraging people. It can be helpful to find a study group, but be sure that the people you're around will encourage a positive attitude. If you spend time with others who are anxious or cynical, this will only contribute to your own anxiety. Look for others who are motivated to study hard from a desire to succeed, not from a fear of failure.

Third, reward yourself. A test is physically and mentally tiring, even without anxiety, and it can be helpful to have something to look forward to. Plan an activity following the test, regardless of the outcome, such as going to a movie or getting ice cream.

When you are taking the test, if you find yourself beginning to feel anxious, remind yourself that you know the material. Visualize successfully completing the test. Then take a few deep, relaxing breaths and return to it. Work through the questions carefully but with confidence, knowing that you are capable of succeeding.

Developing a healthy mental approach to test taking will also aid in other areas of life. Test anxiety affects more than just the actual test—it can be damaging to your mental health and even contribute to depression. It's important to beat test anxiety before it becomes a problem for more than testing.

Review Video: Test Anxiety and Depression
Visit mometrix.com/academy and enter code: 904704

Study Strategy

Being prepared for the test is necessary to combat anxiety, but what does being prepared look like? You may study for hours on end and still not feel prepared. What you need is a strategy for test prep. The next few pages outline our recommended steps to help you plan out and conquer the challenge of preparation.

Step 1: Scope Out the Test

Learn everything you can about the format (multiple choice, essay, etc.) and what will be on the test. Gather any study materials, course outlines, or sample exams that may be available. Not only will this help you to prepare, but knowing what to expect can help to alleviate test anxiety.

Step 2: Map Out the Material

Look through the textbook or study guide and make note of how many chapters or sections it has. Then divide these over the time you have. For example, if a book has 15 chapters and you have five days to study, you need to cover three chapters each day. Even better, if you have the time, leave an extra day at the end for overall review after you have gone through the material in depth.

If time is limited, you may need to prioritize the material. Look through it and make note of which sections you think you already have a good grasp on, and which need review. While you are studying, skim quickly through the familiar sections and take more time on the challenging parts. Write out your plan so you don't get lost as you go. Having a written plan also helps you feel more in control of the study, so anxiety is less likely to arise from feeling overwhelmed at the amount to cover. A sample plan may look like this:

- Day 1: Skim chapters 1–4, study chapter 5 (especially pages 31–33)
- Day 2: Study chapters 6–7, skim chapters 8–9
- Day 3: Skim chapter 10, study chapters 11–12 (especially pages 87–90)
- Day 4: Study chapters 13–15
- Day 5: Overall review (focus most on chapters 5, 6, and 12), take practice test

Step 3: Gather Your Tools

Decide what study method works best for you. Do you prefer to highlight in the book as you study and then go back over the highlighted portions? Or do you type out notes of the important information? Or is it helpful to make flashcards that you can carry with you? Assemble the pens, index cards, highlighters, post-it notes, and any other materials you may need so you won't be distracted by getting up to find things while you study.

If you're having a hard time retaining the information or organizing your notes, experiment with different methods. For example, try color-coding by subject with colored pens, highlighters, or post-it notes. If you learn better by hearing, try recording yourself reading your notes so you can listen while in the car, working out, or simply sitting at your desk. Ask a friend to quiz you from your flashcards, or try teaching someone the material to solidify it in your mind.

Step 4: Create Your Environment

It's important to avoid distractions while you study. This includes both the obvious distractions like visitors and the subtle distractions like an uncomfortable chair (or a too-comfortable couch that makes you want to fall asleep). Set up the best study environment possible: good lighting and a comfortable work area. If background music helps you focus, you may want to turn it on, but otherwise keep the room quiet. If you are using a computer to take notes, be sure you don't have any other windows open, especially applications like social media, games, or anything else that could distract you. Silence your phone and turn off notifications. Be sure to keep water close by so you stay hydrated while you study (but avoid unhealthy drinks and snacks).

Also, take into account the best time of day to study. Are you freshest first thing in the morning? Try to set aside some time then to work through the material. Is your mind clearer in the afternoon or evening? Schedule your study session then. Another method is to study at the same time of day that you will take the test, so that your brain gets used to working on the material at that time and will be ready to focus at test time.

STEP 5: STUDY!

Once you have done all the study preparation, it's time to settle into the actual studying. Sit down, take a few moments to settle your mind so you can focus, and begin to follow your study plan. Don't give in to distractions or let yourself procrastinate. This is your time to prepare so you'll be ready to fearlessly approach the test. Make the most of the time and stay focused.

Of course, you don't want to burn out. If you study too long you may find that you're not retaining the information very well. Take regular study breaks. For example, taking five minutes out of every hour to walk briskly, breathing deeply and swinging your arms, can help your mind stay fresh.

As you get to the end of each chapter or section, it's a good idea to do a quick review. Remind yourself of what you learned and work on any difficult parts. When you feel that you've mastered the material, move on to the next part. At the end of your study session, briefly skim through your notes again.

But while review is helpful, cramming last minute is NOT. If at all possible, work ahead so that you won't need to fit all your study into the last day. Cramming overloads your brain with more information than it can process and retain, and your tired mind may struggle to recall even previously learned information when it is overwhelmed with last-minute study. Also, the urgent nature of cramming and the stress placed on your brain contribute to anxiety. You'll be more likely to go to the test feeling unprepared and having trouble thinking clearly.

So don't cram, and don't stay up late before the test, even just to review your notes at a leisurely pace. Your brain needs rest more than it needs to go over the information again. In fact, plan to finish your studies by noon or early afternoon the day before the test. Give your brain the rest of the day to relax or focus on other things, and get a good night's sleep. Then you will be fresh for the test and better able to recall what you've studied.

STEP 6: TAKE A PRACTICE TEST

Many courses offer sample tests, either online or in the study materials. This is an excellent resource to check whether you have mastered the material, as well as to prepare for the test format and environment.

Check the test format ahead of time: the number of questions, the type (multiple choice, free response, etc.), and the time limit. Then create a plan for working through them. For example, if you have 30 minutes to take a 60-question test, your limit is 30 seconds per question. Spend less time on the questions you know well so that you can take more time on the difficult ones.

If you have time to take several practice tests, take the first one open book, with no time limit. Work through the questions at your own pace and make sure you fully understand them. Gradually work up to taking a test under test conditions: sit at a desk with all study materials put away and set a timer. Pace yourself to make sure you finish the test with time to spare and go back to check your answers if you have time.

After each test, check your answers. On the questions you missed, be sure you understand why you missed them. Did you misread the question (tests can use tricky wording)? Did you forget the information? Or was it something you hadn't learned? Go back and study any shaky areas that the practice tests reveal.

Taking these tests not only helps with your grade, but also aids in combating test anxiety. If you're already used to the test conditions, you're less likely to worry about it, and working through tests until you're scoring well gives you a confidence boost. Go through the practice tests until you feel comfortable, and then you can go into the test knowing that you're ready for it.

Test Tips

On test day, you should be confident, knowing that you've prepared well and are ready to answer the questions. But aside from preparation, there are several test day strategies you can employ to maximize your performance.

First, as stated before, get a good night's sleep the night before the test (and for several nights before that, if possible). Go into the test with a fresh, alert mind rather than staying up late to study.

Try not to change too much about your normal routine on the day of the test. It's important to eat a nutritious breakfast, but if you normally don't eat breakfast at all, consider eating just a protein bar. If you're a coffee drinker, go ahead and have your normal coffee. Just make sure you time it so that the caffeine doesn't wear off right in the middle of your test. Avoid sugary beverages, and drink enough water to stay hydrated but not so much that you need a restroom break 10 minutes into the test. If your test isn't first thing in the morning, consider going for a walk or doing a light workout before the test to get your blood flowing.

Allow yourself enough time to get ready, and leave for the test with plenty of time to spare so you won't have the anxiety of scrambling to arrive in time. Another reason to be early is to select a good seat. It's helpful to sit away from doors and windows, which can be distracting. Find a good seat, get out your supplies, and settle your mind before the test begins.

When the test begins, start by going over the instructions carefully, even if you already know what to expect. Make sure you avoid any careless mistakes by following the directions.

Then begin working through the questions, pacing yourself as you've practiced. If you're not sure on an answer, don't spend too much time on it, and don't let it shake your confidence. Either skip it and come back later, or eliminate as many wrong answers as possible and guess among the remaining ones. Don't dwell on these questions as you continue—put them out of your mind and focus on what lies ahead.

Be sure to read all of the answer choices, even if you're sure the first one is the right answer. Sometimes you'll find a better one if you keep reading. But don't second-guess yourself if you do immediately know the answer. Your gut instinct is usually right. Don't let test anxiety rob you of the information you know.

If you have time at the end of the test (and if the test format allows), go back and review your answers. Be cautious about changing any, since your first instinct tends to be correct, but make sure you didn't misread any of the questions or accidentally mark the wrong answer choice. Look over any you skipped and make an educated guess.

At the end, leave the test feeling confident. You've done your best, so don't waste time worrying about your performance or wishing you could change anything. Instead, celebrate the successful completion of this test. And finally, use this test to learn how to deal with anxiety even better next time.

Review Video: 5 Tips to Beat Test Anxiety
Visit mometrix.com/academy and enter code: 570656

Important Qualification

Not all anxiety is created equal. If your test anxiety is causing major issues in your life beyond the classroom or testing center, or if you are experiencing troubling physical symptoms related to your anxiety, it may be a sign of a serious physiological or psychological condition. If this sounds like your situation, we strongly encourage you to seek professional help.

Tell Us Your Story

We at Mometrix would like to extend our heartfelt thanks to you for letting us be a part of your journey. It is an honor to serve people from all walks of life, people like you, who are committed to building the best future they can for themselves.

We know that each person's situation is unique. But we also know that, whether you are a young student or a mother of four, you care about working to make your own life and the lives of those around you better.

That's why we want to hear your story.

We want to know why you're taking this test. We want to know about the trials you've gone through to get here. And we want to know about the successes you've experienced after taking and passing your test.

In addition to your story, which can be an inspiration both to us and to others, we value your feedback. We want to know both what you loved about our book and what you think we can improve on.

The team at Mometrix would be absolutely thrilled to hear from you! So please, send us an email at tellusyourstory@mometrix.com or visit us at mometrix.com/tellusyourstory.php and let's stay in touch.

Additional Bonus Material

Due to our efforts to try to keep this book to a manageable length, we've created a link that will give you access to all of your additional bonus material:

mometrix.com/bonus948/ncmhce

Made in the USA
Monee, IL
04 January 2024